DISSENT IN AMERICA

Since 1865

VOLUME II

Ralph F. Young

Temple University

PEARSON
Longman

New York   San Francisco   Boston
London   Toronto   Sydney   Tokyo   Singapore   Madrid
Mexico City   Munich   Paris   Cape Town   Hong Kong   Montreal

To the memory of Robert E. Wall, Jr., Teacher, Scholar, Friend

And to my students at Temple University whose intellectual curiosity, sensitivity, and search for answers continues to inspire me

Vice President and Publisher: *Priscilla McGeehon*
Marketing Manager: *Elizabeth Fogarty*
Supplements Editor: *Kristi Olson*
Senior Media Editor: *Patrick McCarthy*
Production Manager: *Ellen MacElree*
Project Coordination, Text Design, and Electronic Page Makeup: *Stratford Publishing Services*
Cover Designer/Manager: *Wendy Ann Fredericks*
Cover Photo: *Courtesy of the National Archives and Records Administration, Records of the U.S. Information Agency*
Photo Researcher: *Stratford Publishing Services*
Senior Manufacturing Buyer: *Dennis J. Para*
Printer and Binder: *Hamilton Printing Company*
Cover Printer: *Phoenix Color Corps.*

For permission to use copyrighted material, grateful acknowledgment is made to the copyright holders on pp. 475–476, which are hereby made part of this copyright page.

The Library of Congress Cataloging-in-Publication Data

Dissent in America / [edited by] Ralph F. Young.
 p.   cm.
  Contents: v. 2. Since 1865. Reconstruction, 1865–1877. Industry and reform, 1877–1912. Conflict and depression, 1912–1945. The affluent society, 1945–1966. Mobilization: Vietnam and the counterculture, 1964–1975. Contemporary dissent, 1975–
  ISBN 0-321-17976-5 (v.1) — ISBN 0-321-22451-5 (V.2)
  1. United States—Politics and government—Sources.   2. United States—Social conditions—Sources.   3. Dissenters—United States—History—Sources.   4. Social reformers—United States—History—Sources.   5. Democracy—United States—History—Sources.   6. Social problems—United States—History—Sources.   I. Young, Ralph F.
  E183.D57 2004
  303.48'4' 0973—dc22   2004007552

Photo Credits

Page 1   Frederick Douglass, photograph courtesy of Bettmann/Corbis
Page 27   Emma Goldman, photograph courtesy of Bettmann/Corbis
Page 111 Margaret Sanger, photograph courtesy of Bettmann/Corbis
Page 225 Allen Ginsberg, photograph courtesy of the Associated Press
Page 313 March on the Pentagon, photograph courtesy of Bettmann/Corbis
Page 385 Julia Butterfly Hill, photograph courtesy of the Associated Press

Please visit us at http://www.ablongman.com

ISBN 0-321-22451-5

1 2 3 4 5 6 7 8 9 10—HT—07 06 05 04

CONTENTS

PART FIVE   # Mobilization: Vietnam and the Counterculture, 1964–1975   313

Introduction: The Movement   313

PREFACE

If a man does not keep pace with his companions, perhaps it is because he hears a different drummer. Let him step to the music which he hears, however measured or far away.
———*Henry David Thoreau*

You don't need a weatherman to know which way the wind blows . . . .
———*Bob Dylan*

———————————

Between 1955 and 1975, the United States underwent a profound change, from a nation that (somewhat naively and arrogantly) believed in its own myths to a nation that (somewhat naively and angrily) began to question those very myths.

For some citizens, the 1960s and the five years on either side of the decade were profoundly disturbing. For others, they were a breath of fresh air. For everyone, no matter what their perspective, it seemed that protest and dissent had reached a high-water mark. But the years that brought the Montgomery bus boycott, the lunch counter sit-ins, the Freedom Rides, the March on Washington, the Berkeley Free Speech Movement, the March on the Pentagon, Woodstock, Altamont, and Kent State, Allen Ginsberg, Malvina Reynolds, Joan Baez, Bob Dylan, Phil Ochs, Timothy Leary, Abbie Hoffman, Ella Baker, Malcolm X, Bobby Seale, Angela Davis, Betty Friedan, and Elizabeth Martinez, SDS, AIM, NOW, and the GLF were in no way an aberration; in no way were they contrary to American ideals and American principles. In fact, the political, cultural, and social upheavals of the 1960s were simply a culmination of the very spirit upon which this country was founded—the spirit of dissent.

All of a sudden, or so it seemed, civil rights activists, antiwar liberals, and song-writers took seriously the injunctions of John Locke and Thomas Jefferson that all of us were endowed with inalienable natural rights. They took seriously the lesson taught to every primary school pupil that the United States was the greatest country in the world because it stood for the inherent equality of *all* people. And yet when these same pupils, growing into adolescence and young adulthood, saw televised images of soldiers of the 101st Airborne (one of the first divisions to parachute into Normandy on June 6, 1944) protecting black teenagers as they entered Little Rock's Central High School in 1957, it suddenly dawned on many of them that the grand American values that they had been taught had simply not been realized. It was this blatant discrepancy between ideal and reality that had a huge impact on the escalation of dissent in the 1960s.

Between 1965 and 1967, while studying Puritanism as a graduate student at Michigan State University, I attended speeches by Martin Luther King Jr., Stokely Carmichael, Timothy Leary, and (of all people) the Führer of the American Nazi

Party, George Lincoln Rockwell, during their whirlwind visits to campus. All four of these men, in their own way, dissented against the norms of American society and, to varying extents, the values of the "American way of life." Yet each man's convictions had historical antecedents. Martin Luther King Jr. adopted the words and ideas of Henry David Thoreau and Walter Rauschenbusch, Reinhold Niebuhr and Mahatma Gandhi, as well as the Bible and the Declaration of Independence, and applied them to America in the 1950s and 1960s. Stokely Carmichael took Marcus Garvey's expressions of "black power" and "black is beautiful" and applied them to the African American experience as the civil rights movement was entering a more cynical phase in the late 1960s. Timothy Leary harked back to the visionaries and mystics of India and Tibet, to European Romanticism, and to the psychedelic experiences of North American Indian shamanism. George Lincoln Rockwell repeated the anti-Semitic, xenophobic sentiments that have persisted in America ever since the founding of the Grand Order of the Star Spangled Banner and the Know-Nothing Party in the nineteenth century.

What I heard in those speeches at Michigan State University was nothing new. Those who espouse radical (or reactionary) revolutionary (or counterrevolutionary) ideas are carrying on a tradition that began during the earliest days of settlement in the New World. In fact, theirs is a tradition that originated even before the foundation of the permanent English colonies that would eventually become the United States. For four centuries, dissent has played a central role in the American experience.

Acknowledgments

A number of my colleagues at Temple University graciously took time from their busy schedules to read and criticize portions of this book as it evolved. Gregory Urwin, Susan Klepp, Ruth Ost, Jim Hilty, Ken Kusmer, Richard Immerman, Vladislav Zubok, Herbert Ershkowitz, Howard Ohline, and David Farber all gave invaluable suggestions and pointed me in the direction of many important and neglected documents of dissent. Lively discussions with Jay Lockenour, Arthur Schmidt, Howard Spodek, Kathy Walker, Barbara Day-Hickman, Peter Gran, David Watt, Phil Evanson and Wilbert Jenkins were also important in honing my views as the book took shape.

Phyllis Cole of the Pennsylvania State University gave me important insights into the Transcendental movement. Barbara Winslow of Brooklyn College clarified many aspects of early feminism. David Wrobel of the University of Nevada, Las Vegas was instrumental in my thinking about this book from its inception and his advice has greatly improved the finished product. James Loewen offered valuable suggestions about the table of contents, and John Serembus and Craig Eisendrath challenged my thinking about the nature of dissent. Homer Yasui graciously offered expert advice on the Japanese American experience during World War II and furnished me with his brother Minoru's letters.

My students have, of course, influenced my thinking and my approach to dissent and protest. Justin Chapman, Shannon Delaney, Zachary Hanson-Hart, Emily Hard,

Evan Hoffman, Courtney Mendillo, Thomas Mosher Barbara Saba, Adam Squire, Regina Szczesniak, Amanda Winalski, Stefanie Woolridge, and the rest of the students in Dissent in America are just a few of those I've taught over the years who have challenged me, inspired me, encouraged me, and made the classroom experience a sheer joy. Jonas Oesterle was especially helpful in enhancing my insights into contemporary protest music.

Terry Halbert's close reading of the manuscript, enthusiasm for the project, and personal encouragement greatly added to whatever value this work has. Even while in Helsinki, she went through the manuscript with the proverbial fine-tooth comb, tearing it apart and putting it back together again.

Without Ashley Dodge, my editor at Longman, this book would not exist. It was she who first recognized the importance of such a book and the central significance of dissent in American history. Without her insights, encouragement, challenging criticism, and valued friendship, this book would never have gotten off the ground. *Dissent in America* is as much hers as it is mine, for she knew its secret first.

Many others, in their own small ways, have contributed to this project. Thanks to Rafe for his tuna salad, tiramisu, and total zest for life; Norbert for his Vega banjo and Dutch bicycle; Istvan for his slivovitz and the story about that stormy night in Fairmount Park; the Radziwill clan for adopting me; Lucy for teaching loyalty; Vlad for his special horseradish vodka; Chris for being bothered enough to make all those telephone calls from Australia; Rachael for telling me to "go for it"; Tara Nevins for "No Place Like the Right Time"; Bruno et Marie-Camille for the fromage lessons; Annie for those quirky short stories; Tom for proving I really wasn't a computer Luddite; Don for all those all-night Michigan talkathons; Pat for the team teaching suggestion; Peter for the never-ending supply of books and Jerry Garcia ties; Rich for the pesto; Darcie for all those e-mails; Leif for his bullet-proof vest; Beverly and Clare for that fiddle session; Len and Veronika for taking me under their collective wing; Gudrun for the seventeenth of January; Riley and Musette for their meditation lessons; Ann and Jessie for questioning my sanity; and Allen Ginsberg for playing his harmonium and singing Blake's "Tyger, Tyger, Burning Bright" to me in my VW that day we were stuck in a traffic jam in the shadow of the Walt Whitman Bridge.

Finally, I'd like to thank the following reviewers for their valuable comments on drafts of this manuscript: Rafaela Acvedo-Field, Mount San Antonio Community College; Martha Jane Brazy, University of South Alabama; Kathleen S. Carter, High Point University; Lauren Coodley, Napa Valley College; Edward J. Davies, University of Utah; Cole P. Dawson, Warner Pacific College; Tim Lehman, Rocky Mountain College; Johnny S. Moore, Radford University; Anne Paulet, Humboldt State University; Ann DeJesus Riley, Hartnell College; William B. Turner, St. Cloud State University; Mark D. Van Ells, City University of New York, Queens College; Jason Ward, Lee University; and Edmund F. Wehrle, Eastern Illinois University.

Ralph F. Young
Department of History
Temple University
ralph.young@temple.edu

ABOUT THE AUTHOR

Ralph Young is a history professor at Temple University in Philadelphia. He lived in England and Germany for ten years where he taught first at London University and later at Bremen Universität. He has done extensive research on seventeenth-century Puritanism, dissenters in the United States, and international terrorism.

Along with his scholarly research he has written novels on terrorism, one of which, *Crossfire,* won a Suntory Award for Suspense Fiction in Japan. At present, in addition to teaching the Dissent in America course at Temple University, he is developing a monograph on dissent in America and, since September 2001, continuing to lead weekly teach-ins on the historical origins of current American foreign policy.

INTRODUCTION

Cautious, careful people, always casting about to preserve their reputation
and social standing, never can bring about a reform. Those who are really
in earnest must be willing to be anything or nothing in the world's estimation,
and publicly and privately, in season and out, avow their sympathy
with despised and persecuted ideas and their advocates, and bear the
consequences.
                                                    —*Susan B. Anthony*

All we say to America is to be true to what you said on paper. . . . Somewhere
I read [*pause*] of the freedom of speech. Somewhere I read [*pause*] of the
freedom of press. Somewhere I read [*pause*] that the greatness of America is
the right to protest for right.
                                                    —*Martin Luther King, Jr.*

What Is Dissent?

A central aspect of a democratic society is the constitutional guarantee that all citizens possess freedom of speech, thought, and conscience. Throughout American history, individuals and groups of people, oftentimes vociferously, have expressed these freedoms by raising their voices in strident protest. These dissenters went against the grain, disagreeing with the majority view, and their actions have changed and formed our country.

Dissent has been expressed for many reasons and in many different forms. There have been those who sought more equality, more moral rectitude, and more freedom. Some dissenters criticized political issues, and others struggled against societal values and attitudes. There were also reactionaries who resisted change and wanted to maintain the privileges and supremacy of their class, race, or gender, and others simply strove to gain political power.

What is dissent? What makes a person a legitimate and thoughtful critic of our society? Are dissenters only those people who want to see a greater society? What is the difference between someone who wants to improve our society and someone who wants to destroy it? Are those who have purely selfish goals legitimate dissenters? Does dissent imply a broader, more inclusive, worldview? Does dissent ever become treasonous? Is dissent patriotic or unpatriotic? Does dissent ultimately change society by offering new ideas, new perspectives, or does dissent merely confirm the status quo by providing a relatively harmless way of letting off steam?

When abolitionists demanded the end of slavery, antiabolitionists argued vehemently to preserve the institution. Do we regard defenders of slavery who considered their property rights superior to their slaves' human rights as "dissenters"? Feminists sought suffrage and equality for women. Antifeminists sought to preserve male dominance and the subjugation of women. So who are the dissenters? *What* is dissent? Is dissent reserved for those with moral grievances whose chief desire is to persuade the United States to live up to its ideals and to ensure that the nation is truly a land where "all men are created equal"? Or is dissent a broader, more complex issue?

Ultimately, the definition of dissent has to be somewhat fluid, because the political/social/cultural/ideological mainstream of America has been fluid. Dissenters are not always responding to the same mainstream. Dissent against Puritanism is different from dissent against McCarthyism (despite the interesting parallels that historians have drawn between the two with respect to the theme of persecution and unfounded accusations). Anti-Puritan dissenters, such as Anne Hutchinson, were dissenting against the mainstream Puritan (religious/theological/theocratic) regimen. Anti-McCarthy spokespeople, such as Margaret Chase Smith, were dissenting against a politically intolerant mainstream. Hutchinson was protesting against the mainstream of her time, just as Senator Smith protested against the mainstream of hers and Martin Luther King Jr. fought against the racial mainstream of his. This kind of fluid view of dissent (i.e., the expression of antimainstream sentiments) means that even right-wing militia groups are also antimainstream dissenters.

However we define it, dissent has played a prominent and sometimes central role in American history. Indeed, in some ways dissent has been the fuel for the engine of progress. If we keep in mind the importance and, indeed, centrality of dissent and protest in the history of the United States, we begin to have a clearer view of our nation as it continues to define itself. In doing so, perhaps we inch closer to a personal historical awareness.

About the Documents

In tracing the theme of dissent as it weaves its way through the fabric of American history, the foremost difficulty is picking and choosing satisfactory samples that construct an accurate picture of American dissent. For every document chosen, scores of others could easily have been included in this book. Readers who further research any of the issues that seem intriguing or particularly stimulating will find their effort amply rewarded.

Some of the documents here are speeches, petitions, broadsides, posters, and songs that deal with various injustices. Other documents included are interviews, articles, recollections, and memoirs of events by the people involved, in which they retell their experiences in jail or on a protest march or simply their personal agonizing over how far to take their protest. Some of the documents were published at the time of the event; others were published years after the event. In scrutinizing the documents, keep in mind *who* is speaking, *what* that person's involvement is in the issue, and *to whom* the comments are addressed. Consider the person's race, class, and gender in reading the document. An African American, for example, writing about African American experience has a different point of view than either a sympathetic or antagonistic white person. Was the document created in an effort to influence people, or was it simply a neutral examination of the issue? Does the document reveal the writer's bias? The answers to these questions enable us to ascertain the accuracy of a particular document, determine how to interpret it, and assess its historical meaning.

It is also important, especially with the early Native American documents, to remember that many of them are speeches that were translated and transcribed by an English-speaking white Christian European who himself was not a neutral observer and therefore might not accurately reflect the sentiments of the speaker. Some of these transcriptions and memoirs were written years and even decades after the event and were therefore clouded by the passage of time.

Because there is not nearly enough space here to cover more than a few of the dissenters in American history, at the end of each section I provide a sampling of Web sites for further information and links about these, and other, dissenters. Remember that this book is *not* the definitive history of dissent. The documents I have chosen inevitably reflect my own view of dissent, and it is obvious that any other historian assembling such documents would choose alternative items. It is my modest hope that this book serves to illustrate that dissent has been a powerful and defining force throughout American history.

Note to Students

At the end of each section of *Dissent in America* is a list of Web resources. These are up-to-date as of publication, but be aware that these can change.

In using the web as a research tool, the student must be acutely aware of the biases that most Web sites contain and make an effort to evaluate the accuracy and the authority of each site, as well as the evidence used to support any assertions that are made.

George Mason University has a site with links to many sources on American history that is invaluable for all students and teachers:

http://historymatters.gmu.edu

Another good overall source of links to many historical documents is:

www.bedfordstmartins.com/doclinks

An excellent Web page at the George Mason University Web site called "Making Sense of Evidence" offers information on how to analyze primary sources and documents.

http://historymatters.gmu.edu/browse/makesense

For a list of suggested readings, visit the author's Web site at

http://oll.temple.edu/ryoung

PART ONE

Reconstruction, 1865–1877

Frederick Douglass, c. 1870. *"No class of men can, without insulting their own nature, be content with any deprivation of their rights."* After the abolition of slavery, Frederick Douglass insisted that the federal government guarantee the rights (especially the right to vote) of all African Americans.

Introduction: Reuniting a Divided Nation

At the end of the Civil War, as Congress began dealing with the problem of reconstructing the Union, many of those who had fought against slavery now took up the cause of the rights of the freedmen. Civil rights, citizenship, and suffrage all became significant issues. Women, who had championed abolition and black rights, began to lobby more vigorously for women's suffrage and engaged energetically in the debate over the Fifteenth Amendment. There were high hopes that the amendment guaranteeing the right to vote would include *all* citizens. But when the Fifteenth Amendment extended the suffrage only to black men, the women's movement split into moderates who supported the amendment and radicals who denounced it and heatedly agitated against its ratification. For the next 50 years, women like Susan B. Anthony and Elizabeth Cady Stanton, leading the National Woman's Suffrage Association; and Lucy Stone, leading the more moderate American Woman's Suffrage Association, carried on the struggle for suffrage.

During the 1870s, the issue of former slaves' civil and political rights began fading from public awareness. The fact that African American men now had the right to vote seemed to convince even the most ardent former abolitionists and advocates of civil rights that nothing more needed to be done to ease the transition of freedmen into the mainstream. Slaves were now free, black men could vote—what more was necessary? The nation's reply seemed to be "nothing." The presidential election of 1876 settled the issue. Although the Democratic candidate, New York Governor Samuel J. Tilden, won 51 percent of the popular vote, his 184 electoral votes were one shy of the majority he needed to be declared the victor. Twenty electoral votes from Florida, South Carolina, Louisiana, and Oregon were disputed, and those states submitted two sets of returns. From November 1876 to March 1877, an electoral commission debated how to resolve the issue. Democrats finally agreed, a few days before inauguration day, to acquiesce in granting all 20 of the disputed electoral votes to the Republican candidate, Rutherford B. Hayes. In return, Republicans agreed to several conditions, among which was the withdrawal of the remaining federal troops stationed in the South. This in effect ended Reconstruction. It removed the freedmen from the protection of the U.S. Army, put their fate into the hands of local politicians, and put conservative Southern Democrats back in power in the South. Southern state officials lost no time in establishing literacy tests and poll taxes to prevent freedmen from voting. They also set up Jim Crow apartheid, imposing the second-class citizenship on African Americans that would last for nearly a century.

In the aftermath of the Civil War, many Americans began moving west. The Homestead Act of 1862 and the completion of the Transcontinental Railroad in 1869 were two factors that made the West enormously attractive to many who sought to improve their lives after the tumult and dislocation of the Civil War. But as settlers poured into the Great Plains, erecting homesteads, and wantonly killing the buffalo herds, the lives and livelihoods of Native Americans were so disrupted that Indian grievances and protests against white encroachment boiled over. In the Fort Laramie Treaty of 1868, the United States promised—in exchange for Sioux assurances not to attack whites traveling through the Great Plains—that the Black Hills would forever belong to the Sioux. Sitting Bull and Crazy Horse, believing that whites could not be trusted, refused to abide by any treaty. In 1873, Sioux warriors loyal to Sitting Bull and Crazy Horse violated the treaty by hunting on lands off the Sioux reservation and by attacking survey parties belonging to the Northern Pacific Railroad. Lieutenant Colonel George Armstrong Custer skirmished twice with these Indians while escorting Northern Railroad personnel, and because of this, the U.S. government sent him the following year to survey the Black Hills. The encroachment of Custer's Seventh Cavalry Regiment in the Black Hills deeply angered the Sioux, while simultaneously the Grant administration, eager to make the Black Hills safe for gold hunters, issued an ultimatum to all nontreaty Sioux to report to their agencies during the winter of 1875–1876. In March 1876, after a U.S. Army column attacked a Cheyenne camp, the Cheyenne joined up with Crazy Horse and Sitting Bull. The Arapaho also joined the Lakota and Cheyenne once the war had begun. The greatest Indian victory of the plains wars took place in June 1876 on the banks of the Greasy Grass in eastern Montana—whites called it the Little Big Horn—when Custer and his entire command were wiped out by Sitting Bull and Crazy Horse's confederation. But Custer's Last Stand was, in reality, one of the final blows for Indian hopes to maintain their way of life. Washington cracked down so severely that in spite of the Nez Percé's heroic run for freedom in 1877 and continued skirmishes with the Cheyenne and the Apache well into the 1880s, Indian resistance was effectively subdued.

Frederick Douglass (1818–1895)

At the close of the Civil War, Frederick Douglass was no less restrained in his political activism on behalf of African Americans than he was when he traveled throughout the country calling for the abolition of slavery. To be sure, slavery would no longer be legal in the United States, but he was quite aware that there would still be a struggle for equal rights, economic opportunity, and suffrage. Douglass dove into this struggle with the same fervor he displayed for the abolitionist crusade. He delivered this persuasive demand for the rights and privileges of full citizenship for the freedmen at the 1865 annual meeting of the Massachusetts Anti-Slavery Society.

Why should blacks, according to Douglass, have the right to vote immediately? What does he say about women's suffrage? How effective is his use of irony in this speech?

————————————

What the Black Man Wants, April 1865

. . . I have had but one idea for the last three years to present to the American people, and the phraseology in which I clothe it is the old abolition phraseology. I am for the "immediate, unconditional, and universal" enfranchisement of the black man, in every State in the Union. Without this, his liberty is a mockery; without this, you might as well almost retain the old name of slavery for his condition; for in fact, if he is not the slave of the individual master, he is the slave of society, and holds his liberty as a privilege, not as a right. He is at the mercy of the mob, and has no means of protecting himself.

It may be objected, however, that this pressing of the Negro's right to suffrage is premature. Let us have slavery abolished, it may be said, let us have labor organized, and then, in the natural course of events, the right of suffrage will be extended to the Negro. I do not agree with this. The constitution of the human mind is such, that if it once disregards the conviction forced upon it by a revelation of truth, it requires the exercise of a higher power to produce the same conviction afterwards. The American people are now in tears. The Shenandoah has run blood—the best blood of the North. All around Richmond, the blood of New England and of the North has been shed—of your sons, your brothers and your fathers. We all feel, in the existence of this Rebellion, that judgments terrible, wide-spread, far-reaching, overwhelming, are abroad in the land; and we feel, in view of these judgments, just now, a disposition to

SOURCE: Philip S. Foner, *The Life and Writings of Frederick Douglass*, vol. 4 (New York: International Publishers, 1950), 157–165.

learn righteousness. This is the hour. Our streets are in mourning, tears are falling at every fireside, and under the chastisement of this Rebellion we have almost come up to the point of conceding this great, this all-important right of suffrage. I fear that if we fail to do it now, if abolitionists fail to press it now, we may not see, for centuries to come, the same disposition that exists at this moment. Hence, I say, now is the time to press this right.

It may be asked, "Why do you want it? Some men have got along very well without it. Women have not this right." Shall we justify one wrong by another? This is the sufficient answer. Shall we at this moment justify the deprivation of the Negro of the right to vote, because some one else is deprived of that privilege? I hold that women, as well as men, have the right to vote, and my heart and voice go with the movement to extend suffrage to woman; but that question rests upon another basis than which our right rests. We may be asked, I say, why we want it. I will tell you why we want it. We want it because it is our right, first of all. No class of men can, without insulting their own nature, be content with any deprivation of their rights. We want it again, as a means for educating our race. Men are so constituted that they derive their conviction of their own possibilities largely by the estimate formed of them by others. If nothing is expected of a people, that people will find it difficult to contradict that expectation. By depriving us of suffrage, you affirm our incapacity to form an intelligent judgment respecting public men and public measures; you declare before the world that we are unfit to exercise the elective franchise, and by this means lead us to undervalue ourselves, to put a low estimate upon ourselves, and to feel that we have no possibilities like other men. Again, I want the elective franchise, for one, as a colored man, because ours is a peculiar government, based upon a peculiar idea, and that idea is universal suffrage. If I were in a monarchial government, or an autocratic or aristocratic government, where the few bore rule and the many were subject, there would be no special stigma resting upon me, because I did not exercise the elective franchise. It would do me no great violence. Mingling with the mass I should partake of the strength of the mass; I should be supported by the mass, and I should have the same incentives to endeavor with the mass of my fellow-men; it would be no particular burden, no particular deprivation; but here where universal suffrage is the rule, where that is the fundamental idea of the Government, to rule us out is to make us an exception, to brand us with the stigma of inferiority, and to invite to our heads the missiles of those about us; therefore, I want the franchise for the black man. . . .

I know that we are inferior to you in some things—virtually inferior. We walk about you like dwarfs among giants. Our heads are scarcely seen above the great sea of humanity. The Germans are superior to us; the Irish are superior to us; the Yankees are superior to us; they can do what we cannot, that is, what we have not hitherto been allowed to do. But while I make this admission, I utterly deny, that we are originally, or naturally, or practically, or in any way, or in any important sense, inferior to anybody on this globe. This charge of inferiority is an old dodge. It has been made available for oppression on many occasions. It is only about six centuries since the blue-eyed and fair-haired Anglo-Saxons were considered inferior by the haughty Normans, who once trampled upon them. If you read the history of the Norman Conquest, you will find that this proud Anglo-Saxon was once looked upon as of coarser clay than his Norman master, and might be found in the highways and byways of Old England laboring with a brass collar on his neck, and the name of his master marked upon it. You were down then! You are up now. I am glad you are up, and I want you to be glad to help us up also.

The story of our inferiority is an old dodge, as I have said; for wherever men oppress their fellows, wherever they enslave them, they will endeavor to find the needed apology for such enslavement and oppression in the character of the people oppressed and enslaved. When we wanted, a few years ago, a slice of Mexico, it was hinted that the Mexicans were an inferior race, that the old Castilian blood had become so weak that it would scarcely run down hill, and that Mexico needed the long, strong and beneficent arm of the Anglo-Saxon care extended over it. We said that it was necessary to its salvation, and a part of the "manifest destiny" of this Republic, to extend our arm over that dilapidated government. So, too, when Russia wanted to take possession of a part of the Ottoman Empire, the Turks were an "inferior race." So, too, when England wants to set the heel of her power more firmly in the quivering heart of old Ireland, the Celts are an "inferior race." So, too, the Negro, when he is to be robbed of any right which is justly his, is an "inferior man." It is said that we are ignorant; I admit it. But if we know enough to be hung, we know enough to vote. If the Negro knows enough to pay taxes to support the government, he knows enough to vote; taxation and representation should go together. If he knows enough to shoulder a musket and fight for the flag, fight for the government, he knows enough to vote. If he knows as much when he is sober as an Irishman knows when drunk, he knows enough to vote, on good American principles.

But I was saying that you needed a counterpoise in the persons of the slaves to the enmity that would exist at the South after the Rebellion is put down. I hold that the American people are bound, not only in self-defence, to extend this right to the freedmen of the South, but they are bound by their love of country, and by all their regard for the future safety of those Southern States, to do this—to do it as a measure essential to the preservation of peace there. But I will not dwell upon this. I put it to the American sense of honor. The honor of a nation is an important thing. It is said in the Scriptures, "What doth it profit a man if he gain the whole world, and lose his own soul?" It may be said, also, What doth it profit a nation if it gain the whole world, but lose its honor? I hold that the American government has taken upon itself a solemn obligation of honor, to see that this war—let it be long or short, let it cost much or let it cost little—that this war shall not cease until every freedman at the South has the right to vote. It has bound itself to it. What have you asked the black men of the South, the black men of the whole country to do? Why, you have asked them to incur the enmity of their masters, in order to befriend you and to befriend this Government. You have asked us to call down, not only upon ourselves, but upon our children's children, the deadly hate of the entire Southern people. You have called upon us to turn our backs upon our masters, to abandon their cause and espouse yours; to turn against the South and in favor of the North; to shoot down the Confederacy and uphold the flag—the American flag. You have called upon us to expose ourselves to all the subtle machinations of their malignity for all time. And now, what do you propose to do when you come to make peace? To reward your enemies, and trample in the dust your friends? Do you intend to sacrifice the very men who have come to the rescue of your banner in the South, and incurred the lasting displeasure of their masters thereby? Do you intend to sacrifice them and reward your enemies? Do you mean to give your enemies the right to vote, and take it away from your friends? Is that wise policy? Is that honorable? Could American honor withstand such a blow? I do not believe you will do it. I think you will see to it that we have the right to vote. There is something too mean in looking upon the Negro, when you are in trouble, as a citizen, and when you are free from trouble, as an alien. When this nation was in trouble, in its early struggles, it looked upon the Negro as a citizen. In 1776 he was a citizen. At the time of the formation of the Constitution the Negro had the right to vote in eleven States out of the old thirteen. In your trouble you have made us citizens. In 1812 Gen. Jackson addressed us as citizens—"fellow-citizens." He wanted us to fight. We were citizens then! And now, when you come to frame a conscription bill, the Negro is a citizen again. He has been a citizen just three times in the history of this government, and it has always been in time of trouble. In time of trouble we are citizens. Shall we be citizens in war, and aliens in peace? Would that be just?

I ask my friends who are apologizing for not insisting upon this right, where can the black man look, in this country, for the assertion of his right, if he may not look to the Massachusetts Anti-Slavery Society? Where under the whole heavens can he look for sympathy, in asserting this right, if he may not look to this platform? Have you lifted us up to a certain height to see that we are men, and then are any disposed to leave us there, without seeing that we are put in possession of all our rights? We look naturally to this platform for the assertion of all our rights, and for this one especially. I understand the anti-slavery societies of this country to be based on two principles,— first, the freedom of the blacks of this country; and, second, the elevation of them. Let me not be misunderstood here. I am not asking for sympathy at the hands of abolitionists, sympathy at the hands of any. I think the American people are disposed often to be generous rather than just. I look over this country at the present time, and I see Educational Societies, Sanitary Commissions, Freedmen's Associations, and the like,— all very good; but in regard to the colored people there is always more that is benevolent, I perceive, than just, manifested towards us. What I ask for the Negro is not benevolence, not pity, not sympathy, but simply justice. The American people have always been anxious to know what they shall do with us. Gen. Banks was distressed with solicitude as to what he should do with the Negro. Everybody has asked the question, and they learned to ask it early of the abolitionists, "What shall we do with the Negro?" I have had but one answer from the beginning. Do nothing with us! Your doing with us has already played the mischief with us. Do nothing with us! If the apples will not remain on the tree of their own strength, if they are wormeaten at the core, if they are early ripe and disposed to fall, let them fall! I am not for tying or fastening them on the tree in any way, except by nature's plan, and if they will not stay there, let them fall. And if the Negro cannot stand on his own legs, let him fall also. All I ask is, give him a chance to stand on his own legs! Let him alone! If you see him on his way to school, let him alone, don't disturb him! If you see him going to the dinner table at a hotel, let him go! If you see him going to the ballot-box, let him alone, don't disturb him! If you see him going into a work-shop, just let him alone,—your interference is doing him a positive injury. Gen. Banks' "preparation" is of a piece with this attempt to prop up the Negro. Let him fall if he cannot stand alone! If the Negro cannot live by the line of eternal justice, so beautifully pictured to you in the illustration used by Mr. Phillips, the fault will not be yours, it will be his who made the Negro, and established that line for his government. Let him live or die by that. If you will only untie his hands, and give him a chance, I think he will live. He will work as readily for himself as the white man. A great many delusions have been swept away by this war. One was, that the Negro would not work; he has proved his ability to work. Another was, that the Negro would not fight; that he possessed only the most sheepish attributes of humanity; was a perfect lamb, or an "Uncle Tom;" disposed to take off his coat whenever required, fold his hands, and be whipped by anybody who wanted to whip him. But the war has proved that there is a great deal of human nature in the Negro, and that "he will fight," as Mr. Quincy, our President, said, in earlier days than these, "when there is reasonable probability of his whipping anybody."

Zion Presbyterian Church

The African American Zion Presbyterian Church of Charleston, South Carolina, submitted a petition to Congress several months after the end of the Civil War, in which the parishioners demanded that the black people of South Carolina be accorded all the rights and privileges of U.S. citizens.

Upon what documents do the church members base their argument? What does this petition imply about circumstances for African Americans in the South at a time when the Confederacy had been utterly destroyed? Why are they so concerned with the Constitutional right to bear arms?

Petition to the United States Congress, November 24, 1865

Gentlemen:

We, the colored people of the State of South Carolina, in Convention assembled, respectfully present for your attention some prominent facts in relation to our present condition, and make a modest yet earnest appeal to your considerate judgment. . . .

Conscious of the difficulties that surround our position we would ask for no rights or privileges but such as rest upon the strong basis of justice and expediency, in view of the best interests of our entire country.

Source: James S. Allen, *Reconstruction: The Battle for Democracy, 1868–1876* (New York: International Publishers, 1937), 228–229.

We ask first, that the strong arm of law and order be placed alike over the entire people of this State; that life and property be secured, and the laborer free to sell his labor as the merchant his goods.

We ask that a fair and impartial instruction be given to the pledges of the government to us concerning the land question.

We ask that the three great agents of civilized society—the school, the pulpit, the press—be as secure in South Carolina as in Massachusetts or Vermont.

We ask that equal suffrage be conferred upon us, in common with the white men of this State. This we ask, because "all free governments derive their just powers from the consent of the governed"; and we are largely in the majority in this State, bearing for a long period the burden of onerous taxation, without a just representation. We ask for equal suffrage as a protection for the hostility evoked by our known faithfulness to our country and flag under all circumstances.

We ask that colored men shall not in every instance be tried by white men; and that neither by custom nor enactment shall we be excluded from the jury box.

We ask that, inasmuch as the Constitution of the United States explicitly declares that the right to keep and bear arms shall not be infringed and the Constitution is the Supreme law of the land—that the late efforts of the Legislature of this State to pass an act to deprive us of arms be forbidden, as a plain violation of the Constitution, and unjust to many of us in the highest degree, who have been soldiers, and purchased our muskets from the United States Government when mustered out of service.

We protest against any code of black laws the Legislature of this State may enact, and pray to be governed by the same laws that control other men. The right to assemble in peaceful convention, to discuss the political questions of the day; the right to enter upon all the avenues of agriculture, commerce, trade; to amass wealth by thrift and industry; the right to develop our whole being by all the appliances that belong to civilized society, cannot be questioned by any class of intelligent legislators.

We solemnly affirm and desire to live orderly and peacefully with all the people of this State; and commending this memorial to your considerate judgment.

Thus we ever pray.

Charleston, S.C. November 24, 1865
Zion Presbyterian Church

American Equal Rights Association

During congressional debates on the proposed Fifteenth Amendment, many people who had been involved in the abolitionist and feminist crusades argued fervently that the suffrage amendment should include women. The American Equal Rights Association (founded in 1866) issued the following resolution arguing its position on the topic. Although such influential people as Frederick Douglass, Susan B. Anthony, and Elizabeth Cady Stanton signed the resolution, the amendment approved by Congress in 1869 granted the suffrage to only African American men. "The right of citizens of the United States to vote shall not be denied or abridged by the United States or any State on account of race, color, or previous condition of servitude." In a bitter aftermath, the ratification process wound up splitting the feminist movement into those who supported the amendment with the intention of continuing the struggle for women's suffrage and those more radical women (and men) who fought energetically against ratification until women were included. The Fifteenth Amendment was ratified in 1870. It would be another 50 years before the Nineteenth Amendment opened the suffrage to women.

What is the basis for the claim that "republican institutions are based on individual rights"? Why do the writers of the resolution bring up the issue of taxes? Why are men reluctant to grant women suffrage?

National Convention Resolutions, New York, May 1867

RESOLVED, That as republican institutions are based on individual rights, and not on the rights of races or sexes, the first question for the American people to settle in the reconstruction of the government, is the RIGHTS OF INDIVIDUALS.

RESOLVED, That the present claim for "manhood suffrage," marked with the words "equal," "impartial," "universal," is a cruel abandonment of the slave women of the South, a fraud on the tax paying women of the North, and an insult to the civilization of the nineteenth century.

RESOLVED, That the [Republican Party] proposal to reconstruct our government on the basis of manhood suffrage . . . [which] has received the recent sanction of the American Anti-Slavery Society, is but a continuation of the old system of class and caste legislation, always cruel and proscriptive in itself, and ending in all ages in national degradation and revolution.

MEMORIAL OF THE AMERICAN EQUAL RIGHTS ASSOCIATION TO CONGRESS

The undersigned . . . respectfully but earnestly protest against any change in the Constitution of the United States, or legislation by Congress, which shall longer violate the principle of Republican Government, by proscriptive distinctions in rights of suffrage or citizenship, on account of color or sex. Your Memorialists would respectfully represent, that neither the colored man's loyalty, bravery on the battle field and general good conduct, nor woman's heroic devotion to liberty and her country, in peace and war, have yet availed to admit them to equal citizenship. . . .

Source: Retrieved on 3/11/2003 from the nineteenth Century American Women Writers Web Etext Library at http://womenshistory.about.com/gi/dynamic/offsite.htm?site= http:// www.unl.edu/legacy/19cwww/books/elibe/documents/suffrage/PURITAN6.HTM

We believe that humanity is one in all those intellectual, moral and spiritual attributes, out of which grow human responsibilities. The Scripture declaration is, "so God created man in his own image: male and female created he them." And all divine legislation throughout the realm of nature recognizes the perfect equality of the two conditions. For male and female are but different conditions neither color nor sex is ever discharged from obedience to law, natural or moral; written or unwritten. The commands, thou shalt not steal, nor kill, nor commit adultery, know nothing of sex in their demands; nothing in their penalty. And hence we believe that all human legislation which is at variance with the divine code, is essentially unrighteous and unjust. Woman and the colored man are taxed. . . .Woman has been fined, whipped, branded with red-hot irons, imprisoned and hung; but when was woman ever tried by a jury of her peers? . . .

Woman and the colored man are loyal, patriotic, property-holding, tax-paying, liberty-loving citizens; and we can not believe that sex or complexion should be any ground for civil or political degradation. In our government, one-half the citizens are disfranchised by their sex, and about one-eighth by the color of their skin; and thus a large majority have no voice in enacting or executing the laws they are taxed to support and compelled to obey. . . . Against such outrages on the very name of republican freedoms, your memorialists do and must ever protest. And is not our protest pre-eminently as just against the tyranny of "taxation without representation," as was that thundered from Bunker Hill. . . ?

And your Memorialists especially remember . . . that our country is still reeling [from] . . . a terrible civil war. . . . [I]n restoring the foundations of our nationality, [we] . . . pray that all discriminations on account of sex or race may be removed; and that our Government may be republican in fact as well as form; A GOVERNMENT BY THE PEOPLE, AND THE WHOLE PEOPLE; FOR THE PEOPLE, AND THE WHOLE PEOPLE . . .

[Signed by Theodore Tilton, Frederick Douglass, Elizabeth Cady Stanton, Lucretia Mott, and Susan B. Anthony].

Susan B. Anthony (1820–1906)

Susan B. Anthony fought for temperance, abolition, labor reform, educational reform, and most notably women's rights. A close friend of Elizabeth Cady Stanton, she became by mid-century a driving force in nineteenth-century feminism and perhaps the most important person in the struggle for women's suffrage. At the end of the Civil War, she cofounded with Stanton the American Equal Rights Association and campaigned vigorously for women to be included in the amendment that would give black men the vote. In 1870, after the Fifteenth Amendment was ratified, indignant that women had been excluded, Anthony stepped up her campaign. In 1872 she was arrested in

Rochester, New York, when she voted in the presidential election. She was tried and fined $100 in June 1873. When she refused to pay the fine, the judge, not wanting to create more publicity for her cause, shrewdly chose not to sentence her to a jail term. It was Susan B. Anthony who wrote the women's suffrage constitutional amendment that was introduced in Congress, where it was repeatedly debated, tabled, defeated, reintroduced, rejected, and eventually, more than a decade after her death, approved and ratified as the Nineteenth Amendment to the Consitution.

There is no accurate account of her comments at the trial. The first document here is an excerpt from one of three separate accounts reported after the event. The second document is a speech she gave on more than 20 occasions between her arrest and her trial. Is Susan B. Anthony's argument that women have the right to vote based on moral, political, or legal grounds? How effective is her tactic of citing passages of the federal and state constitutions? Does the evidence she uses support her case? What is the basis for her contention that there is no difference between being a woman in the United States and being a slave?

Account of Susan B. Anthony's Trial, July 3, 1873

As a matter of outward form the defendant was asked if she had anything to say why the sentence of the court should not be pronounced upon her.

"Yes, your honor," replied Miss Anthony, "I have many things to say. My every right, constitutional, civil, political and judical has been tramped upon. I have not only had no jury of my peers, but I have had no jury at all."

Court— "Sit down Miss Anthony. I cannot allow you to argue the question."

Miss Anthony— "I shall not sit down. I will not lose my only chance to speak."

Court— "You have been tried, Miss Anthony, by the forms of law, and my decision has been rendered by law."

Miss Anthony— "Yes, but laws made by men, under a government of men, interpreted by men and for the benefit of men. The only chance women have for justice in this country is to violate the law, as I have done, and as I shall *continue* to do," and she struck her hand heavily on the table in emphasis of what she said. "Does your honor suppose that we obeyed the infamous fugitive slave law which forbade to give a cup of cold water to a slave fleeing from his master? I tell you we did not obey it; we fed him and clothed him, and sent him on his way to Canada. *So shall we trample all unjust laws* under foot. I do not ask the clemency

---

Source: Matilda Joslyn Gage to Editor, June 20, 1873, Kansas *Leavenworth Times*, July 3, 1873, SBA scrapbook 6, Rare Books, DLC.

of the court. I came into it to get justice, having failed in this, I demand the full rigors of the law."

COURT— "The sentence of the court is $100 fine and the costs of the prosecution."

MISS ANTHONY— "I have no money to pay with, but am $10,000 in debt."

COURT— "You are not ordered to stand committed till it is paid."

Is It a Crime for a U.S. Citizen to Vote?

Friends and Fellow-citizens: I stand before you to-night, under indictment for the alleged crime of having voted at the last Presidential election, without having a lawful right to vote. It shall be my work this evening to prove to you that in thus voting, I not only committed no crime, but, instead, simply exercised my citizen's right guaranteed to me and all United States citizens by the National Constitution, beyond the power of any State to deny.

Our democratic-republican government is based on the idea of the natural right of every individual member thereof to a voice and a vote in making and executing the laws. We assert the province of government to be to secure the people in the enjoyment of their unalienable rights. We throw to the winds the old dogma that governments can give rights. Before governments were organized, no one denies that each individual possessed the right to protect his own life, liberty and property. And when 100 or 1,000,000 people enter into a free government, they do not barter away their natural rights; they simply pledge themselves to protect each other in the enjoyment of them, through prescribed judicial and legislative tribunals. They agree to abandon the methods of brute force in the adjustment of their differences, and adopt those of civilization.

Nor can you find a word in any of the grand documents left us by the fathers that assumes for government the power to create or to confer rights. The Declaration of Independence, the United States Constitution, the constitutions of the several states and the organic laws of the territories, all alike propose to protect the people in the exercise of their God-given rights. Not one of them pretends to bestow rights.

"All men are created equal, and endowed by their Creator with certain unalienable rights. Among these are life, liberty and the pursuit of happiness. That to secure these, governments are instituted among men, deriving their just powers from the consent of the governed."

Here is no shadow of government authority over rights, nor exclusion of any from their full and equal enjoyment. Here is pronounced the right of all men, and "consequently," as the Quaker preacher said, "of all women," to a voice in the government. And here, in this very first paragraph of the declaration, is the assertion of the

SOURCE: Retrieved on 10/19/2003 from www.pbs.org/stantonanthony/resources/index.html?body=crime_to_vote.html. For the full text of another copy of this address, see Ann D. Gordon, ed., *The Selected Papers of Elizabeth Cady Stanton and Susan B. Anthony*, vol. 2 (New Brunswick, NJ: Rutgers University Press, 2000), 554–583.

natural right of all to the ballot; for, how can "the consent of the governed" be given, if the right to vote be denied? Again: "That whenever any form of government becomes destructive of these ends, it is the right of the people to alter or abolish it, and to institute a new government, laying its foundations on such principles, and organizing its powers in such forms as to them shall seem most likely to effect their safety and happiness."

Surely, the right of the whole people to vote is here clearly implied. For however destructive in their happiness this government might become, a disfranchised class could neither alter nor abolish it, nor institute a new one, except by the old brute force method of insurrection and rebellion. One-half of the people of this nation to-day are utterly powerless to blot from the statute books an unjust law, or to write there a new and a just one. The women, dissatisfied as they are with this form of government, that enforces taxation without representation, that compels them to obey laws to which they have never given their consent, that imprisons and hangs them without a trial by a jury of their peers, that robs them, in marriage, of the custody of their own persons, wages and children, are this half of the people left wholly at the mercy of the other half, in direct violation of the spirit and letter of the declarations of the framers of this government, every one of which was based on the immutable principle of equal rights to all. By those declarations, kings, priests, popes, aristocrats, were all alike dethroned, and placed on a common level politically, with the lowliest born subject or serf. By them, too, men, as such, were deprived of their divine right to rule, and placed on a political level with women. By the practice of those declarations all class and caste distinction will be abolished; and slave, serf, plebeian, wife, woman, all alike, bound from their subject position to the proud platform of equality.

The preamble of the federal constitution says: "We, the people of the United States, in order to form a more perfect union, establish justice, insure domestic tranquility, provide for the common defense, promote the general welfare and secure the blessings of liberty to ourselves and our posterity, do ordain and established this constitution for the United States of America."

It was we, the people, not we, the white male citizens, nor yet we, the male citizens; but we, the whole people, who formed this Union. And we formed it, not to give the blessings of liberty, but to secure them; not to the half of ourselves and the half of our posterity, but to the whole people—women as well as men. And it is downright mockery to talk to women of their enjoyment of the blessings of liberty while they are denied the use of the only means of securing them provided by this democratic-republican government—the ballot.

The early journals of Congress show that when the committee reported to that body the original articles of confederation, the very first article which became the subject of discussion was that respecting equality of suffrage. Article 4th said: "The better to secure and perpetuate mutual friendship and intercourse between the people of the different States of this Union, the free inhabitants of each of the States, (paupers, vagabonds and fugitives from justice excepted,) shall be entitled to all the privileges and immunities of the free citizens of the several States."

Thus, at the very beginning, did the fathers see the necessity of the universal application of the great principle of equal rights to all—in order to produce the desired result—a harmonious union and a homogeneous people. . . .

The preamble of the Constitution of the State of New York declares. . . : "We, the people of the State of New York, grateful to Almighty God for our freedom, in order to secure its blessings, do establish this Constitution."

Here is not the slightest intimation either of receiving freedom from the United States Constitution, or of the State conferring the blessings of liberty upon the people, and the same is true of every one of the thirty-six State Constitutions. Each and all, alike declare rights God-given, and that to secure the people in the enjoyment of their inalienable rights, is their one and only object in ordaining and establishing government. And all of the State Constitutions are equally emphatic in their recognition of the ballot as the means of securing the people in the enjoyment of these rights.

Article 1 of the New York State Constitution says: "No member of this State shall be disfranchised or deprived of the rights or privileges secured to any citizen thereof, unless by the law of the land, or the judgement of his peers."

And so carefully guarded is the citizen's right to vote, that the Constitution makes special mention of all who may be excluded. It says: "Laws may be passed excluding from the right of suffrage all persons who have been or may be convicted of bribery, larceny or any infamous crime."

In naming the various employments that shall not affect the residence of voters the 3d section of article 2d says "that being kept at any alms house, or other asylum, at public expense, nor being confined at any public prison, shall deprive a person of his residence," and hence his vote. Thus is the right of voting most sacredly hedged about. The only seeming permission in the New York State Constitution for the disfranchisement of women is in section 1st of article 2d, which says: "Every male citizen of the age of twenty-one years, shall be entitled to vote."

But I submit that in view of the explicit assertions of the equal right of the whole people, both in the preamble and previous article of the constitution, this omission of the adjective "female" in the second, should not be construed into a denial; but, instead, counted as of no effect. Mark the direct prohibition: "No member of this State shall be disfranchised, unless by the law of the land, or the judgment of his peers." "The law of the land," is the United States Constitution: and there is no provision in that document that can be fairly construed into a permission to the States to deprive any class of their citizens of their right to vote. Hence New York can get no power from that source to disfranchise one entire half of her members. Nor has "the judgment of their peers" been pronounced against women exercising their right to vote; no disfranchised person is allowed to be judge or juror and none but disfranchised persons can be women's peers; nor has the legislature passed laws excluding them on account of idiocy of lunacy; nor yet the courts convicted them of bribery, larceny, or any infamous crime. Clearly, then, there is no constitutional ground for the exclusion of women from the ballot-box in the State of New York. No barriers whatever stand to-day between women and the exercise of their right to vote save those of precedent and prejudice. . . .

The only question left to be settled, now, is: Are women persons? And I hardly believe any of our opponents will have the hardihood to say they are not. Being persons, then, women are citizens, and no state has a right to make any new law, or to enforce any old law, that shall abridge their privileges or immunities. Hence, every discrimination against women in the constitutions and laws of the several states, is to-day null and void, precisely as is every one against negroes. Is the right to vote one of the privileges or immunities of citizens? I think the disfranchised ex-rebels, and the ex-state prisoners will agree with me, that it is not only one of them, but the one without which all the others are nothing. Seek first the kingdom of the ballot, and all things else shall be given thee, is the political injunction.

Webster, Worcester and Bouvier all define citizen to be a person, in the United States, entitled to vote and hold office.

Prior to the adoption of the thirteenth amendment, by which slavery was forever abolished, and black men transformed from property to persons, the judicial opinions of the country had always been in harmony with these definitions. To be a person was to be a citizen, and to be a citizen was to be a voter. . . .

If we once establish the false principle, that United States citizenship does not carry with it the right to vote in every state in this Union, there is no end to the petty freaks and cunning devices, that will be resorted to, to exclude one and another class of citizens from the right of suffrage. It will not always be men combining to disfranchise all women; native born men combining to abridge the rights of all naturalized citizens, as in Rhode Island. It will not always be the rich and educated who may combine to cut off the poor and ignorant; but we may live to see the poor, hardworking, uncultivated day laborers, foreign and native born, learning the power of the ballot and their vast majority of numbers, combine and amend state constitutions so as to disfranchise the Vanderbilts and A. T. Stewarts, the Conklings and Fentons. It is poor rule that won't work more ways than one. Establish this precedent, admit the right to deny suffrage to the states, and there is no power to foresee the confusion, discord and disruption that may await us. There is, and can be, but one safe principle of government—equal righs to all. And any and every discrimination against any class, whether on account of color, race, nativity, sex, property, culture, can but embitter and disaffect that class, and thereby endanger the safety of the whole people.

Clearly, then, the national government must not only define the rights of citizens, but it must stretch out its powerful hand and protect them in every state in this Union.

But if you will insist that the fifteenth amendment's emphatic interdiction against robbing United States citizens of their right to vote, "on account of race, color, or previous condition of servitude," is a recogniton of the right, either of the United States, or any state, to rob citizens of that right, for any or all other reason, I will prove to you that the class of citizens for which I now plead, and to which I belong, may be, by all the principles of our government, and many of the laws of the states, included under the term "previous condition of servitude."

First—The married women and their legal status. What is servitude? "The condition of a slave." What is a slave? "A person who is robbed of the proceeds of his labor; a person who is subject to the will of another."

By the law of Georgia, South Carolina, and all the states of the South, the negro had no right to the custody and control of his person. He belonged to his master. If he was disobedient, the master had the right to use correction. If the negro didn't like the correction, and attempted to run away, the master had a right to use coercion to bring him back.

By the law of every state in this Union to-day, North as well as South, the married woman has no right to the custody and control of her person. The wife belongs to her husband; and if she refuses obedience to his will, he may use moderate correction, and if she doesn't like his moderate correction, and attempts to leave his "bed and board," the husband may use moderate coercion to bring her back. The little word "moderate," you see, is the saving clause for the wife, and would doubtless be over-stepped should offended husband administer his correction with the "cat-o'nine-tails," or accomplish his coercion with blood-hounds.

Again, the slave had no right to the earnings of his hands, they belonged to his master; no right to the custody of his children, they belonged to his master; no right to sue or be sued, or testify in the courts. If he committed a crime, it was the master who must sue or be sued.

In many of the states there has been special legislation, giving to married women the right to property inherited, or received by bequest, or earned by the pursuit of any avocation outside of the home; also, giving her the right to sue and be sued in matters pertaining to such separate property; but not a single state of this Union has ever secured the wife in his enjoyment of her right to the joint ownership of the joint earnings of the marriage copartnership. And since, in the nature of things, the vast majority of married women never earn a dollar, by work outside of their families, nor inherit a dollar from their fathers, it follows that from the day of their marriage to the day of the death of their husbands, not one of them ever has a dollar, except it shall please her husband to let her have it.

In some of the states, also, there have been laws passed giving to the mother a joint right with the father in the guardianship of the children. But twenty years ago, when our woman's rights movement commenced, by the laws of the State of New York, and all the states, the father had the sole custody and control of the children. No matter if he were a brutal, drunken libertine, he had the legal right, without the mother's consent, to apprentice her sons to rumsellers, or her daughters to brothel keepers. He could even will away an unborn child, to some other person than the mother. And in many of the states the law still prevails, and the mothers are still utterly powerless under the common law. . . .

There is an old saying that "a rose by any other name would smell as sweet," and I submit it the deprivation by law of the ownership of one's own person, wages, property, children, the denial of the right as an individual, to sue and be sued, and to testify in the courts, is not a condition of servitude most bitter and absolute, though under the sacred name of marriage?

Does any lawyer doubt my statement of the legal status of married women? I will remind him of the fact that the old common law of England prevails in every State in this Union, except where the Legislature has enacted special laws annulling it. And I am ashamed that not one State has yet blotted from its statute books the old common law of marriage, by which Blackstone, summed up in the fewest words possible, is made to say, "husband and wife are one, and that one is the husband."

Thus may all married women, wives and widows, by the laws of the several States, be technically included in the fifteenth amendment's specification of "condition of servitude," present or previous. And not only married women, but I will also prove to you that by all the great fundamental principles of our free government, the entire womanhood of the nation is in a "condition of servitude" as surely as were our revolutionary fathers, when they rebelled against old King George. Women are taxed without representation, governed without their consent, tried, convicted and punished without a jury of their peers. And is all this tyranny any less humiliating and degrading to women under our democratic-republican government to-day than it was to men under their aristocratic, monarchical government one hundred years ago? There is not an utterance of old John Adams, John Hancock or Patrick Henry, but finds a living response in the soul of every intelligent, patriotic woman of the nation. Bring to me a common-sense woman property holder, and I will show you one whose soul is fired with all the indignation of 1776 every time the tax-gatherer presents himself at her door. You will not find one such but feels her condition of servitude as galling as did James Otis when he said: "The very act of taxing exercised over those who are not represented appears to me to be depriving them of one of their most essential rights, and if continued, seems to be in effect an entire disfranchisement of every civil right. For, what one civil right is worth a rush after a man's property is subject to be taken from him at pleasure without his consent? If a man is not his own assessor in person, or by deputy, his liberty is gone, or he is wholly at the mercy of others." . . .

That liberty or freedom consists in having an actual share in the appointment of those who are to frame the laws, and who are to be the guardians of every man's life, property and peace. For the all of one man is as dear to him as the all of another; and the poor man has an equal right, but more need to have representatives in the Legislature than the rich one. That they who have no voice or vote in the electing of representatives, do not enjoy liberty, but are absolutely enslaved to those who have votes and their representatives; for to be enslaved is to have governors whom other men have set over us, and to be subject to laws made by the representatives of others, without having had representatives of our own to give consent in our behalf."

Suppose I read it with the feminine gender: "That women who have no voice nor vote in the electing of representatives, do not enjoy liberty, but are absolutely enslaved to men who have votes and their representatives; for to be enslaved is to have governors whom men have set over us, and to be subject to the laws made by the representatives of men, without having representatives of our own to give consent in our behalf."

And yet one more authority; that of Thomas Paine, than whom not one of the Revolutionary patriots more ably vindicated the principles upon which our government is founded: "The right of voting for representatives is the primary right by which other rights are protected. To take away this right is to reduce man to a state of slavery; for slavery consists in being subject to the will of another; and he that has not a vote in the election of representatives is in this case. The proposal, therefore, to disfranchise any class of men is as criminal as the proposal to take away property."

Is anything further needed to prove women's condition of servitude sufficiently orthodox to entitle her to the guaranties of the fifteenth amendment?

Is there a man who will not agree with me, that to talk of freedom without the ballot, is mockery—is slavery—to the women of this Republic, precisely as New England's orator Wendell Phillips, at the close of the late war, declared it to be to the newly emancipated black men? . . .

We no longer petition Legislature or Congress to give us the right to vote. We appeal to the women everywhere to exercise their too long neglected "citizen's right to vote." We appeal to the inspectors of election everywhere to receive the votes of all United States citizens as it is their duty to do. We appeal to United States commissioners and marshals to arrest the inspectors who reject the names and votes of United States citizens, as it is their duty to do, and leave those alone who, like our eighth ward inspectors, perform their duties faithfully and well.

We ask the juries to fail to return verdicts of "guilty" against honest, law-abiding, tax-paying United States citizens for offering their votes at our elections. Or against intelligent, worthy young men, inspectors of elections, for receiving and counting such citizens votes.

We ask the judges to render true and unprejudiced opinions of the law, and wherever there is room for a doubt to give its benefit on the side of liberty and equal rights to women, remembering that "the true rule of interpretation under our national constitution, especially since its amendments, is that anything for human rights is constitutional, everything against human right unconstitutional."

And it is on this line that we propose to fight our battle for the ballot—all peaceably, but nevertheless persistently through to complete triumph, when all United States citizens shall be recognized as equals before the law.

Robert B. Elliott (1842–1884)

Born and reared in England, Robert B. Elliott moved to South Carolina in the aftermath of the Civil War, where in 1869 he became the first black commander of the state's national guard. From 1871 to 1874 he served in the U.S. House of Representatives. He became an active participant in the congressional debates on the civil rights bill that was eventually passed in 1875.

What would happen, according to Elliott, if the government respected states' rights above individual rights? How did blacks prove their patriotism and therefore their rights to citizenship and suffrage? Why is the civil rights bill necessary?

Speech in Congress on the Civil Rights Bill, January 6, 1874

. . . While I am sincerely grateful for this high mark of courtesy that has been accorded to me by this House, it is a matter of regret to me that it is necessary at this day that I should rise in the presence of an American Congress to advocate a bill which simply

SOURCE: Retrieved on 3/11/2003 from www.law.nyu.edu/davisp/neglectedvoices/Elliot Jan061874.html

asserts equal rights and equal public privileges for all classes of American citizens. I regret, sir, that the dark hue of my skin may lend a color to the imputation that I am controlled by motives personal to myself in my advocacy of this great measure of national justice. Sir, the motive that impels me is restricted by no such narrow boundary, but is as broad as your Constitution. I advocate it, sir, because it is right. The bill, however, not only appeals to your justice, but it demands a response from your gratitude.

In the events that led to the achievement of American Independence the negro was not an inactive or unconcerned spectator. He bore his part bravely upon many battle-fields, although uncheered by that certain hope of political elevation which victory would secure to the white man. The tall granite shaft, which a grateful State has reared above its sons who fell in defending Fort Griswold against the attack of Benedict Arnold, bears the name of Jordan, Freeman, and other brave men of the African race who there cemented with their blood the corner-stone of the Republic. In the State which I have the honor in part to represent the rifle of the black man rang out against the troops of the British crown in the darkest days of the American revolution. Said General Greene, who has been justly termed the Washington of the North, in a letter written by him to Alexander Hamilton, on the 10th day of January, 1781, from the vicinity of Camden, South Carolina: There is no such thing as national character or national sentiment. The inhabitants are numerous, but they would be rather formidable abroad than at home. There is a great spirit of enterprise among the black people, and those that come out as volunteers are not a little formidable to the enemy.

At the battle of New Orleans, under the immortal Jackson, a colored regiment held the extreme right of the American line unflinchingly, and drove back the British column that pressed upon them, at the point of the bayonet. So marked was their valor on that occasion that it evoked from their great commander the warmest encomiums, as will be seen from his dispatch announcing the brilliant victory.

As the gentleman from Kentucky, [Mr. Beck,] who seems to be the leading exponent on this floor of the party that is arrayed against the principle of this bill; has been pleased, in season and out of season, to cast odium upon the negro and to vaunt the chivalry of his state, I may be pardoned for calling attention to another portion of the same dispatch. Referring to the various regiments under his command, and their conduct on that field which terminated the second war of American Independence, General Jackson says: At the very moment when the entire discomfiture of the enemy was looked for with a confidence amounting to certainty, the Kentucky reinforcements, in whom so much reliance had been placed, ingloriously fled.

In quoting this indisputable piece of history, I do so only by way of admonition and not to question the well-attested gallantry of the true Kentuckian, and to suggest to the gentleman that it would be well that he should not flaunt his heraldry so proudly while he bears this scar—sinister on the military escutcheon of his State— a State which answered the call of the Republic in 1861, when treason thundered at the very gates of the capital by coldly declaring her neutrality in the impending struggle. The negro, true to that patriotism and love of country that have ever characterized and marked his history on this continent, came to the aid of the Government in its efforts to maintain the Constitution. To that Government he now appeals; that Constitution he now invokes for protection against outrage and unjust prejudices founded upon caste.

But, sir, we are told by the distinguished gentleman from Georgia [Mr. Stephens] that Congress has no power under the Constitution to pass such a law, and that the passage of such an act is in direct contravention of the rights of the States. I cannot assent to any such proposition. The constitution of a free government ought always to be construed in favor of human rights. Indeed, the thirteenth, fourteenth, and fifteenth amendments, in positive words, invest Congress with the power to protect the citizen in his civil and political rights. Now, sir, what are civil rights: Rights natural, modified by civil society. . . .

Is it the interest of the Government to sacrifice individual rights to the preservation of the rights of an artificial being called States? There can be no truer principle than this, that every individual of the community at large has an equal right to the protection of Government. Can this be a free Government if partial distinctions are tolerated or maintained? . . .

The process of restoring to their proper relations with the Federal Government and with the other States those which had sided with the rebellion, undertaken under the proclamation of President Johnson in 1865, and before the assembling of Congress, developed the fact that, notwithstanding the formal recognition by those states of the abolition of slavery, the condition of the slave race would, without further protection of the Federal Government, be almost as bad as it was before. Among the first acts of legislation adopted by several of the states in the legislative bodies which claimed to be in their normal relations with the Federal government, were laws which imposed upon the colored race onerous disabilities and burdens, and curtailed their rights in the pursult of life, liberty, and property to such an extent that their freedom was of little value, while they had lost the protection which they had received from their former owners from motives both of interest and humanity.

They were in some States forbidden to appear in the towns in any other character than menial servants. They were required to reside on and cultivate the soil, without the right to purchase or own it. They were excluded from any occupations of gain, and were not permitted to give testimony in the courts in any case where a white man was a party. It was said that their lives were at the mercy of bad men, either because the laws for their protection were insufficient or were not enforced.

These circumstances, whatever of falsehood or misconception may have been mingled with their presentation forced upon the statesmen who had conducted the Federal government in safety through the crisis of the rebellion, and who supposed that by the thirteenth article of amendment they had secured the result of their labors, the conviction that something more was necessary in the way of constitutional protection to the unfortunate race who had suffered so much. They accordingly passed through Congress the proposition for the fourteenth amendment, and they declined to treat as restored to their full participation in the Government of the Union the States which had been in insurrection until they ratified that article by a formal vote of their legislative bodies.

Before we proceed to examine more critically the provisions of this amendment, on which the plaintiffs in error rely, let us complete and dismiss the history of the recent amendments, as that history relates to the general purpose which pervades them all. A few years' experience satisfied the thoughtful men who had been the authors of the other two amendments that, notwithstanding the restraints of those articles on the States and the laws passed under the additional powers granted to Congress, these were inadequate for the protection of life, liberty, and property, without which freedom to the slave was no boon. They were in all those States denied the right of suffrage. The laws were administered by the white man alone. It was urged that a race of men distinctively marked as was the negro, living in the midst of another and dominant race, could never be fully secured in their person and their property without the right of suffrage.

Hence the fifteenth amendment, which declares that "the right of a citizen of the United States to vote shall not be denied or abridged by any state on account of race, color, or previous condition of servitude." The negro having, by the fourteenth amendment, been declared to be a citizen of the United states, is thus made a voter in every State of the Union.

We repeat, then, in the light of this recapitulation of events almost too recent to be called history, but which are familiar to us all, and on the most casual examination of the language of these amendments, no one can fail to be impressed with the one pervading purpose found in them all, lying at the foundation of each, and without which none of them would have been even suggested; we mean the freedom of the slave race, the security and firm establishment of that freedom and the protection of the newly-made freeman and citizen from the oppressions of those who had formerly exercised unlimited dominion over him. It is true that only the fifteenth amendment in terms mentions the negro by speaking of his color and his slavery. But it is just as true that each of the other articles was addressed to the grievances of that race, and designed to remedy them, as the fifteenth.

These amendments, one and all, are thus declared to have as their all-pervading design and end the security to the recently enslaved race, not only their nominal freedom, but their complete protection from those who had formerly exercised unlimited dominion over them. It is in this broad light that all these amendments must be read, the purpose to secure the perfect equality before the law of all citizens of the United states. What you give to one class you must give to all; what you deny to one class you shall deny to all, unless in the exercise of the common and universal police power of the state you find it needful to confer exclusive privileges on certain citizens, to be held and exercised still for the common good of all. . . .

Sir, it is scarcely twelve years since that gentleman [Alexander H. Stephens] shocked the civilized world by announcing the birth of a government which rested on human slavery as its corner-stone. The progress of events has swept away that *pseudo*-government which rested on greed, pride, and tyranny; and the race whom he then ruthlessly spurned and trampled on are here to meet him in debate, and to demand that the rights which are enjoyed by their former oppressors—who vainly sought to overthrow a Government which they could not prostitute to the base uses of slavery—shall be accorded to those who even in the darkness of slavery kept their allegiance true to freedom and the Union. Sir, the gentleman from Georgia has learned much since 1861; but he is still a laggard. Let him put away entirely the false and fatal theories which have so greatly marred an otherwise enviable record. Let him accept, in its fullness and beneficence, the great doctrine that American citizenship carries with it every civil and political right which manhood can confer. Let him lend his influence, with all his masterly ability, to complete the proud structure of legislation which makes his nation worthy of the great declaration which heralded its birth, and he will have done that which will most nearly redeem his reputation in the eyes of the world, and best vindicate the wisdom of that policy which has permitted him to regain his seat upon this floor.

To the diatribe of the gentleman from Virginia, [Mr. Harris,] who spoke on yesterday, and who so far transcended the limits of decency and propriety as to announce upon this floor that his remarks were addressed to white men alone, I shall have no word of reply. Let him feel that a negro was not only too magnanimous to smite him in his weakness, but was even charitable enough to grant him the mercy of his silence. [Laughter and applause on the floor and in the galleries.] I shall, sir, leave to others less charitable the unenviable and fatiguing task of sifting out of that mass of chaff the few grains of sense that may, perchance, deserve notice. Assuring the gentleman that the negro in this country aims at a higher degree of intellect than that exhibited by him in this debate, I cheerfully commend him to the commiseration of all intelligent men the world over—black men as well as white men.

Sir, equality before the law is now the broad, universal, glorious rule and mandate of the Republic. No State can violate that. Kentucky and Georgia may crowd their statute-books with retrograde and barbarous legislation; they may rejoice in the odious eminence of their consistent hostility to all the great steps of human progress which have marked our national history since slavery tore down the stars and stripes on Fort Sumter; but, if Congress shall do its duty, if Congress shall enforce the great guarantees which the Supreme Court has declared to be the one pervading purpose of all the recent amendments, then their unwise and unenlightened conduct will fall with the same weight upon the gentlemen from those States who now lend their influence to defeat this bill, as upon the poorest slave who once had no rights which the honorable gentlemen were bound to respect.

But, sir, not only does the decision in the Slaughter-house[1] cases contain nothing which suggests a doubt of the power of Congress to pass the pending bill, but it contains an express recognition and affirmance of such power. I quote now from page 81 of the volume:

> "Nor shall any State deny to any person within its jurisdiction the equal protection of the laws."
>   In the light of the history of these amendments, and the pervading purpose of them, which we have already discussed, it is not difficult to give a meaning to this

[1]When the city of New Orleans granted a monopoly to a slaughterhouse, other slaughterhouse companies sued that the monopoly was depriving them of their livelihood in violation of the 14th Amendment's due process of law clause. The Supreme Court ruled, in 1873, that the 14th Amendment was written to guarantee the rights of former slaves and did not apply to these companies' grievances. However, the court also affirmed that the amendment did not deny a state's right of jurisdiction over its citizens' civil rights.

clause. The existence of laws in the States where the newly emancipated negroes resided, which discriminated with gross injustice and hardship against them as a class, was the evil to be remedied by this clause, and by it such laws are forbidden.

If, however, the States did not conform their laws to its requirements, then, by the fifth section of the article of amendment, Congress was authorized to enforce it by suitable legislation. We doubt very much whether any action of a State not directed by way of discrimination against the negroes as a class, or on account of their race, will ever be held to come within the purview of this provision. It is so clearly a provision for that race and that emergency, that a strong case would be necessary for its application to any other. But as it is a State that is to be dealt with, and not alone the validity of its laws, we may safely leave that matter until Congress shall have exercised its power, or some case of State oppression, by denial of equal justice in its courts shall, have claimed a decision at our hands.

No language could convey a more complete assertion of the power of Congress over the subject embraced in the present bill than is here expressed. If the States do not conform to the requirements of this clause, if they continue to deny to any person within their jurisdiction the equal protection of the laws, or as the Supreme Court had said, "deny equal justice in its courts," then Congress is here said to have power to enforce the constitutional guarantee by appropriate legislation. That is the power which this bill now seeks to put in exercise. It proposes to enforce the constitutional guarantee against inequality and discrimination by appropriate legislation. It does not seek to confer new rights, nor to place rights conferred by State citizenship under the protection of the United States, but simply to prevent and forbid equality and discrimination on account of race, color, or previous condition of servitude. Never was there a bill more completely within the constitutional power of Congress. Never was there a bill which appealed for support more strongly to that sense of justice and fair-play which has been said, and in the main with justice, to be a characteristic of the Anglo-Saxon race. The Constitution warrants it; the Supreme Court sanctions it; justice demands it.

Sir, I have replied to the extent of my ability to the arguments which have been presented by the opponents of this measure. I have replied also to some of the legal propositions advanced by gentleman on the other side, and now that I am about to conclude, I am deeply sensible of the imperfect manner in which I have performed the task. Technically, this bill is to decide upon the civil status of the colored American citizen: a point disputed at the very formation of our present Government, when by a short-sighted policy, a policy repugnant to true republican government, one negro counted as three-fifths of a man. The logical result of this mistake of the framers of the Constitution strengthened the cancer of slavery, which finally spread its poisonous tentacles over the southern portion of the body-politic. To arrest its growth and save the nation we have passed through the harrowing operation of internecine war, dreaded at all times, resorted to at the last extremity, like the surgeon's knife, but absolutely necessary to extirpate the disease which threatened with the life of the nation the overthrow of civil and political liberty on this continent. In that dire extremity the members of the race which I have the honor in part to represent— the race which pleads for justice at your hands today, forgetful of their inhuman and brutalizing servitude at the South, their degradation and ostracism at the North—flew willingly and gallantly to the support of the national Government. Their sufferings, assistance, privations, and trials in the swamps and in the rice-fields, their valor on the land and on the sea, is a part of the ever-glorious record which makes up the history of a nation preserved, and might, should I urge the claim, incline you to respect and guarantee their rights and privileges as citizens of our common Republic. But I remember that valor, devotion, and loyalty are not always rewarded according to their just deserts, and that after the battle some who have borne the brunt of the fray may, through neglect or contempt, be assigned to a subordinate place, while the enemies in war may be preferred to the sufferers.

The results of the war, as seen in reconstruction, have settled forever the political status of my race. The passage of this bill will determine the civil status, not only of the negro, but of any other class of citizens who may feel themselves discriminated against. It will form the cap-stone of the temple of liberty, begun on this continent under discouraging circumstances, carried on in spite of the sneers of monarchists and the cavils of pretended friends of freedom, until at last it stands in all its beautiful symmetry and proportions, a building the grandest which the world has ever seen, realizing the most sanguine expectations and the highest hopes of those who, in the name of equal, impartial, and universal liberty, laid the foundation stones. . . .

WEB RESOURCES FOR PART ONE

SITES FEATURING A NUMBER OF THE DISSENTERS IN PART ONE:

Frederick Douglass

http://memory.loc.gov/ammem/doughtml/doughome.html

Susan B. Anthony

www.law.umkc.edu/faculty/projects/ftrials/anthony/sbahome.html
http://mep.cla.sc.edu/sa/sa-table.html
http://ecssba.rutgers.edu/

Robert B. Elliott

www.aaregistry.com/african_american_history/490/Robert_B_Elliott_a_talented_political_
force

OTHER DISSENTING VOICES OF THE TIME:

Ku Klux Klan

Although klansmen wanted to turn back the clock and prevent African Americans from attaining their rights, it is possible to consider the Ku Klux Klan as a dissenting organization. Though they were reactionary, members undoubtedly saw themselves as legitimate dissenters resisting the new reality of the postwar world. For information on the early Klan see:

www.pointsouth.com/csanet/kkk.htm
www.tngenweb.org/giles/afro-amer/history/kkk5.html

George Perkins Marsh

For information on this nineteenth-century environmentalist see:

http://bailey.uvm.edu/specialcollections/gpmorc.html

The 1872 Prohibition Party Platform

The Prohibition Party, as its name implies, sought to outlaw alcoholic beverages. Their platform can be found at this site.

www.prohibitionists.org/Background/background.html

PART TWO

Industry and Reform, 1877–1912

Emma Goldman speaking for birth control at Union Square, New York City, May 20, 1916. Goldman was an outspoken advocate of socialism, workers' rights, birth control, full equality of the sexes, and sexual liberation. "If the world is ever to give birth to true companionship and oneness," she once wrote, "not marriage, but love will be the parent." Her support of the Bolshevik revolution in Russia resulted in her arrest and deportation from the United States in 1919.

Introduction: Progress and Discontent

The Gilded Age was an era of unprecedented growth, a time of seemingly unlimited expansion of American business and industry. Huge fortunes were made by such skillful entrepreneurs as Andrew Carnegie and John D. Rockefeller as they expanded their companies into monopolies and trusts that seemed more powerful than the government in Washington. It was an age of innovation and mass marketing in which department stores, professional spectator sports like baseball, and inventions like the telephone, electric streetlights, the phonograph, the motion picture camera, electric trolleys, and subways significantly altered people's daily lives. The nation transformed rapidly from a primarily agrarian and rural society into an industrial and urban society.

Such rapid growth and prosperity, however, was not without serious problems. Workers were forced to exchange their labor for subsistence wages in grueling jobs in unsafe factories. A huge influx of immigrants from eastern and southern Europe flooded into ethnic enclaves in America's cities. Factory owners knew that this vast labor force meant that wages could remain at the subsistence level and that competition among workers would act as a brake on unionization efforts. Jay Gould purportedly boasted that he could easily persuade half the working class to kill the other half. The federal government, in spite of the glaring need to address innumerable complex problems, was unwilling to enact any legislation that would curb business growth.

English philosopher Herbert Spencer and Yale professor William Graham Sumner applied Darwin's theory of evolution to society by arguing that just as in nature, where only the fit survive, so, too, in the social order. The rich, according to these "social Darwinists," were stronger and fitter than their workers. Their proof was that they had, in the struggle for survival, emerged at the top as the owners of businesses; if the workers had been fit, they, too, would have risen. "Millionaires," Sumner confidently declared in *What the Social Classes Owe Each Other,* "are a product of natural selection." This, of course, provided perfect justification to the likes of Rockefeller, Carnegie, Vanderbilt, and Morgan. It meant that whatever their exploitive practices, and however harshly they took advantage of workers, they were thoroughly and "scientifically" justified. Spencer and Sumner argued that any kind of governmental intervention in the economy would, in effect, be going against science and evolution. The poor should not be helped, for in doing so the government would be encouraging the proliferation of the "unfit." "Taxing the wealthy," Sumner reasoned, "would be like killing your generals in time of war." This harsh philosophy underlay many of the congressional debates over proposed social legislation. It was also used to justify the dispossession of the Plains tribes and the conquest of the frontier by "fitter" Americans, to justify the implementation of Jim Crow laws and the emergence of segregation, and to justify imperialism. President Theodore Roosevelt insisted that industrial "civilized" nations had a duty to dominate the backward "uncivilized" nations by bestowing on them the benefits of Western culture and Christianity.

Throughout the era, workers' organizing efforts advanced by fits and starts. Although it lasted only six years, in 1869 the National Labor Union was founded. Also in 1869, the Knights of Labor came into being. Under Terence Powderly's leadership, it became an effective advocate of workers' interests but began to disintegrate in the aftermath of the Haymarket bombing. In May 1886 more than 350,000 workers, in order to force industrialists to consider their demand for an eight-hour workday, declared a general strike. During a rally at Chicago's Haymarket Square, while members of the Knights of Labor were addressing the protestors, the police moved in to disperse the crowd. Someone threw a bomb that killed eight policemen, and in the ensuing melee more than 70 people were injured. Eight anarchists were arrested, and the subsequent trial and executions derailed the labor movement. To most Americans, it seemed proof that unions would lead to anarchy and undermine American values. In the summer of 1892, workers at Carnegie's steel mill in Homestead, Pennsylvania, went on strike, but when Carnegie's partner Henry Clay Frick employed Pinkertons as strikebreakers, violence broke out. After 10 people were killed and more than 60 wounded, the strike was broken, and the effort to unionize the steel industry was set back more than 40 years.

Farmers, too, banded together to promote their interests. Based primarily in the Midwest and South, the Granges and the Alliances were cooperative societies that demanded the federal government reform the currency system through the free and unlimited coinage of silver, as well as regulate banks, insurance companies, railroads, and telegraph companies. In 1892, the Populist Party published a platform urging these reforms as well as women's suffrage and the direct election of senators. It nominated James B. Weaver for president, who astonished complacent Washington by winning more than a million votes.

Workers and farmers were not the only groups protesting against the hardships they faced. Minorities, especially Chinese immigrants on the West Coast, African Americans, and Indians, found that their rights were disregarded—even at times taken away. Ironically, the government treated these three minority groups in three entirely disparate ways: exclusion, assimilation, and separation. The Chinese Exclusion Act, passed in 1882, prohibited further Chinese immigration into the country and denied citizenship to those already living in the United States. The Dawes Act of 1887 was Washington's attempt to assimilate the Indian tribes into the American way of life by distributing land on the reservations to individuals and educating Native American children in such private academies as the Carlisle School in Pennsylvania, where they were immersed in white culture, and the English language and compelled to forget Indian ways. The literacy tests, poll taxes, and Jim Crow laws of the Southern states that prevented African Americans from enjoying the full rights of citizenship were officially validated in 1896 by the *Plessy v. Ferguson* decision, in which the Supreme Court ruled that providing "separate but equal" facilities for blacks was constitutional. Dozens of Chinese protested against policies that discriminated against them, usually unsuccessfully, by taking the government to court. Indians struggled against assimilation and frequently attempted to escape from the reservations. However, when a band of 340 Miniconjou Sioux under Big Foot fled the Pine Ridge Reservation in December 1890, the Seventh Cavalry (Custer's old command) intercepted them a few days after Christmas at Wounded Knee. When the Indians resisted the cavalry's attempt to disarm them, the soldiers returned fire with cannon and Gatling guns. Most of the 146 killed were women and children, and the survivors were forced back onto the reservation. Wounded Knee—designated a "battle" by whites and a "massacre" by Indians—marked the end of Indian resistance. W. E. B. DuBois demanded full and immediate equality for African Americans. He was one of the founders of the Niagara Movement (forerunner of the National Association for the Advancement of Colored People), which began an organized campaign to overturn the *Plessy* decision. African American journalist Ida B. Wells-Barnett campaigned for the federal government to enact and enforce antilynching laws.

Middle-class reformers also spoke out in response to the problems of industrialization. Brown University Professor Lester Frank Ward turned Spencer and Sumner's application of the theory of evolution on its head in a forceful attack on social Darwinism. Because humans have intelligence, Ward wrote in *Mind as a Social Factor,* we are capable of having an effect on natural selection. We can, through government, create economic and social legislation that will benefit the masses, and further the evolution of the human race. In contrast to Spencer's "survival of the fittest," Ward argued for making as many people as possible "fit to survive." The ideas of what became known as reform Darwinism became part of the intellectual underpinnings of many progressive reformers. Jane Addams initiated the settlement house movement. Walter Rauschenbusch, claiming that the elimination of suffering was a moral necessity, applied Christian principles to the everyday work of making life better for the downtrodden. This Social Gospel subsequently had a significant impact in the twentieth century, most notably on Martin Luther King Jr.'s tactics in the civil rights movement.

Alcohol consumption was one of the most popular forms of entertainment in nineteenth-century America. As a result alcoholism, unemployment, spousal abuse, poverty, and crime all came to be viewed as the results of "demon rum." The impetus for reform in the antebellum period gave birth to a temperance movement that grew throughout the century, becoming, by the last quarter of the century, a formidable force. Many women viewed it as a feminist issue equal in importance to women's suffrage. Women were tired of husbands who would come home from work on payday after a stopover at the local saloon, not only inebriated but also with their weekly salaries half-consumed. Many arguments ensued, many wives were beaten, and many men became alcoholics and lost their jobs, plunging their families into poverty. The Women's Christian Temperance Union, under the leadership of Frances Willard, led the fight against alcohol abuse. Temperance was a moral as well as a feminist issue, especially for millions of conservative rural Protestants, but this morality was tightly linked with nativism and xenophobia. As millions of immigrants flocked to the United States from eastern and southern Europe, many temperance advocates believed that prohibiting alcohol would somehow penalize and maybe even discourage immigration from these Roman Catholic, Eastern Orthodox, and Jewish areas.

The census report for 1890 revealed that, for the first time in American history, there was no discernible frontier line beyond which white settlement had not penetrated. By mid-decade, industrialists and politicians, fearing that American expansion had reached a limit that would lead to a severe contraction of economic growth, began to look abroad for markets and raw materials. In 1890 Navy Captain Alfred Thayer Mahan published a widely acclaimed book, *The Influence of Seapower upon History: 1660–1783*, in which he argued that all great empires in world history had controlled the seas. The United States, with a vast coastline on both the Atlantic and Pacific oceans, was in a position to become the dominant world power if the government would expand the navy, acquire overseas bases to furnish supplies for the fleet, and construct a canal through the Isthmus of Panama. Mahan's advice was heeded. The acquisition of Hawaii and Samoa and the Spanish American War of 1898 were the first steps to a new international outlook on the part of a nation that had long remained faithful to George Washington's counsel to avoid entangling itself in long-

term alliances and getting too involved with world affairs. By the turn of the century, the United States had acquired Guantanamo Bay in Cuba, as well as Guam, Puerto Rico, and the Philippine Islands. There was, however, widely based and passionate protest that such exercise of imperialist power so contradicted democratic principles that the United States was in danger of negating its own highly vaunted belief in "government of the people, by the people, and for the people."

Many writers and journalists embarked on intense efforts to expose—frequently with exaggeration and sensationalism—the evils of political corruption, worker exploitation, and conning of consumers. Muckrakers like Lincoln Steffens, Frank Norris, Ida M. Tarbell, and Upton Sinclair influenced local governments to pass regulatory legislation. Indeed, Sinclair's popular novel *The Jungle* persuaded President Theodore Roosevelt to initiate the legislation that created the Food and Drug Administration.

Terence Powderly (1849–1924)

As industrialization developed during the nineteenth century, American workers, in an effort to improve their lot, formed small craft unions. By 1866, many of these small unions had combined to form the National Labor Union (NLU). Although difficulties in maintaining solidarity among NLU members caused it to collapse within seven years, one of those who was influenced by the union movement was Terence Powderly. Believing that better wages and shorter hours would enable workers to live more satisfying lives and participate more fully in the American dream, Powderly joined the Knights of Labor in 1876. As he rose to a leadership position in this national union, Powderly realized that political power was one of the keys to workers' rights. With the support of labor, he was elected mayor of Scranton, Pennsylvania, in 1878 and began serving the first of three terms as a reformer. Also in 1878, he opened up the Knights of Labor, making it a more inclusive union, and helped formulate a new constitution for the organization.

What does the preamble to this document reveal about the plight of workers at the time? How accurate is the statement that "aggregated wealth . . . will inevitably lead to the pauperization and hopeless degradation of the toiling masses"? Are the workers' demands radical or excessive? Have these issues been addressed?

When workers around the country gathered at rallies, they often sang such songs as the one appended here, "Eight Hours," by I. G. Blanchard and Jesse Jones.

Preamble to the Constitution of the Knights of Labor, January 3, 1878

The recent alarming development and aggression of aggregated wealth, which, unless checked, will inevitably lead to the pauperization and hopeless degradation of the toiling masses, render it imperative, if we desire to enjoy the blessings of life, that a check should be placed upon its power and upon unjust accumulation, and a system adopted which will secure to the laborer the fruits of his toil; and as this much-desired object can only be accomplished by the thorough unification of labor, and the united efforts of those who obey the divine injunction that "In the sweat of thy brow shalt thou eat bread," we have formed the [Knights of Labor] with a view of securing the organization and direction, by co-operative effort, of the power of the

SOURCE: Terence V. Powderly, *Thirty Years of Labor, 1859 to 1889* (Philadelphia, 1890), 128–130.

industrial classes; and we submit to the world the objects sought to be accomplished by our organization, calling upon all who believe in securing "the greatest good to the greatest number" to aid and assist us:

I. To bring within the folds of organization every department of productive industry, making knowledge a standpoint for action, and industrial and moral worth, not wealth, the true standard of individual and national greatness.

II. To secure to the toilers a proper share of the wealth that they create; more of the leisure that rightfully belongs to them; more societary advantages; more of the benefits, privileges and emoluments of the world; in a word, all those rights and privileges necessary to make them capable of enjoying, appreciating, defending and perpetuating the blessings of good government.

III. To arrive at the true condition of the producing masses in their educational, moral and financial condition, by demanding from the various governments the establishment of Bureaus of Labor Statistics.

IV. The establishment of co-operative institutions, productive and distributive.

V. The reserving of the public lands—the heritage of the people—for the actual settler; not another acre for railroads or speculators.

VI. The abrogation of all laws that do not bear equally upon capital and labor, the removal of unjust technicalities, delays and discriminations in the administration of justice, and the adopting of measures providing for the health and safety of those engaged in mining, manufacturing or building pursuits.

VII. The enactment of laws to compel chartered corporations to pay their employe[e]s weekly, in full, for labor performed during the preceding week, in the lawful money of the country.

VIII. The enactment of laws giving mechanics and laborers a first lien on their work for their full wages.

IX. The abolishment of the contract system on national, State and municipal work.

X. The substitution of arbitration for strikes, whenever and wherever employers and employe[e]s are willing to meet on equitable grounds.

XI. The prohibition of the employment of children in workshops, mines and factories before attaining their fourteenth year.

XII. To abolish the system of letting out by contract the labor of convicts in our prisons and reformatory institutions.

XIII. To secure for both sexes equal pay for equal work.

XIV. The reduction of the hours of labor to eight per day, so that the laborers may have more time for social enjoyment and intellectual improvement, and be enabled to reap the advantages conferred by the labor-saving machinery which their brains have created.

XV. To prevail upon governments to establish a purely national circulating medium, based upon the faith and resources of the nation, and issued directly to the people, without the intervention of any system of banking corporations, which money shall be a legal tender in payment of all debts, public or private.

"Eight Hours," by I. G. Blanchard and Jesse Jones, 1880s

We mean to make things over,
We are tired of toil for naught
With but bare enough to live upon
And ne'er an hour for thought.
We want to feel the sunshine
And we want to smell the flow'rs
We are sure that God has willed it
And we mean to have eight hours;
We're summoning our forces
From the shipyard, shop and mill

Eight hours for work, eight hours for rest
Eight hours for what we will;
Eight hours for work, eight hours for rest
Eight hours for what we will.

The beasts that graze the hillside,
And the birds that wander free,
In the life that God has meted,
Have a better life than we.
Oh, hands and hearts are weary,
And homes are heavy with dole;
If our life's to be filled with drudg'ry,
What need of a human soul.
Shout, shout the lusty rally,
From shipyard, shop, and mill.

Eight hours for work, eight hours for rest
Eight hours for what we will;
Eight hours for work, eight hours for rest
Eight hours for what we will.

The voice of God within us
Is calling us to stand
Erect as is becoming
To the work of His right hand.
Should he, to whom the Maker
His glorious image gave,
The meanest of His creatures crouch,
A bread-and-butter slave?
Let the shout ring down the valleys
And echo from every hill.

Ye deem they're feeble voices
That are raised in labor's cause,

Source: Margaret Bradford Boni, ed., *The Fireside Book of Favorite American Songs* (New York: Simon and Shuster, 1952).

But bethink ye of the torrent,
And the wild tornado's laws.
We say not toil's uprising
In terror's shape will come,
Yet the world were wise to listen
To the monetary hum.
Soon, soon the deep toned rally
Shall all the nations thrill.

Eight hours for work, eight hours for rest
Eight hours for what we will;
Eight hours for work, eight hours for rest
Eight hours for what we will.

From factories and workshops
In long and weary lines,
From all the sweltering forges,
And from out the sunless mines,
Wherever toil is wasting
The force of life to live
There the bent and battered armies
Come to claim what God doth give
And the blazon on the banner
Doth with hope the nation fill:

Eight hours for work, eight hours for rest
Eight hours for what we will;
Eight hours for work, eight hours for rest
Eight hours for what we will.

Hurrah, hurrah for labor,
For it shall arise in might
It has filled the world with plenty,
It shall fill the world with light
Hurrah, hurrah for labor,
It is mustering all its powers
And shall march along to victory
With the banner of Eight Hours.
Shout, shout the echoing rally
Till all the welkin thrill.

Eight hours for work, eight hours for rest
Eight hours for what we will;
Eight hours for work, eight hours for rest
Eight hours for what we will.

Lyrics by I. G. Blanchard

Music by Rev. Jesse H. Jones

Chief Joseph (1840–1904)

Chief Joseph was the name whites gave Heinmot Tooyalaket (Thunder Coming from the Mountain), chief of the Nez Percé. The Nez Percé had given Lewis and Clark provisions when their expedition crossed the Continental Divide on its way to the Pacific in 1805, and the grateful explorers had promised them that the government in Washington would always be their friend. However, in 1877 the Nez Percé were told they had to leave their homes in the Wallowa Valley of eastern Oregon and settle on the Lapwai reservation in Idaho. They refused to go, and when the U.S. Army tried to force them, Chief Joseph led his tribe on an extraordinary journey of more than a thousand miles in an effort to escape to Canada. Finally overtaken 40 miles from the border, Joseph surrendered to Colonel Nelson B. Miles. "I am tired of fighting," Joseph reputedly said. "Our chiefs are killed. . . . It is cold and we have no blankets. The little children are freezing to death. My people—some of them have run away to the hills and have no blankets and no food. No one knows where they are—perhaps freezing to death. I want to have time to look for my children and see how many of them I can find. Maybe I shall find them among the dead. Hear me, my chiefs, my heart is sick and sad. From where the sun now stands I will fight no more forever." General Miles had promised Joseph that the tribe would be returned to Oregon, but instead they were sent to a reservation in Oklahoma. Within two years, many of the Nez Percé had died in the terribly unhealthy conditions of the reservation, and Chief Joseph went to Washington, where he made the following appeal to President Rutherford B. Hayes, members of his cabinet, and a number of congressmen. Eventually the Nez Percé were returned to the Pacific Northwest, but Joseph himself was sent to a separate reservation in Washington, where, in 1904, he died, it was commonly said, of a broken heart.

Why, according to Chief Joseph, have whites not been able to have peaceful relations with the Indians? What does he want from the federal government?

Appeal to the Hayes Administration, 1879

At last I was granted permission to come to Washington and bring my friend Yellow Bull and our interpreter with me. I am glad I came. I have shaken hands with a good many friends, but there are some things I want to know which no one seems able to explain. I cannot understand how the Government sends a man out to fight us, as it did General Miles, and then breaks his word. Such a government has something wrong about it. I cannot understand why so many chiefs are allowed to talk so many different ways, and promise so many different things. I have seen the Great Father Chief [Hayes] . . . and many other law chiefs, and they all say they are my friends,

SOURCE: *North American Review* 128 (April 1879), 431–432.

and that I shall have justice, but while all their mouths talk right I do not understand why nothing is done for my people.

I have heard talk and talk but nothing is done. Good words do not last long unless they amount to something. Words do not pay for my dead people. They do not pay for my country now overrun by white men. They do not protect my father's grave. They do not pay for my horses and cattle.

Good words do not give me back my children. Good words will not make good the promise of your war chief, General Miles. Good words will not give my people a home where they can live in peace and take care of themselves.

I am tired of talk that comes to nothing. It makes my heart sick when I remember all the good words and all the broken promises. There has been too much talking by men who had no right to talk. Too many misinterpretations have been made; too many misunderstandings have come up between the white men and the Indians.

If the white man wants to live in peace with the Indian he can live in peace. There need be no trouble. Treat all men alike. Give them the same laws. Give them all an even chance to live and grow. All men were made by the same Great Spirit Chief. They are all brothers. The earth is the mother of all people, and all people should have equal rights upon it. You might as well expect all rivers to run backward as that any man who was born a free man should be contented penned up and denied liberty to go where he pleases. If you tie a horse to a stake, do you expect he will grow fat? If you pen an Indian up on a small spot of earth and compel him to stay there, he will not be contented nor will he grow and prosper.

I have asked some of the Great White Chiefs where they get their authority to say to the Indian that he shall stay in one place, while he sees white men going where they please. They cannot tell me.

I only ask of the Government to be treated as all other men are treated. If I cannot go to my own home, let me have a home in a country where my people will not die so fast. I would like to go to Bitter Root Valley. There my people would be happy; where they are now they are dying. Three have died since I left my camp to come to Washington. When I think of our condition, my heart is heavy. I see men of my own race treated as outlaws and driven from country to country, or shot down like animals.

I know that my race must change. We cannot hold our own with the white men as we are. We only ask an even chance to live as other men live. We ask to be recognized as men. We ask that the same law shall work alike on all men. If an Indian breaks the law, punish him by the law. If a white man breaks the law, punish him also.

Let me be a free man—free to travel, free to stop, free to work, free to trade where I choose, free to choose my own teachers, free to follow the religion of my fathers, free to talk, think and act for myself—and I will obey every law or submit to the penalty.

Whenever the white man treats the Indian as they treat each other then we shall have no more wars. We shall be all alike—brothers of one father and mother, with one sky above us and one country around us and one government for all. Then the Great Spirit Chief who rules above will smile upon this land and send rain to wash out the bloody spots made by brothers' hands upon the face of the earth. For this time the Indian race is waiting and praying. I hope no more groans of wounded men and women will ever go to the ear of the Great Spirit Chief above, and that all people may be one people.

Emmeline Wells (1828–1921)

Emmeline Wells was a dedicated advocate of women's rights, as well as a believer in the Mormon practice of polygamy. Women were allowed to vote in Utah territory, but the federal government overturned the Utah law in 1887. Along with several other women, Wells then founded the Woman Suffrage Association of Utah, which fought to restore women's right to vote. The association was successful when, in 1896, Utah was admitted as a state with a women's suffrage clause written into its constitution. As editor of the Mormon magazine *The Woman's Exponent*, she published many articles throughout this campaign to champion women's rights and, to the consternation of many suffragists in the country, ardently defend polygamy. Congress, in 1882, had passed the Edmunds Law, which outlawed plural marriage. Many Mormons viewed this law as a federal attack on the Church of Jesus Christ of Latter-Day Saints. Wells passionately made a case in favor of the custom. To those who condemned plural marriage as equivalent to sexual bondage and therefore destructive of women's rights, Wells argued that the practice actually freed women from the conventional idea that female identity derived from a husband and therefore allowed women to have more freedom and play a more significant role in public life.

How did the practice of plural marriage originate? According to Emmeline Wells, why should the practice be permissible? Does polygamy subjugate or liberate women? Why would so many people object to this Mormon practice?

"Is It Ignorance?" 1883

It seems a very common thing with people unacquainted with the facts to say, it is the ignorance of "Mormon" women "that keeps them in bondage," that "makes them submit to plural marriage," when in truth the very contrary is the case. It is because of the intelligence they possess on subjects connected with their existence here and hereafter, as well as that of their posterity and kindred, the hopes entertained, and the actual knowledge concerning the future that causes them to embrace a doctrine so unpopular and so objectionable in the eyes of the world. Such paragraphs as the following and similar ones abound in the newspapers and journals of the day: "It was hoped by giving the women of Utah the ballot they would use it for the destruction of the monster, which keeps them under its iron heel, in hopeless misery." These people may be well meaning, but they talk nonsense and folly in the extreme. Who are the "Mormon" women, who accepted plural marriage when the principle was first revealed to the Prophet Joseph, and taught to a few of the people called Latter-day Saints?

Source: Emmeline Wells, "Is It Ignorance?" *The Woman's Exponent,* July 1, 1883.

They were just such sound, practical, intelligent women as the foremothers of New England and the women pioneers of those Eastern States. Women prepared to encounter hardships and privation, perils by land and sea for the sake of the religion in which they devoutly and implicitly believed. Aye, more! Determined not only to make the sacrifices incident to all those sufferings, but still further to prove their integrity to God by denying themselves that others might be benefited and exalted. Is not this an actual demonstration of that golden rule the Savior gave to his followers: "Do unto others as ye would they should do unto you." These noble women are like other good, pure, virtuous women, industrially, morally and intellectually. Religiously they are far above them in the graces which elevate and adorn human character. It is no wonder that contemplating these noble-minded women many are let to exclaim, "it is not possible that you are like us, for if you were you could not live in such relationships." To esteem others equally with yourself is necessary; to consider the rights and privileges of those with whom you are associated as is requisite in one great family. The women who entered into these sacred covenants of marriage for time and all eternity accepted this holy order as a divine revelation and commandment, and in all sincerity, with the purest motives obeyed the same. To be sure there has another generation grown up since the establishment of the principle of celestial marriage, but has America any reason to be ashamed of these young people? "By their fruits ye shall know them, said the Savior." Do they lack in natural intelligence, in physical strength or vigor, or in any particular? Have they not all the gifts and attributes that go to make up nobility of character in men and women? No one can say to the contrary and speak truthfully.

Speaking of the emigration from other countries, what difference is there here in Utah more than elsewhere? None, except it be that Mormons do more to assist foreign populations in becoming good citizens, and adapting themselves to the conditions of the country. They are taught more carefully and specifically in relation to the laws and government of the country. This is a result of the perfect and thorough organization of the Church itself, both with men and women; There is every opportunity of becoming enlightened on all general subjects. Mormon girls and women have as sensible ideas upon marriage as any people in the civilized world. They are thoroughly taught and instructed to consider well before accepting this sacred rite, and to choose wisely. More particularly are they cautioned in this regard, because, the covenants they make are not only for time, but reach into eternity. It is an important matter to make choice of a companion for this life, but how much more so does it become when the union is an eternal one. In order to investigate the "Mormon" question it is essentially necessary to know the people themselves, and not accept testimony of reporters, tourists and sensational writers nor yet of political demagogues, whose sole aim is to make capital by the votes of the Territory, and turn everything into the hands of their own party. "Mormon" people have rights under the Constitution, and they will seek to maintain them, women as well as men. If anyone supposes these same women citizens to be ignorant of the rights the ballot gives them, then they know very little about the women of this Territory, and our advice to them is, let the matter rest until you have an opportunity of solving the problem by thorough investigation, and not from one side, and remember the words of the Savior, "Judge not, lest ye be judged."

Mary Elizabeth Lease (1850–1933)

Mary Elizabeth Lease was a charismatic and eloquent political agitator who traveled the country in the 1890s to make stirring inflammatory speeches against the exploitation of farmers and workers by industrialists, bankers, and railroads. She was active in the leadership of the Farmers' Alliance, the Knights of Labor, and the Populist Party, as well as an ardent suffragist who urged women to be politically engaged in anticapitalist agitation. Although it is apparently only a legend that she urged farmers in her speeches to "raise less corn and more hell," she truly was a firebrand, as this speech at a Women's Christian Temperance Union (WCTU) convention attests.

Why would people view her as a hell-raiser? Why, according to Lease, should women commit themselves to political activism? Why were western women more active in the 1890s than women from other parts of the country?

Speech to the WCTU, 1890

Madame President and Fellow Citizens:—

If God were to give me my choice to live in any age of the world that has flown, or in any age of the world yet to be, I would say, O God, let me live here and now, in this day and age of the world's history.

For we are living in a grand and wonderful time—a time when old ideas, traditions and customs have broken loose from their moorings and are hopelessly adrift on the great shoreless, boundless sea of human thought—a time when the gray old world begins to dimly comprehend that there is no difference between the brain of an intelligent woman and the brain of an intelligent man; no difference between the soul-power or brainpower that nerved the arm of Charlotte Corday [the assassin of Jean-Paul Marat during the French Revolution] to deeds of heroic patriotism and the soul-power or brain-power that swayed old John Brown behind his death dealing barricade at Ossawattomie. We are living in an age of thought. The mighty dynamite of thought is upheaving the social and political structure and stirring the hearts of men from centre to circumference. Men, women and children are in commotion, discussing the mighty problems of the day. The agricultural classes, loyal and patriotic, slow to act and slow to think, are to-day thinking for themselves; and their thought has crystallized into action. Organization is the key-note to a mighty movement among the masses which is the protest of the patient burden-bearers of the nation against years of economic and political superstition. . . .

The movement among the masses today is an echo of the life of Jesus of Nazareth, an honest endeavor on the part of the people to put into practical operation the basic

---

SOURCE: Mary Elizabeth Lease, "Speech to the Woman's Christian Temperance Union," in Joan M. Jensen, *With These Hands: Women Working on the Land* (Old Westbury, NY: Feminist Press and McGraw-Hill Book Company, 1981), 154–160.

principles of Christianity: "Whatsoever ye would that men should do unto you, do ye even so unto them."

In an organization founded upon the eternal principles of truth and right, based upon the broad and philanthropic principle, "Injury to one is the concern of all," having for its motto, "Exact justice to all, special privileges to none,"—the farmers and laborers could not well exclude their mothers, wives and daughters, the patient burden bearers of the home, who had been their faithful companions, their tried friends and trusted counselors through long, weary years of poverty and toil. Hence the doors of the Farmers' Alliance were thrown open wide to the women of the land. They were invited into full membership, with all the privileges of promotion; actually recognized and treated as human beings. And not only the mothers, wives and daughters, but "the sisters, the cousins and the aunts," availed themselves of their newly offered liberties, till we find at the present time upward of a half-million women in the Alliance, who, because of their loyalty to home and loved ones and their intuitive and inherent sense of justice, are investigating the condition of the country, studying the great social, economic and political problems, fully realizing that the political arena is the only place where the mighty problems of to-day and tomorrow can be satisfactorily fought and settled, and amply qualified to go hand-in-hand with fathers, husbands, sons and brothers to the polls and register their opinion against legalized robbery and corporate wrong.

George Eliot tells us that "much that we are and have is due to the unhistoric acts of those who in life were ungarlanded and in death sleep in unvisited tombs." So to the women of the Alliance, who bravely trudged twice a week to the bleak country schoolhouse, literally burning midnight oil as they studied with their loved ones the economic and political problems, and helped them devise methods by which the shackels of industrial slavery might be broken, and the authors of the nation's liberties, the creators of the nation's wealth and greatness, might be made free and prosperous—to these women, unknown and uncrowned, belongs the honor of defeating for reelection to the United States Senate that man who for eighteen years has signally failed to represent his constituents, and who during that time has never once identified himself with any legislation for the oppressed and overburdened people.

Three years ago this man [John James] Ingalls [Republican Senator from Kansas] made a speech on woman suffrage at Abilene, Kan., in which he took occasion to speak in the most ignorant and vicious manner of women, declaring that "a woman could not and should not vote because she was a woman." Why? She was a woman, and that was enough; the subject was too delicate for further discussion.

But we treasured up these things in our hearts, and then his famous, or rather, infamous interview in a New York paper appeared, in which he declared that: "It is lawful to hire Hessians to kill, to mutilate, to destroy. Success is the object to be attained; the decalogue and the golden rule have no place in a political campaign; the world has outgrown its Christ and needs a new one." This man, said the law-abiding God fearing women, must no longer be permitted to misrepresent us. So we worked and waited for his defeat. And the cyclone, the political Johnstown, that overtook the enemies of the people's rights last November, proves what a mighty factor the women of the Alliance have been in the political affairs of the nation.

I overheard yesterday morning at the hotel breakfast table a conversation between two gentlemen in regard to Ingalls. "I consider his defeat," said the first speaker, "to be a national calamity." "Your reasons," said the second. "Why, he is such a brilliantly smart man," he replied. "True," said the other; "but he must needs be a smart man to be the consummate rascal he has proven himself to be." And I thought as I heard the remarks, "Our opinion is also shared by men." You wonder, perhaps, at the zeal and enthusiasm of the Western women in this reform movement. Let me tell you why they are interested. Turn to your old school-maps and books of a quarter of a century ago, and you will find that what is now the teeming and fruitful West was then known as the Treeless Plain, the Great American Desert. To this sterile and remote region, infested by savage beasts and still more savage men, the women of the New England States, the women of the cultured East, came with husbands, sons and brothers to help them build up a home upon the broad and vernal prairies of the West. We came with the roses of health on our cheek, the light of hope in our eyes, the fires of youth and hope burning in our hearts. We left the old familiar paths, the associations of home and the friends of childhood. We left schools and churches—all that made life dear—and turned our faces toward the setting sun. We endured hardships, dangers and privations; hours of loneliness, fear and sorrow; our little babes were born upon these wide, unsheltered prairies; and there, upon the sweeping prairies beneath the cedar trees our hands have planted to mark the sacred place, our little ones lie buried. We toiled in the cabin and in the field; we planted trees and orchards; we helped our loved ones to make the prairie blossom as the rose. The neat cottage took the place of the sod shanty, the log-cabin and the humble dug-out.

Yet, after all our years of toil and privation, dangers and hardships upon the Western frontier, monopoly is taking our homes from us by an infamous system of mortgage foreclosure, the most infamous that has ever disgraced the statutes of a civilized nation. It takes from us at the rate of five hundred a month the homes that represent the best years of our life, our toil, our hopes, our happiness. How did it happen? The government, at the bid of Wall Street, repudiated its contracts with the people; the circulating medium was contracted in the interest of Shylock from $54 per capita to less than $8 per capita; or, as Senator [Preston] Plumb [of Kansas] tells us, "Our debts were increased, while the means to pay them was decreased;" or as grand Senator [William Morris] Stewart [of Nevada] puts it, "For twenty years the market value of the dollar has gone up and the market value of labor has gone down, till today the American laborer, in bitterness and wrath, asks which is the worst—the black slavery that has gone or the white slavery that has come?"

Do you wonder the women are joining the Alliance? I wonder if there is a woman in all this broad land who can afford to stay out of the Alliance. Our loyal, white-ribbon women should be heart and hand in this Farmers' Alliance movement, for the men whom we have sent to represent us are the only men in the councils of this nation who have not been elected on a liquor platform; and I want to say here, with exultant pride, that the five farmer Congressmen and the United States Senator we have sent up from Kansas—the liquor traffic, Wall Street, "nor the gates of hell shall not prevail against them."

It would sound boastful were I to detail to you the active, earnest part the Kansas women took in the recent campaign. A Republican majority of 82,000 was reduced to less than 8,000 when we elected 97 representatives, 5 out of 7 Congressmen, and a United States Senator, for to the women of Kansas belongs the credit of defeating John J. Ingalls; he is feeling badly about it yet, too, for he said today that "women and Indians were the only class that would scalp a dead man." I rejoice that he realises that he is politically dead.

I might weary you to tell you in detail how the Alliance women found time from cares of home and children to prepare the tempting, generous viands for the Alliance picnic dinners; where hungry thousands and tens of thousands gathered in the forests and groves to listen to the words of impassioned oratory, ofttimes from woman's lips, that nerved the men of Kansas to forget their party prejudice and vote for "Mollie and the babies." And not only did they find their way to the voters' hearts, through their stomachs, but they sang their way as well. I hold here a book of Alliance songs, composed and set to music by an Alliance woman, Mrs. Florence Olmstead of Butler County, Kan., that did much toward moulding public sentiment. Alliance Glee Clubs composed of women, gave us such stirring melodies as the nation has not heard since the Tippecanoe and Tyler campaign of 1840. And while I am individualizing, let me call your attention to a book written also by an Alliance woman. I wish a copy of it could be placed in the hands of every woman in this land. "The Fate of a Fool" is written by Mrs. Emma G. Curtis of Colorado. This book in the hands of women would teach them to be just and generous toward women, and help them to forgive and condone in each other the sins so sweetly forgiven when committed by men.

Let no one for a moment believe that this uprising and federation of the people is but a passing episode in politics. It is a religious as well as a political movement, for we seek to put into practical operation the teachings and precepts of Jesus of Nazareth. We seek to enact justice and equity between man and man. We seek to bring the nation back to the constitutional liberties guaranteed us by our forefathers. The voice that is coming up today from the mystic chords of the American heart is the same voice that Lincoln heard blending with the guns of Fort Sumter and the Wilderness, and it is breaking into a clarion cry today that will be heard around the world.

Crowns will fall, thrones will tremble, kingdoms will disappear, the divine right of kings and the divine right of capital will fade away like the mists of the morning when the Angel of Liberty shall kindle the fires of justice in the hearts of men. "Exact justice to all, special privileges to none." No more millionaires, and no more paupers; no more gold kings, silver kings and oil kings, and no more little waifs of humanity starving for a crust of bread. No more gaunt faced, hollow-eyed girls in the factories, and no more little boys reared in poverty and crime for the penitentiaries and the gallows. But we shall have the golden age of which Isaiah sang and the prophets have so long foretold; when the farmers shall be prosperous and happy, dwelling under their own vine and fig tree; when the laborer shall have that for which he toils; when occupancy and use shall be the only title to land, and every one shall obey the divine injunction, "In the sweat of thy face shalt thou eat bread." When men shall be just and generous, little less than gods, and women shall be just and charitable toward each other, little less than angels; when we shall have not a government of the people by capitalists, but a government of the people, by the people. . . .

The People's Party, 1892

During the 1880s and 1890s, thousands of small midwestern and southern farmers formed cooperative organizations like the Grange and the Farmers' Alliance as a united front to combat the excesses of big business and demand that the federal government overcome its unwillingness to regulate industrialists, railroads, bankers, and processors. By 1892, their discontent and frustration had led them to form a new political party—the People's Party. In July they convened in Omaha, Nebraska, nominated James B. Weaver for president, and issued the Omaha Platform, in which they proclaimed their grievances and demands as well as their solidarity with exploited industrial workers. Dubbed the Populist Party by the press, their ardent campaign for Weaver made the Populists the most successful third party in the nation up to that time. Weaver received more than a million votes in the November election and won four states with 22 electoral votes, forcing Republicans and Democrats to take notice.

How radical are the planks in the Omaha Platform? Are the Populist demands reasonable or unreasonable? Which ones have been attained? Which ones have not? Were the Populists advocating socialism?

The Omaha Platform, July 1892

Assembled upon the 116th anniversary of the Declaration of Independence, the People's Party of America, in their first national convention, invoking upon their action the blessing of Almighty God, put forth in the name and on behalf of the people of this country, the following preamble and declaration of principles:

PREAMBLE

The conditions which surround us best justify our cooperation; we meet in the midst of a nation brought to the verge of moral, political, and material ruin. Corruption dominates the ballot-box, the Legislatures, the Congress, and touches even the ermine of the bench. The people are demoralized; most of the States have been compelled to isolate the voters at the polling places to prevent universal intimidation and bribery. The newspapers are largely subsidized or muzzled, public opinion silenced, business prostrated, homes covered with mortgages, labor impoverished, and the land concentrating in the hands of capitalists. The urban workmen are denied the right to organize for self-protection, imported pauperized labor beats down their wages, a hireling standing army, unrecognized by our laws, is established to shoot them down, and they are rapidly degenerating into European conditions. The fruits of the toil of millions are badly stolen to build up colossal fortunes for a

SOURCE: "People's Party Platform," *Omaha Morning World-Herald,* July 5, 1892.

few, unprecedented in the history of mankind; and the possessors of these, in turn, despise the Republic and endanger liberty. From the same prolific womb of governmental injustice we breed the two great classes—tramps and millionaires.

The national power to create money is appropriated to enrich bond-holders; a vast public debt payable in legal-tender currency has been funded into gold-bearing bonds, thereby adding millions to the burdens of the people. Silver, which has been accepted as coin since the dawn of history, has been demonetized to add to the purchasing power of gold by decreasing the value of all forms of property as well as human labor, and the supply of currency is purposely abridged to fatten usurers, bankrupt enterprise, and enslave industry. A vast conspiracy against mankind has been organized on two continents, and it is rapidly taking possession of the world. If not met and overthrown at once it forebodes terrible social convulsions, the destruction of civilization, or the establishment of an absolute despotism.

We have witnessed for more than a quarter of a century the struggles of the two great political parties for power and plunder, while grievous wrongs have been inflicted upon the suffering people. We charge that the controlling influences dominating both these parties have permitted the existing dreadful conditions to develop without serious effort to prevent or restrain them. Neither do they now promise us any substantial reform. They have agreed together to ignore, in the coming campaign, every issue but one. They propose to drown the outcries of a plundered people with the uproar of a sham battle over the tariff, so that capitalists, corporations, national banks, rings, trusts, watered stock, the demonetization of silver and the oppressions of the usurers may all be lost sight of. They propose to sacrifice our homes, lives, and children on the altar of mammon; to destroy the multitude in order to secure corruption funds from the millionaires.

Assembled on the anniversary of the birthday of the nation, and filled with the spirit of the grand general and chief who established our independence, we seek to restore the government of the Republic to the hands of "the plain people," with which class it originated. We assert our purposes to be identical with the purposes of the National Constitution; "to form a more perfect union and establish justice, insure domestic tranquillity, provide for the common defense, promote the general welfare, and secure the blessings of liberty for ourselves and our posterity." We declare that this republic can only endure as a free government while built upon the love to the whole people for each other and for the nation; that it cannot be pinned together by bayonets; that the civil war is over, and that every passion and resentment which grew out of it must die with it; and that we must be in fact, as we are in name, one united brotherhood of freemen.

Our country finds itself confronted by conditions for which there is not precedent in the history of the world; our annual agricultural productions amount to billions of dollars in value, which must, within a few weeks or months, be exchanged for billions of dollars' worth of commodities consumed in their production; the existing currency supply is wholly inadequate to make this exchange; the results are falling prices, the formation of combines and rings, the impoverishment of the producing class. We pledge ourselves that if given power we will labor to correct these evils by wise and reasonable legislation, in accordance with the terms of our platform. We believe that the power of government—in other words, of the people—should be expanded (as in the case of the postal service) as rapidly and as far as the good sense of an intelligent people and the teaching of experience shall justify, to the end that oppression, injustice, and poverty shall eventually cease in the land. . . .

PLATFORM

We declare, therefore—

First.—That the union of the labor forces of the United States this day consummated shall be permanent and perpetual; may its spirit enter into all hearts for the salvation of the republic and the uplifting of mankind!

Second.—Wealth belongs to him who creates it, and every dollar taken from industry without an equivalent is robbery. "If any will not work, neither shall he eat." The interests of rural and civil labor are the same; their enemies are identical.

Third.—We believe that the time has come when the railroad corporations will either own the people or the people must own the railroads; and should the government enter upon the work of owning and managing all railroads, we should favor an amendment to the constitution by which all persons engaged in the government service shall be placed under a civil-service regulation of the most rigid character, so as to prevent the increase of the power of the national administration by the use of such additional government employees.

FIRST, *Money*—We demand a national currency, safe, sound, and flexible issued by the general government only, a full legal tender for all debts, public and private, and that without the use of banking corporations; a just, equitable, and efficient means of distribution direct to the people, at a tax not to exceed 2 per cent, per annum, to be provided as set forth in the sub-treasury plan of the Farmers' Alliance, or a better system; also by payments in discharge of its obligations for public improvements.

(a) We demand free and unlimited coinage of silver and gold at the present legal ratio of 16 to 1.

(b) We demand that the amount of circulating medium be speedily increased to not less than $50 per capita.

(c) We demand a graduated income tax.

(d) We believe that the money of the country should be kept as much as possible in the hands of the people, and hence we demand that all State and national revenues shall be limited to the necessary expenses of the government, economically and honestly administered.

(e) We demand that postal savings banks be established by the government for the safe deposit of the earnings of the people and to facilitate exchange.

SECOND, *Transportation*—Transportation being a means of exchange and a public necessity, the government should own and operate the railroads in the interest of the people.

(a) The telegraph and telephone, like the post-office system, being a necessity for the transmission of news, should be owned and operated by the government in the interest of the people.

THIRD, *Land*—The land, including all the natural sources of wealth, is the heritage of the people, and should not be monopolized for speculative purposes, and alien ownership of land should be prohibited. All land now held by railroads and other corporations in excess of their actual needs, and all lands now owned by aliens should be reclaimed by the government and held for actual settlers only.

EXPRESSIONS OF SENTIMENTS

Your Committee on Platform and Resolutions beg leave unanimously to report the following: Whereas, Other questions have been presented for our consideration, we hereby submit the following, not as a part of the Platform of the People's Party, but as resolutions expressive of the sentiment of this Convention.

RESOLVED, That we demand a free ballot and a fair count in all elections and pledge ourselves to secure it to every legal voter without Federal Intervention, through the adoption by the States of the unperverted Australian or secret ballot system.

RESOLVED, That the revenue derived from a graduated income tax should be applied to the reduction of the burden of taxation now levied upon the domestic industries of this country.

RESOLVED, That we pledge our support to fair and liberal pensions to ex-Union soldiers and sailors.

RESOLVED, That we condemn the fallacy of protecting American labor under the present system, which opens our ports to the pauper and criminal classes of the world and crowds out our wage-earners; and we denounce the present ineffective laws against contract labor, and demand the further restriction of undesirable emigration.

RESOLVED, That we cordially sympathize with the efforts of organized working-men to shorten the hours of labor, and demand a rigid enforcement of the existing eight-hour law on Government work, and ask that a penalty clause be added to the said law.

RESOLVED, That we regard the maintenance of a large standing army of mercenaries, known as the Pinkerton system, as a menace to our liberties, and we demand its abolition. . . .

RESOLVED, That we commend to the favorable consideration of the people and the reform press the legislative system known as the initiative and referendum.

RESOLVED, That we favor a constitutional provision limiting the office of President and Vice-President to one term, and providing for the election of Senators of the United States by a direct vote of the people.

RESOLVED, That we oppose any subsidy or national aid to any private corporation for any purpose.

RESOLVED, That this convention sympathizes with the Knights of Labor and their righteous contest with the tyrannical combine of clothing manufacturers of

Rochester, and declare it to be a duty of all who hate tyranny and oppression to refuse to purchase the goods made by the said manufacturers, or to patronize any merchants who sell such goods.

Jane Addams (1860–1935)

In 1889, Jane Addams founded Hull House in Chicago. Hull House was part of the settlement house movement, which provided a place for immigrant women and children to stay while they were trying to adapt to life in the United States. Settlement houses offered English and hygiene lessons, after-school programs for children, and often training in job skills, like sewing and bookbinding. Addams, like many other reformers of her time, believed that philanthropic endeavors, such as Hull House, would ease immigrants into American life and therefore serve as a counterbalance to radical or anarchistic tendencies. Hull House was founded only three years after the Haymarket Riots frightened many middle-class Americans into believing that the influx of foreigners would inevitably lead to violent revolution. Lightening the burdens and hardships immigrants faced would give them reason to believe that they could become part of American society. Reform defuses revolution.

Addams, of course, was not only operating from this conservative view to thwart radical tendencies; she truly believed in helping people for purely humanitarian purposes. Places like Hull House also provided job opportunities for many women, and these reform-minded women later became significant players in the suffrage movement. Jane Addams herself was involved in both the women's suffrage and early civil rights movements. She was one of the cofounders of the National Association for the Advancement of Colored People (NAACP). In 1931, she was awarded the Nobel Peace Prize.

The following excerpts are from an address Jane Addams delivered in 1892 that was later published in her book *Twenty Years at Hull House*. What is the purpose of Hull House? Why does she mention the "Hallelujah Chorus" in her speech?

The Subjective Necessity of Social Settlements, 1892

In a thousand voices singing the Hallelujah Chorus in Handel's "Messiah," it is possible to distinguish the leading voices, but the differences of training and cultivation between them and the voices of the chorus, are lost in the unity of purpose and in the

SOURCE: Jane Addams, *Twenty Years at Hull House* (New York: Macmillan, 1910), 99–100.

fact that they are all human voices lifted by a high motive. This is a weak illustration of what a Settlement attempts to do. It aims, in a measure, to develop whatever of social life its neighborhood may afford, to focus and give form to that life, to bring to bear upon it the results of cultivation and training; but it receives in exchange for the music of isolated voices the volume and strength of the chorus. It is quite impossible for me to say in what proportion or degree the subjective necessity which led to the opening of Hull-House combined the three trends: first, the desire to interpret democracy in social terms; secondly, the impulse beating at the very source of our lives, urging us to aid in the race progress; and; thirdly, the Christian movement toward humanitarianism. . . .

The Settlement then, is an experimental effort to aid in the solution of the social and industrial problems which are engendered by the modern conditions of life in a great city. It insists that these problems are not confined to any one portion of a city. It is an attempt to relieve, at the same time, the overaccumulation at one end of society and the destitution at the other; but it assumes that this overaccumulation and destitution is most sorely felt in the things that pertain to social and educational privileges. From its very nature it can stand for no political or social propaganda. It must, in a sense, give the warm welcome of an inn to all such propaganda, if perchance one of them be found an angel. The only thing to be dreaded in the Settlement is that it lose its flexibility, its power of quick adaptation, its readiness to change its methods as its environment may demand. It must be open to conviction and must have a deep and abiding sense of tolerance. It must be hospitable and ready for experiment. It should demand from its residents a scientific patience in the accumulation of facts and the steady holding of their sympathies as one of the best instruments for that accumulation. It must be grounded in a philosophy whose foundation is on the solidarity of the human race, a philosophy which will not waver when the race happens to be represented by a drunken woman or an idiot boy. Its residents must be emptied of all conceit of opinion and all self-assertion, and ready to arouse and interpret the public opinion of their neighborhood. They must be content to live quietly side by side with their neighbors, until they grow into a sense of relationship and mutual interests. Their neighbors are held apart by differences of race and language which the residents can more easily overcome. They are bound to see the needs of their neighborhood as a whole, to furnish data for legislation, and to use their influence to secure it. In short, residents are pledged to devote themselves to the duties of good citizenship and to the arousing of the social energies which too largely lie dormant in every neighborhood given over to industrialism. They are bound to regard the entire life of their city as organic, to make an effort to unify it, and to protest against its over-differentiation.

It is always easy to make all philosophy point one particular moral and all history adorn one particular tale; but I may be forgiven the reminder that the best speculative philosophy sets forth the solidarity of the human race; that the highest moralists have taught that without the advance and improvement of the whole, no man can hope for any lasting improvement in his own moral or material individual condition; and that the subjective necessity for Social Settlements is therefore identical with that necessity, which urges us on toward social and individual salvation.

Frances E. Willard (1839–1898)

After graduating from Northwestern Female College in 1859, Frances E. Willard taught for several years, traveled abroad, and eventually was offered the presidency of Evanston College for Ladies. When the college was absorbed by Northwestern University, Willard became dean of women. In 1874, however, she gave up her academic career to devote herself to the temperance crusade. As corresponding secretary for the Woman's Christian Temperance Union (WCTU), she became increasingly radical, eventually splitting with the organization's first president, Annie Wittenmeyr, over the issue of women's suffrage. Against Wittenmeyr's opposition, Willard argued that other reforms, especially women's suffrage, should be linked to the temperance issue and therefore be a central plank in the WCTU's platform. By 1879, her political struggle with Wittenmeyr ended triumphantly for Willard, when she was elected the organization's second president. In 1883, Willard founded the World's Woman's Christian Temperance Union, which was the first international women's organization. She also was one of the founders of the Prohibition Party and the National Council of Women. She served as the latter's first president from 1888 to 1890. Her attempt in 1892 to form a coalition with the Populist Party failed, however. Through persistent mobilization, political activism, lobbying of Congress, and political pressure on senators and other influential politicians, the WCTU was eventually instrumental in the passage and ratification in 1919 of the Eighteenth Amendment, which prohibited the sale of alcohol in the United States as of January 1, 1920. The Twenty-first Amendment, in 1933, repealed prohibition.

Willard's motto, "Do everything," which she refers to in this excerpt from her 1893 presidential address to the WCTU, reflects her belief that all reforms were interrelated. Throughout her activist career, she was as ardent an advocate of women's suffrage, equal pay for equal work, and other reforms as she was a champion of temperance. According to Willard, why is it necessary to fight the evils of alcohol? Why are gambling halls, the press, and politicians also to be regarded as targets by the WCTU? Why is prohibition a feminist issue?

Speech to the World's Woman's Christian Temperance Union, 1893

Beloved Comrades of the White Ribbon Army:

When we began the delicate, difficult, and dangerous operation of dissecting out the alcohol nerve from the body politic, we did not realize the intricacy of the undertaking

---

SOURCE: Frances E. Willard, in *Women's Speeches Around the World,* "Gifts of Speech," Sweet Briar College, retrieved 3/14/2003 from http://gos.sbc.edu/.

nor the distances that must be traversed by the scalpel of investigation and research. In about seventy days from now, twenty years will have elapsed since the call of battle sounded its bugle note among the homes and hearts of Hillsboro, Ohio. We have all been refreshing our knowledge of those days by reading the "Crusade Sketches" of its heroic leader, Mrs. Eliza J. Thompson, "the mother of us all," and we know that but one thought, sentiment and purpose animated those saintly "Praying Bands" whose name will never die out from human history. "Brothers, we beg you not to drink and not to sell!" This was the one wailing note of these moral Paganinis, playing on one string. It caught the universal ear and set the key of that mighty orchestra, organised with so much toil and hardship, in which the tender and exalted strain of the Crusade violin still soars aloft, but upborne now by the clanging cornets of science, the deep trombones of legislation, and the thunderous drums of politics and parties. The "Do-Everything-Policy" was not of our choosing, but is an evolution as inevitable as any traced by the naturalist or described by the historian. Woman's genius for details, and her patient steadfastness in following the enemies of those she loves "through every lane of life," have led her to antagonise the alcohol habit and the liquor traffic just where they are, wherever that may be. If she does this, since they are everywhere, her policy will be "Do Everything."

A one-sided movement makes one-sided advocates. Virtues, like hounds, hunt in packs. Total abstinence is not the crucial virtue in life that excuses financial crookedness, defamation of character, or habits of impurity. The fact that one's father was, and one's self is, a bright and shining light in the total abstinence galaxy, does not give one a vantage ground for high-handed behaviour toward those who have not been trained to the special virtue that forms the central idea of the Temperance Movement. We have known persons who, because they had "never touched a drop of liquor," set themselves up as if they belonged to a royal line, but whose tongues were as biting as alcohol itself, and whose narrowness had no competitor save a straight line. An all-round movement can only be carried forward by all-round advocates; a scientific age requires the study of every subject in its correlations. It was once supposed that light, heat, and electricity were wholly separate entities; it is now believed and practically proved that they are but different modes of motion. Standing in the valley we look up and think we see an isolated mountain; climbing to its top we see that it is but one member of a range of mountains many of them of well-nigh equal altitude. . . .

Joseph Cook, that devoted friend of every good cause has wisely said: "If England were at war with Russia, and the latter were to have several allies, it would obviously be necessary for England to attack the allies as well as the principal enemy. Not to do this would be foolishness, and might be suicide. In the conflict with the liquor traffic, the policy of the W.C.T.U. is to attack not only the chief foe, but also its notorious and open allies. This is the course dictated not only by common sense, but by absolute necessity. If the home is to be protected, not only must the dram-shop be made an outlaw, but its allies, the gambling hells, the houses of unreportable infamy, the ignorance of the general population as to alcoholics and other narcotics, the timidity of trade, the venality of portions of the press, and especially the subserviency of political parties to the liquor traffic, must be assailed as confederates of the chief enemy of the home. . . . It is certain that the broad and progressive policy of the W.C.T.U. in the United States makes the whiskey rings and time-serving politicians greatly dread its influence. They honour the Union by frequent and bitter attacks. It is a recognised power in international affairs. If its policy were made narrow and non-partisan, its influence would immensely wane in practical matters of great importance. . . .

Let us not be disconcerted, but stand bravely by that blessed trinity of movements, Prohibition, Woman's Liberation and Labour's uplift.

Everything is not in the Temperance Reform, but the Temperance Reform should be in everything.

There is no better motto for the "Do-Everything-Policy," than this which we are saying by our deeds: "Make a chain, for the land is full of bloody crimes and the city of violence."

If we can remember this simple rule, it will do much to unravel the mystery of the much controverted "Do-Everything-Policy," viz: that every question of practical philanthropy or reform has its temperance aspect, and with that we are to deal. . . .

The Temperance cause started out . . . alone, but mighty forces have joined us in the long march. We are now in the midst of the Waterloo battle, and in the providence of God the Temperance army will not have to fight that out all by itself. For Science has come up with its glittering contingent, political economy deploys its legions, the woman question brings an Amazonian army upon the field, and the stout ranks of labor stretch away far as the eye can reach. As in the old Waterloo against Napoleon, so now against the Napoleon of the liquor traffic, no force is adequate except the allied forces. . . .

The three requisites for success are ability, availability, and responsibility. The first is native, the second acquired, the last conferred. In every White Ribboner, whose work is worth the name, these three must meet, and the greatest outcome of the crusade in its original and organic form was that it gave to women of ability the schooling in which they acquired availability, and helped them to the positions in which, through responsibility, they grew from what they were to what they had the power to be. . . .

The history of the reformer, whether man or woman, on any line of action is but this: when he sees it all alone he is a fanatic; when a good many see it with him they are enthusiasts; when all see it he is a hero. The gradations are as clearly marked by which he ascends from zero to hero, as the lines of latitude from the North Pole to the Equator. . . .

Concerning the Temperance Movement in our land and throughout the world to-day, the pessimist says—and says truly— "There was never so much liquor manufactured in any one year since time began as in the year 1893, and as a consequence never did so much liquor flow down the people's throats as in this same year of grace." "But," says the optimist, "There is each year a larger acreage from which the brewer and distiller may gather the golden grain and luscious fruits, there are more people to imbibe the exhilarating poison; but, per contra, there was never so much intelligent thinking in any one year as to the drink delusion, there were never so many children studying in the schools the laws written in their members, there were never such gatherings together of temperance people to consult on the two great questions what to do and what not to do as in this year; there was never such a volume of experience and expert testimony and knowledge so varied, so complete, as we have had this year at the International Congress; there were never so many total abstainers in proportion to the population, never so many intelligent people who could render a reason scientific, ethical, aesthetic, for their total abstinence faith as now; there were never so many pulpits from which to bombard the liquor traffic and the drink habit; there were never so many journalists who had a friendly word to say for the Temperance Reform; there was never such a stirring up of temperance politics; for the foremost historic nation of the world, Great Britain, has this year, for the first time, adopted as a plank in the platform of the dominant party the principle that the people shall themselves decide whether or not they want the public house; and as a natural consequence of this political action there was never a public sentiment so respectful toward the Temperance Reform. The great world-brain is becoming saturated with the idea that it is reasonable and kind to let strong drink alone. The vastness of these changes can only be measured by the remembrance that a few generations ago these same drinks were the accredited emblems in cot and palace alike, of hospitality, kindness, and good-will.

So far as the White Ribbon movement is concerned, this has been its best and brightest year from the outlook of the World's W.C.T.U., and that is the only point of view that is adequate. How little did they dream, those devoted women of the praying bands, who with their patient footsteps bridged the distance between home and saloon, and in their little despised groups poured out their souls to God, and their pitiful plea into the ears of men, that the "Movement" would be systematized twenty years later into an organization known and loved by the best men and women in every civilized nation on the earth; and that its heroic missionaries would be obliged to circumnavigate the globe in order to visit the outposts of the Society. How little did they dream that in the year of the World's Columbian Exposition well nigh half a million of children would send their autographs on the triple pledge cards of our Loyal Temperance Legions, and Sunday School Department; that we should have a publishing house, owned and conducted by the Society itself, from which more than a hundred million pages of the literature of light and leading should go forth this year; how little could they have conceived of the significance that is wrapt up in the lengthening folds of the Polyglot Petition, signed and circulated in fifty languages, and containing the signatures and attestations of between three and four million of the best people that live, praying for the abolition of the alcohol traffic, the opium traffic, and the licensed traffic in degraded women. How little they dreamed of that great movement by which the study of physiology and hygiene were to bring the arrest of thought to millions of young minds concerning the true inwardness of all narcotic poisons in their effects on the body and the brain. How "far beyond their thought" the enfranchisement of women in New Zealand and Wyoming, Kansas and "Michigan, my Michigan!" How inconceivable to them the vision of our House Beautiful reared in the heart of the world's most electric city, and sending forth its influence to the furthest corner of the globe. How little did they dream that the echo of their hymns should yet be heard and heeded by a woman whose lineage, and the prowess of whose historic name may be traced through centuries, and that not alone from the cottage and the homestead, but from the emblazoned walls of splendid castles, should be driven the cup that seems to cheer, but at the last inebriates. But we must remember that, after all, these are but the days of small beginnings compared with what 20 more years shall show. Doubtless if we could see the power to which this movement of women's hearts for the protection of their hearthstones shall attain in the next generation, the inspiration of that knowledge would exhilarate us beyond that which is good for such steady patient workers as we have been, are, and wish to be; but I dare prophesy that twenty years from now woman will be fully panoplied in the politics and government of all English-speaking nations; she will find her glad footsteps impeded by no artificial barriers, but whatever she can do well she will be free to do in the enlightened age of worship, helpfulness and brotherhood, toward which we move with steps accelerated far beyond our ken. The momentum of the centuries is in the widening, deepening current of 19th century reform; the 20th century's dawn shall witness our compensations and reprisals, and as these increase humanity shall pay back into the mother-heart of woman its unmeasured penitence and unfathomed regret for all that she has missed (and through her, every son and daughter that she has brought into the world), by reason of the awful mistake by which, in the age of force, man substituted his "thus far and no farther," in place of the "thus far and no farther" of God; one founded in a selfish and ignorant view of woman's powers, the other giving her what every sentient being ought to have—a fair field and a free course to run and be glorified.

The Prohibition agitation in America has not been as great in the past year as formerly, and the reasons are not far to seek. A presidential campaign always lowers the moral atmosphere for a year before it begins and a year after it is over. Legislators become timid, politicians proceed to "hedge," journalists, with an eye to the loaves and fishes, furl their sails concerning issues that have at best only a fighting chance; the world, the flesh, and the devil get their innings, and the time is not yet. In the past year the attention of the nation has been focused on the World's Fair and the endless difficulties to which that has given birth. There has been an incalculable amount of ill-will set in motion as the result of personal financial interest and ignoble ambition. All this savours not the things of God or of humanity. The re-adjustment of political parties is still inchoate; men's hearts are failing them for fear; leaders in the traditional party of moral ideas have thrown off all disguises and grounded any weapons of rebellion they may once have lifted against the liquor traffic. The financial panic has riveted the attention of the public on their own dangers and disasters, and the spirit of money-making has lamentably invaded the ranks of the temperance army itself; but prohibition is as lively an issue to-day as emancipation was in 1856; an issue that stirs such deadly hatred is by no means dead. It is still quick with fighting blood, and its enemies know this even better than its friends. . . .

The economic view of prohibition is one that appeals to the largest number of our people, and none will deny that more and more they are separating into two camps, the industrious and thrifty favouring prohibition, the idle and spendthrift class opposing it. This is no doubt the most helpful report that can be made upon the present situation. The general drift, or as a great statesman in England has said, "The flowing tide's with us." Those who let strong drink alone must always be the most forceful and in the long run successful and potential portion of the country. Our fathers were as good as we, but they took no stand against the drink habit or the liquor traffic. There is hardly a woman here upon the side-board of whose grandfather's home would not have been found a decanter if not a demijohn. The same influences that have brought us out of the passive into the active voice may be trusted steadily to swell the number of recruits who shall join their intelligence, energy, talents, and sobriety with ours. The Temperance cause has everything to gain and nothing to lose from free discussion, from experimental study of its results, whether physical or financial, moral or mercantile, ethical or aesthetic. . . .

A Bill has been for many years before Congress for the appointment of a commission on the investigation of the liquor traffic. . . . The vast importance of this measure is demonstrated by the ceaseless efforts of the whiskey power to defeat its passage, in which they have thus far been successful, and are likely to be for many years to come. The power of the saloon is nowhere more conspicuously manifested than in the annual defeat of this great measure. Congress has appointed commissions on well-nigh every conceivable subject,—the investigation of the slums of our cities, of sweating establishments, of agricultural interests, of farm mortgages, of immigration, quarantine, railroads, monetary problems, cattle diseases, fisheries, and I know not what besides; but to investigate the liquor monopoly is to touch the very ark of the covenant with hell, and agreement with damnation to which the American people has been sworn by their political leaders. In spite of all this, we have gained an intelligent idea of the business from the internal revenue reports and from state and police records; but what we want is the attestation of the national government to the truth of these figures of perdition. If Congress persists in its refusal, why shall not the W.C.T.U. make a sweeping, and thorough investigation of the liquor traffic? Undoubtedly the political machinery of state and nation would place all possible obstacles in our way; but we have a personnel in every community throughout the republic, than which none that exists is more intelligent and devoted. Such a commission would be absolutely reliable so far as information could be obtained, and unless Congress in creating such a commission would agree to place upon it two or three prohibitionists or White Ribbon women the returns would be unreliable; for no politicians of the two leading parties would dare to weaken their great stronghold—the saloon. . . .

Mrs. Frances Belford of Denver, Colorado, has tabulated the following suggestive specifications. . . .

COMMISSION TO INVESTIGATE THE LIQUOR TRAFFIC

In relation:

to Crime.
to Divorce.
to Education.
to Alms houses.
to Asylums.
to Charitable Institutions and organized Charities.
to Adulteration.
to Society or the status of social drinking.
to Police expenses.

to Revenue—Municipal, State, Nation.

to Disease—Heredity. Acquired.

to Attitude of the Church by denomination.

to Number of Professors of Religion who are actual Prohibitionists.

to Number who are not.

to Statistics of homes ruined.

to Children at work who ought to be in school, where whiskey is the direct cause of absence.

to Mortgages.

to Number of women impoverished and self-supporting.

to Ownership of Property by professed Christians, who lease it for saloon and other immoral purposes.

to Hindrances to Prohibition.

to Home Missions.

to Sunday Schools.

Booker T. Washington (1856–1915)

Booker T. Washington was one of the leading spokesmen for African Americans in the late nineteenth and early twentieth centuries. Born a slave, Washington believed deeply in the indispensable importance of education for the advancement of freedmen. In 1881, he became the first principal of the Normal School for Negroes in Tuskegee, Alabama. Over the next several years, as Washington presided over the transformation of this school into the Tuskegee Institute, he became one of the most influential voices promoting African American education.

Washington believed, however, that blacks should not seek education for education's sake, and that they should not bother learning Latin, Greek, philosophy, or other esoteric subjects. Rather, they should concern themselves with technical education, so that they could become more productive members of society and enter occupations that would advance them economically. The Tuskegee Institute emphasized mechanics and agricultural economics—subjects that were practical.

In his famous "Atlanta Compromise" speech of 1895 at the Cotton States Exposition, Washington urged blacks to accept the Jim Crow laws and acquiesce in segregation, and he urged whites to encourage black economic opportunity. This would be the surest path to achieving equality in the United States. By concentrating on economic betterment, the former slaves would rise up the ladder to such a degree that whites would eventually bestow political and civil rights upon them. "No race that has anything to contribute to the markets of the world is long in any degree ostracized." This pragmatic, compliant philosophy endeared him to whites but also earned him the opprobrium of many of his African American contemporaries. Black leaders such as Ida B. Wells-Barnett and W. E. B. DuBois, concerned with white racism and the rise in lynchings, believed that Washington's accommodationist philosophy made things worse.

Was Booker T. Washington's stance more likely to create racial harmony or racial discord? How realistic are his recommendations? As blacks improved themselves economically, do you suppose whites would accept them as equals? Is Washington an "Uncle Tom" accommodationist, or is his a subtle, shrewd way to achieve equality?

Cast Down Your Bucket Where You Are, 1895

. . . . One-third of the population of the South is of the Negro race. No enterprise seeking the material, civil, or moral welfare of this section can disregard this element of our population and reach the highest success. I but convey to you, Mr. President and Directors, the sentiment of the masses of my race when I say that in no way have the value and manhood of the American Negro been more fittingly and generously recognized than by the managers of this magnificent Exposition at every stage of its progress. It is a recognition that will do more to cement the friendship of the two races than any occurrence since the dawn of our freedom.

Not only this, but the opportunity here afforded will awaken among us a new era of industrial progress. Ignorant and inexperienced, it is not strange that in the first years of our new life we began at the top instead of at the bottom; that a seat in Congress or the state legislature was more sought than real estate or industrial skill; that the political convention or stump speaking had more attractions than starting a dairy farm or truck garden.

A ship lost at sea for many days suddenly sighted a friendly vessel. From the mast of the unfortunate vessel was seen a signal, "Water, water; we die of thirst!" The answer from the friendly vessel at once came back, "Cast down your bucket where you are." A second time the signal, "Water, water; send us water!" ran up from the distressed vessel, and was answered, "Cast down your bucket where you are." And a third and fourth signal for water was answered, "Cast down your bucket where you are." The captain of the distressed vessel, at last heeding the injunction, cast down his bucket, and it came up full of fresh, sparkling water from the mouth of the Amazon River. To those of my race who depend on bettering their condition in a foreign land or who underestimate the importance of cultivating friendly relations with the Southern white man, who is their next-door neighbor, I would say: "Cast down your bucket where you are"— cast it down in making friends in every manly way of the people of all races by whom we are surrounded.

SOURCE: Louis R. Harlan, ed., *The Booker T. Washington Papers*, vol. 3 (Urbana: University of Illinois Press, 1974), 583–587.

Cast it down in agriculture, mechanics, in commerce, in domestic service, and in the professions. And in this connection it is well to bear in mind that whatever other sins the South may be called to bear, when it comes to business, pure and simple, it is in the South that the Negro is given a man's chance in the commercial world, and in nothing is this Exposition more eloquent than in emphasizing this chance. Our greatest danger is that in the great leap from slavery to freedom we may overlook the fact that the masses of us are to live by the productions of our hands, and fail to keep in mind that we shall prosper in proportion as we learn to dignify and glorify common labour, and put brains and skill into the common occupations of life; shall prosper in proportion as we learn to draw the line between the superficial and the substantial, the ornamental gewgaws of life and the useful. No race can prosper till it learns that there is as much dignity in tilling a field as in writing a poem. It is at the bottom of life we must begin, and not at the top. Nor should we permit our grievances to overshadow our opportunities.

To those of the white race who look to the incoming of those of foreign birth and strange tongue and habits for the prosperity of the South, were I permitted I would repeat what I say to my own race, "Cast down your bucket where you are." Cast it down among the eight millions of Negroes whose habits you know, whose fidelity and love you have tested in days when to have proved treacherous meant the ruin of your firesides. Cast down your bucket among these people who have, without strikes and labour wars, tilled your fields, cleared your forests, built your railroads and cities, and brought forth treasures from the bowels of the earth, and helped make possible this magnificent representation of the progress of the South. Casting down your bucket among my people, helping and encouraging them as you are doing on these grounds, and to education of head, hand, and heart, you will find that they will buy your surplus land, make blossom the waste places in your fields, and run your factories. While doing this, you can be sure in the future, as in the past, that you and your families will be surrounded by the most patient, faithful, law-abiding, and unresentful people that the world has seen. As we have proved our loyalty to you in the past, in nursing your children, watching by the sick-bed of your mothers and fathers, and often following them with tear-dimmed eyes to their graves, so in the future, in our humble way, we shall stand by you with a devotion that no foreigner can approach, ready to lay down our lives, if need be, in defense of yours, interlacing our industrial, commercial, civil, and religious life with yours in a way that shall make the interests of both races one. In all things that are purely social we can be as separate as the fingers, yet one as the hand in all things essential to mutual progress. . . .

The wisest among my race understand that the agitation of questions of social equality is the extremest folly, and that progress in the enjoyment of all the privileges that will come to us must be the result of severe and constant struggle rather than of artificial forcing. No race that has anything to contribute to the markets of the world is long in any degree ostracized. It is important and right that all privileges of the law be ours, but it is vastly more important that we be prepared for the exercise of these privileges. The opportunity to earn a dollar in a factory just now is worth infinitely more than the opportunity to spend a dollar in an opera-house.

In conclusion, may I repeat that nothing in thirty years has given us more hope and encouragement, and drawn us so near to you of the white race, as this opportunity offered by the Exposition; and here bending, as it were, over the altar that represents the results of the struggles of your race and mine, both starting practically empty-handed three decades ago, I pledge that in your effort to work out the great and intricate problem which God has laid at the doors of the South, you shall have at all times the patient, sympathetic help of my race; only let this be constantly in mind, that, while from representations in these buildings of the product of field, of forest, of mine, of factory, letters, and art, much good will come, yet far above and beyond material benefits will be that higher good, that, let us pray God, will come, in a blotting out of sectional differences and racial animosities and suspicions, in a determination to administer absolute justice, in a willing obedience among all classes to the mandates of law. This, coupled with our material prosperity, will bring into our beloved South a new heaven and a new earth.

W. E. B. DuBois (1868–1963)

The first African American to earn a PhD from Harvard, W. E. B. DuBois was one of the most influential figures in the fight for African American rights. Throughout his long life, DuBois fought incessantly against racism and passionately argued that blacks should demand full and immediate political, social, and civil rights. He was a harsh critic of Booker T. Washington's accommodationist philosophy and was instrumental in the founding of the Niagara Movement, out of which the National Association for the Advancement of Colored People (NAACP) was formed in 1909. In his 1903 book, *The Souls of Black Folk*, DuBois called on the "talented tenth" of African Americans not to settle for anything less than a full academic education and to demand what is theirs by right. For 25 years, DuBois was the editor-in-chief of the NAACP publication *The Crisis*, in which his stinging editorials frequently caused division within the organization. DuBois had no objections to whites being active members of the NAACP, but he believed they should be in subordinate, not leadership, roles. As time went by, DuBois felt increasingly alienated in the United States, and toward the end of his life he moved to Ghana, became a Ghanaian citizen, and joined the Communist Party. He died on the eve of the March on Washington in August 1963, and as news of his death spread amid the marchers gathering at the Lincoln Memorial to listen to Martin Luther King Jr.'s "I Have A Dream" speech, there was a sense that the "torch had been passed."

Why, according to DuBois in the first selection, is Washington's philosophy detrimental to African Americans? Is DuBois's view that blacks should opt for a higher academic education more realistic than Washington's belief that they should seek only to develop practical occupational skills? How would white America greet the demands in his "Address to the Niagara Congress?" Have these demands been realized in the United States?

"Of Mr. Booker T. Washington and Others," 1903

. . . . Easily the most striking thing in the history of the American Negro since 1876 is the ascendancy of Mr. Booker T. Washington. It began at the time when war memories and ideals were rapidly passing; a day of astonishing commercial development was dawning; a sense of doubt and hesitation overtook the freedmen's sons,—then it was that his leading began. Mr. Washington came, with a single definite programme, at the psychological moment when the nation was a little ashamed of having bestowed so much sentiment on Negroes, and was concentrating its energies on Dollars. His programme of industrial education, conciliation of the South, and submission and silence as to civil and political rights, was not wholly original; the Free Negroes from 1830 up to wartime had striven to build industrial schools, and the American Missionary Association had from the first taught various trades; and Price and others had sought a way of honorable alliance with the best of the Southerners. But Mr. Washington first indissolubly linked these things; he put enthusiasm, unlimited energy, and perfect faith into this programme, and changed it from a by-path into a veritable Way of Life. And the tale of the methods by which he did this is a fascinating study of human life.

It startled the nation to hear a Negro advocating such a programme after many decades of bitter complaint; it startled and won the applause of the South, it interested and won the admiration of the North; and after a confused murmur of protest, it silenced if it did not convert the Negroes themselves.

To gain the sympathy and cooperation of the various elements comprising the white South was Mr. Washington's first task; and this, at the time Tuskegee was founded, seemed, for a black man, well-nigh impossible. And yet ten years later it was done in the word spoken at Atlanta: "In all things purely social we can be as separate as the five fingers, and yet one as the hand in all things essential to mutual progress." This "Atlanta Compromise" is by all odds the most notable thing in Mr. Washington's career. The South interpreted it in different ways: the radicals received it as a complete surrender of the demand for civil and political equality; the conservatives, as a generously conceived working basis for mutual understanding. So both approved it, and today its author is certainly the most distinguished Southerner since Jefferson Davis, and the one with the largest personal following.

Next to this achievement comes Mr. Washington's work in gaining place and consideration in the North. Others less shrewd and tactful had formerly essayed to sit on these two stools and had fallen between them; but as Mr. Washington knew the heart of the South from birth and training, so by singular insight he intuitively grasped the spirit of the age which was dominating the North. And so thoroughly did he learn the speech and thought of triumphant commercialism, and the ideals of material prosperity that the picture of a lone black boy poring over a French grammar amid the weeds and dirt of a neglected home soon seemed to him the acme of absurdities. One wonders what Socrates and St. Francis of Assisi would say to this.

SOURCE: W. E. B. DuBois, *The Souls of Black Folk*, ed. David W. B light and Robert Gooding-Williams (Boston: Bedford, 1977), 62–72.

And yet this very singleness of vision and thorough oneness with his age is a mark of the successful man. It is as though Nature must needs make men narrow in order to give them force. So Mr. Washington's cult has gained unquestioning followers, his work has wonderfully prospered, his friends are legion, and his enemies are confounded. To-day he stands as the one recognized spokesman of his ten million fellows, and one of the most notable figures in a nation of seventy millions. One hesitates, therefore, to criticise a life which, beginning with so little has done so much. And yet the time is come when one may speak in all sincerity and utter courtesy of the mistakes and shortcomings of Mr. Washington's career, as well as of his triumphs, without being thought captious or envious, and without forgetting that it is easier to do ill than well in the world. . . .

Among his own people . . . Mr. Washington has encountered the strongest and most lasting opposition, amounting at times to bitterness, and even to-day continuing strong and insistent even though largely silenced in outward expression by the public opinion of the nation. Some of this opposition is, of course, mere envy; the disappointment of displaced demagogues and the spite of narrow minds. But aside from this, there is among educated and thoughtful colored men in all parts of the land a feeling of deep regret, sorrow, and apprehension at the wide currency and ascendancy which some of Mr. Washington's theories have gained. These same men admire his sincerity of purpose, and are willing to forgive much to honest endeavor which is doing something worth the doing. They cooperate with Mr. Washington as far as they conscientiously can; and, indeed, it is no ordinary tribute to this man's tact and power that, steering as he must between so many diverse interests and opinions, he so largely retains the respect of all.

But the hushing of the criticism of honest opponents is a dangerous thing. It leads some of the best of the critics to unfortunate silence and paralysis of effort, and others to burst into speech so passionately and intemperately as to lose listeners. Honest and earnest criticism from those whose interests are most nearly touched,—criticism of writers by readers, of government by those governed, of leaders by those led, —this is the soul of democracy and the safeguard of modern society. If the best of the American Negroes receive by outer pressure a leader whom they had not recognized before, manifestly there is here a certain palpable gain. Yet there is also irreparable loss,—a loss of that peculiarly valuable education which a group receives when by search and criticism it finds and commissions its own leaders. The way in which this is done is at once the most elementary and the nicest problem of social growth. History is but the record of such group-leadership; and yet how infinitely changeful is its type and character! And of all types and kinds, what can be more instructive than the leadership of a group within a group?—that curious double movement where real progress may be negative and actual advance be relative retrogression. All this is the social student's inspiration and despair.

Now in the past the American Negro has had instructive experience in the choosing of group leaders, founding thus a peculiar dynasty which in the light of present conditions is worth while studying. When sticks and stones and beasts form the sole environment of a people, their attitude is largely one of determined opposition to and conquest of natural forces. But when to earth and brute is added an environment of men and ideas, then the attitude of the imprisoned group may take three main forms,—a feeling of revolt and revenge; an attempt to adjust all thought and action to the will of the greater group; or, finally, a determined effort at self-realization and self-development despite environing opinion. The influence of all of these attitudes at various times can be traced in the history of the American Negro, and in the evolution of his successive leaders.

Before 1750, while the fire of African freedom still burned in the veins of the slaves, there was in all leadership or attempted leadership but the one motive of revolt and revenge,—typified in the terrible Maroons, the Danish blacks, and Cato of Stono, and veiling all the Americas in fear of insurrection. The liberalizing tendencies of the latter half of the eighteenth century brought, along with kindlier relations between black and white, thoughts of ultimate adjustment and assimilation. Such aspiration was especially voiced in the earnest songs of Phyllis [Wheatley], in the martyrdom of Attucks, the fighting of Salem and Poor, the intellectual accomplishments of Banneker and Derham, and the political demands of the Cuffes.

Stern financial and social stress after the war cooled much of the previous humanitarian ardor. The disappointment and impatience of the Negroes at the persistence of slavery and serfdom voiced itself in two movements. The slaves in the South, aroused undoubtedly by vague rumors of the Haitian revolt, made three fierce attempts at insurrection,—in 1800 under Gabriel in Virginia, in 1822 under Vesey in Carolina, and in 1831 again in Virginia under the terrible Nat Turner. In the Free States, on the other hand, a new and curious attempt at self-development was made. In Philadelphia and New York color-prescription led to a withdrawal of Negro communicants from white churches and the formation of a peculiar socio-religious institution among the Negroes known as the African Church,—an organization still living and controlling in its various branches over a million of men.

Walker's wild appeal against the trend of the times showed how the world was changing after the coming of the cotton-gin. By 1830 slavery seemed hopelessly fastened on the South, and the slaves thoroughly cowed into submission. The free Negroes of the North, inspired by the mulatto immigrants from the West Indies, began to change the basis of their demands; they recognized the slavery of slaves, but insisted that they themselves were freemen, and sought assimilation and amalgamation with the nation on the same terms with other men. Thus, Forten and Purvis of Philadelphia, Shad of Wilmington, Du Bois of New Haven, Barbadoes of Boston, and others, strove singly and together as men, they said, not as slaves; as "people of color," not as "Negroes." The trend of the times, however, refused them recognition save in individual and exceptional cases, considered them as one with all the despised blacks, and they soon found themselves striving to keep even the rights they formerly had of voting and working and moving as freemen. Schemers of migration and colonization arose among them; but these they refused to entertain, and they eventually turned to the Abolition movement as a final refuge.

Here, led by Remond, Nell, Wells-Brown, and Douglass, a new period of self-assertion and self-development dawned. To be sure, ultimate freedom and assimilation was the ideal before the leaders, but the assertion of the manhood rights of the Negro by himself was the main reliance, and John Brown's raid was the extreme of its logic. After the war and emancipation, the great form of Frederick Douglass, the greatest of American Negro leaders, still led the host. Self-assertion, especially in political lines, was the main programme, and behind Douglass came Elliot, Bruce, and Langston, and the Reconstruction politicians, and, less conspicuous but of greater social significance Alexander Crummell and Bishop Daniel Payne.

Then came the Revolution of 1876, the suppression of the Negro votes, the changing and shifting of ideals, and the seeking of new lights in the great night. Douglass, in his old age, still bravely stood for the ideals of his early manhood,— ultimate assimilation through self-assertion, and no other terms. For a time Price arose as a new leader, destined, it seemed, not to give up, but to re-state the old ideals in a form less repugnant to the white South. But he passed away in his prime. Then came the new leader. Nearly all the former ones had become leaders by the silent suffrage of their fellows, had sought to lead their own people alone, and were usually, save Douglass, little known outside their race. But Booker T. Washington arose as essentially the leader not of one race but of two,—a compromiser between the South, the North, and the Negro. Naturally the Negroes resented, at first bitterly, signs of compromise which surrendered their civil and political rights, even though this was to be exchanged for larger chances of economic development. The rich and dominating North, however, was not only weary of the race problem, but was investing largely in Southern enterprises, and welcomed any method of peaceful cooperation. Thus, by national opinion, the Negroes began to recognize Mr. Washington's leadership; and the voice of criticism was hushed.

Mr. Washington represents in Negro thought the old attitude of adjustment and submission; but adjustment at such a peculiar time as to make his programme unique. This is an age of unusual economic development, and Mr. Washington's programme naturally takes an economic cast, becoming a gospel of Work and Money to such an extent as apparently almost completely to overshadow the higher aims of life. Moreover, this is an age when the more advanced races are coming in closer contact with the less developed races, and the race-feeling is therefore intensified; and Mr. Washington's programme practically accepts the alleged inferiority of the Negro races. Again, in our own land, the reaction from the sentiment of war time has given impetus to race-prejudice against Negroes, and Mr. Washington withdraws many of the high demands of Negroes as men and American citizens. In other periods of intensified prejudice all the Negro's tendency to self-assertion has been called forth; at this period a policy of submission is advocated. In the history of nearly all other races and peoples the doctrine preached at such crises has been that manly self-respect is worth more than lands and houses, and that a people who voluntarily surrender such respect, or cease striving for it, are not worth civilizing.

In answer to this, it has been claimed that the Negro can survive only through submission. Mr. Washington distinctly asks that black people give up, at least for the present, three things,—

First, political power,
Second, insistence on civil rights,
Third, higher education of Negro youth,

—and concentrate all their energies on industrial education, the accumulation of wealth, and the conciliation of the South. This policy has been courageously and insistently advocated for over fifteen years, and has been triumphant for perhaps ten years. As a result of this tender of the palm-branch, what has been the return? In these years there have occurred:

1. The disfranchisement of the Negro.
2. The legal creation of a distinct status of civil inferiority for the Negro.
3. The steady withdrawal of aid from institutions for the higher training of the Negro.

These movements are not, to be sure, direct results of Mr. Washington's teachings; but his propaganda has, without a shadow of doubt, helped their speedier accomplishment. The question then comes: Is it possible, and probable, that nine millions of men can make effective progress in economic lines if they are deprived of political rights, made a servile caste, and allowed only the most meagre chance for developing their exceptional men? If history and reason give any distinct answer to these questions, it is an emphatic No. And Mr. Washington thus faces the triple paradox of his career:

1. He is striving nobly to make Negro artisans business men and property-owners; but it is utterly impossible, under modern competitive methods, for workingmen and property-owners to defend their rights and exist without the right of suffrage.

2. He insists on thrift and self-respect, but at the same time counsels a silent submission to civic inferiority such as is bound to sap the manhood of any race in the long run.

3. He advocates common-school and industrial training, and depreciates institutions of higher learning; but neither the Negro common-schools, nor Tuskegee itself, could remain open a day were it not for teachers trained in Negro colleges, or trained by their graduates.

This triple paradox in Mr. Washington's position is the object of criticism by two classes of colored Americans. One class is spiritually descended from Toussaint the Savior, through Gabriel, Vesey, and Turner, and they represent the attitude of revolt and revenge; they hate the white South blindly and distrust the white race generally, and so far as they agree on definite action, think that the Negro's only hope lies in emigration beyond the borders of the United States. And yet, by the irony of fate, nothing has more effectually made this programme seem hopeless than the recent course of the United States toward weaker and darker peoples in the West Indies, Hawaii, and the Philippines,—for where in the world may we go and be safe from lying and brute Force?

The other class of Negroes who cannot agree with Mr. Washington has hitherto said little aloud. They deprecate the sight of scattered counsels, of internal disagreement; and especially they dislike making their just criticism of a useful and earnest man an excuse for a general discharge of venom from small-minded opponents. Nevertheless, the questions involved are so fundamental and serious that it is difficult to see how men like the Grimkes, Kelly Miller, J. W. E. Bowen, and other representatives of this group, can much longer be silent. Such men feel in conscience bound to ask of this nation three things.

1. The right to vote.
2. Civic equality.
3. The education of youth according to ability.

They acknowledge Mr. Washington's invaluable service in counselling patience and courtesy in such demands; they do not ask that ignorant black men vote when ignorant whites are debarred, or that any reasonable restrictions in the suffrage should not be applied; they know that the low social level or the mass of the race is responsible for much discrimination against it, but they also know, and the nation knows, that relentless color-prejudice is more often a cause than a result of the Negro's degradation; they seek the abatement of this relic or barbarism, and not its systematic encouragement and pampering by all agencies of social power from the Associated Press to the Church of Christ. They advocate, with Mr. Washington, a broad system of Negro common schools supplemented by thorough industrial training; but they are surprised that a man of Mr. Washington's insight cannot see that no such educational system ever has rested or can rest on any other basis than that of the well-equipped college and university, and they insist that there is a demand for a few such institutions throughout the South to train the best of the Negro youth as teachers, professional men, and leaders.

This group of men honor Mr. Washington for his attitude of conciliation toward the white South; they accept the "Atlanta Compromise" in its broadest interpretation; they recognize, with him, many signs of promise, many men of high purpose and fair judgment, in this section; they know that no easy task has been laid upon a region already tottering under heavy burdens. But, nevertheless, they insist that the way to truth and right lies in straightforward honesty, not in indiscriminate flattery; in praising those of the South who do well and criticising uncompromisingly those who do ill; in taking advantage of the opportunities at hand and urging their fellows to do the same, but at the same time in remembering that only a firm adherence to their higher ideals and aspirations will ever keep those ideals within the realm of possibility. They do not expect that the free right to vote, to enjoy civic rights, and to be educated, will come in a moment; they do not expect to see the bias and prejudices of years disappear at the blast of a trumpet; but they are absolutely certain that the way for a people to gain their reasonable rights is not by voluntarily throwing them away and insisting that they do not want them; that the way for a people to gain respect is not by continually belittling and ridiculing themselves; that, on the contrary, Negroes must insist continually, in season and out of season, that voting is necessary to modern manhood, that color discrimination is barbarism, and that black boys need education as well as white boys.

In failing thus to state plainly and unequivocally the legitimate demands of their people, even at the cost of opposing an honored leader, the thinking classes of American Negroes would shirk a heavy responsibility,—a responsibility to themselves, a responsibility to the struggling masses, a responsibility to the darker races of men whose future depends so largely on this American experiment, but especially a responsibility to this nation,—this common Fatherland. It is wrong to encourage a man or a people in evil-doing; it is wrong to aid and abet a national crime simply because it is unpopular not to do so. The growing spirit of kindliness and reconciliation between the North and South after the frightful difference of a generation ago ought to be a source of deep congratulation to all, and especially to those whose mistreatment caused the war; but if that reconciliation is to be marked by the industrial slavery and civic death of those same black men, with permanent legislation into a position of inferiority, then those black men, if they are really men, are called upon by every consideration of patriotism and loyalty to oppose such a course by all civilized methods, even though such opposition involves disagreement with Mr. Booker T. Washington. We have no right to sit silently by while the inevitable seeds are sown for a harvest of disaster to our children, black and white.

First, it is the duty of black men to judge the South discriminatingly. The present generation of Southerners are not responsible for the past, and they should not be blindly hated or blamed for it. Furthermore, to no class is the indiscriminate endorsement of the recent course of the South toward Negroes more nauseating than to the best thought of the South. The South is not "solid"; it is a land in the ferment of social change, wherein forces of all kinds are fighting for supremacy; and to praise the ill the South is to-day perpetrating is just as wrong as to condemn the good. Discriminating and broad-minded criticism is what the South needs,—needs it for the sake of her own white sons and daughters, and for the insurance of robust, healthy mental and moral development.

To-day even the attitude of the Southern whites toward the blacks is not, as so many assume, in all cases the same; the ignorant Southerner hates the Negro, the workingmen fear his competition, the money-makers wish to use him as a laborer, some of the educated see a menace in his upward development, while others—usually the sons of the masters—wish to help him to rise. National opinion has enabled this last class to maintain the Negro common schools, and to protect the Negro partially in property, life, and limb. Through the pressure of the money-makers, the Negro is in danger of being reduced to semi-slavery, especially in the country districts; the workingmen, and those of the educated who fear the Negro, have united to disfranchise him, and some have urged his deportation; while the passions of the ignorant are easily aroused to lynch and abuse any black man. To praise this intricate whirl of thought and prejudice is nonsense; to inveigh indiscriminately against "the South" is unjust; but to use the same breath in praising Governor Aycock, exposing Senator Morgan, arguing with Mr. Thomas Nelson Page, and denouncing Senator Ben Tillman, is not only sane, but the imperative duty of thinking black men.

It would be unjust to Mr. Washington not to acknowledge that in several instances he has opposed movements in the South which were unjust to the Negro; he sent memorials to the Louisiana and Alabama constitutional conventions, he has spoken against lynching, and in other ways has openly or silently set his influence against sinister schemes and unfortunate happenings. Notwithstanding this, it is equally true to assert that on the whole the distinct impression left by Mr. Washington's propaganda is, first, that the South is justified in its present attitude toward the Negro because of the Negro's degradation; secondly, that the prime cause of the Negro's failure to rise more quickly is his wrong education in the past; and, thirdly, that his future rise depends primarily on his own efforts. Each of these propositions is a dangerous half-truth. The supplementary truths must never be lost sight of: first, slavery and race-prejudice are potent if not sufficient causes of the Negro's position; second, industrial and common-school training were necessarily slow in planting because they had to await the black teachers trained by higher institutions,—it being extremely doubtful if any essentially different development was possible, and certainly a Tuskegee was unthinkable before 1880; and, third, while it is a great truth to say that the Negro must strive and strive mightily to help himself, it is equally true that unless his striving be not simply seconded, but rather aroused and encouraged, by the initiative of the richer and wiser environing group, he cannot hope for great success.

In his failure to realize and impress this last point, Mr. Washington is especially to be criticised. His doctrine has tended to make the whites, North and South, shift the burden of the Negro problem to the Negro's shoulders and stand aside as critical and rather pessimistic spectators; when in fact the burden belongs to the nation, and the hands of none of us are clean if we bend not our energies to righting these great wrongs.

The South ought to be led, by candid and honest criticism, to assert her better self and do her full duty to the race she has cruelly wronged and is still wronging. The North—her co-partner in guilt—cannot salve her conscience by plastering it with gold. We cannot settle this problem by diplomacy and suaveness, by "policy" alone. If worse comes to worst, can the moral fibre of this country survive the slow throttling and murder of nine millions of men?

The black men of America have a duty to perform, a duty stern and delicate,—a forward movement to oppose a part of the work of their greatest leader. So far as Mr. Washington preaches Thrift, Patience, and Industrial Training for the masses, we must hold up his hands and strive with him, rejoicing in his honors and glorying in the strength of this Joshua called of God and of man to lead the headless host. But so far as Mr. Washington apologizes for injustice, North or South, does not rightly value the privilege and duty of voting, belittles the emasculating effects of caste distinctions, and opposes the higher training and ambition of our brighter minds,—so far as he, the South, or the Nation, does this,—we must unceasingly and firmly oppose them. By every civilized and peaceful method we must strive for the rights which the world accords to men, clinging unwaveringly to those great words which the sons of the Fathers would fain forget: "We hold these truths to be self-evident: That all men are created equal; that they are endowed by their Creater with certain unalienable rights; that among these are life, liberty, and the pursuit of happiness."

Address to the Niagara Conference, Harpers Ferry, West Virginia, 1906

. . . . In the past year the work of the Negro-hater has flourished in the land. Step by step the defenders of the rights of American citizens have retreated. The work of stealing the black man's ballot has progressed and the fifty and more representatives of stolen votes still sit in the nation's capital. Discrimination in travel and public

SOURCE: W. E. B. DuBois, "Niagara Address of 1906," W. E. B. DuBois Manuscripts, University of Massachusetts, Amherst, Massachusetts.

accommodation has so spread that some of our weaker brethren are actually afraid to thunder against color discrimination as such and are simply whispering for ordinary decencies.

Against this the Niagara Movement eternally protests. We will not be satisfied to take one jot or tittle less than our full manhood rights. . . . [We] claim for ourselves every single right that belongs to a freeborn American, political, civil and social; and until we get these rights we will never cease to protest and assail the ears of America. The battle we wage is not for ourselves alone but for all true Americans. It is a fight for ideals, lest this, our common fatherland, false to its founding, become in truth, the land of the thief and the home of the slave, a byword and a hissing among the nations for its sounding pretensions and pitiful accomplishments.

Never before in the modern age has a great and civilized folk threatened to adopt so cowardly a creed in the treatment of its fellow citizens born and bred on its soil. Stripped of verbiage and subterfuge and in its naked nastiness, the new American creed says: "Fear to let black men even try to rise lest they become the equals of the white." And this is the land that professes to follow Jesus Christ! The blasphemy of such a course is only matched by its cowardice.

In detail, our demands are clear and unequivocal. First, we would vote; with the right to vote goes everything: freedom, manhood, the honor of your wives, the chastity of your daughters, the right to work, and the chance to rise, and let no man listen to those who deny this.

We want full manhood suffrage, and we want it now, henceforth and forever!

Second. We want discrimination in public accommodation to cease. Separation in railway and street cars, based simply on race and color, is un-American, undemocratic, and silly. We protest against all such discrimination.

Third. We claim the right of freemen to walk, talk, and be with them that wish to be with us. No man has a right to choose another man's friends, and to attempt to do so is an impudent interference with the most fundamental human privilege.

Fourth. We want the laws enforced against rich as well as poor; against capitalist as well as laborer; against white as well as black. We are not more lawless than the white race: We are more often arrested, convicted and mobbed. We want Congress to take charge of Congressional elections. We want the Fourteenth Amendment carried out to the letter and every state disfranchised in Congress which attempts to disfranchise its rightful voters. We want the Fifteenth Amendment enforced and no state allowed to base its franchise simply on color. . . .

Fifth. We want our children educated. The school system in the country districts of the South is a disgrace, and in few towns and cities are the Negro schools what they ought to be. We want the national government to step in and wipe out illiteracy in the South. Either the United States will destroy ignorance, or ignorance will destroy the United States.

And when we call for education we mean real education. We believe in work. We ourselves are workers, but work is not necessarily education. Education is the development of power and ideal. We want our children trained as intelligent human beings should be, and we will fight for all time against any proposal to educate black boys and girls simply as servants and underlings, or simply for the use of other people. They have a right to know, to think, to aspire.

These are some of the chief things which we want. How shall we get them? By voting where we may vote, by persistent, unceasing agitation, by hammering at the truth, by sacrifice and work.

We do not believe in violence, neither in the despised violence of the raid nor the lauded violence of the soldier, nor the barbarous violence of the mob, but we do believe in John Brown, in that incarnate spirit of justice, that hatred of a lie, that willingness to sacrifice money, reputation, and life itself on the altar of right. And here on the scene of John Brown's martyrdom, we reconsecrate ourselves, our honor, our property to the final emancipation of the race which John Brown died to make free.

Our enemies, triumphant for the present, are fighting the stars in their courses. Justice and humanity must prevail. We live to tell these dark brothers of ours—scattered in counsel, wavering, and weak—that no bribe of money or notoriety, no promise of wealth or fame, is worth the surrender of a people's manhood or the loss of a man's self-respect. We refuse to surrender the leadership of this race to cowards and trucklers. We are men; we will be treated as men. On this rock we have planted our banners. We will never give up, though the trump of doom finds us still fighting.

And we shall win! The past promised it. The present foretells it. Thank God for John Brown. Thank God for Garrison and Douglass, Sumner and Phillips, Nat Turner and Robert Gould Shaw, and all the hallowed dead who died for freedom. Thank God for all those today, few though their voices be, who have not forgotten the divine brotherhood of all men, white and black, rich and poor, fortunate and unfortunate.

We appeal to the young men and women of this nation, to those whose nostrils are not yet befouled by greed and snobbery and racial narrowness: Stand up for the right, prove yourselves worthy of your heritage and, whether born North or South, dare to treat men as men. Cannot the nation that has absorbed ten-million foreigners into its political life without catastrophe absorb ten-million Negro Americans into that same political life at less cost than their unjust and illegal exclusion will involve?

Courage, brothers! The battle for humanity is not lost or losing. All across the skies sit signs of promise! The Slav is rising in his might, the yellow millions are tasting liberty, the black Africans are writhing toward the light, and everywhere the laborer, with ballot in his hand, is voting open the gates of opportunity and peace.

The morning breaks over blood-stained hills. We must not falter, we may not shrink. Above are the everlasting stars.

Ida B. Wells-Barnett (1862–1931)

Ida B. Wells-Barnett was born a slave in Mississippi during the Civil War. She attended Rust University in Mississippi and later Fisk University in Memphis. After she earned her college degree, she became first a teacher and, by the end of the 1880s, a journalist. In 1889, she began working as an editor of the *Memphis Free Speech*, a weekly newspaper, for which she contributed many articles on education and self-help for African Americans. Living in the South, she was, of course, afflicted by the Jim Crow laws. Once in 1884, she refused to sit in the black car of a train and was consequently physically ejected from the train. She sued the railroad and eventually lost her case.

Segregation laws were hardly the only evils African Americans had to endure. In 1892, three of Wells-Barnett's friends who owned a small, prosperous grocery store were lynched. Booker T. Washington had argued that if blacks would achieve economic success, they would be respected by whites and eventually achieve civil and political equality. The lynching of small business owners was an appalling and indisputable refutation of this notion. This event had a powerful impact on Wells-Barnett, and from this point on, she began using her position as a writer to denounce lynching and expose the truth behind the racial stereotypes that whites used to subjugate blacks. She contended that whites' reliance on the charge of rape as a justification for lynching black men was a lie. It was merely a subterfuge, both an excuse to murder African Americans who were becoming an economic threat for whites and a very effective way to keep them down. Her editorials in the *Free Speech* antagonized the white community so thoroughly that the offices and presses of the newspaper were destroyed and Wells-Barnett driven out of town. She moved to New York, where she began writing primarily investigative articles on lynching for the *New York Age*. By the end of 1892, she had published a pamphlet, "Southern Horrors," and had begun giving speeches in both the United States and Europe in which she militantly protested against lynching and advocated that the federal government enact strong laws against the practice. In 1895 she published A *Red Record* and in 1899, *Lynch Law in Georgia*. Through her determined antilynching campaign Ida B. Wells-Barnett became a prominent and effective figure in the early civil rights movement.

What is the cause of lynching? What impact would this document have on whites reading it?

Lynch Law in Georgia, June 20, 1899

Consider The Facts.

During six weeks of the months of March and April just past, twelve colored men were lynched in Georgia, the reign of outlawry culminating in the torture and hanging of the colored preacher, Elijah Strickland, and the burning alive of Samuel Wilkes, alias Hose, Sunday, April 23, 1899.

The real purpose of these savage demonstrations is to teach the Negro that in the South he has no rights that the law will enforce. Samuel Hose was burned to teach the Negroes that no matter what a white man does to them, they must not resist. Hose, a servant, had killed Cranford, his employer. An example must be made. Ordinary punishment was deemed inadequate. This Negro must be burned alive. To make the burning a certainty the charge of outrage was invented, and added to the charge of murder. The daily press offered reward for the capture of Hose and then openly incited the people to burn him as soon as caught. The mob carried out the plan in every savage detail.

Of the twelve men lynched during that reign of unspeakable barbarism, only one was even charged with an assault upon a woman. Yet Southern apologists justify their savagery on the ground that Negroes are lynched only because of their crimes against women.

The Southern press champions burning men alive, and says, "Consider the facts." The colored people join issue and also say, "Consider the fact." The colored people of Chicago employed a detective to go to Georgia, and his report in this pamphlet gives the facts. We give here the details of the lynching as they were reported in the Southern papers, then follows the report of the true facts as to the cause of the lynchings, as learned by the investigation. We submit all to the sober judgment of the Nation, confident that, in this cause, as well as all others, "Truth is mighty and will prevail."

Ida B. Wells-Barnett
2939 Princeton Avenue, Chicago, June 20, 1899

"Tortured and Burned Alive"

. . . . The burning of Samuel Hose, or, to give his right name, Samuel Wilkes, gave to the United States the distinction of having burned alive seven human beings during the past ten years. The details of this deed of unspeakable barbarism have shocked the civilized world, for it is conceded universally that no other nation on earth, civilized or savage, has put to death any human being with such atrocious cruelty as that inflicted upon Samuel Hose by the Christian white people of Georgia.

Source: Ida B. Wells-Barnett, *Lynch Law in Georgia: A Six-Weeks' Record in the Center of Southern Civilization, As Faithfully Chronicled by the "Atlanta Journal" and the "Atlanta Constitution." Also the Full Report of Louis P. Le Vin, The Chicago Detective Sent to Investigate the Burning of Samuel Hose, the Torture and Hanging of Elijah Strickland, the Colored Preacher, and the Lynching of Nine Men for Alleged Arson* (Chicago: Chicago Colored Citizens, 1899), 1–11.

The charge is generally made that lynch law is condemned by the best white people of the South, and that lynching is the work of the lowest and lawless class. Those who seek the truth know the fact to be, that all classes are equally guilty, for what the one class does the other encourages, excuses and condones.

This was clearly shown in the burning of Hose. This awful deed was suggested, encouraged and made possible by the daily press of Atlanta, Georgia, until the burning actually occurred, and then it immediately condoned the burning by a hysterical plea to "consider the facts."

Samuel Hose killed Alfred Cranford Wednesday afternoon, April 12, 1899, in a dispute over the wages due Hose. The dispatch which announced the killing of Cranford stated that Hose had assaulted Mrs. Cranford and that bloodhounds had been put on his track.

The next day the Atlanta Constitution, in glaring double headlines, predicted a lynching and suggested burning at the stake. This it repeated in the body of the dispatch in the following language: "When Hose is caught he will either be lynched and his body riddled with bullets or he will be burned at the stake." And further in the same issue the Constitution suggests torture in these words: "There have been whisperings of burning at the stake and of torturing the fellow, and so great is the excitement, and so high the indignation, that this is among the possibilities."

In the issue of the 15th, in another double-column display heading, the Constitution announces: "Negro will probably be burned," and in the body of the dispatch burning and torture is confidently predicted in these words: "Several modes of death have been suggested for him, but it seems to be the universal opinion that he will be burned at the stake and probably tortured before burned."

The next day, April 16th, the double-column head still does its inflammatory work. Never a word for law and order, but daily encouragement for burning. The headlines read: "Excitement still continues intense, and it is openly declared that if Sam Hose is brought in alive he will be burned," and in the dispatch it is said: "The residents have shown no disposition to abandon the search in the immediate neighborhood of Palmetto; their ardor has in no degree cooled, and if Sam Hose is brought here by his captors he will be publicly burned at the stake as an example to members of his race who are said to have been causing the residents of this vicinity trouble for some time."

On the 19th the Constitution assures the public that interest in the pursuit of Hose does not lag, and in proof of the zeal of the pursuers said: "'If Hose is on earth I'll never rest easy until he's caught and burned alive. And that's the way all of us feel,' said one of them last night."

Clark Howell, editor, and W. A. Hemphill, business manager, of the Constitution, had offered through their paper a reward of five hundred dollars for the arrest of the fugitive. This reward, together with the persistent suggestion that the Negro be burned as soon as caught, make it plain as day that the purpose to burn Hose at the stake was formed by the leading citizens of Georgia. The Constitution offered the reward to capture him, and then day after day suggested and predicted that he be burned when caught. The Chicago anarchists [at Haymarket Square] were hanged, not because they threw the bomb, but because they incited to that act the unknown man who did throw it. Pity that the same law cannot be carried into force in Georgia!

Hose was caught Saturday night, April 23, and let the Constitution tell the story of his torture and death.

From the issue of April 24th the following account is condensed: Newman, Ga., April 23.—(Special.)—Sam Hose, the Negro murderer of Alfred Cranford and the assailant of Cranford's wife, was burned at the stake one mile and a quarter from this place this afternoon at 2:30 o'clock. Fully 2,000 people surrounded the small sapling to which he was fastened and watched the flames eat away his flesh, saw his body mutilated by knives and witnessed the contortions of his body in his extreme agony.

Such suffering has seldom been witnessed, and through it all the Negro uttered hardly a cry. During the contortions of his body several blood vessels bursted. The spot selected was an ideal one for such an affair, and the stake was in full view of those who stood about and with unfeigned satisfaction saw the Negro meet his death and saw him tortured before the flames killed him.

A few smoldering ashes scattered about the place, a blackened stake, are all that is left to tell the story. Not even the bones of the Negro were left in the place, but were eagerly snatched by a crowd of people drawn here from all directions, who almost fought over the burning body of the man, carving it with knives and seeking souvenirs of the occurrence.

Preparations for the execution were not necessarily elaborate, and it required only a few minutes to arrange to make Sam Hose pay the penalty of his crime. To the sapling Sam Hose was tied, and he watched the cool, determined men who went about arranging to burn him.

First he was made to remove his clothing, and when the flames began to eat into his body it was almost nude. Before the fire was lighted his left ear was severed from his body. Then his right ear was cut away. During this proceeding he uttered not a groan. Other portions of his body were mutilated by the knives of those who gathered about him, but he was not wounded to such an extent that he was not fully conscious and could feel the excruciating pain. Oil was poured over the wood that was placed about him and this was ignited.

The scene that followed is one that never will be forgotten by those who saw it, and while Sam Hose writhed and performed contortions in his agony, many of those present turned away from the sickening sight, and others could hardly look at it. Not a sound but the crackling of the flames broke the stillness of the place, and the situation grew more sickening as it proceeded.

The stake bent under the strains of the Negro in his agony and his sufferings cannot be described, although he uttered not a sound. After his ears had been cut off he was asked about the crime, and then it was he made a full confession. At one juncture, before the flames had begun to get in their work well, the fastenings that held him to the stake broke and he fell forward partially out of the fire.

He writhed in agony and his sufferings can be imagined when it is said that several blood vessels burst during the contortions of his body. When he fell from the stake he was kicked back and the flames renewed. Then it was that the flames consumed his body and in a few minutes only a few bones and a small part of the body was all that was left of Sam Hose.

One of the most sickening sights of the day was the eagerness with which the people grabbed after souvenirs, and they almost fought over the ashes of the dead criminal. Large pieces of his flesh were carried away, and persons were seen walking through the streets carrying bones in their hands.

When all the larger bones, together with the flesh, had been carried away by the early comers, others scraped in the ashes, and for a great length of time a crowd was about the place scraping in the ashes. Not even the stake to which the Negro was tied when burned was left, but it was promptly chopped down and carried away as the largest souvenir of the burning.

Carl Schurz (1829–1906)

Carl Schurz was a German immigrant who served as a brigadier general during the Civil War, Republican senator from Missouri during Reconstruction, and secretary of the interior during the Hayes administration. He later moved to New York, where he helped found the *New York Evening Post* and wrote extensive political columns for *Harper's Weekly*. At the turn of the century, just as the United States was beginning to redefine its notion of manifest destiny, Schurz became an outspoken critic of American expansionism. "My Country!" he once wrote, "when right keep it right; when wrong, set it right!" In June 1898, believing that the war with Spain was wrong, he became very active (along with such diverse celebrated individuals as Jane Addams, Andrew Carnegie, William James, and Mark Twain) in the Anti-Imperialist League. Early in 1899, he delivered a speech at the University of Chicago in which he emphatically denounced the acquisition of the Philippines and Puerto Rico as a result of the Spanish-American War.

What, according to Schurz, are the United States's motives in acquiring colonies? Is his assumption correct that we would no longer be a democracy "of the people, by the people, for the people" if we became an imperial power? How have his views played out in the twentieth century, and how do they relate to recent American diplomacy?

Address at the University of Chicago Denouncing U.S. Imperialism, January 4, 1899

It is proposed to embark this republic in a course of imperialistic policy by permanently annexing to it certain islands taken, or partly taken, from Spain in the late war. The matter is near its decision, but not yet ratified by the Senate; but even if it were, the question whether those islands, although ceded by Spain, shall be permanently incorporated in the territory of the United States would still be open for final determination by Congress. As an open question therefore I shall discuss it.

SOURCE: *Speeches, Correspondence, and Political Papers of Carl Schurz,* ed. by Frederic Bancroft, vol.6 (New York: G. P. Putnam's Sons, 1913), 2, 4, 6, 8,10–11, 14–15, 26–29.

If ever, it behooves the American people to think and act with calm deliberation, for the character and future of the republic and the welfare of its people now living and yet to be born are in unprecedented jeopardy. . . .

According to the solemn proclamation of our government, [the Spanish War] had been undertaken solely for the liberation of Cuba, as a war of humanity and not of conquest. But our easy victories had put conquest within our reach, and when our arms occupied foreign territory, a loud demand arose that, pledge or no pledge to the contrary, the conquests should be kept, even the Philippines on the other side of the globe, and that as to Cuba herself, independence would only be a provisional formality. Why not? was the cry. Has not the career of the republic almost from its very beginning been one of territorial expansion? . . .

Compare now with our old acquisitions as to all these important points those at present in view.

They are not continental, not contiguous to our present domain, but beyond seas, the Philippines many thousand miles distant from our coast. They are all situated in the tropics, where people of the northern races, such as Anglo-Saxons, or generally speaking, people of Germanic blood, have never migrated in mass to stay; and they are more or less densely populated, parts of them as densely as Massachusetts—their populations consisting almost exclusively of races to whom the tropical climate is congenial—Spanish creoles mixed with negroes in the West Indies, and Malays, Tagals, Filipinos, Chinese, Japanese, Negritos, and various more or less barbarous tribes in the Philippines. . . .

Whatever we may do for their improvement the people of the Spanish Antilles will remain in overwhelming numerical predominance . . . , some of them quite clever in their way, but the vast majority utterly alien to us not only in origin and language, but in habits, traditional ways of thinking, principles, ambitions—in short, in most things that are of the greatest importance in human intercourse and especially in political cooperation. And under the influences of their tropical climate they will prove incapable of becoming assimilated to the Anglo-Saxon. They would, therefore, remain in the population of this republic a hopelessly heterogeneous element—in some respects more hopeless even than the colored people now living among us. . . .

If we [become an imperialist power], we shall transform the government of the people, for the people, and by the people, for which Abraham Lincoln lived, into a government of one part of the people, the strong, over another part, the weak. Such an abandonment of a fundamental principle as a permanent policy may at first seem to bear only upon more or less distant dependencies, but it can hardly fail in its ultimate effects to disturb the rule of the same principle in the conduct of democratic government at home. And I warn the American people that a democracy cannot so deny its faith as to the vital conditions of its being—it cannot long play the king over subject populations without creating within itself ways of thinking and habits of action most dangerous to its own vitality. . . .

Conservative citizens will tell [us] that thus the homogeneousness of the people of the republic, so essential to the working of our democratic institutions, will be irretrievably lost; that our race troubles, already dangerous, will be infinitely aggravated, and that the government of, by, and for the people will be in imminent danger of fatal demoralization. . . . The American people will be driven on and on by the force of events as Napoleon was when started on his career of limitless conquest. This is imperialism as now advocated. Do we wish to prevent its excesses? Then we must stop at the beginning, before taking Porto Rico. If we take that island, not even to speak of the Philippines, we shall have placed ourselves on the inclined plane, and roll on and on, no longer masters of our own will, until we have reached the bottom. And where will that bottom be? Who knows? . . .

What can there be to justify a change of policy fraught with such direful consequences? Let us pass the arguments of the advocates of such imperialism candidly in review.

The cry suddenly raised that this great country has become too small for us is too ridiculous to demand an answer, in view of the fact that our present population may be tripled and still have ample elbow-room, with resources to support many more. But we are told that our industries are gasping for breath; that we are suffering from over production; that our products must have new outlets, and that we need colonies and dependencies the world over to give us more markets. More markets? Certainly. But do we, civilized beings, indulge in the absurd and barbarous notion that we must own the countries with which we wish to trade? . . .

"But the Pacific Ocean," we are mysteriously told, "will be the great commercial battlefield of the future, and we must quickly use the present opportunity to secure our position on it. The visible presence of great power is necessary for us to get our share of the trade of China. Therefore, we must have the Philippines." Well, the China trade is worth having, although for a time out of sight the Atlantic Ocean will be an infinitely more important battlefield of commerce. . . . But does the trade of China really require that we should have the Philippines and make a great display of power to get our share? . . .

"But we must have coaling stations for our navy!" Well, can we not get as many coaling stations as we need without owning populous countries behind them that would entangle us in dangerous political responsibilities and complications? Must Great Britain own the whole of Spain in order to hold Gibraltar?

"But we must civilize those poor people!" Are we not ingenious and charitable enough to do much for their civilization without subjugating and ruling them by criminal aggression?

The rest of the pleas for imperialism consist mostly of those high-sounding catch-words of which a free people when about to decide a great question should be especially suspicious. We are admonished that it is time for us to become a "world power." Well, we are a world power now, and have been for many years. What is a world power? A power strong enough to make its voice listened to with deference by the world whenever it chooses to speak. Is it necessary for a world power, in order to be such, to have its finger in every pie? Must we have the Philippines in order to become a world power? To ask the question is to answer it.

The American flag, we are told, whenever once raised, must never be hauled down. Certainly, every patriotic citizen will always be ready, if need be, to fight and to die under his flag wherever it may wave in justice and for the best interests of the country. But I say to you, woe to the republic if it should ever be without citizens patriotic and brave enough to defy the demagogues' cry and to haul down the flag wherever it may be raised not in justice and not for the best interests of the country. Such a republic would not last long. . . .

William Jennings Bryan (1860–1925)

The 1900 presidential election was a rematch between Democrat William Jennings Bryan and the incumbent president, William McKinley. Both elections were hard-fought campaigns, and both saw Bryan narrowly defeated by the Republicans. In 1896, the primary issue was silver. In 1900, however, a new issue had arisen: imperialism. The United States had just acquired Guam, Puerto Rico, and the Philippines from Spain, and although a great deal of pride had swept the country as a result of American expansion, a significant minority believed the United States was turning its back on its own democratic values by emulating European imperialism.

As soon as the United States began exerting authority in the Philippines, Filipino nationalist Emilio Aguinaldo resumed his guerrilla activity. This time, instead of fighting the Spanish, Aguinaldo led the fight against the American occupying forces. As the Filipino insurrection picked up steam, Bryan and the Democratic Party took up the anti-imperialist cause. Bryan believed that the American attempt to conquer the Philippines and impose American principles and democracy on an unwilling people was contrary to the values of the founding fathers and the very principles on which this nation was founded.

According to this Democratic National Convention speech by Bryan, how did the United States justify the acquisition of the Philippines? Many historians have compared the American military presence in the Philippines to our course of action 65 years later in Vietnam. In what ways is this comparison accurate, and in what ways is it not? Would Bryan's argument be applicable to other American military ventures?

The Paralyzing Influence of Imperialism, July 1900

. . . Someone has said that a truth once spoken can never be recalled. It goes on and on, and no one can set a limit to its ever widening influence. But if it were possible to obliterate every word written or spoken in defense of the principles set forth in the Declaration of Independence, a war of conquest would still leave its legacy of perpetual hatred, for it was God Himself who placed in every human heart the love of liberty. He never made a race of people so low in the scale of civilization or intelligence that it would welcome a foreign master.

Those who would have this nation enter upon a career of empire must consider not only the effect of imperialism on the Filipinos but they must also calculate its effects upon our own nation. We cannot repudiate the principle of self-government in the Philippines without weakening that principle here.

SOURCE: *Official Proceedings of the Democratic National Convention Held in Kansas City, MO., July 4, 5 and 6, 1900* (Chicago, 1900), 205–227.

Lincoln said that the safety of this nation was not in its fleets, its armies, its forts, but in the spirit which prizes liberty as the heritage of all men, in all lands, everywhere, and he warned his countrymen that they could not destroy this spirit without planting the seeds of despotism at their own doors.

Even now we are beginning to see the paralyzing influence of imperialism. Heretofore this nation has been prompt to express its sympathy with those who were fighting for civil liberty. While our sphere of activity has been limited to the Western Hemisphere, our sympathies have not been bounded by the seas. We have felt it due to ourselves and to the world, as well as to those who were struggling for the right to govern themselves, to proclaim the interest which our people have, from the date of their own independence, felt in every contest between human rights and arbitrary power. . . .

A colonial policy means that we shall send to the Philippine Islands a few traders, a few taskmasters, and a few officeholders, and an army large enough to support the authority of a small fraction of the people while they rule the natives.

If we have an imperial policy we must have a great standing army as its natural and necessary complement. The spirit which will justify the forcible annexation of the Philippine Islands will justify the seizure of other islands and the domination of other people, and with wars of conquest we can expect a certain, if not rapid, growth of our military establishment.

That a large permanent increase in our regular army is intended by Republican leaders is not a matter of conjecture but a matter of fact. In his message of Dec. 5, 1898, the President asked for authority to increase the standing army to 100,000. In 1896 the army contained about 25,000. Within two years the President asked for four times that many, and a Republican House of Representatives complied with the request after the Spanish treaty had been signed, and when no country was at war with the United States.

If such an army is demanded when an imperial policy is contemplated but not openly avowed, what may be expected if the people encourage the Republican Party by endorsing its policy at the polls?

A large standing army is not only a pecuniary burden to the people and, if accompanied by compulsory service, a constant source of irritation but it is even a menace to a republican form of government. The army is the personification of force, and militarism will inevitably change the ideals of the people and turn the thoughts of our young men from the arts of peace to the science of war. The government which relies for its defense upon its citizens is more likely to be just than one which has at call a large body of professional soldiers.

A small standing army and a well-equipped and well-disciplined state militia are sufficient at ordinary times, and in an emergency the nation should in the future as in the past place its dependence upon the volunteers who come from all occupations at their country's call and return to productive labor when their services are no longer required—men who fight when the country needs fighters and work when the country needs workers. . . .

The Republican platform promises that some measure of self-government is to be given the Filipinos by law; but even this pledge is not fulfilled. Nearly sixteen months elapsed after the ratification of the treaty before the adjournment of Congress last

June and yet no law was passed dealing with the Philippine situation. The will of the President has been the only law in the Philippine Islands wherever the American authority extends.

Why does the Republican Party hesitate to legislate upon the Philippine question? Because a law would disclose the radical departure from history and precedent contemplated by those who control the Republican Party. The storm of protest which greeted the Puerto Rican bill was an indication of what may be expected when the American people are brought face to face with legislation upon this subject.

If the Puerto Ricans, who welcomed annexation, are to be denied the guarantees of our Constitution, what is to be the lot of the Filipinos, who resisted our authority? If secret influences could compel a disregard of our plain duty toward friendly people living near our shores, what treatment will those same influences provide for unfriendly people 7,000 miles away? If, in this country where the people have a right to vote, Republican leaders dare not take the side of the people against the great monopolies which have grown up within the last few years, how can they be trusted to protect the Filipinos from the corporations which are waiting to exploit the islands?

Is the sunlight of full citizenship to be enjoyed by the people of the United States and the twilight of semi-citizenship endured by the people of Puerto Rico, while the thick darkness of perpetual vassalage covers the Philippines? The Puerto Rico tariff law asserts the doctrine that the operation of the Constitution is confined to the forty-five states.

The Democratic Party disputes this doctrine and denounces it as repugnant to both the letter and spirit of our organic law. There is no place in our system of government for the deposit of arbitrary and irresistible power. That the leaders of a great party should claim for any President or Congress the right to treat millions of people as mere "possessions" and deal with them unrestrained by the Constitution or the Bill of Rights shows how far we have already departed from the ancient landmarks and indicates what may be expected if this nation deliberately enters upon a career of empire.

The territorial form of government is temporary and preparatory, and the chief security a citizen of a territory has is found in the fact that he enjoys the same constitutional guarantees and is subject to the same general laws as the citizen of a state. Take away this security and his rights will be violated and his interests sacrificed at the demand of those who have political influence. This is the evil of the colonial system, no matter by what nation it is applied.

What is our title to the Philippine Islands? Do we hold them by treaty or by conquest? Did we buy them or did we take them? Did we purchase the people? If not, how did we secure title to them? Were they thrown in with the land? Will the Republicans say that inanimate earth has value but that when that earth is molded by the Divine Hand and stamped with the likeness of the Creator it becomes a fixture and passes with the soil? If governments derive their just powers from the consent of the governed, it is impossible to secure title to people, either by force or by purchase.

We could extinguish Spain's title by treaty, but if we hold title we must hold it by some method consistent with our ideas of government. When we made allies of the Filipinos and armed them to fight against Spain, we disputed Spain's title. If we buy

Spain's title, we are not innocent purchasers. There can be no doubt that we accepted and utilized the services of the Filipinos and that when we did so we had full knowledge that they were fighting for their own independence; and I submit that history furnishes no example of turpitude baser than ours if we now substitute our yoke for the Spanish yoke. . . .

Some argue that American rule in the Philippine Islands will result in the better education of the Filipinos. Be not deceived. If we expect to maintain a colonial policy, we shall not find it to our advantage to educate the people. The educated Filipinos are now in revolt against us, and the most ignorant ones have made the least resistance to our domination. If we are to govern them without their consent and give them no voice in determining the taxes which they must pay, we dare not educate them lest they learn to read the Declaration of Independence and the Constitution of the United States and mock us for our inconsistency.

The principal arguments, however, advanced by those who enter upon a defense of imperialism are:

First, that we must improve the present opportunity to become a world power and enter into international politics.

Second, that our commercial interests in the Philippine Islands and in the Orient make it necessary for us to hold the islands permanently.

Third, that the spread of the Christian religion will be facilitated by a colonial policy.

Fourth, that there is no honorable retreat from the position which the nation has taken.

The first argument is addressed to the nation's pride and the second to the nation's pocketbook. The third is intended for the church member and the fourth for the partisan.

It is sufficient answer to the first argument to say that for more than a century this nation has been a world power. For ten decades it has been the most potent influence in the world. Not only has it been a world power but it has done more to affect the policies of the human race than all the other nations of the world combined. Because our Declaration of Independence was promulgated, others have been promulgated. Because the patriots of 1776 fought for liberty, others have fought for it. Because our Constitution was adopted, other constitutions have been adopted.

The growth of the principle of self-government, planted on American soil, has been the overshadowing political fact of the 19th century. It has made this nation conspicuous among the nations and given it a place in history, such as no other nation has ever enjoyed. Nothing has been able to check the onward march of this idea. I am not willing that this nation shall cast aside the omnipotent weapon of truth to seize again the weapons of physical warfare. I would not exchange the glory of this republic for the glory of all the empires that have risen and fallen since time began.

The permanent chairman of the last Republican National Convention presented the pecuniary argument in all its baldness when he said:

We make no hypocritical pretense of being interested in the Philippines solely on account of others. While we regard the welfare of those people as a sacred trust, we regard the welfare of the American people first. We see our duty to ourselves as well as to others. We believe in trade expansion. By every legitimate means within the province of government and constitution we mean to stimulate the expansion of our trade and open new markets.

This is the commercial argument. It is based upon the theory that war can be rightly waged for pecuniary advantage and that it is profitable to purchase trade by force and violence. Franklin denied both of these propositions. When Lord Howe asserted that the acts of Parliament which brought on the Revolution were necessary to prevent American trade from passing into foreign channels, Franklin replied:

> To me it seems that neither the obtaining nor retaining of any trade, howsoever valuable, is an object for which men may justly spill each other's blood; that the true and sure means of extending and securing commerce are the goodness and cheapness of commodities, and that the profits of no trade can ever be equal to the expense of compelling it and holding it by fleets and armies. I consider this war against us, therefore, as both unjust and unwise.

I place the philosophy of Franklin against the sordid doctrine of those who would put a price upon the head of an American soldier and justify a war of conquest upon the ground that it will pay. The Democratic Party is in favor of the expansion of trade. It would extend our trade by every legitimate and peaceful means; but it is not willing to make merchandise of human blood.

But a war of conquest is as unwise as it is unrighteous. A harbor and coaling station in the Philippines would answer every trade and military necessity and such a concession could have been secured at any time without difficulty. It is not necessary to own people in order to trade with them. We carry on trade today with every part of the world, and our commerce has expanded more rapidly than the commerce of any European empire. We do not own Japan or China, but we trade with their people. We have not absorbed the republics of Central and South America, but we trade with them. Trade cannot be permanently profitable unless it is voluntary.

When trade is secured by force, the cost of securing it and retaining it must be taken out of the profits, and the profits are never large enough to cover the expense. Such a system would never be defended but for the fact that the expense is borne by all the people while the profits are enjoyed by a few.

Imperialism would be profitable to the Army contractors; it would be profitable to the shipowners, who would carry live soldiers to the Philippines and bring dead soldiers back; it would be profitable to those who would seize upon the franchises, and it would be profitable to the officials whose salaries would be fixed here and paid over there; but to the farmer, to the laboring man, and to the vast majority of those engaged in other occupations, it would bring expenditure without return and risk without reward.

Farmers and laboring men have, as a rule, small incomes, and, under systems which place the tax upon consumption, pay much more than their fair share of the expenses of government. Thus the very people who receive least benefit from imperialism will be injured most by the military burdens which accompany it.

In addition to the evils which he and the former share in common, the laboring man will be the first to suffer if Oriental subjects seek work in the United States; the first to suffer if American capital leaves our shores to employ Oriental labor in the Philippines to supply the trade of China and Japan; the first to suffer from the violence which the military spirit arouses, and the first to suffer when the methods of imperialism are applied to our own government. . . .

The religious argument varies in positiveness from a passive belief that Providence delivered the Filipinos into our hands for their good and our glory to the exultation of the minister who said that we ought to "thrash the natives (Filipinos) until they understand who we are," and that "every bullet sent, every cannon shot, and every flag waved means righteousness."

We cannot approve of this doctrine in one place unless we are willing to apply it everywhere. If there is poison in the blood of the hand, it will ultimately reach the heart. It is equally true that forcible Christianity, if planted under the American flag in the far-away Orient, will sooner or later be transplanted upon American soil. . . .

If true Christianity consists of carrying out in our daily lives the teachings of Christ, who will say that we are commanded to civilize with dynamite and proselyte with the sword? . . .

There is an easy, honest, honorable solution of the Philippine question . . . first, to establish a stable form of government in the Philippine Islands, just as we are now establishing a stable form of government in Cuba; second, to give independence to the Filipinos as we have promised to give independence to the Cubans; third, to protect the Filipinos from outside interference while they work out their destiny, just as we have protected the republics of Central and South America, and are, by the Monroe Doctrine, pledged to protect Cuba.

A European protectorate often results in the plundering of the ward by the guardian. An American protectorate gives to the nation protected the advantage of our strength without making it the victim of our greed. For three-quarters of a century the Monroe Doctrine has been a shield to neighboring republics and yet it has imposed no pecuniary burden upon us. After the Filipinos had aided us in the war against Spain, we could not honorably turn them over to their former masters; we could not leave them to be the victims of the ambitious designs of European nations, and since we do not desire to make them a part of us or to hold them as subjects, we propose the only alternative, namely, to give them independence and guard them against molestation from without.

When our opponents are unable to defend their position by argument, they fall back upon the assertion that it is destiny and insist that we must submit to it no matter how much it violates our moral precepts and our principles of government. This is a complacent philosophy. It obliterates the distinction between right and wrong and makes individuals and nations the helpless victims of circumstances.

Destiny is the subterfuge of the invertebrate, who, lacking the courage to oppose error, seeks some plausible excuse for supporting it. Washington said that the destiny of the republican form of government was deeply, if not finally, staked on the experiment entrusted to the American people. How different Washington's definition of destiny from the Republican definition! . . .

The Republicans say that this nation is in the hands of destiny; Washington believed that not only the destiny of our own nation but the destiny of the republican form of government throughout the world was entrusted to American hands. Immeasurable responsibility!

The destiny of this republic is in the hands of its own people, and upon the success of the experiment here rests the hope of humanity. No exterior force can disturb this republic, and no foreign influence should be permitted to change its course. What the future has in store for this nation no one has authority to declare, but each individual has his own idea of the nation's mission, and he owes it to his country as well as to himself to contribute as best he may to the fulfillment of that mission. . . .

Mother Jones (1830–1930)

Throughout her long life, Mary Harris (Mother) Jones was a leading activist in the labor movement. When she was 37, her husband and four children died in a yellow fever epidemic. Soon thereafter, she involved herself in the union cause and became active as a strike organizer with the Knights of Labor and the United Mine Workers. By the twentieth century, she had joined the Socialist Party, and was one of the founders of the Industrial Workers of the World. Even in her nineties, she was still active in helping to organize strikes. As she strove to alleviate the hardships faced by all victims of industrialization, she became especially dedicated to the abolition of child labor. In 1903, at the age of 73, she led a march of more than a hundred miles from Philadelphia to Sagamore Hill to confront President Theodore Roosevelt with the harsh realities of the exploitation of children, which she describes in the following reading.

What does Mother Jones's account reveal about the working conditions these children faced? Why did politicians and the public ignore the exploitation of children?

"The March of the Mill Children," 1903

In the spring of 1903 I went to Kensington, Pennsylvania, where seventy-five thousand textile workers were on strike. Of this number at least ten thousand were little children. The workers were striking for more pay and shorter hours. Every day little children came into Union Headquarters, some with their hands off, some with the thumb missing, some with their fingers off at the knuckle. They were stooped things, round shouldered and skinny. Many of them were not over ten years of age, the state law prohibited their working before they were twelve years of age.

SOURCE: *The Autobiography of Mother Jones*, 4th ed. (Chicago: Charles H. Kerr, 1990), chapter 10.

The law was poorly enforced and the mothers of these children often swore falsely as to their children's age. In a single block in Kensington, fourteen women, mothers of twenty-two children all under twelve, explained it was a question of starvation or perjury. That the fathers had been killed or maimed at the mines.

I asked the newspaper men why they didn't publish the facts about child labor in Pennsylvania. They said they couldn't because the mill owners had stock in the papers.

"Well, I've got stock in these little children," said I, "and I'll arrange a little publicity."

We assembled a number of boys and girls one morning in Independence Park and from there we arranged to parade with banners to the court house where we would hold a meeting. A great crowd gathered in the public square in front of the city hall. I put the little boys with their fingers off and hands crushed and maimed on a platform. I held up their mutilated hands and showed them to the crowd and made the statement that Philadelphia's mansions were built on the broken bones, the quivering hearts and drooping heads of these children. That their little lives went out to make wealth for others. That neither state or city officials paid any attention to these wrongs. That they did not care that these children were to be the future citizens of the nation.

The officials of the city hall were standing in the open windows. I held the little ones of the mills high up above the heads of the crowd and pointed to their puny arms and legs and hollow chests. They were light to lift.

I called upon the millionaire manufactures to cease their moral murders, and I cried to the officials in the open windows opposite, "Some day the workers will take possession of your city hall, and when we do, no child will be sacrificed on the altar of profit."

The officials quickly closed the windows, as they had closed their eyes and hearts.

The reporters quoted my statement that Philadelphia mansions were built on the broken bones and quivering hearts of children. The Philadelphia papers and the New York papers got into a squabble with each other over the question. The universities discussed it. Preachers began talking. That was what I wanted. Public attention on the subject of child labor.

The matter quieted down for a while and I concluded the people needed stirring up again. The Liberty Bell that a century ago rang out for freedom against tyranny was touring the country and crowds were coming to see it everywhere. That gave me an idea. These little children were striking for some of the freedom that childhood ought to have, and I decided that the children and I would go on a tour.

I asked some of the parents if they would let me have their little boys and girls for a week or ten days, promising to bring them back safe and sound. They consented. A man named Sweeny was marshal for our "army." A few men and women went with me to help with the children. They were on strike and I thought, they might well have a little recreation.

The children carried knapsacks on their backs which had a knife and fork, a tin cup and plate. We took along a wash boiler in which to cook the food on the road. One little fellow had drum and another had a fife. That was our band. We carried banners that said, "We want more schools and less hospitals." "We want time to play." "Prosperity is here. Where is ours?"

We started from Philadelphia where we held a great mass meeting. I decided to go with the children to see President Roosevelt to ask him to have Congress pass a law prohibiting the exploitation of childhood. I thought that President Roosevelt might see these mill children and compare them with his own little ones who were spending the summer on the seashore at Oyster Bay. I thought too, out of politeness, we might call on Morgan in Wall Street who owned the mines where many of these children's fathers worked.

The children were very happy, having plenty to eat, taking baths in the brooks and rivers every day. I thought when the strike is over and they go back to the mills, they will never have another holiday like this. All along the line of march the farmers drove out to meet us with wagon loads of fruit and vegetables. Their wives brought the children clothes and money. The interurban trainmen would stop their trains and give us free rides.

Marshal Sweeny and I would go ahead to the towns and arrange sleeping quarters for the children, and secure meeting halls. As we marched on, it grew terribly hot. There was no rain and the roads were heavy with dust. From time to time we had to send some of the children back to their homes. They were too weak to stand the march.

We were on the outskirts of New Trenton, New Jersey, cooking our lunch in the wash boiler, when the conductor on the interurban car stopped and told us the police were coming down to notify us that we could not enter the town. There were mills in the town and the mill owners didn't like our coming.

I said, "All right, the police will be just in time for lunch."

Sure enough, the police came and we invited them to dine with us. They looked at the little gathering of children with their tin plates and cups around the wash boiler. They just smiled and spoke kindly to the children, and said nothing at all about not going into the city.

We went in, held our meeting, and it was the wives of the police who took the little children and cared for them that night, sending them back in the morning with a nice lunch rolled up in paper napkins.

Everywhere we had meetings, showing up with living children, the horrors of child labor. . . .

I called on the mayor of Princeton and asked for permission to speak opposite the campus of the University. I said I wanted to speak on higher education. The mayor gave me permission. A great crowd gathered, professors and students and the people; and I told them that the rich robbed these little children of any education of the lowest order that they might send their sons and daughters to places of higher education. That they used the hands and feet of little children that they might buy automobiles for their wives and police dogs for their daughters to talk French to. I said the mill owners take babies almost from the cradle. And I showed those professors children in our army who could scarcely read or write because they were working ten hours a day in the silk mills of Pennsylvania.

"Here's a text book on economics," I said pointing to a little chap, James Ashworth, who was ten years old and who was stooped over like an old man from carrying bundles of yarn that weighed seventy-five pounds. "He gets three dollars a week and his sister who is fourteen gets six dollars. They work in a carpet factory ten hours a day while the children of the rich are getting their higher education.". . .

I sent a committee over to the New York Chief of Police, Ebstein, asking for permission to march up Fourth Avenue to Madison Square where I wanted to hold a meeting. The chief refused and forbade our entrance to the city.

I went over myself to New York and saw Mayor Seth Low. The mayor was most courteous but he said he would have to support the police commissioner. I asked him what the reason was for refusing us entrance to the city and he said that we were not citizens of New York.

"Oh, I think we will clear that up, Mr. Mayor," I said. "Permit me to call your attention to an incident which took place in this nation just a year ago. A piece of rotten royalty came over here from Germany, called Price Henry. The Congress of the United States voted $45,000 to fill that fellow's stomach three weeks and to entertain him. His highness was getting $4,000,000 dividends out of the blood of the workers in this country. Was he a citizen of this land?"

"And it was reported, Mr. Mayor, that you and all the officials of New York and the University Club entertained that chap." And repeated, "Was he a citizen of New York!"

"No, Mother," said the mayor, "he was not." . . .

"Well, Mr. Mayor, these are the little citizens of the nation and they also produce its wealth. Aren't we entitled to enter your city?" . . .

We marched to Twentieth Street. I told an immense crowd of the horrors of child labor in the mills around the anthracite region and I showed them some of the children. I showed them Eddie Dunphy, a little fellow of twelve, whose job it was to sit all day on a high stool, handing in the right thread to another worker. Eleven hours a day he sat on the high stool with dangerous machinery all about him. All day long, winter and summer, spring and fall, for three dollars a week.

And then I showed them Gussie Rangnew, a little girl from whom all the childhood had gone. Her face was like an old woman's. Gussie packed stockings in a factory, eleven hours a day for a few cents a day.

We raised a lot of money for the strikers and hundreds of friends offered their homes to the little ones while we were in the city.

The next day we went to Coney Island at the invitation of Mr. Bostick who owned the wild animal show The children had a wonderful day such as they never had in all their lives. After the exhibition of the trained animals, Mr. Bostick let me speak to the audience. . . . Right in front of the emperors were the empty iron cages of the animals. I put my little children in the cages and they clung to the iron bars while I talked.

I told the crowd that the scene was typical of the aristocracy of employers with their thumb down to the little ones of the mills and factories, and people sitting dumbly by.

"We want President Roosevelt to hear the wail of the children who never have a chance to go to school but work eleven and twelve hours a day in the textile mills of Pennsylvania; who weave the carpets that he and you walk upon and the lace curtains in your windows, and the clothes of the people. Fifty years ago there was a cry against slavery and men gave up their lives to stop the selling of black children on the block. Today the white child is sold for two dollars a week to the manufacturers. Fifty years ago the black babies were sold C.O.D. Today the white baby is sold on the installment plan.

"In Georgia where children work day and night in the cotton mills they have just passed a bill to protect song birds. What about little children from whom all song is gone?

"I shall ask the president in the name of the aching hearts of these little ones that he emancipate them from slavery. I will tell the president that the prosperity he boasts of is the prosperity of the rich wrung from the poor and the helpless.

"The trouble is that no one in Washington cares. I saw our legislators in one hour pass three bills for the relief of the railways but when labor cries for aid for the children they will not listen.

"I asked a man in prison once how he happened to be there and he said he had stolen a pair of shoes. I told him if he had stolen a railroad he would be a United States Senator.

"We are told that every American boy has the chance of being president. I tell you that these little boys in the iron cages would sell their chance any day for good square meals and a chance to play. These little toilers whom I have taken from the mills—deformed, dwarfed in body and soul, with nothing but toil before them— have never heard that they have a chance, the chance of every American male citizen, to become the president.

"You see those monkeys in those cages over there." I pointed to a side cage. "The professors are trying to teach them to talk. The monkeys are too wise for they fear that the manufacturers would buy them for slaves in their factories." . . .

The next day we left Coney Island for Manhattan Beach to visit Senator Platt, who had made an appointment to see me at nine o'clock in the morning. The children got stuck in the sand banks and I had a time cleaning the sand off the littlest ones. So we started to walk on the railroad track. I was told it was private property and we had to get off. Finally a saloon keeper showed us a short cut into the sacred grounds of the hotel and suddenly the army appeared in the lobby. The little fellows played "Hail, hail, the gang's all here" their fifes and drums, and Senator Platt when he saw the little army ran away through the back door to New York.

I asked the manager if he would give children breakfast and charge it up to Senator as we had an invitation to breakfast that morning with him. He gave us a private room and he gave those children such a breakfast as they had never had in all their lives. I had breakfast too, and a reporter from of the Hearst papers and I charged it all to Senator Platt.

We marched down to Oyster Bay but the president refused to see us and he would not answer my letters. But our march had done its work. We had drawn the attention of the nation to the crime of child labor. And while the strike of the textile workers in Kensington was lost and the children driven back to work, not long afterward the Pennsylvania legislature passed a child labor law that sent thousands of children home from the mills, and kept thousands of others from entering the factory until they were fourteen years of age.

John Muir (1838–1914)

Born in Scotland and reared in Wisconsin, John Muir became one of the leading exponents and founders of the ecological movement. As a young man, he traveled extensively around the United States, and after his first visit to the Hetch Hetchy Valley in 1868, he made up his mind to settle in California. Concerned that loggers, miners, cattlemen, and sheepherders were despoiling the meadows and mountainsides of the Sierra Nevada, he began writing articles extolling the beauties of nature and advocating the preservation of the wilderness. By the end of the 1870s, his reputation had spread, not only throughout the United States but also around the world. In 1890, along with *Century* magazine editor Robert Underwood Johnson and several other supporters, Muir convinced Congress to preserve the Hetch Hetchy Valley and the surrounding area by passing an act establishing Yosemite National Park. Later he was influential in the creation of the Sequoia and Grand Canyon national parks, which earned him the nickname of "Father" of the national park system.

Determined to prevent ranchers from encroaching on the new park, Muir founded the Sierra Club in 1892 to protect the Sierras and the redwoods. In 1903, President Theodore Roosevelt camped out with Muir in Yosemite and began to shape his own conservation and preservation policy. Claiming that "everybody needs beauty as well as bread, places to play in and pray in, where nature may heal and give strength to body and soul alike," Muir campaigned ardently, until his death in 1914, against business interests and politicians who would destroy the natural beauty of the forests and wilderness. The year before his death, he fought a losing and disheartening battle against the proposal to dam the Hetch Hetchy Valley to create a reservoir for San Francisco. Still, his efforts to preserve the redwoods and create a national park system bore fruit. One of the most beautiful state parks in California, in Marin County just north of the Golden Gate Bridge, is Muir Woods, and nearby is Muir Beach. Participants in the environmental movement that emerged from 1960s activism still regard Muir's writings to be as relevant and applicable today as they were a century ago.

Why is it so crucial, as John Muir contends in "The Hetch Hetchy Valley," to fight against the proposal to dam this pristine valley in order to create a reservoir for San Francisco? What are the arguments favoring the dam? In the posthumously published article "Save the Redwoods," Muir deplores what has happened to the redwood forests. Why is it better to preserve these ancient trees than harvest them for lumber? How can we balance the obvious need for such natural resources as lumber, iron ore, and coal with the need to preserve natural beauty? What would the effect have been if John Muir and others had not protested against the unrestricted exploitation of natural resources?

"The Hetch Hetchy Valley," January 1908

It is impossible to overestimate the value of wild mountains and mountain temples as places for people to grow in, recreation grounds for soul and body. They are the greatest of our natural resources, God's best gifts, but none, however high and holy, is beyond reach of the spoiler. In these ravaging money-mad days monopolizing San Francisco capitalists are now doing their best to destroy the Yosemite Park, the most wonderful of all our great mountain national parks. Beginning on the Tuolumne side, they are trying with a lot of sinful ingenuity to get the Government's permission to dam and destroy the Hetch-Hetchy Valley for a reservoir, simply that comparatively private gain may be made out of universal public loss, while of course the Sierra Club is doing all it can to save the valley. The Honorable Secretary of the Interior has not yet announced his decision in the case, but in all that has come and gone nothing discouraging is yet in sight on our side of the fight.

As long as the busy public in general knew little or nothing about the Hetch-Hetchy Valley, the few cunning drivers of the damming scheme, working in darkness like moles in a low-lying meadow, seemed confident of success; but when light was turned on and the truth became manifest that next to Yosemite, Hetch-Hetchy is the most wonderful and most important feature of the great park, that damming it would destroy it, render it inaccessible, and block the way through the wonderful Tuolumne Cañon to the grand central campground in the upper Tuolumne Valley, thousands from near and far came to our help,—mountaineers, nature-lovers, naturalists. Most of our thousand club members wrote to the President or Secretary protesting against the destructive reservoir scheme while other sources of city water as pure or purer than the Hetch-Hetchy were available; so also did the Oregon and Washington mountaineering clubs and the Appalachian of Boston and public-spirited citizens everywhere. And the President, recognizing the need of beauty as well as bread and water in the life of the nation, far from favoring the destruction of any of our country's natural wonder parks and temples, is trying amid a host of other cares to save them all. Within a very short time he has saved the petrified forests of Arizona and the Grand Cañon, and in our own State the jagged peaks of San Benito county known as "The Pinnacles," making them national monuments or parks to be preserved for the people forever. None, therefore, need doubt that everything possible will be done to save Hetch-Hetchy.

After my first visit, in the autumn of 1871, I have always called it the Tuolumne Yosemite, for it is a wonderfully exact counterpart of the great Yosemite, not only in its crystal river and sublime rocks and waterfalls, but in the gardens, groves, and meadows of its flower park-like floor. The floor of Yosemite is about 4000 feet above the sea, the Hetch-Hetchy floor about 3700; the walls of both are of gray granite, rise abruptly out of the flowery grass and groves are sculptured in the same style, and in both every rock is a glacial monument.

Standing boldly out from the south wall is a strikingly picturesque rock called "Kolana" by the Indians, the outermost of a group 2300 feet high, corresponding with the Cathedral Rocks of Yosemite both in relative position and form. On the

Source: *Sierra Club Bulletin*, vol. 6, no. 4, January, 1908.

opposite side of the Valley, facing Kolana, there is a counterpart of the El Capitan of Yosemite rising sheer and plain to a height of 1800 feet, and over its massive brow flows a stream which makes the most graceful fall I have ever seen. From the edge of the cliff it is perfectly free in the air for a thousand feet, then breaks up into a ragged sheet of cascades among the boulders of an earthquake talus. It is in all its glory in June, when the snow is melting fast, but fades and vanishes toward the end of summer. The only fall I know with which it may fairly be compared is the Yosemite Bridal Veil; but it excels even that favorite fall both in height and fineness of fairy-airy beauty and behavior. Lowlanders are apt to suppose that mountain streams in their wild career over cliffs lose control of themselves and tumble in a noisy chaos of mist and spray. On the contrary, on no part of their travels are they more harmonious and self-controlled. Imagine yourself in Hetch Hetchy on a sunny day in June, standing waist-deep in grass and flowers (as I have oftentimes stood), while the great pines sway dreamily with scarce perceptible motion. Looking northward across the Valley you see a plain, gray granite cliff rising abruptly out of the gardens and groves to a height of 1800 feet, and in front of it Tueeulala's silvery scarf burning with irised sun-fire in every fiber. In the first white outburst of the stream at the head of the fall there is abundance of visible energy, but it is speedily hushed and concealed in divine repose, and its tranquil progress to the base of the cliff is like that of downy feathers in a still room. Now observe the fineness and marvelous distinctness of the various sun-illumined fabrics into which the water is woven; they sift and float from form to form down the face of that grand gray rock in so leisurely and unconfused a manner that you can examine their texture, and patterns and tones of color as you would a piece of embroidery held in the hand. Near the head of the fall you see groups of booming, comet-like masses, their solid, white heads separate, their tails like combed silk interlacing among delicate shadows, ever forming and dissolving, worn out by friction in their rush through the air. Most of these vanish a few hundred feet below the summit, changing to the varied forms of cloud-like drapery. Near the bottom the width of the fall has increased from about twenty-five to a hundred feet. Here it is composed of yet finer tissues, and is still without a trace of disorder—air, water and sunlight woven into stuff that spirits might wear.

So fine a fall might well seem sufficient to glorify any valley; but here, as in Yosemite, Nature seems in nowise moderate, for a short distance to the eastward of Tueeulala booms and thunders the great Hetch Hetchy Fall, Wapama, so near that you have both of them in full view from the same standpoint. It is the counterpart of the Yosemite Fall, but has a much greater volume of water, is about 1700 feet in height, and appears to be nearly vertical, though considerably inclined, and is dashed into huge outbounding bosses of foam on the projecting shelves and knobs of its jagged gorge. No two falls could be more unlike—Tueeulala out in the open sunshine descending like thistledown; Wapama in a jagged, shadowy gorge roaring and plundering, pounding its way with the weight and energy of an avalanche. Besides this glorious pair there is a broad, massive fall on the main river a short distance above the head of the Valley. Its position is something like that of the Vernal in Yosemite, and its roar as it plunges into a surging trout-pool may be heard a long way, though it is only about twenty feet high. There is also a chain of magnificent cascades at the head of the valley on a stream that comes in from the northeast, mostly silvery plumes, like the one between the Vernal and Nevada falls of Yosemite, half-sliding, half-leaping on bare glacier polished granite, covered with crisp clashing spray into which the sunbeams pour with glorious effect. And besides all these a few small streams come over the walls here and there, leaping from ledge to ledge with birdlike song and watering many a hidden cliff-garden and fernery, but they are too unshowy to be noticed in so grand a place.

The correspondence between the Hetch Hetchy walls in their trends, sculpture, physical structure, and general arrangement of the main rock-masses has excited the wondering admiration of every observer. We have seen that the El Capitan and Cathedral rocks occupy the same relative positions in both valleys; so also do their Yosemite Points and North Domes. Again that part of the Yosemite north wall immediately to the east of the Yosemite Fall has two horizontal benches timbered with golden-cup oak about 500 and 1500 feet above the floor. Two benches similarly situated and timbered occur on the same relative portion of the Hetch Hetchy north wall, to the east of Wapama Fall, and on no other. The Yosemite is bounded at the head by the great Half Dome. Hetch Hetchy is bounded in the same way though its head rock is far less wonderful and sublime in form.

The floor of the Valley is about three and a half miles long and from a fourth to half a mile wide. The lower portion is mostly a level meadow about a mile long, with the trees restricted to the sides, and partially separated from the upper forested portion by a low bar of glacier-polished granite across which the river breaks in rapids.

The principal trees are the yellow and sugar pines, Sabine pine, incense cedar, Douglas spruce, silver fir, the California and gold-cup oaks, balm of Gilead poplar, Nuttall's flowering dogwood, alder, maple, laurel, tumion, etc. The most abundant and influential are the great yellow pines, the tallest over two hundred feet in height, and the oaks with massive rugged trunks four to six or seven feet in diameter, and broad arching heads, assembled in magnificent groves. The shrubs forming conspicuous flowery clumps and tangles are manzanita, azalea, spiraea, brier-rose, ceanothus, calycanthus, philadelphus, wild cherry, etc.; with abundance of showy and fragrant herbaceous plants growing about them or out in the open in beds by themselves— lilies, Mariposa tulips, brodiaeas, orchids—several species of each,—iris, spraguea, draperia, collomia, collinsia, castilleia, nemophila, larkspur, columbine, goldenrods, sunflowers, and mints of many species, honeysuckle, etc. etc. Many fine ferns dwell here also, especially the beautiful and interesting rock-ferns—pellaea, and cheilanthes of several species—fringing and rosetting dry rock-piles and ledges; woodwardia and asplenium on damp spots with fronds six or seven feet high; the delicate maidenhair in mossy nooks by the falls, and the sturdy, broad-shouldered pteris beneath the oaks and pines.

It appears therefore that Hetch-Hetchy Valley, far from being a plain, common, rock-bound meadow, as many who have not seen it seem to suppose, is a grand landscape garden, one of Nature's rarest and most precious mountain mansions. As in Yosemite, the sublime rocks of its walls seem to the nature-lover to glow with life, whether leaning back in repose or standing erect in thoughtful attitudes, giving welcome to storms and calms alike. And how softly these mountain rocks are adorned, and how fine and reassuring the company they keep—their brows in the sky, their feet set in groves and gay emerald meadows, a thousand flowers leaning confidingly against their adamantine bosses, while birds, bees, and butterflies help the river and waterfalls to stir all the air into music—things frail and fleeting and types of permanence meeting here and blending, as if into this glorious mountain temple Nature had gathered here choicest treasures, whether great or small, to draw her lovers into close confiding communion with her.

Strange to say, this is the mountain temple that is now in danger of being dammed and made into a reservoir to help supply San Francisco with water and light. This use of the valley, so destructive and foreign to its proper park use, has long been planned and prayed for, and is still being prayed for by the San Francisco board of supervisors, not because water as pure and abundant cannot be got from adjacent sources outside the park—for it can,—but seemingly only because of the comparative cheapness of the dam required.

Garden- and park-making goes on everywhere with civilization, for everybody needs beauty as well as bread, places to play in and pray in, where Nature may heal and cheer and give strength to body and soul. This natural beauty-hunger is displayed in poor folks' window-gardens made up of a few geranium slips in broken cups, as well as in the costly lily gardens of the rich, the thousands of spacious city parks and botanical gardens, and in our magnificent National parks—the Yellowstone, Yosemite, Sequoia, etc.—Nature's own wonderlands, the admiration and joy of the world. Nevertheless, like everything else worth while, however sacred and precious and well-guarded, they have always been subject to attack, mostly by despoiling gainseekers,—mischief-makers of every degree from Satan to supervisors, lumbermen, cattlemen, farmers, etc., eagerly trying to make everything dollarable, often thinly disguised in smiling philanthropy, calling pocket-filling plunder "Utilization of beneficent natural resources, that man and beast may be fed and the dear Nation grow great." Thus long ago a lot of enterprising merchants made part of the Jerusalem temple into a place of business instead of a place of prayer, changing money, buying and selling cattle and sheep and doves. And earlier still, the Lord's garden in Eden, and the first forest reservation, including only one tree, was spoiled. And so to some extent have all our reservations and parks. Ever since the establishment of the Yosemite National Park by act of Congress, October 8, 1890, constant strife has been going on around its borders and I suppose this will go on as part of the universal battle between right and wrong, however its boundaries may be shorn or its wild beauty destroyed. The first application to the Government by the San Francisco Supervisors for the use of Lake Eleanor and the Hetch Hetchy Valley was made in 1903, and denied December 22nd of that year by the Secretary of the Interior. In his report on this case he well says: "Presumably the Yosemite National Park was created such by law because of the natural objects, of varying degrees of scenic importance, located within its boundaries, inclusive alike of its beautiful small lakes, like Eleanor, and its majestic wonders, like Hetch-Hetchy and Yosemite Valley. It is the aggregation of such natural scenic features that makes the Yosemite Park a wonderland which the Congress of the United States sought by law to preserve for all coming time as nearly as practicable in the condition fashioned by the hand of the Creator—a worthy object of national pride and a source of healthful pleasure and rest for the thousands of people who may annually sojourn there during the heated months."

The most delightful and wonderful campgrounds in the Park are the three great valleys—Yosemite, Hetch-Hetchy, and Upper Tuolumne; and they are also the most important places with reference to their positions relative to the other great features—the Merced and Tuolumne Cañons, and the High Sierra peaks and glaciers, etc., at the head of the rivers. The main part of the Tuolumne Valley is a beautiful spacious flowery lawn four or five miles long, surrounded by magnificent snowy mountains. It is about 8500 feet above the sea, and forms the grand central High Sierra camp ground from which excursions are made to the noble mountains, domes, glaciers, etc.; across the Range to the Mono Lake and volcanoes and down the Tuolumne Cañon to Hetch Hetchy. But should Hetch Hetchy be submerged, as proposed, not only would it be made utterly inaccessible, but the sublime cañon way to the heart of the High Sierra would be hopelessly blocked. None, as far as I have learned, of all the thousands who have seen the park is in favor of this destructive water scheme.

My last visit to the Valley was made in the autumn of last year, with William Keith, the artist. The leaf-colors were then ripe, and the great godlike rocks in repose seemed to glow with life. The artist, under their spell, wandered day after day along the beautiful river and through the groves and gardens, studying the wonderful scenery; and, after making about forty sketches, declared with enthusiasm that in picturesque beauty and charm Hetch Hetchy surpassed even Yosemite.

That any one would try to destroy such a place seemed impossible; but sad experience shows that there are people good enough and bad enough for anything. The proponents of the dam scheme bring forward a lot of bad arguments to prove that the only righteous thing for Hetch-Hetchy is its destruction. These arguments are curiously like those of the devil devised for the destruction of the first garden—so much of the very best Eden fruit going to waste; so much of the best Tuolumne water. Very few of their statements are even partly true, and all are misleading. Thus, Hetch Hetchy, they say, is a "low-lying meadow."

On the contrary, it is a high-lying natural landscape garden.

"It is a common minor feature, like thousands of others."

On the contrary, it is a very uncommon feature; after Yosemite, the rarest and in many ways the most important in the park.

"Damming and submerging it 175 feet deep would enhance its beauty by forming a crystal-clear lake."

Landscape gardens, places of recreation and worship, are never made beautiful by destroying and burying them. The beautiful lake, forsooth, should be only an eyesore, a dismal blot on the landscape, like many others to be seen in the Sierra. For, instead of keeping it at the same level all the year, allowing Nature to make new shores, it would, of course, be full only a month or two in the spring, when the snow is melting fast; then it would be gradually drained, exposing the slimy sides of the basin and shallower parts of the bottom, with the gathered drift and waste, death and decay of the upper basins, caught here instead of being swept on to decent natural burial along the banks of the river or in the sea. Thus the Hetch Hetchy dam-lake would be only a rough imitation of a natural lake for a few of the spring months, an open mountain sepulcher for the others.

"Hetch Hetchy water is the purest, wholly unpolluted, and forever unpollutable."

On the contrary, excepting that of the Merced below Yosemite, it is less pure than that of most of the other Sierra streams, because of the sewerage of campgrounds draining into it, especially of the Big Tuolumne Meadows campgrounds, where hundreds of tourists and mountaineers, with their animals, are encamped for months every summer, soon to be followed by thousands of travelers from all the world.

These temple destroyers, devotees of ravaging commercialism, seem to have a perfect contempt for Nature, and, instead of lifting their eyes to the mountains, lift them to dams and town skyscrapers.

Dam Hetch-Hetchy! As well dam for water-tanks the people's cathedrals and churches, for no holier temple has ever been consecrated by the heart of man.

"Save the Redwoods," January 1920

We are often told that the world is going from bad to worse, sacrificing everything to mammon. But this righteous uprising in defense of God's trees in the midst of exciting politics and wars is telling a different story, and every Sequoia, I fancy, has heard the good news and is waving its branches for joy. The wrongs done to trees, wrongs of every sort, are done in the darkness of ignorance and unbelief, for when light comes the heart of the people is always right. Forty-seven years ago one of these Calaveras King Sequoias was laboriously cut down, that the stump might be had for a dancing-floor. Another, one of the finest in the grove, more than three hundred feet high, was skinned alive to a height of one hundred and sixteen feet from the ground and the bark sent to London to show how fine and big that Calaveras tree was—as sensible a scheme as skinning our great men would be to prove their greatness. This grand tree is of course dead, a ghastly disfigured ruin, but it still stands erect and holds forth its majestic arms as if alive and saying, "Forgive them; they know not what they do." Now some millmen want to cut all the Calaveras trees into lumber and money. But we have found a better use for them. No doubt these trees would make good lumber after passing through a sawmill, as George Washington after passing through the hands of a French cook would have made good food. But both for Washington and the tree that bears his name higher uses have been found.

Could one of these Sequoia Kings come to town in all its godlike majesty so as to be strikingly seen and allowed to plead its own cause, there would never again be any lack of defenders. And the same may be said of all the other Sequoia groves and forests of the Sierra with their companions and the noble *Sequoia sempervirens,* or redwood, of the coast mountains.

In a general view we find that the *Sequoia gigantea,* or Big Tree, is distributed in a widely interrupted belt along the west flank of the Sierra, from a small grove on the middle fork of the American River to the head of Deer Creek, a distance of about two hundred and sixty miles, at an elevation of about five thousand to a little over eight thousand feet above the sea. From the American River grove to the forest on Kings River the species occurs only in comparatively small isolated patches or groves so sparsely distributed along the belt that three of the gaps in it are from forty to

SOURCE: *Sierra Club Bulletin,* vol. 11, no.1, January 1920, 1–4.

sixty miles wide. From Kings River southward the Sequoia is not restricted to mere groves, but extends across the broad rugged basins of the Kaweah and Tule rivers in majestic forests a distance of nearly seventy miles, the continuity of this portion of the belt being but slightly broken save by the deep cañons.

In these noble groves and forests to the southward of the Calaveras Grove the axe and saw have long been busy, and thousands of the finest Sequoias have been felled, blasted into manageable dimensions, and sawed into lumber by methods destructive almost beyond belief, while fires have spread still wider and more lamentable ruin. In the course of my explorations twenty-five years ago, I found five sawmills located on or near the lower margin of the Sequoia belt, all of which were cutting more or less Big Tree lumber, which looks like the redwood of the coast, and was sold as redwood. One of the smallest of these mills in the season of 1874 sawed two million feet of Sequoia lumber. Since that time other mills have been built among the Sequoias, notably the large ones on Kings River and the head of the Fresno. The destruction of these grand trees is still going on.

On the other hand, the Calaveras Grove for forty years has been faithfully protected by Mr. Sperry, and with the exception of the two trees mentioned above is still in primeval beauty. The Tuolumne and Merced groves near Yosemite, the Dinky Creek grove, those of the General Grant National Park and the Sequoia National Park, with several outstanding groves that are nameless on the Kings, Kaweah, and Tule river basins, and included in the Sierra forest reservation, have of late years been partially protected by the Federal Government; while the well-known Mariposa Grove has long been guarded by the State.

For the thousands of acres of Sequoia forest outside of the reservation and national parks, and in the hands of lumbermen, no help is in sight. Probably more than three times as many Sequoias as are contained in the whole Calaveras Grove have been cut into lumber every year for the last twenty-six years without let or hindrance, and with scarce a word of protest on the part of the public, while at the first whisper of the bonding of the Calaveras Grove to lumbermen most everybody rose in alarm. This righteous and lively indignation on the part of Californians after the long period of deathlike apathy, in which they have witnessed the destruction of other groves unmoved, seems strange until the rapid growth that right public opinion has made during the last few years is considered and the peculiar interest that attaches to the Calaveras giants. They were the first discovered and are best known. Thousands of travelers from every country have come to pay them tribute of admiration and praise, their reputation is world-wide, and the names of great men have long been associated with them—Washington, Humboldt, Torrey and Gray, Sir Joseph Hooker, and others. These kings of the forest, the noblest of a noble race, rightly belong to the world, but as they are in California we cannot escape responsibility as their guardians. Fortunately the American people are equal to this trust, or any other that may arise, as soon as they see it and understand it.

Any fool can destroy trees. They cannot defend themselves or run away. And few destroyers of trees ever plant any; nor can planting avail much toward restoring our grand aboriginal giants. It took more than three thousand years to make some of the oldest of the Sequoias, trees that are still standing in perfect strength and beauty, waving and singing in the mighty forests of the Sierra. Through all the eventful centuries since Christ's time, and long before that, God has cared for these trees, saved them from drought, disease, avalanches, and a thousand storms; but he cannot save them from sawmills and fools; this is left to the American people. . . .

Emma Goldman (1869–1940)

Emma Goldman, a Lithuanian Jew, spent much of her youth in St. Petersburg, Russia, at a time when Jews were persecuted and the political philosophy of anarchism was having a huge impact on revolutionary students. In 1881, revolutionary factions had become so sure of the righteousness of their cause that they assassinated Czar Alexander III. In the aftermath of the authoritarian crackdown on anarchists, 16-year-old Emma Goldman emigrated to the United States in 1885. She must have had a sense that she would find a golden land of opportunity in the New World—at least that there would be more opportunities for a young woman than there were in czarist Russia. But it did not take her long to realize that life in her new home was not exactly a bed of roses. She took a low-paying job in a factory in Rochester, New York, and began to engage in political activities. Influenced by newspaper accounts of the trial, conviction, and execution of the anarchists who had been accused of killing several police officers at Haymarket Square in Chicago, Goldman left her job in 1889, moved to New York City, and joined an anarchist association. Within a few short years, she became one of the most outspoken and notorious anarchist-feminists in the nation. Believing that a society could be created in which there would be no private property or repression and in which absolute freedom would exist for all individuals, she became an activist campaigning for women's rights to birth control, full equality, and sexual liberation, as well as the rights of workers to unionize. In 1892, she went so far as to aid and abet her lover (and fellow anarchist) Alexander Berkman in his unsuccessful attempt to assassinate the chairman of the Carnegie Steel Company, Henry Clay Frick, during the Homestead Strike. During the First World War, her protests against conscription and her speeches praising the Bolshevik revolution in Russia led to her arrest and, after two years in jail, her eventual deportation in 1919.

The institution of marriage, Goldman believed, was nothing but legalized prostitution. In a patriarchic society that deprived them of social and economic equality, women were forced to "sell themselves" into marriage to survive. The only way women would ever achieve equality was not through gaining political power or the right to vote but through abolishing the institution of marriage altogether and securing absolute control over their own bodies. "True emancipation," she declared, "begins neither at the polls nor in court. It begins in a woman's soul." The goal was complete and total emotional and sexual liberation.

In her writings, Emma Goldman argues persuasively for the creation of a society in which democracy and freedom are truly realized and in which distinctions of gender and race have been obliterated. What does Goldman believe is the cause of exploitation? What does the institution of marriage do for women? Why should marriage be abolished? Can the type of society she envisions succeed?

"Marriage and Love," 1911

The popular notion about marriage and love is that they are synonymous, that they spring from the same motives, and cover the same human needs. Like most popular notions this also rests not on actual facts, but on superstition.

Marriage and love have nothing in common; they are as far apart as the poles; are, in fact, antagonistic to each other. No doubt some marriages have been the result of love. Not, however, because love could assert itself only in marriage; much rather is it because few people can completely outgrow a convention. There are to-day large numbers of men and women to whom marriage is naught but a farce, but who submit to it for the sake of public opinion. At any rate, while it is true that some marriages are based on love, and while it is equally true that in some cases love continues in married life, I maintain that it does so regardless of marriage, and not because of it.

On the other hand, it is utterly false that love results from marriage. On rare occasions one does hear of a miraculous case of a married couple falling in love after marriage, but on close examination it will be found that it is a mere adjustment to the inevitable. Certainly the growing used to each other is far away from the spontaneity, the intensity, and beauty of love, without which the intimacy of marriage must prove degrading to both the woman and the man.

Marriage is primarily an economic arrangement, an insurance pact. It differs from the ordinary life insurance agreement only in that it is more binding, more exacting. Its returns are insignificantly small compared with the investments. In taking out an insurance policy one pays for it in dollars and cents, always at liberty to discontinue payments. If, however, woman's premium is a husband, she pays for it with her name, her privacy, her self-respect, her very life, "until death doth part." Moreover, the marriage insurance condemns her to life-long dependency, to parasitism, to complete uselessness, individual as well as social. Man, too, pays his toll, but as his sphere is wider, marriage does not limit him as much as woman. He feels his chains more in an economic sense.

Thus Dante's motto over Inferno applies with equal force to marriage: "Ye who enter here leave all hope behind."

That marriage is a failure none but the very stupid will deny. One has but to glance over the statistics of divorce to realize how bitter a failure marriage really is. . . . [S]cores of . . . writers are discussing the barrenness, the monotony, the sordidness, the inadequacy of marriage as a factor for harmony and understanding.

SOURCE: Emma Goldman, *Anarchism and Other Essays*, 2nd ed. (New York & London: Mother Earth Publishing Association, 1911), 233–245.

The thoughtful social student will not content himself with the popular superficial excuse for this phenomenon. He will have to dig down deeper into the very life of the sexes to know why marriage proves so disastrous.

Edward Carpenter says that behind every marriage stands the life-long environment of the two sexes; an environment so different from each other that man and woman must remain strangers. Separated by an insurmountable wall of superstition, custom, and habit, marriage has not the potentiality of developing knowledge of, and respect for, each other, without which every union is doomed to failure.

Henrik Ibsen, the hater of all social shams, was probably the first to realize this great truth. Nora leaves her husband, not—as the stupid critic would have it—because she is tired of her responsibilities or feels the need of woman's rights, but because she has come to know that for eight years she had lived with a stranger and borne him children. Can there be any thing more humiliating, more degrading than a life-long proximity between two strangers? No need for the woman to know anything of the man, save his income. As to the knowledge of the woman—what is there to know except that she has a pleasing appearance? We have not yet outgrown the theologic myth that woman has no soul, that she is a mere appendix to man, made out of his rib just for the convenience of the gentleman who was so strong that he was afraid of his own shadow.

Perchance the poor quality of the material whence woman comes is responsible for her inferiority. At any rate, woman has no soul—what is there to know about her? Besides, the less soul a woman has the greater her asset as a wife, the more readily will she absorb herself in her husband. It is this slavish acquiescence to man's superiority that has kept the marriage institution seemingly intact for so long a period. Now that woman is coming into her own, now that she is actually growing aware of herself as a being outside of the master's grace, the sacred institution of marriage is gradually being undermined, and no amount of sentimental lamentation can stay it.

From infancy, almost, the average girl is told that marriage is her ultimate goal; therefore her training and education must be directed towards that end. Like the mute beast fattened for slaughter, she is prepared for that. Yet, strange to say, she is allowed to know much less about her function as wife and mother than the ordinary artisan of his trade. It is indecent and filthy for a respectable girl to know anything of the marital relation. Oh, for the inconsistency of respectability, that needs the marriage vow to turn something which is filthy into the purest and most sacred arrangement that none dare question or criticize. Yet that is exactly the attitude of the average upholder of marriage. The prospective wife and mother is kept in complete ignorance of her only asset in the competitive field—sex. Thus she enters into life-long relations with a man only to find herself shocked, repelled, outraged beyond measure by the most natural and healthy instinct, sex. It is safe to say that a large percentage of the unhappiness, misery, distress, and physical suffering of matrimony is due to the criminal ignorance in sex matters that is being extolled as a great virtue. Nor is it at all an exaggeration when I say that more than one home has been broken up because of this deplorable fact.

If, however, woman is free and big enough to learn the mystery of sex without the sanction of State or Church, she will stand condemned as utterly unfit to become the wife of a "good" man, his goodness consisting of an empty head and plenty of money. Can there be anything more outrageous than the idea that a healthy, grown woman, full of life and passion, must deny nature's demand, must subdue her most intense craving, undermine her health and break her spirit, must stunt her vision, abstain from the depth and glory of sex experience until a "good" man comes along to take her unto himself as a wife? That is precisely what marriage means. How can such an arrangement end except in failure? This is one, though not the least important, factor of marriage, which differentiates it from love.

Ours is a practical age. . . . If, on rare occasions young people allow themselves the luxury of romance they are taken in care by the elders, drilled and pounded until they become "sensible."

The moral lesson instilled in the girl is not whether the man has aroused her love, but rather is it, "How much?" The important and only God of practical American life: Can the man make a living? Can he support a wife? That is the only thing that justifies marriage. Gradually this saturates every thought of the girl; her dreams are not of moonlight and kisses, of laughter and tears; she dreams of shopping tours and bargain counters. This soul-poverty and sordidness are the elements inherent in the marriage institution. The State and the Church approve of no other ideal, simply because it is the one that necessitates the State and Church control of men and women.

Doubtless there are people who continue to consider love above dollars and cents. Particularly is this true of that class whom economic necessity has forced to become self-supporting. The tremendous change in woman's position, wrought by that mighty factor, is indeed phenomenal when we reflect that it is but a short time since she has entered the industrial arena. Six million women wage-earners; six million women, who have the equal right with men to be exploited, to be robbed, to go on strike; aye, to starve even. Anything more, my lord? Yes, six million wage-workers in every walk of life, from the highest brain work to the most difficult menial labor in the mines and on the railroad tracks; yes, even detectives and policemen. Surely the emancipation is complete.

Yet with all that, but a very small number of the vast army of women wage-workers look upon work as a permanent issue, in the same light as does man. No matter how decrepit the latter, he has been taught to be independent, self-supporting. Oh, I know that no one is really independent in our economic tread mill; still, the poorest specimen of a man hates to be a parasite; to be known as such, at any rate.

The woman considers her position as worker transitory, to be thrown aside for the first bidder. That is why it is infinitely harder to organize women than men. "Why should I join a union? I am going to get married, to have a home." Has she not been taught from infancy to look upon that as her ultimate calling? She learns soon enough that the home, though not so large a prison as the factory, has more solid doors and bars. It has a keeper so faithful that naught can escape him. The most tragic part, however, is that the home no longer frees her from wage slavery; it only increases her task.

According to the latest statistics submitted before a Committee "on labor and wages, and congestion of Population," ten per cent. of the wage workers in New York City alone are married, yet they must continue to work at the most poorly paid labor in the world. Add to this horrible aspect the drudgery of house work, and what remains of the protection and glory of the home? As a matter of fact, even the middle class girl in marriage can not speak of her home, since it is the man who creates her sphere. It is not important whether the husband is a brute or a darling. What I wish to prove is that marriage guarantees woman a home only by the grace of her husband. There she moves about in *his* home, year after year until her aspect of life and human affairs becomes as flat, narrow, and drab as her surroundings. Small wonder if she becomes a nag, petty, quarrelsome, gossipy, unbearable, thus driving the man from the house. She could not go, if she wanted to; there is no place to go. Besides, a short period of married life, of complete surrender of all faculties, absolutely incapacitates the average woman for the outside world. She becomes reckless in appearance, clumsy in her movements, dependent in her decisions, cowardly in her judgment, a weight and a bore, which most men grow to hate and despise. Wonderfully inspiring atmosphere for the bearing of life, is it not?

But the child, how is it to be protected, if not for marriage? After all, is not that the most important consideration? The sham, the hypocrisy of it! Marriage protecting the child, yet thousands of children destitute and homeless. Marriage protecting the child, yet orphan asylums and reformatories over crowded, the Society for the Prevention of Cruelty to Children keeping busy in rescuing the little victims from "loving" parents, to place them under more loving care, the Gerry Society. Oh, the mockery of it! . . .

As to the protection of the woman,—therein lies the curse of marriage. Not that it really protects her, but the very idea is so revolting, such an outrage and insult on life, so degrading to human dignity, as to forever condemn this parasitic institution.

It is like that other paternal arrangement—capitalism. It robs man of his birthright, stunts his growth, poisons his body, keeps him in ignorance, in poverty and dependence, and then institutes charities that thrive on the last vestige of man's self-respect.

The institution of marriage makes a parasite of woman, an absolute dependent. It incapacitates her for life's struggle, annihilates her social consciousness, paralyzes her imagination, and then imposes its gracious protection, which is in reality a snare, a travesty on human character.

If motherhood is the highest fulfillment of woman's nature, what other protection does it need save love and freedom? Marriage but defiles, outrages, and corrupts her fulfillment. Does it not say to woman, Only when you follow me shall you bring forth life? Does it not condemn her to the block, does it not degrade and shame her if she refuses to buy her right to motherhood by selling herself? Does not marriage only sanction motherhood, even though conceived in hatred, in compulsion? Yet, if motherhood be of free choice, of love, of ecstasy, of defiant passion, does it not place a crown of thorns upon an innocent head and carve in letters of blood the hideous epithet, Bastard? Were marriage to contain all the virtues claimed for it, its crimes against motherhood would exclude it forever from the realm of love.

Love, the strongest and deepest element in all life, the harbinger of hope, of joy, of ecstasy; love, the defier of all laws, of all conventions; love, the freest, the most powerful moulder of human destiny; how can such an all-compelling force be synonymous with that poor little State and Church-begotten weed, marriage?

Free love? As if love is anything but free! Man has bought brains, but all the millions in the world have failed to buy love. Man has subdued bodies, but all the power on earth has been unable to subdue love. Man has conquered whole nations, but all his armies could not conquer love. Man has chained and fettered the spirit, but he has been utterly helpless before love. High on a throne, with all the splendor and pomp his gold can command, man is yet poor and desolate, if love passes him by. And if it stays, the poorest hovel is radiant with warmth, with life and color. Thus love has the magic power to make of a beggar a king. Yes, love is free; it can dwell in no other atmosphere. In freedom it gives itself unreservedly, abundantly, completely. All the laws on the statutes, all the courts in the universe, cannot tear it from the soil, once love has taken root. If, however, the soil is sterile, how can marriage make it bear fruit? It is like the last desperate struggle of fleeting life against death.

Love needs no protection; it is its own protection. So long as love begets life no child is deserted, or hungry, or famished for the want of affection. I know this to be true. I know women who became mothers in freedom by the men they loved. Few children in wedlock enjoy the care, the protection, the devotion free motherhood is capable of bestowing.

The defenders of authority dread the advent of a free motherhood, lest it will rob them of their prey. Who would fight wars? Who would create wealth? Who would make the policeman, the jailer, if woman were to refuse the indiscriminate breeding of children? The race, the race! shouts the king, the president, the capitalist, the priest. The race must be preserved, though woman be degraded to a mere machine,—and the marriage institution is our only safety valve against the pernicious sex-awakening of woman. But in vain these frantic efforts to maintain a state of bondage. In vain, too, the edicts of the Church, the mad attacks of rulers, in vain even the arm of the law. Woman no longer wants to be a party to the production of a race of sickly, feeble, decrepit, wretched human beings, who have neither the strength nor moral courage to throw off the yoke of poverty and slavery. Instead she desires fewer and better children, begotten and reared in love and through free choice; not by compulsion, as marriage imposes. Our pseudo-moralists have yet to learn the deep sense of responsibility toward the child, that love in freedom has awakened in the breast of woman. Rather would she forego forever the glory of motherhood than bring forth life in an atmosphere that breathes only destruction and death. And if she does become a mother, it is to give to the child the deepest and best her being can yield. To grow with the child is her motto; she knows that in that manner alone can she help build true manhood and womanhood. . . .

In our present pygmy state love is indeed a stranger to most people. Misunderstood and shunned, it rarely takes root; or if it does, it soon withers and dies. Its delicate fiber can not endure the stress and strain of the daily grind. Its soul is too complex to adjust itself to the slimy woof of our social fabric. It weeps and moans and suffers with those who have need of it, yet lack the capacity to rise to love's summit.

Some day, some day men and women will rise, they will reach the mountain peak, they will meet big and strong and free, ready to receive, to partake, and to bask in the golden rays of love. What fancy, what imagination, what poetic genius can foresee even approximately the potentialities of such a force in the life of men and women. If the world is ever to give birth to true companionship and oneness, not marriage, but love will be the parent.

Walter Rauschenbusch (1861–1918)

Throughout history, when the destitute sought solace and relief from hardship from their clergy, they were usually advised to pray and look forward to their reward in the next life. Walter Rauschenbusch, however, believed that it was as important to address people's needs in this life as it was to minister to their spiritual needs. After studying in Germany and England, where he was influenced by the Fabian socialist movement, he returned to the United States and became pastor of the Second German Baptist Church in New York City. While ministering to the German immigrants in the Hell's Kitchen section of the city, he began to develop the Social Gospel. By applying Christian principles to his critique of capitalism and Spencer and Sumner's social Darwinism, he, in effect, brought a moral dimension to the progressive movement. It was not enough to approach the problems of society from a political or social standpoint, for the problems were also, in Rauschenbusch's eyes, moral ones. By bringing morality into the discussion, he had a profound impact on many other reformers at the beginning of the twentieth century. His Social Gospel's appeal to Christian ethics brought many people who had previously been apathetic to the plight of the poor into the progressive movement. One of Rauschenbusch's contemporaries, Charles Sheldon, wrote a popular and influential book, In His Steps, in which he urged businessmen and politicians, whenever they were confronted with a decision that would affect the lives of workers, always to ask themselves one simple question before making that decision: "What would Jesus do?" Later in the century, another clergyman, Martin Luther King Jr., would apply a moral dimension to the civil rights movement.

In this excerpt, Rauschenbusch applies Christianity to the social order. What is the cause, according to Rauschenbusch, of society's problems? What is a Christian's responsibility to society?

From *Christianizing the Social Order*, 1912

The chief purpose of the Christian Church in the past has been the salvation of individuals. But the most pressing task of the present is not individualistic. Our business is to make over an antiquated and immoral economic system: to get rid of laws, customs, maxims, and philosophies inherited from an evil and despotic past; to create just and brotherly relations between great groups and classes of society; and thus to lay a social foundation on which modern men individually can live and work in a fashion that will not outrage all the better elements in them. . . .

The Christian Church in the past has taught us to work with our eyes fixed on another world and a life to come. But the business before us is concerned with refashioning the present world, making this earth clean and sweet and habitable. . . .

Twenty-five years ago the social wealth of the Bible was almost undiscovered to most of us. . . . Even Jesus talked like an individualist in those days and seemed to repudiate the social interest when we interrogated him. He said his kingdom was not of this world; the things of God had nothing to do with the things of Caesar; the poor we would always have with us; and his ministers must not be judges and dividers when Labor argued with Capital about the division of the inheritance. Today he has resumed the spiritual leadership of social Christianity, of which he was the founder. It is a new tribute to his mastership that the social message of Jesus was the first great possession which social Christianity rediscovered. . . .

With true Christian instinct men have turned to the Christian law of love as the key to the situation. If we all loved our neighbor, we should "treat him right," pay him a living wage, give sixteen ounces to the pound, and not charge so much for beef. But this appeal assumes that we are still living in the simple personal relations of the good old times, and that every man can do the right thing when he wants to do it. But suppose a business man would be glad indeed to pay his young women the $12 a week which they need for a decent living, but all his competitors are paying from $7 down to $5. Shall he love himself into bankruptcy? . . . The old advice of love breaks down before the hugeness of modern relations. . . . It is indeed love that we want, but it is socialized love. Blessed be the love that holds a cup of water to thirsty lips. . . . What we most need today is not the love that will break its back drawing water for a growing factory town from a well that was meant to supply a village, but a love so large and intelligent that it will persuade an ignorant people to build a system of waterworks up in the hills, and that will get after the thoughtless farmers who contaminate the brooks with typhoid bacilli, and after the lumber concern that is denuding the watershed of its forests. We want a new avatar of love. . . .

The Socialist Party

In 1912, the Socialist Party's presidential candidate, Eugene V. Debs, received a remarkable 6 percent of the popular vote. Democrats, Republicans, industrial leaders, and bankers were shocked that nearly a million men voted for a party that wanted to abolish capitalism and turn the United States into

Source: Walter Rauschenbusch, *Christianizing the Social Order* (New York: Macmillan, 1912), 41–44.

a socialist society. In the ensuing years, especially after the Bolshevik revolution in Russia in 1917, opposition to socialism increased dramatically, as politicians and businessmen did everything in their power to discredit the Socialist Party, as well as all other left-wing political organizations.

How is the Socialist Party platform here similar to the Populists'? In what way is it different? Why is socialism viewed as such a threat to American principles? Which American values and ideals would be diminished under a socialist government? Are the socialists' demands still viewed as radical today?

Socialist Party Platform, May 12, 1912

The Socialist party declares that the capitalist system has outgrown its historical function, and has become utterly incapable of meeting the problems now confronting society. We denounce this outgrown system as incompetent and corrupt and the source of unspeakable misery and suffering to the whole working class.

Under this system the industrial equipment of the nation has passed into the absolute control of a plutocracy which exacts an annual tribute of hundreds of millions of dollars from the producers. Unafraid of any organized resistance, it stretches out its greedy hands over the still undeveloped resources of the nation— the land, the mines, the forests and the water powers of every State of the Union.

In spite of the multiplication of laborsaving machines and improved methods in industry which cheapen the cost of production, the share of the producers grows ever less, and the prices of all the necessities of life steadily increase. The boasted prosperity of this nation is for the owning class alone. To the rest it means only greater hardship and misery. The high cost of living is felt in every home. Millions of wage-workers have seen the purchasing power of their wages decrease until life has become a desperate battle for mere existence.

Multitudes of unemployed walk the streets of our cities or trudge from State to State awaiting the will of the masters to move the wheels of industry.

The farmers in every state are plundered by the increasing prices exacted for tools and machinery and by extortionate rents, freight rates and storage charges.

Capitalist concentration is mercilessly crushing the class of small business men and driving its members into the ranks of propertyless wage-workers. The overwhelming majority of the people of America are being forced under a yoke of bondage by this soulless industrial despotism.

It is this capitalist system that is responsible for the increasing burden of armaments, the poverty, slums, child labor, most of the insanity, crime and prostitution, and much of the disease that afflicts mankind.

Under this system the working class is exposed to poisonous conditions, to frightful and needless perils to life and limb, is walled around with court decisions,

---

Source: Retrieved on 12/22/2003 from www.utdallas.edu/~pryan/4378%20Readings/socialist.html.

injunctions and unjust laws, and is preyed upon incessantly for the benefit of the controlling oligarchy of wealth. Under it also, the children of the working class are doomed to ignorance, drudging toil and darkened lives.

In the face of these evils, so manifest that all thoughtful observers are appalled at them, the legislative representatives of the Republican and Democratic parties remain the faithful servants of the oppressors. Measures designed to secure to the wage-earners of this Nation as humane and just treatment as is already enjoyed by the wage-earners of all other civilized nations have been smothered in committee without debate, the laws ostensibly designed to bring relief to the farmers and general consumers are juggled and transformed into instruments for the exaction of further tribute. The growing unrest under oppression has driven these two old parties to the enactment of a variety of regulative measures, none of which has limited in any appreciable degree the power of the plutocracy, and some of which have been perverted into means of increasing that power. Anti-trust laws, railroad restrictions and regulations, with the prosecutions, indictments and investigations based upon such legislation, have proved to be utterly futile and ridiculous.

Nor has this plutocracy been seriously restrained or even threatened by any Republican or Democratic executive. It has continued to grow in power and insolence alike under the administration of Cleveland, McKinley, Roosevelt and Taft.

We declare, therefore, that the longer sufferance of these conditions is impossible, and we purpose to end them all. We declare them to be the product of the present system in which industry is carried on for private greed, instead of for the welfare of society. We declare, furthermore, that for these evils there will be and can be no remedy and no substantial relief except through Socialism under which industry will be carried on for the common good and every worker receive the full social value of the wealth he creates.

Society is divided into warring groups and classes, based upon material interests. Fundamentally, this struggle is a conflict between the two main classes, one of which, the capitalist class, owns the means of production, and the other, the working class, must use these means of production, on terms dictated by the owners.

The capitalist class, though few in numbers, absolutely controls the government, legislative, executive and judicial. This class owns the machinery of gathering and disseminating news through its organized press. It subsidizes seats of learning—the colleges and schools—and even religious and moral agencies. It has also the added prestige which established customs give to any order of society, right or wrong.

The working class, which includes all those who are forced to work for a living whether by hand or brain, in shop, mine or on the soil, vastly outnumbers the capitalist class. Lacking effective organization and class solidarity, this class is unable to enforce its will. Given such a class solidarity and effective organization, the workers will have the power to make all laws and control all industry in their own interest. All political parties are the expression of economic class interests. All other parties than the Socialist party represent one or another group of the ruling capitalist class. Their political conflicts reflect merely superficial rivalries between competing capitalist groups. However they result, these conflicts have no issue of real value to the workers. Whether the Democrats or Republicans win politically, it is the capitalist class that is victorious economically.

The Socialist party is the political expression of the economic interests of the workers. Its defeats have been their defeats and its victories their victories. It is a party founded on the science and laws of social development. It proposes that, since all social necessities to-day are socially produced, the means of their production and distribution shall be socially owned and democratically controlled.

In the face of the economic and political aggressions of the capitalist class the only reliance left the workers is that of their economic organizations and their political power. By the intelligent and class conscious use of these, they may resist successfully the capitalist class, break the fetters of wage slavery, and fit themselves for the future society, which is to displace the capitalist system. The Socialist party appreciates the full significance of class organization and urges the wage-earners, the working farmers and all other useful workers to organize for economic and political action, and we pledge ourselves to support the toilers of the fields as well as those in the shops, factories and mines of the nation in their struggles for economic justice.

In the defeat or victory of the working class party in this new struggle for freedom lies the defeat or triumph of the common people of all economic groups, as well as the failure or triumph of popular government. Thus the Socialist party is the party of the present day revolution which makes the transition from economic individualism to socialism, from wage slavery to free co-operation, from capitalist oligarchy to industrial democracy.

WORKING PROGRAM

As measures calculated to strengthen the working class in its fight for the realization of its ultimate aim, the co-operative commonwealth, and to increase its power against capitalist oppression, we advocate and pledge ourselves and our elected officers to the following program:

COLLECTIVE OWNERSHIP

1. The collective ownership and democratic management of railroads, wire and wireless telegraphs and telephones, express service, steamboat lines, and all other social means of transportation and communication and of all large scale industries.
2. The immediate acquirement by the municipalities, the states or the federal government of all grain elevators, stock yards, storage warehouses, and other distributing agencies, in order to reduce the present extortionate cost of living.
3. The extension of the public domain to include mines, quarries, oil wells, forests and water power.
4. The further conservation and development of natural resources for the use and benefit of all the people. . .
5. The collective ownership of land wherever practicable, and in cases where such ownership is impracticable, the appropriation by taxation of the annual rental value of all the land held for speculation and exploitation.
6. The collective ownership and democratic management of the banking and currency system.

UNEMPLOYMENT

The immediate government relief of the unemployed by the extension of all useful public works. All persons employed on such works to be engaged directly by the government under a work day of not more than eight hours and at not less than the prevailing union wages. The government also to establish employment bureaus; to lend money to states and municipalities without interest for the purpose of carrying on public works, and to take such other measures within its power as will lessen the widespread misery of the workers caused by the misrule of the capitalist class.

INDUSTRIAL DEMANDS

The conservation of human resources, particularly of the lives and well-being of the workers and their families:

1. By shortening the work day in keeping with the increased productiveness of machinery.
2. By securing for every worker a rest period of not less than a day and a half in each week.
3. By securing a more effective inspection of workshops, factories and mines.
4. By forbidding the employment of children under sixteen years of age.
5. By the co-operative organization of the industries in the federal penitentiaries for the benefit of the convicts and their dependents.
6. By forbidding the interstate transportation of the products of child labor, of convict labor and of all uninspected factories and mines.
7. By abolishing the profit system in government work and substituting either the direct hire of labor or the awarding of contracts to co-operative groups of workers.
8. By establishing minimum wage scales.
9. By abolishing official charity and substituting a non-contributary system of old age pensions, a general system of insurance by the State of all its members against unemployment and invalidism and a system of compulsory insurance by employers of their workers, without cost to the latter, against industrial diseases, accidents and death.

POLITICAL DEMANDS

1. The absolute freedom of press, speech and assemblage.
2. The adoption of a graduated income tax and the extension of inheritance taxes, graduated in proportion to the value of the estate and to nearness of kin—the proceeds of these taxes to be employed in the socialization of industry.
3. The abolition of the monopoly ownership of patents and the substitution of collective ownership, with direct rewards to inventors by premiums or royalties.
4. Unrestricted and equal suffrage for men and women.
5. The adoption of the initiative, referendum and recall and of proportional representation, nationally as well as locally.
6. The abolition of the Senate and of the veto power of the President.

7. The election of the President and Vice-President by direct vote of the people.

8. The abolition of the power usurped by the Supreme Court of the United States to pass upon the constitutionality of the legislation enacted by Congress. National laws to be repealed only by act of Congress or by a referendum vote of the whole people.

9. Abolition of the present restrictions upon the amendment of the constitution, so that instrument may be made amendable by a majority of the voters in a majority of the States.

10. The granting of the right of suffrage in the District of Columbia with representation in Congress and a democratic form of municipal government for purely local affairs.

11. The extension of democratic government to all United States territory.

12. The enactment of further measures for the conservation of health. The creation of an independent bureau of health, with such restrictions as will secure full liberty to all schools of practice.

13. The enactment of further measures for general education and particularly for vocational education in useful pursuits. The Bureau of Education to be made a department.

14. The separation of the present Bureau of Labor from the Department of Commerce and Labor and its elevation to the rank of a department.

15. Abolition of all federal district courts and the United States circuit court of appeals. State courts to have jurisdiction in all cases arising between citizens of several states and foreign corporations. The election of all judges for short terms.

16. The immediate curbing of the power of the courts to issue injunctions.

17. The free administration of the law.

18. The calling of a convention for the revision of the constitution of the U.S.

Such measures of relief as we may be able to force from capitalism are but a preparation of the workers to seize the whole powers of government, in order that they may thereby lay hold of the whole system of socialized industry and thus come to their rightful inheritance.

WEB RESOURCES FOR PART TWO

SITES FEATURING A NUMBER OF THE DISSENTERS IN PART TWO:

Indian Land Cessions
www.tngenweb.org/cessions/ms-west/

Chief Joseph
www.pbs.org/weta/thewest/people/a_c/chiefjoseph.htm

Terence Powderly
www.takver.com/history/secsoc02.htm

Emmeline Wells
www.pbs.org/weta/thewest/people/s_z/wells.htm

Mary Elizabeth Lease
http://projects.vassar.edu/1896/lease.html
www.law.stanford.edu/library/wlhbp/profiles/LeaseMary.shtml

Susan B. Anthony
www.law.umkc.edu/faculty/projects/ftrials/anthony/sbahome.html
http://mep.cla.sc.edu/sa/sa-table.html
http://ecssba.rutgers.edu/

Jane Addams
www.lkwdpl.org/wihohio/adda-jan.htm

Frances Willard
http://gos.sbc.edu/w/willard.html

Booker T. Washington
www.historycooperative.org/btw/

W. E. B. DuBois
http://faculty.millikin.edu/~rbrooks.hum.faculty.mu/MApoetry/Duboissite.html
www.dc.peachnet.edu/~shale/humanities/composition/assignments/dubois.html

Ida B. Wells-Barnett
www.webster.edu/~woolflm/idabwells.html
www.duke.edu/~ldbaker/classes/AAIH/caaih/ibwells/ibwbkgrd.html

Carl Schurz
www.balchinstitute.org/manuscript_guide/html/schurz.html

William Jennings Bryan
www.boondocksnet.com/ai/ail/bryan.html

Mother Jones
www.eclipse.net/~basket42/mojones.htm
www.kentlaw.edu/ilhs/majones.htm

John Muir
www.sierraclub.org/john_muir_exhibit/

Emma Goldman
http://sunsite.berkeley.edu/Goldman/

Walter Rauschenbusch
http://spider.georgetowncollege.edu/htallant/courses/his338/students/kpotter/

OTHER DISSENTING VOICES OF THE TIME:

John Burroughs
John Burroughs was a naturalist who wrote many essays extolling the environment.

http://cdl.library.cornell.edu/moa/browse.author/b.206.html

The Haymarket Affair, 1886

For information about the Haymarket demonstration and the subsequent trials of the anarchists, see:

http://memory.loc.gov/ammem/award98/ichihtml/hayhome.html

The Homestead Strike, 1892

This strike was an attempt of steel workers to unionize at the Carnegie Plant in Pennsylvania.

www.pbs.org/wgbh/amex/carnegie/peopleevents/pande04.html

Molly Maguires

These Pennsylvania coal miners attempted, sometimes through violence, to organize a union.

www.dep.state.pa.us/dep/PA_env-Her/history_1681_1945/molliemaguires.htm

Henry George

Information and links to the works of this economist and political philosopher can be found at:

www.progress.org/books/george.htm

Lester Frank Ward

Lester Frank Ward was not only one of the first sociologists but also a major critic of the social Darwinist philosophies of Herbert Spencer and William Graham Sumner. Ward argued for reform Darwinism in which the state would step in and create a society that would enable as many people as possible to be "fit to survive."

www.cityofjoliet.com/halloffame/scientists/lesterfward.htm
www.si.edu/archives/archives/findingaids/FARU7321.htm

Mark Twain

This is an excellent site dealing with Twain's anti-war writings.

www.boondocksnet.com/ai/twain/index.html

Charles Eliot Norton

Norton, an anti-imperialist, felt a true patriot is not afraid to criticize the government.

http://47.1911encyclopedia.org/N/NO/NORTON_CHARLES_ELIOT.htm
www.boondocksnet.com/ai/ailtexts/norton98.html

Samuel Gompers

This Web site is a valuable resource for information on this important labor leader.

www.history.umd.edu/Gompers/

Lincoln Steffens

For information about this crusading, muckraking journalist, see:

http://historymatters.gmu.edu/d/5733/

Upton Sinclair

For information and links to this famous muckraker's works, see:

http://sunsite.berkeley.edu/Literature/Sinclair/

William James

This is an excellent site with information about and writings by this philosopher of pragmatism.

www.emory.edu/EDUCATION/mfp/james.html

PART THREE

Conflict and Depression, 1912–1945

Margaret Sanger, feminist and birth control advocate, was a powerful voice for womens' reproductive rights. "No woman," she proclaimed. "can call herself free who does not own and control her body. No women can call herself free until she can choose consciously whether she will or will not be a mother."

Introduction: Becoming a World Power

During the first two decades of the twentieth century, women were ever more insistently demanding suffrage. Woodrow Wilson's inauguration as president raised hopes that a Democrat would now, finally, support the suffragist cause. It was soon apparent, however, that Wilson had no intention to fight for women's suffrage, and so militants, led by Alice Paul, increased their pressure by picketing the White

House six days a week. Their signs displayed passages from Wilson's speeches justifying America's entry into the Great War as part of the nation's mission to spread democracy to people who had no say in their government; suffragists demanded to know why the president was blind to the fact that 50 percent of America's citizens were denied a say in their own government. By 1918, Wilson gave in and began to urge congressional Democrats to vote for the suffrage amendment. With the ratification of the Nineteenth Amendment in 1920, women had finally won the right to vote, 144 years after Abigail Adams had exhorted her husband "not to forget the ladies" and 72 years after Lucretia Mott and Elizabeth Cady Stanton had written the "Declaration of Sentiments" at Seneca Falls. Still, the vote did not bring equality for women, and in 1923 Alice Paul began a new campaign for an equal rights amendment that would give women full economic and social rights.

Simultaneous with the battle for political rights, Margaret Sanger led the feminist movement into new territory by championing a woman's right to have complete control over her body. Sanger's successful assault on the Comstock Law, which equated the promotion of birth control with pornography, resulted in the repeal of the law and the opening of the first clinics that would later become known as Planned Parenthood.

Women were not the only people fighting the status quo. A growing number of radical dissenters were also agitating for reform and, in some cases, for outright revolution. Radicals like Joe Hill, Big Bill Haywood, and Eugene V. Debs condemned capitalism itself and argued for a new economic system based on socialism. Hill and Haywood were major forces in the socialist Industrial Workers of the World union (the Wobblies), which demanded worker ownership of the means of production. In 1915, because of his ties to the Wobblies, Joe Hill was tried, convicted, and executed for murder on dubious circumstantial evidence. Eugene V. Debs, the Socialist Party's presidential candidate in 1920, had to run his campaign from a jail cell because of his outspoken criticism of the U.S. entry into the war. As we have seen, anarchist Emma Goldman spoke out for many radical causes, especially complete sexual freedom for women and the right to birth control, and she continued to do so even after she was deported to the Soviet Union in the 1920s.

Theodore Roosevelt had set the United States on a course of increasing international involvement well before the war. By 1917, Washington was exerting more influence in Latin America, but it was the First World War that finally gave rise to the United States as a world power. But entering the war was not easy for the Wilson administration because antiwar sentiment ran high. German Americans, Irish Americans, Quakers, intellectuals like Randolph Bourne, politicians like Robert M. LaFollette, and radicals like Eugene V. Debs all spoke out strongly against the war. As a result, Congress enacted the Espionage and Sedition Acts in an attempt to stifle dissent and authorized the Committee on Public Information to implement a full-scale propaganda campaign to convince skeptical Americans of the necessity to unite against the barbaric "Huns." Somes states outlawed the teaching of the German language and banned German books (in some instances, books were even burned), frankfurters became hot dogs, hamburgers became Salisbury steak, sauerkraut became "liberty cabbage," and people who publicly expressed opposition to the war were summarily arrested.

While escalating class and gender tensions were causing alarm in the United States, the level of anxiety increased exponentially in the wake of the Russian revolution. Fear of communism, socialism, and anarchy led Attorney General A. Mitchell Palmer to initiate a campaign of wholesale arrests of thousands of left-wing sympathizers around the country. This "Red Scare" lasted well into the 1920s and resulted in innumerable civil liberties violations. As was the case when Lincoln suspended habeas corpus during the Civil War, hundreds of Americans and aliens were held without charges filed against them. The most notorious civil liberties violation was the murder trial of Nicola Sacco and Bartolomeo Vanzetti, two Italian immigrants who were convicted and executed because of their anarchist philosophy and not because of incontestable evidence proving their guilt. Tied in with the Red Scare was a surge of xenophobia and nativism that reached fever pitch in the 1920s. A second incarnation of the Ku Klux Klan (KKK) appealed to a far wider audience than the Reconstruction era Klan. This KKK, whose membership was just as extensive in the North and Midwest as it was in the South, added foreigners, Jews, Catholics, communists, modernists, divorcees, and feminists to their list of those who were not "100% pure American" and who therefore should not be tolerated. Congress, responding to these concerns, passed immigration acts that set strict quotas which drastically reduced the number of immigrants from Eastern Europe, Asia, and Latin America.

As young men were sent off to fight in Europe, industry in the northern United States needed more workers, so industrialists began actively to entice southern blacks to move north and fill the laboring ranks. The lure of economic improvement, combined with the indignities suffered in the Jim Crow South, led many impoverished African Americans to move north. This Great Migration, which continued for the next several decades, created a demographic shift that raised racial tensions in many northern cities. At the conclusion of the war, as one contemporary observed, "Americans stopped hating the Germans and started hating each other," and in this climate, racial violence, brutal lynchings, and rioting occurred in Omaha, Tulsa, Washington, Chicago, and in many other cities. Despite the violence, there were many positive developments for African Americans. The Harlem Renaissance brought black writers, artists, and musicians great acclaim in the 1920s. The popular enthusiasm for jazz and the blues created an awareness on the part of whites of the vibrancy and originality of African American culture and, at the same time, created a deeper sense of racial pride, racial awareness, and racial solidarity in blacks. Marcus Garvey inspired many African Americans with his view that "black is beautiful" and his admonition that social and economic advancement would only come through "black power."

Before the war, there had been a nearly universal belief in progress. The nineteenth century had witnessed so many scientific advances that people assumed that society itself was evolving toward a bright future. The dawn of the twentieth century was hailed as the beginning of an era of peace, progress, and prosperity. However, the war shook this conviction, and it suddenly seemed to many people that so much of what had been taken for granted was no longer certain. Freud's theories of the unconscious and his contention that "man is wolf to man" seemed confirmed by the terrible slaughter of a war in which science and technology were employed to increase human killing. Heisenberg's principle of uncertainty and Einstein's theory of relativity raised doubts about the inviolability of science itself. Darwin's theory of evolution cast doubt on the existence of God. Was nothing certain? In a sense, the 1920s can be best understood as a clash between the emergence of this new modern skepticism and the traditionalists who fought desperately to restore the old ways. The rise of Protestant fundamentalism attempted to restore God to a central place in the American ideology, the John Scopes "Monkey Trial" in mid-decade was a battle between science and old-time religion, the strict new immigration laws that limited the number of non-Western European immigrants were an attempt to turn the United States back to a purer, more Anglo-Saxon time, and the Ku Klux Klan fought to return to an all-white America that had never really existed.

President Calvin Coolidge said, "The business of America is business." In the great financial boom of the Roaring Twenties, mass consumption became central to the American way of life, but it was based on an insufficiently well-rounded economy. There was a maldistribution of purchasing power and not enough diversification. Most discretionary income was in the hands of the wealthy, and too much of the economy was dependent on the success of Henry Ford's Model T. In 1929 the boom crashed, and within three years the nation, as well as much of the Western world, was mired in the Great Depression. The inauguration of Franklin Delano Roosevelt in March 1933 helped to restore confidence to a desperate people, but all of the resourcefulness and ingenuity of the new president's New Deal programs were not enough to turn the economy around. It was the Second World War that would end the depression. Nevertheless, despite the intense criticism of an antagonistic business community, the New Deal was ultimately successful in saving capitalism from itself. But the New Deal's essentially pro-capitalist stance gave rise to left-wing critics who vigorously attacked the Roosevelt administration for not going far enough to reform society. In the Communist Party of the USA, membership rose dramatically, making it the bastion of the Old Left in its call for a Marxist revision of American society. Retired physician Francis Townsend strongly criticized the administration and called for a national pension plan for all citizens over age 65 (Roosevelt later used a modified version of Townsend's plan as the springboard for Social Security.) Senator Huey Long of Louisiana demanded a redistribution of wealth by which taxation of the rich would guarantee an annual income of $2500 to each citizen. And Father Charles Coughlin condemned the president for not cracking down hard enough on the excessive influence and power of unscrupulous eastern industrial and banking elites.

While most Americans suffered terribly during the Depression, minority groups were especially hard hit. If a job was to be had at a time when the unemployment rate soared to 25 percent, an African American, for example, had little chance of being hired. Still, even while enduring such circumstances, African Americans were heartened to see that First Lady Eleanor Roosevelt was very much on their side. The president's wife was an influential advocate for equal treatment and helped raise African American expectations that the future would bring better times. Her promotion of equal rights was dramatically spotlighted when she organized African American opera singer Marian Anderson's historic recital on the steps of the Lincoln Memorial in 1939, an event that prefigured the modern civil rights movement that would emerge after World War II. As the United States entered the war, there were other signs that the times were changing. African American leader A. Philip Randolph convinced President Roosevelt to sign executive orders opening up defense contract jobs to all people on an equal opportunity basis. More than 750,000 black men and women served in the armed forces during World War II, an experience that increased their self-esteem and opened up a wider world of possibilities.

Although the Second World War is frequently referred to as the "good war," and few people today doubt that the defeat of Hitler and Tojo was a positive undertaking, there was nevertheless significant antiwar sentiment throughout the conflict. Even before the war, the America First Committee and its most famous spokesman, Charles Lindbergh, denounced policies that most people correctly sensed would inevitably draw the United States into the war. In fact, antiwar sentiment was so strong that, had the Japanese not attacked Pearl Harbor, it is highly doubtful that even 50 percent of the American people would have united behind the war effort. Of course, the Japanese did attack, and a high level of unity was achieved. Still, many conscientious objectors—both religious and political—protested and refused to fight, and for many of these people (as well as for Japanese Americans, who would discover that American citizenship was not sufficient protection for their civil liberties), the war was a particularly traumatic time. When the long-awaited peace finally arrived in the summer of 1945, a new crisis emerged from the ashes of the old, and the world entered a new, and seemingly more dangerous era.

Joe Hill (1879–1915)

Born Joel Haggland in Sweden, Joe Hill emigrated to the United States in 1902. A great deal of mythologizing surrounds him, for little is known about his adventures in America during the first years after his arrival, other than that his expectations of finding the streets paved with gold were, as they were with so many other immigrants, quickly dashed. For several years, he traveled around the country, trying to make a living at various odd jobs and, perhaps, engaging in petty thievery. Sometime during these years, he changed his name—perhaps to keep one step ahead of the law—to Joseph Hillstrom. He is known to have joined the Industrial Workers of the World (IWW) in San Pedro, California, in 1910. Popularly known as the Wobblies, the IWW was part of the early socialist movement in the United States that called for a radical transformation of the capitalist system. Soon after joining the Wobblies, he changed his name again (to Joe Hill) and quickly became an important recruiter, organizer, and agitator for this radical union.

One of the most effective means Hill used to spread the Wobbly gospel was through song. He wrote dozens of pro-union, anticapitalist songs that were eventually published in the IWW's *Little Red Song Book*. In 1913, Hill went to Utah, a notoriously conservative and antiunion state, in order to organize mine workers. Early in 1914, Hill was arrested for murdering two men during a grocery store holdup. Although he claimed his innocence, Hill was tried, convicted, and sentenced to death. Big Bill Haywood, the leader of the IWW, immediately denounced the verdict and declared that business interests were out to destroy Hill and the Wobblies. For several months, workers around the world, as well as such national figures as Elizabeth Gurley Flynn, Helen Keller, and even President Woodrow Wilson, appealed to the governor of Utah to free Joe Hill. Despite the public outcry, Hill was executed by firing squad in November 1915. Just before his execution, he sent a telegram to Haywood urging the IWW and his supporters worldwide, "Don't waste time mourning, organize!" Joe Hill has, in subsequent years, become semideified in the pantheon of the labor movement's heroes.

"We Will Sing One Song" is one of many songs Hill wrote to urge workers to organize. "The Preacher and the Slave Girl," is Hill's denunciation of the role organized religion plays in supporting big business. During the struggle to unionize, music played a significant role, as it did later in the century in the civil rights movement and in antiwar protests. What makes music an effective device for protestors and dissidents?

"We Will Sing One Song"

We will sing one song of the meek and humble slave,
The horn-handed son of the soil,
He's toiling hard from the cradle to the grave,
But his master reaps the profits from his toil.
Then we'll sing one song of the greedy master class,
They're vagrants in broadcloth, indeed,
They live by robbing the ever-toiling mass,
Human blood they spill to satisfy their greed.

Organize! Oh, toilers, come organize your might;
Then we'll sing one song of the workers' commonwealth,
Full of beauty, full of love and health.

We will sing one song of the politician sly,
He's talking of changing the laws;
Election day all the drinks and smokes he'll buy,
While he's living from the sweat of your brow.
Then we'll sing one song of the girl below the line,
She's scorned and despised everywhere,
While in their mansions the "keepers" wine and dine
From the profits that immoral traffic bear.

Organize! Oh, toilers, come organize your might;
Then we'll sing one song of the workers' commonwealth,
Full of beauty, full of love and health.

We will sing one song of the preacher, fat and sleek,
He tells you of homes in the sky.
He says, "Be generous, be lowly, and be meek,
If you don't you'll sure get roasted when you die."
Then we'll sing one song of the poor and ragged tramp,
He carries his home on his back;
Too old to work, he's not wanted 'round the camp,
So he wanders without aim along the track.

Organize! Oh, toilers, come organize your might;
Then we'll sing one song of the workers' commonwealth,
Full of beauty, full of love and health.

We will sing one song of the children in the mills,
They're taken from playgrounds and schools,
In tender years made to go the pace that kills,
In the sweatshops, 'mong the looms and the spools.

SOURCE: The Industrial Workers of the World, *Little Red Songbook* (I.W.W., March 6, 1913).

Then we'll sing one song of the One Big Union Grand,
The hope of the toiler and slave,
It's coming fast; it is sweeping sea and land,
To the terror of the grafter and the knave.

Organize! Oh, toilers, come organize your might;
Then we'll sing one song of the workers' commonwealth,
Full of beauty, full of love and health.

"The Preacher and the Slave Girl"

Long haired preachers come out ev'ry night,
Try to tell you what's wrong and what's right;
But when asked, how 'bout something to eat, (Let us eat)
They will answer with voices so sweet; (Oh so sweet)

You will eat, (You will eat)
Bye and bye, (Bye and bye) in that glorious land above the sky;
(way up high)
work and pray, (work and pray) live on hay, (Live on hay)
you'll get pie in the sky when you die. (That's a lie)

And the starvation army they play,
And they sing and they clap and they pray.
Till they get all your coin on the drum,
Then they'll tell you when you're on the bum:

You will eat, (You will eat)
Bye and bye, (Bye and bye) in that glorious land above the sky;
(way up high)
work and pray, (work and pray) live on hay, (Live on hay)
you'll get pie in the sky when you die. (That's a lie)

Holy Rollers and Jumpers come out,
And they holler, they jump and they shout
"Give your money to Jesus," they say,
"He will cure all diseases today."

You will eat, (You will eat)
Bye and bye, (Bye and bye) in that glorious land above the sky;
(way up high)
work and pray, (work and pray) live on hay, (Live on hay)
you'll get pie in the sky when you die. (That's a lie)

If you fight hard for children and wife—
Try to get something good in this life—
You're a sinner and bad man, they tell,
When you die you will sure go to hell.

You will eat, (You will eat)
Bye and bye, (Bye and bye) in that glorious land above the sky;
(way up high)
work and pray, (work and pray) live on hay, (Live on hay)
you'll get pie in the sky when you die. (That's a lie)

Workingmen of all countries unite,
Side by side we for freedom will fight!
When the world and its wealth we have gained,
To the grafters we'll sing this refrain:

You will eat, bye and bye,
When you've learned how to cook and to fry.
Chop some wood, 'twill do you good,
And you'll eat in the sweet bye and bye.

Robert M. LaFollette (1855–1925)

Wisconsin Republican Robert M. LaFollette served his state first as governor
and later as U.S. senator. Claiming that his role as a politician was to "protect
the people" from exploitive industrialists and businessmen, LaFollete gained
prominence as one of the most progressive and reform-minded politicians of
the early twentieth century. He championed such radical causes as racial
equality, women's suffrage, and the right of workers to organize unions. He
supported the Democratic presidential candidate, Woodrow Wilson, in 1912
because of Wilson's program of social reform and regulation of big business.
However, he parted ways with Wilson in 1917 when the president asked
Congress for a declaration of war. He became even more critical when the
Conscription Act was passed. The administration's attempt to stifle dissent
with the passage of the Espionage and Sedition Acts, which made even
questioning the government's war policy a federal crime, drew LaFollette's
most scathing criticism and led to accusations of treason against him. After he
voted against the declaration of war, which the Senate overwhelmingly
approved, someone handed him a coil of rope as he was leaving the chamber,
presumably so he could save the country the cost of a trial for treason.

According to LaFollette, in these two speeches delivered to the U.S. Senate,
what is the basic error in Wilson's argument for going to war? Does the senator
agree that the war would be to "make the world safe for democracy," as Wilson
often asserted, or does LaFollette identify other reasons behind the push for
war? Why does LaFollete argue that free speech is absolutely necessary,
especially in time of war?

Antiwar Speech, April 4, 1917

The poor, sir, who are the ones called upon to rot in the trenches, have no organized power, have no press to voice their will upon this question of peace or war; but, oh, Mr. President, at some time they will be heard. I hope and I believe they will be heard in an orderly and a peaceful way. I think they may be heard from before long. I think, sir, if we take this step, when the people to-day who are staggering under the burden of supporting families at the present prices of the necessaries of life find those prices multiplied, when they are raised a hundred percent, or 200 percent, as they will be quickly, aye, sir, when beyond that those who pay taxes come to have their taxes doubled and again doubled to pay the interest on the nontaxable bonds held by Morgan and his combinations, which have been issued to meet this war, there will come an awakening; they will have their day and they will be heard. It will be as certain and as inevitable as the return of the tides, and as resistless. . . .

If we are to enter upon this war in the manner the President demands, let us throw pretense to the winds, let us be honest, let us admit that this is a ruthless war against not only Germany's Army and her Navy but against her civilian population as well, and frankly state that the purpose of Germany's hereditary European enemies has become our purpose.

Again, the President says "we are about to accept the gauge of battle with this natural foe of liberty and shall, if necessary, spend the whole force of the nation to check and nullify its pretensions and its power." That much, at least, is clear; that program is definite. The whole force and power of this nation, if necessary, is to be used to bring victory to the Entente Allies, and to us as their ally in this war. Remember, that not yet has the "whole force" of one of the warring nations been used.

Countless millions are suffering from want and privation; countless other millions are dead and rotting on foreign battlefields; countless other millions are crippled and maimed, blinded, and dismembered; upon all and upon their children's children for generations to come has been laid a burden of debt which must be worked out in poverty and suffering, but the "whole force" of no one of the warring nations has yet been expended; but our "whole force" shall be expended, so says the President. We are pledged by the President, so far as he can pledge us, to make this fair, free, and happy land of ours the same shambles and bottomless pit of horror that we see in Europe today.

Just a word of comment more upon one of the points in the President's address. He says that this is a war "for the things which we have always carried nearest to our hearts—for democracy, for the right of those who submit to authority to have a voice in their own government." In many places throughout the address is this exalted sentiment given expression.

SOURCE: Ronald F. Reid, *American Rhetorical Discourse*, 2nd ed. (Prospect Heights, IL: Waveland Press), 702–705.

It is a sentiment peculiarly calculated to appeal to American hearts and, when accompanied by acts consistent with it, is certain to receive our support; but in this same connection, and strangely enough, the President says that we have become convinced that the German government as it now exists—"Prussian autocracy" he calls it—can never again maintain friendly relations with us. His expression is that "Prussian autocracy was not and could never be our friend," and repeatedly throughout the address the suggestion is made that if the German people would overturn their government, it would probably be the way to peace. So true is this that the dispatches from London all hailed the message of the President as sounding the death knell of Germany's government.

But the President proposes alliance with Great Britain, which, however liberty-loving its people, is a hereditary monarchy, with a hereditary ruler, with a hereditary House of Lords, with a hereditary landed system, with a limited and restricted suffrage for one class and a multiplied suffrage power for another, and with grinding industrial conditions for all the wageworkers. The President has not suggested that we make our support of Great Britain conditional to her granting home rule to Ireland, or Egypt, or India. We rejoice in the establishment of a democracy in Russia, but it will hardly be contended that if Russia was still an autocratic government, we would not be asked to enter this alliance with her just the same. . . .

Is it not a remarkable democracy which leagues itself with allies already far overmatching in strength the German nation and holds out to such beleaguered nation the hope of peace only at the price of giving up their Government? I am not talking now of the merits or demerits of any government, but I am speaking of a profession of democracy that is linked in action with the most brutal and domineering use of autocratic power. Are the people of this country being so well represented in this war movement that we need to go abroad to give other people control of their governments? Will the President and the supporters of this war bill submit it to a vote of the people before the declaration of war goes into effect? Until we are willing to do that, it ill becomes us to offer as an excuse for our entry into the war the unsupported claim that this war was forced upon the German people by their Government "without their previous knowledge or approval."

Who has registered the knowledge or approval of the American people of the course this Congress is called upon in declaring war upon Germany? Submit the question to the people, you who support it. You who support it dare not do it, for you know that by a vote of more than ten to one the American people as a body would register their declaration against it.

In the sense that this war is being forced upon our people without their knowing why and without their approval, and that wars are usually forced upon all peoples in the same way, there is some truth in the statement; but I venture to say that the response which the German people have made to the demands of this war shows that it has a degree of popular support which the war upon which we are entering has not and never will have among our people. The espionage bills, the conscription bills, and other forcible military measures which we understand are being ground out of the war machine in this country is the complete proof that those responsible for this war fear that it has no popular support and that armies sufficient to satisfy the demand of the entente allies can not be recruited by voluntary enlistments.

Defense of Free Speech, October 6, 1917

Mr. President:

. . . Six Members of the Senate and fifty Members of the House voted against the declaration of war. Immediately there was let loose upon those Senators and Representatives a flood of invective and abuse from newspapers and individuals who had been clamoring for war, unequalled, I believe, in the history of civilized society.

Prior to the declaration of war every man who had ventured to oppose our entrance into it had been condemned as a coward or worse, and even the President had by no means been immune from these attacks.

Since the declaration of war, the triumphant war press has pursued those Senators and Representatives who voted against war with malicious falsehood and recklessly libelous attacks, going to the extreme limit of charging them with treason against their country.

This campaign of libel and character assassination directed against the Members of Congress who opposed our entrance into the war has. . . . continued . . . One of these newspaper reports most widely circulated represents a Federal judge in the State of Texas as saying, in a charge of a grand jury—I read the article as it appeared in the newspaper. . . .

> Houston, Texas, October 1, 1917. Judge Waller T. Burns, of the United States district court, in charging a Federal grand jury at the beginning of the October term today, after calling by name Senators Stone of Missouri, Hardwick of Georgia, Vardaman of Mississippi, Gronna of North Dakota, Gore of Oklahoma, and LaFollette of Wisconsin, said: "If I had a wish, I would wish that you men had jurisdiction to return bills of indictment against these men. They ought to be tried promptly and fairly, and I believe this court could administer the law fairly; but I have a conviction, as strong as life, that this country should stand them up against an adobe wall tomorrow and give them what they deserve. If any man deserves death, it is a traitor. I wish that I could pay for the ammunition. I would like to attend the execution, and if I were in the firing squad I would not want to be the marksman who had the blank shell.". . .

If this newspaper clipping were a single or exceptional instance of lawless defamation, I should not trouble the Senate with a reference to it. But, Mr. President, it is not.

In this mass of newspaper clippings which I have here upon my desk, and which I shall not trouble the Senate to read unless it is desired, and which represent but a small part of the accumulation clipped from the daily press of the country in the last three months, I find other Senators, as well as myself, accused of the highest crimes of which any man can be guilty—treason and disloyalty—and, sir, accused not only with no evidence to support the accusation, but without the suggestion that such evidence anywhere exists. . . .

I am aware, Mr. President, that in pursuance of this campaign of vilification and attempted intimidation, requests from various individuals and certain organizations have been submitted to the Senate for my expulsion from this body, and that such requests have been referred to and considered by one of the committees of the Senate.

If I alone had been made the victim of these attacks, I should not take one moment of the Senate's time for their consideration, and I believe that other Senators who have been unjustly and unfairly assailed, as I have been, hold the same attitude upon this that I do. Neither the clamor of the mob nor the voice of power will ever turn me by the breadth of a hair from the course I mark out for myself, guided by such knowledge as I can obtain and controlled and directed by a solemn conviction of right and duty.

But, sir, it is not alone Members of Congress that the war party in this country has sought to intimidate. The mandate seems to have gone forth to the sovereign people of this country that they must be silent while those things are being done by their Government which most vitally concern their well-being, their happiness, and their lives.

Today, and for weeks past, honest and law-abiding citizens of this country are being terrorized and outraged in their rights by those sworn to uphold the laws and protect the rights of the people. I have in my possession numerous affidavits establishing the fact that people are being unlawfully arrested, thrown into jail, held incommunicado for days, only to be eventually discharged without ever having been taken into court, because they have committed no crime. Private residences are being invaded, loyal citizens of undoubted integrity and probity arrested, cross-examined, and the most sacred constitutional rights guaranteed to every American citizen are being violated.

It appears to be the purpose of those conducting this campaign to throw the country into a state of terror, to coerce public opinion, to stifle criticism, and suppress discussion of the great issues involved in this war.

I think all men recognize that in time of war the citizen must surrender some rights for the common good which he is entitled to enjoy in time of peace. *But, sir, the right to control their own Government according to constitutional forms is not one of the rights that the citizens of this country are called upon to surrender in time of war.*

Rather, in time of war, the citizen must be more alert to the preservation of his right to control his Government. He must be most watchful of the encroachment of the military upon the civil power. He must beware of those precedents in support of arbitrary action by administration officials which, excused on the pleas of necessity in war time, become the fixed rule when the necessity has passed and normal conditions have been restored.

More than all, the citizen and his representative in Congress in time of war must maintain his right of free speech. More than in times of peace it is necessary that the channels for free public discussion of governmental policies shall be open and unclogged.

I believe, Mr. President, that I am now touching upon the most important question in this country today—and that is the right of the citizens of this country and their representatives in Congress to discuss in an orderly way, frankly and publicly and without fear, from the platform and through the press, every important phase of this war; its causes, and manner in which it should be conducted, and the terms upon which peace should be made.

The belief which is becoming widespread in this land that this most fundamental right is being denied to the citizens of this country is a fact, the tremendous significance of which those in authority have not yet begun to appreciate. I am contending, Mr. President, for the great fundamental right of the sovereign people of this country to make their voice heard and have that voice heeded upon the great questions arising out of this war, including not only how the war shall be prosecuted but the conditions upon which it may be terminated with a due regard for the rights and the honor of this Nation and the interests of humanity.

I am contending for this right because the exercise of it is necessary to the welfare, to the existence of this Government, to the successful conduct of this war, and to a peace which shall be enduring and for the best interests of this country.

Suppose success attends the attempt to stifle all discussion of the issues of this war, all discussions of the terms upon which it should be concluded, all discussion of the objects and purposes to be accomplished by it, and concede the demand of the war-mad press and war extremists that they monopolize the right of public utterance upon these questions unchallenged. What think you would be the consequences to this country not only during the war but after the war?

Mr. President, our Government, above all others, is founded on the right of the people freely to discuss all matters pertaining to their Government, in war not less than in peace. . . . How can that popular will express itself between elections except by meetings, by speeches, by publications, by petitions, and by addresses to the representatives of the people?

Any man who seeks to set a limit upon those rights, whether in war or peace, aims a blow at the most vital part of our Government. And then, as the time for election approaches and the official is called to account for his stewardship—not a day, not a week, not a month, before the election, but a year or more before it, if the people choose—they must have the right to the freest possible discussion of every question upon which their representative has acted, of the merits of every measure he has supported or opposed, of every vote he has cast, and every speech that he has made. And before this great fundamental right every other must, if necessary, give way. For in no other manner can representative government be preserved.

Eugene V. Debs (1855–1926)

As a young man, Eugene V. Debs worked in the railroad industry and became active in the Brotherhood of Locomotive Firemen. In 1893 he organized the American Railway Union and in 1894 helped lead the Pullman strike. For his part in this strike, he was imprisoned for six months, during which time he became a socialist. After his release, he was instrumental in founding the American Socialist Party. He also was involved with organizing the Industrial Workers of the World and associated with other radical activists such as Emma Goldman and Margaret Sanger. For the remainder of his life, he worked hard for the workingman and for socialist principles. In 1900, 1904, 1908, 1912, and 1920, he was the Socialist Party's candidate for president, and as the United States moved ever closer to entering the Great War, he became an articulate antiwar critic. A few months after the United States declared war on Germany, Debs was arrested under the Sedition and Espionage Acts for delivering an antiwar speech and for hindering the draft. These acts of Congress, in addition to singling out actions that would aid the enemy, interfere with conscription, or encourage soldiers to desert, also condemned anyone who would "willfully utter, print, write, or publish any disloyal, profane, scurrilous, or abusive language about the form of government of the United States, or the Constitution of the United States, or the military or naval forces of the United States, or the flag of the United States . . . or shall willfully utter, print, write, or publish any language intended to incite, provoke, or encourage resistance to the United States, or . . . willfully advocate, teach, defend, or suggest the doing of any of the acts or things in this section enumerated." Debs was convicted, sentenced to ten years in prison, and stripped of his American citizenship. He served nearly three years of this sentence and, despite losing his American citizenship, he was nominated as the Socialist Party's candidate for President; he conducted his entire 1920 campaign from behind bars. He was released on Christmas in 1921, when President Warren G. Harding commuted his sentence, and eventually, in 1976 (50 years after his death), his citizenship was restored. Though his health had deteriorated in prison, he spent the remaining five years of his life continuing to fight to make life better for American workers. "While there is a lower class," Debs proclaimed, "I am in it; while there is a criminal element, I am of it; while there is a soul in prison, I am not free!"

What does the following speech reveal about the state of freedom of speech in the United States? Why is Debs opposed to the war? What does his arrest for delivering this speech reveal about the state of civil liberties in the United States in 1918? Is it constitutional for Congress to limit freedom of speech in times of war? In light of the USA PATRIOT Act (Uniting and Strengthening America by Providing Appropriate Tools Required to Intercept and Obstruct Terrorism Act), would Debs have been arrested if he had given this speech in 2003 during the war with Iraq? Is restricting civil liberties necessary in times of crisis?

Antiwar Speech, Canton, Ohio, June 1918

Comrades, friends and fellow-workers, for this very cordial greeting, this very hearty reception, I thank you all with the fullest appreciation of your interest in and your devotion to the cause for which I am to speak to you this afternoon.

To speak for labor; to plead the cause of the men and women and children who toil; to serve the working class, has always been to me a high privilege; a duty of love.

I have just returned from a visit over yonder, where three of our most loyal comrades are paying the penalty for their devotion to the cause of the working class. They have come to realize, as many of us have, that it is extremely dangerous to exercise the constitutional right of free speech in a country fighting to make democracy safe in the world.

I realize that, in speaking to you this afternoon, there are certain limitations placed upon the right of free speech. I must be exceedingly careful, prudent, as to what I say, and even more careful and prudent as to how I say it. I may not be able to say all I think; but I am not going to say anything that I do not think. I would rather a thousand times be a free soul in jail than to be a sycophant and coward in the streets. They may put those boys in jail—and some of the rest of us in jail—but they cannot put the Socialist movement in jail. Those prison bars separate their bodies from ours, but their souls are here this afternoon. They are simply paying the penalty that all men have paid in all the ages of history for standing erect, and for seeking to pave the way to better conditions for mankind.

If it had not been for the men and women who, in the past, have had the moral courage to go to jail, we would still be in the jungles. . . .

There is but one thing you have to be concerned about, and that is that you keep foursquare with the principles of the international Socialist movement. It is only when you begin to compromise that trouble begins. So far as I am concerned, it does not matter what others may say, or think, or do, as long as I am sure that I am right with myself and the cause. There are so many who seek refuge in the popular side of a great question. As a Socialist, I have long since learned how to stand alone. For the last month I have been traveling over the Hoosier State; and, let me say to you, that, in all my connection with the Socialist movement, I have never seen such meetings, such enthusiasm, such unity of purpose; never have I seen such a promising outlook as there is today, notwithstanding the statement published repeatedly that our leaders have deserted us. Well, for myself, I never had much faith in leaders. I am willing to be charged with almost anything, rather than to be charged with being a leader. I am suspicious of leaders, and especially of the intellectual variety. Give me the rank and file every day in the week. If you go to the city of Washington, and you examine the pages of the Congressional Directory, you will find that almost all of those corporation lawyers and cowardly politicians, members of Congress, and misrepresentatives of the masses—you will find that almost all of them claim, in glowing terms, that they have risen from the ranks to places of eminence and

Source: *The Call*, 1918, online version: E. V. Debs Internet Archive, 2001. Retrieved on 8/11/2003 from www.marxists.org/archive/debs/works/1918/canton.htm.

distinction. I am very glad I cannot make that claim for myself. I would be ashamed to admit that I had risen from the ranks. When I rise it will be with the ranks, and not from the ranks. . . .

Why should a Socialist be discouraged on the eve of the greatest triumph in all the history of the Socialist movement? It is true that these are anxious, trying days for us all—testing days for the women and men who are upholding the banner of labor in the struggle of the working class of all the world against the exploiters of all the world; a time in which the weak and cowardly will falter and fail and desert. They lack the fiber to endure the revolutionary test; they fall away; they disappear as if they had never been. On the other hand, they who are animated by the unconquerable spirit of the social revolution; they who have the moral courage to stand erect and assert their convictions; stand by them; fight for them; go to jail or to hell for them, if need be—they are writing their names, in this crucial hour—they are writing their names in faceless letters in the history of mankind.

Those boys over yonder—those comrades of ours—and how I love them! Aye, they are my younger brothers; their very names throb in my heart, thrill in my veins, and surge in my soul. I am proud of them; they are there for us; and we are here for them. Their lips, though temporarily mute, are more eloquent than ever before; and their voice, though silent, is heard around the world.

Are we opposed to Prussian militarism? Why, we have been fighting it since the day the Socialist movement was born; and we are going to continue to fight it, day and night, until it is wiped from the face of the earth. Between us there is no truce—no compromise. . . .

To whom do the Wall Street Junkers [aristocrats] in our country marry their daughters? After they have wrung their countless millions from your sweat, your agony and your life's blood, in a time of war as in a time of peace, they invest these untold millions in the purchase of titles of broken-down aristocrats, such as princes, dukes, counts and other parasites and no-accounts. Would they be satisfied to wed their daughters to honest workingmen? To real democrats? Oh, no! They scour the markets of Europe for vampires who are titled and nothing else. And they swap their millions for the titles, so that matrimony with them becomes literally a matter of money.

These are the gentry who are today wrapped up in the American flag, who shout their claim from the housetops that they are the only patriots, and who have their magnifying glasses in hand, scanning the country for evidence of disloyalty, eager to apply the brand of treason to the men who dare to even whisper their opposition to Junker rule in the United Sates. No wonder Sam Johnson declared that "patriotism is the last refuge of the scoundrel." He must have had this Wall Street gentry in mind, or at least their prototypes, for in every age it has been the tyrant, the oppressor and the exploiter who has wrapped himself in the cloak of patriotism, or religion, or both to deceive and overawe the people.

They would have you believe that the Socialist Party consists in the main of disloyalists and traitors. It is true in a sense not at all to their discredit. We frankly admit that we are disloyalists and traitors to the real traitors of this nation. . . .

How stupid and shortsighted the ruling class really is! Cupidity is stone blind. It has no vision. The greedy, profit-seeking exploiter cannot see beyond the end of his nose. He can see a chance for an "opening"; he is cunning enough to know what graft is and where it is, and how it can be secured, but vision he has none—not the slightest. He knows nothing of the great throbbing world that spreads out in all directions. He has no capacity for literature; no appreciation of art; no soul for beauty. That is the penalty the parasites pay for the violation of the laws of life. The Rockefellers are blind. Every move they make in their game of greed but hastens their own doom. Every blow they strike at the Socialist movement reacts upon themselves. Every time they strike at us they hit themselves. It never fails. Every time they strangle a Socialist paper they add a thousand voices proclaiming the truth of the principles of socialism and the ideals of the Socialist movement. They help us in spite of themselves.

Socialism is a growing idea; an expanding philosophy. It is spreading over the entire face of the earth: It is as vain to resist it as it would be to arrest the sunrise on the morrow. It is coming, coming, coming all along the line. Can you not see it? If not, I advise you to consult an oculist. There is certainly something the matter with your vision. It is the mightiest movement in the history of mankind. What a privilege to serve it! I have regretted a thousand times that I can do so little for the movement that has done so much for me. The little that I am, the little that I am hoping to be, I owe to the Socialist movement. It has given me my ideas and ideals; my principles and convictions, and I would not exchange one of them for all of Rockefeller's bloodstained dollars. It has taught me how to serve—a lesson to me of priceless value. It has taught me the ecstasy in the handclasp of a comrade. It has enabled me to hold high communion with you, and made it possible for me to take my place side by side with you in the great struggle for the better day; to multiply myself over and over again, to thrill with a fresh-born manhood; to feel life truly worthwhile; to open new avenues of vision; to spread out glorious vistas; to know that I am kin to all that throbs; to be class-conscious, and to realize that, regardless of nationality, race, creed, color or sex, every man, every woman who toils, who renders useful service, every member of the working class without an exception, is my comrade, my brother and sister—and that to serve them and their cause is the highest duty of my life.

And in their service I can feel myself expand; I can rise to the stature of a man and claim the right to a place on earth—a place where I can stand and strive to speed the day of industrial freedom and social justice.

Wars throughout history have been waged for conquest and plunder. In the Middle Ages when the feudal lords who inhabited the castles whose towers may still be seen along the Rhine concluded to enlarge their domains, to increase their power, their prestige and their wealth they declared war upon one another. But they themselves did not go to war any more than the modern feudal lords, the barons of Wall Street go to war. The feudal barons of the Middle Ages, the economic predecessors of the capitalists of our day, declared all wars. And their miserable serfs fought all the battles. The poor, ignorant serfs had been taught to revere their masters; to believe that when their masters declared war upon one another, it was their patriotic duty to fall upon one another and to cut one another's throats for the profit and glory of the lords and barons who held them in contempt. And that is war in a nutshell. The master class has always declared the wars; the subject class has always fought the battles. The master class has had all to gain and nothing to lose, while the subject class has had nothing to gain and all to lose—especially their lives.

They have always taught and trained you to believe it to be your patriotic duty to go to war and to have yourselves slaughtered at their command. But in all the history of the world you, the people, have never had a voice in declaring war, and strange as it certainly appears, no war by any nation in any age has ever been declared by the people.

And here let me emphasize the fact—and it cannot be repeated too often—that the working class who fight all the battles, the working class who make the supreme sacrifices, the working class who freely shed their blood and furnish the corpses, have never yet had a voice in either declaring war or making peace. It is the ruling class that invariably does both. They alone declare war and they alone make peace.

> *Yours not to reason why;*
> *Yours but to do and die.*

That is their motto and we object on the part of the awakening workers of this nation.

If war is right let it be declared by the people. You who have your lives to lose, you certainly above all others have the right to decide the momentous issue of war or peace. . . .

What a compliment it is to the Socialist movement to be . . . persecuted for the sake of the truth! The truth alone will make the people free. And for this reason the truth must not be permitted to reach the people. The truth has always been dangerous to the rule of the rogue, the exploiter, the robber. So the truth must be ruthlessly suppressed. That is why they are trying to destroy the Socialist movement; and every time they strike a blow they add a thousand new voices to the hosts proclaiming that socialism is the hope of humanity and has come to emancipate the people from their final form of servitude. . . .

It is the minorities who have made the history of this world. It is the few who have had the courage to take their places at the front; who have been true enough to themselves to speak the truth that was in them; who have dared oppose the established order of things; who have espoused the cause of the suffering, struggling poor; who have upheld without regard to personal consequences the cause of freedom and righteousness. It is they, the heroic, self-sacrificing few who have made the history of the race and who have paved the way from barbarism to civilization. The many prefer to remain upon the popular side. They lack the courage and vision to join a despised minority that stands for a principle; they have not the moral fiber that withstands, endures and finally conquers. They are to be pitied and not treated with contempt for they cannot help their cowardice. But, thank God, in every age and in every nation there have been the brave and self-reliant few, and they have been sufficient to their historic task; and we, who are here today, are under infinite obligations to them because they suffered, they sacrificed, they went to jail, they had their bones broken upon the wheel, they were burned at the stake and their ashes scattered to the winds by the hands of hate and revenge in their struggle to leave the world better for us than they found it for themselves. We are under eternal obligations to them because of what they did and what they suffered for us and the only way we can discharge that obligation is by doing the best we can for those who are to come after us. And this is the high purpose of every Socialist on earth. Everywhere they are animated by the same lofty principles; everywhere they have the same noble ideals; everywhere they are clasping hands across national boundary lines; everywhere they are calling one another Comrade, the blessed word that springs from the heart of unity and bursts into blossom upon the lips. Each passing day they are getting into closer touch all along the battle line, waging the holy war of the working class of the world against the ruling and exploiting class of the world. They make many mistakes and they profit by them all. They encounter numerous defeats, and grow stronger through them all. They never take a backward step.

The heart of the international Socialist never beats a retreat. . . .

Do you wish to hasten the day of victory? Join the Socialist Party! Don't wait for the morrow. Join now! Enroll your name without fear and take your place where you belong. You cannot do your duty by proxy. You have got to do it yourself and do it squarely and then as you look yourself in the face you will have no occasion to blush. You will know what it is to be a real man or woman. You will lose nothing; you will gain everything. Not only will you lose nothing but you will find something of infinite value, and that something will be yourself. And that is your supreme need—to find yourself—to really know yourself and your purpose in life.

You need at this time especially to know that you are fit for something better than slavery and cannon fodder. You need to know that you were not created to work and produce and impoverish yourself to enrich an idle exploiter. You need to know that you have a mind to improve, a soul to develop, and a manhood to sustain. . . .

Anybody can be nobody; but it takes a man to be somebody.

To turn your back on the corrupt Republican Party and the still more corrupt Democratic Party—the gold-dust lackeys of the ruling class counts for still more after you have stepped out of those popular and corrupt capitalist parties to join a minority party that has an ideal, that stands for a principle, and fights for a cause. This will be the most important change you have ever made and the time will come when you will thank me for having made the suggestion. . . .

Randolph Bourne (1886–1918)

A man of extraordinary intellect, Randolph Bourne's life was problematic from the beginning. His face was misshapen at birth by a botched forceps delivery, and before the age of five, he had contracted spinal tuberculosis, which dwarfed him and gave him a hunchbacked appearance. Growing up very much an outsider in suburban Bloomfield, New Jersey, he suffered inordinately from his physical disability and from his awareness of being a social outcast. But his remarkable intellect blossomed when he entered Columbia University in 1909. There he became editor of the *Columbia Monthly* and wrote numerous articles on radical politics. After graduation, he became an articulate and influential spokesman for his generation. He contributed articles to

The Atlantic, The New Republic, The Dial, and *Seven Arts,* in which he encouraged the nation's youth to question conventional social roles, personal relationships, and American values. He also angrily criticized corporate capitalism and condemned the Wilson administration's policy of suppressing dissent. His strident opposition to U.S. entry into the First World War went so far against the grain of his more complacent contemporaries that he was fired from *The New Republic* and put under surveillance by the Wilson administration. Bourne could never accept President Wilson's conviction that the war would be the "war to end wars" or that it would "make the world safe for democracy," nor could he accept the intellectuals who supported and condoned the war, especially those who wrote propaganda for the Committee on Public Information. To Bourne, American participation in the Great War revealed that the United States, despite its deeply held belief in the virtues of democracy, was no different from any other nation. The state, Bourne declared, is simply "the organization of the herd to act offensively or defensively against another herd similarly organized."

"War Is the Health of the State," an unfinished essay published after Bourne's death in the 1918 flu epidemic at the age of 32, is a provocative and compelling indictment of the First World War that seems applicable to any war. What, according to Bourne, is the state? How does he distinguish it from the government? The nation? What responsibility do intellectuals have in a time of war? Is Bourne's analysis still valid in the 21st century?

"War Is the Health of the State," 1918

To most Americans of the classes which consider themselves significant the war brought a sense of the sanctity of the State which, if they had had time to think about it, would have seemed a sudden and surprising alteration in their habits of thought. In times of peace, we usually ignore the State in favor of partisan political controversies, or personal struggles for office, or the pursuit of party policies. It is the Government rather than the State with which the politically minded are concerned. The State is reduced to a shadowy emblem which comes to consciousness only on occasions of patriotic holiday.

Government is obviously composed of common and unsanctified men, and is thus a legitimate object of criticism and even contempt. If your own party is in power, things may be assumed to be moving safely enough; but if the opposition is in, then clearly all safety and honor have fled the State. Yet you do not put it to yourself in quite that way. What you think is only that there are rascals to be turned out of a very practical machinery of offices and functions which you take for granted. When we say that Americans are lawless, we usually mean that they are less conscious

---

SOURCE: Bourne's unfinished essay, "War Is the Health of the State." The original manuscript is in the Bourne MSS, Columbia University Libraries.

than other peoples of the august majesty of the institution of the State as it stands behind the objective government of men and laws which we see. In a republic the men who hold office are indistinguishable from the mass. Very few of them possess the slightest personal dignity with which they could endow their political role; even if they ever thought of such a thing. And they have no class distinction to give them glamour. In a republic the Government is obeyed grumblingly, because it has no bedazzlements or sanctities to gild it. If you are a good old-fashioned democrat, you rejoice at this fact, you glory in the plainness of a system where every citizen has become a king. If you are more sophisticated you bemoan the passing of dignity and honor from affairs of State. But in practice, the democrat does not in the least treat his elected citizen with the respect due to a king, nor does the sophisticated citizen pay tribute to the dignity even when he finds it. The republican State has almost no trappings to appeal to the common man's emotions. What it has are of military origin, and in an unmilitary era such as we have passed through since the Civil War, even military trappings have been scarcely seen. In such an era the sense of the State almost fades out of the consciousness of men.

With the shock of war, however, the State comes into its own again. The Government, with no mandate from the people, without consultation of the people, conducts all the negotiations, the backing and filling, the menaces and explanations, which slowly bring it into collision with some other Government, and gently and irresistibly slides the country into war. For the benefit of proud and haughty citizens, it is fortified with a list of the intolerable insults which have been hurled toward us by the other nations; for the benefit of the liberal and beneficent, it has a convincing set of moral purposes which our going to war will achieve; for the ambitious and aggressive classes, it can gently whisper of a bigger role in the destiny of the world. The result is that, even in those countries where the business of declaring war is theoretically in the hands of representatives of the people, no legislature has ever been known to decline the request of an Executive, which has conducted all foreign affairs in utter privacy and irresponsibility, that it order the nation into battle. Good democrats are wont to feel the crucial difference between a State in which the popular Parliament or Congress declares war, and the State in which an absolute monarch or ruling class declares war. But, put to the stern pragmatic test, the difference is not striking. In the freest of republics as well as in the most tyrannical of empires, all foreign policy, the diplomatic negotiations which produce or forestall war, are equally the private property of the Executive part of the Government, and are equally exposed to no check whatever from popular bodies, or the people voting as a mass themselves.

The moment war is declared, however, the mass of the people, through some spiritual alchemy, become convinced that they have willed and executed the deed themselves. They then, with the exception of a few malcontents, proceed to allow themselves to be regimented, coerced, deranged in all the environments of their lives, and turned into a solid manufactory of destruction toward whatever other people may have, in the appointed scheme of things, come within the range of the Government's disapprobation. The citizen throws off his contempt and indifference to Government, identifies himself with its purposes, revives all his military memories and symbols, and the State once more walks, an august presence, through the imaginations of men. Patriotism becomes the dominant feeling, and produces immediately that intense and hopeless confusion between the relations which the individual bears and should bear toward the society of which he is a part.

The patriot loses all sense of the distinction between State, nation, and government. In our quieter moments, the Nation or Country forms the basic idea of society. We think vaguely of a loose population spreading over a certain geographical portion of the earth's surface, speaking a common language, and living in a homogeneous civilization. Our idea of Country concerns itself with the non-political aspects of a people, its ways of living, its personal traits, its literature and art, its characteristic attitudes toward life. We are Americans because we live in a certain bounded territory, because our ancestors have carried on a great enterprise of pioneering and colonization, because we live in certain kinds of communities which have a certain look and express their aspirations in certain ways. We can see that our civilization is different from contiguous civilizations like the Indian and Mexican. The institutions of our country form a certain network which affects us vitally and intrigues our thoughts in a way that these other civilizations do not. We are a part of Country, for better or for worse. We have arrived in it through the operation of physiological laws, and not in any way through our own choice. By the time we have reached what are called years of discretion, its influences have molded our habits, our values, our ways of thinking, so that however aware we may become, we never really lose the stamp of our civilization, or could be mistaken for the child of any other country. Our feeling for our fellow countrymen is one of similarity or of mere acquaintance. We may be intensely proud of and congenial to our particular network of civilization, or we may detest most of its qualities and rage at its defects. This does not alter the fact that we are inextricably bound up in it. The Country, as an inescapable group into which we are born, and which makes us its particular kind of a citizen of the world, seems to be a fundamental fact of our consciousness, an irreducible minimum of social feeling.

Now this feeling for country is essentially noncompetitive; we think of our own people merely as living on the earth's surface along with other groups, pleasant or objectionable as they may be, but fundamentally as sharing the earth with them. In our simple conception of country there is no more feeling of rivalry with other peoples than there is in our feeling for our family. Our interest turns within rather than without, is intensive and not belligerent. We grow up and our imaginations gradually stake out the world we live in, they need no greater conscious satisfaction for their gregarious impulses than this sense of a great mass of people to whom we are more or less attuned, and in whose institutions we are functioning. The feeling for country would be an uninflatable maximum were it not for the ideas of State and Government which are associated with it. Country is a concept of peace, of tolerance, of living and letting live. But State is essentially a concept of power, of competition: it signifies a group in its aggressive aspects. And we have the misfortune of being born not only into a country but into a State, and as we grow up we learn to mingle the two feelings into a hopeless confusion.

The State is the country acting as a political unit, it is the group acting as a repository of force, determiner of law, arbiter of justice. International politics is a "power politics" because it is a relation of States and that is what States infallibly and calamitously are, huge aggregations of human and industrial force that may be hurled against each other in war. When a country acts as a whole in relation to another country, or in imposing laws on its own inhabitants, or in coercing or punishing individuals or minorities, it is acting as a State. The history of America as a country is quite different from that of America as a State. In one case it is the drama of the pioneering conquest of the land, of the growth of wealth and the ways in which it was used, of the enterprise of education, and the carrying out of spiritual ideals, of the struggle of economic classes. But as a State, its history is that of playing a part in the world, making war, obstructing international trade, preventing itself from being split to pieces, punishing those citizens whom society agrees are offensive, and collecting money to pay for all.

Government on the other hand is synonymous with neither State nor Nation. It is the machinery by which the nation, organized as a State, carries out its State functions. Government is a framework of the administration of laws, and the carrying out of the public force. Government is the idea of the State put into practical operation in the hands of definite, concrete, fallible men. It is the visible sign of the invisible grace. It is the word made flesh. And it has necessarily the limitations inherent in all practicality. Government is the only form in which we can envisage the State, but it is by no means identical with it. That the State is a mystical conception is something that must never be forgotten. Its glamour and its significance linger behind the framework of Government and direct its activities.

Wartime brings the ideal of the State out into very clear relief, and reveals attitudes and tendencies that were hidden. In times of peace the sense of the State flags in a republic that is not militarized. For war is essentially the health of the State. The ideal of the State is that within its territory its power and influence should be universal. As the Church is the medium for the spiritual salvation of man, so the State is thought of as the medium for his political salvation. Its idealism is a rich blood flowing to all the members of the body politic. And it is precisely in war that the urgency for union seems greatest, and the necessity for universality seems most unquestioned. The State is the organization of the herd to act offensively or defensively against another herd similarly organized. The more terrifying the occasion for defense, the closer will become the organization and the more coercive the influence upon each member of the herd. War sends the current of purpose and activity flowing down to the lowest level of the herd, and to its most remote branches. All the activities of society are linked together as fast as possible to this central purpose of making a military offensive or a military defense, and the State becomes what in peacetimes it has vainly struggled to become—the inexorable arbiter and determinant of men's business and attitudes and opinions. The slack is taken up, the crosscurrents fade out, and the nation moves lumberingly and slowly, but with ever accelerated speed and integration, toward the great end, toward the "peacefulness of being at war . . . "

The classes which are able to play an active and not merely a passive role in the organization for war get a tremendous liberation of activity and energy. Individuals are jolted out of their old routine, many of them are given new positions of responsibility, new techniques must be learned. Wearing home ties are broken and women who would have remained attached with infantile bonds are liberated for service overseas. A vast sense of rejuvenescence pervades the significant classes, a sense of new importance in the world. Old national ideals are taken out, re-adapted to the purpose and used as universal touchstones, or molds into which all thought is poured. Every individual citizen who in peacetimes had no function to perform by which he could imagine himself an expression or living fragment of the State becomes an active amateur agent of the Government in reporting spies and disloyalists, in raising Government funds, or in propagating such measures as are considered necessary by officialdom. Minority opinion, which in times of peace, was only irritating and could not be dealt with by law unless it was conjoined with actual crime, becomes, with the outbreak of war, a case for outlawry. Criticism of the State, objections to war, lukewarm opinions concerning the necessity or the beauty of conscription, are made subject to ferocious penalties, far exceeding in severity those affixed to actual pragmatic crimes. Public opinion, as expressed in the newspapers, and the pulpits and the schools, becomes one solid block. "Loyalty," or rather war orthodoxy, becomes the sole test for all professions, techniques, occupations. Particularly is this true in the sphere of the intellectual life. There the smallest taint is held to spread over the whole soul, so that a professor of physics is *ipso facto* disqualified to teach physics or to hold honorable place in a university—the republic of learning—if he is at all unsound on the war. Even mere association with persons thus tainted is considered to disqualify a teacher. Anything pertaining to the enemy becomes taboo. His books are suppressed wherever possible, his language is forbidden. His artistic products are considered to convey in the subtlest spiritual way taints of vast poison to the soul that permits itself to enjoy them. So enemy music is suppressed, and energetic measures of opprobrium taken against those whose artistic consciences are not ready to perform such an act of self-sacrifice. The rage for loyal conformity works impartially, and often in diametric opposition to other orthodoxies and traditional conformities, or even ideals. The triumphant orthodoxy of the State is shown at its apex perhaps when Christian preachers lose their pulpits for taking in more or less literal terms the Sermon on the Mount, and Christian zealots are sent to prison for twenty years for distributing tracts which argue that war is unscriptural.

War is the health of the State. It automatically sets in motion throughout society those irresistible forces for uniformity, for passionate cooperation with the Government in coercing into obedience the minority groups and individuals which lack the larger herd sense. The machinery of government sets and enforces the drastic penalties; the minorities are either intimidated into silence, or brought slowly around by a subtle process of persuasion which may seem to them really to be converting them. Of course, the ideal of perfect loyalty, perfect uniformity is never really attained. The classes upon whom the amateur work of coercion falls are unwearied in their zeal, but often their agitation instead of converting, merely serves to stiffen their resistance. Minorities are rendered sullen, and some intellectual opinion bitter and satirical. But in general, the nation in wartime attains a uniformity of feeling, a hierarchy of values culminating at the undisputed apex of the State ideal, which could not possibly be produced through any other agency than war. Loyalty—or mystic devotion to the State—becomes the major imagined human value. Other values, such as artistic creation, knowledge, reason, beauty, the enhancement of life, are instantly and almost unanimously sacrificed, and the significant classes who have constituted themselves the amateur agents of the State are engaged not only in sacrificing these values for themselves but in coercing all other persons into sacrificing them.

War—or at least modern war waged by a democratic republic against a powerful enemy—seems to achieve for a nation almost all that the most inflamed political idealist could desire. Citizens are no longer indifferent to their Government, but each cell of the body politic is brimming with life and activity. We are at last on the way to full realization of that collective community in which each individual some-how contains the virtue of the whole. In a nation at war, every citizen identifies himself with the whole, and feels immensely strengthened in that identification. The purpose and desire of the collective community live in each person who throws himself wholeheartedly into the cause of war. The impeding distinction between society and the individual is almost blotted out. At war, the individual becomes almost identical with his society. He achieves a superb self-assurance, an intuition of the rightness of all his ideas and emotions, so that in the suppression of opponents or heretics he is invincibly strong; he feels behind him all the power of the collective community. The individual as social being in war seems to have achieved almost his apotheosis. Not for any religious impulse could the American nation have been expected to show such devotion *en masse,* such sacrifice and labor. Certainly not for any secular good, such as universal education or the subjugation of nature, would it have poured forth its treasure and its life, or would it have permitted such stern coercive measures to be taken against it, such as conscripting its money and its men. But for the sake of a war of offensive self-defense, undertaken to support a difficult cause to the slogan of "democracy," it would reach the highest level ever known of collective effort.

For these secular goods, connected with the enhancement of life, the education of man and the use of the intelligence to realize reason and beauty in the nation's communal living, are alien to our traditional ideal of the State. The State is inti-mately connected with war, for it is the organization of the collective community when it acts in a political manner, and to act in a political manner towards a rival group has meant, throughout all history—war.

There is nothing invidious in the use of the term "herd" in connection with the State. It is merely an attempt to reduce closer to first principles the nature of this institution in the shadow of which we all live, move, and have our being. Ethnolo-gists are generally agreed that human society made its first appearance as the human pack and not as a collection of individuals or of couples. The herd is in fact the original unit, and only as it was differentiated did personal individuality develop. All the most primitive surviving tribes of men are shown to live in a very complex but very rigid social organization where opportunity for individuation is scarcely given. These tribes remain strictly organized herds, and the difference between them and the modern State is one of degree of sophistication and variety of organization, and not of kind.

Psychologists recognize the gregarious impulse as one of the strongest primitive pulls which keeps together the herds of the different species of higher animals. Mankind is no exception. Our pugnacious evolutionary history has prevented the impulse from ever dying out. This gregarious impulse is the tendency to imitate, to conform, to coalesce together, and is most powerful when the herd believes itself threatened with attack. Animals crowd together for protection, and men become most conscious of their collectivity at the threat of war. Consciousness of collectivity brings confidence and a feeling of massed strength, which in turn arouses pugnacity and the battle is on. In civilized man, the gregarious impulse acts not only to produce concerted action for defense, but also to produce identity of opinion. Since thought is a form of behavior, the gregarious impulse floods up into its realms and demands that sense of uniform thought which wartime produces so successfully. And it is in this flooding of the conscious life of society that gregariousness works its havoc.

For just as in modern societies the sex instinct is enormously oversupplied for the requirements of human propagation, so the gregarious impulse is enormously oversupplied for the work of protection which it is called upon to perform. It would be quite enough if we were gregarious enough to enjoy the companionship of others, to be able to cooperate with them, and to feel a slight malaise at solitude. Unfortunately, however, this impulse is not content with these reasonable and healthful demands, but insists that like-mindedness shall prevail everywhere, in all departments of life. So that all human progress, all novelty, and nonconformity, must be carried against the resistance of this tyrannical herd instinct which drives the individual into obedience and conformity with the majority. Even in the most modern and enlightened societies this impulse shows little sign of abating. As it is driven by inexorable economic demand out of the sphere of utility, it seems to fasten itself ever more fiercely in the realm of feeling and opinion, so that conformity comes to be a thing aggressively desired and demanded.

The gregarious impulse keeps its hold all the more virulently because when the group is in motion or is taking any positive action, this feeling of being with and supported by the collective herd very greatly feeds that will to power, the nourishment of which the individual organism so constantly demands. You feel powerful by conforming, and you feel forlorn and helpless if you are out of the crowd. While even if you do not get any access of power by thinking and feeling just as everybody else in your group does, you get at least the warm feeling of obedience, the soothing irresponsibility of protection.

Joining as it does to these very vigorous tendencies of the individual—the pleasure in power and the pleasure in obedience—this gregarious impulse becomes irresistible in society. War stimulates it to the highest possible degree, sending the influences of its mysterious herd-current with its inflations of power and obedience to the farthest reaches of the society, to every individual and little group that can possibly be affected. And it is these impulses which the State—the organization of the entire herd, the entire collectivity—is founded on and makes use of.

There is, of course, in the feeling toward the State a large element of pure filial mysticism. The sense of insecurity, the desire for protection, sends one's desire back to the father and mother, with whom is associated the earliest feelings of protection. It is not for nothing that one's State is still thought of as Father or Motherland, that one's relation toward it is conceived in terms of family affection. The war has shown that nowhere under the shock of danger have these primitive childlike attitudes failed to assert themselves again, as much in this country as anywhere. If we have not the intense Father-sense of the German who worships his Vaterland, at least in

Uncle Sam we have a symbol of protecting, kindly authority, and in the many Mother-posters of the Red Cross, we see how easily in the more tender functions of war service, the ruling organization is conceived in family terms. A people at war have become in the most literal sense obedient, respectful, trustful children again, full of that naïve faith in the all-wisdom and all-power of the adult who takes care of them, imposes his mild but necessary rule upon them and in whom they lose their responsibility and anxieties. In this recrudescence of the child, there is great comfort, and a certain influx of power. . . .

In this great herd machinery, dissent is like sand in the bearings. The State ideal is primarily a sort of blind animal push toward military unity. Any difference with that unity turns the whole vast impulse toward crushing it. Dissent is speedily outlawed, and the Government, backed by the significant classes and those who in every locality, however small, identify themselves with them, proceeds against the outlaws, regardless of their value to the other institutions of the nation, or to the effect their persecution may have on public opinion. The herd becomes divided into the hunters and the hunted, and war enterprise becomes not only a technical game but a sport as well.

It must never be forgotten that nations do not declare war on each other, nor in the strictest sense is it nations that fight each other. Much has been said to the effect that modern wars are wars of whole peoples and not of dynasties. Because the entire nation is regimented and the whole resources of the country are levied on for war, this does not mean that it is the country *qua* country which is fighting. It is the country organized as a State that is fighting, and only as a State would it possibly fight. So literally it is States which make war on each other and not peoples. Governments are the agents of States, and it is Governments which declare war on each other, acting truest to form in the interests of the great State ideal they represent. There is no case known in modern times of the people being consulted in the initiation of a war. The present demand for "democratic control" of foreign policy indicates how completely, even in the most democratic of modern nations, foreign policy has been the secret private possession of the executive branch of the Government.

However representative of the people Parliaments and Congresses may be in all that concerns the internal administration of a country's political affairs, in international relations it has never been possible to maintain that the popular body acted except as a wholly mechanical ratifier of the Executive's will. The formality by which Parliaments and Congresses declare war is the merest technicality. Before such a declaration can take place, the country will have been brought to the very brink of war by the foreign policy of the Executive. A long series of steps on the downward path, each one more fatally committing the unsuspecting country to a warlike course of action, will have been taken without either the people or its representatives being consulted or expressing its feeling. When the declaration of war is finally demanded by the Executive, the Parliament or Congress could not refuse it without reversing the course of history, without repudiating what has been representing itself in the eyes of the other States as the symbol and interpreter of the nation's will and animus. To repudiate an Executive at that time would be to publish to the entire world the evidence that the country had been grossly deceived by its own Government, that the country with an almost criminal carelessness had allowed its

Government to commit it to gigantic national enterprises in which it had no heart. In such a crisis, even a Parliament which in the most democratic States represents the common man and not the significant classes who most strongly cherish the State ideal, will cheerfully sustain the foreign policy which it understands even less than it would care for if it understood, and will vote almost unanimously for an incalculable war, in which the nation may be brought well nigh to ruin. That is why the referendum which was advocated by some people as a test of American sentiment in entering the war was considered even by thoughtful democrats to be something subtly improper. The die had been cast. Popular whim could only derange and bungle monstrously the majestic march of State policy in its new crusade for the peace of the world. The irresistible State ideal got hold of the bowels of men. Whereas up to this time, it had been irreproachable to be neutral in word and deed, for the foreign policy of the State had so decided it, henceforth it became the most arrant crime to remain neutral. The Middle West, which had been soddenly pacifistic in our days of neutrality, became in a few months just as soddenly bellicose, and in its zeal for witch-burnings and its scent for enemies within gave precedence to no section of the country. The herd-mind followed faithfully the State-mind and, the agitation for a referendum being soon forgotten, the country fell into the universal conclusion that, since its Congress had formally declared the war, the nation itself had in the most solemn and universal way devised and brought on the entire affair. Oppression of minorities became justified on the plea that the latter were perversely resisting the rationally constructed and solemnly declared will of a majority of the nation. The herd coalescence of opinion which became inevitable the moment the State had set flowing the war attitudes became interpreted as a prewar popular decision, and disinclination to bow to the herd was treated as a monstrously antisocial act. So that the State, which had vigorously resisted the idea of a referendum and clung tenaciously and, of course, with entire success to its autocratic and absolute control of foreign policy, had the pleasure of seeing the country, within a few months, given over to the retrospective impression that a genuine referendum had taken place. When once a country has lapped up these State attitudes, its memory fades; it conceives itself not as merely accepting, but of having itself willed, the whole policy and technique of war. The significant classes, with their trailing satellites, identify themselves with the State, so that what the State, through the agency of the Government, has willed, this majority conceives itself to have willed.

All of which goes to show that the State represents all the autocratic, arbitrary, coercive, belligerent forces within a social group, it is a sort of complexus of everything most distasteful to the modern free creative spirit, the feeling for life, liberty, and the pursuit of happiness. War is the health of the State. Only when the State is at war does the modern society function with that unity of sentiment, simple uncritical patriotic devotion, cooperation of services, which have always been the ideal of the State lover. With the ravages of democratic ideas, however, the modern republic cannot go to war under the old conceptions of autocracy and death-dealing belligerency. If a successful animus for war requires a renaissance of State ideals, they can only come back under democratic forms, under this retrospective conviction of democratic control of foreign policy, democratic desire for war, and particularly of this identification of the democracy with the State. How unregenerate the ancient State may be, however, is indicated by the laws against sedition, and by the Government's unreformed attitude on foreign policy. One of the first demands of the more farseeing democrats in the democracies of the Alliance was that secret diplomacy must go. The war was seen to have been made possible by a web of secret agreements between States, alliances that were made by Governments without the shadow of popular support or even popular knowledge, and vague, half-understood commitments that scarcely reached the stage of a treaty or agreement, but which proved binding in the event. Certainly, said these democratic thinkers, war can scarcely be avoided unless this poisonous underground system of secret diplomacy is destroyed, this system by which a nation's power, wealth, and manhood may be signed away like a blank check to an allied nation to be cashed in at some future crisis. Agreements which are to affect the lives of whole peoples must be made between peoples and not by Governments, or at least by their representatives in the full glare of publicity and criticism.

Such a demand for "democratic control of foreign policy" seemed axiomatic. Even if the country had been swung into war by steps taken secretly and announced to the public only after they had been consummated, it was felt that the attitude of the American State toward foreign policy was only a relic of the bad old days and must be superseded in the new order. The American President himself, the liberal hope of the world, had demanded, in the eyes of the world, open diplomacy, agreements freely and openly arrived at. Did this mean a genuine transference of power in this most crucial of State functions from Government to people? Not at all. When the question recently came to a challenge in Congress, and the implications of open discussion were somewhat specifically discussed, and the desirabilities frankly commended, the President let his disapproval be known in no uncertain way. No one ever accused Mr. Wilson of not being a State idealist, and whenever democratic aspirations swung ideals too far out of the State orbit, he could be counted on to react vigorously. Here was a clear case of conflict between democratic idealism and the very crux of the concept of the State. However unthinkingly he might have been led on to encourage open diplomacy in his liberalizing program, when its implication was made vivid to him, he betrayed how mere a tool the idea had been in his mind to accentuate America's redeeming role. Not in any sense as a serious pragmatic technique had he thought of a genuinely open diplomacy. And how could he? For the last stronghold of State power is foreign policy. It is in foreign policy that the State acts most concentratedly as the organized herd, acts with fullest sense of aggressive-power, acts with freest arbitrariness. In foreign policy, the State is most itself. States, with reference to each other, may be said to be in a continual state of latent war. The "armed truce," a phrase so familiar before 1914, was an accurate description of the normal relation of States when they are not at war. Indeed, it is not too much to say that the normal relation of States is war. Diplomacy is a disguised war, in which States seek to gain by barter and intrigue, by the cleverness of wits, the objectives which they would have to gain more clumsily by means of war. Diplomacy is used while the States are recuperating from conflicts in which they have exhausted themselves. It is the wheedling and the bargaining of the worn-out bullies as they rise from the ground and slowly restore their strength to begin fighting again. If diplomacy had been a moral equivalent for war, a higher stage in human progress, an inestimable means of making words prevail instead of blows, militarism would have broken down and given place to it. But since it is a mere temporary substitute, a mere appearance of war's energy under another form, a surrogate effect is almost exactly proportioned to the armed force behind it. When it fails, the recourse is immediate to the military technique whose thinly veiled arm it has been. A diplomacy that was the agency of popular democratic forces in their non-State manifestations would be no diplomacy at all. It would be no better than the Railway or Education commissions that are sent from one country to another with rational constructive purpose. The State, acting as a diplomatic-military ideal, is eternally at war. Just as it must act arbitrarily and autocratically in time of war, it must act in time of peace in this particular role where it acts as a unit. Unified control is necessarily autocratic control. Democratic control of foreign policy is therefore a contradiction in terms. Open discussion destroys swiftness and certainty of action. The giant State is paralyzed. Mr. Wilson retains his full ideal of the State at the same time that he desires to eliminate war. He wishes to make the world safe for democracy as well as safe for diplomacy. When the two are in conflict, his clear political insight, his idealism of the State, tells him that it is the naïver democratic values that must be sacrificed. The world must primarily be made safe for diplomacy. The State must not be diminished.

What is the State essentially? The more closely we examine it, the more mystical and personal it becomes. On the Nation we can put our hand as a definite social group, with attitudes and qualities exact enough to mean something. On the Government we can put our hand as a certain organization of ruling functions, the machinery of lawmaking and law-enforcing. The Administration is a recognizable group of political functionaries, temporarily in charge of the government. But the State stands as an idea behind them all, eternal, sanctified, and from it Government and Administration conceive themselves to have the breath of life. Even the nation, especially in times of war—or at least, its significant classes—considers that it derives its authority and its purpose from the idea of the State. Nation and State are scarcely differentiated, and the concrete, practical, apparent facts are sunk in the symbol. We reverence not our country but the flag. We may criticize ever so severely our country, but we are disrespectful to the flag at our peril. It is the flag and the uniform that make men's heart beat high and fill them with noble emotions, not the thought of and pious hopes for America as a free and enlightened nation.

It cannot be said that the object of emotion is the same, because the flag is the symbol of the nation, so that in reverencing the American flag we are reverencing the nation. For the flag is not a symbol of the country as a cultural group, following certain ideals of life, but solely a symbol of the political State, inseparable from its prestige and expansion. The flag is most intimately connected with military achievement, military memory. It represents the country not in its intensive life, but in its far-flung challenge to the world. The flag is primarily the banner of war; it is allied with patriotic anthem and holiday. It recalls old martial memories. A nation's patriotic history is solely the history of its wars, that is, of the State in its health and glorious functioning. So in responding to the appeal of the flag, we are responding to the appeal of the State, to the symbol of the herd organized as an offensive and defensive body, conscious of its prowess and its mystical herd strength.

Even those authorities in the present Administration, to whom has been granted autocratic control over opinion, feel, though they are scarcely able to philosophize over, this distinction. It has been authoritatively declared that the horrid penalties against seditious opinion must not be construed as inhibiting legitimate, that is, partisan criticism of the Administration. A distinction is made between the Administration and the Government. It is quite accurately suggested by this attitude that the Administration is a temporary band of partisan politicians in charge of the machinery of Government, carrying out the mystical policies of State. The manner in which they operate this machinery may be freely discussed and objected to by their political opponents. The Governmental machinery may also be legitimately altered, in case of necessity. What may not be discussed or criticized is the mystical policy itself or the motives of the State in inaugurating such a policy. The President, it is true, has made certain partisan distinctions between candidates for office on the ground of support or nonsupport of the Administration, but what he means was really support or nonsupport of the State policy as faithfully carried out by the Administration. Certain of the Administration measures were devised directly to increase the health of the State, such as the Conscription and the Espionage laws. Others were concerned merely with the machinery. To oppose the first was to oppose the State and was therefore not tolerable. To oppose the second was to oppose fallible human judgment, and was therefore, though to be depreciated, not to be wholly interpreted as political suicide.

The distinction between Government and State, however, has not been so carefully observed. In time of war it is natural that Government as the seat of authority should be confused with the State or the mystic source of authority. You cannot very well injure a mystical idea which is the State, but you can very well interfere with the processes of Government. So that the two become identified in the public mind, and any contempt for or opposition to the workings of the machinery of Government is considered equivalent to contempt for the sacred State. The State, it is felt, is being injured in its faithful surrogate, and public emotion rallies passionately to defend it. It even makes any criticism of the form of Government a crime. . . .

Such attitudes are inevitable as arising from the devotees of the State. For the State is a personal as well as a mystical symbol, and it can only be understood by tracing its historical origin. The modern State is not the rational and intelligent product of modern men desiring to live harmoniously together with security of life, property, and opinion. It is not an organization which has been devised as pragmatic means to a desired social end. All the idealism with which we have been instructed to endow the State is the fruit of our retrospective imaginations. What it does for us in the way of security and benefit of life, it does incidentally as a by-product and development of its original functions, and not because at any time men or classes in the full possession of their insight and intelligence have desired that it be so. It is very important that we should occasionally lift the incorrigible veil of that *ex post facto* idealism by which we throw a glamour of rationalization over what is, and pretend in the ecstasies of social conceit that we have personally invented and set up for the glory of God and man the hoary institutions which we see around us. Things are what they are, and come down to us with all their thick encrustations of error and malevolence. Political philosophy can delight us with fantasy and convince us who need illusion to live that the actual is a fair and approximate copy—full of failings, of course, but approximately sound and sincere—of that ideal society which we can imagine ourselves as creating. From this it is a step to the tacit assumption that we have somehow had a hand in its creation and are responsible for its maintenance and sanctity.

Nothing is more obvious, however, than that every one of us comes into society as into something in whose creation we had not the slightest hand. . . . By the time we find ourselves here we are caught in a network of customs and attitudes, the major directions of our desires and interests have been stamped on our minds, and by the time we have emerged from tutelage and reached the years of discretion when we might conceivably throw our influence to the reshaping of social institutions, most of us have been so molded into the society and class we live in that we are scarcely aware of any distinction between ourselves as judging, desiring individuals and our social environment. We have been kneaded so successfully that we approve of what our society approves, desire what our society desires, and add to the group our own passionate inertia against change, against the effort of reason, and the adventure of beauty.

Every one of us, without exception, is born into a society that is given, just as the fauna and flora of our environment are given. Society and its institutions are, to the individual who enters it, as much naturalistic phenomena as is the weather itself. There is, therefore, no natural sanctity in the State any more than there is in the weather. We may bow down before it, just as our ancestors bowed before the sun and moon, but it is only because something in us unregenerate finds satisfaction in such an attitude, not because there is anything inherently reverential in the institution worshiped. Once the State has begun to function, and a large class finds its interest and its expression of power in maintaining the State, this ruling class may compel obedience from any uninterested minority. The State thus becomes an instrument by which the power of the whole herd is wielded for the benefit of a class. The rulers soon learn to capitalize the reverence which the State produces in the majority, and turn it into a general resistance toward a lessening of their privileges. The sanctity of the State becomes identified with the sanctity of the ruling class, and the latter are permitted to remain in power under the impression that in obeying and serving them, we are obeying and serving society, the nation, the great collectivity of all of us. . . .

A. Philip Randolph (1889–1979)

Suffering from the injustices of living in the Jim Crow South, Asa Philip Randolph moved to New York City in 1911. The vibrant culture of the Harlem Renaissance was liberating for Randolph, and soon he became involved in class and race issues. Impressed by the efforts of the socialist Industrial Workers of the World to free all workers from "wage slavery," Randolph began promoting the union cause and, in 1916, joined the Socialist Party. Socialism, he believed, was the solution to the inequities and exploitation inherent in the capitalist system. Through socialism, a society would be created that would provide full equality to all citizens, including African Americans. In 1917, in collaboration with Chandler Owen, Randolph began publishing *The Messenger*, a radical magazine urging blacks to join unions and convert to socialism if they wanted economic, social, and political equality.

Although he later moderated his socialist views, Randolph worked throughout his life as a civil rights activist. In 1925 he founded the Brotherhood of Sleeping Car Porters, which, after 12 years of effort, finally achieved the Pullman company's recognition and improved job security and higher wages for its members. This success augmented his reputation as an African American leader and gained him an audience with President Franklin D. Roosevelt in 1941. At this meeting, Randolph threatened that he and his union would lead a march on Washington if the president did not do something about racial discrimination in the defense industry. Not wishing to expose to the rest of the world the inequality that existed in the United States at a time when the nation was being drawn into a war against fascism and racism, Roosevelt signed an executive order stipulating that federally-funded defense jobs must be made available on an equal-opportunity basis. When Roosevelt signed the executive order, Randolph called off the march. After the war, he continued to press for civil rights and, in 1963, proposed a march on Washington to pressure Congress to pass President Kennedy's Civil Rights Bill. And so it was that, at age 74, he was the first speaker on the steps of the Lincoln Memorial on August 28, 1963. And it was A. Philip Randolph who introduced the next speaker: Martin Luther King Jr.

In what way, according to this *Messenger* article by Randolph, does capitalism promote racism? How does socialism correct this?

"On Socialism," 1919

Socialism would deprive individuals of the power to make fortunes out of the labor of other individuals by virtue of their ownership of the machinery which the worker must use in order to live. When an individual or class may make profits out of the labor of black and white workers, it is to his or to the interest of the class to use any means to keep them (the workers) from combining in order to raise wages, to lower their hours of work or to demand better working conditions. This is the only reason why prejudice is fostered in the South. Of course, it may not be possible to trace every lynching or act of prejudice to a direct economic cause, but the case may be explained by the law of habit. When social practices are once set they act or recur with a dangerous accuracy. So that it is now a social habit to lynch Negroes. But

SOURCE: The *Messenger*, March 1919.

when the motive for promoting race prejudice is removed, viz., profits, by the social ownership, control and operation of the machinery and sources of production through the government, the government being controlled by the workers; the effects of prejudice, race riots, lynching, etc., will also be removed.

For instance, if railroads were owned and democratically managed by the government, its collective and social service function would not be prostituted to jim-crow cars in order to pander and cater to race prejudice. No individuals would be making profits out of them and consequently there would be no interest in promoting race antagonisms. Lynchings, the product of capitalism, would pass as the burning of heretics and the Spanish Inquisition, the product of religious intolerance, passed.

Besides Socialism would arm every man and woman with the ballot. Education would be compulsory and universal. The vagrancy law, child labor and peonage would no longer exist. Tenant-farming and the crop-lien system would be discarded. And every worker would receive the full product of his toil.

This is the goal of Socialism. This is why every Negro should be a Socialist.

Marcus Garvey (1887–1940)

In 1914, Marcus Garvey founded the Universal Negro Improvement Association (UNIA) in his native Jamaica. Garvey believed that blacks around the world would only ever rise up out of oppression by uniting in a powerful worldwide movement. Much like Booker T. Washington's Tuskegee Institute, UNIA's mission was to promote education in practical skills so that blacks could advance themselves economically. But, significantly, Garvey was a vocal champion of racial pride. In 1916, seeking to create an international movement, Garvey went to New York and began promoting the UNIA in Harlem. Claiming that America was a white man's country that would never fully accept blacks, he urged African Americans not to cooperate with whites but to work only for their own power. Coining the phrase "black power," he advocated the creation of a separate nation for blacks in Africa. He also argued that, in their efforts to achieve black power, blacks should abandon the effort to fit into white society and recognize instead the beauty and uniqueness of their racial heritage. "Black," Garvey proclaimed, "is beautiful," and African Americans should proudly accentuate their Africanness. He composed an anthem and designed a red, green, and white flag that would symbolize the Pan-Africa movement, and he organized and sold shares in a steamship company, the Black Star Line (a play on England's White Star Line), that would be an example of a successful black business venture. The scheme, however, failed in 1922, and in 1927, after being convicted and serving time for mail fraud, he was deported. Although he had been vehemently disparaged as a charlatan by A. Philip Randolph and W. E. B. DuBois, among others, and although many of his followers deserted him in the end, he had awakened African American racial pride and helped to create a deep sense of racial solidarity that would have an enormous impact during the civil rights movement.

In the following two excerpts, what is Garvey's argument for black separation? Why would Garvey's ideas have achieved such popularity in the 1920s? Have conditions changed sufficiently that today such views would no longer be so highly regarded?

―――――――――――

Speech to the Universal Negro Improvement Association, Philadelphia, 1919

We have lived upon the farce of brotherhood for hundreds of years, and if there is anybody who has suffered from that farce it is the Negro. The white man goes forth with the Bible and tells us that we are all brothers, but it is against the world to believe, against all humanity to believe, that really there is but one brotherhood. And if there are six brothers in any family, at least those six brothers from natural ties ought to be honest in their dealings with each other to the extent of not seeing any of the six starve. If one has not a job, naturally the others would see to it that the one that is out of a job gets something to eat and a place to sleep so as to prevent him from starving and dying. This is brotherhood. Now there is one brother with all the wealth; he has more than he wants and there is the other brother. What is he doing to the other brother? He is murdering the other brother. He is lynching the other brother, and still they are brothers. Now, if I have any brother in my family who has no better love for me than to starve me, to whip me and to burn me, I say, brother, I do not want your relationship at all. To hell with it. . . .

Tonight the Universal Negro Improvement Association is endeavoring to teach Negroes that the time has come for them to help themselves. We have helped the white man in this Western Hemisphere for over three hundred years until he has become so almighty that he respects not even God himself. The white man believes that there is only one God, and that is the white man. We have a different idea about God. We believe that there is but one God, and he is in a place called heaven. There is a heaven, we believe, and a God presides over that heaven, and as far as the Negro is concerned that God is the only being in the world whom we respect. We believe with Theodore Roosevelt, "Fear God and know no other fear." And if every Negro in Philadelphia could just get that one thought into his or her mind, to fear God and him alone and let the world take care of itself, the better it would be for each and every one.

The white man comes before you in his imperial and majestic pomp and tries to impress upon you the idea that he is your superior. Who made him your superior? You stick his face with a pin and blood runs out. Starve the white man and he dies. Starve the black man and he dies. What difference is there, therefore, in black and

―――――――

SOURCE: *Negro World*, November 1, 1919.

white. If you stick the white man, blood comes out. If you starve the white man he dies. The same applies to the black man. They said the white man was the superior being and the black man was the inferior being. That is the old time notion, but today the world knows that all men were created equal. We were created equal and were put into this world to possess equal rights and equal privileges, and the time has come for the black man to get his share. . . .

[T]he Universal Negro Improvement Association is no joke. It is a serious movement. It is as serious a movement as the movement of the Irish today to have a free Ireland; as the determination of the Jew to recover Palestine. The Negro peoples of the world should be so determined to reclaim Africa and found a government there, so that if any black man in any part of the world is abused we can call the mighty power of Africa to come to our aid. Men, a Negro government we had once, and a Negro government we must have again. Tell me that I must live everlastingly under the domination of a white man, that I must bequeath to my children white overlordship, then I say, let me die now, Almighty God. If there is no better future in the world for me than to be the slave of a white man, I say, take the life you gave me. I do not want it. You would not be my God if you created me to be a slave to other men; but you are my God and will continue to be my God if you created me an equal of all men. . . .

Again I want you to understand that economically we are flirting with our graves if we do not start out to make ourselves economically independent. This war brought about new conditions in America and all over the world. America sent hundreds of thousands of colored soldiers to fight the white man's battles, during which time she opened the doors of industry to millions of white American men and women and created a new problem in the industrial market. And now the war is over and those millions who took the places of the soldiers who have returned home say: "We are not going to give up our jobs. We are going to remain in the industrial life of the world." This makes it difficult for returned soldiers to get work now. There will be sufficient jobs now for returned soldiers and for white men, because abnormal conditions are still in existence, but in the next two years these abnormal conditions will pass away and the industries will not be opened up for so long. It means that millions are going to starve. Do you think the white industrial captains are going to allow the white men and the white women to starve and give you bread? To the white man blood is thicker than water.

Therefore, in the next two years there is going to be an industrial boomerang in this country, and if the Negroes do not organize now to open up economic and industrial opportunities for themselves there will be starvation among all Negroes. It is because we want to save the situation when this good time shall have passed by and the white man calls you, "My dear John, I haven't any job for you today," and you can leave the white man's job as a porter and go into the Negro factory as a clerk, you can leave the white man's kitchen and go into your home as the wife of a big Negro banker or a corporation manager.

Appeal to the Soul of White America, 1923

The Negro needs a nation and a country of his own, where he can best show evidence of his own ability in the art of human progress. Scattering him as an unmixed and unrecognized part of alien nations and civilizations is but to demonstrate his imbecility, and point him out as an unworthy derelict, fit neither for the society of Greek, Jew nor Gentile. It is unfortunate that we should so drift apart, as a race, as not to see that we are but perpetuating our own sorrow and disgrace in failing to appreciate the first requisite of all peoples—organization. . . .

No Negro, let him be American, European, West Indian or African, shall be truly respected until his race as a whole has emancipated itself, through self-achievement and progress, from universal prejudice. The Negro will have to build his own government, industry, art, science, literature and culture, before the world will stop to consider him. Until then, we are but wards of a superior race and civilization, and the outcasts of a standard social system. The race needs workers at this time, not plagiarists, copyists and mere imitators, but men and women who are able to create, to originate and improve, and thus make an independent racial contribution to the world and civilization.

The unfortunate thing about it is that we take the monkey apings of our so-called "leading men" for progress. There is no real progress in Negroes aping white people and telling us that they represent the best in the race, for in that respect any dressed monkey would represent the best of its species, irrespective of the creative matter of the monkey instinct. The best in a race is not reflected through or by the action of its apes, but by its ability to create of and by itself. It is such creation that our organization seeks. Let us not try to be the best or worst of others, but let us make the effort to be the best of ourselves. Our own racial critics criticize us as dreamers and fanatics, and call us benighted and ignorant, because they lack backbone. They are unable to see themselves creators of their own needs. The slave instinct has not yet departed from them. They still believe that they can only live or exist through the good graces of their "masters." The good slaves have not yet thrown off their shackles; thus to them, the U.N.I.A. is an "impossibility.". . .

SOURCE: *Negro World*, October 2, 1923.

Margaret Sanger (1879–1966)

While the battle for women's suffrage was being waged, Margaret Sanger fought a different fight, but one that was just as important for women in the United States. Living in New York City and associating with such intellectuals as John Reed, Emma Goldman, and Max Eastman, she began participating in Socialist Party and Industrial Workers of the World activities. Becoming especially concerned with the plight of women, in 1912 she launched a column, "What Every Girl Should Know," in the *New York Call*. Although one of her articles on venereal disease was suppressed by the censors, giving her her first run-in with authorities, she was in no way discouraged from continuing to educate women about their sexual health. She also worked in a clinic in the lower East Side, where she was confronted daily with the plight of poor women suffering from the results of illegal and often self-induced abortions. Sanger later wrote in her autobiography that one of her patients, Sadie Sachs, asked the doctor, as she was about to return home, how she could avoid pregnancy. The doctor flippantly advised the woman to tell her husband to "sleep on the roof." When Mrs. Sachs returned a year later, dying from a botched abortion, Sanger decided she had no alternative but to act. Claiming this event changed her life, Sanger committed herself to fight for contraception for women. In 1914, she began publication of *The Woman Rebel*, a radical feminist magazine (its masthead proclaiming "No Gods, No Masters") that advocated women's rights, especially the right to birth control, and provided explicit information on contraception. She was arrested for violating the Comstock Law and for breaking postal obscenity laws. Unwilling to go to prison, she jumped bail and went to England for a year.

When she returned, charges against her were dropped, and she continued to agitate for birth control by going on a national speaking tour. In 1916, she opened a clinic in Brooklyn where women could be advised on contraception, but the clinic was raided and Sanger spent a month in jail. In 1921, Sanger founded the American Birth Control League, and eventually enough people supported her position that Congress finally acceded to the idea that physicians, if medical reasons warranted, could disseminate birth control information. This led Sanger to open a legal clinic staffed with female doctors in 1923. In 1939, she founded the Birth Control Federation of America, later renamed the Planned Parenthood Federation of America. In the 1950s, Sanger was instrumental in the development of the birth control pill.

Among Margaret Sanger's many publications, *Woman and the New Race* (1920) puts forth many cogent arguments supporting women's reproductive rights. Why, according to Sanger, should women break laws that forbid contraceptives?

Why is birth control a fundamental right for women? Why is it that "man has not protected woman in matters most vital to her"? What tactics should women use to claim this basic right?

"Legislating Woman's Morals," 1920

One of the important duties before those women who are demanding birth control as a means to a New Race is the changing of our so-called obscenity laws. This will be no easy undertaking; it is usually much easier to enact statutes than to revise them. Laws are seldom exactly what they seem, rarely what their advocates claim for them. The "obscenity" statutes are particularly deceptive.

Enacted, avowedly, to protect society against the obscene and the lewd, they make no distinction between the scientific works of human emancipators like Forel and Ellis and printed matter such as they are ostensibly aimed at. Naturally enough, then, detectives and narrow-minded judges and prosecutors who would chuckle over pictures that would make a clean-minded woman shudder, unite to suppress the scientific works and the birth-control treatises which would enable men and women to attain higher physical, mental, moral and spiritual standards.

Woman, bent upon her freedom and seeking to make a better world, will not permit the indecent and unclean forces of reaction to mask themselves forever behind the plea that it is necessary to keep her in ignorance to preserve her purity. In the birth-control movement, she has already begun to fight for her right to have, without legal interference, all knowledge pertaining to her sex nature. This is the third and most important of the epoch-making battles for general liberty upon American soil. It is most important because it is to purify the very fountain of the race and make the race completely free.

The first and most dramatic of the three great struggles for liberty reached its apex, as we know, in the American Revolution. It had for its object the right to hold such political beliefs as one might choose, and to act in accordance with those beliefs. If this political freedom is now lost to us, it is because we did not hold strongly enough to those liberties fought for by our forefathers.

Nearly a hundred years after the Revolution the battle for religious liberty came to a climax in the career of Robert G. Ingersoll. His championship of the much vaunted and little exercised freedom of religious opinion swept the blasphemy laws into the lumber room of outworn tyrannies. Those yet remaining upon the statute books are invoked but rarely, and then the effort to enforce them is ridiculous.

Within a few years the tragic combination of false moral standards and infamous obscenity laws will be as ridiculous in the public mind as are the now all but forgotten blasphemy laws. If the obscenity laws are not radically revised or repealed, few reactionaries will dare to face the public derision that will greet their attempts to use them to stay woman's progress.

SOURCE: Margaret Sanger, *Woman and the New Race* (New York: Brentano's, 1920), chapters 15 and 18.

The French have a saying concerning "mort main"—the dead hand. This hand of the past reaches up into the present to smother the rising flame of modern ideals, to reforge our chains when we have broken them, to arrest progress. It is the hand of such as have lived on earth but have not loved humanity. At the call of those who fear progress and freedom, it rises from the gloom of forgotten things to oppress the living.

It is the dead hand that holds imprisoned within the obscenity laws all direct information concerning birth control. It is the dead hand that thus compels millions of American women to remain in the bondage of maternity.

Previous to the year 1868, the obscenity laws of the various states in the Union contained no specific prohibition of information concerning contraceptives. In that year, however, the General Assembly of New York passed an act which specifically included the subject of contraceptives. The act made it exactly as great an offense to give such information as to exhibit the sort of pictures and writings at which the legislation was ostensibly aimed.

In 1873, the late Anthony Comstock, who with a list of contributors, most of whom did not realize the real effects of his work, constituted the so-called Society for the Suppression of Vice, succeeded in obtaining the passage of the federal obscenity act. This act was presented as one to prevent the circulation of pornographic literature and pictures among school children. As such, it was rushed through with two hundred sixty other acts in the closing hours of the Congress. This act made it a crime to use the mails to convey contraceptives or information concerning contraceptives. Other acts later made the original law applicable to express companies and other common carriers, as well as to the mails.

With this precedent established—a precedent which a majority of the congressmen could hardly have understood because of the hasty passage of the act—Comstock secured the enactment of state laws to the same effect. Meanwhile, the provisions regarding contraceptives had been dropped from the amended New York State law of 1872. In 1873, however, a new section, said to have been drafted by Comstock himself, was substituted for the one enacted in 1872, and that section is essentially the substance of the present law. None of these acts made it an offense to prevent conception—all of them provided punishment for anyone disseminating information concerning the prevention of conception. In the federal statutes, the maximum penalties were fixed at a fine of $5,000 or five years imprisonment, or both. The usual maximum penalty under a state law is a fine of $1,000 or one year's imprisonment, or both.

Comstock has passed out of public notice. His body has been entombed but the evil that he did lives after him. His dead hand still reaches forth to keep the subject of prevention of conception where he placed it—in the same legal category with things unclean and vile. Forty years ago the laws were changed and the chief work of Comstock's life accomplished. Those laws still live, legal monuments to ignorance and to oppression. Through those laws reaches the dead hand to bring to the operating table each year hundreds of thousands of women who undergo the agony of abortion. Each year this hand reaches out to compel the birth of hundreds of thousands of infants who must die before they are twelve months old.

Like many laws upon our statute books, these are being persistently and intelligently violated. Few members of the well-to-do and wealthy classes think for a single moment of obeying them. They limit their families to one, two or three well-cared-for children Usually the prosecutor who presents the case against a birth-control advocate, trapped by a detective hired by the Comstock Society, has no children at all or a small family. The family of the judge who passes upon the case is likely to be smaller still. The words "It is the law" sums it all up for these officials when they pass sentence in court. But these words, so magical to the official mind, have no weight when these same officials are adjusting their own private lives. They then obey the higher laws of their own beings—they break the obsolete statutes for themselves while enforcing them for others.

This is not the situation with the poorer people of the United States, however. Millions of them know nothing of reliable contraceptives. When women of the impoverished strata of society do not break these laws against contraceptives, they violate those laws of their inner beings which tell them not to bring children into the world to live in want, disease and general misery. They break the first law of nature, which is that of self preservation. Bound by false morals, enchained by false conceptions of religion, hindered by false laws, they endure until the pressure becomes so great that morals, religion and laws alike fail to restrain them. Then they for a brief respite resort to the surgeon's instruments.

For many years the semi-official witch hunting of the Comstock organization had a remarkable and a deadly effect. Everyone, whether it was novelist, essayist, publicist, propagandist or artist, who sought to throw definite light upon the forbidden subject of sex, or upon family limitation, was prosecuted if detected. Among the many books suppressed were works by physicians designed to warn young men and women away from the pitfalls of venereal diseases and sexual errors. The darkness that surrounded the whole field of sex was made as complete as possible.

Since then the feeling of the awakened women of America has intensified. The rapidity with which women are going into industry, the increasing hardship and poverty of the lower strata of society, the arousing of public conscience, have all operated to give force and volume to the demand for woman's right to control her own body that she may work out her own salvation.

Those who believe in strictly legal measures, as well as those who believe both in legal measures and in open defiance of these brutal and unjust laws, are demanding amendments to the obscenity statutes, which shall remove information concerning contraceptives from its present classification among things filthy and obscene.

An amendment typical of those offered is that drawn up for the New York statutes under the direction of Samuel McClure Lindsey, of Columbia University. The words and sentences in italics are those which it proposed to add:

(Section 1145.) Physicians' instruments *and information*. An article or instrument used or applied by physicians lawfully practicing, or by their direction or prescription, for the cure or prevention of disease, is not an article of indecent or immoral nature or use, within this article. The supplying of such articles to such physicians or by their direction or prescription, is not an offense under this article. *The giving by a duly licensed physician or registered nurse lawfully practicing, of information or advice in regard to, or the supplying to any person of any article or medicine for the prevention of, conception is not a violation of any provision of this article.*

This proposed amendment should without doubt include midwives as well as nurses. There are thousands of women who never see a nurse or a physician. Under this section, even as it now stands, physicians have a right to prescribe contraceptives, but few of them have claimed that right or have even known that it has existed. It does exist, however, and was specifically declared by the New York State Court of Appeals, as we shall see when we consider that court's opinion in the Sanger case, farther on in the book. It can do no harm to make the intent of the law as regards physicians plainer, and it would be an immense step forward to include nurses and midwives in the section. With this addition it would remove one of the most serious obstacles to the freedom and advancement of American womanhood. Every woman interested in the welfare of women in general should make it her business to agitate for such a change in the obscenity laws.

The above provision would take care of the case of the woman who is ill, or who is plainly about to become ill, but it does not take care of the vast body of women who have not yet ruined their health by childbearing and who are not yet suffering from diseases complicated by pregnancy. If this amendment had been attached to the laws in all the states, there would still remain much to be done.

Shall we go on indefinitely driving the now healthy mother of two children into the hands of the abortionist, where she goes in preference to constant ill health, overwork and the witnessing of dying and starving babies? It is each woman's duty to herself and to society to hasten the repeal of all laws against the communication of birth-control information. Now that she has the vote, she should use her political influence to strike, first of all, at these restrictive statutes. It is not to her credit that a district attorney, arguing against a birth control advocate, is able to show that women have made no effort to wipe out such laws in states where they have had the ballot for years.

It is time that women assert themselves upon this fundamental right, and the first and best use they can make of the ballot is in this direction. These laws were made by men and have been instruments of martyrdom and death for unnumbered thousands of women. Women now have the opportunity to sweep them into the trash heap. They will do it at once unless, like men, they use the ballot for those political honors which many years of experience have taught men to be hollow.

It is only a question of how long it will take women to make up their minds to this result. The law of woman's being is stronger than any statute, and the man-made law must sooner or later give way to it. Man has not protected woman in matters most vital to her—but she is awaking and will sooner or later realize this and assert herself. If she acts in mass now, it will be another cheering evidence that she is moving consciously toward her goal.

"The Goal," 1920

What is the goal of woman's upward struggle? Is it voluntary motherhood? Is it general freedom? Or is it the birth of a new race? For freedom is not fruitless, but prolific of higher things. Being the most sacred aspect of woman's freedom, voluntary motherhood is motherhood in its highest and holiest form. It is motherhood unchained—motherhood ready to obey its own urge to remake the world.

Voluntary motherhood implies a new morality—a vigorous, constructive, liberated morality. That morality will, first of all, prevent the submergence of womanhood into motherhood. It will set its face against the conversion of women into mechanical maternity and toward the creation of a new race.

Woman's role has been that of an incubator and little more. She has given birth to an incubated race. She has given to her children what little she was permitted to give, but of herself, of her personality, almost nothing. In the mass, she has brought forth quantity, not quality. The requirement of a male dominated civilization has been numbers. She has met that requirement.

It is the essential function of voluntary motherhood to choose its own mate, to determine the time of childbearing and to regulate strictly the number of offspring. Natural affection upon her part, instead of selection dictated by social or economic advantage, will give her a better fatherhood for her children. The exercise of her right to decide how many children she will have and when she shall have them will procure for her the time necessary to the development of other faculties than that of reproduction. She will give play to her tastes, her talents and her ambitions. She will become a full-rounded human being.

Thus and only thus will woman be able to transmit to her offspring those qualities which make for a greater race.

The importance of developing these qualities in the mothers for transmission to the children is apparent when we recall certain well-established principles of biology. In all of the animal species below the human, motherhood has a clearly discernible superiority over fatherhood. It is the first pulse of organic life. Fatherhood is the fertilizing element. Its development, compared to that of the mother cell, is comparatively new. Likewise, its influence upon the progeny is comparatively small. There are weighty authorities who assert that through the female alone comes those modifications of form, capacity and ability which constitute evolutionary progress. It was the mothers who first developed cunning in chase, ingenuity in escaping enemies, skill in obtaining food, and adaptability. It was they also who attained unfailing discretion in leadership, adaptation to environment and boldness in attack. When the animal kingdom as a whole is surveyed, these stand out as distinctly feminine traits. They stand out also as the characteristics by which the progress of species is measured.

Why is all this true of the lower species yet not true of human beings? The secret is revealed by one significant fact—the female's functions in these animal species are not limited to motherhood alone. Every organ and faculty is fully employed and perfected. Through the development of the individual mother, better and higher types of animals are produced and carried forward. In a word, natural law makes the female the expression and the conveyor of racial efficiency.

Birth control itself, often denounced as a violation of natural law, is nothing more or less than the facilitation of the process of weeding out the unfit, of preventing the birth of defectives or of those who will become defectives. So, in compliance with nature's working plan, we must permit womanhood its full development before we can expect of it efficient motherhood. If we are to make racial progress, this development of womanhood must precede motherhood in every individual woman. Then and then only can the mother cease to be an incubator and be a mother indeed. Then only can she transmit to her sons and daughters the qualities which make strong individuals and, collectively, a strong race.

Voluntary motherhood also implies the right of marriage without maternity. Two utterly different functions are developed in the two relationships. In order to give the mate relationship its full and free play, it is necessary that no woman should be a mother against her will. There are other reasons, of course—reasons more frequently emphasized—but the reason just mentioned should never be overlooked. It is as important to the race as to the woman, for through it is developed that high love impulse which, conveyed to the child, attunes and perfects its being.

Marriage, quite aside from parentage, also gives two people invaluable experience. When parentage follows in its proper time, it is a better parentage because of the mutual adjustment and development—because of the knowledge thus gained. Few couples are fitted to understand the sacred mystery of child life until they have solved some of the problems arising out of their own love lives.

Maternal love, which usually follows upon a happy, satisfying mate love, becomes a strong and urgent craving. It then exists for two powerful, creative functions. First, for its own sake, and then for the sake of further enriching the conjugal relationship. It is from such soil that the new life should spring. It is the inherent right of the new life to have its inception in such physical ground, in such spiritual atmosphere. The child thus born is indeed a flower of love and tremendous joy. It has within it the seeds of courage and of power. This child will have the greatest strength to surmount hardships, to withstand tyrannies, to set still higher the mark of human achievement.

Shall we pause here to speak again of the rights of womanhood, in itself and of itself, to be absolutely free? We have talked of this right so much in these pages, only to learn that in the end, a free womanhood turns of its own desire to a free and happy motherhood, a motherhood which does not submerge the woman, but which is enriched because she is unsubmerged. When we voice, then, the necessity of setting the feminine spirit utterly and absolutely free, thought turns naturally not to rights of the woman, nor indeed of the mother, but to the rights of the child—of all children in the world. For this is the miracle of free womanhood, that in its freedom it becomes the race mother and opens its heart in fruitful affection for humanity.

How narrow, how pitifully puny has become motherhood in its chains! The modern motherhood enfolds one or two adoring children of its own blood, and cherishes, protects and loves them. It does not reach out to all children. When motherhood is a high privilege, not a sordid, slavish requirement, it will encircle all. Its deep, passionate intensity will overflow the limits of blood relationship. Its beauty will shine upon all, for its beauty is of the soul, whose power of enfoldment is unbounded.

When motherhood becomes the fruit of a deep yearning, not the result of ignorance or accident, its children will become the foundation of a new race. There will be no killing of babies in the womb by abortion, nor through neglect in foundling homes, nor will there be infanticide. Neither will children die by inches in mills and factories. No man will dare to break a child's life upon the wheel of toil.

Voluntary motherhood will not be passive, resigned, or weak. Out of its craving will come forth a fierceness of love for its fruits that will make such men as remain unawakened stand aghast at its fury when offended. The tigress is less terrible in defense of her offspring than will be the human mother. The daughters of such women will not be given over to injustice and to prostitution; the sons will not perish in industry nor upon the battle field. Nor could they meet these all too common fates if an undaunted motherhood were there to defend. Childhood and youth will be too valuable in the eyes of society to waste them in the murderous mills of blind greed and hate.

This is the dawn. Womanhood shakes off its bondage. It asserts its right to be free. In its freedom, its thoughts turn to the race. Like begets like. We gather perfect fruit from perfect trees. The race is but the amplification of its mother body, the multiplication of flesh habitations—beautified and perfected for souls akin to the mother soul.

The relentless efforts of reactionary authority to suppress the message of birth control and of voluntary motherhood are futile. The powers of reaction cannot now prevent the feminine spirit from breaking its bonds. When the last fetter falls the evils that have resulted from the suppression of woman's will to freedom will pass. Child slavery, prostitution, feeblemindedness, physical deterioration, hunger, oppression and war will disappear from the earth.

In their subjection women have not been brave enough, strong enough, pure enough to bring forth great sons and daughters. Abused soil brings forth stunted growths. An abused motherhood has brought forth a low order of humanity. Great beings come forth at the call of high desire. Fearless motherhood goes out in love and passion for justice to all mankind. It brings forth fruits after its own kind. When the womb becomes fruitful through the desire of an aspiring love, another Newton will come forth to unlock further the secrets of the earth and the stars. There will come a Plato who will be understood, a Socrates who will drink no hemlock, and a Jesus who will not die upon the cross. These and the race that is to be in America await upon a motherhood that is to be sacred because it is free.

H. L. Mencken (1880–1956)

Baltimore journalist Henry Louis Mencken's dissenting voice was laced with vitriol. A master of withering sarcasm and mocking satire, Mencken was perhaps the most perceptive, humorous, and outrageous critic of all aspects of American society in the first half of the twentieth century. Nothing, with the exception of free speech, was too sacred to escape his derision. Republicans, Democrats, Socialists, presidents, Congress, the common man, women, democracy, religion, Victorian morality, politicos, the American South, prohibition—all fell victim to the finely honed scalpel of his ridicule. He paid tribute to intelligence and critical thinking for the simple reason that "the most dangerous man, to any government, is the man who is able to think things out for himself, without regard to the prevailing superstitions and taboos. Almost inevitably he comes to the conclusion that the government he lives under is dishonest, insane and intolerable."

Mencken wrote thousands of articles for newspapers, including the *Baltimore Sun* and the *Baltimore Herald Tribune*, and his own magazine, *The American Mercury*. Frequently his articles oozed with such impudence that it was difficult to distinguish between a facetious tongue-in-cheek commentary and a thought-provoking appraisal of the subject at hand. Claiming that Americans (the "Booboisie") were uncivilized idiots, the most gullible people in the world who readily believed everything advertisers and politicians told them, he argued that this was the natural consequence of democracy. "We live in a land of abounding quackeries," Mencken wrote, "and if we do not learn how to laugh we succumb to the melancholy disease which afflicts the race of viewers-with-alarm. . . . I do not believe in democracy, but I am perfectly willing to admit that it provides the only really amusing form of government ever endured by mankind." By today's standards, his disparaging comments about blacks and Jews have raised the accusation that he was a bigot, but no group was spared Mencken's satire, especially white males. A detractor once demanded to know why, if he was so disenchanted with the United States, he did not move to some other country. Mencken's response: "Why do people like to visit the zoo?"

In these excerpts from Mencken's writings, what does his satirical eye reveal about life in the United States in the 1920s? Do his comments have any relevance to today's society? What place does humor have in critiquing society? Can it bring about change? Was Mencken looking to alter the conditions he mocked? Was he advocating change?

"On Being an American," 1922

All the while I have been forgetting the third of my reasons for remaining so faithful a citizen of the Federation, despite all the lascivious inducements from expatriates to follow them beyond the seas, and all the surly suggestions from patriots that I succumb. It is the reason which grows out of my mediaeval but unashamed taste for the bizarre and indelicate, my congenital weakness for comedy of the grosser varieties. The United States, to my eye, is incomparably the greatest show on earth. It is a show which avoids diligently all the kinds of clowning which tire me most quickly—for example, royal ceremonials, the tedious hocus-pocus of haut politique, the taking of politics seriously—and lays chief stress upon the kinds which delight me unceasingly—for example, the ribald combats of demagogues, the exquisitely ingenious operations of master rogues, the pursuit of witches and heretics, the desperate struggles of inferior men to claw their way into Heaven. We have clowns in constant practice among us who are as far above the clowns of any other great state as a Jack Dempsey is above a paralytic—and not a few dozen or score of them, but whole droves and herds. Human enterprises which, in all other Christian countries, are resigned despairingly to an incurable dullness—things that seem devoid of exhilarating amusement, by their very nature—are here lifted to such vast heights of buffoonery that contemplating them strains the midriff almost to breaking. I cite

Source: H. L. Mencken, *Prejudices, Third Series* (New York: Knopf, 1922), 57–64.

an example: the worship of God. Everywhere else on earth it is carried on in a solemn and dispiriting manner; in England, of course, the bishops are obscene, but the average man seldom gets a fair chance to laugh at them and enjoy them. Now come home. Here we not only have bishops who are enormously more obscene than even the most gifted of the English bishops; we have also a huge force of lesser specialists in ecclesiastical mountebankery—tin-horn Loyolas, Savonarolas and Xaviers of a hundred fantastic rites, each performing untiringly and each full of a grotesque and illimitable whimsicality. Every American town, however small, has one of its own: a holy clerk with so fine a talent for introducing the arts of jazz into the salvation of the damned that his performance takes on all the gaudiness of a four-ring circus, and the bald announcement that he will raid Hell on such and such a night is enough to empty all the town blind-pigs and bordellos and pack his sanctuary to the doors. And to aid him and inspire him there are travelling experts to whom he stands in the relation of a wart to the Matterhorn—stupendous masters of theological imbecility, contrivers of doctrines utterly preposterous, heirs to the Joseph Smith, Mother Eddy and John Alexander Dowie tradition—[William Jennings]Bryan, [Billy]Sunday, and their like. These are the eminences of the American Sacred College. I delight in them. Their proceedings make me a happier American.

Turn, now, to politics. Consider, for example, a campaign for the Presidency. Would it be possible to imagine anything more uproariously idiotic—a deafening, nerve-wracking battle to the death between Tweedledum and Tweedledee . . . — the unspeakable, with fearful snorts, gradually swallowing the inconceivable? I defy any one to match it elsewhere on this earth. In other lands, at worst, there are at least intelligible issues, coherent ideas, salient personalities. Somebody says something, and somebody replies. But what did Harding say in 1920, and what did Cox reply? Who was Harding, anyhow, and who was Cox? Here, having perfected democracy, we lift the whole combat to symbolism, to transcendentalism, to metaphysics. Here we load a pair of palpably tin cannon with blank cartridges charged with talcum power, and so let fly. Here one may howl over the show without any uneasy reminder that it is serious, and that some one may be hurt. I hold that this elevation of politics to the plane of undiluted comedy is peculiarly American, that no-where else on this disreputable ball has the art of the sham-battle been developed to such fineness. . . .

Here politics is purged of all menace, all sinister quality, all genuine significance, and stuffed with such gorgeous humors, such inordinate farce that one comes to the end of a campaign with one's ribs loose, and ready for "King Lear," or a hanging, or a course of medical journals.

But feeling better for the laugh. *Ridi si sapis,* said Martial. Mirth is necessary to wisdom, to comfort, above all to happiness. Well, here is the land of mirth, as Germany is the land of metaphysics and France is the land of fornication. Here the buffoonery never stops. What could be more delightful than the endless struggle of the Puritan to make the joy of the minority unlawful and impossible? The effort is itself a greater joy to one standing on the side-lines than any or all of the carnal joys it combats. Always, when I contemplate an uplifter at his hopeless business, I recall a scene in an old-time burlesque show, witnessed for hire in my days as a dramatic critic. A chorus girl executed a fall upon the stage, and Rudolph Krausemeyer, the Swiss comedian, rushed to her aid. As he stooped painfully to succor her, Irving Rabinovitz, the Zionist comedian, fetched him a fearful clout across the cofferdam with a slap-stick. So the uplifter, the soul-saver, the Americanizer, striving to make the Republic fit for Y.M.C.A. secretaries. He is the eternal American, ever moved by the best of intentions, ever running a la Krausemeyer to the rescue of virtue, and ever getting his pantaloons fanned by the Devil. I am naturally sinful, and such spectacles caress me. If the slap-stick were a sash-weight, the show would be cruel, and I'd probably complain to the Polizei. As it is, I know that the uplifter is not really hurt, but simply shocked. The blow, in fact, does him good, for it helps get him into Heaven, as exegetes prove from Matthew v, 11: *Hereux serez-vous, lorsqu'on vous outragera, qu'on vous persecutera,* and so on. As for me, it makes me a more contented man, and hence a better citizen. One man prefers the Republic because it pays better wages than Bulgaria. Another because it has laws to keep him sober and his daughter chaste. Another because the Woolworth Building is higher than the cathedral at Chartres. Another because, living here, he can read the New York Evening Journal. Another because there is a warrant out for him somewhere else. Me, I like it because it amuses me to my taste. I never get tired of the show. It is worth every cent it costs.

That cost, it seems to me is very moderate. Taxes in the United States are not actually high. I figure, for example, that my private share of the expense of maintaining the Hon. Mr. Harding in the White House this year will work out to less than 80 cents. Try to think of better sport for the money: in New York it has been estimated that it costs $8 to get comfortably tight, and $17.50, on an average, to pinch a girl's arm. The United States Senate will cost me perhaps $11 for the year, but against that expense set the subscription price of the Congressional Record, about $15, which, as a journalist, I receive for nothing. For $4 less than nothing I am thus entertained as Solomon never was by his hooch dancers. Col. George Brinton McClellan Harvey costs me but 25 cents a year; I get Nicholas Murray Butler free. Finally, there is young Teddy Roosevelt, the naval expert. Teddy costs me, as I work it out, about 11 cents a year, or less than a cent a month. More, he entertains me doubly for the money, first as a naval expert, and secondly as a walking attentat upon democracy, a devastating proof that there is nothing, after all, in that superstition. We Americans subscribe to the doctrine of human equality—and the *Rooseveltii* reduce it to an absurdity as brilliantly as the sons of Veit Bach. Where is your equal opportunity now? Here in this Eden of clowns, with the highest rewards of clowning theoretically open to every poor boy—here in the very citadel of democracy we found and cherish a clown dynasty!

"Last Words," 1926

I have alluded somewhat vaguely to the merits of democracy. One of them is quite obvious: it is, perhaps, the most charming form of government ever devised by man. The reason is not far to seek. It is based upon propositions that are palpably not true

---

SOURCE: H. L. Mencken, *Last Words* (1926). Retrieved on 3/11/2004 from www.bigeye. com/mencken.htm.

and what is not true, as everyone knows, is always immensely more fascinating and satisfying to the vast majority of men than what is true. Truth has a harshness that alarms them, and an air of finality that collides with their incurable romanticism. They turn, in all the great emergencies of life, to the ancient promises, transparently false but immensely comforting, and of all those ancient promises there is none more comforting than the one to the effect that the lowly shall inherit the earth. It is at the bottom of the dominant religious system of the modern world, and it is at the bottom of the dominant political system. The latter, which is democracy, gives it an even higher credit and authority than the former, which is Christianity. More, democracy gives it a certain appearance of objective and demonstrable truth. The mob man, functioning as citizen, gets a feeling that he is really important to the world—that he is genuinely running things. Out of his maudlin herding after rogues and mountebanks there comes to him a sense of vast and mysterious power—which is what makes archbishops, police sergeants, the grand goblins of the Ku Klux and other such magnificoes happy. And out of it there comes, too, a conviction that he is somehow wise, that his views are taken seriously by his betters—which is what makes United States Senators, fortune tellers and Young Intellectuals happy. Finally, there comes out of it a glowing consciousness of a high duty triumphantly done which is what makes hangmen and husbands happy.

All these forms of happiness, of course, are illusory. They don't last. The democrat, leaping into the air to flap his wings and praise God, is for ever coming down with a thump. The seeds of his disaster, as I have shown, lie in his own stupidity: he can never get rid of the naive delusion—so beautifully Christian—that happiness is something to be got by taking it away from the other fellow. But there are seeds, too, in the very nature of things: a promise, after all, is only a promise, even when it is supported by divine revelation, and the chances against its fulfillment may be put into a depressing mathematical formula. Here the irony that lies under all human aspiration shows itself: the quest for happiness, as always, brings only unhappiness in the end. But saying that is merely saying that the true charm of democracy is not for the democrat but for the spectator. That spectator, it seems to me, is favoured with a show of the first cut and calibre. Try to imagine anything more heroically absurd! What grotesque false pretenses! What a parade of obvious imbecilities! What a welter of fraud! But is fraud unamusing? Then I retire forthwith as a psychologist. The fraud of democracy, I contend, is more amusing than any other, more amusing even, and by miles, than the fraud of religion. Go into your praying-chamber and give sober thought to any of the more characteristic democratic inventions: say, Law Enforcement. Or to any of the typical democratic prophets: say, the late Archangel[William Jennings] Bryan. If you don't come out paled and palsied by mirth then you will not laugh on the Last Day itself, when Presbyterians step out of the grave like chicks from the egg, and wings blossom from their scapulae, and they leap into interstellar space with roars of joy.

I have spoken hitherto of the possibility that democracy may be a self-limiting disease, like measles. It is, perhaps, something more: it is self-devouring. One cannot observe it objectively without being impressed by its curious distrust of itself—its apparently ineradicable tendency to abandon its whole philosophy at the first sign of strain. I need not point to what happens invariably in democratic states when the national safety is menaced. All the great tribunes of democracy, on such occasions, convert themselves, by a process as simple as taking a deep breath, into despots of an almost fabulous ferocity. Lincoln, Roosevelt and Wilson come instantly to mind: Jackson and Cleveland are in the background, waiting to be recalled. Nor is this process confined to times of alarm and terror: it is going on day in and day out. Democracy always seems bent upon killing the thing it theoretically loves. I have rehearsed some of its operations against liberty, the very cornerstone of its political metaphysic. It not only wars upon the thing itself; it even wars upon mere academic advocacy of it. I offer the spectacle of Americans jailed for reading the Bill of Rights as perhaps the most gaudily humorous ever witnessed in the modern world. Try to imagine monarchy jailing subjects for maintaining the divine right of Kings! Or Christianity damning a believer for arguing that Jesus Christ was the Son of God! This last, perhaps, has been done: anything is possible in that direction. But under democracy the remotest and most fantastic possibility is a common-place of every day. All the axioms resolve themselves into thundering paradoxes, many amounting to downright contradictions in terms. The mob is competent to rule the rest of us—but it must be rigorously policed itself. There is a government, not of men, but of laws—but men are set upon benches to decide finally what the law is and may be. The highest function of the citizen is to serve the state—but the first assumption that meets him, when he essays to discharge it, is an assumption of his disingenuousness and dishonour. Is that assumption commonly sound? Then the farce only grows the more glorious.

I confess, for my part, that it greatly delights me. I enjoy democracy immensely. It is incomparably idiotic, and hence incomparably amusing. Does it exalt dunderheads, cowards, trimmers, frauds, cads? Then the pain of seeing them go up is balanced and obliterated by the joy of seeing them come down. Is it inordinately wasteful, extravagant, dishonest? Then so is every other form of government: all alike are enemies to laborious and virtuous men. Is rascality at the very heart of it? Well, we have borne that rascality since 1776, and continue to survive. In the long run, it may turn out that rascality is necessary to human government, and even to civilization itself—that civilization, at bottom, is nothing but a colossal swindle. I do not know: I report only that when the suckers are running well the spectacle is infinitely exhilarating. But I am, it may be, a somewhat malicious man: my sympathies, when it comes to suckers, tend to be coy. What I can't make out is how any man can believe in democracy who feels for and with them, and is pained when they are debauched and made a show of. How can any man be a democrat who is sincerely a democrat?

"Mencken's Creed"

I believe that religion, generally speaking, has been a curse to mankind—that its modest and greatly overestimated services on the ethical side have been more than overcome by the damage it has done to clear and honest thinking.

SOURCE: Retrieved on 3/11/2004 from www.crispinsartwell.com/mencken.htm.

I believe that no discovery of fact, however trivial, can be wholly useless to the race, and that no trumpeting of falsehood, however virtuous in intent, can be anything but vicious.

I believe that all government is evil, in that all government must necessarily make war upon liberty. . . .

I believe that the evidence for immortality is no better than the evidence of witches, and deserves no more respect.

I believe in the complete freedom of thought and speech. . . .

I believe in the capacity of man to conquer his world, and to find out what it is made of, and how it is run.

I believe in the reality of progress. . . .

I believe that it is better to tell the truth than to lie. I believe that it is better to be free than to be a slave. And I believe that it is better to know than be ignorant.

Langston Hughes (1902–1967)

One of the seminal figures in the Harlem Renaissance of the 1920s, Langston Hughes has had a significant impact on American literature, as well as influence in the civil rights movement. His essays, poems, short stories, novels, and plays sensitively portrayed the experience of being black in white America. He wrote for *The Nation*, the NAACP's *Crisis Magazine*, and many other publications. His first book of poetry, *The Weary Blues*, was published in 1926 and his first novel, *Not Without Laughter*, in 1930. He claimed that in his effort to write of the real experiences of real black people that he approached his writing as the blues and jazz musician approaches music.

In a 1926 essay, "The Negro Artist and the Racial Mountain," he revealed that he, just like any other serious writer, was not worried about bringing himself into his writing. The key to great writing is to write fearlessly and above all to be honest, he said. "We younger Negro artists," he wrote, "now intend to express our individual dark-skinned selves without fear or shame. If white people are pleased we are glad. If they aren't, it doesn't matter. We know we are beautiful. And ugly too. . . . If colored people are pleased we are glad. If they are not, their displeasure doesn't matter either. We build our temples for tomorrow, as strong as we know how and we stand on the top of the mountain, free within ourselves."

What do the following poems reveal about equality in the United States? Is race the only basis for discrimination? In what ways do the experiences of African Americans differ from those of white Americans?

"I, Too, Sing America," 1925

I, too, sing America.

I am the darker brother.
They send me to eat in the kitchen
When company comes,
But I laugh,
And eat well,
And grow strong.

Tomorrow,
I'll be at the table
When company comes.
Nobody'll dare
Say to me,
"Eat in the kitchen,"
Then.

Besides,
They'll see how beautiful I am
And be ashamed—

I, too, am America.

"One-Way Ticket," 1949

I pick up my life
And take it with me
And I put it down in
Chicago, Detroit,
Buffalo, Scranton,
Any place that is
North and East—
And not Dixie.

I pick up my life
And take it on the train
To Los Angeles, Bakersfield,
Seattle, Oakland, Salt Lake,
Any place that is
North and West—
And not South.

SOURCE: Langston Hughes, *The Collected Poems of Langston Hughes*, ed. by Arnold Rampersad (New York: Knopf, 1994), 46, 361.

I am fed up
With Jim Crow laws,
People who are cruel
And afraid,
Who lynch and run,
Who are scared of me
And me of them.

I pick up my life
And take it away
On a one-way ticket—
Gone up North,
Gone out West,
Gone!

Father Charles Coughlin (1891–1979)

Father Charles Coughlin, a Catholic priest in Detroit, Michigan, emerged during the 1930s as an important and notorious radical demagogue. The "Radio Priest's" weekly radio broadcasts attracted an estimated 30 million listeners around the nation who believed that he was fighting for the interests of the common man against the power of Wall Street. Coughlin was against capitalism, socialism, and communism—all, in his eyes, were equally evil. He attacked business leaders, but he was so suspicious of bureaucratic elites and politicians that he had no respect for Roosevelt or the Democratic administration, even though he had at first supported Roosevelt in 1932. He founded the National Union for Social Justice in 1934 to promote his ideas about reforming the economy. By the late 1930s, Coughlin's comments were taking on an increasingly bigoted and anti-Semitic tone, as he regularly condemned the New Deal as the "Jew Deal" and scorned the president for being a mere puppet dancing to the tunes of international Jewish bankers and industrialists. Eventually, when he began praising Hitler and Mussolini, the archbishop of Detroit forbade him to continue his radio broadcasts. Along with his undoubted impact on millions of Americans, his rabble-rousing diatribes also had an influence on Roosevelt, goading the president into a more combative stance against powerful business leaders.

What was the cause, as Coughlin views it in these radio addresses, of the Great Depression? Why had Franklin D. Roosevelt failed as the savior of the nation? What does Coughlin's statement that Republicans have bred more radicals than Marx and Lenin ever did reveal about discontent in the 1930s?

National Radio Address, November 1934

"Increase and multiply" was the command of God—a command that has been steril-ized in the heart of every thinking young man who dares not marry because he dares not inflict poverty upon his children.

And this in a nation where the birth rate and the death rate are sparring for supremacy; this in a nation that dares not invite the immigrant to enter because already there is too much unemployment!

Yes, "increase and multiply" was the command which echoed over the flowering fields and the towering forests. It was heard in the sheep-folds and on the pasture-lands. It broke forth in holy emotions as lovers clasped in fond embrace.

"Increase and multiply and I shall kiss your fields with the lips of the sun and water them with the fountains of rain. I will unfold to you the secrets of nature. And I shall teach your nimble fingers to work and labor as I do the wings of a bird to fly."

Oh! how this Sacred Scripture has become perverted as, in the midst of plenty, we struggle to create want—we struggle to create profits—all for the purpose of per-petuating a slavery which has been so often described as the concentration of wealth in the hands of a few!

My friends, the outworn creed of capitalism is done for. The clarion call of com-munism has been sounded. I can support one as easily as the other. They are both rotten! But it is not necessary to suffer any longer the slings and arrows of modern capitalism any more than it is to surrender our rights to life, to liberty and to the cherished bonds of family to communism.

The high priests of capitalism bid us beware of the radical and call upon us to expel him from our midst. There will be no expulsion of radicals until the causes which breed radicals will first be destroyed!

The apostles of Lenin and Trotsky bid us forsake all rights to private ownership and ask us to surrender our liberty for that mess of pottage labeled "prosperity," while it summons us to worship at the altar where a dictator of flesh and blood is enthroned as our god and the citizens are branded as his slaves.

Away with both of them! But never into the discard with the liberties which we have already won and the economic liberty which we are about to win—or die in the attempt!

My friends, I have spent many hours during these past two weeks—hours, far into the night, reading thousands of letters which have come to my office from the young folks and the old folks of this nation. I believe that in them I possess the great-est human document written within our times.

I am not boasting when I say to you that I know the pulse of the people. I know it better than all your newspaper men. I know it better than do all your industrialists with your paid-for advice. I am not exaggerating when I tell you of their demand for social justice which, like a tidal wave, is sweeping over this nation.

Nor am I happy to think that, through my broadcasts, I have placed myself today in a position to accept the challenge which these letters carry to me—a challenge for

Source: Retrieved on 8/11/2003 from www.ssa.gov/history/fcspeech.html.

me to organize these men and women of all classes not for the protection of property rights as does the American Liberty League; not for the protection of political spoils as do the henchmen of the Republican or Democratic parties. Away with them too!

But, happy or unhappy as I am in my position, I accept the challenge to organize for obtaining, for securing and for protecting the principles of social justice.

To organize for action, if you will! To organize for social united action which will be founded on God-given social truths which belong to Catholic and Protestant, to Jew and Gentile, to black and white, to rich and poor, to industrialist and to laborer.

I realize that I am more or less a voice crying in the wilderness. I realize that the doctrine which I preach is disliked and condemned by the princes of wealth. What care I for that! And, more than all else, I deeply appreciate how limited are my qualifications to launch this organization which shall be known as the NATIONAL UNION FOR SOCIAL JUSTICE.

But the die is cast! The word has been spoken! And by it I am prepared either to stand or to fall; to fall, if needs be, and thus, to be remembered as an arrant upstart who succeeded in doing nothing more than stirring up the people.

National Radio Address, June 1936

Ladies and gentlemen:

In the Autumn of 1932, it was my privilege to address the American people on the causes of the so-called depression and upon the obvious remedies required to bring about a permanent recovery.

Those were days which witnessed a complete breakdown of the financial system under which our Western civilization had been developed. It was also evident that under this financial system there resulted a concentration of wealth and a multiplication of impoverished families. Unjust wages and unreasonable idleness were universally recognized as contradictions in an age of plenty.

To my mind it was inconceivable that irrational and needless want should exist in an age of plenty. Were there not plenty of raw materials in America? Were not our citizens and our countryside inhabited by plenty of skilled inventors, engineers, executives, workmen and farmers? At no time in the history of civilization was it possible for man to produce such an abundant supply, thanks to the benedictions of mass production machinery. At no time within the last two centuries was there such a demand on the part of our population for the thousands of good things capable of being produced in our fields and in our factories.

What was the basic cause which closed factories, which created idleness, which permitted weeds to overrun our golden fields and plowshares to rust? There was and is but one answer. Some call it lack of purchasing power. Others, viewing the problem in a more philosophic light, recognize that the financial system which was able to function in an age of scarcity was totally inadequate to operate successfully in an age of plenty.

SOURCE: Retrieved on 8/11/2003 from www.pbs.org/greatspeeches/timeline/c_ coughlin_s2.html

Let me explain this statement briefly: Before the nineteenth century, the ox-cart, the spade and the crude instruments of production were handicaps to the rapid creation of real wealth.

By 1932, a new era of production had come into full bloom. It was represented by the motor car, the tractor and the power lathe, which enabled the laborer to produce wealth ten times more rapidly than was possible for his ancestors. Within the short expanse of 150 years, the problem of production had been solved, due to the ingenuity of men like Arkwright and his loom, Fulton and his steam engine, and Edison and his dynamo. These and a thousand other benefactors of mankind made it possible for the teeming millions of people throughout the world to transfer speedily the raw materials into the thousand necessities and conveniences which fall under the common name of wealth.

Thus, with the advent of our scientific era, with its far-flung fields, its spacious factories, its humming motors, its thundering locomotives, its highly trained mechanics, it is inconceivable how such a thing as a so-called depression should blight the lives of an entire nation when there was a plenitude of everything surrounding us, only to be withheld from us because the so-called leaders of high finance persisted in clinging to an outworn theory of privately issued money, the medium through which wealth is distributed. . . .

Before the year 1932, very few persons fully realized the existence of this financial bondage. Millions of citizens began asking the obvious questions: "Why should the farmer be forced to follow his plow at a loss?" "Why should the citizens—at least 90 per cent of them—be imprisoned behind the cruel bars of want when, within their grasp, there are plenty of shoes, of clothing, of motor cars, of refrigerators, to which they are entitled?" At last, when the most brilliant minds amongst the industrialists, bankers and their kept politicians had failed to solve the cause of the needless depression, there appeared upon the scene of our national life a new champion of the people, Franklin Delano Roosevelt! He spoke golden words of hope. He intimated to the American people that the system of permitting a group of private citizens to create money, then to issue it to the government as if it were real money, then to exact payment from the entire nation through a system of taxation earned by real labor and service, was immoral. With the whip of his scorn he castigated these usurers who exploited the poor. With his eloquent tongue he lashed their financial system which devoured the homes of widows and orphans. No man in modern times received such plaudits from the poor as did Franklin Roosevelt when he promised to drive the money-changers from the temple—the money-changers who had clipped the coins of wages, who had manufactured spurious money, and who had brought proud America to her knees.

March 4, 1933! I shall never forget the inaugural address, which seemed to re-echo the very words employed by Christ Himself as He actually drove the money-changers from the temple. The thrill that was mine was yours. Through dim clouds of the depression, this man Roosevelt was, as it were, a new savior of his people! Oh, just a little longer shall there be needless poverty! Just another year shall there be naked backs! Just another moment shall there be dark thoughts of revolution! Never again will the chains of economic poverty bite into the hearts of simple folks, as they did in the past days of the Old Deal! Such were our hopes in the springtime of 1933. It is not pleasant for me who coined the phrase "Roosevelt *or* ruin"—a phrase fashioned upon promises—to voice such passionate words. But I am constrained to admit that "Roosevelt *and* ruin" is the order of the day, because the money-changers have not been driven from the temple.

My friends, I come before you tonight not to ask you to return to . . . the Hoovers, to the Old Deal exploiters, who honestly defended the dishonest system of gold standardism and rugged individualism. Their sun has set never to rise again. America has turned its back definitely upon the platitudinous platforms of "rugged individualism." These Punch and Judy Republicans, whose actions and words were dominated by the ventriloquists of Wall Street, are so blind that they do not recognize, even in this perilous hour, that their gold basis and their private coinage of money have bred more radicals than did Karl Marx or Lenin. To their system or ox-cart financialism we must never return!

On the other hand, the Democratic platform is discredited before it is published. Was there not a 1932 platform? By Mr. Roosevelt and his colleagues, was it not regarded as a solemn pledge to the people? Certainly! [But] it was plowed under like the cotton, slaughtered like the pigs. . . . Therefore, the veracity of the future upstage pledges must be judged by the echoings of the golden voice of a lost leader.

Said he, when the flag of hope was proudly unfurled on March 4, 1933: "Plenty is at our doorsteps, but the generous use of it languished in the very sight of the supply. Primarily, this is because the rulers of the exchange of mankind's goods have failed through their own stubbornness and their own incompetence—have admitted their failure and abdicated. Practices of the unscrupulous money-changers stand indicted in the court of public opinion, rejected by the hearts and minds of men. . . . "

These words, my friends, are not mine. These are the caustic, devastating words uttered by Franklin Delano Roosevelt on March 4, 1933, condemning Franklin Delano Roosevelt in November of 1936.

Alas! The temple still remains the private property of the money-changers. The golden key has been handed over to them for safekeeping—the key which now is fashioned in the shape of a double cross!

Huey Long (1893–1935)

Democrat Huey ("Kingfish") Long was one of the most controversial and colorful figures of the 1920s and 1930s. Elected governor of Louisiana in 1928 (his campaign slogan was "every man a king, but no one wears a crown"), Long's populist policies—his reform efforts in education, road construction and internal improvements in the state, and notions of taxing big business more heavily—earned him a national reputation. Although he was extraordinarily popular with his constituents, his dictatorial rule and questionable morals (he was known to extort bribes and pay graft) created formidable enemies. People either loved or hated Huey Long. In 1930, he was elected to the U.S. Senate but still controlled Louisiana politics through his hand-picked successor. Within two years of the election of Franklin Delano Roosevelt, Long, although he was a Democrat, became one of the president's most vocal critics. Gearing himself for a run at the presidency in 1936, Long criticized the New Deal as not going far enough to alleviate poverty and injustice and devised his own "Share Our Wealth" program. This program, guaranteeing an annual income of $2500 for every citizen in the nation, went down well with voters, especially those who were unemployed or otherwise experiencing the hardships of the Depression. Before the "Kingfish" could challenge FDR for the Democratic nomination or make a run for the presidency on a third-party ticket, however, one of his enemies caught up with him in the state capitol building in September 1935 and assassinated him.

The first reading is the 1934 Senate speech in which Huey Long proposes his Share Our Wealth program. The second is a 1935 national radio address in which Long criticizes Roosevelt and reiterates his own plan. What are the specifics of the Share Our Wealth program? Who would be helped by it? Who would be harmed? How practical is it? What commonality is there between Long's plan and Father Coughlin's "Social Justice" program? Does the senator's speech reveal a compassionate man who was truly interested in the plight of the poor or a demagogue who was merely interested in becoming president?

Speech in the U.S. Senate, February 5, 1934

People of America: In every community get together at once and organize a share-our-wealth society—Motto: Every man a king.

Principles and platform:

1. To limit poverty by providing that every deserving family shall share in the wealth of America for not less than one third of the average wealth, thereby to possess not less than $5,000 free of debt.

2. To limit fortunes to such a few million dollars as will allow the balance of the American people to share in the wealth and profits of the land.

3. Old-age pensions of $30 per month to persons over 60 years of age who do not earn as much as $1,000 per year or who possess less than $10,000 in cash or property, thereby to remove from the field of labor in times of unemployment those who have contributed their share to the public service.

4. To limit the hours of work to such an extent as to prevent overproduction and to give the workers of America some share in the recreations, conveniences, and luxuries of life.

Source: Retrieved on 8/14/2003 from www.ssa.gov/history/longsen.html.

5. To balance agricultural production with what can be sold and consumed according to the laws of God, which have never failed.

6. To care for the veterans of our wars.

7. Taxation to run the Government to be supported, first, by reducing big fortunes from the top, thereby to improve the country and provide employment in public works whenever agricultural surplus is such as to render unnecessary, in whole or in part, any particular crop.

SIMPLE AND CONCRETE—NOT AN EXPERIMENT

To share our wealth by providing for every deserving family to have one third of the average wealth would mean that, at the worst, such a family could have a fairly comfortable home, an automobile, and a radio, with other reasonable home conveniences, and a place to educate their children. Through sharing the work, that is, by limiting the hours of toil so that all would share in what is made and produced in the land, every family would have enough coming in every year to feed, clothe, and provide a fair share of the luxuries of life to its members. Such is the result to a family, at the worst.

From the worst to the best there would be no limit to opportunity. One might become a millionaire or more. There would be a chance for talent to make a man big, because enough would be floating in the land to give brains its chance to be used. As it is, no matter how smart a man may be, everything is tied up in so few hands that no amount of energy or talent has a chance to gain any of it.

Would it break up big concerns? No. It would simply mean that, instead of one man getting all the one concern made, that there might be 1,000 or 10,000 persons sharing in such excess fortune, any one of whom, or all of whom, might be millionaires and over.

I ask somebody in every city, town, village, and farm community of America to take this as my personal request to call a meeting of as many neighbors and friends as will come to it to start a share-our-wealth society. Elect a president and a secretary and charge no dues. The meeting can be held at a courthouse, in some town hall or public building, or in the home of someone.

It does not matter how many will come to the first meeting. Get a society organized, if it has only two members.

Then let us get to work quick, quick, quick to put an end by law to people starving and going naked in this land of too much to eat and too much to wear. The case is all with us. It is the word and work of the Lord. The Gideons had but two men when they organized. Three tailors of Tooley Street drew the Magna Carta of England.

The Lord says: "For where two or three are gathered together in My name, there am I in the midst of them."

We propose to help our people into the place where the Lord said was their rightful own and no more.

We have waited long enough for these financial masters to do these things. They have promised and promised.

Now we find our country $10 billion further in debt on account of the depression, and big lenders even propose to get 90 percent of that out of the hides of the common people in the form of a sales tax.

There is nothing wrong with the United States. We have more food than we can eat. We have more clothes and things out of which to make clothes than we can wear. We have more houses and lands than the whole 120 million can use if they all had good homes. So what is the trouble? Nothing except that a handful of men have everything and the balance of the people have nothing if their debts were paid. There should be every man a king in this land flowing with milk and honey instead of the lords of finance at the top and slaves and peasants at the bottom.

Now be prepared for the slurs and snickers of some high-ups when you start your local spread-our-wealth society. Also when you call your meeting be on your guard for some smart-aleck tool of the interests to come in and ask questions. Refer such to me for an answer to any question, and I will send you a copy. Spend your time getting the people to work to save their children and to save their homes, or to get a home for those who have already lost their own.

To explain the title, motto, and principles of such a society I give the full information, viz:

Title: Share-our-wealth society is simply to mean that God's creatures on this lovely American continent have a right to share in the wealth they have created in this country. They have the right to a living, with the conveniences and some of the luxuries of this life, so long as there are too many or enough for all. They have a right to raise their children in a healthy, wholesome atmosphere and to educate them, rather than to face the dread of their under-nourishment and sadness by being denied a real life.

Motto: "Every man a king" conveys the great plan of God and of the Declaration of Independence, which said: "All men are created equal." It conveys that no one man is the lord of another, but that from the head to the foot of every man is carried his sovereignty.

Now to cover the principles of the share-our-wealth society, I give them in order:

1. To limit poverty: We propose that a deserving family shall share in our wealth of America at least for one third the average. An average family is slightly less than five persons. The number has become less during depression. The United States total wealth in normal times is about $400 billion or about $15,000 to a family. If there were fair distribution of our things in America, our national wealth would be three or four or five times the $400 billion, because a free, circulating wealth is worth many times more than wealth congested and frozen into a few hands as is America's wealth. But, figuring only on the basis of wealth as valued when frozen into a few hands, there is the average of $15,000 to the family. We say that we will limit poverty of the deserving people. One third of the average wealth to the family, or $5,000, is a fair limit to the depths we will allow any one man's family to fall. None too poor, none too rich.

2. To limit fortunes: The wealth of this land is tied up in a few hands. It makes no difference how many years the laborer has worked, nor does it make any difference

how many dreary rows the farmer has plowed, the wealth he has created is in the hands of manipulators. They have not worked any more than many other people who have nothing. Now we do not propose to hurt these very rich persons. We simply say that when they reach the place of millionaires they have everything they can use and they ought to let somebody else have something. As it is, 0.1 of 1 percent of the bank depositors nearly half of the money in the banks, leaving 99.9 of bank depositors owning the balance. Then two thirds of the people do not even have a bank account. The lowest estimate is that 4 percent of the people own 85 percent of our wealth. The people cannot ever come to light unless we share our wealth, hence the society to do it.

3. Old-age pensions: Everyone has begun to realize something must be done for our old people who work out their lives, feed and clothe children and are left penniless in their declining years. They should be made to look forward to their mature years for comfort rather than fear. We propose that, at the age of 60, every person should begin to draw a pension from our Government of $30 per month, unless the person of 60 or over has an income of over $1,000 per year or is worth $10,000, which is two thirds of the average wealth in America, even figured on a basis of it being frozen into a few hands. Such a pension would retire from labor those persons who keep the rising generations from finding employment.

4. To limit the hours of work: This applies to all industry. The longer hours the human family can rest from work, the more it can consume. It makes no difference how many labor-saving devices we may invent, just as long as we keep cutting down the hours and sharing what those machines produce, the better we become. Machines can never produce too much if everybody is allowed his share, and if it ever got to the point that the human family could work only 15 hours per week and still produce enough for everybody, then praised be the name of the Lord. Heaven would be coming nearer to earth. All of us could return to school a few months every year to learn some things they have found out since we were there: All could be gentlemen: Every man a king.

5. To balance agricultural production with consumption: About the easiest of all things to do when financial masters and market manipulators step aside and let work the law of the Lord. When we have a supply of anything that is more than we can use for a year or two, just stop planting that particular crop for a year either in all the country or in a part of it. Let the Government take over and store the surplus for the next year. If there is not something else for the farmers to plant or some other work for them to do to live on for the year when the crop is banned, then let that be the year for the public works to be done in the section where the farmers need work. There is plenty of it to do and taxes of the big fortunes at the top will supply plenty of money without hurting anybody. In time we would have the people not struggling to raise so much when all were well fed and clothed. Distribution of wealth almost solves the whole problem without further trouble.

6. To care for the veterans of our wars: A restoration of all rights taken from them by recent laws and further, a complete care of any disabled veteran for any ailment, who has no means of support.

7. Taxation: Taxation is to be levied first at the top for the Government's support and expenses. Swollen fortunes should be reduced principally through taxation. The Government should be run through revenues it derives after allowing persons to become well above millionaires and no more. In this manner the fortunes will be kept down to reasonable size and at the same time all the works of the Government kept on a sound basis, without debts.

Things cannot continue as they now are. America must take one of three choices, viz:

1. A monarchy ruled by financial masters—a modern feudalism.
2. Communism.
3. Sharing of the wealth and income of the land among all the people by limiting the hours of toil and limiting the size of fortunes.

The Lord prescribed the last form. It would preserve all our gains, share them among our population, guarantee a greater country and a happy people.

The need for such share-our-wealth society is to spread the truth among the people and to convey their sentiment to their Members of Congress.

Whenever such a local society has been organized, please send me notice of the same, so that I may send statistics and data which such local society can give out in their community, either through word of mouth in meetings, by circulars, or, when possible, in local newspapers.

Please understand that the Wall Street controlled public press will give you as little mention as possible and will condemn and ridicule your efforts. Such makes necessary the organizations to share the wealth of this land among the people, which the financial masters are determined they will not allow to be done. Where possible, I hope those organizing a society in one community will get in touch with their friends in other communities and get them to organize societies in them. Anyone can have copies of this article reprinted in circular form to distribute wherever they may desire, or, if they want me to have them printed for them, I can do so and mail them to any address for 60 cents per hundred or $4 per thousand copies.

I introduced in Congress and supported other measures to bring about the sharing of our wealth when I first reached the United States Senate in January 1932. The main efforts to that effect polled about six votes in the Senate at first. Last spring my plan polled the votes of nearly twenty United States Senators, becoming dangerous in proportions to the financial lords. Since then I have been abused in the newspapers and over the radio for everything under the sun. Now that I am pressing this program, the lies and abuse in the big newspapers and over the radio are a matter of daily occurrence. It will all become greater with this effort. Expect that. Meantime go ahead with the work to organize a share-our-wealth society.

Sincerely,
Huey P. Long,
United States Senator.

Radio Address, January 1935

President Roosevelt was elected on November 8, 1932. People look upon an elected President as the President. This is January 1935. We are in our third year of the Roosevelt depression, with the conditions growing worse. . . .

We must now become awakened! We must know the truth and speak the truth. There is no use to wait three more years. It is not Roosevelt or ruin; it is Roosevelt's ruin.

Now, my friends, it makes no difference who is President or who is senator. America is for 125 million people and the unborn to come. We ran Mr. Roosevelt for the presidency of the United States because he promised to us by word of mouth and in writing:

That the size of the big man's fortune would be reduced so as to give the masses at the bottom enough to wipe out all poverty; and
That the hours of labor would be so reduced that all would share in the work to be done and in consuming the abundance mankind produced.

Hundreds of words were used by Mr. Roosevelt to make these promises to the people, but they were made over and over again. He reiterated these pledges even after he took his oath as President. Summed up, what these promises meant was: "Share our wealth."

When I saw him spending all his time of ease and recreation with the business partners of Mr. John D. Rockefeller, Jr., with such men as the Astors, etc., maybe I ought to have had better sense than to have believed he would ever break down their big fortunes to give enough to the masses to end poverty—maybe some will think me weak for ever believing it all, but millions of other people were fooled the same as myself. I was like a drowning man grabbing at a straw, I guess. The face and eyes, the hungry forms of mothers and children, the aching hearts of students denied education were before our eyes, and when Roosevelt promised, we jumped for that ray of hope.

So therefore I call upon the men and women of America to immediately join in our work and movement to share our wealth.

There are thousands of share-our-wealth societies organized in the United States now. We want 100,000 such societies formed for every nook and corner of this country—societies that will meet, talk, and work, all for the purpose that the great wealth and abundance of this great land that belongs to us may be shared and enjoyed by all of us.

We have nothing more for which we should ask the Lord. He has allowed this land to have too much of everything that humanity needs.

So in this land of God's abundance we propose laws, viz.:

1. The fortunes of the multimillionaires and billionaires shall be reduced so that no one person shall own more than a few million dollars to the person. We would do

Source: Retrieved on 8/14/2003 from www.americanrhetoric.com/speeches/hueyplongshare. htm.

this by a capital levy tax. On the first million that a man was worth, we would not impose any tax. We would say, "All right for your first million dollars, but after you get that rich you will have to start helping the balance of us." So we would not levy any capital levy tax on the first million one owned. But on the second million a man owns, we would tax that 1 percent, so that every year the man owned the second million dollars he would be taxed $10,000. On the third million we would impose a tax of 2 percent. On the fourth million we would impose a tax of 4 percent. On the fifth million we would impose a tax of 8 percent. On the sixth million we would impose a tax of 16 percent. On the seventh million we would impose a tax of 32 percent. On the eighth million we would impose a tax of 64 percent; and on all over the eighth million we would impose a tax of 100 percent.

What this would mean is that the annual tax would bring the biggest fortune down to $3 or $4 million to the person because no one could pay taxes very long in the higher brackets. But $3 to $4 million is enough for any one person and his children and his children's children. We cannot allow one to have more than that because it would not leave enough for the balance to have something.

2. We propose to limit the amount any one man can earn in one year or inherit to $1 million to the person.

3. Now, by limiting the size of the fortunes and incomes of the big men, we will throw into the government Treasury the money and property from which we will care for the millions of people who have nothing; and with this money we will provide a home and the comforts of home, with such common conveniences as radio and automobile, for every family in America, free of debt.

4. We guarantee food and clothing and employment for everyone who should work by shortening the hours of labor to thirty hours per week, maybe less, and to eleven months per year, maybe less. We would have the hours shortened just so much as would give work to everybody to produce enough for everybody; and if we were to get them down to where they were too short, then we would lengthen them again. As long as all the people working can produce enough of automobiles, radios, homes, schools, and theaters for everyone to have that kind of comfort and convenience, then let us all have work to do and have that much of heaven on earth.

5. We would provide education at the expense of the states and the United States for every child, not only through grammar school and high school but through to a college and vocational education. We would simply extend the Louisiana plan to apply to colleges and all people. Yes; we would have to build thousands of more colleges and employ 100,000 more teachers; but we have materials, men, and women who are ready and available for the work. Why have the right to a college education depend upon whether the father or mother is so well-to-do as to send a boy or girl to college? We would give every child the right to education and a living at birth.

6. We would give a pension to all persons above sixty years of age in an amount sufficient to support them in comfortable circumstances, excepting those who earn $1,000 per year or who are worth $10,000.

7. Until we could straighten things out—and we can straighten things out in two months under our program—we would grant a moratorium on all debts which people owe that they cannot pay.

And now you have our program, none too big, none too little, but every man a king.

We owe debts in America today, public and private, amounting to $252 billion. That means that every child is born with a $2,000 debt tied around his neck to hold him down before he gets started. Then, on top of that, the wealth is locked in a vise owned by a few people. We propose that children shall be born in a land of opportunity, guaranteed a home, food, clothes, and the other things that make for living, including the right to education.

Our plan would injure no one. It would not stop us from having millionaires—it would increase them tenfold, because so many more people could make $1 million if they had the chance our plan gives them. Our plan would not break up big concerns.

The only difference would be that maybe 10,000 people would own a concern instead of 10 people owning it.

But, my friends, unless we do share our wealth, unless we limit the size of the big man so as to give something to the little man, we can never have a happy or free people. God said so! He ordered it.

We have everything our people need. Too much of food, clothes, and houses—why not let all have their fill and lie down in the ease and comfort God has given us? Why not? Because a few own everything—the masses own nothing.

I wonder if any of you people who are listening to me were ever at a barbecue! We used to go there—sometimes 1,000 people or more. If there were 1,000 people, we would put enough meat and bread and everything else on the table for 1,000 people. Then everybody would be called and everyone would eat all they wanted. But suppose at one of these barbecues for 1,000 people that one man took 90 percent of the food and ran off with it and ate until he got sick and let the balance rot. Then 999 people would have only enough for 100 to eat and there would be many to starve because of the greed of just one person for something he couldn't eat himself.

Well, ladies and gentlemen, America, all the people of America, have been invited to a barbecue. God invited us all to come and eat and drink all we wanted. He smiled on our land and we grew crops of plenty to eat and wear. He showed us in the earth the iron and other things to make everything we wanted. He unfolded to us the secrets of science so that our work might be easy. God called: "Come to my feast."

Then what happened? Rockefeller, Morgan, and their crowd stepped up and took enough for 120 million people and left only enough for 5 million for all the other 125 million to eat. And so many millions must go hungry and without these good things God gave us unless we call on them to put some of it back.

Emma Goldman (1869–1940)

Emma Goldman (see also Part Two, pp. 96–102) published a pamphlet in 1936, *The Individual Society, and the State,* in which she explicitly outlines her anarchistic views. According to Goldman, what is the importance of the individual? What is the purpose of the state? Can democracy fulfill this role? Why is the individual a threat to the state? Why does she believe an anarchistic society is superior to a Marxist society?

The Individual, Society and the State, 1936

The minds of men are in confusion, for the very foundations of our civilization seem to be tottering. People are losing faith in the existing institutions, and the more intelligent realize that capitalist industrialism is defeating the very purpose it is supposed to serve.

The world is at a loss for a way out. Parliamentarism and democracy are on the decline. Salvation is being sought in Fascism and other forms of "strong" government.

The struggle of opposing ideas now going on in the world involves social problems urgently demanding a solution. The welfare of the individual and the fate of human society depend on the right answer to those questions The crisis, unemployment, war, disarmament, international relations, etc., are among those problems.

The State, government with its functions and powers, is now the subject of vital interest to every thinking man. Political developments in all civilized countries have brought the questions home. Shall we have a strong government? Are democracy and parliamentary government to be preferred, or is Fascism of one kind or another, dictatorship—monarchical, bourgeois or proletarian—the solution of the ills and difficulties that beset society today?

In other words, shall we cure the evils of democracy by more democracy, or shall we cut the Gordian knot of popular government with the sword of dictatorship?

My answer is neither the one nor the other. I am against dictatorship and Fascism as I am opposed to parliamentary regimes and so-called political democracy.

Nazism has been justly called an attack on civilization. This characterization applies with equal force to every form of dictatorship; indeed, to every kind of suppression and coercive authority. For what is civilization in the true sense? All progress has been essentially an enlargement of the liberties of the individual with a corresponding decrease of the authority wielded over him by external forces. This holds good in the realm of physical as well as of political and economic existence. In the physical world man has progressed to the extent in which he has subdued the forces of nature and made them useful to himself. Primitive man made a step on the road to progress when he first produced fire and thus triumphed over darkness, when he chained the wind or harnessed water.

Source: Emma Goldman, *The Individual, Society, and the State* (Chicago: Free Society Forum Pamphlet, 1936).

What role did authority or government play in human endeavor for betterment, in invention and discovery? None whatever, or at least none that was helpful. It has always been the individual that has accomplished every miracle in that sphere, usually in spite of the prohibition, persecution and interference by authority, human and divine.

Similarly, in the political sphere, the road of progress lay in getting away more and more from the authority of the tribal chief or of the clan, of prince and king, of government, of the State. Economically, progress has meant greater well-being of ever larger numbers. Culturally, it has signified the result of all the other achievements—greater independence, political, mental and psychic.

Regarded from this angle, the problems of man's relation to the State assumes an entirely different significance. It is no more a question of whether dictatorship is preferable to democracy, or Italian Fascism superior to Hitlerism. A larger and far more vital question poses itself: Is political government, is the State beneficial to mankind, and how does it affect the individual in the social scheme of things?

The individual is the true reality in life. A cosmos in himself, he does not exist for the State, nor for that abstraction called "society," or the "nation," which is only a collection of individuals. Man, the individual, has always been and, necessarily is the sole source and motive power of evolution and progress. Civilization has been a continuous struggle of the individual or of groups of individuals against the State and even against "society," that is, against the majority subdued and hypnotized by the State and State worship. Man's greatest battles have been waged against man-made obstacles and artificial handicaps imposed upon him to paralyze his growth and development. Human thought has always been falsified by tradition and custom, and perverted false education in the interests of those who held power and enjoyed privileges. In other words, by the State and the ruling classes. This constant incessant conflict has been the history of mankind.

Individuality may be described as the consciousness of the individual as to what he is and how he lives. It is inherent in every human being and is a thing of growth. The State and social institutions come and go, but individuality remains and persists. The very essence of individuality is expression; the sense of dignity and independence is the soil wherein it thrives. Individuality is not the impersonal and mechanistic thing that the State treats as an "individual." The individual is not merely the result of heredity and environment, of cause and effect. He is that and a great deal more, a great deal else. The living man cannot be defined; he is the fountain-head of all life and all values; he is not a part of this or of that; he is a whole, an individual whole, a growing, changing, yet always constant whole.

Individuality is not to be confused with the various ideas and concepts of Individualism; much less with that "rugged individualism" which is only a masked attempt to repress and defeat the individual and his individuality. So-called Individualism is the social and economic *laissez faire:* the exploitation of the masses by the classes by means of legal trickery, spiritual debasement and systematic indoctrination of the servile spirit, which process is known as "education." That corrupt and perverse "individualism" is the strait-jacket of individuality. It has converted life into a degrading race for externals, for possession, for social prestige and supremacy. Its highest wisdom is "the devil take the hindmost."

This "rugged individualism" has inevitably resulted in the greatest modern slavery, the crassest class distinctions, driving millions to the breadline. "Rugged individualism" has meant all the "individualism" for the masters, while the people are regimented into a slave caste to serve a handful of self-seeking "supermen." America is perhaps the best representative of this kind of individualism, in whose name political tyranny and social oppression are defended and held up as virtues; while every aspiration and attempt of man to gain freedom and social opportunity to live is denounced as "unAmerican" and evil in the name of that same individualism.

There was a time when the State was unknown. In his natural condition man existed without any State or organized government. People lived as families in small communities; they tilled the soil and practiced the arts and crafts. The individual, and later the family, was the unit of social life where each was free and the equal of his neighbor. Human society then was not a State but an *association;* a *voluntary* association for mutual protection and benefit. The elders and more experienced members were the guides and advisers of the people. They helped to manage the affairs of life, not to rule and dominate the individual.

Political government and the State were a much later development, growing out of the desire of the stronger to take advantage of the weaker, of the few against the many. The State, ecclesiastical and secular, served to give an appearance of legality and right to the wrong done by the few to the many. That appearance of right was necessary the easier to rule the people, because no government can exist without the consent of the people, consent open, tacit or assumed. Constitutionalism and democracy are the modern forms of that alleged consent; the consent being inoculated and indoctrinated by what is called "education," at home, in the church, and in every other phase of life.

That consent is the belief in authority, in the necessity for it. At its base is the doctrine that man is evil, vicious, and too incompetent to know what is good for him. On this all government and oppression is built. God and the State exist and are supported by this dogma.

Yet the State is nothing but a name. It is an abstraction. Like other similar conceptions—nation, race, humanity—it has no organic reality. To call the State an organism shows a diseased tendency to make a fetish of words.

The State is a term for the legislative and administrative machinery whereby certain business of the people is transacted, and badly so. There is nothing sacred, holy or mysterious about it. The State has no more conscience or moral mission than a commercial company for working a coal mine or running a railroad.

The State has no more existence than gods and devils have. They are equally the reflex and creation of man, for man, the individual, is the only reality. The State is but the shadow of man, the shadow of his opaqueness of his ignorance and fear.

Life begins and ends with man, the individual. Without him there is no race, no humanity, no State. No, not even "society" is possible without man. It is the individual who lives, breathes and suffers. His development, his advance, has been a continuous struggle against the fetishes of his own creation and particularly so against the "State."

In former days religious authority fashioned political life in the image of the Church. The authority of the State, the "rights" of rulers came from on high; power, like faith, was divine. Philosophers have written thick volumes to prove the sanctity of the State; some have even clad it with infallibility and with god-like attributes. Some have talked themselves into the insane notion that the State is "superhuman," the supreme reality, "the absolute."

Enquiry was condemned as blasphemy. Servitude was the highest virtue. By such precepts and training certain things came to be regarded as self-evident, as sacred of their truth, but because of constant and persistent repetition.

All progress has been essentially an unmasking of "divinity" and "mystery," of alleged sacred, eternal "truth"; it has been a gradual elimination of the abstract and the substitution in its place of the real, the concrete. In short, of facts against fancy, of knowledge against ignorance, of light against darkness.

That slow and arduous liberation of the individual was not accomplished by the aid of the State. On the contrary, it was by continuous conflict, by a life-and-death struggle with the State, that even the smallest vestige of independence and freedom has been won. It has cost mankind much time and blood to secure what little it has gained so far from kings, tsars and governments.

The great heroic figure of that long Golgotha has been Man. It has always been the individual, often alone and singly, at other times in unity and co-operation with others of his kind, who has fought and bled in the age-long battle against suppression and oppression, against the powers that enslave and degrade him.

More than that and more significant: It was man, the individual, whose soul first rebelled against injustice and degradation; it was the individual who first conceived the idea of resistance to the conditions under which he chafed. In short, it is always the individual who is the parent of the liberating thought as well as of the deed.

This refers not only to political struggles, but to the entire gamut of human life and effort, in all ages and climes. It has always been the individual, the man of strong mind and will to liberty, who paved the way for every human advance, for every step toward a freer and better world; in science, philosophy and art, as well as in industry, whose genius rose to the heights, conceiving the "impossible," visualizing its realization and imbuing others with his enthusiasm to work and strive for it. Socially speaking, it was always the prophet, the seer, the idealist, who dreamed of a world more to his heart's desire and who served as the beacon light on the road to greater achievement.

The State, every government whatever its form, character or color—be it absolute or constitutional, monarchy or republic, Fascist, Nazi or Bolshevik—is by its very nature conservative, static, intolerant of change and opposed to it. Whatever changes it undergoes are always the result of pressure exerted upon it, pressure strong enough to compel the ruling powers to submit peaceably or otherwise, generally "otherwise"—that is, by revolution. Moreover, the inherent conservatism of government, of authority of any kind, unavoidably becomes reactionary. For two reasons: first, because it is in the nature of government not only to retain the power it has, but also to strengthen, widen and perpetuate it, nationally as well as internationally. The stronger authority grows, the greater the State and its power, the less it can tolerate a similar authority or political power along side of itself. The psychology of government demands that its influence and prestige constantly grow, at home and abroad, and it exploits every opportunity to increase it. This tendency is motivated by the financial and commercial interests back of the government, represented and served by it. The fundamental *raison d'etre* of every government to which, incidentally, historians of former days wilfully shut their eyes, has become too obvious now even for professors to ignore.

The other factor which impels governments to become even more conservative and reactionary is their inherent distrust of the individual and fear of individuality. Our political and social scheme cannot afford to tolerate the individual and his constant quest for innovation. In "self-defense" the State therefore suppresses, persecutes, punishes and even deprives the individual of life. It is aided in this by every institution that stands for the preservation of the existing order. It resorts to every form of violence and force, and its efforts are supported by the "moral indignation" of the majority against the heretic, the social dissenter and the political rebel—the majority for centuries drilled in State worship, trained in discipline and obedience and subdued by the awe of authority in the home, the school, the church and the press.

The strongest bulwark of authority is uniformity; the least divergence from it is the greatest crime. The wholesale mechanisation of modern life has increased uniformity a thousandfold. It is everywhere present, in habits, tastes, dress, thoughts and ideas. Its most concentrated dullness is "public opinion." Few have the courage to stand out against it. He who refuses to submit is at once labelled "queer," "different," and decried as a disturbing element in the comfortable stagnancy of modern life.

Perhaps even more than constituted authority, it is social uniformity and sameness that harass the individual most. His very "uniqueness," "separateness" and "differentiation" make him an alien, not only in his native place, but even in his own home. Often more so than the foreign born who generally falls in with the established.

In the true sense one's native land, with its back ground of tradition, early impressions, reminiscences and other things dear to one, is not enough to make sensitive human beings feel at home. A certain atmosphere of "belonging," the consciousness of being "at one" with the people and environment, is more essential to one's feeling of home. This holds good in relation to one's family, the smaller local circle, as well as the larger phase of the life and activities commonly called one's country. The individual whose vision encompasses the whole world often feels nowhere so hedged in and out of touch with his surroundings than in his native land.

In pre-war time the individual could at least escape national and family boredom. The whole world was open to his longings and his quests. Now the world has become a prison, and life continual solitary confinement. Especially is this true since the advent of dictatorship, right and left.

Friedrich Nietzsche called the State a cold monster. What would he have called the hideous beast in the garb of modern dictatorship? Not that government had ever allowed much scope to the individual; but the champions of the new State ideology do not grant even that much. "The individual is nothing," they declare, "it is the collectivity which counts." Nothing less than the complete surrender of the individual will satisfy the insatiable appetite of the new deity.

Strangely enough, the loudest advocates of this new gospel are to be found among the British and American intelligentsia. Just now they are enamored with the "dictatorship of the proletariat." In theory only, to be sure. In practice, they still prefer the few liberties in their own respective countries. They go to Russia for a short visit or as salesmen of the "revolution," but they feel safer and more comfortable at home.

Perhaps it is not only lack of courage which keeps these good Britishers and Americans in their native lands rather than in the millenium come. Subconsciously there may lurk the feeling that individuality remains the most fundamental fact of all human association, suppressed and persecuted yet never defeated, and in the long run the victor.

The "genius of man," which is but another name for personality and individuality, bores its way through all the caverns of dogma, through the thick walls of tradition and custom, defying all taboos, setting authority at naught, facing contumely and the scaffold—ultimately to be blessed as prophet and martyr by succeeding generations. But for the "genius of man," that inherent, persistent quality of individuality, we would be still roaming the primeval forests.

Peter Kropotkin has shown what wonderful results this unique force of man's individuality has achieved when strengthened by *co-operation* with other individualities. The one-sided and entirely inadequate Darwinian theory of the struggle for existence received its biological and sociological completion from the great Anarchist scientist and thinker. In his profound work, *Mutual Aid,* Kropotkin shows that in the animal kingdom, as well as in human society, co-operation—as opposed to internecine strife and struggle—has worked for the survival and evolution of the species. He demonstrated that only mutual aid and voluntary co-operation—not the omnipotent, all-devastating State—can create the basis for a free individual and associational life.

At present the individual is the pawn of the zealots of dictatorship and the equally obsessed zealots of "rugged individualism." The excuse of the former is its claim of a new objective. The latter does not even make a pretense of anything new. As a matter of fact "rugged individualism" has learned nothing and forgotten nothing. Under its guidance the brute struggle for physical existence is still kept up. Strange as it may seem, and utterly absurd as it is, the struggle for physical survival goes merrily on though the necessity for it has entirely disappeared. Indeed, the struggle is being continued apparently because there is no necessity for it. Does not so-called overproduction prove it? Is not the world-wide economic crisis an eloquent demonstration that the struggle for existence is being maintained by the blindness of "rugged individualism" at the risk of its own destruction?

One of the insane characteristics of this struggle is the complete negation of the relation of the producer to the things he produces. The average worker has no inner point of contact with the industry he is employed in, and he is a stranger to the process of production of which he is a mechanical part. Like any other cog of the machine, he is replaceable at any time by other similar depersonalized human beings.

The intellectual proletarian, though he foolishly thinks himself a free agent, is not much better off. He, too, has a little choice or self-direction, in his particular metier as his brother who works with his hands. Material considerations and desire for greater social prestige are usually the deciding factors in the vocation of the intellectual. Added to it is the tendency to follow in the footsteps of family tradition, and become doctors, lawyers, teachers, engineers, etc. The groove requires less effort and personality. In consequence nearly everybody is out of place in our present scheme of things. The masses plod on, partly because their senses have been dulled by the deadly routine of work and because they must eke out an existence. This applies with even greater force to the political fabric of today. There is no place in its texture for free choice of independent thought and activity. There is a place only for voting and tax-paying puppets.

The interests of the State and those of the individual differ fundamentally and are antagonistic. The State and the political and economic institutions it supports can exist only by fashioning the individual to their particular purpose; training him to respect "law and order"; teaching him obedience, submission and unquestioning faith in the wisdom and justice of government; above all, loyal service and complete self-sacrifice when the State commands it, as in war. The State puts itself and its interests even above the claims of religion and of God. It punishes religious or conscientious scruples against individuality because there is no individuality without liberty, and liberty is the greatest menace to authority.

The struggle of the individual against these tremendous odds is the more difficult—too often dangerous to life and limb—because it is not truth or falsehood which serves as the criterion of the opposition he meets. It is not the validity or usefulness of his thought or activity which rouses against him the forces of the State and of "public opinion." The persecution of the innovator and protestant has always been inspired by fear on the part of constituted authority of having its infallibility questioned and its power undermined.

Man's true liberation, individual and collective, lies in his emancipation from authority and from the belief in it. All human evolution has been a struggle in that direction and for that object. It is not invention and mechanics which constitute development. The ability to travel at the rate of 100 miles an hour is no evidence of being civilized. True civilization is to be measured by the individual, the unit of all social life; by his individuality and the extent to which it is free to have its being to grow and expand unhindered by invasive and coercive authority.

Socially speaking, the criterion of civilization and culture is the degree of liberty and economic opportunity which the individual enjoys; of social and international unity and co-operation unrestricted by man-made laws and other artificial obstacles; by the absence of privileged castes and by the reality of liberty and human dignity; in short, by the true emancipation of the individual.

Political absolutism has been abolished because men have realized in the course of time that absolute power is evil and destructive. But the same thing is true of all power, whether it be the power of privilege, of money, of the priest, of the politician or of so-called democracy. In its effect on individuality it matters little what the particular character of coercion is—whether it be as black as Fascism, as yellow as Nazism or as pretentiously red as Bolshevism. It is power that corrupts and degrades both master and slave and it makes no difference whether the power is wielded by an autocrat, by parliament or Soviets. More pernicious than the power of a dictator is that of a class; the most terrible—the tyranny of a majority.

The long process of history has taught man that division and strife mean death, and that unity and cooperation advance his cause, multiply his strength and further his welfare. The spirit of government has always worked against the social application of this vital lesson, except where it served the State and aided its own particular interests. It is this anti-progressive and anti-social spirit of the State and of the privileged castes back of it which has been responsible for the bitter struggle between man and man. The individual and ever larger groups of individuals are beginning to see beneath the surface of the established order of things. No longer are they so blinded as in the past by the glare and tinsel of the State idea, and of the "blessings" of "rugged individualism." Man is reaching out for the wider scope of human relations which liberty alone can give. For true liberty is not a mere scrap of paper called "constitution," "legal right" or "law." It is not an abstraction derived from the non-reality known as "the State." It is not the *negative* thing of being free *from* something, because with such freedom you may starve to death. Real freedom, true liberty *is positive:* it is freedom *to* something; it is the liberty to be, to do; in short, the liberty of actual and active opportunity.

That sort of liberty is not a gift: it is the natural right of man, of every human being. It cannot be given: it cannot be conferred by any law or government. The need of it, the longing for it, is inherent in the individual. Disobedience to every form of coercion is the instinctive expression of it. Rebellion and revolution are the more or less conscious attempt to achieve it. Those manifestations, individual and social, are fundamentally expressions of the values of man. That those values may be nurtured, the community must realize that its greatest and most lasting asset is the unit—the individual.

In religion, as in politics, people speak of abstractions and believe they are dealing with realities. But when it does come to the real and the concrete, most people seem to lose vital touch with it. It may well be because reality alone is too matter-of-fact, too cold to enthuse the human soul. It can be aroused to enthusiasm only by things out of the commonplace, out of the ordinary. In other words, the Ideal is the spark that fires the imagination and hearts of men. Some ideal is needed to rouse man out of the inertia and humdrum of his existence and turn the abject slave into an heroic figure.

Right here, of course, comes the Marxist objector who has outmarxed Marx himself. To such a one, man is a mere puppet in the hands of that metaphysical Almighty called economic determinism or, more vulgarly, the class struggle. Man's will, individual and collective, his psychic life and mental orientation count for almost nothing with our Marxist and do not affect his conception of human history.

No intelligent student will deny the importance of the economic factor in the social growth and development of mankind. But only narrow and wilful dogmatism can persist in remaining blind to the important role played by an idea as conceived by the imagination and aspirations of the individual.

It were vain and unprofitable to attempt to balance one factor as against another in human experience. No one single factor in the complex of individual or social behavior can be designated as the factor of decisive quality. We know too little, and may never know enough, of human psychology to weigh and measure the relative values of this or that factor in determining man's conduct. To form such dogmas in their social connotation is nothing short of bigotry; yet, perhaps, it has its uses, for the very attempt to do so proved the persistence of the human will and confutes the Marxists.

Fortunately even some Marxists are beginning to see that all is not well with the Marxian creed. After all, Marx was but human—all too human—hence by no means infallible. The practical application of economic determinism in Russia is helping to clear the minds of the more intelligent Marxists. This can be seen in the transvaluation of Marxian values going on in Socialist and even Communist ranks in some European countries. They are slowly realising that their theory has overlooked the human element, *den Menschen,* as a Socialist paper put it. Important as the economic factor is, it is not enough. The rejuvenation of mankind needs the inspiration and energising force of an ideal.

Such an ideal I see in Anarchism. To be sure, not in the popular misrepresentations of Anarchism spread by the worshippers of the State and authority. I mean the philosophy of a new social order based on the released energies of the individual and the free association of liberated individuals.

Of all social theories Anarchism alone steadfastly proclaims that society exists for man, not man for society. The sole legitimate purpose of society is to serve the needs and advance the aspiration of the individual. Only by doing so can it justify its existence and be an aid to progress and culture.

The political parties and men savagely scrambling for power will scorn me as hopelessly out of tune with our time. I cheerfully admit the charge. I find comfort in the assurance that their hysteria lacks enduring quality. Their hosanna is but of the hour.

Man's yearning for liberation from all authority and power will never be soothed by their cracked song. Man's quest for freedom from every shackle is eternal. It must and will go on.

Woody Guthrie (1912–1967)

Woodrow Wilson Guthrie, born in Oklahoma the year of his namesake's election to the presidency, was a rambler, a musician, a critical observer of American society, a union organizer, and a radical, who, through hundreds of protest songs, left behind an exceptional legacy of dissent that is still felt today. At the age of 23, he left his wife and three children and, along with thousands of other Okies fleeing the dust bowl of Oklahoma, bummed his way to the "promised land" of California. There he ran head-on into the anti-Okie discrimination and hatred that greeted all desperate migrant workers during the dislocation of the Great Depression. Although he was living on the outside of society, he was able to make a living singing songs of social protest on the radio. "Goin' Down the Road Feelin' Bad," "Hard Travelin'," and many of the other songs he called his dust bowl ballads virtually became anthems for those who, like Guthrie, also felt like outcasts. He wrote union songs like "Union Maid," antiestablishment songs like "Philadelphia Lawyer," children's songs like "Car, Car," and droll songs like "Do Re Me." Frequently, he visited the government camps and Hoovervilles in California to sing to migrant workers.

His most famous song, "This Land is Your Land," was Guthrie's response to Irving Berlin's "God Bless America," a song which Guthrie loathed as the epitome of American self-righteousness. In the original draft, Guthrie penned several radical verses (later eliminated) that revealed his belief that America was for the common people, the ordinary people, and that it belonged to everyone, not just the wealthy, or the pious, or the powerful. In one verse he wonders, while observing his fellow Americans standing on line at the relief office, "if God blessed America for me." In another verse he sings about "a sign that says 'private property,'" on one side while on the other side it says nothing. He felt the implication was clear: "that side was made for you and me."

At the end of the decade, he was living in New York, where he teamed up with Pete Seeger, Lee Hayes, Leadbelly, Cisco Houston, and other leftist musicians and songwriters and, with the outbreak of the Second World War, added antifascist songs to his repertoire. He was against "Hitlerism and fascism homemade and imported," he wrote in his autobiography, "and made up songs to pay honor and tribute to the story of the trade union workers around the world." In 1943 he joined the merchant marine and in 1945 was drafted into the army.

Though he had inscribed on the front of his guitar "this machine kills fascists," many critics detested his radical lyrics and questioned his patriotism. Once, when asked if he was a "Red," he replied that he did not know if he would call himself a "Red," although he had to admit that he had always been "in the red" all his life.

Guthrie did a number of recordings for the Library of Congress and also performed and recorded with the Almanac Singers, a group that was the forerunner of the Weavers. In 1943, he published *Bound for Glory*, an autobiographical account of his life. Although he continued to travel about the country writing, performing, and recording, his health began to fail on account of a debilitating hereditary nerve disease, Huntington's chorea. In the last 13 years of his life, he was unable to sing, and he spent most of his time in and out of hospitals as the disease gradually consumed him. In 1961, a young musician-songwriter who had grown up listening to Woody Guthrie's records and who had begun to model his own approach to music on Guthrie's example made a pilgrimage to New York to pay homage to his hero. During his visits Robert Zimmerman of Hibbings, Minnesota, would sit with Woody while reading some of his own poetry and playing both his and Woody's songs to the invalid. It was during this time that Zimmerman began to perform at a Manhattan folk club, Gerde's Folk City, going by the name of Bob Dylan.

"The Ballad of Pretty Boy Floyd" turns a notorious bank robber who was hunted down by the FBI into a modern-day Robin Hood. In "Jesus Christ," Guthrie portrays Jesus Christ as an activist. How radical are Guthrie's songs? Were his critics correct in labeling him a communist? Who are the villains in his songs? The heroes?

"The Ballad of Pretty Boy Floyd"

If you'll gather 'round me, children,
A story I will tell
'Bout Pretty Boy Floyd, an outlaw,
Oklahoma knew him well.

It was in the town of Shawnee,
A Saturday afternoon,
His wife beside him in his wagon
As into town they rode.

There a deputy sheriff approached him
In a manner rather rude,
Vulgar words of anger,
An' his wife she overheard.

Pretty Boy grabbed a log chain,
And the deputy grabbed his gun;
In the fight that followed
He laid that deputy down.

Then he took to the trees and timber
To live a life of shame;
Every crime in Oklahoma
Was added to his name.

There's many a starving farmer
The same old story told
How the outlaw paid their mortgage
And saved their little home.

Others tell you of a stranger
That came to beg a meal,
Underneath his napkin
Left a thousand dollar bill.

It was in Oklahoma City,
It was on a Christmas Day,
There was a whole car load of groceries
Come with a note to say:

"Well, you say that I'm an outlaw,
You say that I'm a thief.
Here's a Christmas dinner
For the families on relief."

SOURCE: Harold Leventhal and Marjorie Guthrie, eds., *The Woody Guthrie Songbook* (New York: Grosset and Dunlap, 1976), 186–187.

Now as through this world I ramble
I see lots of funny men;
Some will rob you with a six-gun,
And some with a fountain pen.

And as through your life you travel,
Yes, as through your life you roam,
You won't never see an outlaw
Drive a family from their home.

"Jesus Christ"

Jesus Christ was a man who traveled through the land,
A hard working man and brave.
He said to the rich "Give your goods to the poor."
But they laid Jesus Christ in His grave.

Jesus was a man, a carpenter by hand,
His followers true and brave,
One dirty little coward called Judas Iscariot
Has laid Jesus Christ in His grave.

He went to the preacher, He went to the sheriff,
He told them all the same,
"Sell all of your jewelry and give it to the poor,"
And they laid Jesus Christ in his grave.

When Jesus come to town, all the working folks around
Believed what He did say,
But bankers and the preachers they nailed Him on a cross.
And they laid Jesus Christ in His grave.

And the people held their breath when they heard about His death,
Everybody wondered why.
It was the big landlord and the soldiers that they hired
To nail Jesus Christ in the sky.

This song it was wrote in New York City,
Of rich man, preacher and slave,
If Jesus was to preach what He preached in Galilee,
They would lay poor Jesus Christ in His grave.

SOURCE: Harold Leventhal and Marjorie Guthrie, eds., *The Woody Guthrie Songbook* (New York: Grosset and Dunlap 1976),153–155. JESUS CHRIST, words and music by Woody Guthrie. TRO— © 1961(renewed) 1963 (renewed) Ludlow Music, Inc., New York, NY. Used by permission.

J. Saunders Redding and Charles F. Wilson

The First World War was a bitterly disillusioning experience for African Americans. Many had joined the army in hopes that their patriotism and gallantry in battle would guarantee equal treatment for them after the war. But racism was in no way diminished following the war—in fact, there were a number of bloody race riots in several cities—and African Americans were still treated as second-class citizens. When the Second World War broke out, there was concern that this time there should be a different outcome. The first selection here is J. Saunders Redding's attempt to analyze the meaning of the war for African Americans. Why does Redding support the war effort? Did the civil rights movement prove him right? The second selection, by Charles F. Wilson, an African American private in the Army Air Corps, is a letter to President Roosevelt in which he protests the undemocratic nature of the segregated U.S. Army. How does Wilson suggest the president should solve the problem?

J. Saunders Redding, "A Negro Looks at This War," 1942

War had no heroic traditions for me. Wars were white folks'. All wars in historical memory. The last war, and the Spanish-American War before that, and the Civil War. I had been brought up in a way that admitted of no heroics. I think my parents were right. Life for them was a fierce, bitter, soul-searching war of spiritual and economic attrition; they fought it without heroics, but with stubborn heroism. Their heroism was screwed up to a pitch of idealism so intense that it found a safety valve in cynicism about the heroics of white folks' war. This cynicism went back at least as far as my paternal grandmother, whose fierce eyes used to lash the faces of her five grandchildren as she said, "An' he done som'pin big an' brave away down dere to Chickymorgy an' dey made a iron image of him 'cause he got his head blowed off an' his stomick blowed out fightin' to keep his slaves." I cannot convey the scorn and the cynicism she put into her picture of that hero-son of her slave-master, but I have never forgotten.

I was nearly ten when we entered the last war in 1917. The European fighting, and the sinking of the Lusitania, had seemed as remote, as distantly meaningless to us, as the Battle of Hastings. Then we went in and suddenly the city was flag-draped, slogan-plastered, and as riotously gay as on circus half-holidays. I remember one fine Sunday we came upon an immense new billboard with a new slogan: GIVE! TO

SOURCE: J. Saunders Redding, "A Negro Looks at This War," *American Mercury* 55 (November 1942): 585–592.

MAKE THE WORLD SAFE FOR DEMOCRACY. My brother, who was the oldest of us, asked what making the world safe for democracy meant. My father frowned, but before he could answer, my mother broke in.

"It's just something to say, like . . . "—and then she was stuck until she hit upon one of the family's old jokes—"like 'Let's make a million dollars.'" We all laughed, but the bitter core of her meaning lay revealed, even for the youngest of us, like the stone in a halved peach. . . .

And so, since I have reached maturity and thought a man's thoughts and had a man's—a Negro man's—experiences, I have thought that I could never believe in war again. Yet I believe in this one.

There are many things about this war that I do not like, just as there are many things about "practical" Christianity that I do not like. But I believe in Christianity, and if I accept the shoddy and unfulfilling in the conduct of this war, I do it as voluntarily and as purposefully as I accept the trash in the workings of "practical" Christianity. I do not like the odor of political pandering that arises from some groups. I do not like these "race incidents" in the camps. I do not like the world's not knowing officially that there were Negro soldiers on Bataan with General Wainwright. I do not like the constant references to the Japs as "yellow bastards," "yellow bellies," and "yellow monkeys," as if color had something to do with treachery, as if color were the issue and the thing we are fighting rather than oppression, slavery, and a way of life hateful and nauseating. These and other things I do not like, yet I believe in the war. . . .

This is a war to keep men free. The struggle to broaden and lengthen the road of freedom—our own private and important war to enlarge freedom here in America—will come later. That this private, intra-American war will be carried on and won is the only real reason we Negroes have to fight. We must keep the road open. Did we not believe in a victory in that intra-American war, we could not believe in nor stomach the compulsion of this. If we could not believe in the realization of democratic freedom for ourselves, certainly no one could ask us to die for the preservation of that ideal for others. But to broaden and lengthen the road of freedom is different from preserving it. And our first duty is to keep the road of freedom open. It must be done continuously. It is the duty of the whole people to do this. Our next duty (and this, too, is the whole people's) is to broaden the road so that more people can travel it without snarling traffic. To die in these duties is to die for something. . . .

I believe in this war, finally, because I believe in the ultimate vindication of the wisdom of the brotherhood of man. This is not foggy idealism. I think that the growing manifestations of the interdependence of all men is an argument for the wisdom of brotherhood. I think that the shrunk compass of the world is an argument. I think that the talk of united nations and of planned interdependence is an argument.

More immediately, I believe in this war because I believe in America. I believe in what America professes to stand for. Nor is this, I think, whistling in the dark. There are a great many things wrong here. There are only a few men of good will. I do not lose sight of that. I know the inequalities, the outraged hopes and faith, the inbred hate; and I know that there are people who wish merely to lay these by in the closet of the national mind until the crisis is over. But it would be equally foolish for me to lose sight of the advances that are made, the barriers that are leveled, the privileges that grow. Foolish, too, to remain blind to the distinction that exists between simple race prejudice, already growing moribund under the impact of this war, and theories of racial superiority as a basic tenet of a societal system—theories that at bottom are the avowed justification for suppression, defilement and murder.

I will take this that I have here. I will take the democratic theory. The bit of road of freedom that stretches through America is worth fighting to preserve. The very fact that I, a Negro in America, can fight against the evils in America is worth fighting for. This open fighting against the wrongs one hates is the mark and the hope of democratic freedom. I do not underestimate the struggle. I know the learning that must take place, the evils that must be broken, the depths that must be climbed. But I am free to help in doing these things. I count. I am free (though only a little as yet) to pound blows at the huge body of my American world until, like a chastened mother, she gives me nurture with the rest.

Charles F. Wilson, Letter to President Roosevelt, 1944

Dear President Roosevelt:

It was with extreme pride that I, a soldier in the Armed Forces of our country, read the following affirmation of our war aims, pronounced by you at a recent press conference:

> "The United Nations are fighting to make a world in which tyranny, and aggression cannot exist; a world based upon freedom, equality, and justice; a world in which all persons, regardless of race, color and creed, may live in peace, honor and dignity." . . .

But the picture in our country is marred by one of the strangest paradoxes in our whole fight against world fascism. The United States Armed Forces, to fight for World Democracy, is within itself undemocratic. The undemocratic policy of Jim Crow and segregation is practiced by our Armed Forces against its Negro members. Totally inadequate opportunities are given to the Negro members of our Armed Forces, nearly one tenth of the whole, to participate with "equality" . . . "regardless of race and color" in the fight for our war aims. In fact it appears that the army intends to follow the very policy that the FEPC [Fair Employment Practices Committee] is battling against in civilian life, the pattern of assigning Negroes to the lowest types of work.

Let me give you an example of the lack of democracy in our Field, where I am now stationed. Negro soldiers are completely segregated from the white soldiers on the base. And to make doubly sure that no mistake is made about this, the barracks and other housing facilities (supply room, mess hall, etc.) of the Negro section C are covered with black tar paper, while all other barracks and housing facilities on the base are painted white.

Source: Phillip McGuire, ed. *Taps for a Jim Crow Army: Letters from Black Soldiers in World War II* (Santa Barbara, CA: ABC-CLIO, 1983), 134–139.

It is the stated policy of the Second Air Force that "every potential fighting man must be used as a fighting man. If you have such a man in a base job, you have no choice. His job must be eliminated or be filled by a limited service man, WAC, or civilian." And yet, leaving out the Negro soldiers working with the Medical Section, fully 50% of the Negro soldiers are working in base jobs, such as, for example, at the Resident Officers' Mess, Bachelor Officers' Quarters, and Officers' Club, as mess personnel, BOQ orderlies, and bar tenders. Leaving out the medical men again, based on the section C average only 4% of this 50% would not be "potential fighting men." . . .

How can we convince nearly one tenth of the Armed Forces, the Negro members, that your pronouncement of the war aims of the United Nations means what it says, when their experience with one of the United Nations, the United States of America, is just the opposite? . . .

With your issuance of Executive Order 8802, and the setting up of the Fair Employment Practices Committee, you established the foundation for fighting for democracy in the industrial forces of our country, in the interest of victory for the United Nations. In the interest of victory for the United Nations, another Executive Order is now needed. An Executive Order which will lay the base for fighting for democracy in the Armed Forces of our country. An Executive Order which would bring about the result here at Davis-Monthan Field whereby the Negro soldiers would be integrated into all of the Sections on the base, as fighting men, instead of in the segregated Section C as housekeepers.

Then and only then can your pronouncement of the war aims of the United Nations mean to all that we "are fighting to make a world in which tyranny, and aggression cannot exist; a world based upon freedom, equality and justice; a world in which all persons, regardless of race, color and creed, may live in peace, honor and dignity."

Respectfully yours,
Charles F. Wilson, 36794590
Private, Air Corps

David Dellinger (1915–2004)

A year before the United States entered the Second World War, Congress passed the Selective Training and Service Act, establishing the first peacetime draft in the nation's history. A person given the 1-A classification was at the top of the conscription list; 4-F meant the person was physically unable to enter the military. The act also assigned two classifications for those opposed to the war: 1-AO, for people who would be willing to work in the medical corps, and 4-E, for those who would not accept any assignment connected to the military but who would agree to do alternative civilian work. Selective Service records show that about 12,000 men refused to fight in the "good war" and were classified as conscientious objectors. Another 6000 men refused to participate in any way in the war effort and wound up serving prison terms. They came from all backgrounds: Quakers, Jehovah's Witnesses, Seventh Day Adventists, Buddhists, pacifists, and others.

David Dellinger, who later was prominent in the 1960s antiwar movement and was tried as one of the Chicago Seven for his role in the demonstrations at the 1968 Democratic convention, believed deeply that the only viable method of fighting evil was through nonviolence. Inspired by the example of Mahatma Gandhi and disgusted with U.S. bankers and industrialists' complicity in the rise of Adolf Hitler, Dellinger was sent to prison for his refusal to register for the draft. The following document is Dellinger's firsthand account of his experience. What was his main objection to the war? If he was so opposed to Nazism and Fascism, why would he refuse to fight against it?

Why I Refused to Register in the October 1940 Draft and a Little of What It Led To

I believe that there are mysterious spiritual factors that influence who we are and what we do. For me, beginning in early childhood, these were the solitary experiences of the ecstasies of Nature and having to deal with the racism and classism of many of the well-to-do adults in the suburb of Boston where I grew up (even as I saw indications that they were not as happy as they would have been had they lived a more egalitarian and sharing life-style). I can think of four other influences that led me to become an objector to World War II long before the United States officially entered.

First, I was influenced by my exposure to the lies and failures of World War I and the examples of persons who fought in that war or went to prison for resisting it. A second influence included my visits to Nazi Germany in 1936 and 1937 when I was anti-Nazi and the U.S. government, banks, and major corporations were supporting Hitler. A third was my experience, after returning from Europe, going "on the road," penniless, riding the rails, and staying at missions and hobo jungles. The fourth influence was the inspiring example of grass-roots practitioners of nonviolent resistance to oppression and injustice. The practitioners included radical Christians, Jews, Budhists, atheists, anarchists, Native Americans, African Americans, the labor organizers with whom I worked in the thirties, and Gandhians in India. I mention Buddhists, anarchists, and Native Americans, even though I knew none of them personally. But I read widely, and all the major influences I have listed were broadened and deepened by this.

SOURCE: Larry Gara and Lenna Mae Gara, eds., *A Few Small Candles: War Resisters of World War II Tell Their Stories* (Kent, OH: Kent State University Press, 1999), 20–37.

One of my most vivid memories is of the widespread rejoicing I observed—and felt—when World War I came to an end in November 1918, about three months after my third birthday. "Now no one will have to kill other people," is the way my father put it at the time. When I was thirteen, a German officer from that war was invited to speak in our Wakefield, Massachusetts, town hall in a celebration of the tenth anniversary of the ending of the war. Many people spoke out against allowing an "enemy" to speak, but my father and I went to hear him. I was profoundly moved by the German's appeal for the people of the world to work across national boundaries to solve their differences rather than going to war and doing the terrible things that he had done. And it was an early lesson on the gains to be made by following one's own common sense and conscience, rather than being intimidated by self-styled patriots.

Sometime during college I read a book that contained a moving account of something that happened during the Christmas season among soldiers in rival trenches. One night the Germans, as I remember it, started singing Christmas carols. After a while the British also began singing carols. Soon a few soldiers started climbing out of their trenches and singing on the strip of land that separated them. Others joined in and together they shared the Christmas spirit. When dawn came they climbed back into their trenches. I don't remember if the story relates whether or when they resumed shooting at one another. But soldiers in many wars often shoot over the heads of their enemies when they receive orders to fire. My guess is that that's what most of those soldiers did.

Harry Rudin, a history teacher at Yale, participated in that war. He was the first person who told me that quite a few disillusioned soldiers made a point of firing over the heads of opponents rather than trying to kill them. He didn't do this at first, but he soon became horrified enough by the senseless slaughter to start doing so. Though I had no courses with Rudin, we became good friends and he strengthened my determination never to support war. He also had a historical perspective that supported my early antinazism.

An even more inspiring example to me than Gandhi (who offered military support to the British during World War I) was Eugene Victor Debs, the charismatic labor leader who was sentenced to ten years in federal prison for his antiwar speeches. In the end he served only three years because the country had begun to realize that entering the war had been a terrible mistake. Even Woodrow Wilson, the president who had demanded U.S. participation in "A War to Make the World Safe for Democracy," reached a point of utter disillusionment when he said, "Is there any man, woman or child in America—let me repeat, is there any child—who does not know that this was an industrial and commercial war?"

I knew those words by heart long before the United States came close to entering what is known as the Second World War. And I also knew the words of Debs which told me that going to prison could have desirable spiritual consequences. At the time of his sentencing he said, "While there is a lower class I am in it; while there is a criminal element I am of it; while there is a soul in prison I am not free." Debs also said something that encouraged me long before World War II to develop my own conscience and to follow it rather than becoming a follower of role models; "I would not be a Moses to lead you into the Promised Land, because if I could lead you into it someone else could lead you out of it." This became especially relevant when most of the peace leaders from whom I had learned valuable lessons tried to persuade me to register for the 1940 draft.

Even Roger Baldwin, the head of the American Civil Liberties Union who had been jailed in the earlier war, appealed to me to register. Otherwise, he said, I would embarrass the peace organizations that had secured passage of a special nonmilitary assignment for draftees whose religious training forbade them to kill. Primarily the exemption was for Quakers, Mennonites, and Brethren, the so-called "peace churches." And indeed, the head of the American Friends Service Committee, whom I had long admired, tried to persuade me to register so that I could become the director of one of the camps for such draftees. Under my leadership, he argued, it could become a worldwide example of the importance of nonviolence. But I was working with youth gangs in a racially conflicted inner city, and to leave that to supervise nonviolent religionists raking leaves in an isolated geographical area wasn't the kind of nonviolence I believed in. To make it even worse, the rules were set by Gen. Lewis B. Hershey, and he forbade the residents to use their weekends or other spare time to go where other people lived and speak against the war. For a final example, Reinhold Niebuhr, who had inspired me at Yale with his brilliant, deeply religious, anti-imperialist pacifist sermons, went through a subsequent spiritual crisis. He became obsessed with the sinfulness of human beings, including himself, and condemned sinful "addiction" to nonviolent soul force as "arrogant utopianism." The day that I and seven other students at Union were carted off to prison, he preached a sermon in the chapel saying that his greatest failure as a Christian had been his inability to educate us as to the true nature of Christianity.

Shortly after Hitler came to power, I became an anti-Nazi. One of my favorite poets at the time was Archibald MacLeish, who expressed his condemnation of fascism in 1933, both verbally and in his "frescoes for Mr. Rockefeller's City." But there were other influences as well: Jewish friends; E. Fay Campbell, an adult adviser at the University Christian Association; and other radicals I have mentioned. And opposition to nazism flowed naturally from my early opposition to lynching and other racial oppressions. This had developed as a result of the "mistake" I made in junior high school of falling in love with a poor Irish girl and having a poor Italian boy for my best friend. That was in the twenties, when there were no Negroes in town; but in my neighborhood the Irish and Italians were treated as if they were inherently inferior members of worthless races.

When I graduated from Yale in 1936, I had won a graduate fellowship to study at Oxford University for two or three years. Before I entered Oxford, I made two trips to Nazi Germany, with a visit to Spain and Italy in between. In Spain I was so impressed with the grass-roots soldiers who had been attending the People's University in Madrid, where I stayed for a time, that I seriously considered joining them in fighting Franco. This is how I put it in my book *From Yale to Jail:* "If my friends were going to die I was ready to die with them, and who knows, maybe we'll win. But by then I knew that the Communists were shooting the Trotskyists, both were shooting the anarchists, and the anarchists had shot at the car in which I had been riding in Barcelona when it made a wrong turn into their sector. Whoever won that way it wouldn't be the people. I knew that I had to find a better way of fighting, a nonviolent way."

Earlier that summer I had read the book *The Conquest of Violence,* which gave historic examples of how even idealists who pick up the gun for a just cause tend to become corrupted, much as some of the Communists, Trotskyists, and anarchists had. The book was written by a Dutch anarchist named Bart de Ligt, who advocated the kind of nonviolent anarchism I soon became attracted to.

Between Spain and Germany I spent a week or more tracing one of the routes of Francis of Assisi through southern Italy, stopping to spend solitary time in each of the little chapels identified with him. Like me, Francis was the son of a rich man but became committed to nonviolence, justice, and sharing. Of course, he went much further than I have in sharing worldly goods with the poor. But after Spain, and from what I had already learned about the challenges of being an anti-Nazi in Germany, I wanted to absorb as much as I could of Francis's spirit before going back for a second visit.

Before my first trip to Germany, I knew that the U.S. government and banks were supporting and arming Adolf Hitler, much as in later years they armed and supported Saddam Hussein before waging war against Iraq. As Thomas Mann wrote in his diary in 1934, "Russian socialism has a powerful opponent in the West, Hitler, and this is more important to Britain's ruling class than the moral . . . climate of the continent . . . the governor of the Bank of England was sent to the United States to obtain credits for war materials for Germany, armament credits."

I also knew that a number of major U.S. corporations had set up plants in Nazi Germany for reasons similar to those that more recently have led corporations to set up plants in dictatorships supported by the United States in Central and South America. General Motors, ITT, and Ford come most readily to mind as having plants protected by Hitler, but there were others. In all my visits the pro-Nazis used these activities by the United States as an example of why I should support the Nazis, while the anti-Nazis cited them as an example of what they were up against in their efforts to get rid of Hitler. Some middle-of-the-roaders agreed with some of my complaints about the Nazis, but said that if Hitler was as dangerous as I claimed, the United States would not support him as strongly as it did. Others argued that Hitler's main purpose was to get rid of the Versailles Treaty, which extorted German reparations long after the end of World War I, imposed repressive restrictions on the German economy and armed forces, and robbed Germany of some of its traditional territories.

When I first entered Germany, I went to bookstores and asked for the works of Heinrich Heine, one of my favorite poets, whose works were banned because he was Jewish. This led to some fascinating discussions. One was with a Jewish manager who, after getting the book from the store's cellar, suggested that I stay in a bed-and-breakfast near his home in the ghetto. After that I often stayed in similar places in other cities. Especially in the ghettoes, but elsewhere as well, I was asked why the United States had a limited quota on German immigrants and was turning away Jewish refugees and other anti-Nazis, except for well-known individuals like Thomas Mann and Albert Einstein. Many times I was urged to go back to the United States to work against this and other evil practices that supported the Nazis. Later I canceled the last two years at Oxford in order to do some of these things while also working against lynching. Lynching was on the increase during that period, and the pro-Nazis frequently cited it as the American equivalent of their country's occasional mistreatment of Jews.

When I finally got to Oxford, I learned that Jobst von der Gröben, a German Rhodes scholar, was a member of my residential college, New College. Since the Nazis had not vetoed his selection, I assumed that he was pro-Nazi. But when we met, I found that Jobst was strongly anti-Nazi. Apparently he came from a leading family and had a brilliant record. So, for public relations reasons, the Nazis decided not to oppose his selection. We became good friends, discussing, among other things, what we could do to strengthen the anti-Nazi movement inside Germany, which was far stronger than most Americans realized, then or to this day. Also, what we could do to get the United States to work with the anti-Nazi movement rather than the Nazis. When I went back to Germany in the spring and summer of 1937, Jobst felt that because of his publicized anti-Nazi activities in England it was not safe for him to return to Germany. He did give me the names and addresses of a number of anti-Nazis, and I was able to carry a few messages from those in one city to those in another. He also told me that a number of anti-Nazis worked in the German Foreign Ministry, and he gave me the names of two or three who were apt to be sent to the United States from time to time, in case I could help them in any way. The only one I ever saw in the United States said that the U.S. officials he talked with liked the similarities between German fascism and the U.S. system, so they didn't want to hear any of his criticisms of the Nazis.

It was clear to me during this period that England, France, and the United States were working with Hitler not only for the profits to be gained by U.S. banks and corporations, but also with the major aim of influencing the Nazis to expand militarily to the east, destroying, or at least crippling, the Communist enemy. On the other hand, the Soviet Union was wooing the Nazis in the hope that they would expand westward and engage in a war with its capitalist enemies. When the Nazi-Soviet Pact was signed in August 1939, the United States knew that it had lost this diplomatic war and for the first time Roosevelt and other top capitalists began to prepare for war against their German ally. . . .

The thirties was a time when the nonviolent Gandhian movement against the British occupation and rule in India was heavily publicized in the U.S. media. In part this was because the revolt was against the British rather than against U.S. imperialism in Cuba, Puerto Rico, Central America, and the Philippines. Also, the rulers of the United States were already aiming to replace British colonialism in much of the world by "more enlightened, more democratic" American imperialism, which was the underlying reason they entered both world wars. In any event, I got more extensive details of the spirit, methods, defeats, and triumphs of the Gandhian campaigns than today's media ever prints about nonviolent campaigns for justice within the United States or its territories. In addition, there were radical visitors from the United States to India who supplied additional information that I savored. Primary among them were Richard Gregg and a number of nonviolent activists who, as teaching missionaries, became a part of the Gandhian movement. These included Ralph Templin and Jay Holmes Smith, who were expelled from India when they refused to sign the oath of allegiance that the British rulers required of all foreigners in 1939. When they returned to this country, I learned from them of a number of books by Indian nonviolent activists that had a profound influence on me. I particularly remember *War Without Violence* by Krishnalal Shridharani. So, whereas U.S. Communist party members were thrilled to "know" (despite evidence to the contrary) that the Soviet Union was a shining example of Leninist successes, I was thrilled to know that a creative and powerful nonviolent movement for justice and equality existed in India, even if it had not yet achieved most of its objectives. And soon the radical intentional pacifist community that I was a part of in the inner city of Newark was sharing experiences with the Nonviolent Ashram that Smith had helped start in Harlem and with the communitarians in Yellow Springs, Ohio, with whom Templin was working. . . .

. . . During every April since 1934, there was a day whose growing list of sponsors called for a National Student Strike Against War. Originally it was in response to the Oxford Pledge, in which a large number of students at Oxford pledged that they would never take part in an international war. Soon the pledge and the day of observance grew in this country and became very powerful. I can't remember whether I began to observe this strike in my sophomore year at Yale or slightly later. But for many years before the draft law was passed, many of my friends and I stayed away from classes on that day, holding a variety of public vigils, rallies, and demonstrations. And of course we did this in prison in April 1940, with the ultimately exciting results noted by George Houser.

We eight Union Seminary students spent the first week of our imprisonment in New York City's West Street Jail. There we mingled with Leo Lepke, the head of the Mafia, and several of his adjutants. To our surprise, they were friendly to us while saying to me such things as "I am in jail for killing people but you are here for refusing to kill anyone. It doesn't make sense." Or, "I just gave my lawyer a few thousand dollars to give to the judge to lessen my sentence, but all you guys had to do was to sign a paper that wouldn't have required you to do anything, and yet you refused. WOW!" Later, after one of my arrests, I stepped between another Mafioso and a guard who was roughing him up. He thanked me and said something like this: "Like us, you know that the system is based on stealing as much as you can from anyone you can, but unlike us you are trying to work out a better way of living." That was before I temporarily shared a cell with a bank robber, who told me that with the right pieces of paper (stocks, bonds, property deeds) he wouldn't have had to use guns, knives, and jimmies. Instead of becoming a bank robber, he could have been a banker who robbed people legally.

After West Street, we were transferred to the Federal Correctional Institution at Danbury, Connecticut. None of the top officials there showed any interest in making it a genuine correctional institution. I walked into the first Saturday night movie with a black man with whom I had been talking. The guard pointed to the white section for me and the black section for him, but I sat next to my friend in the black section. It was not a planned protest, just the instinctive, natural thing to do. Soon I was carried out and placed in a solitary cell in the maximum security "troublemakers" cell block. Later, war objectors organized a number of protests against racial segregation, both at Danbury and in other prisons, including Lewisburg Penitentiary, where I did two years. When we took such actions, or did other things that I thought were in accord with the best teachings of Jesus and the Jewish prophets, we never received any support or understanding from the Christian chaplains at either Danbury or Lewisburg. But I developed a fruitful relationship with the rabbi at Danbury, who stimulated me spiritually and encouraged me to be true to what I saw as the prophetic heritage.

One aspect of my working with John L. Lewis was that Eleanor Roosevelt proposed that I be included in the list of organizers of the biggest antiwar demonstration where Lewis would speak. After the event she invited me into the White House and we had a friendly talk in which she expressed her support for my nonviolent efforts for justice and equality and for changing from a greedy, selfishly competitive society to a more communal one. After I had been in Danbury a short while, I got a letter from my brother, who was a student at Swarthmore College. He had been part of a committee that had lunch with Mrs. Roosevelt when she came to the college to speak. When she heard his name she asked if I were his brother and pumped him for prison news about me. She also said, "When you write Dave, tell him that I admire him. Tell him that I think he is right in the stand he had taken." Knowing the attacks she was under for attitudes and practices that differed from those of her opportunistic husband, I decided to view this as a personal message that I would not publicize because of the difficulties it might cause her. I did this because of my belief that true nonviolence requires special sensitivities not only toward one's opponents but also toward persons with whom one shares many convictions but who have to decide for themselves when they will go public about some of them. I don't know if my decision was a correct one, but looking back now I wonder if she might have sent the message both personally and with the hope that I would release it and put her antiwar sentiments in the context that she associated with me, instead of the selfish isolationism of those who wanted to let the Europeans fight while the United States profited. Perhaps I lacked the faith in Mrs. Roosevelt that I should have had.

The other reason I mention the message is that the censors had decreed that I should not see the letter in which my younger brother wrote the words that Mrs. Roosevelt had asked him to send me. When his letter arrived, I was in solitary confinement, but a lieutenant with whom I had become friends showed it to me, saying that I should read it but never tell anyone that he had shown it to me. If I did, he would be in dire trouble, perhaps discharged or worse. His willingness to show me the letter came out of a friendship that we had gradually developed as he and I each tried to live up to our best selves. For the lieutenant that meant not blindly accepting the prison system's condemnation of criminals as evil subhumans who could never be trusted. For me it meant trying to treat each prison guard as an individual with a potential humanity that lay beneath the surface but was usually frustrated by the routine cruelties he was supposed to inflict on prisoners. I understood why so many prisoners called the guards "hacks"and why they would not consider being friends with any of them, except as a way to obtain dope or other forbidden items. But, in addition to my understanding of the need to treat every person, in or out of prison, as a potential friend, I also realized that most of the guards were working-class people who had taken the job as the only way they could earn a living and support their families, especially during the depression. So sometimes I tried to get into a discussion about that aspect of their employment, hoping that later I would be able to suggest that even as they were sometimes forced to do terrible things that the prison system required, similarly many of the prisoners were there because they had done terrible things that society required in order for them to feed their families or provide them with other forms of security. This led to several good friendships with guards who did their best to be as decent as possible with their "fellow prisoners."

My belief in the submerged humanity of prisoners who had committed the most heinous crimes was strengthened in a Hudson County, New Jersey, jail shortly before I landed at Lewisburg's maximum security prison. I was in the jail because I had refused to pay bail during the period between my arraignment and trial. I do this as often as I can because I don't believe that the inability to raise money for bail should force people to spend weeks, months, sometimes a year or more in jail before they have even been tried. This time my wife, Elizabeth, called the judge after a week or two and explained why I had refused bail. He responded by releasing me on my own recognizance. And when he sentenced me to two years, which was less time than the court sentenced most war objectors at that time, he suggested that I spend the evening at home with my wife and voluntarily return to the federal building the next morning to meet a sheriff who would drive me to Lewisburg.

But at my arrival at the New Jersey jail, the officials had concluded that I must be "yellow," since I was refusing to defend my country militarily. Saying this to my face and to the prisoners in my assigned cell, they asked the prisoners to "take care of this unpatriotic guy." The men they said this to were in a small, overcrowded cell where the most violent prisoners were kept. Later, when I was leaving on my own recognizance, a slightly nicer guard said that he hadn't approved of where I had been put but hoped that I had learned how evil prisoners and Nazis can be and had given up my ideas that nonviolence is a practical way of combating them. Despite all this, I was clearly saved from what might have happened to me—not by my own efforts, but because this was the prison where, on my arrival, I had intervened when a Mafioso was being roughed up by a guard. Word of what had happened came rather quickly to the "worthless, evil" prisoners in the cell where I had been assigned and, step by step, several of them became my friends.

Not long after I arrived at Lewisburg, five of us conducted a long hunger strike for abolishing "the Hole" and eliminating the censorship of mail, books, and magazines. Winning the issue on censorship and feeling that the issue of the Hole had reached a fairly wide audience on the outside through prison visitors and progressive publicity, we stopped the strike on the sixty-fifth day (after a month of force feeding). The next day I was put in the "fuck-up dorm," which had a high percentage of southern military prisoners who had committed violent crimes. One of the two guards who took me there addressed the prisoners as follows: "This guy is one of those phonies who says he's too good to be in regular prison with you." This was a total lie. Unlike a few war objectors, I had always opposed special classification and treatment as a political prisoner. "He's a nigger-lover who says that you guys should eat and sleep with the niggers and use the same toilets and showers as niggers do." True. "And he's a Nazi who spits on the flag and refuses to fight for our country." And, after a pause, as if to let his words sink in, "We're leaving now so that you guys can take care of him." Just before they closed the door, the other guard spoke for the first time: "When we come back, we hope you give him to us with his head in his hands."

Here I will have to paraphrase what I said because I don't remember it word for word the way I remember what the guards had said; but this was the general line of attack, using street language and drawing on things I had learned from my earlier prison experiences: "You guys know enough not to believe those hacks. That's a lot of bullshit they're trying to shove down your throats and you know it. It's the hacks who act like Nazis, not me. You know how they treat you. I've been up there in solitary fightin' for you guys. Five of us have been up there fightin' to get rid of the goddam Hole. We're fightin' for the cons and the hacks don't like it. I know a lot of you guys have been in the Hole, so I don't have to tell you what it's like. I don't have to tell you why we've been on hunger strike demanding that they stop acting like Nazis and do away with the Hole once and for all. You want to know why they're tellin' all those lies about me? To get you and me fightin' amongst ourselves instead of stickin' together against them. Anyone who has been doin' time like you guys have won't fall for that shit. You know the score. And so do I."

I survived, though there were times, especially that night after the lights went out, when I didn't expect to. But it was more than a month before I made a request to be transferred to a cellblock, where I desperately needed the relative quiet of a cell after that noisy "fuck-up dorm." I waited that long because the one thing you can't do as a serious nonviolent activist, especially in prison, is to run away from threats or danger. If you do, the wrong reputation will follow you wherever you go or are moved.

This was only one of several times in Lewisburg when prisoners were asked to "take care of Dellinger," sometimes with the offer of parole if they did. But this was the most difficult occasion for me to handle because of my exhaustion from the long hunger strike. A few years later I wasn't surprised at something Dorothy Day, the cofounder of the Catholic Worker movement, said when she visited me and Elizabeth at our intentional pacifist community. It was the day after William Remington, a former commerce department official who was a victim of the McCarthy era, had been killed at Lewisburg. "You don't believe the official version, do you?" she asked. "That he was killed by a prisoner who was stealing his cigarettes when Remington came back to his cell and caught him?" Based on our similar prison experiences, we agreed that the officials had asked some prisoners to kill him, probably saying something like, "He's a dirty Communist, so why don't you get rid of him. If you do, we'll reward you with parole, or time off your long sentence."

Is it any wonder that in my resume I included under "Education" the following: "Three years' imprisonment at Danbury, Connecticut, Federal Correctional Institution (1940–41) and Lewisburg, Pennsylvania, Federal Penitentiary (1942–45)...."

Minoru Yasui (1916–1986)

In the panic following Pearl Harbor, anti-Japanese sentiment in the United States rose to a fever pitch. Washington's first reaction, in Public Proclamation Number 3, was to establish a curfew for all people of Japanese ethnic origin living on the West Coast. Subsequently, in February 1942, President Roosevelt signed Executive Order 9066, which authorized Secretary of War Henry Stimson to delegate to a responsible military authority the discretionary right to exclude or remove anybody from certain designated "military areas." Lieutenant General John L. DeWitt, commanding general of the Western

Defense Command and of the Fourth Army, promptly did so. All people of one-sixteenth Japanese descent or more were evacuated and removed to internment camps. Thus, not only were the Issei (those who were born in Japan) subject to incarceration in the camps but so too were the Nisei (those who were born in the United States and were American citizens). In 1943 and 1944, Japanese Americans protested the order by taking cases to the Supreme Court. The constitutionality of the order was upheld in three cases: *Hirabayashi v. United States* (1943), *Yasui v. United States* (1943), and *Korematsu v. United States* (1944). Minoru Yasui, who was born in the United States in 1916 and earned his law degree from the University of Oregon in 1939, broke the curfew law and refused to report for evacuation. He served nine months in solitary confinement and, in 1943, took his case to the Supreme Court. The Supreme Court upheld the evacuation order, and Yasui lost his case. Although wartime hysteria cost so many Japanese Americans their homes, occupations, and self-esteem, not one case of espionage or sabotage was brought against any of them.

On what grounds did Yasui fight the curfew and evacuation orders? What does the treatment of Japanese Americans indicate about the state of mind of Americans during the Second World War? Is it appropriate, in order to achieve wartime security, to suspend any of the basic civil liberties guaranteed by the Constitution?

Reflections on Executive Order 9066

The evacuation came out of Executive Order 9066. The thing that struck me immediately was that the military was ordering the civilian to do something. In my opinion, that's the way dictatorships are formed. And if I, as an American citizen stood still for this, I would be derogating the rights of all citizens. By God, I had to stand up and say, "That's wrong." I refused to report for evacuation. Sure enough, within the week, I got a telephone call from the military police saying, "We're coming to get you." I was thrown into the North Portland Livestock Pavilion where Japanese Americans had been put. In September, they started moving us into the desert camps. You were surrounded with barbed-wire fences. There were armed guards, search lights, and machine-gun nests. We wondered how long we were going to be there. What was going to happen? No one knew. By then, we had heard rumors of forced labor camps in Germany. Were they, indeed, as Westbrook Pegler and others were suggesting, going to castrate the men and ship them back to Japan? These things were in the paper constantly: Make them suffer. Make them hurt. *And you keep thinking, "What did I do?"*

SOURCE: Retrieved on 7/26/2003 from www.hrcr.org/ccr/yasui.html.

Resistance

In mid-December, 1941, I received official orders to report for active duty with the United States Army at Camp Vancouver, Washington. I held a reserve commission as a second lieutenant in the U.S. Army. The instructions ordered me to report for duty on January 19, 1942. So I went down to the Union Pacific Railroad station to purchase a ticket back to Portland, Oregon. But the ticket agent wanted to know if I were a "Jap." When I foolishly answered truthfully that I was of Japanese ancestry, he responded that he could not sell transportation to a "Jap." Despite my showing him travel orders from the U.S. Army, I could not persuade him to issue me a railroad ticket. I finally had to make an appointment to see one of the attorneys in the general counsel's office for the Union Pacific Railroad in Chicago to obtain authorization for me to buy a ticket to report for active duty with the U.S. Army. I had to point to the Fourteenth Amendment to the Constitution of the United States to persuade that lawyer that I was a citizen of the United States, on the basis of my birth certificate alone.

. . . at 8:00 P.M., March 28, 1942, after having asked Rae Shimojima, my assistant, to notify the FBI and the local Portland police, I started to walk the streets of Portland in deliberate violation of Military Proclamation No. 3. The principle involved was whether the military could single out a specific group of U.S. citizens on the basis of ancestry and require them to do something not required of other U.S. citizens. As a lawyer, I knew that unless legal protest is made at the time of injury, the doctrine of laches or indeed the statute of limitations would forever bar a remedy. . . .

So on March 28, 1942, I began to walk the streets of Portland, up and down Third Avenue until about 11:00 P.M., and I was getting tired of walking. I stopped a Portland police officer, and I showed him a copy of Military Proclamation No. 3, prohibiting persons of Japanese ancestry from being away from their homes after 8:00 P.M.; and I pulled out my birth certificate to show him that I was a person of Japanese ancestry. When I asked him to arrest me, he replied, "Run along home, sonny boy, or you'll get in trouble." So I had to go on down to the Second Avenue police station and argue myself into jail. I pulled this thing on a Saturday and didn't get bailed out until the following Monday.

. . . At the end of April 1942, military orders were posted for all residents of Japanese ancestry, aliens and nonaliens (a euphemism for citizens), calling for them to report for evacuation and processing at the North Portland Livestock Pavilion.

. . . So before the deadline to report to the North Portland Livestock Pavilion, I packed my files and my few belongings and left for Hood River. I had given the military my address and invited them to arrest me. . . . After I was home for a few days, I received a call from the military offices in Portland saying that the MPs would be coming to get me on May 12, 1942, and that they would escort me to the North Portland Livestock Pavilion. I indicated that I would cooperate but would go under coercion only. Sure enough, on May 12, 1942, a sedan with a second lieutenant, a driver, and a jeep with four MPs came to our home in Hood River at the appointed time. The lieutenant said, "Let's go," and I complied in my 1935 Chevy.

SOURCE: John Tateishi, ed. *And Justice for All* (New York: Random House, 1984). Retrieved on 7/26/2003 from www.geocities.com/Athens/8420/memories.html.

. . . At the North Portland Assembly Center I . . . remember Benny Higashi's and Don Sugai's families. Both men were married to local Chinese American women, and both had two children. The wives, LaLun Higashi and Pil Sugai, endured camp with us. Even though they themselves would have been exempt, their children would not, because they were half Japanese. The children, in each case, were two and four years old.

. . . Judge [James Alger] Fee sentenced me to one year in jail and a five-thousand dollar fine. . . . I wanted my attorneys to apply for an appeal bond so I could be free pending appeal. (They subsequently did, and it was refused.)

. . . At first the guards would not let me out long enough to take a bath or to get a haircut or shave. At the end of several months I was stinking dirty, although I tried to wash myself in the washbasin with rags. My hair was growing long and shaggy, unkempt and tangled. My facial hair was growing in all directions, untrimmed. And my nails were growing so long that they began to curl over on themselves, both on my hands and feet. I found I could chew off my fingernails, but the nails on my toes gave me trouble. It was not until after Christmas that I was given permission to take a bath and get a haircut and shave, and that seemed like such a luxury then. Thereafter, they permitted me monthly baths and monthly hair trims.

. . . I learned that during my absence the military draft had been reopened for Nisei, and further volunteers were being sought for both the 442nd Infantry Combat Team and for the Camp Savage military intelligence school in Minnesota. Because of my infantry training, I immediately volunteered for the infantry, and many months later was advised that I had been rejected.

. . . I had not seen my father since February 1942, nor my mother and younger brother since May 1942, or my younger sister since Christmas of 1939. . . . I applied for a temporary leave from Minidoka for thirty days to visit them.

My official records at the Minidoka WRA[War Relocation Authority] administration evidently indicated I was not a very desirable individual. . . . A charade of a hearing was held for me, and the result was mixed, with the civilian hearing officer recommending that temporary leave be granted and the two military officials recommending that I be kept in custody. I offered to test this matter by a habeas corpus proceeding, and the project director relented by issuing me a thirty-day temporary leave in October 1943.

. . . I remember going with Joe Grant to the FCI [Federal Correctional Institution] and meeting a young Nisei who had just turned eighteen years of age, who had refused to register and refused to conform to draft-board orders. He had been indicted, arrested, and was being held, pending trial.

We said to him, "Son, you're ruining your life. You're still a young man, and you'll have a criminal record that will hold you back for the rest of your life. Please reconsider and cooperate with your draft board."

He replied, "Why should I when the government has taken away our rights and locked us up like a bunch of criminals anyway?"

We responded, "But, you've got to fulfill your obligations to the government. When you fulfill your responsibilities, you'll be in a much stronger position to demand your rights."

To which he said, "Look, the government took my father away, and interned him someplace. My mother is alone at the Granada camp with my younger sister who is only fourteen. If the government would take care of them here in America, I'd feel like going out to fight for my country, but this country is treating us worse than shit!"

Statement upon Sentencing, 1942

Your Honor—if the Court please, I should like to say a few words. There is no intent to plead for leniency for myself or to request a mitigation of the punishment that is about to be inflicted upon me.

Despite the circumstances, I am compelled to pay tribute and give my unreserved respect to this honorable court for its clear-cut and courageous reaffirmation of the inviolability of the fundamental civil rights and liberties of an American citizen.

As an American citizen, it was for a clarification and the preservation of those rights that I undertook this case, confident that the American judiciary would zealously defend those rights, war or no war, in order to preserve the fundamental democratic doctrines of our nation and to perpetuate the eternal truths of America.

My confidence has been justified and I feel the greatest satisfaction and patriotic uplift in the decision of this honorable court, for it is full of significance for every American, be he humble or mighty.

I say that I am glad, regardless of the personal consequences to me, because I believe in the future and in the ultimate destiny of America. Ever since I was a child, I have been inculcated in the basic concepts and the traditions of those great patriots who founded our nation.

I have lived, believed, worked and aspired as an American. With due respect to this honorable court, in all good conscience, I can say that I have never, and will never, voluntarily relinquish my American citizenship.

The decision of this honorable court to the contrary notwithstanding, I am confident that I can establish in law and in fact that I am an American citizen, who is not only proud of that fact, but who is willing to defend that right.

When I attained majority, I swore allegiance to the United States of America, renouncing any and all other allegiances that I may have unknowingly owed. That solemn obligation to my native land has motivated me during the past 12 months upon three separate and distinct occasions to volunteer for active service in the United States army, wheresoever it may be fighting to preserve the American way of life.

For I would a thousand times prefer to die on a battlefront as an American soldier in defense of freedom and democracy, for the principles which I believe, rather than to live in relative comfort as an interned alien Jap.

The treacherous attack on Pearl Harbor, the bombing of Manila, the aggressor policies of the warlords of Japan are just as reprehensible to me as to any American citizen.

—————
SOURCE: Gordon B. Dodds, ed., *Varieties of Hope—An Anthology of Oregon Prose* (Corvallis: Oregon State University Press, 1993), 117–119. Retrieved on 7/26/2003 from www. minoruyasui.com/history_4.htm.

If America were invaded today, I and 70,000 other loyal American citizens of Japanese ancestry would be willing, eager, to lay down our lives in the streets, down in the gutters, to defend our homes, our country, and our liberties!

Be that as it may; I reiterate, regardless of the personal consequences, even though it entail the sacrifice of my American citizenship which I regard as sacred and more dear than life itself I pay homage and salute this honorable court and my country, the United States of America, for the gallant stand that has been taken for the preservation of the fundamental principles of democracy and freedom!

Letters from Jail to His Sister Yuka Yasui, 1942–1943

Min (to Yuka, in Denver)
Multnomah County Jail
April 5, 1942

. . . Anyway, I'm sure that the case is now in good hands. I've been re-reading "The Federalist" written by Alexander Hamilton, John Jay and James Madison in 1787–1788, and I find much which is encouraging, so far as the theories of government are concerned. And too, I'm particularly thankful for Jefferson's democratic principles and safeguards that were included in the first 10 amendments. The more I think about the fundamental issues involved, the more sure I feel that the principles advanced in my case are *RIGHT*, and the more confident I am that the Supreme Court will re-affirm my beliefs.

It seems funny that a Nihonjin should be the instrument for bringing about a supreme judicial declaration of Americanism. I guess that's only possible in America. . . .

Min (to Yuka, in Denver)
Multnomah County Jail
November 30, 1942

. . . I am glad to read Mom's concept of America. I realize all that she and Dad has [*sic*] done for our country, and particularly for Hood River. It is my proud boast that Dad is a better American than I am, and I consider myself a pretty fine American too! I know too that both Dad and Mom raised us to be good American citizens, and I felt that as an American, I should personally do something to prevent the deterioration of the fundamental principles which made America great. I felt that I was compelled to do so if I were to be a worthy son of a worthy father.

The insidious danger of creating a precedent of confining American citizens behind barbed wire fences and machine guns when they have committed no crime seemed reprehensible to me. Perhaps the analogy is far fetched, but surely as the attack on Pearl Harbor endangered our democracy, evacuation of American citizens on the basis of race is just as dangerous a threat to democracy!

SOURCE: Letters in Yuka Yasui Fujikura's private collection. Used with permission.

I have always contended, and shall continue to maintain, that if it be repugnant to the Constitution of the United States of America, then it is tyrannical, dictatorial and unreasonable to impose restrictive and discriminatory measures upon the basis of race, and moreover, it is just as shameful and disgraceful for proud and loyal American citizens to submit to such dictatorial measures without a legal reservation [?] of their rights!

I feel and I know that Caucasian Americans are no better nor worse than I, for we are all human beings. It is only the principles of liberty, democracy and justice, and the adherence to these principles that made America great, and as a loyal American who can suffer his native land to do no wrong, I must hold true to those principles.

Obviously, we are regarded with suspicion and distrust, but can we call ourselves worthy Americans if we tolerate the destruction of those eternal truths of America without an effort to preserve them?

But, all of this you know and fully appreciate. I only wish that 130,000,000 [other] Americans would too! . . .

Min (to Yuka, in Denver)
Multnomah County Jail
March 5, 1943

. . . Nope, I've been here in the Multnomah County "College for Criminals" as per usual. Suma Tsuboi was mistaken about my going to San Francisco. All of my hopes and prayers were there though! [This was in reference to a hoped-for appeal to the U.S. Ninth Circuit Court of Appeals.] Gee, I wish I could have gone to argue my case! But no such luck, I'm still sitting here like a canary in a bird cage only I can't sing.

Because my attorney went back East on another case, I'm probably going to be here for some little time yet. Aw, if I left now, the cockroaches might miss me! But, I'm still hoping for some type of conditional release, either on bail, or by parole to the relocation center. After all, I'm not going to run away anywhere! Besides, instead of sitting here like bump on a log (and twice as useless) I could be doing something worthwhile elsewhere. As for the Circuit Court decision, I'm afraid that it will be a long time before they will come to any conclusion. Probably, it will be some 3 or 4 months. But, cheer up, if I lose there, it will be about a year before the U.S. Supreme Court will get around to it. Meanwhile, I'd hate to be sitting in jail. I'd rather be packing a rifle for Uncle Sam, somewhere out in the deserts of the Sahara, just to prove to Judge Fee that, by golly, I'm a man! And not only that, an American that has a stake in America too! This case, I hope, will secure legal recognition of that fact. Yep, and it's for you too, Punkus, as well as for every American, white, yellow, or black, that these principles *must* be recognized. I think that they will be.

But, my ideas aren't very interesting. I generate them looking at the same 4 walls every day. . . . Anyway, Yuka, when you're going to school, learn well the lessons of democracy; learn them well so that you will love them too, and be prepared to defend them. After going through Pinedale, and Tule Lake, you might be inclined to think that all the idealistic principles of democracy are hooey, but that isn't so! Some of those principles in practice have been distorted by men who have not thought deeply enough, who have failed to appreciate their full significance; but those principles, I believe, are true. At least, that is what I'm trying to establish by my case.

Henry Miller (1891–1980)

Because of his sexually explicit autobiographical novels *Tropic of Cancer, Tropic of Capricorn, Sexus,* and *Quiet Days in Clichy,* Henry Miller's name has become almost synonymous with the sexual revolution. However, these few novels have created an aura of notoriety that obfuscates the true nature of Miller's contribution to American literature. While he was labeled as a writer of obscenity, Miller was an inward-looking man whose numerous essays explored such matters as art, spirituality, creativity, psychology, Buddhism, politics, and, above all, his never-ending and agonizing struggle to be true to himself and to find his own way to express that truth. Life, to Miller, in spite of its hardships, was to be lived fully and joyously each moment of the day. He spent his first 42 years trying to "find his voice," as he put it, and struggling to become a writer. In 1930 he went to Paris—the gathering place for between-the-wars American literati—because he felt that the atmosphere in America stifled creativity. After several failed attempts, he finally gave up the effort to be "literary" and wrote an autobiographical novel, *Tropic of Cancer,* which was published in Paris in 1934. In 1939, after ten years in Paris, he traveled to Corfu to visit his friend, the English writer Lawrence Durrell. While Miller was in Greece, Hitler's army invaded Poland, and the Second World War began. In December, the American embassy in Athens ordered all Americans to return to the United States because of the war. Reluctantly, Miller set sail for New York. With Pearl Harbor, the United States was brought into the war, but despite the fact that American forces were fighting against the Axis powers in the Pacific and in Europe, Miller took the unpopular stance of opposing what most Americans believed was a "just" war. "Murder the Murderer" is a lengthy letter that Miller wrote to an Austrian friend, Alfred Perles, whom he had met in Paris. It is a vitriolic, sarcastic, Milleresque diatribe on the follies of those who believe that war is a viable means to bring about peace.

Miller writes: "Nations make war upon one another on the assumption that the views of the people and those who govern them are one. The moment war is declared it is impossible to dissent. . . . Nor is there ever the remotest possibility of establishing a situation whereby those in favor of war go to war and those not in favor remain passive. The unanimity of a nation, in times of war, is brought about by coercion pure and simple." Notice the similarity of Miller's view with that of Randolph Bourne's 1918 essay "War Is the Health of the State." What authorities does Miller use to back up his argument? In what ways, in "Murder the Murderer," does Miller echo other war dissenters? In what ways does he go beyond traditional political or religious objections to war? How effective is the sarcasm he frequently employs?

———————————

Murder the Murderer, 1944

June 25, 1944.

A period of darkness has set in. The world seems determined to resolve its problems by force. No single individual can stem the tide of hate. We are in the grip of cosmic forces and each one does what he can, or must.

To each man the conflict assumes a different face. Millions of men and women will sacrifice their lives; millions more will be maimed and mutilated. The innocent will suffer with the guilty, the wise with the foolish. It is beyond control now; we are in the hands of Fate.

Useless to say now that it need not have happened. It is not for us to question what happens; it is for us to accept. But there are a thousand ways of accepting the inevitable. In the way we accept lies our ability to transform a situation. No disaster is irremediable. The whole meaning of life is contained in the word suffering. That all the world can be suffering at one time is a fact of tremendous significance. (Not quite the whole world!—the "civilized" peoples mostly.) It never has happened before. It is an opportunity which we can reject or use to advantage.

Since I am having my say, I want to reveal what I sincerely believe this opportunity may be. We, the American people, having resisted war to the very last, have now thrown ourselves into the universal conflict. Whether we admit it to ourselves or not, whether or not we have lived up to that faith which the other peoples of the world have in us, *we are the hope of the world*. That is the rock on which America was founded. Let it be our rock now!

Are we at war to extend our empire, to increase our possessions, to gain ascendancy over the other nations of this earth? I believe the great body of American people would answer NO! Like other peoples, we have been misguided. Above all, we had grown callous and indifferent. That was our crime. To-day we are ready to accept our share of suffering, along with the righteous and the unrighteous. Moreover, we are determined to endure what we have never endured before. That was evident the day war was declared.

What can we as a people do beyond anything our allies may expect of us? We can be magnanimous and far-sighted, we can be patient and full of understanding; we can be hard as steel, yet wise and full of tenderness when the time is ripe. We can be all these things because we are the favored people of the earth. Our forefathers, when first they came to this country, were hailed as gods. To our disgrace they behaved as demons. They asked for gold instead of grace. To-day their sins are visited upon us. We are paying now for the crimes committed by our ancestors. They fled their self-imposed prisons because they had a vision of Paradise. Had they acted as the gods they were mistaken for by the aborigines of this continent they could have realized the Paradise which they were seeking. But they were only men and they were weak, and because they were weak the dream of Paradise was forgotten. Dreams are hard to kill; they linger on even when the memory of them is faded. The

Source: Henry Miller, "Murder the Murderer," in *Remember to Remember* (New York: New Directions, 1947), 164–169, 191–196, 198–199, 204–216.

dream of golden opportunity still clings to the name America no matter what part of the world you may go to. It is regrettable that we, the American people, have fostered a false interpretation of that dream and thereby helped to further poison the world. We have given the impression that America was a place in which to grow rich. We have emphasized gold instead of opportunity. Out of greed we killed the goose that laid the golden egg. Yet, despite the tragic error, we all know that there *was* a golden goose. We are now at the point where we are obliged to interpret the fable intelligently.

What *was* the golden opportunity which was offered the American pilgrim? The opportunity to serve the world, the opportunity to bring about enlightenment and justice. Since the inception of this republic we had no enemies save the mother country, England. We were surrounded by friends. The only great struggle we had was an internal one. Then, in the last war, we were dragged into a world-wide conflict whose significance we only partially understood. The war over, we tried to take refuge again in our comfortable shell, unwilling to accept the responsibilities we had assumed as participants of that great conflict. We refused to sit at the Hague Tribunal and assist in the first crude attempt to establish some kind of international law and order. We refused for years to recognize the one government which had taken the lesson of the war to heart and was endeavoring to bring about a more intelligent and equitable order of human society. With the emergence of the dictators we sat by and watched one little nation after the other swallowed up and enslaved. When France fell we were full of bitterness. We cried "Shame!" though we hadn't lifted a finger to help her. We would have suffered England to undergo the same fate, but the English were made of different stuff. Until the treacherous attack by Japan, which we should have anticipated, considering all the lessons we had been given, we were undecided what course to pursue. Now suddenly we are united and, as in the last war, we are pretending that we are fighting to free the world. The newspapers are doing their best to make the American people believe this beautiful legend, knowing well that the psychology of the American people is based on a sense of utter unreality, that only when we visualize ourselves as saviours and crusaders can we kill with fury and efficiency. . . .

It is unthinkable that we shall lose. But what do we hope to win? Or better, what do we hope to win to? That is the question which the editorial gentry cleverly evade by grandiloquent phrases such as "ridding the world forever of the Nazi pestilence," and so on. Are we microbe hunters and bug exterminators? Are we merely going to preserve the *tomb* of Christ from the desecrating paw of the infidel? For two thousand years the world has been squabbling over the dead body of Christ. The Christians themselves will admit that God sent his son, a *living* Christ, to redeem the world. He didn't send us a corpse to fight over. In effect, however, that is what the Christian world has done: it has welcomed every excuse to fight in the name of Christ who came to bring peace on earth. There can be no end to this repetitious pattern until each and every one of us become as Christ, until belief and devotion transform our words into deeds and thus make of myth reality.

. . . We are all interested in what lies beyond the war. Nobody is any longer interested in war for the sake of war. But what comes after the war depends altogether on the spirit in which we wage war. We will accomplish exactly what we aim to accomplish, and no more. In this respect war is no different from peace. The fact that we are desperate instead of lethargic means nothing, if we are not clear as to what we wish to attain. To defeat Hitler and his gang is not a particularly brilliant goal to set oneself. Hitler and his gang could have been defeated without war had we possessed the intelligence, the will, and the purity to undertake the task. Wherever there is indecision, confusion, dalliance and an atmosphere of unreality, you have Hitler. Just as Judas was necessary in order for Christ to enact the drama which was ordained, so Hitler was necessary for this age in order that the world might enact the drama of unification and regeneration. Christ chose Judas to betray him; we have chosen Hitler. All the intermediary figures, the supernumeraries, so to speak, good, honest gentlemen though they be, are dwarfed by this Satanic figure which looms across the horizon. Churchill, Roosevelt, Stalin, none of these is big enough to cope with the monster alone. It is fortunate that they are not, for now it devolves upon the little men, the poor anonymous figures who make up the great mass of humanity, to answer the challenge. Christ chose twelve little men to do his work—not great world figures.

I come back to that idea which America has always inspired in the minds of other peoples, the idea that the lowest man may rise and "make his place" in the world. (It would have been better had we inspired the idea of "finding one's place" in the world.) I repeat that the behavior of the American people has brought about a distortion of that idea. We have shown in ways too numerous to specify that we have reduced the conception of freedom and service to mankind to a poverty-stricken notion of power and riches. Power and riches, not for *all* Americans—that would be bad enough!—but for the few. Our democracy has been the worst democracy that has ever been tried out. It has never had anything to do with freedom, has never been anything more than a name. . . .

Nobody can deny that we're the most philanthropic-minded people in the world. A few months ago there were eight or nine million people unemployed in this wonder-working land. Now it's down to about a million, an irreducible minimum, I believe it's called. We work fast, I'll say. And all because that half-witted Hirohito stabbed us in the back. Some say we had no right to be taken by surprise—criminal negligence they call it. Others seem pleased that it turned out so—it proved that we were angels, that we had no intention of going to war with Japan, that our fleet and our fortifications were created only to *frighten* the enemy away. It's six one way and a half dozen the other. I was always of the opinion that if you make cannon you've got to use them some time or other. I'm never surprised when a gun goes off unexpectedly. I expect the unexpected. What does surprise me is that people who believe in making cannon should be aggrieved to see them used so effectively. "In time of peace prepare for war," said the Father of this beloved country. He was a realist, just as Stalin is to-day. He didn't get himself elected a third time by promising to keep his people out of war. He was no half-wit. No sir, he was an aristocrat, a great land-holder with slaves and port and sherry in the cellar. The people were so grateful to him for making this country a democracy that they almost made him a king. About seventy years later there appeared in the State of Massachusetts, noted even then for its hypocrisy, repression and iniquity, a troublesome character who sensed that all was not well with the government of these United States. What's more, he had the courage to say so. He wrote a paper called "Civil Disobedience" which we look upon to-day as a monument to the democratic spirit. Here is a citation from this beautifully embalmed document:

"The progress from an absolute to a limited monarchy, from a limited monarchy to a democracy, is a progress towards a true respect for the individual. Even the Chinese philosopher was wise enough to regard the individual as the basis of the empire. Is a democracy, such as we know it, the last improvement possible in government? Is it not possible to take a step further towards recognizing and organizing the rights of man? There will never be a really free and enlightened State until the State comes to recognize the individual as a higher and independent power, from which all its own power and authority are derived, and treats him accordingly. I please myself with imagining a State at last which can afford to be just to all men, and to treat the individual with respect as a neighbor; which even would not think it inconsistent with its own repose if a few were to live aloof from it, not meddling with it, nor embraced by it, who fulfilled all the duties of neighbors and fellowmen. A State which bore this kind of fruit, and suffered it to drop off as fast as it ripened, would prepare the way for a still more perfect and glorious State, which also I have imagined, but not yet anywhere seen."

That was Henry David Thoreau, author of *Walden* and defender of John Brown, speaking. No doubt the only excuse we can make to-day for such a treasonable anarchistic utterance is to palm him off as a half-witted graduate of the then Transcendentalist School of Philosophy. About the only person I can think of who would have dared to defend him, in our time, had he openly expressed his desire to live a life apart from the most holy and sacrosanct State, is the recently defunct Justice of the Supreme Court, Louis D. Brandeis. In the case of Whitney versus the State of California, Brandeis, whose vote was overruled, wrote a brief in which there appeared these words:

"Those who won our independence by revolution were not cowards. They did not fear political change. They did not exalt order at the cost of liberty. To courageous, self-reliant men, with confidence in the power of free and fearless reasoning applied through the processes of popular government, no danger flowing from speech can be deemed clear and present, unless the incidence of evil apprehended is so imminent that it may befall before there is opportunity for full discussion. If there be time to expose through discussion the falsehood and fallacies, to avert the evil by the processes of education, the remedy to be applied is more speech, not enforced silence. Only an emergency can justify repression. Such must be the rule if authority is to be reconciled with freedom. Such, in my opinion, is the command of the Constitution. It is, therefore, always open to Americans to challenge a law abridging free speech and assembly by showing that there was no emergency justifying it."

Nevertheless, when the good shoe-maker and the poor fish-peddler found themselves at the bar of justice in the benighted State of Massachusetts some few years ago, they were unable to get a fair, honest hearing. Despite all the noble words handed down by the upstanding members of the judiciary, and they are the wordiest people on God's green earth, Sacco and Vanzetti were foully murdered. But just before he went to the chair Vanzetti gave birth to a few lines which are destined to be as immortal as any of Lincoln's or Jefferson's . . .

"If it had not been for these thing, I might have live out my life talking at street corners to scorning men. I might have died, unmarked, unknown, a failure. Now we are not a failure. This is our career and our triumph. Never in our full life could we hope to do such work for tolerance, for justice, for man's understanding of man as now we do by accident. Our words—our lives—our pains—nothing! The taking of our lives—lives of a good shoemaker and a poor fish-peddler—all. That last moment belongs to us—that agony is our triumph."

A few days ago, moved by the President's declaration of war the newspapers gave some space to the remarks made by John Haynes Holmes, Minister of the Community Church, N. Y., in tendering his resignation. He had just finished a sermon, it seems, on the 150th anniversary of the Bill of Rights. Mr. Holmes is quoted as saying that "neither as clergyman nor as citizen would he participate in the war," adding however that "neither would he oppose, obstruct or interfere with officials, soldiers or citizens in the performance of what they regard as their patriotic duty."

Then he threw this bombshell:

"I will be loyal and obedient to my government, and loyal and obedient to my God; and when these loyalties conflict, I will choose, as did the Apostles, to 'obey God rather than men.'"

I wait to see if Mr. Holmes will be condemned to prison. In the last world war there were three great figures who, because they openly announced their opposition to war, suffered dire persecution. They were Romain Rolland, Bertrand Russell and Eugene V. Debs. Unimpeachable characters, all three. I'm going to give you Debs' speech on being condemned to prison, but before I do so I want to mention the Very Reverend Dean Inge's statement about a German theologian named Harnack. "War," writes the gloomy Dean, "is a very horrible thing, an unmixed evil, a reversion to barbarism no less than cannibalism, human sacrifice and judicial torture. Most of us think that we were obliged to resist German agression, which threatens to extinguish liberty, and with liberty all that makes life worth living, over the whole continent of Europe. But no good can ever come out of war. It is a flat negation of Christianity. Even Harnack, a Prussian and the most learned theologian in Europe, said that it is futile to deny that Christ condemned war absolutely." He adds that the Quakers believe they are the only consistent Christians. And what is the history of the Quaker movement? According to recent authority on the subject, the Quaker movement was met with terrific persecution, first from mob violence and later from organized legal procedure. George Fox himself endured eight imprisonments, and more than fifteen thousand Quakers were imprisoned in England before the period of toleration, of whom three hundred and sixty-six died under their sufferings. Four Quakers were hanged on Boston Common and a great number in the American Colonies endured beatings and mutilation.

To-day the Quakers are exempt from military service, in these United States. But what a battle! A man who is not a Quaker, like Eugene V. Debs for example, gets it in the neck. Yet no Quaker could have made a more simple, honest, dignified statement of his views than did Eugene V. Debs. Here are his beautiful, moving words:

"Gentleman of the Jury, I am accused of having obstructed the war. I admit it. Gentlemen, I abhor war. I would oppose the war if I stood alone. When I think of a cold, glittering steel bayonet being plunged in the white, quivering flesh of a human being, I recoil with horror.

"Men talk about holy wars. There are none. War is the trade of unholy savages and barbarians. . . .

"Gentlemen of the Jury, I am accused of being unpatriotic. I object to that accusation. It is not true. I believe in patriotism. I have never uttered a word against the flag. I love the flag as a symbol of freedom. . . .

"I believe, however, in a wider patriotism. Thomas Paine said, 'My country is the world. To do good is my religion.' That is the sort of patriotism I believe in. I am an Internationalist. I believe that nations have been pitted against nations long enough in hatred, in strife, in warfare. I believe there ought to be a bond of unity between all of these nations. I believe that the human race consists of one great family. I love the people of this country, but I don't hate a human being because he happens to be born in some other country. Why should I? Like myself, he is the image of his Creator. I would infinitely rather serve him and love him than to hate him and kill him. . . .

"Yes, I am opposed to killing him. I am opposed to war. I am perfectly willing on that account to be branded as a traitor. And if it is a crime under the American law to be opposed to human bloodshed, I am perfectly willing to be branded as a criminal and to end my days in a prison cell. . . .

"And now, Gentlemen of the Jury, I am prepared for the sentence. I will accept your verdict. What you will do to me does not matter much. Years ago I recognized my kinship with all living beings, and I made up my mind that I was not one whit better than the meanest of earth. I said then, and I say now, that while there is a lower class, I am in it; while there is a criminal element, I am of it; while there is a soul in prison, I am not free."

. . . War now means just as it did in the past, "blood, sweat and tears"—oodles of it. Not blood, sweat and tears for those who launch it, but for those who have to go through with it. And that means practically everybody, except, as I said before, the favored few who direct the show. The latter are just as eager to give their lives as the little fellows, don't make any mistake about that. Only, because of the peculiar set-up involved in these fracases, they are somehow never privileged to enjoy this supreme sacrifice. They must be protected in order that the others can be most efficiently sacrificed. You can understand what anguish this causes the political and military leaders of any war. (Yet few of them ever pine away because of it. On the contrary, they seem to grow tough as steel.) However, if it were possible to take them by surprise, assure them that nothing they said would be held against them, it's just possible you'd discover that they were fed up with it too. A moment later, to be sure, they would be ready to deny such weak sentiments. "What would the people think?" they'd say. Always that to fall back on. *The people!* It was the people who wanted the war. Of course. Yes, when they're stabbed in the back the people may cry for war, *but*—how does it happen that they get stabbed in the back, and at just the right moment? And so, right or wrong, willing or unwilling, "the war must be fought to a just and victorious conclusion!" From time immemorial every leader has proclaimed that high and mighty truth. That's why the future is always so full of death. Right or wrong, the war must be continued, always. No looking back. No looking forward. *Head down and charge!* That's the order of the day. Victory? Just around the corner. And if not victory, death. Death, death, death. Always death. Or, if you're lucky, your old job back in the mines. The future? It never begins. You had your future yesterday, don't you remember? There is only the present, and the present is never pleasant. Only the future is bright. But then, the future never takes place. The future always recedes, that's the law. When the original Fascists have been vanquished, or exterminated, we'll all be Fascists—that's what the future, if there is to be any future, promises. And that means more death, more blood, sweat and tears, more Churchills, more Roosevelts, more Hitlers, more Stalins. . . .

With the conclusion of this war it is not even probable that we shall see the dissolution of national boundaries. To eliminate race prejudice no one can say how many more wars it will require. There are thousands of problems for which men will find no solution but war. No system of government now in vogue offers the slightest hope of a future free of war. The remedy for dissent is still, as it was in the past, subjugation or extirpation. The government has never existed which recognizes the freedom and equality of all men. As for freedom of thought, freedom to express one's ideas—not to speak of living them out—where is the government which ever permitted this? Conformity is the rule, and conformity will be the rule as long as men believe in governing one another.

Men of good-will need no government to regulate their affairs. In every age there is a very small minority which lives without thought of, or desire for, government. These men never brought about a war. So long as civilization lasts it is quite possible that this minority will never be substantially increased. Such men are not the products of our religious organizations or our educational systems; they live outside the cultural pattern of the times. The most we can say, in explanation of their appearance and existence, is that they are evolved beings. And here we must needs touch on the drawback to all schemes, Utopian or otherwise, for the improvement of human society: the failure inherent in all of them to recognize that the human race does not evolve at the same speed nor with the same rhythm. Where there is dream and wish fulfillment merely—and what else can there be if one focuses on society instead of the individual?—there is confusion and disillusionment. Even with redhot bayonets up their rear, men cannot be prodded all at the same time into Paradise. It is this fact, of course, which the so-called realists, who are always defeatists, seize upon with grim relish in order to excuse and perpetuate the business of murder. With each war they pretend that they are preserving society from a dire fate, or that they are protecting the weak and the helpless. The men of wisdom, who are really the men of good-will, and who are found in every stratum of society and not in any particular class, never make such pretences. They are often accused of being aloof, remote, out of touch with the world. Yet it is to them that all men turn for comfort and guidance in their hour of need. For, even the clod seems to sense that genuine disinterestedness is a source of strength.

If any particular set of men were destined to rule the world it would seem logical that it should be ruled by the men of wisdom. But that is not the case, and there is good reason for it. No one man, no set of men, is capable of ruling the world. The world is ruled by its own inner, mysterious laws. It evolves according to a logic which defies our man-made logic. The higher the type of man, moreover, the less inclined he feels to rule others; he lives in harmony with the world despite the fact that he is in total disagreement with the vast majority, as well as with the leaders of the world. Were there good reason to kill, he could find a thousand justifications to the ordinary man's one. The principal reason, however, for his failure to become embroiled in world conflicts is his absence of fear. Accustomed as he is to live habitually in the world of ideas, he is not frightened when he learns that his neighbor thinks differently from him. Indeed, he might really become alarmed if he found that his neighbors were in agreement with him. The average man, on the contrary, is more frightened of alien ideas than of cold steel or flame throwers. He has spent most of his empty life getting adjusted to the few simple ideas which were thrust on him by his elders or superiors. Anything which menaces this precarious adjustment, which he calls his liberty, throws him into a panic. Let an alien idea become active, and the transition from fear to hate proceeds like clock-work. Trot out the word "enemy," and the whole bloody race behaves as if it had the blind staggers. The nit-wits who never showed the least ability to govern themselves suddenly get the idea that their last mission on earth is to teach the enemy good government. It makes no difference whether this nit-wit be a Communist, Fascist, or Democrat: the reaction is always the same. Just tell him that the other fellow is threatening his liberty, and he reaches for his gun—*automatically*.

And what is the little bundle of ideas around which this precious notion of liberty is formed? Private property, the sanctity of the home, the church he belongs to, the preservation of the political party, or the system, which gives him the privilege of being a drudge all his life. If he could but take one sweeping view of the planet, see what different things the same words mean everywhere, see how all men, including the primitives, believe that whatever they believe is right and just, and of course supremely intelligent, would he be so quick to reach for the sword or the gun? Yes, he would, because he has been educated to understand with his head but not with the rest of his being. As a civilized creature, a man can study and know the ways and customs of a thousand different peoples, yet insist on defending the ways of his own, even though he knows them to be stupid, inadequate or wrong. He will describe with irony and subtle discrimination the reasons why other peoples make war, but he will go to war himself when the time comes, even though he does not believe in killing. He will kill rather than be humiliated by his own people.

In how many wars have people killed who had no desire to kill? Many who killed one another had more in common than with their own compatriots. Were men to seek their real enemies they would have only to turn round and examine the ranks behind them. If men were to realize who their true enemies were, what a scrimmage would ensue! But again, one of the disadvantages of living under civilized rule is that only those may be considered as enemies, and therefore killed or enslaved, whom the governments designate as such. To kill your commanding officer, for example, even though he be the bitterest enemy you have, is strictly taboo. So it goes . . . scholars killing scholars, poets killing poets, workers killing workers, teachers killing teachers, and no one killing the munitions makers, the politicians, the priests, the military idiots or any of the other criminals who sanction war and egg one on to kill one another off.

Just to take one element, the munitions makers, for example: who could be more international-minded than they? Come war and they will sell to any side that has the money to buy. Strictly neutral, these birds, until they see which way the wind blows. No amount of taxation impoverishes them; the longer the war lasts, the more the dead pile up, the fatter they grow. Imagine the colossal absurdity of supporting a body of men whose mission in life it is to supply us with the means of self-destruction. (Whereas it is a crime to attempt to take one's own life by one's own means, no matter how unbearable life becomes!) Nobody considers the munitions maker—not even the Communist, mind you—as an enemy. Yet he is the greatest enemy man has. He sits like a vulture and waits and prays for the day to come when we shall lose our reason and beg him to furnish us with his most expensive lethal products. Instead of being looked upon as a leper he is given a place of honor in human society; often he is knighted for his indubitably dubious services. On the other hand, Monsieur le Paris[the executioner], who really performs a service for society, albeit a most disagreeable one, is shunned like a pariah. Strange paradox. If there is any logic to it it is thus: the man who by our own sanction justly removes a murderer from the ranks of society is a worthless wretch, whereas the man who provides the means of killing en masse, for no matter what reason good or bad, deserves a place of honor in our midst. Corollary logic: murder on a wholesale scale is always justifiable, as well as profitable and honorable, but ordinary murder, whether for passion or greed, is so disgraceful that even the man whose duty it is to make way with the culprit appears to us as tainted.

And what of all the plans fond parents make for their children's sake? Why bother to make plans when we know for a certainty that in each generation there will be one or more wars? Why not plan to make no plans at all, to just vegetate until the bugle calls? What a waste of time, money and effort to prepare your son for the ministry or the law, or any other pursuit, when you know that the army or navy will get him, and if not the army or navy, then the marines. Why think of training your boy to go into business when the only important business of every new generation is to make war? Talk about common sense . . . what sense is there in pretending that one will engage in peaceful pursuits when the only pursuit we ever enter whole-heartedly, and with vim and vigor, is the pursuit of war? Why not train your son from the beginning to be a killer, an expert killer? Why delude yourself and him too? Sooner or later your boy must learn to kill; the quicker he learns the less pain and disillusionment he will suffer. Don't teach him how to live, teach him how to die! Prepare him not for the pleasures of this world, for the chances are he will never taste them; prepare him for the pleasures of the afterworld. If you find that he is hypersensitive, kill him while he is still young. Better to kill him with your own hands than to let him die at the hands of a ruthless enemy. Kill off all the males, if possible, and let only the females survive. And if the females begin warring with one another, kill them off at birth too. In any case, believe no one who promises you peace and prosperity unless all the munitions makers have been killed off and the machines they employ destroyed.

If the idea that your son must become a killer as well as a provider is abhorrent to you, if you believe that death-dealing weapons should not continue to be manufactured, even if never used, then make a new world in which killing will be unnecessary. Concentrate all your energies upon that, and that alone. If you had a home which you were fond of, and it were suddenly invaded by rats, would you not set everything aside to eliminate the pest? War is the greatest plague that civilized man has had to contend with. And what has he done in all these thousands of years to grapple with the problem? Nothing, really. With the passage of time he has devoted increasing effort, ingenuity and money towards aggrandizing the horrors of war, as though pretending to himself that if war became too horrible it might cease of itself. The greatest nations have ruined themselves in preparing for and making war. Nevertheless the whole civilized world deludes itself into believing (by what amazing self-hypnosis!) that men are becoming better, more humane, more intelligent, more considerate of one another. The truth is that the farther along the path of civilization we go the more diabolical men seem to become. The torture inflicted upon one another by savages is nothing compared to the torture which civilized beings inflict upon one another. (This is true even in times of peace.) Add to this, that in taking over the so-called inferior peoples of the earth, in adapting them to our ways, the price we demand of them is that they become good auxiliary fighters. When there is a particularly dirty job of butchering to be done, we throw in the colonial troops. Progress! Progress!

Moreover, and above all, and to add to the illogical, the inconsistent and the paradoxical—does any serious-minded person believe for one moment that a victorious China, Russia, America, England will not become more militant, more ready and prepared for war, more suited to find fresh problems to quarrel over? Germany and Japan *may* be put out of harm's way. Agreed. But what then? Are they the only enemies man will ever have or could have? Since when have Big Powers agreed with one another, or laid down their arms and become as lambs? Since when have the Big Powers treated Little Powers with equal tact and consideration? And what of the Little Powers, when we have liberated them by our victorious but ruinous campaigns? Will they be grateful and ready to fall in line with our way of life when their people return to the desolate, ruined lands which we turned into a stupendous proving ground? Will they perhaps differ with us as to how life and liberty is to be maintained in the future?

Who will rule the coming world? The strong ones. And who are the strong? America, Russia, England, China. . . .

The great question, to be sure, which will come up as soon as the war ends, is: who will buy whose goods and how? As for the debt problem, that is easily solved. The people will pay off the debts. The people always pay. Though the people never start a war, nor even a revolution, the government somehow always convinces the people that they must pay for these adventures, both before and after. A war is fought for the benefit of the people. By the time the war is over, however, there are no benefits, just debts, death and desolation. All of which has to be paid for.

This time the peoples who make up the victorious nations won't mind the cost because they will have the Four Freedoms[freedom of speech, freedom of worship, freedom from want, freedom from fear]. They will also have all sorts of new machines, new labor-saving devices, which will make work a pleasure. (And the harder they work the faster the debts will be paid off; the more ready they will be, too, for the next war.)

Yes, there will be all sorts of new inventions, which, if they are not used destructively, will bring untold bliss. There will be, among other things, new airplanes capable of taking us back and forth to China in twenty-four hours—and for a song! Week-ends the workers of the world will be flying around the globe greeting their fellow-workers in Java, Borneo, Mozambique, Saskatchewan, Tierra del Fuego and such places. No need to go to Coney Island any more, or Deauville, or Brighton—there will be far more interesting places at which to spend the week-end. There will be television, too, don't forget. If you don't care to fly around the world in your spare time you can sit quietly by the hearth and watch the Eskimos climbing up and down the slippery icebergs, or look at the primitive peoples in the jungle busy gathering rice, ivory, coffee, tea, rubber, chicle and other useful commodities for our delectation. Every one will be working blissfully, even the Chinese coolies. For, by that time the vast and all-powerful Chiang Kai-shek dynasty will be operating with the smoothness of a highpowered dynamo. The opium traffic will be wiped out, and the heretofore ignorant coolies will be able to understand and appreciate American movies, which are an excellent substitute for opium. We will probably make special Grade D pictures for them at a figure so absurd that even the lowest coolie will be able to afford the price of admission. We will have Grade K or J pictures for "our little brown brothers" too. We will make chewing gum in greater quantities, and Eskimo pies, and malted milk shakes, to say nothing of can openers and other gadgets, so that the little people everywhere may enjoy some of the luxuries of our economic millennium.

The thing to guard against, however, is that the little peoples of the world should not be infected with Communism. Russia will have to be content to communize Siberia, Mongolia, and possibly Japan. But not China! And not the Malay archipelago, nor Africa, nor South America. South America will be somewhat of a problem, especially as miscegenation assumes increasing proportions. It won't do for the peoples of North America, "the melting pot," to begin intermarrying with the black, brown and yellow races. Marrying red-skins is quite another matter; the Indian, it seems, is a hundred percent American, and we don't mind any more if they have a touch of color. But don't let any one think, especially south of the Mason-Dixon line, that the Four Freedoms means freedom for blacks and whites to intermarry! That belongs to the fifth or sixth freedom, and will probably demand another war.

With a plethora of new labor-saving devices flooding the market there will no longer be any question of who is to do the dirty work of the world. *The machine will do it!* No one will need to soil his hands. The machines will work with such efficiency, in fact, that there may be danger of the workers growing bored. Unless the master minds introduce new forms of creative activity. It is quite possible that in the next few hundred years we shall see everybody turning artist. An hour or two at the machine each day, and the rest of the day for art! Perhaps that will be the new order in the world to come. How glorious! *The joy of creation:* something man has never known before, at least not the civilized races. Suddenly, thanks to the ubiquity and the domination of the machine, we will become again as the primitives, only wiser, happier, conscious at last of our blessedness. Everybody dancing, singing, painting, carying, fiddling, drumming, strumming . . . so marvelous! All due to the machine. How simple!

Finally, when every one has become a genius, when genius becomes the norm, there will be no room for envy or rivalry. Art will be truly universal. There will be no need for critics or interpreters; the dealers and middle men will perish, and with them the publishers and editors, the lawyers, the bookkeepers, the politicians, perhaps even the police. Every one will have the kind of home he chooses to live in, and with it a frigidaire, a radio, a telephone, a vacuum cleaner, a washing machine, an automobile, an airplane, a parachute, *and*—a full set of Dr. Cowen's light-weight platinum teeth. The cripples will all have the most wonderful, the most extraordinary, light-weight artificial limbs, which will enable them to run, skip, dance, jump or walk with perfect ease. The insane will have better lunatic asylums, and more humane, more intelligent keepers. The prisons will be more spacious, more sanitary, more comfortable in every way. There will be hospitals in abundance, on every street, and ambulances fitted up like Pullmans. There will be such a variety of pain removers that no one need ever suffer any more, not even the throes of death. Add to this, that when all the world learns English, which will happen inevitably, there won't be the least possibility of a misunderstanding any more. One language, one flag, one way of life. The machine doing all the dirty work, the master minds doing all the thinking: an Entente Cordiale with a vengeance.

That's how it looks for the next five hundred years or so. *Or doesn't it?* Anyway, that's how it *could* look, you must admit. And what's to hinder? Well, we don't know yet, but undoubtedly there will arise some idiot, some fanatic, who will have a better idea to foist upon us. And that will cause trouble. Trouble always starts with "a better idea." It's too soon to predict the nature of the monkey wrench which will wreck the Utopian machine we have just described, but that there will be such a joy-killer we have no doubt. It's in the cards.

So, just to play safe, hold on to your battle-ships and battle wagons, your tanks, your flame-throwers, your bombing machines and everything super-duper in the way of destructive devices—we may have need for them again. One day, out of a clear sky—always a clear sky, mind you!—some fanatic will make an issue of some unforeseeable little incident, magnify it to the proportions of a calamity, and then a fresh catastrophe will be at our door. But if we are armed to the teeth, if we are better prepared than we were this last time, perhaps we shall get it over with more quickly. We must never relinquish the Four Freedoms, remember that! If possible, we must pave the way for a fifth and sixth freedom. Because, the more freedoms we pile up, the nearer we will be to freedom in the abstract.

Each new freedom, to be sure, will entail a few million deaths, as well as the destruction of our principal cities. But, if we achieve ten or twelve freedoms, we won't mind how many millions of lives are sacrificed, nor will we care how many cities are destroyed. After all, we can always make babies, and we can always build new cities—better babies, better cities. If we were able to discover a way to homogenize and irradiate cow's milk we surely will find the way to homogenize and irradiate the minds of our children. If we have to destroy everything now standing, including the Vatican, it will be worth it. What we want is a world in which war will be unthinkable. And, by God, if we have to wipe out the human race in order to achieve it, we will. *Mieux vaut revenir en fantôme que jamais,* as the French say.

So, until that blessed day looms upon the horizon, do please go on murdering one another. Murder as you have never murdered before. Murder the murderers, murder murder, but murder! murder! murder! Murder for God and country! Murder for peace! Murder for sweet murder's sake! Don't stop murdering ever! Murder! Murder! Murder! Murder your mother! Murder your brother! Murder the animals of the field, murder the insects, the birds, the flowers, the grass! Murder the microbes! Murder the molecule and the atom! Murder the electron! Murder the stars, and the sun and moon, if you can get at them! Murder everything off, so that we shall have at last a bright, pure, clean world in which to live in peace, bliss and security until the end of time!

WEB RESOURCES FOR PART THREE

SITES FEATURING A NUMBER OF THE DISSENTERS IN PART THREE:

Joe Hill
www.pbs.org/joehill/

Robert M. LaFollette
www.library.wisc.edu/etext/WIReader/WER0661.html

Eugene V. Debs
www.eugenevdebs.com

Randolph Bourne
www.bigeye.com/rbourne.htm
http://randolphbourne.org/

A. Philip Randolph
www.apri.org

Marcus Garvey
www.africawithin.com/garvey/garvey.htm

Margaret Sanger
www.MSU.edu/course/mc/112/1920s/Sanger/
www.nyu.edu/projects/sanger/AboutMS.htm

H. L. Mencken
www.io.com/~gibbonsb/mencken.html

Langston Hughes
www.poets.org/poets/poets.cfm?45442B7C000C0E01

Father Charles Coughlin
www.ssa.gov/history/cough.html
www.spartacus.schoolnet.co.uk/USAcoughlinE.htm

Huey Long
www.sec.state.la.us/60.htm

Emma Goldman
http://sunsite.berkeley.edu/Goldman/

Woody Guthrie
http://fortunecity.com/tinpan/parton/2/guthrie.html

World War Two Pacifism
www.pbs.org/itvs/thegoodwar/ww2pacifists.html

Japanese Americans Resisting Internment
www.geocities.com/Athens/8420/main.html

Henry Miller
www.henrymiller.org

OTHER DISSENTING VOICES OF THE TIME:

Elizabeth Gurley Flynn
For biographical information on union organizer Elizabeth Gurley Flynn, see:

www.pbs.org/joehill/faces/flynn.html

William Haywood
For information on the leader of the I.W.W., see:

http://members.tripod.com/~RedRobin2/index-46.html
www.pbs.org/joehill/faces/bill_haywood.html

The Industrial Workers of the World
These two sites have information on the "Wobblies."

www.iww.org/
http://vision-nary.com/spwa/iww.html

Alice Paul
For information on suffragist Alice Paul and the fight for the nineteenth amendment, see:

http://womenshistory.about.com/library/bio/blbio_paul_alice.htm
www.moondance.org/1998/winter98/nonfiction/alice.html

Amy Jacques Garvey
Marcus Garvey's wife, Amy, was also a significant Black Nationalist.

http://5 × 5media.com/bhp/pages/agarvey.shtml

Mary Church Terrell
For information on this important NAACP activist, see:

http://womenshistory.about.com/cs/terrell/

Mary McLeod Bethune

For information on the founder of the National Council of Negro Women, see:

www.floridamemory.com/OnlineClassroom/MaryBethune/
http://womenshistory.about.com/cs/bethune/

Highlander Folk School

The Highlander Folk School was a significant and influential training school for union and civil rights activists.

http://hrec.org/a-history.asp

CPUSA

The Communist Party of the USA was very active during the 1930s. They were especially vocal in matters relating to unions and racism. For general information on the Communist Party and also its involvement in the Scottsboro Boys case, see:

www.cpusa.org/article/frontpage/1
www.courttv.com/archive/greatesttrials/scottsboro/trials.html
www.pbs.org/wnet/jimcrow/stories_org_communist.html

Vito Marcantonio

For information on Congressman Vito Marcantonio, member of the American Labor Party, see these Web sites. The second Web site contains the FBI files (released under the Freedom of Information Act) when Marcantonio was being investigated for supposed Communist ties.

http://users.rcn.com/redpost/life.html
http://foia.fbi.gov/vitomarc.htm

PART FOUR

The Affluent Society, 1945–1966

Beat poet and social and political critic Allen Ginsberg championed civil rights, criticized the "split-level American dream," demonstrated against the Vietnam War, nuclear proliferation, and President Reagan's Latin American policy, and protested against a society that sought to marginalize free spirits. "Are you going to let your emotional life," he asked drolly in his poem "America", "be run by Time *magazine?"*

Introduction: The Crack in the Picture Window

As GIs came back from Europe and the Pacific to the euphoric welcome of an exultant nation, there was already a sense that "returning home" would be anything but normal. With the defeat of Germany and Japan, the division of Europe, and the dawn of the Atomic Age, the world had irrevocably changed. Uncertainty was in the air. The Soviet Union, its massive armies occupying Eastern Europe, loomed as a menace.

Even during the war, much of President Roosevelt (FDR) and Prime Minister Churchill's military strategy and diplomatic policy was determined by their recognition that the war would result in the emergence of the United States and the Soviet Union as the two major super powers. Although he did not fully trust Stalin, at Tehran and again at Yalta FDR was convinced he could work out an adequate understanding with the Soviet leader. However, Roosevelt's successor, Harry Truman, did not trust Stalin at all and was adamant about holding the line against what was perceived as Soviet imperialism. Stalin's actions fed these suspicions. Not only were the Soviets in control of Eastern Europe but also Stalin presented an ultimatum to Turkey and attempted to carve a sphere of influence in Iran. In 1946, Churchill gave his famous "iron curtain" speech, which seemed to draw the line in the sand, dividing West from East. And so, less than a year after the war's end, the cold war was a reality.

Historians have debated at length the question "who started the cold war?" Some have argued that it was the result of Soviet expansion and U.S. resistance to that expansion. Others have contended that it was the U.S. wish to expand capitalism and control markets and raw materials around the world that was the cause. Still others have claimed that the cold war was simply a result of misunderstanding on the part of the two great powers: If only the United States had realized that the Soviet grip on Eastern Europe had less to do with imperialism and expansion and was more a matter of Russia's attempt to create a secure buffer zone on its western flank to guard against the possibility of yet another German invasion. (Millions of people in the Soviet Union had experienced two German invasions, and millions had died as a result—approximately 27 million in World War II alone!) However one interprets its origins, the cold war was the determining factor presiding over international relations for the next 46 years.

Because it was not possible to unseat the Soviets from the positions they already occupied, Truman's response was the policy of "containment." Communism must not be allowed to spread; it must be contained. After 1947, the Marshall Plan, channeling billions of dollars into the rebuilding of Europe, became one of the more successful devices for containing communism. In 1948, the United States set the wheels in motion to unify the three allied occupied sectors of Germany into the Federal Republic of Germany (which came into being in 1949). In response, the Soviets initiated the Berlin blockade to force the allies out of West Berlin. The Americans and British reacted with the Berlin airlift.

In 1949, the North Atlantic Treaty Organization (NATO) was founded to defend Western Europe from Soviet aggression. Even earlier, the Soviet Union created its own bloc through the system of separate military-political alliances with Eastern European countries. (Later, in 1955, the Soviets initiated the Warsaw Pact, uniting the Soviet Union with East Germany, Hungary, Czechoslovakia, Poland, Romania, and Bulgaria in a defense pact against capitalist aggression.) Also in 1949, the Soviets successfully tested their first atomic bomb, and in October the Chinese communist revolution became a victorious reality. The North Korean invasion of South Korea followed closely in June 1950, bringing a wave of anxiety across the United States. Just five years after having won the biggest war in history, how could we suddenly be living in such a perilous, uncertain world, in which our mortal enemies seemed to be building in strength? Fear of Soviet expansion abroad was accompanied by an equally deep fear of communism at home. The Alger Hiss case, which brought national attention to a young, previously unknown congressman from California—Richard Nixon—and the trial of the Communist Party in 1948–1949 was part of the spy mania that beset the nation after the war. The House Committee on Un-American Activities (HUAC) held scores of hearings in an effort to unmask Americans working to spread communist propaganda within the United States. Because Hollywood had a powerful influence on American attitudes, HUAC concentrated much of its efforts on the "Hollywood Ten" and others in the entertainment industry. Unions and other "left-wing" organizations were also targeted. In 1950, Senator Joseph McCarthy, proclaiming there were 205 card-carrying members of the Communist Party employed by the State Department, began his infamous witch hunt that would last for the next four years. This Red Scare reached such proportions that it stifled legitimate political discourse and debate, even within the Capitol. Senators and congressmen were afraid to voice criticism of American policy, lest they be labeled "soft on communism" or "pinko." As those investigated by HUAC and McCarthy quickly discovered, such allegations destroyed reputations and careers. There were many, however, who did take a stand against the hysteria. Senator Margaret Chase Smith of Maine issued a "declaration of conscience" to warn about the destruction of civil liberties. Even though it got them blacklisted, Paul Robeson, Pete Seeger, John Howard Lawson, and others being investigated stood up for the Bill of Rights and condemned the committee itself for being un-American.

With the American and Soviet development of the hydrogen bomb (a thousand times more powerful than the atomic bomb dropped on Hiroshima), the nuclear arms race took a more alarming, more terrifying turn. Fears rose that a simple miscalculation, a failure of the United States and Soviet Union to communicate, could lead to Armageddon—the destruction of the world. The fact that the Eisenhower administration was relying more on the development of nuclear weapons than on stockpiling conventional weapons made the situation more unsettling. Secretary of State John Foster Dulles's diplomatic strategy was "brinkmanship." When negotiating with the Soviets over a crisis, let them know that if a compromise could not be reached, we would be prepared to launch an attack. The policy at the negotiating table was therefore to force the issue to the brink of catastrophe and then wait for someone to pull back. In this way, it seemed, every confrontation could lead to the end of the world. Every school in America began instituting regular air raid drills (along with the customary fire drills). National air raid drills were also introduced, with members of Congress and even the president participating. Underground areas in every city were designated as fallout shelters. Many citizens built their own private fallout shelters in backyards or basements and stockpiled water, canned food, and weapons so that, if the worst happened, they could fend off those who would try to seize their shelter. Anxiety was on the rise.

Cold war reality, along with anticommunist hysteria, was one fundamental development that shaped 1950s America. The other was the booming economy. After 15 years of depression and war, Americans were, at first, nervous that the wartime economy would collapse and the nation would sink once again into depression. Indeed, strikes and labor unrest for the first three years after the war were ominous warnings that a recession could ensue. However, the return of GIs eager to start families (leading to the baby boom), the burgeoning housing industry (to accommodate growing families), the production of consumer goods (especially automobiles), and the nuclear arms race all led to a soaring economy, creating such a sense of progress and affluence that it became a widely accepted belief that the American dream was within the reach of every citizen. With an attitude bordering on arrogance, Americans were convinced that the United States was the greatest country on earth. Part of this patriotic pride, of course, was in reaction to the Soviet threat. Patriotic Americans, viewing the two sides through somewhat distorted lenses, compared the free, democratic United States with the atheistic, totalitarian Soviet Union and saw obvious, unacceptable differences. Anticommunist attitudes combined with the postwar economic miracle to encourage conformity. The cultural mantra became: Everyone should be prosperous, everyone should have a good job, everyone should have a nice house in the suburbs with a nice picture window, everyone should value the American way of life, and everyone should oppose communism. Television, the new technological innovation that burst on the scene in the 1950s, underscored and enabled this ideology. Every night, people were glued to their television sets watching *Gunsmoke, Have Gun Will Travel,* and *The Rifleman* extolling the virtues of the rugged individuals who made America great. Or they were watching *Leave It to Beaver, The Donna Reed Show, Father Knows Best,* or *Ozzie and Harriet* extolling the virtues of white, middle-class, male-dominated America. The message was clear. This is the way it ought to be for every American.

But, as writer John Keats observed, there was a "crack in the picture window" of suburbia. Not everyone was happy with the American dream. Not everyone, indeed, was able to participate in that dream. Vance Packard passed judgment on the advertising industry and the urge so many Americans had to achieve status in his widely read books *The Hidden Persuaders* and *The Status Seekers.* Sociologists David Riesman, in *The Lonely Crowd,* and William Whyte, in *The Organization Man,* critically analyzed the conformity that seemed so attractive to so many people. Americans, Whyte maintained, were no longer concerned with standing out, thinking for themselves, and being innovative; rather, they were more inclined to "fit in" to become part of the corporate team. Riesman argued that Americans were no longer "inner-directed" individuals, guided by inner principles and morality, but were becoming "other directed," more concerned with what others thought of them and with pleasing others than with being faithful to their own principles.

To be sure, there were many who did not conform to conventional standards. In art, there was the abstract expressionism of Jackson Pollock, Robert Motherwell, and Mark Rothko that mystified and bewildered critics. In music, there was bebop, an unwaveringly individualistic, improvisational style of jazz performed by Charlie Parker,

Thelonious Monk, Dizzy Gillespie, and others. In literature, J. D. Salinger's *Catcher in the Rye* criticized the shallowness and phoniness of American society, and Arthur Miller's *The Crucible* compared the McCarthy hearings to the Salem witchcraft trials. Thus in some ways it can be argued that the conformity of the 1950s was not so widespread and deeply ingrained as some historians and sociologists have maintained—otherwise, how does one explain the rebellion of the 1960s? The rise of the Beat Movement and the sudden popularity of rock and roll are two developments often viewed as "seeds of the sixties." William Burroughs, Allen Ginsberg, Jack Kerouac, and others attacked pervasive conformist values in their books. Teenagers devoured the music of Chuck Berry, Little Richard, Elvis Presley, Jerry Lee Lewis, Fats Domino, and many others with such enthusiasm that their parents began to worry that rock and roll was part of the international communist conspiracy to corrupt America's youth and eventually destroy the United States. The fact that the nation's youth took to rock and roll so quickly and passionately suggested that there was an indefinable hunger for something else, something that the material comforts of the affluent 1950s were not providing.

The most obvious indication of the crack in the American picture window—in fact, a development that significantly challenged the fundamental assumption that the United States was a democracy—was the emergence of the civil rights movement. After the 1954 *Brown v. Board of Education* decision outlawing segregation in public schools, African Americans began to hope that nearly a century of discrimination and second-class citizenship would finally come to an end. However, southern states and school districts resisted implementation of the decision and in some cases delayed school integration, for many years. Blacks understood that achieving parity with whites would involve more than the long struggle to change racist laws; they understood that the rights of American citizenship were not simply going to be given to them; they would have to struggle to claim them. In 1955, Rosa Parks refused to give up her seat on a Montgomery, Alabama, bus, thus leading to the 11-month Montgomery bus boycott and the rise of Dr. Martin Luther King Jr. to national prominence. In 1957, Governor Orval Faubus ordered the Arkansas National Guard to prevent nine black students from entering Little Rock Central High School. After a tense confrontation, a reluctant President Eisenhower was eventually forced to send in the U.S. Army to enforce compliance with the *Brown* decision. (Ironically he sent in the 101st Airborne Division, the elite division that parachuted into Normandy in the predawn hours of June 6, 1944. Some thought it appropriate that the 101st, which helped restore freedom to France in 1944, would also facilitate bringing freedom to Arkansas in 1957.) These events, broadcast on national television, awakened many people to the reality that the United States had not yet lived up to its ideal that "all men are created equal." In 1960 black students in Greensboro, North Carolina, and Nashville, Tennessee, began a new campaign of sit-ins at segregated lunch counters, and in 1961 CORE and SNCC activists launched the Freedom Rides to push the new Kennedy administration to enforce the Supreme Court's decision outlawing bus segregation. A pivotal year for the civil rights movement was 1963. In April and May, Martin Luther King Jr. initiated a series of demonstrations in Birmingham, Alabama, during which the police and fire departments attacked the demonstrators with dogs and fire hoses. The shock of this violent reaction to nonviolent protest generated so much positive publicity for the civil rights movement that Kennedy finally threw the weight of the Oval Office behind the movement, calling civil rights a "moral issue" and forwarding a bill to Congress that would outlaw segregation in workplaces, public housing, and public accommodation. In August, the Freedom Now movement sponsored the historic March on Washington, where King delivered his celebrated "I Have a Dream" speech to an orderly crowd of more than 250,000 people. King, although the most famous of the civil rights leaders, was only one of hundreds of deeply dedicated individuals who risked their lives for the cause. Though they had differing points of view on how best to achieve their rights as American citizens, Robert Moses, John Lewis, Ella Baker, Malcolm X, Anne Moody, Stokely Carmichael, Floyd McKissick, and countless others were profoundly committed to transforming race relations in the United States.

In 1964, when the Civil Rights Act became law, hundreds of white and black students participated in Freedom Summer—a voter registration drive for Mississippi blacks. Although three civil rights workers were killed during the first week of the campaign, volunteers kept arriving in Mississippi. In 1965, the Voting Rights Bill, providing for federal overseers to monitor voter registration to make sure no citizen was prevented from registering, was signed into law by President Johnson. As the civil rights movement moved north, however, it began to splinter between advocates of King's nonviolent resistance and supporters of Black Power.

When Democrat John F. Kennedy became president, it was not only civil rights activists who had high hopes for the country. Young people generally were idealistic and hopeful, especially after Kennedy exhorted them, in his inaugural address, to "ask not what your country can do for you, ask what you can do for your country!" Thousands joined the Peace Corps or involved themselves in the civil rights movement. At the University of Michigan, a group of students formed Students for a Democratic Society and, in 1962, issued the Port Huron Statement, in which they questioned cold war assumptions, analyzed American capitalism from a Marxist perspective, criticized racial bigotry, and called for a "participatory democracy" in which all Americans would work for bringing about a more just society. In 1963, in *The Feminine Mystique,* Betty Friedan wrote that for American women, being trapped in the only accepted role—of homemaker—was frustrating and unfulfilling. This "problem that has no name," she insisted, needed to be addressed. That same year, the President's Commission on the Status of Women (which Kennedy had set up in 1961) reported that there was indeed pervasive discrimination against women in education, in jobs, and in salaries. As a result, Kennedy backed the Equal Pay Act of 1963 and signed an executive order that civil service hiring must be done "without regard to sex." A feeling of change was in the air.

The idealism that Kennedy and the civil rights struggle had generated in the nation's young baby boomers, however, was dealt a severe blow on November 22, 1963. As news of Kennedy's assassination in Dallas flashed over the airwaves, the country ground to a halt. For four days, the sense of grief was overwhelming. For those young idealists Kennedy had inspired, the assassination was especially devastating. Many sensed, just as those in the current generation did on September 11, 2001, that somehow their lives would unfold differently because of this event. The historical and the personal had come together in a way that no one could have imagined.

In the aftermath of the assassination, great numbers of young people, no longer quite so naive, tried to work out how they might carry on what was perceived as Kennedy's legacy. Even though Kennedy himself had been very slow to endorse civil rights, the fact that he had finally done so during his last months convinced many that he would have become a major force in accomplishing the movement's goals. Over the next few years, many young men, also beguiled by Kennedy's inaugural injunction to "pay any price, bear any burden," eagerly enlisted in the Armed Forces in order to fight communists in Vietnam. Ironically, in the end, Vietnam became the final spark igniting the student movement.

John Howard Lawson (1894–1977)

John Howard Lawson, a Hollywood screenwriter and president of the Screen Writers Guild, was brought before the House Committee on Un-American Activities (HUAC) in 1947 to respond to questions about his communist activity and his efforts to put communist propaganda into his film scripts. HUAC was convinced that there was an international communist conspiracy to overthrow the American government and that the media and Hollywood had a particularly powerful influence on public thinking. If communists infiltrated the film industry or the media, they could "brainwash" Americans with insidious, subversive pro-leftist ideas. The committee therefore singled out Hollywood for investigation. During the hearings, Lawson, who had joined the Communist Party in 1934, attempted to read a statement into the record that accused the committee of undermining the Bill of Rights. Lawson's strategy was to get the Supreme Court to rule that HUAC was violating the free speech amendment of the Constitution and therefore overturn the committee's rulings. In 1949, however, the court refused to hear the appeal, and Lawson (along with the other nine members of the Hollywood Ten, Herbert Biberman, Albert Maltz, Lester Cole, Dalton Trumbo, Alvah Bessie, Samuel Ornitz, Edward Dmytryk, Adrian Scott, and Ring Lardner Jr.) was blacklisted and imprisoned.

The first document here is Lawson's HUAC testimony, during which he tried to read his statement into the record. The second document is the disallowed statement. Does the give-and-take between Lawson and the chairman support Lawson's view that the committee was jeopardizing free speech? Were Lawson's communist ideas more of a threat to the United States than the alleged suspension of the Bill of Rights?

Testimony Before the House Committee on Un-American Activities, 1947

Mr. LAWSON: Mr. Chairman, I have a statement here which I wish to make—
The CHAIRMAN: Well, all right, let me see your statement.
(Statement handed to the chairman.)

Source: From Congress, House, Committee on Un-American Activities, *Hearings Regarding the Communist Infiltration of the Motion Picture Industry*, 80th Congress, 1st Session, October 1947 (Washington: Government Printing Office, 1947); "A Statement by John Howard Lawson," in Gordon Kahn, ed., *Hollywood on Trial* (New York, 1948); quoted in *Thirty Years of Treason: Excerpts from Hearings before the House Committee on Un-American Activities, 1938–1968*, Eric Bentley, ed. (New York: Viking Press, 1971), 161–165.

THE CHAIRMAN: I don't care to read any more of the statement. The statement will not be read. I read the first line.

MR. LAWSON: You have spent one week vilifying me before the American public—

THE CHAIRMAN: Just a minute—

MR. LAWSON: And you refuse to allow me to make a statement on my rights as an American citizen.

THE CHAIRMAN: I refuse you to make the statement, because of the first sentence in your statement. That statement is not pertinent to the inquiry.

Now, this is a congressional committee— a congressional committee set up by law. We must have orderly procedure, and we are going to have orderly procedure.

Mr. Stripling, identify the witness.

MR. LAWSON: The rights of American citizens are important in this room here, and I intend to stand up for those rights, Congressman Thomas.

MR. STRIPLING: Mr. Lawson, will you state your full name, please?

MR. LAWSON: I wish to protest against the unwillingness of this committee to read a statement, when you permitted Mr. Warner, Mr. Mayer, and others to read statements in this room.

My name is John Howard Lawson. . . .

MR. STRIPLING: What is your occupation, Mr. Lawson?

MR. LAWSON. I am a writer.

MR. STRIPLING: How long have you been a writer?

MR. LAWSON: All my life—at least 35 years—my adult life.

MR. STRIPLING: Are you a member of the Screen Writers Guild?

MR. LAWSON: The raising of any question here in regard to membership, political beliefs, or affiliation—

MR. STRIPLING: Mr. Chairman—

MR. LAWSON: Is absolutely beyond the powers of this committee.

MR. STRIPLING: Mr. Chairman—

MR. LAWSON: But—

(The chairman pounding gavel.)

MR. LAWSON: It is a matter of public record that I am a member of the Screen Writers Guild.

MR. STRIPLING: I ask—

(Applause.)

THE CHAIRMAN: I want to caution the people in the audience: You are the guests of this committee and you will have to maintain order at all times. I do not care for any applause or any demonstrations of one kind or another.

MR. STRIPLING: Now, Mr. Chairman, I am also going to request that you instruct the witness to be responsive to the questions.

THE CHAIRMAN: I think the witness will be more responsive to the questions.

MR. LAWSON: Mr. Chairman, you permitted—

THE CHAIRMAN (POUNDING GAVEL): Never mind—

MR. LAWSON (CONTINUING): Witnesses in this room to make answers of three or four or five hundred words to questions here.

THE CHAIRMAN: Mr. Lawson, you will please be responsive to these questions and not continue to try to disrupt these hearings.

MR. LAWSON: I am not on trial here, Mr. Chairman. This committee is on trial here before the American people. Let us get that straight.

THE CHAIRMAN: We don't want you to be on trial.

MR. STRIPLING: Mr. Lawson, how long have you been a member of the Screen Writers Guild?

MR. LAWSON: Since it was founded in its present form, in 1933.

MR. STRIPLING: Have you ever held any office in the guild?

MR. LAWSON: The question of whether I have held office is also a question which is beyond the purview of this Committee.

(The chairman pounding gavel.)

MR. LAWSON: It is an invasion of the right of association under the Bill of Rights of this country.

THE CHAIRMAN: Please be responsive to the question.

MR. LAWSON: It is also a matter—

(The chairman pounding gavel.)

MR. LAWSON: Of public record—

THE CHAIRMAN: You asked to be heard. Through your attorney, you asked to be heard, and we want you to be heard. And if you don't care to be heard, then we will excuse you and we will put the record in without your answers.

MR. LAWSON: I wish to frame my own answers to your questions, Mr. Chairman, and I intend to do so.

. . .

MR. LAWSON: It is absolutely beyond the power of this committee to inquire into my association in any organization.

THE CHAIRMAN: Mr. Lawson, you will have to stop or you will leave the witness stand. And you will leave the witness stand because you are in contempt. That is why you will leave the witness stand. And if you are just trying to force me to put you in contempt, you won't have to try much harder. You know what has happened to a lot of people that have been in contempt of this committee this year, don't you?

MR. LAWSON: I am glad you have made it perfectly clear that you are going to threaten and intimidate the witnesses, Mr. Chairman.

(The chairman pounding gavel.)

MR. LAWSON: I am an American and I am not at all easy to intimidate, and don't think I am.

(The chairman pounding gavel.) . . .

THE CHAIRMAN (POUNDING GAVEL): Mr. Lawson, just quiet down again.

Mr. Lawson, the most pertinent question that we can ask is whether or not you have ever been a member of the Communist Party. Now, do you care to answer that question?

MR. LAWSON: You are using the old technique, which was used in Hitler Germany in order to create a scare here—

THE CHAIRMAN (POUNDING GAVEL): Oh—

MR. LAWSON: In order to create an entirely false atmosphere in which this hearing is conducted—

(The chairman pounding gavel.)

THE **CHAIRMAN** (POUNDING GAVEL): Excuse the witness—

MR. **LAWSON:** As they do from what I have written.

THE **CHAIRMAN** (POUNDING GAVEL): Stand away from the stand—

MR. **LAWSON:** I have written Americanism for many years, and I shall continue to fight for the Bill of Rights, which you are trying to destroy.

THE **CHAIRMAN:** Officers, take this man away from the stand—

(Applause and boos.)

THE **CHAIRMAN** (POUNDING GAVEL): There will be no demonstrations. No demonstrations, for or against. Everyone will please be seated. . . .

Lawson's Statement That Was Excluded from the Public Record, 1947

For a week, this Committee has conducted an illegal and indecent trial of American citizens, whom the Committee has selected to be publicly pilloried and smeared. I am not here to defend myself, or to answer the agglomeration of falsehoods that has been heaped upon me, I believe lawyers describe this material, rather mildly, as "hearsay evidence." To the American public, it has a shorter name: dirt. Rational people don't argue with dirt. I feel like a man who has had truckloads of filth heaped upon him; I am now asked to struggle to my feet and talk while more truckloads pour more filth around my head.

No, you don't argue with dirt. But you try to find out where it comes from. And to stop the evil deluge before it buries you—and others. The immediate source is obvious. The so-called "evidence" comes from a parade of stool-pigeons, neurotics, publicity-seeking clowns, Gestapo agents, paid informers, and a few ignorant and frightened Hollywood artists. I am not going to discuss this perjured testimony. Let these people live with their consciences, with the knowledge that they have violated their country's most sacred principles.

These individuals are not important. As an individual, I am not important. The obvious fact that the Committee is trying to destroy me personally and professionally, to deprive me of my livelihood and what is far dearer to me—my honor as an American—gains significance only because it opens the way to similar destruction of any citizen whom the Committee selects for annihilation.

I am not going to touch on the gross violation of the Constitution of the United States, and especially of its First and Fifth Amendments, that is taking place here. The proof is so overwhelming that it needs no elaboration. The Un-American Activities Committee stands convicted in the court of public opinion.

I want to speak here as a writer and a citizen. . . .

My political and social views are well known. My deep faith in the motion picture as a popular art is also well known. I don't "sneak ideas" into pictures. I never make a contract to write a picture unless I am convinced that it serves democracy and the interests of the American people. I will never permit what I write and think to be subject to the orders of self-appointed dictators, ambitious politicians, thought-control gestapos, or any other form of censorship this Un-American Committee may attempt to devise. My freedom to speak and write is not for sale in return for a card signed by J. Parnell Thomas saying "O.K. for employment until further notice."

Pictures written by me have been seen and approved by millions of Americans. A subpoena for me is a subpoena for all those who have enjoyed these pictures and recognized them as an honest portrayal of our American life.

Thus, my integrity as a writer is obviously an integral part of my integrity as a citizen. As a citizen I am not alone here. I am not only one of nineteen men who have been subpoenaed. I am forced to appear here as a representative of one hundred and thirty million Americans because the illegal conduct of this Committee has linked me with every citizen. If I can be destroyed no American is safe. You can subpoena a farmer in a field, a lumberjack in the woods, a worker at a machine, a doctor in his office—you can deprive them of a livelihood, deprive them of their honor as Americans.

Let no one think that this is an idle or thoughtless statement. This is the course that the Un-American Activities Committee has charted. Millions of Americans who may as yet be unconscious of what may be in store for them will find that the warning I speak today is literally fulfilled. No American will be safe if the Committee is not stopped in its illegal enterprise.

I am like most Americans in resenting interference with my conscience and belief. I am like most Americans in insisting on my right to serve my country in the way that seems to me most helpful and effective. I am like most Americans in feeling that loyalty to the United States and pride in its traditions is the guiding principle of my life. I am like most Americans in believing that divided loyalty—which is another word for treason—is the most despicable crime of which any man or woman can be accused.

It is my profound conviction that it is precisely because I hold these beliefs that I have been hailed before this illegal court. These are the beliefs that the so-called Un-American Activities Committee is seeking to root out in order to subvert orderly government and establish an autocratic dictatorship.

I am not suggesting that J. Parnell Thomas aspires to be the man on horseback. He is a petty politician, serving more powerful forces. Those forces are trying to introduce fascism in this country. They know that the only way to trick the American people into abandoning their rights and liberties is to manufacture an imaginary danger, to frighten the people into accepting repressive laws which are supposedly for their protection.

. . . Today, we face a serious crisis in the determination of national policy. The only way to solve that crisis is by free discussion. Americans must know the facts. The only plot against American safety is the plot to conceal facts. I am plastered with mud because I happen to be an American who expresses opinions that the House Un-American Activities Committee does not like. But my opinions are not an issue in this case. The issue is my right to have opinions. The Committee's logic is obviously: Lawson's opinions are properly subject to censorship; he writes for the motion picture industry, so the industry is properly subject to censorship; the industry makes pictures for the American people, so the minds of the people must be censored and controlled.

Why? What are J. Parnell Thomas and the Un-American interests he serves, afraid of? They're afraid of the American people. They don't want to muzzle me. They want to muzzle public opinion. They want to muzzle the great Voice of democracy. Because they're conspiring against the American way of life. They want to cut living standards, introduce an economy of poverty, wipe out labor's rights, attack Negroes, Jews, and other minorities, drive us into a disastrous and unnecessary war.

The struggle between thought-control and freedom of expression is the struggle between the people and a greedy unpatriotic minority which hates and fears the people. I wish to present as an integral part of this statement, a paper which I read at a Conference on Thought Control in the United States held in Hollywood on July 9th to 13th. The paper presents the historical background of the threatening situation that we face today, and shows that the attack on freedom of communication is, and has always been, an attack on the American people.

The American people will know how to answer that attack. They will rally, as they have always rallied, to protect their birthright.

Margaret Chase Smith (1897–1995)

Maine's Margaret Chase Smith was the first woman to be elected to both houses of Congress. She was a representative from 1940 to 1949 and U. S. senator from 1949 to 1973. In 1963 she declared her candidacy for the Republican presidential nomination and was thus the first woman to have her name put forth at a national convention. She came to prominence during the height of Senator Joseph McCarthy's anticommunist crusade and in 1950 was the first senator to speak out against him. Her "Declaration of Conscience" speech denouncing McCarthy's smear campaign and his recklessness in trying to uncover communists in the federal government is a classic statement of the constitutionally guaranteed right to dissent and protest. Senator Smith claimed that McCarthy's campaign was endangering the central principle of American democracy: freedom of conscience. As a result, Smith's "Declaration of Conscience" can be viewed as an early seed of the more radical dissent of the 1960s.

According to Smith, is McCarthy trying to expose communists, or is he just attempting to build political advantage? How does she see McCarthy's "witch hunt" as endangering American democracy? Do you agree with the declaration's assertion that McCarthy is playing into the hands of the communists?

Declaration of Conscience, 1950

For Release upon Delivery
Statement of Senator Margaret Chase Smith
June 1, 1950

Mr. President:

I would like to speak briefly and simply about a serious national condition. It is a national feeling of fear and frustration that could result in national suicide and the end of everything that we Americans hold dear. It is a condition that comes from the lack of effective leadership in either the Legislative Branch or the Executive Branch of our Government.

That leadership is so lacking that serious and responsible proposals are being made that national advisory commissions be appointed to provide such critically needed leadership.

I speak as briefly as possible because too much harm has already been done with irresponsible words of bitterness and selfish political opportunism. I speak as simply as possible because the issue is too great to be obscured by eloquence. I speak simply and briefly in the hope that my words will be taken to heart.

I speak as a Republican, I speak as a woman. I speak as a United States Senator. I speak as an American.

The United States Senate has long enjoyed worldwide respect as the greatest deliberative body in the world. But recently that deliberative character has too often been debased to the level of a forum of hate and character assassination sheltered by the shield of congressional immunity.

It is ironical that we Senators can in debate in the Senate directly or indirectly, by any form of words impute to any American, who is not a Senator, any conduct or motive unworthy or unbecoming an American—and without that non-Senator American having any legal redress against us—yet if we say the same thing in the Senate about our colleagues we can be stopped on the grounds of being out of order.

It is strange that we can verbally attack anyone else without restraint and with full protection and yet we hold ourselves above the same type of criticism here on the Senate Floor. Surely the United States Senate is big enough to take self-criticism and self-appraisal. Surely we should be able to take the same kind of character attacks that we dish out to outsiders.

I think that it is high time for the United States Senate and its members to do some soul searching—for us to weigh our consciences—on the manner in which we are performing our duty to the people of America—on the manner in which we are using or abusing our individual powers and privileges.

I think that it is high time that we remembered that we have sworn to uphold and defend the Constitution. I think that it is high time that we remembered; that

SOURCE: "Declaration of Conscience" by Senator Margaret Chase Smith and "Statement of Seven Senators," June 1, 1950, *Congressional Record*, 82nd Congress. 1st Session, in Arthur M. Schlesinger Jr. and Roger Burns, *Congress Investigates: A Documented History, 1792–1974* (New York: Chelsea House, 1963), 84–88.

the Constitution, as amended, speaks not only of the freedom of speech but also of trial by jury instead of trial by accusation.

Whether it be a criminal prosecution in court or a character prosecution in the Senate, there is little practical distinction when the life of a person has been ruined.

Those of us who shout the loudest about Americanism in making character assassinations are all too frequently those who, by our own words and acts, ignore some of the basic principles of Americanism—

The right to criticize;
The right to hold unpopular beliefs;
The right to protest;
The right of independent thought.

The exercise of these rights should not cost one single American citizen his reputation or his right to a livelihood nor should he be in danger of losing his reputation or livelihood merely because he happens to know some one who holds unpopular beliefs. Who of us doesn't? Otherwise none of us could call our souls our own. Otherwise thought control would have set in.

The American people are sick and tired of being afraid to speak their minds lest they be politically smeared as "Communists" or "Fascists" by their opponents. Freedom of speech is not what it used to be in America. It has been so abused by some that it is not exercised by others. The American people are sick and tired of seeing innocent people smeared and guilty people whitewashed. But there have been enough proved cases to cause nationwide distrust and strong suspicion that there may be something to the unproved, sensational accusations.

As a Republican, I say to my colleagues on this side of the aisle that the Republican Party faces a challenge today that is not unlike the challenge that it faced back in Lincoln's day. The Republican Party so successfully met that challenge that it emerged from the Civil War as the champion of a united nation—in addition to being a Party that unrelentingly fought loose spending and loose programs.

Today our country is being psychologically divided by the confusion and the suspicions that are bred in the United States Senate to spread like cancerous tentacles of "know nothing, suspect everything" attitudes. Today we have a Democratic Administration that has developed a mania for loose spending and loose programs. History is repeating itself—and the Republican Party again has the opportunity to emerge as the champion of unity and prudence.

The record of the present Democratic Administration has provided us with sufficient campaign issues without the necessity of resorting to political smears. America is rapidly losing its position as leader of the world simply because the Democratic Administration has pitifully failed to provide effective leadership.

The Democratic Administration has completely confused the American people by its daily contradictory grave warnings and optimistic assurances—that show the people that our Democratic Administration has no idea of where it is going.

The Democratic Administration has greatly lost the confidence of the American people by its complacency to the threat of communism here at home and the leak of vital secrets to Russia through key officials of the Democratic Administration. There are enough proved cases to make this point without diluting our criticism with unproved charges.

Surely these are sufficient reasons to make it clear to the American people that it is time for a change and that a Republican victory is necessary to the security of this country. Surely it is clear that this nation will continue to suffer as long as it is governed by the present ineffective Democratic Administration.

Yet to displace it with a Republican regime embracing a philosophy that lacks political integrity or intellectual honesty would prove equally disastrous to this nation. The nation sorely needs a Republican victory. But I don't want to see the Republican Party ride to political victory on the Four Horsemen of Calumny—Fear, Ignorance, Bigotry and Smear.

I doubt if the Republican Party could—simply because I don't believe the American people will uphold any political party that puts political exploitation above national interest. Surely we Republicans aren't that desperate for victory.

I don't want to see the Republican Party win that way. While it might be a fleeting victory for the Republican Party, it would be a more lasting defeat for the American people. Surely it would ultimately be suicide for the Republican Party and the two-party system that has protected our American liberties from the dictatorship of a one party system.

As members of the Minority Party, we do not have the primary authority to formulate the policy of our Government. But we do have the responsibility of rendering constructive criticism, of clarifying issues, of allaying fears by acting as responsible citizens.

As a woman, I wonder how the mothers, wives, sisters and daughters feel about the way in which members of their families have been politically mangled in Senate debate—and I use the word "debate" advisedly.

As a United States Senator, I am not proud of the way in which the Senate has been made a publicity platform for irresponsible sensationalism. I am not proud of the reckless abandon in which unproved charges have been hurled from this side of the aisle. I am not proud of the obviously staged, undignified countercharges that have been attempted in retaliation from the other side of the aisle.

I don't like the way the Senate has been made a rendezvous for vilification, for selfish political gain at the sacrifice of individual reputations and national unity. I am not proud of the way we smear outsiders from the Floor of the Senate and hide behind the cloak of congressional immunity and still place ourselves beyond criticism on the Floor of the Senate.

As an American, I am shocked at the way Republicans and Democrats alike are playing directly into the Communist design of "confuse, divide and conquer." As an American, I don't want a Democratic Administration "white wash" or "cover up" any more than I want a Republican smear or witch hunt.

As an American, I condemn a Republican "Fascist" just as much as I condemn a Democrat "Communist." I condemn a Democrat "Fascist" just as much as I condemn a Republican "Communist." They are equally dangerous to you and me and to our country. As an American, I want to see our nation recapture the strength and unity it once had when we fought the enemy instead of ourselves.

It is with these thoughts I have drafted what I call a "Declaration of Conscience." I am gratified that Senator Tobey, Senator Aiken, Senator Morse, Senator Ives, Senator Thye and Senator Hendrickson, have concurred in that declaration and have authorized me to announce their concurrence.

STATEMENT OF THE SEVEN REPUBLICAN SENATORS; 1950

1. We are Republicans. But we are Americans first. It is as Americans that we express our concern with the growing confusion that threatens the security and stability of our country. Democrats and Republicans alike have contributed to that confusion.

2. The Democratic administration has initially created the confusion by its lack of effective leadership, by its contradictory grave warnings and optimistic assurances, by its complacency to the threat of communism here at home, by its oversensitiveness to rightful criticism, by its petty bitterness against its critics.

3. Certain elements of the Republican Party have materially added to this confusion in the hopes of riding the Republican party to victory through the selfish political exploitation of fear, bigotry, ignorance, and intolerance. There are enough mistakes of the Democrats for Republicans to criticize constructively without resorting to political smears.

4. To this extent, Democrats and Republicans alike have unwittingly, but undeniably, played directly into the Communist design of "confuse, divide and conquer."

5. It is high time that we stopped thinking politically as Republicans and Democrats about elections and started thinking patriotically as Americans about national security based on individual freedom. It is high time that we all stopped being tools and victims of totalitarian techniques—techniques that, if continued here unchecked, will surely end what we have come to cherish as the American way of life.

Paul Robeson (1898–1976)

When the distinguished African American actor and concert singer Paul Robeson visited the Soviet Union in the 1930s, he was so impressed by the unprejudiced treatment he received that he became convinced that a communist society was more egalitarian and less racist than the democratic society of the United States. By the time he returned home, he had embraced communist ideology and had begun promoting communism as well as actively protesting against racism. In 1949, he advised African Americans not to fight in an "imperialist war" if the United States should go to war against the Soviet Union. As a result, Robeson was investigated by the House Committee on Un-American Activities, and his passport was revoked. Members of the committee browbeat Robeson in an effort to get him to admit that he was a member of the Communist Party, but Robeson repeatedly invoked the Fifth Amendment.

How accurate is Robeson's charge that the committee itself is unpatriotic? According to Robeson, what is the real reason his loyalty to the United States is being questioned? Why does he lecture the committee on African American history?

Testimony Before the House Committee on Un-American Activities, June 12, 1956

THE **CHAIRMAN:** The Committee will be in order. This morning the Committee resumes its series of hearings on the vital issue of the use of American passports as travel documents in furtherance of the objectives of the Communist conspiracy. . . .

MR. **ARENS:** Now, during the course of the process in which you were applying for this passport, in July of 1954, were you requested to submit a non-Communist affidavit?

MR. **ROBESON:** We had a long discussion—with my counsel, who is in the room, Mr. [Leonard B.] Boudin—with the State Department, about just such an affidavit and I was very precise not only in the application but with the State Department, headed by Mr. Henderson and Mr. McLeod, that under no conditions would I think of signing any such affidavit, that it is a complete contradiction of the rights of American citizens.

MR. **ARENS:** Did you comply with the requests?

MR. **ROBESON:** I certainly did not and I will not.

MR. **ARENS:** Are you now a member of the Communist Party?

MR. **ROBESON:** Oh please, please, please.

MR. **SCHERER:** Please answer, will you, Mr. Robeson?

MR. **ROBESON:** What is the Communist Party? What do you mean by that?

MR. **SCHERER:** I ask that you direct the witness to answer the question.

MR. **ROBESON:** What do you mean by the Communist Party? As far as I know it is a legal party like the Republican Party and the Democratic Party. Do you mean a party of people who have sacrificed for my people, and for all Americans and workers, that they can live in dignity? Do you mean that party?

MR. **ARENS:** Are you now a member of the Communist Party?

MR. **ROBESON:** Would you like to come to the ballot box when I vote and take out the ballot and see?

SOURCE: Congress, House, Committee on Un-American Activities, *Investigation of the Unauthorized Use of U.S. Passports,* 84th Congress, Part 3, June 12, 1956; in *Thirty Years of Treason: Excerpts from Hearings Before the House Committee on Un-American Activities, 1938–1968,* Eric Bentley, ed. (New York: Viking Press, 1971), 770.

Mr. ARENS: Mr. Chairman, I respectfully suggest that the witness be ordered and directed to answer that question.

The CHAIRMAN: You are directed to answer the question.

(*The witness consulted with his counsel.*)

Mr. ROBESON: I stand upon the Fifth Amendment of the American Constitution.

Mr. ARENS: Do you mean you invoke the Fifth Amendment?

Mr. ROBESON: I invoke the Fifth Amendment.

Mr. ARENS: Do you honestly apprehend that if you told this Committee truthfully—

Mr. ROBESON: I have no desire to consider anything. I invoke the Fifth Amendment, and it is none of your business what I would like to do, and I invoke the Fifth Amendment. And forget it.

The CHAIRMAN: You are directed to answer that question.

Mr. ROBESON: I invoke the Fifth Amendment, and so I am answering it, am I not?

Mr. ARENS: I respectfully suggest the witness be ordered and directed to answer the question as to whether or not he honestly apprehends, that if he gave us a truthful answer to this last principal question, he would be supplying information which might be used against him in a criminal proceeding.

(*The witness consulted with his counsel.*)

The CHAIRMAN: You are directed to answer that question, Mr. Robeson.

Mr. ROBESON: Gentlemen, in the first place, wherever I have been in the world, Scandinavia, England, and many places, the first to die in the struggle against Fascism were the Communists and I laid many wreaths upon graves of Communists. It is not criminal, and the Fifth Amendment has nothing to do with criminality. The Chief Justice of the Supreme Court, Warren, has been very clear on that in many speeches, that the Fifth Amendment does not have anything to do with the inference of criminality. I invoke the Fifth Amendment.

Mr. ARENS: Have you ever been known under the name of "John Thomas"?

Mr. ROBESON: Oh, please, does somebody here want—are you suggesting—do you want me to be put up for perjury some place? "John Thomas"! My name is Paul Robeson, and anything I have to say, or stand for, I have said in public all over the world, and that is why I am here today.

Mr. SCHERER: I ask that you direct the witness to answer the question. He is making a speech.

Mr. FRIEDMAN: Excuse me, Mr. Arens, may we have the photographers take their pictures, and then desist, because it is rather nerve-racking for them to be there.

The CHAIRMAN: They will take the pictures.

Mr. ROBESON: I am used to it and I have been in moving pictures. Do you want me to pose for it good? Do you want me to smile? I cannot smile when I am talking to him.

Mr. ARENS: I put it to you as a fact, and ask you to affirm or deny the fact, that your Communist Party name was "John Thomas."

Mr. ROBESON: I invoke the Fifth Amendment. This is really ridiculous.

Mr. ARENS: Now, tell this Committee whether or not you know Nathan Gregory Silvermaster.

Mr. SCHERER: Mr. Chairman, this is not a laughing matter.

Mr. ROBESON: It is a laughing matter to me, this is really complete nonsense.

Mr. **ARENS:** Have you ever known Nathan Gregory Silvermaster?

(*The witness consulted with his counsel.*)

Mr. **ROBESON:** I invoke the Fifth Amendment.

Mr. **ARENS:** Do you honestly apprehend that if you told whether you know Nathan Gregory Silvermaster you would be supplying information that could be used against you in a criminal proceeding?

Mr. **ROBESON:** I have not the slightest idea what you are talking about. I invoke the Fifth—

Mr. **ARENS:** I suggest, Mr. Chairman, that the witness be directed to answer that question.

The CHAIRMAN: You are directed to answer the question.

Mr. **ROBESON:** I invoke the Fifth.

Mr. **SCHERER:** The witness talks very loud when he makes a speech, but when he invokes the Fifth Amendment I cannot hear him.

Mr. **ROBESON:** I invoked the Fifth Amendment very loudly. You know I am an actor, and I have medals for diction.

. . .

Mr. **ROBESON:** Oh, gentlemen, I thought I was here about some passports.

Mr. **ARENS:** We will get into that in just a few moments.

Mr. **ROBESON:** This is complete nonsense.

. . .

The CHAIRMAN: This is legal. This is not only legal but usual. By a unanimous vote, this Committee has been instructed to perform this very distasteful task.

Mr. **ROBESON:** To whom am I talking?

The CHAIRMAN: You are speaking to the Chairman of this Committee.

Mr. **ROBESON:** Mr. Walter?

The CHAIRMAN: Yes.

Mr. **ROBESON:** The Pennsylvania Walter?

The CHAIRMAN: That is right.

Mr. **ROBESON:** Representative of the steelworkers?

The CHAIRMAN: That is right.

Mr. **ROBESON:** Of the coal-mining workers and not United States Steel, by any chance? A great patriot.

The CHAIRMAN: That is right.

Mr. **ROBESON:** You are the author of all of the bills that are going to keep all kinds of decent people out of the country.

The CHAIRMAN: No, only your kind.

Mr. **ROBESON:** Colored people like myself, from the West Indies and all kinds. And just the Teutonic Anglo-Saxon stock that you would let come in.

The CHAIRMAN: We are trying to make it easier to get rid of your kind, too.

Mr. **ROBESON:** You do not want any colored people to come in?

The CHAIRMAN: Proceed. . . .

Mr. **ROBESON:** Could I say that the reason that I am here today, you know, from the mouth of the State Department itself, is: I should not be allowed to travel because I have struggled for years for the independence of the colonial peoples of Africa. For many years I have so labored and I can say modestly that my name is very much honored all over Africa, in my struggles for their independence. That is the kind of independence like Sukarno got in Indonesia. Unless we are double-talking, then these efforts in the interest of Africa would be in the same context. The other reason that I am here today, again from the State Department and from the court record of the court of appeals, is that when I am abroad I speak out against the injustices against the Negro people of this land. I sent a message to the Bandung Conference and so forth. That is why I am here. This is the basis, and I am not being tried for whether I am a Communist, I am being tried for fighting for the rights of my people, who are still second-class citizens in this United States of America. My mother was born in your state, Mr. Walter, and my mother was a Quaker, and my ancestors in the time of Washington baked bread for George Washington's troops when they crossed the Delaware, and my own father was a slave. I stand here struggling for the rights of my people to be full citizens in this country. And they are not. They are not in Mississippi. And they are not in Montgomery, Alabama. And they are not in Washington. They are nowhere, and that is why I am here today. You want to shut up every Negro who has the courage to stand up and fight for the rights of his people, for the rights of workers, and I have been on many a picket line for the steelworkers too. And that is why I am here today. . . .

Mr. ARENS: Did you make a trip to Europe in 1949 and to the Soviet Union?

Mr. ROBESON: Yes, I made a trip. To England. And I sang.

Mr. ARENS: Where did you go?

Mr. ROBESON: I went first to England, where I was with the Philadelphia Orchestra, one of two American groups which was invited to England. I did a long concert tour in England and Denmark and Sweden, and I also sang for the Soviet people, one of the finest musical audiences in the world. Will you read what the *Porgy and Bess* people said? They never heard such applause in their lives. One of the most musical peoples in the world, and the great composers and great musicians, very cultured people, and Tolstoy, and—

The CHAIRMAN: We know all of that.

Mr. ROBESON: They have helped our culture and we can learn a lot.

Mr. ARENS: Did you go to Paris on that trip?

Mr. ROBESON: I went to Paris.

Mr. ARENS: And while you were in Paris, did you tell an audience there that the American Negro would never go to war against the Soviet government?

Mr. ROBESON: May I say that is slightly out of context? May I explain to you what I did say? I remember the speech very well, and the night before, in London, and do not take the newspaper, take me: I made the speech, gentlemen, Mr. So-and-So. It happened that the night before, in London, before I went to Paris . . . and will you please listen?

Mr. ARENS: We are listening.

Mr. ROBESON: Two thousand students from various parts of the colonial world, students who since then have become very important in their governments, in places like Indonesia and India, and in many parts of Africa, two thousand students asked me and Mr. [Dr. Y. M.] Dadoo, a leader of the Indian people in South Africa, when we addressed this conference, and remember I was speaking to a peace conference, they asked me and Mr. Dadoo to say there that they were struggling for peace, that they did not want war against anybody. Two thousand students who came from populations that would range to six or seven hundred million people.

Mr. KEARNEY: Do you know anybody who wants war?

Mr. ROBESON: They asked me to say in their name that they did not want war. That is what I said. No part of my speech made in Paris says fifteen million American Negroes would do anything. I said it was my feeling that the American people would struggle for peace, and that has since been underscored by the President of these United States. Now, in passing, I said—

Mr. KEARNEY: Do you know of any people who want war?

Mr. ROBESON: Listen to me. I said it was unthinkable to me that any people would take up arms, in the name of an Eastland, to go against anybody. Gentlemen, I still say that. This United States Government should go down to Mississippi and protect my people. That is what should happen.

The CHAIRMAN: Did you say what was attributed to you?

Mr. ROBESON: I did not say it in that context.

Mr. ARENS: I lay before you a document containing an article, "I Am Looking for Full Freedom," by Paul Robeson, in a publication called the *Worker*, dated July 3, 1949. "At the Paris Conference I said it was unthinkable that the Negro people of America or elsewhere in the world could be drawn into war with the Soviet Union."

Mr. ROBESON: Is that saying the Negro people would *do* anything? I said it is unthinkable. I did not say that there [in Paris]: I said that in the *Worker.*

Mr. ARENS: "I repeat it with hundredfold emphasis: they will not." Did you say that?

Mr. ROBESON: I did not say that in Paris, I said that in America. And, gentlemen, they have not yet done so, and it is quite clear that no Americans, no people in the world probably, are going to war with the Soviet Union. So I was rather prophetic, was I not?

Mr. ARENS: On that trip to Europe, did you go to Stockholm?

Mr. ROBESON: I certainly did, and I understand that some people in the American Embassy tried to break up my concert. They were not successful.

Mr. ARENS: While you were in Stockholm, did you make a little speech?

Mr. ROBESON: I made all kinds of speeches, yes.

Mr. ARENS: Let me read you a quotation.

Mr. ROBESON: Let me listen.

Mr. ARENS: Do so, please.

Mr. ROBESON: I am a lawyer.

Mr. KEARNEY: It would be a revelation if you would listen to counsel.

Mr. ROBESON: In good company, I usually listen, but you know people wander around in such fancy places. Would you please let me read my statement at some point?

The CHAIRMAN: We will consider your statement.

Mr. ARENS: "I do not hesitate one second to state clearly and unmistakably: I belong to the American resistance movement which fights against American imperialism, just as the resistance movement fought against Hitler."

Mr. ROBESON: Just like Frederick Douglass and Harriet Tubman were underground railroaders, and fighting for our freedom, you bet your life.

THE CHAIRMAN: I am going to have to insist that you listen to these questions.

MR. ROBESON: I am listening.

MR. ARENS: "If the American warmongers fancy that they could win America's millions of Negroes for a war against those countries (i.e., the Soviet Union and the peoples' democracies) then they ought to understand that this will never be the case. Why should the Negroes ever fight against the only nations of the world where racial discrimination is prohibited, and where the people can live freely? Never! I can assure you, they will never fight against either the Soviet Union or the peoples' democracies." Did you make that statement?

MR. ROBESON: I do not remember that. But what is perfectly clear today is that nine hundred million other colored people have told you that *they* will not. Four hundred million in India, and millions everywhere, have told you, precisely, that the colored people are not going to die for anybody: they are going to die for their independence. We are dealing not with fifteen million colored people, we are dealing with hundreds of millions.

MR. KEARNEY: The witness has answered the question and he does not have to make a speech. . . .

MR. ROBESON: In Russia I felt for the first time like a full human being. No color prejudice like in Mississippi, no color prejudice like in Washington. It was the first time I felt like a human being. Where I did not feel the pressure of color as I feel [it] in this Committee today.

MR. SCHERER: Why do you not stay in Russia?

MR. ROBESON: Because my father was a slave, and my people died to build this country, and I am going to stay here, and have a part of it just like you. And no Fascist-minded people will drive me from it. Is that clear? I am for peace with the Soviet Union, and I am for peace with China, and I am not for peace or friendship with the Fascist Franco, and I am not for peace with Fascist Nazi Germans. I am for peace with decent people.

MR. SCHERER: You are here because you are promoting the Communist cause.

MR. ROBESON: I am here because I am opposing the neo-Fascist cause which I see arising in these committees. You are like the Alien [and] Sedition Act, and Jefferson could be sitting here, and Frederick Douglass could be sitting here, and Eugene Debs could be here.

. . .

THE CHAIRMAN: Now, what prejudice are you talking about? You were graduated from Rutgers and you were graduated from the University of Pennsylvania. I remember seeing you play football at Lehigh.

MR. ROBESON: We beat Lehigh.

THE CHAIRMAN: And we had a lot of trouble with you.

MR. ROBESON: That is right. DeWysocki was playing in my team.

THE CHAIRMAN: There was no prejudice against you. Why did you not send your son to Rutgers?

MR. ROBESON: Just a moment. This is something that I challenge very deeply, and very sincerely: that the success of a few Negroes, including myself or Jackie Robinson can make up—and here is a study from Columbia University—for seven hundred dollars a year for thousands of Negro families in the South. My father was a slave, and I have cousins who are sharecroppers, and I do not see my success in terms of myself. That is the reason my own success has not meant what it should mean: I have sacrificed literally hundreds of thousands, if not millions, of dollars for what I believe in.

MR. ARENS: While you were in Moscow, did you make a speech lauding Stalin?

MR. ROBESON: I do not know.

MR. ARENS: Did you say, in effect, that Stalin was a great man, and Stalin had done much for the Russian people, for all of the nations of the world, for all working people of the earth? Did you say something to that effect about Stalin when you were in Moscow?

MR. ROBESON: I cannot remember.

MR. ARENS: Do you have a recollection of praising Stalin?

MR. ROBESON: I said a lot about Soviet people, fighting for the peoples of the earth.

MR. ARENS: Did you praise Stalin?

MR. ROBESON: I do not remember.

MR. ARENS: Have you recently changed your mind about Stalin?

MR. ROBESON: Whatever has happened to Stalin, gentlemen, is a question for the Soviet Union, and I would not argue with a representative of the people who, in building America, wasted sixty to a hundred million lives of my people, black people drawn from Africa on the plantations. You are responsible, and your forebears, for sixty million to one hundred million black people dying in the slave ships and on the plantations, and don't ask me about anybody, please.

MR. ARENS: I am glad you called our attention to that slave problem. While you were in Soviet Russia, did you ask them there to show you the slave labor camps?

THE CHAIRMAN: You have been so greatly interested in slaves, I should think that you would want to see that.

MR. ROBESON: The slaves I see are still in a kind of semiserfdom. I am interested in the place I am, and in the country that can do something about it. As far as I know, about the slave camps, they were Fascist prisoners who had murdered millions of the Jewish people, and who would have wiped out millions of the Negro people, could they have gotten a hold of them. That is all I know about that.

MR. ARENS: Tell us whether or not you have changed your opinion in the recent past about Stalin.

MR. ROBESON: I have told you, mister, that I would not discuss anything with the people who have murdered sixty million of my people, and I will not discuss Stalin with you.

MR. ARENS: You would not, of course, discuss with us the slave labor camps in Soviet Russia.

MR. ROBESON: I will discuss Stalin when I may be among the Russian people some day, singing for them, I will discuss it there. It is their problem. . . .

MR. ARENS: Now I would invite your attention, if you please, to the *Daily Worker* of June 29, 1949, with reference to a get-together with you and Ben Davis. Do you know Ben Davis?

MR. ROBESON: One of my dearest friends, one of the finest Americans you can imagine, born of a fine family, who went to Amherst and was a great man.

THE CHAIRMAN: The answer is yes?

MR. ROBESON: Nothing could make me prouder than to know him.

THE **CHAIRMAN:** That answers the question.

MR. **ARENS:** Did I understand you to laud his patriotism?

MR. **ROBESON:** I say that he is as patriotic an American as there can be, and you gentlemen belong with the Alien and Sedition Acts, and you are the nonpatriots, and you are the un-Americans, and you ought to be ashamed of yourselves.

THE **CHAIRMAN:** Just a minute, the hearing is now adjourned.

MR. **ROBESON:** I should think it would be.

THE **CHAIRMAN:** I have endured all of this that I can.

MR. **ROBESON:** Can I read my statement?

THE **CHAIRMAN:** No, you cannot read it. The meeting is adjourned.

MR. **ROBESON:** I think it should be, and you should adjourn this forever, that is what I would say. . . .

Harry Hay (1912–2002)

Harry Hay is considered by many to be the founder of the modern gay movement in the United States. He was active in progressive politics for many years, promoted trade unionism in the 1930s and 1940s, was associated with radical songwriters Woody Guthrie and Pete Seeger, and joined the Communist Party (which resulted in his being interrogated by the House Committee on Un-American Activities in 1955). Calling for others of the "androgynous minority" to form a political organization, he founded Bachelors Anonymous primarily to promote the 1948 presidential campaign of Progressive Party candidate Henry Wallace. In 1950, he founded the Mattachine Society in California, which was the first state organization designed to promote gay rights. Although the oppressive homophobia of the 1950s compelled the Mattachine Society to be a secret organization, it rapidly expanded by forming chapters in many cities throughout the nation. Because of his communist affiliation, however, Hays became a liability to the Mattachine Society, and he wound up leaving the organization. Ironically, because of his homosexuality, he was also booted out of the Communist Party. In 1969, when the Stonewall riots spawned the more radical gay civil rights movement of the 1970s, it was Hay's Mattachine Society and its sister organization, the lesbian Daughters of Bilitis (founded in San Francisco in 1955), that provided examples on which other gay organizations could model themselves. In 1979, he was a founder of the Radical Faeries, which advocated that gays should stress the differences between themselves and hetero-sexuals because, as Hay believed, the alternative gay perception of the world enabled them to offer a new range of insights and responses that could help solve society's problems. Hay opposed the view that many other gay rights activists held, that gays were just like everyone else and should therefore be assimilated into American society. Instead, he proclaimed that gays and lesbians were a distinct minority and should be treated as such. He believed that gay activists should not be merely concerned with electing gay politicians to office but should be more concerned about changing the basic structure of a consumerist society that systematically treated all people as objects and as a result demeaned the human spirit. He did not want gays to be assimilated into such a society but instead aimed to create a more humane society that was not controlled by corporate industrialism.

In 1990, Hay reflected on the historical background of the gay movement in a speech he gave at the Gay Spirit Visions Conference in Highlands, North Carolina. What is his distinction between a political organization and a social organization? Which does he prefer and why? What is the problem with the modern gay rights movement, according to Hay? What is his purpose in quoting Julian Huxley?

Speech at the Gay Spirit Visions Conference, Highlands, North Carolina, November 1990

"Where have we been and where are we now?" is an interesting topic because it is one of the places where my head is at the moment. One of the places in my Consciousness where my preparations for the two addresses I made at the university this week took me, has made me realize that we—as a distinct biologically determined human variant—have been developing our own collection of Gay Consciousness (by inventing it as we went along) for a long, long, long time. Maybe for as far back as when Species Homo began to emerge as hominids.

Taking the liberty of citing Sir Julian Huxley, the great biologist of the century, who said, "No negative trait" (and as you know, a negative trait in biology is one which does not reproduce itself) "appears in a given species millennia after millennia after millennia unless it in some way insures the survival of that species." (Parenthetically, we should hardly be expecting that the heteros have been hastening to discover how we Queers are about to insure THEIR survival. If anyone's going to discover it, it obviously is going to have to be US!). . . .

One of the most obvious observations might be how often, at not only previous Faerie gatherings but even at the planning sessions for this one, that it is our Faerie collective inclination to be functioning by consensus—to reflect on how it really is, for us, rather distasteful to engage in the endless bickering and to placate ego-posturings in the give-and-take of so-called democratic procedures. Recognizing—in a rush—those of us here tonight who were at the First Radical Faerie gathering eleven years ago in 1979, that the galvanizing revelation that overtook us all on that

Source: Retrieved on 12/18/2003 from www.geocities.com/WestHollywood/Heights/5347/gsv.html. For more on Hay, see Harry Hay and Will Roscoe, *Radically Gay: Gay Liberation in the Words of Its Founder* (Boston: Beacon Press, 1997).

occasion was the instant centrifugal rush by which we all realized how we had been longing (maybe all our lives hitherto) to connect in a circular celebration of our Faerie inclination to loving, sharing, consensual interaction with one another. For me, this has always been intensely interesting and important, because that was exactly the way it was with the first discussion groups first coming together in my first Mattachine Society 40 years ago. That same breathless, nameless excitement, as though it was something we'd always known, something that must have happened long ago of which we were a part. And now it was about to happen again. . . .

[P]erhaps the most important thing encompassed by my Mattachine Society was that for the first time in American homosexual experience our guild brother-hoods developed BEING GAY into a POSITIVE SELF-LOVING identity. Up until then, we had been only perverted heteros—EVEN IN OUR OWN EYES. According to every known social REFERENT, we were heteros who occasionally degraded our-selves through degenerate behavior. The best that I would hear in the 1930s was that maybe I, someday, would discover words which could explain to heteros just how beautiful our deviant voices and visions really were. But that we might be a different people altogether wouldn't be a concept until the 1970s. Although sometimes I'd wonder if, in the ballads of Thomas the Rhymer, I wasn't hearing of the Faerie People as being a different race.

In 1969, the Stonewall Rebellion exploded. The powder-train which my Mattachine . . . had been laying across the country in the 60's took off like a barrage of Roman candles. The "I" in the positive Gay identity changed to "WE," and sud-denly from everywhere Gay Brothers and Sisters were on the march, making the first lap of that social and political change which had always been implicit in the original dream of Mattachine—the vision of a social, minority who had contributions to share. At this point I need to point out the huge difference between the American Gay Movement and all the movements that came previously in Europe, as well as those which still exist in Europe. The Mattachine Society, as I conceived it, and all the others who have developed subsequently, have been perceived as politically-based, so that we all have continually perceived ourselves as being on the cutting edge of change. The European groups, of both the 19th and 20th centuries, have perceived themselves as "social" in orientation and therefore were and are con-cerned, not with political and social change, but with "accommodations" just as our middle-class "sell-out" assimilationists are now.

In the early '70s, the Gay and Lesbian Brothers and Sisters, exploding out of the Stonewall rage, screamed and hollered and zapped their way into the public media in ways never before experienced by the Gay Movement. But for all its rhetoric and thunder, and the political friends it was making in high places, the Movement remained essentially lily-white and middle-class. And hetero-imitative like you wouldn't believe. By 1978, the steam which had impelled the earlier zapping fury had mostly dissipated—apathy was everywhere in Gay and Lesbian land. The first Radical Faerie Gathering was a call to the Radical Brothers to see what all we might have developed and experienced since Stonewall. Also, I had this wonderful vision about a new type of consciousness which I felt we had been carrying with us down through the millennia, waiting for that time when the hetero "subject-object" way of growing and developing would be obsolete, and new directions would have to be taken if the race were to survive. The murderous nuclear competition between U.S. Imperialism and Soviet Imperialism had become so lethal that the fate of the planet seemed at stake. I felt that those Gay Brothers who could share my new vision of what I was calling "subject-subject" consciousness, might be able to begin to learn to turn the tide.

This is what we've been experimenting with for these last ten years. Radical Faerie experience has spread across this country and Canada. It has made its way to Australia and New Zealand, and in the last several years it has spread into England, Scotland and Ireland, with occasional echoes in Scandinavia. The most immediate result of our work has been in the conscious encouragement of the use of the loving-sharing consensus. Our occasional impatiences that our subject-subject way of perceiving, and our work in the loving-sharing consensus, does not spread as fast and as far as our impatience does is political naïveté. The hetero-male subject-object mind set is supported by the hierarchical dominant-male competition by which men developed the incentives needed to spur themselves to achievement. It was, of course, the social process par excellence whereby the hominid strain, having devised as yet ONLY an oral culture was able to train all its offspring and so remember EVERY-THING discovered by the ancestors because anything forgotten is lost forever. . . .

In the two million years during which our hominid ancestors were slowly evolving, our planet was also evolving in terms of its spherically volcanic nature. When cracks and crevices in the walls of a given social climate permitted, when a given culture required new solutions which the hetero ice-age originating MIND-SET couldn't assess, the phylogenetically inherited potentials to perceive and invent (what we today recognize as Gay Consciousness) have indeed appeared. They appeared briefly and brilliantly at given junctures in history: in Ancient Imperial China for three or four hundred years; in the great Songhai educational center of the Western Sudan for a century; or on a Chimu village pot whose myth stretches back into the mist. Each of these episodes is, in turn, followed by long ages of blank—ages not so much of silence as of VOID! And yet, WE WERE THERE! Silenced, muzzled, driven out of villages and towns again and again and again in myth and story; burned at stakes and in wicker baskets, and giggling at some hysterical absurdity even as the flames began to leap; drowned face down in bogs; obliterated by being thrown off cliffs. Yet we continued to appear in this generation or that, as though to assure the cosmos we were still a viable syndrome in the hominid biological make-up. Remember my earlier quotation from Sir Julian Huxley, "No negative trait appears in a given species millennia after millennia after millennia unless it in some way contributes to the survival or that species?"

. . . John (Burnside) and I felt in the late '70s that the obsession of the Harvard sociobiologists to find THE gene which makes us all Queer was much too simplistic. We felt that the ongoing discoveries on the brain's several hemispheres, and its mysterious intercameral connections, were marking not only new territories to be perceived, but new dimensions of territoriality to be perceived. We felt that all the new and exciting discoveries in Ethnology—the recognitions of Lorenz and Tinberggen and Fox and Morris and others—indicated that in our own phylogenetic inheritances we would have received many of the traits we would need for survival, and for learning to adapt to what had earlier been threatening and alien. We would have acquired that which—in the course of evolutionary development, reassembled in consciousness—would be the one new dimension Humans had evolved through natural selection. It would be only natural to call upon the newer disciplines—Ethnology or Sociobiology—to supply new models by which to encompass it.

We proposed Gay Consciousness needed to be perceived as a syndrome, a sheaf of hundreds of traits inherited from ancestors weaving together in hominid psychosexual natures so as to develop, in a small percentage of humans, what is known in physics and chemistry as "the critical mass." This biologically inherited, as well as phylogenetically inherited, "critical mass" in turn precipitates out a separate strain of people, a mutant strain of people psychically as well as emotionally different enough from their Parent Society. A strain that could devise ways of being totally self-reliant in situations where the Parent Society—as presently constituted—couldn't survive. The psychic and emotional differences of these Separate People had combined to create a spiritual difference and the key to their new dimensions of vision was their lovely deviant sexuality. . . .

Meantime, for us Radical Faeries here and now, I would like to suggest that in our last eleven years we have, through our Country Gatherings and City Circles, been devising ways and means to cut through the many layers of guilt and shame our Parent Society has forced us to disguise our Separate and Deviant lives within. And now many of us are experiencing even newer pressures to begin releasing visions of memories of ancient discoveries in physical and spirit hearings which we were forced to silence and subvert and bury and pretend to forget in order for us to survive. Some of us feel we are occasionally visited by spatial blurs, things that seem to have sought crevices in past times and perhaps, were partially or even wholly denied. Last summer, for example, John and I began a sex magic ritual, brain storming workshop, (a week-long session as we envisioned it) that has been pressing on me to explore for many years. . . .

In these next few days, here at Highlands, a number of us have brought new Faerie Spirit Visions to share. I fervently pray that what we bring is pure Faerie in Spirit, and not reworked or warmed-over Hetero material garnished with a little glitter here and there. The Radical Faeries, and all Gay spirit-seeking groups, need to attempt to keep as pure and as untrammeled as possible those channels from our precious secrets that have been long guarded at the cost of lives if they are to now be brought into service as powerfully and as brilliantly as they have long deserved.

Allen Ginsberg (1926–1997)

Allen Ginsberg was one of the most gifted and influential American poets of the twentieth century. His influence, however, was not limited to poetry and literature, for he was a deeply engaged social, cultural, and political activist. He, along with Jack Kerouac, William Burroughs, Lawrence Ferlinghetti, Gregory Corso, and others, were the focal points of the Beat Movement that emerged in the 1950s in response to the stultifying, suffocating conformity of the times. Decrying the "split-level American dream," Beats called for a more honest, introspective morality. Ginsberg once declared in an interview that the Beats' response to the pervasive American values and morality of the 1950s was to discard the old morality and build a new one from scratch. "The generation that was responsible for the Holocaust and Hiroshima had no right to tell us what was moral. So we threw it all out." Ginsberg first achieved national prominence in 1955, when he performed his iconoclastic poem *Howl* at the Six Gallery in San Francisco. After City Lights Press published *Howl*, the book was promptly banned and confiscated as obscene. The resulting court case wound up a publicity bonanza, and when the court ruled that *Howl* was indeed constitutionally protected "literature," everyone, it seemed, wanted to read it. Ginsberg's notoriety was assured, and his influence continued to be felt for the remainder of the 1950s, and in the early 1960s he in a sense became the godfather of the emerging counterculture. Ginsberg's use of words and imagery had an influence on Bob Dylan's song lyrics; Ginsberg's advocacy of marijuana and peyote and his LSD experiments with Timothy Leary influenced millions of people to explore drugs as a means to self-discovery; Ginsberg's sojourn in India and his espousal of Buddhism offered an alternative philosophy to those Americans who were beginning to question the validity and relevance of Christianity and Judaism; Ginsberg's unconventional appearance and his unashamed open homosexuality encouraged many others to "do their own thing." Throughout the 1960s and 1970s Ginsberg, in his beard, long hair, and black-framed glasses was a highly visible figure at antiwar demonstrations in San Francisco, New York, Chicago, London, Prague, and many other cities.

In the 1970s, Ginsberg founded the Jack Kerouac School of Disembodied Poetics at the Naropa Institute in Boulder, Colorado. By the 1980s and 1990s he was an antinuclear protestor and unwaveringly continued his social activism right up to his death in 1997. "I want to be known," Ginsberg wrote in *Ego Confessions* in 1974, "as the most brilliant man in America . . . [As the man who] Prepared the way for Dharma in America without mentioning Dharma . . . distributed monies to poor poets & nourished imaginative genius of the land. Sat silent in jazz roar writing poetry with an ink pen—wasn't afraid of God or Death after his 48th year."

In "America," Ginsberg, with characteristic humor, takes on consumerism and the superficiality of American values. What is the effect of Ginsberg's citation of historical persons and events? What does he think is wrong with *Time* magazine?

"America"

America I've given you all and now I'm nothing.
America two dollars and twenty-seven cents January 17, 1956.
I can't stand my own mind.
America when will we end the human war?
Go fuck yourself with your atom bomb
I don't feel good don't bother me.
I won't write my poem till I'm in my right mind.
America when will you be angelic?
When will you take off your clothes?
When will you look at yourself through the grave?
When will you be worthy of your million Trotskyites?
America why are your libraries full of tears?
America when will you send your eggs to India?
I'm sick of your insane demands.
When can I go into the supermarket and buy what I need with my good looks?
America after all it is you and I who are perfect not the next world.
Your machinery is too much for me.
You made me want to be a saint.
There must be some other way to settle this argument.
Burroughs is in Tangiers I don't think he'll come back it's sinister.
Are you being sinister or is this some form of practical joke?
I'm trying to come to the point.
I refuse to give up my obsession.
America stop pushing I know what I'm doing.
America the plum blossoms are falling.
I haven't read the newspapers for months, everyday somebody goes on trial for murder.
America I feel sentimental about the Wobblies.
America I used to be a communist when I was a kid and I'm not sorry.
I smoke marijuana every chance I get.
I sit in my house for days on end and stare at the roses in the closet.
When I go to Chinatown I get drunk and never get laid.
My mind is made up there's going to be trouble.
You should have seen me reading Marx.
My psychoanalyst thinks I'm perfectly right.
I won't say the Lord's Prayer.
I have mystical visions and cosmic vibrations.
America I still haven't told you what you did to Uncle Max after he came over from Russia.
I'm addressing you.
Are you going to let your emotional life be run by Time *magazine?*
I'm obsessed by Time *magazine.*

SOURCE: Allen Ginsberg, *Howl and Other Poems* (San Francisco: City Lights Press, 1956), 31–34.

I read it every week.

Its cover stares at me every time I slink past the corner candystore.

I read it in the basement of the Berkeley Public Library.

It's always telling me about responsibility. Businessmen are serious. Movie producers are serious. Everybody's serious but me.

It occurs to me that I am America.

I am talking to myself again.

Asia is rising against me.

I haven't got a chinaman's chance.

I'd better consider my national resources.

My national resources consist of two joints of marijuana millions of genitals an unpublishable private literature that goes 1400 miles an hour and twentyfivethousand mental institutions.

I say nothing about my prisons nor the millions of underpriviliged who live in my flowerpots under the light of five hundred suns.

I have abolished the whorehouses of France, Tangiers is the next to go.

My ambition is to be President despite the fact that I'm a Catholic.

America how can I write a holy litany in your silly mood?

I will continue like Henry Ford my strophes are as individual as his automobiles more so they're all different sexes

America I will sell you strophes $2500 apiece $500 down on your old strophe

America free Tom Mooney

America save the Spanish Loyalists

America Sacco & Vanzetti must not die

America I am the Scottsboro boys.

America when I was seven momma took me to Communist Cell meetings they sold us garbanzos a handful per ticket a ticket costs a nickel and the speeches were free everybody was angelic and sentimental about the workers it was all so sincere you have no idea what a good thing the party was in 1935 Scott Nearing was a grand old man a real mensch Mother Bloor made me cry I once saw Israel Amter plain. Everybody must have been a spy.

America you don't really want to go to war.

America it's them bad Russians.

Them Russians them Russians and them Chinamen. And them Russians.

The Russia wants to eat us alive. The Russia's power mad. She wants to take our cars from out our garages.

Her wants to grab Chicago. Her needs a Red Reader's Digest. *Her wants our auto plants in Siberia. Him big bureaucracy running our fillingstations.*

That no good. Ugh. Him makes Indians learn read. Him need big black niggers.

Hah. Her make us all work sixteen hours a day. Help.

America this is quite serious.

America this is the impression I get from looking in the television set.

America is this correct?

I'd better get right down to the job.

It's true I don't want to join the Army or turn lathes in precision parts factories, I'm nearsighted and psychopathic anyway.

America I'm putting my queer shoulder to the wheel.

Songs of the Civil Rights Movement

Songs that grow out of protests and demonstrations have a significant impact in two main ways. First, they get a message across, not only to those in power but also to those who are either unaware of the issue or have not yet made up their minds where they stand on it. A second and equally important effect the songs have is that they create a level of consciousness and solidarity among the demonstrators themselves. This was particularly true in the civil rights movement. A song like "We Shall Overcome," as sung by thousands of marchers during a demonstration, was a powerful galvanizer of unity and resolve. Daniel Wood was a student from Beloit College when he participated in the third Selma march in 1965. He remembers that as the demonstrators were crossing the Edmund Pettis Bridge leading out of Selma, they were singing "We Shall Overcome." When they noticed that the policemen lining the roadway were all armed with semiautomatic weapons trained on the marchers, the activists sang the "we are not afraid" verse of the song. As Wood puts it, "we were scared shitless, but still we sang it anyway!" Fortunately, no weapons were discharged, and the march proceeded toward Montgomery.

The civil rights movement embraced hundreds of songs. Some were adaptations of old slave songs; some were made up on the spot with lyrics referring to a town or a governor or a sheriff opposing the demonstrators; some were carefully crafted by popular musicians like Bob Dylan or Phil Ochs. There are rich resources on the Internet where you can read protest lyrics and even hear these songs.

The first two songs here emerged from civil rights demonstrations. "I Ain't Scared of Your Jail," as Pete Seeger explained during his June 1963 Carnegie Hall concert, was a spontaneous ditty that grew out of the Birmingham protests of the previous month. As the young people were beginning to march, Reverend King had told them that it was to be a silent demonstration that day, and that singing could begin only if arrests were made. This, indeed, did happen, and as the police moved in and began making arrests, the marchers all begin singing, "I ain't scared of your jail." The second song, "If You Miss Me at the Back of the Bus," refers to several events: the Montgomery bus boycott, the Freedom Rides, and voter registration drives. The last song is Bob Dylan's response to the assassination of Medgar Evers.

During an interview on German radio in 1988, Pete Seeger was asked: "Mr. Seeger can you change the world with a song?" "No," Seeger responded, "I can't change the world with a song. But if I write a song, and someone else designs a poster, and someone else gives a speech, and someone else organizes a teach-in, and someone else leads a demonstration, *together* we can change the world." What impact do these songs have on people who are sympathetic to the African American struggle to achieve equal rights? What impact do they have on those opposed to this struggle? Can songs like this change people's minds? Can a song change the world?

"I Ain't Scared of Your Jail"

I ain't scared of your jail
Because I want my freedom,
I want my freedom,
I want my freedom.
I ain't scared of your jail
Because I want my freedom,
I want my freedom,
Now!

"If You Miss Me at the Back of the Bus"

If you miss me at the back of the bus
You can't find me nowhere
Oh come on over to the front of the bus
I'll be riding up there
I'll be riding up there, I'll be riding up there
Oh come on over to the front of the bus
Because I'll be riding up there

If you miss me on the picket line
You can't find me nowhere
Come on over to the city jail
Because I'll be rooming over there
I'll be rooming over there
I'll be rooming over there oh
Come on over to the city jail
Because I'll be rooming over there

If you miss me at the Mississippi river
You can't find me nowhere
Come on over to the swimming pool
Because I'll be swimming over there
I'll be swimming over there, over there
I'll be swimming right there
Come on over to the swimming pool
Because I'll be swimming over there

If you miss me in the cotton fields
You can't find me nowhere
Come on over to the voting booth

Source: Pete Seeger, *We Shall Overcome: The Carnegie Hall Concert*, Columbia 1963.

Because I'll be a voting right there
I'll be voting right there, right there
I'll be voting right there
Well come on over to the voting booth
Because I'll be voting right there

"Only a Pawn in Their Game"

A bullet from the back of a bush took Medgar Evers' blood.
A finger fired the trigger to his name.
A handle hid out in the dark
A hand set the spark
Two eyes took the aim
Behind a man's brain
But he can't be blamed
He's only a pawn in their game.

A South politician preaches to the poor white man,
"You got more than the blacks, don't complain.
You're better than them, you been born with white skin," they explain.
And the Negro's name
Is used it is plain
For the politician's gain
As he rises to fame
And the poor white remains
On the caboose of the train
But it ain't him to blame
He's only a pawn in their game.

The deputy sheriffs, the soldiers, the governors get paid,
And the marshals and cops get the same,
But the poor white man's used in the hands of them all like a tool.
He's taught in his school
From the start by the rule
That the laws are with him
To protect his white skin
To keep up his hate
So he never thinks straight
'Bout the shape that he's in
But it ain't him to blame
He's only a pawn in their game.

SOURCE: Bob Dylan, *The Times They Are A-Changin'*, Columbia 1964.

From the poverty shacks, he looks from the cracks to the tracks,
And the hoof beats pound in his brain.
And he's taught how to walk in a pack
Shoot in the back
With his fist in a clinch
To hang and to lynch
To hide 'neath the hood
To kill with no pain
Like a dog on a chain
He ain't got no name
But it ain't him to blame
He's only a pawn in their game.

Today, Medgar Evers was buried from the bullet he caught.
They lowered him down as a king.
But when the shadowy sun sets on the one
That fired the gun
He'll see by his grave
On the stone that remains
Carved next to his name
His epitaph plain:
Only a pawn in their game.

Martin Luther King Jr. (1929–1968)

This icon of American history, recognized as one of the most influential and significant figures of the twentieth century, had a career on the public stage—from the beginning of the Montgomery bus boycott in December 1955 to his assassination in April 1968—that spanned less than 13 years.

Developing his own weltanschauung as he studied for the ministry, Martin Luther King Jr. drew his inspiration from many sources—from the teachings of Christ and the Social Gospel, from Locke, Jefferson, and Lincoln, from Henry David Thoreau, Mahatma Gandhi, Walter Rauschenbusch, and Reinhold Niebuhr. He first came to public attention during the 11-month Montgomery bus boycott. In 1957 he founded the Southern Christian Leadership Conference (SCLC), a grassroots civil rights organization whose membership consisted primarily of members of black congregations, as distinct from the earlier National Association for the Advancement of Colored People (NAACP), which had been founded by intellectuals and lawyers in order to overturn segregation through the legal system. After less than a decade of political activism, by 1963 (the centennial year of Lincoln's Emancipation Proclamation) King was widely understood to be the leader of the civil rights movement. That year he urged President Kennedy to issue a new emancipation proclamation and to come out forcefully for civil rights, and he was deeply disappointed when Kennedy, at first, did nothing.

In April 1963, King brought the movement to Birmingham—the most segregated city in the South. The events that followed proved the catalyst for finally convincing the president to use the power of the Oval Office to guarantee civil rights for *all* Americans. Newsreel footage coming out of Birmingham—of Police Chief Bull Connor's men loosing dogs on the demonstrators, of the city's fire department hosing protestors with enough force to roll them down the street—convinced many that segregation had to go. These disturbing images made civil rights supporters of people who had known virtually nothing about the plight of African Americans. In a nationally televised address, President Kennedy called civil rights a "moral issue as old as the scriptures" and declared "race has no place in American society." He announced that he would send a sweeping civil rights bill to Congress that would outlaw segregation. This, of course, is what King and the movement had been hoping to accomplish throughout their long campaign.

At one point during the Birmingham demonstrations, King was arrested and jailed for eight days. Meanwhile, a group of white Alabama ministers put an ad in the *New York Times* condemning King as an "outside agitator" whose poorly timed campaign was itself the cause of violence. King's eloquent reply, written in the margins of a newspaper and on scraps of paper, is a persuasive statement of the necessity of nonviolent direct action. Like Thoreau more than a century earlier, he argues that while just laws must be obeyed, unjust laws must be broken. What is the distinction between a just law and an unjust law? How does King respond to the charge that the nonviolent civil rights movement is the cause of violence?

———————————

Letter from a Birmingham Jail, April 16, 1963

My Dear Fellow Clergymen:

While confined here in the Birmingham City Jail, I came across your recent statement calling our present activities "unwise and untimely." Seldom, if ever, do I pause to answer criticism of my work and ideas. If I sought to answer all the criticisms that cross my desk, my secretaries would be engaged in little else in the course of the day, and I would have no time for constructive work. But since I feel that you are men of genuine goodwill and your criticisms are sincerely set forth, I would like to answer your statement in what I hope will be patient and reasonable terms.

I think I should give the reason for my being in Birmingham, since you have been influenced by the argument of "outsiders coming in." I have the honor of serving as president of the Southern Christian Leadership Conference, an organization operating in every Southern state, with headquarters in Atlanta, Georgia. We have some eighty-five affiliate organizations all across the South—one being the Alabama Christian Movement for Human Rights. Whenever necessary and possible we share staff, educational and financial resources with our affiliates. Several months ago our local affiliate here in Birmingham invited us to be on call to engage in a nonviolent direct action program if such were deemed necessary. We readily consented and when the hour came we lived up to our promises. So I am here, along with several members of my staff, because I have basic organizational ties here.

Beyond this, I am in Birmingham because injustice is here. Just as the eighth century prophets left their little villages and carried their "thus saith the Lord" far beyond the boundaries of their home towns; and just as the Apostle Paul left his little village of Tarsus and carried the gospel of Jesus Christ to practically every hamlet and city of the Graeco-Roman world, I too am compelled to carry the gospel of freedom beyond my particular home town. Like Paul, I must constantly respond to the Macedonian call for aid.

Moreover, I am cognizant of the interrelatedness of all communities and states. I cannot sit idly by in Atlanta and not be concerned about what happens in Birmingham. Injustice anywhere is a threat to justice everywhere. We are caught in an inescapable network of mutuality, tied in a single garment of destiny. Whatever affects one directly affects all indirectly. Never again can we afford to live with the narrow, provincial "outside agitator" idea. Anyone who lives inside the United States can never be considered an outsider anywhere in this country.

———

Source: Martin Luther King Jr., *Why We Can't Wait* (New York: Mentor, 1963), 76–95.

You deplore the demonstrations that are presently taking place in Birmingham. But I am sorry that your statement did not express a similar concern for the conditions that brought the demonstrations into being. I am sure that each of you would want to go beyond the superficial social analyst who looks merely at effects, and does not grapple with underlying causes. I would not hesitate to say that it is unfortunate that so-called demonstrations are taking place in Birmingham at this time, but I would say in more emphatic terms that it is even more unfortunate that the white power structure of this city left the Negro community with no other alternative.

In any nonviolent campaign there are four basic steps: 1) Collection of the facts to determine whether injustices are alive. 2) Negotiation. 3) Self-purification and 4) Direct action. We have gone through all of these steps in Birmingham. There can be no gainsaying of the fact that racial injustice engulfs this community.

Birmingham is probably the most thoroughly segregated city in the United States. Its ugly record of police brutality is known in every section of this country. Its unjust treatment of Negroes in the courts is a notorious reality. There have been more unsolved bombings of Negro homes and churches in Birmingham than any city in this nation. These are the hard, brutal and unbelievable facts. On the basis of these conditions, Negro leaders sought to negotiate with the city fathers. But the political leaders consistently refused to engage in good faith negotiation.

Then came the opportunity last September to talk with some of the leaders of the economic community. In these negotiating sessions certain promises were made by the merchants—such as the promise to remove the humiliating racial signs from the stores. On the basis of these promises Rev. Shuttlesworth and the leaders of the Alabama Christian Movement for Human Rights agreed to call a moratorium on any type of demonstrations. As the weeks and months unfolded we realized that we were the victims of a broken promise. The signs remained. Like so many experiences of the past we were confronted with blasted hopes, and the dark shadow of a deep disappointment settled upon us. So we had no alternative except that of preparing for direct action, whereby we would present our very bodies as a means of laying our case before the conscience of the local and national community. We were not unmindful of the difficulties involved. So we decided to go through a process of self-purification. We started having workshops on nonviolence and repeatedly asked ourselves the questions: "Are you able to accept blows without retaliating?" "Are you able to endure the ordeals of jail?" We decided to set our direct-action program around the Easter season, realizing that with the exception of Christmas, this was the largest shopping period of the year. Knowing that a strong economic withdrawal program would be the by-product of direct action, we felt that this was the best time to bring pressure on the merchants for the needed changes. Then it occurred to us that the March election was ahead and so we speedily decided to postpone action until after election day. When we discovered that Mr. Connor was in the run-off, we decided again to postpone action so that the demonstrations could not be used to cloud the issues. At this time we agreed to begin our nonviolent witness the day after the run-off.

This reveals that we did not move irresponsibly into direct action. We too wanted to see Mr. Connor defeated; so we went through postponement after postponement to aid in this community need. After this we felt that direct action could be delayed no longer.

You may well ask: "Why direct action? Why sit-ins, marches, etc.? Isn't negotiation a better path?" You are exactly right in your call for negotiation. Indeed, this is the purpose of direct action. Nonviolent direct action seeks to create such a crisis and establish such creative tension that a community that has constantly refused to negotiate is forced to confront the issue. It seeks so to dramatize the issue that it can no longer be ignored. I just referred to the creation of tension as a part of the work of the nonviolent resister. This may sound rather shocking. But I must confess that I am not afraid of the word tension. I have earnestly worked and preached against violent tension, but there is a type of constructive nonviolent tension that is necessary for growth. Just as Socrates felt that it was necessary to create a tension in the mind so that individuals could rise from the bondage of myths and half-truths to the unfettered realm of creative analysis and objective appraisal, we must see the need of having nonviolent gadflies to create the kind of tension in society that will help men to rise from the dark depths of prejudice and racism to the majestic heights of understanding and brotherhood. So the purpose of the direct action is to create a situation so crisis-packed that it will inevitably open the door to negotiation. We, therefore, concur with you in your call for negotiation. Too long has our beloved Southland been bogged down in the tragic attempt to live in monologue rather than dialogue.

One of the basic points in your statement is that our acts are untimely. Some have asked, "Why didn't you give the new administration time to act?" The only answer that I can give to this inquiry is that the new Birmingham administration must be prodded about as much as the outgoing one before it acts. We will be sadly mistaken if we feel that the election of Mr. Boutwell will bring the millennium to Birmingham. While Mr. Boutwell is much more articulate and gentle than Mr. Connor, they are both segregationists, dedicated to the task of maintaining the status quo. The hope I see in Mr. Boutwell is that he will be reasonable enough to see the futility of massive resistance to desegregation. But he will not see this without pressure from the devotees of civil rights. My friends, I must say to you that we have not made a single gain in civil rights without determined legal and nonviolent pressure. History is the long and tragic story of the fact that privileged groups seldom give up their privileges voluntarily. Individuals may see the moral light and voluntarily give up their unjust posture; but as Reinhold Niebuhr has reminded us, groups are more immoral than individuals.

We know through painful experience that freedom is never voluntarily given by the oppressor; it must be demanded by the oppressed. Frankly, I have never yet engaged in a direct action movement that was "well timed," according to the timetable of those who have not suffered unduly from the disease of segregation. For years now I have heard the words [*sic*] "Wait!" It rings in the ear of every Negro with a piercing familiarity. This "Wait" has almost always meant "Never." We must come to see with the distinguished jurist of yesterday that "justice too long delayed is justice denied."

We have waited for more than three hundred and forty years for our constitutional and God-given rights. The nations of Asia and Africa are moving with jet-like speed toward the goal of political independence, and we still creep at horse and buggy pace toward the gaining of a cup of coffee at a lunch counter. I guess it is easy for those who have never felt the stinging darts of segregation to say, "Wait." But when you have seen vicious mobs lynch your mothers and fathers at will and drown your sisters and brothers at whim; when you have seen hate filled policemen curse, kick, brutalize and even kill your black brothers and sisters with impunity; when you see the vast majority of your twenty million Negro brothers smothering in an air-tight cage of poverty in the midst of an affluent society; when you suddenly find your tongue twisted and your speech stammering as you seek to explain to your six-year-old daughter why she can't go to the public amusement park that has just been advertised on television, and see tears welling up in her eyes when she is told that Funtown is closed to colored children, and see the depressing clouds of inferiority begin to form in her little mental sky, and see her begin to distort her little personality by unconsciously developing a bitterness toward white people; when you have to concoct an answer for a five-year-old son asking in agonizing pathos: "Daddy, why do white people treat colored people so mean?"; when you take a cross-country drive and find it necessary to sleep night after night in the uncomfortable corners of your automobile because no motel will accept you; when you are humiliated day in and day out by nagging signs reading "white" and "colored"; when your first name becomes "nigger," your middle name becomes "boy" (however old you are) and your last name becomes "John," and your wife and mother are never given the respected title "Mrs."; when you are harried by day and haunted by night by the fact that you are a Negro, living constantly at tip-toe stance never quite knowing what to expect next, and plagued with inner fears and outer resentments; when you are forever fighting a degenerating sense of "nobodiness"; then you will understand why we find it difficult to wait. There comes a time when the cup of endurance runs over, and men are no longer willing to be plunged into an abyss of despair. I hope, sirs, you can understand our legitimate and unavoidable impatience.

You express a great deal of anxiety over our willingness to break laws. This is certainly a legitimate concern. Since we so diligently urge people to obey the Supreme Court's decision of 1954 outlawing segregation in the public schools, it is rather strange and paradoxical to find us consciously breaking laws. One may well ask: "How can you advocate breaking some laws and obeying others?" The answer is found in the fact that there are two types of laws: There are *just* and there are *unjust* laws. I would agree with Saint Augustine that "An unjust law is no law at all."

Now, what is the difference between the two? How does one determine when a law is just or unjust? A just law is a man-made code that squares with the moral law or the law of God. An unjust law is a code that is out of harmony with the moral law. To put it in the terms of Saint Thomas Aquinas, an unjust law is a human law that is not rooted in eternal and natural law. Any law that uplifts human personality is just. Any law that degrades human personality is unjust. All segregation statutes are unjust because segregation distorts the soul and damages the personality. It gives the segregator a false sense of superiority, and the segregated a false sense of inferiority. To use the words of Martin Buber, the Jewish philosopher, segregation substitutes an "I-it" relationship for an "I-thou" relationship, and ends up relegating persons to the status of things. So segregation is not only politically, economically and sociologically unsound, but it is morally wrong and sinful. Paul Tillich has said that sin is separation. Isn't segregation an existential expression of man's tragic separation, an expression of his awful estrangement, his terrible sinfulness? So I can urge men to disobey segregation ordinances because they are morally wrong.

Let us turn to a more concrete example of just and unjust laws. An unjust law is a code that a majority inflicts on a minority that is not binding on itself. This is difference made legal. On the other hand a just law is a code that a majority compels a minority to follow that it is willing to follow itself. This is sameness made legal.

Let me give another explanation. An unjust law is a code inflicted upon a minority which that minority had no part in enacting or creating because they did not have the unhampered right to vote. Who can say that the legislature of Alabama which set up the segregation laws was democratically elected? Throughout the state of Alabama all types of conniving methods are used to prevent Negroes from becoming registered voters and there are some counties without a single Negro registered to vote despite the fact that the Negro constitutes a majority of the population. Can any law set up in such a state be considered democratically structured?

These are just a few examples of unjust and just laws. There are some instances when a law is just on its face and unjust in its application. For instance, I was arrested Friday on a charge of parading without a permit. Now there is nothing wrong with an ordinance which requires a permit for a parade, but when the ordinance is used to preserve segregation and to deny citizens the First-Amendment privilege of peaceful assembly and peaceful protest, then it becomes unjust.

I hope you can see the distinction I am trying to point out. In no sense do I advocate evading or defying the law as the rabid segregationist would do. This would lead to anarchy. One who breaks an unjust law must do it *openly, lovingly* (not hatefully as the white mothers did in New Orleans when they were seen on television screaming "nigger, nigger, nigger") and with a willingness to accept the penalty. I submit that an individual who breaks a law that conscience tells him is unjust, and willingly accepts the penalty by staying in jail to arouse the conscience of the community over its injustice, is in reality expressing the very highest respect for law.

Of course, there is nothing new about this kind of civil disobedience. It was seen sublimely in the refusal of Shadrach, Meshach and Abednego to obey the laws of Nebuchadnezzar because a higher moral law was involved. It was practiced superbly by the early Christians who were willing to face hungry lions and the excruciating pain of chopping blocks, before submitting to certain unjust laws of the Roman empire. To a degree academic freedom is a reality today because Socrates practiced civil disobedience.

We can never forget that everything Hitler did in Germany was "legal" and everything the Hungarian freedom fighters did in Hungary was "illegal." It was "illegal" to aid and comfort a Jew in Hitler's Germany. But I am sure that if I had lived in Germany during that time I would have aided and comforted my Jewish brothers even though it was illegal. If I lived in a Communist country today where certain principles dear to the Christian faith are suppressed, I believe I would openly advocate disobeying these anti-religious laws. I must make two honest confessions to you, my Christian and Jewish brothers. First, I must confess that over the last few years I have been gravely disappointed with the white moderate. I have almost reached the regrettable conclusion that the Negro's great stumbling block in the stride toward freedom is not the White Citizen's Counciler or the Ku Klux Klanner, but the white moderate who is more devoted to "order" than to justice; who prefers a negative peace which is the absence of tension to a positive peace which is the presence of justice; who constantly says "I agree with you in the goal you seek, but I can't agree with your methods of direct action"; who paternalistically feels he can set the timetable for another man's freedom; who lives by the myth of time and who constantly advises the Negro to wait until a "more convenient season." Shallow understanding from people of goodwill is more frustrating than absolute misunderstanding from people of ill will. Lukewarm acceptance is much more bewildering than outright rejection.

I had hoped that the white moderate would understand that law and order exist for the purpose of establishing justice, and that when they fail to do this they become dangerously structured dams that block the flow of social progress. I had hoped that the white moderate would understand that the present tension in the South is merely a necessary phase of the transition from an obnoxious negative peace, where the Negro passively accepted his unjust plight, to a substance-filled positive peace, where all men will respect the dignity and worth of human personality. Actually, we who engage in nonviolent direct action are not the creators of tension. We merely bring to the surface the hidden tension that is already alive. We bring it out in the open where it can be seen and dealt with. Like a boil that can never be cured as long as it is covered up but must be opened with all its pus-flowing ugliness to the natural medicines of air and light, injustice must likewise be exposed, with all of the tension its exposing creates, to the light of human conscience and the air of national opinion before it can be cured.

In your statement you asserted that our actions, even though peaceful, must be condemned because they precipitate violence. But can this assertion be logically made? Isn't this like condemning the robbed man because his possession of money precipitated the evil act of robbery? Isn't this like condemning Socrates because his unswerving commitment to truth and his philosophical delvings precipitated the misguided popular mind to make him drink the hemlock? Isn't this like condemning Jesus because His unique God-Consciousness and never-ceasing devotion to His will precipitated the evil act of crucifixion? We must come to see, as the federal courts have consistently affirmed, that it is immoral to urge an individual to withdraw his efforts to gain his basic constitutional rights because the quest precipitates violence. Society must protect the robbed and punish the robber.

I had also hoped that the white moderate would reject the myth of time. I received a letter this morning from a white brother in Texas which said: "All Christians know that the colored people will receive equal rights eventually, but it is possible that you are in too great of a religious hurry. It has taken Christianity almost 2000 years to accomplish what it has. The teachings of Christ take time to come to earth." All that is said here grows out of a tragic misconception of time. It is the strangely irrational notion that there is something in the very flow of time that will inevitably cure all ills. Actually time is neutral. It can be used either destructively or constructively. I am coming to feel that the people of ill-will have used time much more effectively than the people of good will. We will have to repent in this generation not merely for the vitriolic words and actions of the bad people, but for the appalling silence of the good people. We must come to see that human progress never rolls in on wheels of inevitability. It comes through the tireless efforts and persistent work of men willing to be co-workers with God, and without this hard work time itself becomes an ally of the forces of social stagnation. We must use time creatively, and forever realize that the time is always ripe to do right. Now is the time to make real the promise of democracy, and transform our pending national elegy into a creative psalm of brotherhood. Now is the time to lift our national policy from the quicksand of racial injustice to the solid rock of human dignity.

You spoke of our activity in Birmingham as extreme. At first I was rather disappointed that fellow clergymen would see my nonviolent efforts as those of the extremist. I started thinking about the fact that I stand in the middle of two opposing forces in the Negro community. One is a force of complacency made up of Negroes who, as a result of long years of oppression, have been so completely drained of self-respect and a sense of "somebodiness" that they have adjusted to segregation, and, of a few Negroes in the middle class who, because of a degree of academic and economic security, and because at points they profit by segregation, have unconsciously become insensitive to the problems of the masses. The other force is one of bitterness, and hatred comes perilously close to advocating violence. It is expressed in the various black nationalist groups that are springing up over the nation, the largest and best-known being Elijah Muhammad's Muslim movement. This movement is nourished by the contemporary frustration over the continued existence of racial discrimination. It is made up of people who have lost faith in America, who have absolutely repudiated Christianity, and who have concluded that the white man is an incurable "devil." I have tried to stand between these two forces saying that we need not follow the "do-nothingism" of the complacent or the hatred and despair of the black nationalist. There is the more excellent way of love and nonviolent protest. I'm grateful to God that, through the Negro church, the dimension of nonviolence entered our struggle. If this philosophy had not emerged, I am convinced that by now many streets of the South would be flowing with floods of blood. And I am further convinced that if our white brothers dismiss as "rabble rousers" and "outside agitators" those of us who are working through the channels of nonviolent direct action and refuse to support our nonviolent efforts, millions of Negroes, out of frustration and despair, will seek solace and security in black-nationalist ideologies, a development that will lead inevitably to a frightening racial nightmare.

Oppressed people cannot remain oppressed forever. The urge for freedom will eventually come. This is what happened to the American Negro. Something within has reminded him of his birthright of freedom; something without has reminded him that he can gain it. Consciously and unconsciously, he has been swept in by what the Germans call the *Zeitgeist,* and with his black brothers of Africa, and his brown and yellow brothers of Asia, South America and the Caribbean, he is moving with a sense of cosmic urgency toward the promised land of racial justice. Recognizing this vital urge that has engulfed the Negro community, one should readily understand public demonstrations. The Negro has many pent up resentments and latent frustrations. He has to get them out. So let him march sometime; let him have his prayer pilgrimages to the city hall; understand why he must have sit-ins and freedom rides. If his repressed emotions do not come out in these nonviolent ways, they will come out in ominous expressions of violence. This is not a threat; it is a fact of history. So I have not said to my people "get rid of your discontent." But I have tried to say that this normal and healthy discontent can be channelized through the creative outlet of nonviolent direct action. Now this approach is being dismissed as extremist. I must admit that I was initially disappointed in being so categorized.

But as I continued to think about the matter I gradually gained a bit of satisfaction from being considered an extremist. Was not Jesus an extremist for love—"Love your enemies, bless them that curse you, pray for them that despitefully use you." Was not Amos an extremist for justice—"Let justice roll down like waters and righteousness like a mighty stream." Was not Paul an extremist for the gospel of Jesus Christ—"I bear in my body the marks of the Lord Jesus." Was not Martin Luther an extremist—"Here I stand; I can do none other so help me God." Was not John Bunyan an extremist —"I will stay in jail to the end of my days before I make a butchery of my conscience." Was not Abraham Lincoln an extremist—"This nation cannot survive half slave and half free." Was not Thomas Jefferson an extremist—"We hold these truths to be self-evident, that all men are created equal." So the question is not whether we will be extremist but what kind of extremist will we be. Will we be extremists for hate or will we be extremists for love? Will we be extremists for the preservation of injustice—or will we be extremists for the cause of justice? In that dramatic scene on Calvary's hill, three men were crucified. We must not forget that all three were crucified for the same crime—the crime of extremism. Two were extremists for immorality, and thusly fell below their environment. The other, Jesus Christ, was an extremist for love, truth and goodness, and thereby rose above his environment. So, after all, maybe the South, the nation and the world are in dire need of creative extremists.

I had hoped that the white moderate would see this. Maybe I was too optimistic. Maybe I expected too much. I guess I should have realized that few members of a race that has oppressed another race can understand or appreciate the deep groans and passionate yearnings of those that have been oppressed and still fewer have the vision to see that injustice must be rooted out by strong, persistent and determined action. I am thankful, however, that some of our white brothers have grasped the meaning of this social revolution and committed themselves to it. They are still all too small in quantity, but they are big in quality. Some like Ralph McGill, Lillian Smith, Harry Golden and James Dabbs have written about our struggle in eloquent, prophetic and understanding terms. Others have marched with us down nameless streets of the South. They have languished in filthy roach-infested jails, suffering the abuse and brutality of angry policemen who see them as "dirty nigger lovers." They, unlike so many of their moderate brothers and sisters, have recognized the urgency of the moment and sensed the need for powerful "action" antidotes to combat the disease of segregation.

Let me rush on to mention my other disappointment. I have been so greatly disappointed with the white church and its leadership. Of course, there are some notable exceptions. I am not unmindful of the fact that each of you has taken some significant stands on this issue. I commend you, Rev. Stallings, for your Christian stand on this past Sunday, in welcoming Negroes to your worship service on a non-segregated basis. I commend the Catholic leaders of this state for integrating Spring Hill College several years ago.

But despite these notable exceptions I must honestly reiterate that I have been disappointed with the church. I do not say that as one of those negative critics who can always find something wrong with the church. I say it as a minister of the gospel, who loves the church; who was nurtured in its bosom; who has been sustained by its spiritual blessings and who will remain true to it as long as the cord of life shall lengthen.

I had the strange feeling when I was suddenly catapulted into the leadership of the bus protest in Montgomery several years ago, that we would have the support of the white church. I felt that the white ministers, priests and rabbis of the South would be some of our strongest allies. Instead, some have been outright opponents, refusing to understand the freedom movement and misrepresenting its leaders; all too many others have been more cautious than courageous and have remained silent behind the anesthetizing security of the stained-glass windows.

In spite of my shattered dreams of the past, I came to Birmingham with the hope that the white religious leadership of this community would see the justice of our cause, and with deep moral concern, serve as the channel through which our just grievances would get to the power structure. I had hoped that each of you would understand. But again I have been disappointed. I have heard numerous religious leaders of the South call upon their worshippers to comply with a desegregation decision because it is the *law,* but I have longed to hear white ministers say, "follow this decree because integration is morally *right* and the Negro is your brother." In the midst of blatant injustices inflicted upon the Negro, I have watched white churches stand on the sideline and merely mouth pious irrelevancies and sanctimonious trivialities. In the midst of a mighty struggle to rid our nation of racial and economic injustice, I have heard so many ministers say, "Those are social issues with which the gospel has no real concern." And I have watched so many churches commit themselves to a completely other-worldly religion which made a strange distinction between body and soul, the sacred and the secular.

So here we are moving toward the exit of the twentieth century with a religious community largely adjusted to the status quo, standing as a tail-light behind other community agencies rather than a headlight leading men to higher levels of justice.

I have traveled the length and breadth of Alabama, Mississippi and all the other southern states. On sweltering summer days and crisp autumn mornings I have looked at her beautiful churches with their lofty spires pointing heavenward. I have beheld the impressive outlay of her massive religious education buildings. Over and over again I have found myself asking: "What kind of people worship here? Who is their God? Where were their voices when the lips of Governor Barnett dripped with words of interposition and nullification? Where were they when Governor Wallace gave the clarion call for defiance and hatred? Where were their voices of support when tired, bruised and weary Negro men and women decided to rise from the dark dungeons of complacency to the bright hills of creative protest?"

Yes, these questions are still in my mind. In deep disappointment, I have wept over the laxity of the church. But be assured that my tears have been tears of love. There can be no deep disappointment where there is not deep love. Yes, I love the church; I love her sacred walls. How could I do otherwise? I am in the rather unique position of being the son, the grandson and the great-grandson of preachers. Yes,

I see the church as the body of Christ. But, oh! How we have blemished and scarred that body through social neglect and fear of being nonconformists.

There was a time when the church was very powerful. It was during that period when the early Christians rejoiced when they were deemed worthy to suffer for what they believed. In those days the church was not merely a thermometer that recorded the ideas and principles of popular opinion; it was a thermostat that transformed the mores of society. Whenever the early Christians entered a town the power structure got disturbed and immediately sought to convict them for being "disturbers of the peace" and "outside agitators." But they went on with the conviction that they were "a colony of heaven," and had to obey God rather than man. They were small in number but big in commitment. They were too God-intoxicated to be "astronomically intimidated." They brought an end to such ancient evils as infanticide and gladiatorial contest.

Things are different now. The contemporary church is often a weak, ineffectual voice with an uncertain sound. It is so often the arch supporter of the status quo. Far from being disturbed by the presence of the church, the power structure of the average community is consoled by the church's silent and often vocal sanction of things as they are.

But the judgement of God is upon the church as never before. If the church of today does not recapture the sacrificial spirit of the early church, it will lose its authentic ring, forfeit the loyalty of millions, and be dismissed as an irrelevant social club with no meaning for the twentieth century. I am meeting young people every day whose disappointment with the church has risen to outright disgust.

Maybe again, I have been too optimistic. Is organized religion too inextricably bound to the status quo to save our nation and the world? Maybe I must turn my faith to the inner spiritual church, the church within the church, as the true *ecclesia* and the hope of the world. But again I am thankful to God that some noble souls from the ranks of organized religion have broken loose from the paralyzing chains of conformity and joined us as active partners in the struggle for freedom. They have left their secure congregations and walked the streets of Albany, Georgia, with us. They have gone through the highways of the South on tortuous rides for freedom. Yes, they have gone to jail with us. Some have been kicked out of their churches, and lost support of their bishops and fellow ministers. But they have gone with the faith that right defeated is stronger than evil triumphant. These men have been the leaven in the lump of the race. Their witness has been the spiritual salt that has preserved the true meaning of the Gospel in these troubled times. They have carved a tunnel of hope though the dark mountain of disappointment.

I hope the church as a whole will meet the challenge of this decisive hour. But even if the church does not come to the aid of justice, I have no despair about the future. I have no fear about the outcome of our struggle in Birmingham, even if our motives are presently misunderstood. We will reach the goal of freedom in Birmingham and all over the nation, because the goal of America is freedom. Abused and scorned though we may be, our destiny is tied up with the destiny of America. Before the pilgrims landed at Plymouth we were here. Before the pen of Jefferson etched across the pages of history the majestic words of the Declaration of Independence, we were here. For more than two centuries our fore-parents labored in this country without wages; they made cotton king; and they built the homes of their masters in the midst of brutal injustice and shameful humiliation—and yet out of a bottomless vitality they continued to thrive and develop. If the inexpressible cruelties of slavery could not stop us, the opposition we now face will surely fail. We will win our freedom because the sacred heritage of our nation and the eternal will of God are embodied in our echoing demands.

I must close now. But before closing I am impelled to mention one other point in your statement that troubled me profoundly. You warmly commended the Birmingham police force for keeping "order" and "preventing violence." I don't believe you would have so warmly commended the police force if you had seen its angry violent dogs literally biting six unarmed, nonviolent Negroes. I don't believe you would so quickly commend the policemen if you would observe their ugly and inhuman treatment of Negroes here in the city jail; if you would watch them push and curse old Negro women and young Negro girls; if you would see them slap and kick old Negro men and young boys; if you will observe them, as they did on two occasions, refuse to give us food because we wanted to sing our grace together. I'm sorry that I can't join you in your praise for the police department.

It is true that they have been rather disciplined in their public handling of the demonstrators. In this sense they have been rather publicly "nonviolent." But for what purpose? To preserve the evil system of segregation. Over the last few years I have consistently preached that nonviolence demands that the means we use must be as pure as the ends we seek. So I have tried to make it clear that it is wrong to use immoral means to attain moral ends. But now I must affirm that it is just as wrong, or even more so, to use moral means to preserve immoral ends. Maybe Mr. Connor and his policemen have been rather publicly nonviolent, as Chief Pritchett was in Albany, Georgia, but they have used the moral means of nonviolence to maintain the immoral end of flagrant racial injustice. T. S. Eliot has said that there is no greater treason than to do the right deed for the wrong reason.

I wish you had commended the Negro sit-inners and demonstrators of Birmingham for their sublime courage, their willingness to suffer and their amazing discipline in the midst of the most inhuman provocation. One day the South will recognize its real heroes. They will be the James Merediths, courageously and with a majestic sense of purpose, facing jeering and hostile mobs and with the agonizing loneliness that characterizes the life of the pioneer. They will be old oppressed, battered Negro women, symbolized in a seventy-two year old woman of Montgomery, Alabama, who rose up with a sense of dignity and with her people decided not to ride the segregated buses, and responded to one who inquired about her tiredness with ungrammatical profundity: "my feet is tired, but my soul is rested." They will be the young high school and college students, young ministers of the gospel and a host of their elders courageously and nonviolently sitting-in at lunch counters and willingly going to jail for conscience's sake. One day the South will know that when these disinherited children of God sat down at lunch counters they were in reality standing up for the best in the American dream and the most sacred values in our Judaeo-Christian heritage, and thusly, carrying our whole nation back to those great wells of democracy which were dug deep by the founding fathers in the formulation of the Constitution and the Declaration of Independence.

Never before have I written a letter this long (or should I say a book?). I'm afraid it is much too long to take your precious time. I can assure you that it would have been much shorter if I had been writing from a comfortable desk, but what else is there to do when you are alone for days in the dull monotony of a narrow jail cell other than write long letters, think strange thoughts, and pray long prayers?

If I have said anything in this letter that is an overstatement of the truth and is indicative of an unreasonable impatience, I beg you to forgive me. If I have said anything in this letter that is an understatement of the truth and is indicative of my having a patience that makes me patient with anything less than brotherhood, I beg God to forgive me.

I hope this letter finds you strong in the faith. I also hope that circumstances will soon make it possible for me to meet each of you, not as an integrationist or a civil rights leader, but as a fellow clergyman and a Christian brother. Let us all hope that the dark clouds of racial prejudice will soon pass away and the deep fog of mis-understanding will be lifted from our fear-drenched communities and in some not too distant tomorrow the radiant stars of love and brotherhood will shine over our great nation with all their scintillating beauty.

Yours for the cause of Peace and Brotherhood,

Martin Luther King, Jr.

Fannie Lou Hamer (1917–1977)

Black and white civil rights activists spent the summer of 1964 in Mississippi registering African Americans to vote. Three civil rights volunteers, James Chaney, Andrew Goodman, and Michael Schwerner, were murdered during that "Freedom Summer." The Mississippi Freedom Democratic Party (MFDP) sent a delegation to the Democratic National Convention in Atlantic City in August, hoping that liberals in the party who supported the civil rights movement would seat them rather than the regular, all-white Mississippi delegation. Student Nonviolent Coordinating Committee (SNCC) worker Fannie Lou Hamer, granddaughter of a slave, was a member of the delegation. The credentials committee held a televised hearing, and while Fannie Lou Hamer's gripping testimony was being aired, President Johnson, angry that the issue would divide the Democratic Party, deliberately preempted the proceedings by holding a spur-of-the-moment press conference. Hamer's testimony was aired later that evening by the networks, and although it was no longer prime time, millions of viewers around the country then heard of the injustices faced by blacks in Mississippi. Johnson and the Democratic leadership still refused to seat the MFDP, although they offered a compro-mise: admitting two MFDP members as delegates-at-large and agreeing that at the next convention in 1968 delegations from states that denied citizens suffrage would not be seated. The MFDP rejected the compromise: "We didn't come all this way for no two seats," Fannie Lou Hamer indignantly announced. An important result of this episode was that many African Americans began losing faith in the political process. Over the next few years, the civil rights movement itself fragmented as advocates of Black Power became critical of the moderate approach of such leaders as Martin Luther King Jr. and Roy Wilkins of the NAACP.

What does Hamer's testimony before the credentials committee reveal about conditions African Americans faced in Mississippi in 1964?

Testimony Before the Credentials Committee of the Democratic National Convention, 1964

Mr. Chairman, and the Credentials Committee, my name is Mrs. Fanny Lou Hamer, and I live at 626 East Lafayette Street, Ruleville, Mississippi, Sunflower County, the home of Senator James O. Eastland, and Senator Stennis.

It was the 31st of August in 1962 that 18 of us traveled 26 miles to the county courthouse in Indianola to try to register to try to become first-class citizens. We was met in Indianola by Mississippi men, Highway Patrolmens and they only allowed two of us in to take the literacy test at the time. After we had taken this test and started back to Ruleville, we was held up by the City Police and the State Highway Patrolmen and carried back to Indianola where the bus driver was charged that day with driving a bus the wrong color.

After we paid the fine among us, we continued on to Ruleville, and Reverend Jeff Sunny carried me four miles in the rural area where I had worked as a time-keeper and sharecropper for 18 years. I was met there by my children, who told me that the plantation owner was angry because I had gone down to try to register. After they told me, my husband came, and said that the plantation owner was raising cain because I had tried to register, and before he quit talking the plantation owner came, and said, "Fanny Lou, do you know—did Pap tell you what I said?"

And I said, "yes, sir."

He said, "I mean that," he said, "If you don't go down and withdraw your registration, you will have to leave," said, "Then if you go down and withdraw," he said, "You will—you [still] might have to go because we are not ready for that in Mississippi."

And I addressed him and told him and said, "I didn't try to register for you. I tried to register for myself." I had to leave that same night.

On the 10th of September 1962, 16 bullets was fired into the home of Mr. and Mrs. Robert Tucker for me. That same night two girls were shot in Ruleville, Mississippi. Also Mr. Joe McDonald's house was shot in.

And in June the 9th, 1963, I had attended a voter registration workshop, was returning back to Mississippi. Ten of us was traveling by the Continental Trailway bus.

SOURCE: Reprinted in Peter B. Levy, ed., *Documentary History of the Modern Civil Rights Movement* (New York: Greenwood Press, 1992), 139–141.

When we got to Winona, Mississippi, which is in Montgomery County, four of the people got off to use the washroom, and two of the people—to use the restaurant—two of the people wanted to use the washroom. The four people that had gone in to use the restaurant was ordered out. During this time I was on the bus. But when I looked through the window and saw they had rushed out I got off of the bus to see what had happened, and one of the ladies said, "It was a State Highway Patrolman and a Chief of Police ordered us out."

I got back on the bus and one of the persons had used the washroom got back on the bus, too. As soon as I was seated on the bus, I saw when they began to get the four people in a highway patrolman's car, I stepped off of the bus to see what was happening and somebody screamed from the car that the four workers was in and said, "Get that one there," and when I went to get in the car, when the man told me I was under arrest, he kicked me.

I was carried to the county jail, and put in the booking room. They left some of the people in the booking room and began to place us in cells. I was placed in a cell with a young woman called Miss Ivesta Simpson. After I was placed in the cell I began to hear the sound of kicks and horrible screams, and I could hear somebody say, "Can you say, yes, sir, nigger? Can you say yes, sir?"

And they would say other horrible names. She would say, "Yes, I can say yes, sir."

"So say it."

She says, "I don't know you well enough."

They beat her, I don't know how long, and after a while she began to pray, and asked God to have mercy on those people.

And it wasn't too long before three white men came to my cell. One of these men was a State Highway Patrolman and he asked me where I was from, and I told him Ruleville, he said, "We are going to check this." And they left my cell and it wasn't too long before they came back. He said, "You are from Ruleville all right," and he used a curse word, and he said, "We are going to make you wish you was dead."

I was carried out of that cell into another cell where they had two Negro prisoners. The State Highway Patrolmen ordered the first Negro to take the blackjack. The first Negro prisoner ordered me, by orders from the State Highway Patrolman for me, to lay down on a bunk bed on my face, and I laid on my face. The first Negro began to beat, and I was beat by the first Negro until he was exhausted, and I was holding my hands behind me at that time on my left side because I suffered from polio when I was six years old. After the first Negro had beat until he was exhausted the State Highway Patrolman ordered the second Negro to take the blackjack.

The second Negro began to beat and I began to work my feet, and the State Highway Patrolman ordered the first Negro who had beat me to sit upon my feet to keep me from working my feet. I began to scream and one white man got up and began to beat me my head and told me to hush. One white man—since my dress had worked up high, walked over and pulled my dress down and he pulled my dress back, back up. . . .

All of this is on account of us wanting to register, to become first-class citizens, and if the freedom Democratic Party is not seated now, I question America, is this America, the land of the free and the home of the brave where we have to sleep with our telephones off of the hooks because our lives be threatened daily because we want to live as decent human beings, in America?

Malcolm X (1925–1965)

By the time Malcolm Little was a teenager, he was involved in drugs, pimping, and burglary. He was finally arrested and sent to prison. While incarcerated, he began reading avidly and converted to Elijah Muhammad's Nation of Islam. Having learned that all African Americans had lost their original African names when they were forced into slavery, he dropped his own surname upon his release in 1952. He called himself Malcolm X—the X representing his lost African name.

During the next several years, his eloquence and personal charisma brought Malcolm X to the fore in the Nation of Islam, and he spent most of his time giving speeches that condemned white America and urged blacks to convert to Islam. His message contrasted sharply with Martin Luther King Jr.'s advocacy of nonviolent direct action as a means to achieve integration. Malcolm X believed that all whites were racists and that there was no way white America would ever respect black America's rights; rejecting integration as a goal, he called instead for black separatism. In 1964, however, after his hajj to Mecca, where he met many white Muslims who were not racist, he began to believe that there was some hope of working together with whites to eradicate racism. By this time, he had had a falling out with Elijah Muhammad and founded his own Organization of Afro-American Unity. In February 1965, Nation of Islam gunmen assassinated him while he was addressing supporters in the Avalon Ballroom in Harlem.

What is Malcolm's definition of black nationalism? Under what circumstances does he advocate violence? Is his approach more realistic than Martin Luther King Jr.'s philosophy?

The Black Revolution, 1964

Friends and enemies, tonight I hope that we can have a little fireside chat with as few sparks as possible being tossed around. . . . I hope that this little conversation tonight about the black revolution won't cause many of you to accuse us of igniting it when you find it at your doorstep. . . . I'm still a Muslim but I'm also a nationalist, meaning that my political philosophy is black nationalism, my economic philosophy is black nationalism, my social philosophy is black nationalism. And when I say that this philosophy is black nationalism, to me this means that the political philosophy of black nationalism is that which is designed to encourage our people, the black people, to gain complete control over the politics and the politicians of our own community.

Our economic philosophy is that we should gain economic control over the economy of our own community, the businesses and the other things which create employment so that we can provide jobs for our own people instead of having to picket and

---

SOURCE: Malcolm X, "The Black Revolution," in *Two Speeches by Malcolm X* (New York: Merit, 1965), 5, 14.

boycott and beg someone else for a job. And, in short, our social philosophy means that we feel that it is time to get together among our own kind and eliminate the evils that are destroying the moral fiber of our society, like drug addiction, drunkenness, adultery that leads to an abundance of bastard children, welfare problems. We believe that we should lift the level or the standard of our own society to a higher level wherein we will be satisfied and then not inclined toward pushing ourselves into other societies where we are not wanted.

Why is America in a position to bring about a bloodless revolution? Because the Negro in this country holds the balance of power and if the Negro in this country were given what the Constitution says he is supposed to have, the added power of the Negro in this country would sweep all of the racists and the segregationists out of office. It would change the entire political structure of the country. It would wipe out the Southern segregationism that now controls America's foreign policy, as well as America's domestic policy.

And the only way without bloodshed that this can be brought about is that the black man has to be given full use of the ballot in every one of the 50 states. But if the black man doesn't get the ballot, then you are going to be faced with another man who forgets the ballot and starts using the bullet.

Revolutions are fought to get control of land, to remove the absentee landlord and gain control of the land and the institutions that flow from that land. The black man has been in a very low condition because he has had no control whatsoever over any land. He has been a beggar economically, a beggar politically, a beggar socially, a beggar even when it comes to trying to get some education. So that in the past the type of mentality that was developed in this colonial system among our people, today is being overcome. And as the young ones come up they know what they want. And as they listen to your beautiful preaching about democracy and all those other flowery words, they know what they're supposed to have.

So you have a people today who not only know what they want, but also know what they are supposed to have. And they themselves are clearing another generation that is coming up that not only will know what it wants and know what it should have, but also will be ready and willing to do whatever is necessary to see that what they should have materializes immediately. Thank you.

Stokely Carmichael (1941–1998)

By 1965, the civil rights movement was entering the final stages of overturning segregation in the Jim Crow South. There had been boycotts, freedom rides, and sit-ins. The Civil Rights Bill became law in 1964. Jim Crow was dying. In the aftermath of the Selma march, in March 1965, President Johnson submitted the Voting Rights Bill to Congress, which, when it was passed, sent federal examiners into the South to make sure that all citizens, regardless of race, would be permitted to register to vote. Over the next few years, political power in the South began to shift away from white segregationists, and all politicians were forced, if they hoped to be elected, to address the needs of *all* their constituents. However, there were many civil rights activists who believed the federal government had not responded to the campaign quickly or effectively enough and that many important issues still needed to be tackled.

African Americans living in the North had also been closely watching the fight for equality in the South, and although many successes could be claimed, those in the ghettos of Detroit, Chicago, New York, and other cities did not perceive that their lives had in any way changed or improved. Civil rights activists like Stokely Carmichael of the Student Nonviolent Coordinating Committee (SNCC), Floyd McKissick of the Congress of Racial Equality (CORE), and many others grew impatient with Reverend King's nonviolent passive resistance and began advocating that blacks no longer turn the other cheek. African Americans, they proclaimed, should and must fight back. Recovering Marcus Garvey's phrase from the 1920s, Stokely Carmichael called for black power. Equality was not going to be handed to African Americans by benevolent whites. It had to be seized. Black power "is a call for black people in this country to unite," Carmichael and Charles Hamilton wrote in their book, *Black Power*, "to recognize their heritage, to build a sense of community. It is a call for black people to define their own goals, to lead their own organizations." These radicals also questioned the basic premise of Martin Luther King Jr.'s assumption that integration was a worthy goal. White society had nothing to offer blacks, so why, then, should they want to be integrated into it? Rejecting both segregation and integration, black power militants demanded separation. After he became chairman of SNCC in 1966, Carmichael began a speaking tour at universities around the country, urging blacks to build their own "independent political, economic, and cultural institutions."

In this speech, is Carmichael threatening white America with violence? Is he correct when he claims that whites have controlled African Americans' identity and that African Americans must define themselves on their own terms and not on white America's terms? Why does Carmichael object to integration as a solution? Which approach, Carmichael's or King's, is more effective in achieving civil rights? Is there a place in the civil rights movement for whites or should *only* blacks be involved in the struggle? Is black power, as many critics claimed, merely racism in reverse?

Berkeley Speech, October 1966

It's a privilege and an honor to be in the white intellectual ghetto of the West. This is a student conference, as it should be, held on a campus, and we'll never be caught up in intellectual masturbation on the question of Black Power. That's the function of the

SOURCE: Stokely Carmichael, "Berkeley Speech," in *Contemporary American Voices*, ed. James R. Andrews and David Zarefsky (White Plains, NY: Longman, 1992), 100–107.

people who are advertisers but call themselves reporters. Incidentally, for my friends and members of the press, my self-appointed white critics, I was reading Mr. Bernard Shaw two days ago, and I came across a very important quote that I think is most apropos to you. He says, "All criticism is an autobiography." Dig yourself. Ok.

The philosophers Camus and Sartre raise the question of whether or not a man can condemn himself. The black existentialist philosopher who is pragmatic, Frantz Fanon, answered the question. He said that man could not. Camus and Sartre don't answer the question. We in SNCC tend to agree with Fanon—a man cannot condemn himself. If he did, he would then have to inflict punishment upon himself. An example is the Nazis. Any of the Nazi prisoners who, after he was caught and incarcerated, admitted that he committed crimes, that he killed all the many people he killed, had to commit suicide. The only ones able to stay alive were the ones who never admitted that they committed a crime against people—that is, the ones who rationalized that Jews were not human beings and deserved to be killed, or that they were only following orders. There's another, more recent example provided by the officials and the population—the white population—of Neshoba County, Mississippi (that's where Philadelphia is). They could not condemn Sheriff Rainey, his deputies, and the other fourteen men who killed three human beings. They could not because they elected Mr. Rainey to do precisely what he did; and condemning him would be condemning themselves.

In a much larger view, SNCC says that white America cannot condemn herself for her criminal acts against black America. So black people have done it—you stand condemned. The institutions that function in this country are clearly racist; they're built upon racism. The questions to be dealt with then are: how can black people inside this country move? How can white people who say they're not part of those institutions begin to move? And how then do we begin to clear away the obstacles that we have in this society, to make us live like human beings?

Several people have been upset because we've said that integration was irrelevant when initiated by blacks, and that in fact it was an insidious subterfuge for the maintenance of white supremacy. In the past six years or so, this country has been feeding us a "thalidomide drug of integration," and some negroes have been walking down a dream street talking about sitting next to white people. That does not begin to solve the problem. We didn't go to Mississippi to sit next to Ross Barnett [former governor of Mississippi], we did not go to sit next to Jim Clark [sheriff of Selma, Alabama], we went to get them out of our way. People ought to understand that; we were never fighting for the right to integrate, we were fighting against white supremacy. In order to understand white supremacy we must dismiss the fallacious notion that white people can give anybody his freedom. A man is born free. You may enslave a man after he is born free, and that is in fact what this country does. It enslaves blacks after they're born. The only thing white people can do is stop denying black people their freedom.

I maintain that every civil rights bill in this country was passed for white people, not for black people. For example, I am black. I know that. I also know that while I am black I am a human being. Therefore I have the right to go into any public place. White people don't know that. Every time I tried to go into a public place they stopped me. So some boys had to write a bill to tell that white man, "He's a human being; don't stop him." That bill was for the white man, not for me. I knew I could vote all the time and that it wasn't a privilege but my right. Every time I tried I was shot, killed or jailed, beaten or economically deprived. So somebody had to write a bill to tell white people, "When a black man comes to vote, don't bother him." That bill was for white people. I know I can live anyplace I want to live. It is white people across this country who are incapable of allowing me to live where I want. You need a civil rights bill, not me. The failure of the civil rights bill isn't because of Black Power or because of the Student Nonviolent Coordinating Committee or because of the rebellions that are occurring in the major cities. That failure is due to the white's incapacity to deal with their own problems inside their own communities.

And so in a sense we must ask, How is it that black people move? And what do we do? But the question in a much greater sense is, How can white people who are the majority, and who are responsible for making democracy work, make it work? They have never made democracy work, be it inside the United States, Vietnam, South Africa, the Philippines, South America, Puerto Rico, or wherever America has been. We not only condemn the country for what it has done internally, but we must condemn it for what it does externally. We see this country trying to rule the world, and someone must stand up and start articulating that this country is not God, and that it cannot rule the world.

The white supremacist attitude, which you have either consciously or subconsciously, is running rampant through society today. For example, missionaries were sent to Africa with the attitude that blacks were automatically inferior. As a matter of fact, the first act the missionaries did when they got to Africa was to make us cover up our bodies, because they said it got them excited. We couldn't go bare-breasted any more because they got excited! When the missionaries came to civilize us because we were uncivilized, to educate us because we were uneducated, and to give us some literate studies because we were illiterate, they charged a price. The missionaries came with the Bible, and we had the land: When they left, they had the land, and we still have the Bible. That's been the rationalization for Western civilization as it moves across the world—stealing, plundering, and raping everybody in its path. Their one rationalization is that the rest of the world is uncivilized and they are in fact civilized. But the West is un-civ-i-lized. And that still runs on today, you see, because now we have "modern-day missionaries," and they come into our ghettos—they Head Start, Upward Lift, Bootstrap, and Upward Bound us into white society. They don't want to face the real problem. A man is poor for one reason and one reason only—he does not have money. If you want to get rid of poverty, you give people money. And you ought not tell me about people who don't work, and that you can't give people money if they don't work, because if that were true, you'd have to start stopping Rockefeller, Kennedy, Lyndon Baines Johnson, Lady Bird Johnson, the whole of Standard Oil, the Gulf Corporation, all of them, including probably a large number of the board of trustees of this university. The question, then, is not whether or not one can work; it's Who has power to make his or her acts legitimate? That is all. In this country that power is invested in the hands of white people, and it makes their acts legitimate.

We are now engaged in a psychological struggle in this country about whether or not black people have the right to use the words they want to use without white people giving their sanction. We maintain the use of the words Black Power—let them address themselves to that. We are not going to wait for white people to sanction Black Power. We're tired of waiting; every time black people try to move in this country, they're forced to defend their position beforehand. It's time that white people do that. They ought to start defending themselves as to why they have oppressed and exploited us. A man was picked as a slave for one reason—the color of his skin. Black was automatically inferior, inhuman. And therefore fit for slavery, so the question of whether or not we are individually suppressed is nonsensical, and it's a downright lie. We are oppressed as a group because we are black, not because we are lazy or apathetic, not because we're stupid or we stink, not because we eat watermelon or have good rhythm. We are oppressed because we are black.

In order to escape that oppression we must wield the group power we have, not the individual power that this country sets as the criterion under which a man may come into it. That's what is called integration. "You do what I tell you to do and we'll let you sit at the table with us." Well, if you believe in integration, you can come live in Watts, send your children to the ghetto schools. Let's talk about that. If you believe in integration, then we're going to start adopting us some white people to live in our neighborhoods. So it is clear that this question is not one of integration or segregation. We cannot afford to be concerned about the 6 percent black children in this country whom you allow to enter white schools. We are going to be concerned about the 94 percent. You ought to be concerned about them too. But are we willing to be concerned about the black people who will never get to Berkeley, never get to Harvard, and cannot get an education, the ones you'll never get a chance to rub shoulders with and say, "Why, he's almost as good as we are; he's not like the others"? The question is, How can white society begin to move to see black people as human beings? I am black, therefore I am. Not I am black and I must go to college to prove myself. I am black, therefore I am. And don't deprive me of anything and say to me that you must go to college before you gain access to X, Y, and Z. That's only a rationalization for suppression.

The political parties of this country do not meet the needs of the people on a day-to-day basis. How can we build new political institutions that will become the political expressions of people? How can you build political institutions that will begin to meet the needs of Oakland, California? The need of Oakland, California, is not 1,000 policemen with submachine guns. They need that least of all. How can we build institutions that will allow those people to function on a day-to-day basis, so that they can get decent jobs and have decent houses, and they can begin to participate in the policy and make the decisions that affect their lives? That's what they need, not Gestapo troops, because this is not 1942, and if you play like Nazis, we're not going to play Jew this time around. Get hip to that. Can white people move inside their own community and start tearing down racism where in fact it exists? It is you who live in Cicero and stopped us from living there. White people stopped us from moving into Grenada, Mississippi. White people make sure that we live in the ghettos of this country. White institutions do that. They must change. In order for America to really live on a basic principle of human relationships, a new society must be born. Racism must die. The economic exploitation by this country of non-white people around the world must also die.

There are several programs in the South where whites are trying to organize poor whites so they can begin to move around the question of economic exploitation and political disfranchisement. We've all heard the theory several times. But few people are willing to go into it. The question is, Can the white activist stop trying to be a Pepsi generation who comes alive in the black community, and be a man who's willing to move into the white community and start organizing where the organization is needed? Can he do that? Can the white activist disassociate himself from the clowns who waste time parrying with each other and start talking about the problems that are facing people in this state? You must start inside the white community. Our political position is that we don't think the Democratic Party represents the needs of black people. We know that it does not. If, in fact, white people believe that they're going to move inside that structure, how are they going to organize around a concept of whiteness based on true brotherhood and on stopping economic exploitation in order to form a coalition base for black people to hook up with? You cannot build a coalition based on national sentiment. If you want a coalition to address itself to real changes in this country, white people must start building those institutions inside the white community. And that's the real question facing the white activists today. Can they tear down the institutions that have put us all in the trick bag we've been into for the last hundreds of years? Frederick Douglass said that the youth should fight to be leaders today. God knows we need to be leaders today, because the men who run this country are sick. We must begin to start building those institutions and to fight to articulate our position, to fight to be able to control our universities (we need to be able to do that), to fight to control the basic institutions that perpetuate racism by destroying them and building new ones. That's the real question that faces us today, and it is a dilemma because most of us don't know how to work.

Most white activists run into the black community as an excuse. We cannot have white people working in the black community—on psychological grounds. The fact is that all black people question whether or not they are equal to whites, since every time they start to do something, white people are around showing them how to do it. If we are going to eliminate that for the generation that comes after us, then black people must be in positions of power, doing and articulating for themselves. That's not reverse racism; it is moving onto healthy ground; it is becoming what the philosopher Sartre says, an "antiracist racist." And this country can't understand that. If everybody who's white sees himself as racist and sees us against him, he's speaking from his own guilt.

We do not have the power in our hands to change the institution of war in this country—to begin to recreate it so that they can learn to leave the Vietnamese people alone. The only power we have is the power to say, "Hell, no!" to the draft.

The war in Vietnam is illegal and immoral. The question is, What can we do to stop that war? What can we do to stop the people who, in the name of America, are killing babies, women, and children? We have to say to ourselves that there's a higher law than the law of a fool named Rusk; there's a higher law than the law of a buffoon named Johnson. It's the law of each of us. We will not murder anybody who they say kill, and if we decide to kill, "we're" going to decide who it shall be. This country will only stop the war in Vietnam when the young men who are made to fight it begin to say, "Hell, no, we aren't going."

The peace movement has been a failure because it hasn't gotten off the college campuses where everybody has a 2S and is not afraid of being drafted anyway. The problem is how you can move out of that into the white ghettos of this country and articulate a position for those white youth who do not want to go. You cannot do that. It is sometimes ironic that many of the peace groups have begun to call SNCC violent and they say they can no longer support us, when we are in fact the most militant organization for peace or civil rights or human rights against the war in Vietnam in this country today. There isn't one organization that has begun to meet our stand on the war in Vietnam. We not only say we are against the war in Vietnam; we are against the draft. No man has the right to take a man for two years and train him to be a killer. Any black man fighting in the war in Vietnam is nothing but a black mercenary. Any time a black man leaves the country where he can't vote to supposedly deliver the vote to somebody else, he's a black mercenary. Any time a black man leaves this country, gets shot in Vietnam on foreign ground, and returns home and you won't give him a burial place in his own homeland, he's a black mercenary. Even if I believed the lies of Johnson, that we're fighting to give democracy to the people of Vietnam, as a black man living in this country I wouldn't fight to give this to anybody. We have to use our bodies and our minds in the only way that we see fit. We must begin, as the philosopher Camus says, to come alive by saying "no." This country is a nation of thieves. It stole everything it has, beginning with black people. The U.S. cannot justify its existence as the policeman of the world any longer. The marines are at ready disposal to bring democracy, and if the Vietnamese don't want democracy, well then, "We'll just wipe them out, because they don't deserve to live if they won't have our way of life."

There is a more immediate question: What do you do on your campus? Do you raise questions about the hundred black students who were kicked off campus a couple of weeks ago? Eight hundred? And how does that question begin to move? Do you begin to relate to people outside the ivory tower and university walls? Do you think you're capable of building those human relationships based on humanity when the country is the way it is, when the institutions are clearly against us.

We have found all the myths of the country to be nothing but downright lies. We were told that if we worked hard we would succeed, and if that were true we would own this country lock, stock, and barrel. We have picked the cotton for nothing; we are the maids in the kitchens of liberal white people; we are the janitors, the porters, the elevator men; we sweep up your college floors. We are the hardest workers and the lowest paid. It is nonsensical for people to talk about human relationships until they are willing to build new institutions. Black people are economically insecure. White liberals are economically secure. Can you begin to build an economic coalition? Are the liberals willing to share their salaries with the economically insecure black people they so much love? Then if you're not, are you willing to start building new institutions that will provide economic security for black people? That's the question we want to deal with!

American students are perhaps the most politically unsophisticated students in the world. Across every country of the world, while we were growing up, students were leading the major revolutions of their countries. We have not been able to do that. They have been politically aware of their existence. In South America our neighbors have one every 24 hours just to remind us that they are politically aware. But we have been unable to grasp it because we've always moved in the field of morality and love while people have been politically jiving with our lives. You can't move morally against men like Brown and Reagan. You can't move morally against Lyndon Baines Johnson because he is an immoral man. He doesn't know what it's all about. So you've got to move politically. We have to develop a political sophistication that doesn't parrot "the two-party system is the best system in the world." We have to raise questions about whether we need new types of political institutions in this country, and we in SNCC maintain that we need them now. Any time Lyndon Baines Johnson can head a party that has in it Bobby Kennedy, Wayne Morse, Eastland, Wallace, and all those other supposed-to-be-liberal cats, there's something wrong with that party. They're moving politically, not morally. If that party refuses to seat black people from Mississippi and goes ahead and seats racists like Eastland and his clique, it's clear to me that they're moving politically, and that one cannot begin to talk morality to people like that.

We must question the values of this society, and I maintain that black people are the best people to do that since we have been excluded from that society. We ought to think whether or not we want to become a part of that society. That's precisely what the Student Nonviolent Coordinating Committee is doing. We are raising questions about this country. I do not want to be a part of the American pie. The American pie means raping South Africa, beating Vietnam, beating South America, raping the Philippines, raping every country you've been in. I don't want any of your blood money. I don't want to be part of that system. We are the generation who has found this country to be a world power and the wealthiest country in the world. We must question whether or not we want this country to continue being the wealthiest country in the world at the price of raping everybody else. And because black people are saying we do not now want to become a part of you, we are called reverse racists. Ain't that a gas?

White society has caused the failure of nonviolence. I was always surprised at Quakers who came to Alabama and counseled me to be nonviolent, but didn't have the guts to tell James Clark to be nonviolent. That's where nonviolence needs to be preached—to Jim Clark, not to black people. White people should conduct their nonviolent schools in Cicero where they are needed, not among black people in Mississippi. Six-foot-two men kick little black children in Grenada—can you conduct nonviolent schools there? Can you name one black man today who has killed anybody white and is still alive? Even after a rebellion, when some black brothers throw bricks and bottles, ten thousand of them have to pay the price. When the white policeman comes in, anybody who's black is arrested because we all look alike.

The youth of this country must begin to raise those questions. We are going to have to change the foreign policy of this country. One of the problems with the peace movement is that it is too caught up in Vietnam, and if America pulled out the troops from Vietnam this week, next week you'd have to get another peace movement for Santo Domingo. We have to hook up with black people around the world; and that hookup must not only be psychological, but real. If South America were to rebel today, and black people were to shoot the hell out of all the white people there, as they should, Standard Oil would crumble tomorrow. If South Africa were to go today,

Chase Manhattan Bank would crumble tomorrow. If Zimbabwe, which is called Rhodesia by white people, were to go tomorrow, General Electric would cave in on the East Coast. How do we stop those institutions that are so willing to fight against "Communist aggression" but close their eyes against racist oppression? We're not talking about a policy of aid or sending Peace Corps people in to teach people how to read and write and build houses while we steal their raw materials from them. Because that's all this country does. What underdeveloped countries need is information about how to become industrialized, so they can keep their raw materials where they have them, produce goods, sell them to this country for the price it's supposed to pay. Instead, America keeps selling goods back to them for a profit and keeps sending our modern day missionaries there, calling them the sons of Kennedy. And if the youth are going to participate in that program, how do you begin to control the Peace Corps.

This country assumes that if someone is poor, they are poor because of their own individual blight, or because they weren't born on the right side of town, or they had too many children, or went in the army too early, or because their father was a drunk, or they didn't care about school—they made a mistake. That's a lot of nonsense. Poverty is well calculated in this country, and the reason why the poverty program won't work is because the calculators of poverty are administering it.

How can you, as the youth in this country, move to start carrying those things out? Move into the white community. We have developed a movement in the black community. The white activist has miserably failed to develop the movement inside of his community. Will white people have the courage to go into the white communities and start organizing them? That's the question for the white activist. We won't get caught up in questions about power. This country knows what power is. It knows what Black Power is because it deprived black people of it for over four hundred years. White people associate Black Power with violence because of their own inability to deal with blackness. If we had said "Negro power" nobody would get scared. Everybody would support it. If we said power for colored people, everybody'd be for that, but it is the word "black" that bothers people in this country, and that's their problem, not mine. That's the lie that says anything black is bad.

You're all a college and university crowd. You've taken your basic logic course. You know about major premise, minor premise. People have been telling you anything all black is bad. Let's make that our major premise.

Major premise: Anything all black is bad. Minor premise or particular premise: I am all black. Therefore . . . I'm never going to be put in that bag; I'm all black and I'm all good. Anything all black is not necessarily bad. Anything all black is only bad when you use force to keep whites out. Now that's what white people have done in this country, and they're projecting their same fears and guilt on us, and we won't have it. Let them handle their own affairs and their own guilt. Let them find their own psychologists. We refuse to be the therapy for white society any longer. We have gone stark, raving mad trying to do it.

I look at Dr. King on television every single day, and I say to myself: "Now there is a man who's desperately needed in this country. There is a man full of love. There is a man full of mercy. There is a man full of compassion." But every time I see Lyndon on television, I say, "Martin, baby, you got a long way to go."

If we were to be real and honest, we would have to admit that most people in this country see things black and white. We live in a country that's geared that way. White people would have to admit that they are afraid to go into a black ghetto at night. They're afraid because they'd be "beat up," "lynched," "looted," "cut up," etc. It happens to black people inside the ghetto every day, incidentally. Since white people are afraid of that, they get a man to do it for them—a policeman. Figure his mentality. The first time a black man jumps, that white man's going to shoot him. Police brutality is going to exist on that level. The only time I hear people talk about nonviolence is when black people move to defend themselves against white people. Black people cut themselves every night in the ghetto—nobody talks about nonviolence. White people beat up black people every day—nobody talks about nonviolence. But as soon as black people start to move, the double standard comes into being. You can't defend yourself. You show me a black man who advocates aggressive violence who would be able to live in this country. Show him to me. Isn't it hypocritical for Lyndon to talk about how you can't accomplish anything by looting and you must accomplish it by the legal ways? What does he know about legality? Ask Ho Chi Minh.

We must wage a psychological battle on the right for black people to define themselves as they see fit, and organize themselves as they see fit. We don't know whether the white community will allow for that organizing, because once they do they must also allow for the organizing inside their own community. It doesn't make a difference, though—we're going to organize our way. The question is how we're going to organize our way. The question is how we're going to facilitate those matters, whether it's going to be done with a thousand policemen with submachine guns, or whether it's going to be done in a context where it's allowed by white people warding off those policemen. Are white people who call themselves activists ready to move into the white communities on two counts, on building new political institutions to destroy the old ones that we have, and to move around the concept of white youth refusing to go into the army? If so, then we can start to build a new world. We must urge you to fight now to be the leaders of today, not tomorrow. This country is a nation of thieves. It stands on the brink of becoming a nation of murderers. We must stop it. We must stop it.

We are on the move for our liberation. We're tired of trying to prove things to white people. We are tired of trying to explain to white people that we're not going to hurt them. We are concerned with getting the things we want, the things we have to have to be able to function. The question is, Will white people overcome their racism and allow for that to happen in this country? If not, we have no choice but to say very clearly, "Move on over, or we're going to move over you."

The Black Panther Party

As the civil rights movement entered the Black Power phase, Bobby Seale and Huey Newton founded the Black Panther Party in Oakland, California. The Panthers attempted to apply Marxist principles to the idea of black nationalism and called for black autonomy in the United States. Spurning

Martin Luther King Jr.'s nonviolent approach and proclaiming that all black people should be allowed to defend themselves against the establishment, they patrolled the streets of Oakland in black berets and leather jackets while openly carrying arms. If police officers stopped an African American on the street and questioned him, within minutes a group of armed Black Panthers would appear to guarantee that the police refrained from any sort of brutality or provocative action.

White Americans reacted strongly, afraid of the violent message the Panthers seemed to be advocating. Armed Panthers, to be sure, were very intimidating, but they seldom provoked violence. In spite of this, the FBI and police forces around the country targeted them, and by the early 1970s there had been a number of shootouts (mostly provoked by the FBI and the police), during which many Black Panther leaders were killed. As a result the party disintegrated in the early 1970s.

According to their platform, what is the Black Panthers' main program? Does this document promote violence? Are their demands unreasonable?

Black Panther Party Platform, 1966

1. We want freedom. We want power to determine the destiny of our Black Community. We believe that black people will not be free until we are able to determine our destiny.

2. We want full employment for our people. We believe that the federal government is responsible and obligated to give every man employment or a guaranteed income. We believe that if the white American businessmen will not give full employment, then the means of production should be taken from the businessmen and placed in the community so that the people of the community can organize and employ all of its people and give a high standard of living.

3. We want an end to the robbery by the white man of our Black Community. We believe that this racist government has robbed us and now we are demanding the overdue debt of forty acres and two mules. Forty acres and two mules was promised 100 years ago as restitution for slave labor and mass murder of black people. We will accept the payment as currency which will be distributed to our many communities. The Germans are now aiding the Jews in Israel for the genocide of the Jewish people. The Germans murdered six million Jews. The American racist has taken part in the slaughter of over twenty million black people; therefore, we feel that this is a modest demand that we make.

Source: The Black Panther Party, "Platform and Program of the Black Panther Party" (October 1966). Retrieved on 3/7/2004 from www.stanford.edu/group/blackpanthers/history.shtml.

4. We want decent housing, fit for shelter of human beings. We believe that if the white landlords will not give decent housing to our black community, then the housing and the land should be made into cooperatives so that our community, with government aid, can build and make decent housing for its people.

5. We want education for our people that exposes the true nature of this decadent American society. We want education that teaches us our true history and our role in the present-day society. We believe in an educational system that will give to our people a knowledge of self. If a man does not have knowledge of himself and his position in society and the world, then he has little chance to relate to anything else.

6. We want all black men to be exempt from military service. We believe that Black people should not be forced to fight in the military service to defend a racist government that does not protect us. We will not fight and kill other people of color in the world who, like black people, are being victimized by the white racist government of America. We will protect ourselves from the force and violence of the racist police and the racist military, by whatever means necessary.

7. We want an immediate end to POLICE BRUTALITY and MURDER of black people. We believe we can end police brutality in our black community by organizing black self-defense groups that are dedicated to defending our black community from racist police oppression and brutality. The Second Amendment to the Constitution of the United States gives a right to bear arms. We therefore believe that all black people should arm themselves for self defense.

8. We want freedom for all black men held in federal, state, county and city prisons and jails. We believe that all black people should be released from the many jails and prisons because they have not received a fair and impartial trial.

9. We want all black people when brought to trial to be tried in court by a jury of their peer group or people from their black communities, as defined by the Constitution of the United States. We believe that the courts should follow the United States Constitution so that black people will receive fair trials. The 14th Amendment of the U.S. Constitution gives a man a right to be tried by his peer group. A peer is a person from a similar economic, social, religious, geographical, environmental, historical and racial background. To do this the court will be forced to select a jury from the black community from which the black defendant came. We have been, and are being tried by all-white juries that have no understanding of the "average reasoning man" of the black community.

10. We want land, bread, housing, education, clothing, justice and peace. And as our major political objective, a United Nations–supervised plebiscite to be held throughout the black colony in which only black colonial subjects will be allowed to participate for the purpose of determining the will of black people as to their national destiny.

When in the course of human events, it becomes necessary for one people to dissolve the political bands which have connected them with another, and to assume, among the powers of the earth, the separate and equal station to which the laws of nature and nature's God entitle them, a decent respect to the opinions of mankind requires that they should declare the causes which impel them to the separation.

We hold these truths to be self-evident, that all men are created equal; that they are endowed by their Creator with certain unalienable rights; that among these are life, liberty, and the pursuit of happiness. That, to secure these rights, governments are instituted among men, deriving their just powers from the consent of the governed; that, whenever any form of government becomes destructive of these ends, it is the right of the people to alter or to abolish it, and to institute a new government, laying its foundation on such principles, and organizing its powers in such form, as to them shall seem most likely to effect their safety and happiness. Prudence, indeed, will dictate that governments long established should not be changed for light and transient causes; and accordingly, all experience hath shown, that mankind are more disposed to suffer, while evils are sufferable, than to right themselves by abolishing the forms to which they are accustomed. But, when a long train of abuses and usurpations, pursuing invariable the same object, evinces a design to reduce them under absolute despotism, it is their right, it is their duty, to throw off such government, and to provide new guards for their future security.

Students for a Democratic Society

Robert Haber, Tom Hayden, Sharon Jeffrey, Robert Ross, and other students at the University of Michigan formed Students for a Democratic Society (SDS) in 1960. Influenced by the civil rights movement and specifically by sit-ins organized by black students in Greensboro, North Carolina, SDS sought to address many diverse issues that the United States was confronting at the end of the complacent 1950s. Basing much of their thinking on the writings of Marx, Lenin, Fanon, Marcuse, and other left-wing philosophers, SDS wanted the United States to live up to its lofty ideals of equality and freedom for all. In 1962, at a convention in Port Huron, Michigan, they released the following statement, written primarily by Tom Hayden, in which they called for a participatory democracy. For the rest of the decade, as the civil rights movement progressed and the Vietnam War eventually took center stage, SDS grew rapidly and had a huge impact on radicals. Unlike the Old Left, this New Left organization was not content merely to change the power structure but urged people to change their values, to change their consciousness. Only in this way could a true revolution come to fruition. SDS provided much of the intellectual foundation for the emerging student movement.

What, according to this SDS statement, is the source of problems in the United States? What glaring paradoxes must be rectified? What is meant by "participatory democracy"?

The Port Huron Statement, 1962

We are people of this generation, bred in at least modest comfort, housed now in universities, looking uncomfortably to the world we inherit.

When we were kids the United States was the wealthiest and strongest country in the world; the only one with the atom bomb, the least scarred by modern war, an initiator of the United Nations that we thought would distribute Western influence throughout the world. Freedom and equality for each individual, government of, by, and for the people—these American values we found good, principles by which we could live as men. Many of us began maturing in complacency.

As we grew, however, our comfort was penetrated by events too troubling to dismiss. First, the permeating and victimizing fact of human degradation, symbolized by the Southern struggle against racial bigotry, compelled most of us from silence to activism. Second, the enclosing fact of the Cold War, symbolized by the presence of the Bomb, brought awareness that we ourselves, and our friends, and millions of abstract "others" we knew more directly because of our common peril, might die at any time. We might deliberately ignore, or avoid, or fail to feel all other human problems, but not these two, for these were too immediate and crushing in their impact, too challenging in the demand that we as individuals take the responsibility for encounter and resolution.

While these and other problems either directly oppressed us or rankled our consciences and became our own subjective concerns, we began to see complicated and disturbing paradoxes in our surrounding America. The declaration "all men are created equal . . . " rang hollow before the facts of Negro life in the South and the big cities of the North. The proclaimed peaceful intentions of the United States contradicted its economic and military investments in the Cold War status quo.

We witnessed, and continue to witness, other paradoxes. With nuclear energy whole cities can easily be powered, yet the dominant nation-states seem more likely to unleash destruction greater than that incurred in all wars of human history. Although our own technology is destroying old and creating new forms of social organization, men still tolerate meaningless work and idleness. While two-thirds of mankind suffers undernourishment, our own upper classes revel amidst superfluous abundance. Although world population is expected to double in forty years, the nations still tolerate anarchy as a major principle of international conduct and uncontrolled exploitation governs the sapping of the earth's physical resources. Although mankind desperately needs revolutionary leadership, America rests in national stalemate, its goals ambiguous and tradition-bound instead of informed and clear, its democratic system apathetic and manipulated rather than "of, by, and for the people."

Not only did tarnish appear on our image of American virtue, not only did disillusion occur when the hypocrisy of American ideals was discovered, but we began to sense that what we had originally seen as the American Golden Age was actually the decline of an era. The worldwide outbreak of revolution against

SOURCE: James Miller, *"Democracy Is In the Streets:" From Port Huron to the Siege of Chicago* (Cambridge, MA: Harvard University Press, 1987), 329–345.

colonialism and imperialism, the entrenchment of totalitarian states, the menace of war, overpopulation, international disorder, supertechnology—these trends were testing the tenacity of our own commitment to democracy and freedom and our abilities to visualize their application to a world in upheaval.

Our work is guided by the sense that we may be the last generation in the experiment with living. But we are a minority—the vast majority of our people regard the temporary equilibriums of our society and world as eternally functional parts. In this is perhaps the outstanding paradox; we ourselves are imbued with urgency, yet the message of our society is that there is no viable alternative to the present. Beneath the reassuring tones of the politicians, beneath the common opinion that America will "muddle through," beneath the stagnation of those who have closed their minds to the future, is the pervading feeling that there simply are no alternatives, that our times have witnessed the exhaustion not only of Utopias, but of any new departures as well.

Feeling the press of complexity upon the emptiness of life, people are fearful of the thought that at any moment things might be thrust out of control. They fear change itself, since change might smash whatever invisible framework seems to hold back chaos for them now.

For most Americans, all crusades are suspect, threatening. The fact that each individual sees apathy in his fellows perpetuates the common reluctance to organize for change. The dominant institutions are complex enough to blunt the minds of their potential critics, and entrenched enough to swiftly dissipate or entirely repel the energies of protest and reform, thus limiting human expectancies. Then, too, we are a materially improved society, and by our own improvements we seem to have weakened the case for further change.

Some would have us believe that Americans feel contentment amidst prosperity—but might it not better be called a glaze above deeply felt anxieties about their role in the new world? And if these anxieties produce a developed indifference to human affairs, do they not as well produce a yearning to believe that there is an alternative to the present, that something can be done to change circumstances in the school, the workplaces, the bureaucracies, the government?

It is to this latter yearning, at once the spark and engine of change, that we direct our present appeal. The search for truly democratic alternatives to the present, and a commitment to social experimentation with them, is a worthy and fulfilling human enterprise, one which moves us and, we hope, others today.

On such a basis do we offer this document of our convictions and analysis: as an effort in understanding and changing the conditions of humanity in the late twentieth century, an effort rooted in the ancient, still unfulfilled conception of man attaining determining influence over his circumstances of life. . . .

Making values explicit—an initial task in establishing alternatives—is an activity that has been devalued and corrupted. The conventional moral terms of the age, the politician moralities—"free world," "people's democracies"—reflect realities poorly, if at all, and seem to function more as ruling myths than as descriptive principles. But neither has our experience in the universities brought us moral enlightenment. Our professors and administrators sacrifice controversy to public relations; their curriculums change more slowly than the living events of the world; their skills and silence are purchased by investors in the arms race; passion is called unscholastic. The questions we might want raised—what is really important? can we live in a different and better way? if we wanted to change society, how would we do it?—are not thought to be questions of a "fruitful, empirical nature," and thus are brushed aside. . . .

Theoretic chaos has replaced the idealistic thinking of old—and, unable to reconstitute theoretic order, men have condemned idealism itself. Doubt has replaced hopefulness—and men act out a defeatism that is labeled realistic. The decline of utopia and hope is in fact one of the defining features of social life today. The reasons are various: the dreams of the older left were perverted by Stalinism and never re-created; the congressional stalemate makes men narrow their view of the possible; the specialization of human activity leaves little room for sweeping thought; the horrors of the twentieth century symbolized in the gas ovens and concentration camps and atom bombs, have blasted hopefulness. To be idealistic is to be considered apocalyptic, deluded. To have no serious aspirations, on the contrary, is to be "tough-minded."

In suggesting social goals and values, therefore, we are aware of entering a sphere of some disrepute. Perhaps matured by the past, we have no formulas, no closed theories—but that does not mean values are beyond discussion and tentative determination. A first task of any social movement is to convince people that the search for orienting theories and the creation of human values is complex but worthwhile. We are aware that to avoid platitudes we must analyze the concrete conditions of social order. But to direct such an analysis we must use the guideposts of basic principles. Our own social values involve conceptions of human beings, human relationships, and social systems.

We regard men as infinitely precious and possessed of unfulfilled capacities for reason, freedom, and love. In affirming these principles we are aware of countering perhaps the dominant conceptions of man in the twentieth century: that he is a thing to be manipulated, and that he is inherently incapable of directing his own affairs. We oppose the depersonalization that reduces human being to the status of things—if anything, the brutalities of the twentieth century teach that means and ends are intimately related, that vague appeals to "posterity" cannot justify the mutilations of the present. We oppose, too, the doctrine of human incompetence because it rests essentially on the modern fact that men have been "competently" manipulated into incompetence—we see little reason why men cannot meet with increasing the skill the complexities and responsibilities of their situation, if society is organized not for minority, but for majority, participation in decision-making.

Men have unrealized potential for self-cultivation, self-direction, self-understanding, and creativity. It is this potential that we regard as crucial and to which we appeal, not to the human potentiality for violence, unreason, and submission to authority. The goal of man and society should be human independence: a concern not with image of popularity but with finding a meaning in life that is personally authentic; a quality of mind not compulsively driven by a sense of powerlessness, nor one which unthinkingly adopts status values, nor one which represses all threats to its habits, but one which has full, spontaneous access to present and past experiences, one which easily unites the fragmented parts of personal history, one which openly faces problems which are troubling and unresolved; one with an intuitive awareness of possibilities, an active sense of curiosity, an ability and willingness to learn.

This kind of independence does not mean egotistic individualism—the object is not to have one's way so much as it is to have a way that is one's own. Nor do we deify man—we merely have faith in his potential.

Human relationships should involve fraternity and honesty. Human interdependence is contemporary fact; human brotherhood must be willed, however, as a condition of future survival and as the most appropriate form of social relations. Personal links between man and man are needed, especially to go beyond the partial and fragmentary bonds of function that bind men only as worker to worker, employer to employee, teacher to student, American to Russian.

Loneliness, estrangement, isolation describe the vast distance between man and man today. These dominant tendencies cannot be overcome by better personnel management, nor by improved gadgets, but only when a love of man overcomes the idolatrous worship of things by man. As the individualism we affirm is not egoism, the selflessness we affirm is not self-elimination. On the contrary, we believe in generosity of a kind that imprints one's unique individual qualities in the relation to other men, and to all human activity. Further, to dislike isolation is not to favor the abolition of privacy; the latter differs from isolation in that it occurs or is abolished according to individual will.

Finally, we would replace power rooted in possession, privilege, or circumstance by power and uniqueness rooted in love, reflectiveness, reason, and creativity. As a *social system* we seek the establishment of a democracy of individual participation, governed by two central aims: that the individual share in those social decisions determining the quality and direction of his life; that society be organized to encourage independence in men and provide the media for their common participation.

In a participatory democracy, the political life would be based in several root principles: that decision-making of basic social consequence be carried on by public groupings; that politics be seen positively, as the art of collectively creating an acceptable pattern of social relations; that politics has the function of bringing people out of isolation and into community, thus being a necessary, though not sufficient, means of finding meaning in personal life; that the political order should serve to clarify problems in a way instrumental to their solution; it should provide outlets for the expression of personal grievance and aspiration; opposing views should be organized so as to illuminate choices and facilitate the attainment of goals; channels should be commonly available to relate men to knowledge and to power so that private problems—from bad recreation facilities to personal alienation—are formulated as general issues.

The economic sphere would have as its basis the principles: that work should involve incentives worthier than money or survival. It should be educative, not stultifying; creative, not mechanical; self-directed, not manipulated, encouraging independence, a respect for others, a sense of dignity, and a willingness to accept social responsibility, since it is this experience that has crucial influence on habits, perceptions and individual ethics; that the economic experience is so personally decisive that the individual must share in its full determination; that the economy itself is of such social importance that its major resources and means of production should be open to democratic participation and subject to democratic social regulation.

Like the political and economic ones, major social institutions—cultural, educational, rehabilitative, and others—should be generally organized with the well-being and dignity of man as the essential measure of success.

In social change or interchange, we find violence to be abhorrent because it requires generally the transformation of the target, be it a human being or a community of people, into a depersonalized object of hate. It is imperative that the means of violence be abolished and the institutions—local, national, international—that encourage non-violence as a condition of conflict be developed. These are our central values, in skeletal form. It remains vital to understand their denial or attainment in the context of the modern world. . . .

Betty Friedan (1921–)

Freelance writer Betty Friedan, a 1942 graduate of Smith College, sent out a questionnaire on the occasion of her fifteenth class reunion to her fellow alumna to evaluate how successful they had become. The replies suggested that though most of them were doing quite well materially, a substantial number felt deeply discontented with how their lives had turned out. This prompted Friedan to do extensive research and a series of in-depth interviews to write about what she called the "problem that has no name." When she had finished, she submitted the article to *McCall's* and *Ladies' Home Journal*. Both magazines rejected it. Though frustrated about the rejections, she continued and expanded her research, and in 1963 the article was finally published as a book. *The Feminine Mystique* was an immediate best seller and a significant factor in launching the modern feminist movement. It was foolish, Friedan wrote, for people to believe in the feminine mystique—the assumption that women could achieve happiness only by waxing the kitchen floor, scrubbing the bathtub, and taking care of husband and children. Many of her classmates from Smith were living in nice suburbs, with nice husbands, and nice children. To Friedan, however, these suburbs were nothing more than "comfortable concentration camps" in which women's creativity was stifled. The time had now come, she claimed, for women to cast off the false ideology and values that stultified their ambitions and opportunities.

Though Friedan had been active, before she wrote *The Feminine Mystique*, in the labor movement, left-wing politics, and the civil rights movement, she was criticized for concentrating mostly on middle-class white women in her analysis. In 1966 she founded the National Organization for Women (NOW), which campaigned, during the ensuing years, for equal opportunities for women in the workplace and in education, as well as for the adoption of the Equal Rights Amendment to the U.S. Constitution.

The first document here is an excerpt from the first chapter of *The Feminine Mystique*. The second is the National Organization for Women's "Statement of Purpose." What is "the problem that has no name"? What caused it? How can it be solved? Are there any noticeable similarities between the "Statement of Purpose" and the "Declaration of Sentiments" of 1848? What does NOW see as the root of the problem that women face? Are women's roles determined by biology or by society? We still have no Equal Rights Amendment. Should we?

From *The Feminine Mystique*, 1963

The problem lay buried, unspoken, for many years in the minds of American women. It was a strange stirring, a sense of dissatisfaction, a yearning that women suffered in the middle of the twentieth century in the United States. Each suburban wife struggled with it alone. As she made the beds, shopped for groceries, matched slipcover material, ate peanut butter sandwiches with her children, chauffeured Cub Scouts and Brownies, lay beside her husband at night—she was afraid to ask even of herself the silent question—"Is this all?"

For over fifteen years there was no word of this yearning in the millions of words written about women, for women, in all the columns, books and articles by experts telling women their role was to seek fulfillment as wives and mothers. Over and over women heard in voices of tradition and of Freudian sophistication that they could desire no greater destiny than to glory in their own femininity. Experts told them how to catch a man and keep him, how to breastfeed children and handle their toilet training, how to cope with sibling rivalry and adolescent rebellion; how to buy a dishwasher, bake bread, cook gourmet snails, and build a swimming pool with their own hands; how to dress, look, and act more feminine and make marriage more exciting; how to keep their husbands from dying young and their sons from growing into delinquents. They were taught to pity the neurotic, unfeminine, unhappy women who wanted to be poets or physicists or presidents. They learned that truly feminine women do not want careers, higher education, political rights—the independence and the opportunities that the old-fashioned feminists fought for. Some women, in their forties and fifties, still remembered painfully giving up those dreams, but most of the younger women no longer even thought about them. A thousand expert voices applauded their femininity, their adjustment, their new maturity. All they had to do was devote their lives from earliest girlhood to finding a husband and bearing children.

By the end of the nineteen-fifties, the average marriage age of women in America dropped to 20, and was still dropping, into the teens. Fourteen million girls were engaged by 17. The proportion of women attending college in comparison with men dropped from 47 percent in 1920 to 35 percent in 1958. A century earlier, women had fought for higher education; now girls went to college to get a husband. By the

SOURCE: Betty Friedan, *The Feminine Mystique* (New York: Norton, 1963), 15–20.

mid-fifties, 60 percent dropped out of college to marry, or because they were afraid too much education would be a marriage bar. Colleges built dormitories for "married students," but the students were almost always the husbands. A new degree was instituted for the wives—"Ph.T." (Putting Husband Through).

Then American girls began getting married in high school. And the women's magazines, deploring the unhappy statistics about these young marriages, urged that courses on marriage, and marriage counselors, be installed in the high schools. Girls started going steady at twelve and thirteen, in junior high. Manufacturers put out brassieres with false bosoms or foam rubber for little girls of ten. And an advertisement for a child's dress, size 3–6s, in the New York Times in the fall of 1960, said: "She Too Can Join the Man-Trap Set."

By the end of the fifties, the United States birthrate was overtaking India's. The birth-control movement, renamed Planned Parenthood, was asked to find a method whereby women who had been advised that a third or fourth baby would be born dead or defective might have it anyhow. Statisticians were especially astounded at the fantastic increase in the number of babies among college women. Where once they had two children, now they had four, five, six. Women who had once wanted careers were now making careers out of having babies. So rejoiced Life magazine in a 1956 paean to the movement of American women back to the home.

In a New York hospital, a woman had a nervous breakdown when she found she could not breastfeed her baby. In other hospitals, women dying of cancer refused a drug which research had proved might save their lives: its side effects were said to be unfeminine. "If I have only one life, let me live it as a blonde," a larger-than-life-sized picture of a pretty, vacuous woman proclaimed from newspaper, magazine, and drugstores ads. And across America, three out of every ten women dyed their hair blonde. They ate a chalk called Metrecal, instead of food, to shrink to the size of the thin young models. Department-store buyers reported that American women, since 1939, had become three and four sizes smaller, "Women are out to fit the clothes, instead of vice-versa," one buyer said.

Interior decorators were designing kitchens with mosaic murals and original paintings, for kitchens were once again the center of women's lives. Home sewing became a million-dollar industry. Many women no longer left their homes, except to shop, chauffeur their children, or attend a social engagement with their husbands. Girls were growing up in America without ever having jobs outside the home. In the late fifties, a sociological phenomenon was suddenly remarked: a third of American women now worked, but most were no longer young and very few were pursuing careers. They were married women who held part-time jobs, selling or secretarial, to put their husbands through school, their sons through college, or to help pay the mortgage. Or they were widows supporting families. Fewer and fewer women were entering professional work. The shortages in the nursing, social work, and teaching professions caused crises in almost every American city. Concerned over the Soviet Union's lead in the space race, scientists noted the America's greatest source of unused brainpower was women. But girls would not study physics: it was "unfeminine." A girl refused a science fellowship at Johns Hopkins to take a job in a real-estate office. All she wanted, she said, was what every other American girl wanted—to get married, have four children and live in a nice house in a nice suburb.

The suburban housewife—she was the dream image of the young American women and the envy, it was said, of women all over the world. The American housewife—freed by science and labor-saving appliances from the drudgery, the angers of childbirth and the illnesses of her grandmother. She was healthy, beautiful, educated, concerned only about her husband, her children, her home. She had found true feminine fulfillment. As a housewife and mother, she was respected as a full and equal partner to man in his world. She was free to choose automobiles, clothes, appliances, supermarkets; she had everything that women ever dreamed of.

In the fifteen years after World War II, this mystique of feminine fulfillment became the cherished and self-perpetuating core of contemporary American culture. Millions of women lived their lives in the image of those pretty pictures of the American suburban housewife, kissing their husbands goodbye in front of the picture window, depositing their station wagons full of children at school, and smiling as they ran the new electric waxer over the spotless kitchen floor. They baked their own bread, sewed their own and their children's clothes, kept their new washing machines and dryers running all day. They changed the sheets on the beds twice a week instead of once, took the rug-hooking class in adult education, and pitied their poor frustrated mothers, who had dreamed of having a career. Their only dream was to be perfect wives and mothers; their highest ambition to have five children and a beautiful house, their only fight to get and keep their husbands. They had no thought for the unfeminine problems of the world outside the home; they wanted the men to make the major decisions. They gloried in their role as women, and wrote proudly on the census blank: "Occupation: housewife."

For over fifteen years, the words written for women, and the words women used when they talked to each other, while their husbands sat on the other side of the room and talked shop or politics or septic tanks, were about problems with their children, or how to keep their husbands happy, or improve their children's school or cook chicken or make slipcovers. Nobody argued whether women were inferior or superior to men; they were simply different. Words like "emancipation" and "career" sounded strange and embarrassing; no one had used them for years. When a Frenchwoman named Simone de Beauvoir wrote a book called *The Second Sex,* an American critic commented that she obviously "didn't know what life was all about," and besides, she was talking about French women. The "woman problem" in America no longer existed.

If a woman had a problem in the 1950's and 1960's she knew that something must be wrong with her marriage, or with herself. Other women were satisfied with their lives, she thought. What kind of woman was she if she did not feel this mysterious fulfillment waxing the kitchen floor? She was so ashamed to admit her dissatisfaction that she never knew how many other women shared it. If she tried to tell her husband, he didn't understand what she was talking about. She did not really understand it herself. For over fifteen years women in America found it harder to talk about this problem than about sex. Even the psychoanalysts had no name for it. When a woman went to a psychiatrist for help, as many women did, she would say, "I'm so ashamed," or "I must be hopelessly neurotic." "I don't know what's wrong with women today," a suburban psychiatrist said uneasily. "I only know something is wrong because most of my patients happen to be women. And their problem isn't sexual." Most women with this problem did not go to see a psychoanalyst, however. "There's nothing wrong really," they kept telling themselves. "There isn't any problem."

But on an April morning in 1959, I heard a mother of four, having coffee with four other mothers in a suburban development fifteen miles from New York, say in a tone of quiet desperation, "the problem." And the others knew, without words, that she was not talking about a problem with her husband, or her children, or her home. Suddenly they realized they all shared the same problem, the problem that has no name. They began, hesitantly, to talk about it. Later, after they had picked up their children at nursery school and taken them home to nap, two of the women cried, in sheer relief, just to know they were not alone.

Gradually I came to realize that the problem that has no name was shared by countless women in America. As a magazine writer I often interviewed women about problems with their children, or their marriages, or their houses, or their communities. But after a while I began to recognize the telltale signs of this other problem. I saw the same signs in suburban ranch houses and split-levels on Long Island and in New Jersey and Westchester County; in colonial houses in the small Massachusetts town; on patios in Memphis; in suburban and city apartments; in living rooms in the Midwest. Sometimes I sensed the problem, not as a reporter, but as a suburban housewife, for during this time I was also bringing up my own three children in Rockland County, New York. I heard echoes of the problem in college dormitories and semi-private maternity wards, at PTA meetings and luncheons of the League of Women Voters, at suburban cocktail parities, in station wagons waiting for trains, and in snatches of conversation overheard at Schrafft's. The groping words I heard from other women, on quiet afternoons when children were at school or on quiet evenings when husbands worked late, I think I understood first as a woman long before I understood their larger social and psychological implications.

Statement of Purpose, National Organization for Women, 1966

We, men and women who hereby constitute ourselves as the National Organization for Women, believe that the time has come for a new movement toward true equality for all women in America, and toward a fully equal partnership of the sexes, as part of the world-wide revolution of human rights now taking place within and beyond our national borders.

The purpose of NOW is to take action to bring women into full participation in the mainstream of American society now, exercising all the privileges and responsibilities thereof in truly equal partnership with men.

We believe the time has come to move beyond the abstract argument, discussion and symposia over the status and special nature of women which has raged in America

---

SOURCE: Betty Friedan, "Statement of Purpose, National Organization of Women," from *It Changed My Life: Writings on the Women's Movement,* originally published by Random House. © 1963, 1964, 1966, 1970, 1971, 1972, 1973, 1974, 1975, 1976, 1985, 1991, 1998 by Betty Friedan. Reprinted by permission of Curtis Brown, Ltd.

in recent years; the time has come to confront, with concrete action, the conditions that now prevent women from enjoying the equality of opportunity and freedom of choice which is their right, as individual Americans, and as human beings.

NOW is dedicated to the proposition that women, first and foremost, are human beings, who, like all other people in our society, must have the chance to develop their fullest human potential. We believe that women can achieve such equality only by accepting to the full the challenges and responsibilities they share with all other people in our society, as part of the decision-making mainstream of American political, economic and social life.

We organize to initiate or support action, nationally, or in any part of this nation, by individuals or organizations, to break through the silken curtain of prejudice and discrimination against women in government, industry, the professions, the churches, the political parties, the judiciary, the labor unions, in education, science, medicine, law, religion and every other field of importance in American society.

Enormous changes taking place in our society make it both possible and urgently necessary to advance the unfinished revolution of women toward true equality, now. With a life span lengthened to nearly 75 years it is no longer either necessary or possible for women to devote the greater part of their lives to child-rearing; yet childbearing and rearing which continues to be a most important part of most women's lives—still is used to justify barring women from equal professional and economic participation and advance.

Today's technology has reduced most of the productive chores which women once performed in the home and in mass-production industries based upon routine unskilled labor. This same technology has virtually eliminated the quality of muscular strength as a criterion for filling most jobs, while intensifying American industry's need for creative intelligence. In view of this new industrial revolution created by automation in the mid-twentieth century, women can and must participate in old and new fields of society in full equality—or become permanent outsiders.

Despite all the talk about the status of American women in recent years, the actual position of women in the United States has declined, and is declining, to an alarming degree throughout the 1950's and 60's. Although 46.4% of all American women between the ages of 18 and 65 now work outside the home, the overwhelming majority—75%—are in routine clerical, sales, or factory jobs, or they are household workers, cleaning women, hospital attendants. About two-thirds of Negro women workers are in the lowest paid service occupations. Working women are becoming increasingly—not less—concentrated on the bottom of the job ladder. As a consequence full-time women workers today earn on the average only 60% of what men earn, and that wage gap has been increasing over the past twenty-five years in every major industry group. In 1964, of all women with a yearly income, 89% earned under $5,000 a year; half of all full-time year round women workers earned less than $3,690; only 1.4% of full-time year round women workers had an annual income of $10,000 or more.

Further, with higher education increasingly essential in today's society, too few women are entering and finishing college or going on to graduate or professional school. Today, women earn only one in three of the B.A.'s and M.A.'s granted, and one in ten of the Ph.D.'s.

In all the professions considered of importance to society, and in the executive ranks of industry and government, women are losing ground. Where they are present it is only a token handful. Women comprise less than 1% of federal judges; less than 4% of all lawyers; 7% of doctors. Yet women represent 51% of the U.S. population. And, increasingly, men are replacing women in the top positions in secondary and elementary schools, in social work, and in libraries—once thought to be women's fields.

Official pronouncements of the advance in the status of women hide not only the reality of this dangerous decline, but the fact that nothing is being done to stop it. The excellent reports of the President's Commission on the Status of Women and of the State Commissions have not been fully implemented. Such Commissions have power only to advise. They have no power to enforce their recommendation; nor have they the freedom to organize American women and men to press for action on them. The reports of these commissions have, however, created a basis upon which it is now possible to build. Discrimination in employment on the basis of sex is now prohibited by federal law, in Title VII of the Civil Rights Act of 1964. But although nearly one-third of the cases brought before the Equal Employment Opportunity Commission during the first year dealt with sex discrimination and the proportion is increasing dramatically, the Commission has not made clear its intention to enforce the law with the same seriousness on behalf of women as of other victims of discrimination. Many of these cases were Negro women, who are the victims of double discrimination of race and sex. Until now, too few women's organizations and official spokesmen have been willing to speak out against these dangers facing women. Too many women have been restrained by the fear of being called "feminist." There is no civil rights movement to speak for women, as there has been for Negroes and other victims of discrimination. The National Organization for Women must therefore begin to speak.

WE BELIEVE that the power of American law, and the protection guaranteed by the U.S. Constitution to the civil rights of all individuals, must be effectively applied and enforced to isolate and remove patterns of sex discrimination, to ensure equality of opportunity in employment and education, and equality of civil and political rights and responsibilities on behalf of women, as well as for Negroes and other deprived groups.

We realize that women's problems are linked to many broader questions of social justice; their solution will require concerted action by many groups. Therefore, convinced that human rights for all are indivisible, we expect to give active support to the common cause of equal rights for all those who suffer discrimination and deprivation, and we call upon other organizations committed to such goals to support our efforts toward equality for women.

WE DO NOT ACCEPT the token appointment of a few women to high-level positions in government and industry as a substitute for serious continuing effort to recruit and advance women according to their individual abilities. To this end, we urge American government and industry to mobilize the same resources of ingenuity and command with which they have solved problems of far greater difficulty than those now impeding the progress of women.

WE BELIEVE that this nation has a capacity at least as great as other nations, to innovate new social institutions which will enable women to enjoy the true equality of opportunity and responsibility in society, without conflict with their responsibilities as mothers and homemakers. In such innovations, America does not lead the Western world, but lags by decades behind many European countries. We do not accept the traditional assumption that a woman has to choose between marriage and mother-hood, on the one hand, and serious participation in industry or the professions on the other. We question the present expectation that all normal women will retire from job or profession for 10 or 15 years, to devote their full time to raising children, only to reenter the job market at a relatively minor level. This, in itself, is a deterrent to the aspirations of women, to their acceptance into management or professional training courses, and to the very possibility of equality of opportunity or real choice, for all but a few women. Above all, we reject the assumption that these problems are the unique responsibility of each individual woman, rather than a basic social dilemma which society must solve. True equality of opportunity and freedom of choice for women requires such practical, and possible innovations as a nationwide network of child-care centers, which will make it unnecessary for women to retire completely from society until their children are grown, and national programs to provide retraining for women who have chosen to care for their children full-time.

WE BELIEVE that it is as essential for every girl to be educated to her full poten-tial of human ability as it is for every boy—with the knowledge that such education is the key to effective participation in today's economy and that, for a girl as for a boy, education can only be serious where there is expectation that it will be used in society. We believe that American educators are capable of devising means of imparting such expectations to girl students. Moreover, we consider the decline in the proportion of women receiving higher and professional education to be evidence of discrimination. This discrimination may take the form of quotas against the admission of women to colleges, and professional schools; lack of encouragement by parents, counselors and educators; denial of loans or fellowships; or the traditional or arbitrary procedures in graduate and professional training geared in terms of men, which inadvertently discriminate against women. We believe that the same serious attention must be given to high school dropouts who are girls as to boys.

WE REJECT the current assumptions that a man must carry the sole burden of supporting himself, his wife, and family, and that a woman is automatically entitled to lifelong support by a man upon her marriage, or that marriage, home and family are primarily woman's world and responsibility—hers, to dominate—his to support. We believe that a true partnership between the sexes demands a different concept of marriage, an equitable sharing of the responsibilities of home and children and of the economic burdens of their support. We believe that proper recognition should be given to the economic and social value of homemaking and child-care. To these ends, we will seek to open a reexamination of laws and mores governing marriage and divorce, for we believe that the current state of "half-equity" between the sexes discriminates against both men and women, and is the cause of much unnecessary hostility between the sexes.

WE BELIEVE that women must now exercise their political rights and respon-sibilities as American citizens. They must refuse to be segregated on the basis of sex into separate-and-not-equal ladies' auxiliaries in the political parties, and they must demand representation according to their numbers in the regularly constituted party committees—at local, state, and national levels—and in the informal power structure, participating fully in the selection of candidates and political decision-making, and running for office themselves.

IN THE INTERESTS OF THE HUMAN DIGNITY OF WOMEN, we will protest, and endeavor to change, the false image of women now prevalent in the mass media, and in the texts, ceremonies, laws, and practices of our major social institutions. Such images perpetuate contempt for women by society and by women for themselves. We are similarly opposed to all policies and practices—in church, state, college, factory, or office—which, in the guise of protectiveness, not only deny opportunities but also foster in women self-denigration, dependence, and evasion of responsibility, undermine their confidence in their own abilities and foster contempt for women.

NOW WILL HOLD ITSELF INDEPENDENT OF ANY POLITICAL PARTY in order to mobilize the political power of all women and men intent on our goals. We will strive to ensure that no party, candidate, president, senator, governor, congressman, or any public official who betrays or ignores the principle of full equality between the sexes is elected or appointed to office. If it is necessary to mobilize the votes of men and women who believe in our cause, in order to win for women the final right to be fully free and equal human beings, we so commit ourselves.

WE BELIEVE THAT women will do most to create a new image of women by acting now, and by speaking out in behalf of their own equality, freedom, and human dignity—not in pleas for special privilege, nor in enmity toward men, who are also victims of the current, half-equality between the sexes—but in an active, self-respecting partnership with men. By so doing, women will develop confidence in their own ability to determine actively, in partnership with men, the conditions of their life, their choices, their future and their society.

Protest Music I

During the latter half of the 1950s a number of coffee houses and folk clubs opened in New York and San Francisco. This was partly an outgrowth of the popularity of the Weavers folk group as well as the growing Beat Movement. Beat poets (and would-be poets) often gathered in these smoke-filled clubs to exchange ideas, denounce the conformist social atmosphere of the 1950s, read their poetry, and, in some cases, sing their songs. The result was the folk music revival. In 1958, when the Kingston Trio's "Tom Dooley" raced to the top of the charts, folk music became a force in popular culture. By the early 1960s, numerous performers such as Peter, Paul, and Mary, Joan Baez, Phil Ochs, and Bob Dylan were appealing to a rapidly growing audience of baby boomers. At first these musicians recorded and performed traditional songs; the songs of Woody Guthrie, Leadbelly, and Pete Seeger; or songs from 1920s blues artists like Mississippi John Hurt or Robert Johnson. Soon, however, many folk artists began writing their own songs. This was especially true of Bob Dylan and Phil Ochs, who had such an influence that by 1965 it was almost a requirement for any would-be folksingers to be writing their own songs.

Folk songs tell a story. A story can be political. Many of the songs performed at the clubs (and later at larger venues like Carnegie Hall) were critical and probing explorations of the problems facing the nation: civil rights, the cold war, the uptight conformity of crew-cut, gray-flannel-suit America, and the arms race that seemed to be pushing the world to the brink of Armageddon.

Phil Ochs presents his version of history here in his antiwar "I Ain't Marchin' Anymore," and Malvina Reynolds takes on conventionality and "fitting in" in "Little Boxes." Bob Dylan's "The Times They Are A-Changin'" has become one of the anthems of the 1960s and in "It's Alright Ma (I'm Only Bleeding)" Dylan seems to take on everything. What do these songs say about American life in the late 1950s and early 1960s? What impact do you suppose they had on audiences at the time? Are the lyrics still relevant today?

"I Ain't Marching Anymore"

Oh I marched to the battle of New Orleans
At the end of the early British war
The young land started growing
The young blood started flowing
But I ain't marching anymore

For I've killed my share of Indians
In a thousand different fights
I was there at the Little Big Horn
I heard many men lying
I saw many more dying
But I ain't marching anymore

It's always the old to lead us to the war
It's always the young to fall
Now look at all we've won with the sabre and the gun
Tell me is it worth it all

For I stole California from the Mexican land
Fought in the bloody Civil War
Yes I even killed my brother
And so many others
And I ain't marching anymore

SOURCE: Phil Ochs, *I Ain't Marching Anymore*, Hannibal 1965.

For I marched to the battles of the German trench
In a war that was bound to end all wars
Oh I must have killed a million men
And now they want me back again
But I ain't marching anymore

For I flew the final mission in the Japanese sky
Set off the mighty mushroom roar
When I saw the cities burning
I knew that I was learning
That I ain't marching anymore

Now the labor leader's screamin' when they close the missile plants,
United Fruit screams at the Cuban shore,
Call it "Peace" or call it "Treason,"
Call it "Love" or call it "Reason,"
But I ain't marching any more.

"Little Boxes"

Little boxes on the hillside,
Little boxes made of ticky tacky
Little boxes on the hillside,
Little boxes all the same,
There's a green one and a pink one
And a blue one and a yellow one
And they're all made out of ticky tacky
And they all look just the same.

And the people in the houses
All went to the university
Where they were put in boxes
And they came out all the same
And there's doctors and lawyers
And business executives
And they're all made out of ticky tacky
And they all look just the same.

And they all play on the golf course
And drink their martinis dry
And they all have pretty children
And the children go to school,
And the children go to summer camp
And then to the university

SOURCE: Pete Seeger, *We Shall Overcome: The Carnegie Hall Concert*, Columbia 1963.

Where they are put in boxes
And they come out all the same.

And the boys go into business
And marry and raise a family
In boxes made of ticky tacky
And they all look just the same,
There's a green one and a pink one
And a blue one and a yellow one
And they're all made out of ticky tacky
And they all look just the same.

"The Times They Are A-Changin'"

Come gather 'round people
Wherever you roam
And admit that the waters
Around you have grown
And accept it that soon
You'll be drenched to the bone.
If your time to you
Is worth savin'
Then you better start swimmin'
Or you'll sink like a stone
For the times they are a-changin'.

Come writers and critics
Who prophesize with your pen
And keep your eyes wide
The chance won't come again
And don't speak too soon
For the wheel's still in spin
And there's no tellin' who
That it's namin'.
For the loser now
Will be later to win
For the times they are a-changin'.

Come senators, congressmen
Please heed the call
Don't stand in the doorway
Don't block up the hall
For he that gets hurt
Will be he who has stalled

SOURCE: Bob Dylan, *The Times They are A-Changin'*, Columbia 1964.

There's a battle outside
And it is ragin'.
It'll soon shake your windows
And rattle your walls
For the times they are a-changin'.

Come mothers and fathers
Throughout the land
And don't criticize
What you can't understand
Your sons and your daughters
Are beyond your command
Your old road is
Rapidly agin'.
Please get out of the new one
If you can't lend your hand
For the times they are a-changin'.

The line it is drawn
The curse it is cast
The slow one now
Will later be fast
As the present now
Will later be past
The order is
Rapidly fadin'.
And the first one now
Will later be last
For the times they are a-changin'.

"It's Alright Ma (I'm Only Bleeding)"

Darkness at the break of noon
Shadows even the silver spoon
The handmade blade, the child's balloon
Eclipses both the sun and moon
To understand you know too soon
There is no sense in trying.

Pointed threats, they bluff with scorn
Suicide remarks are torn
From the fool's gold mouthpiece
The hollow horn plays wasted words
Proves to warn

SOURCE: Bob Dylan. *Bringing It All Back Home,* Columbia 1965.

That he not busy being born
Is busy dying.

Temptation's page flies out the door
You follow, find yourself at war
Watch waterfalls of pity roar
You feel to moan but unlike before
You discover
That you'd just be
One more person crying.

So don't fear if you hear
A foreign sound to your ear
It's alright, Ma, I'm only sighing.

As some warn victory, some downfall
Private reasons great or small
Can be seen in the eyes of those that call
To make all that should be killed to crawl
While others say don't hate nothing at all
Except hatred.

Disillusioned words like bullets bark
As human gods aim for their mark
Made everything from toy guns that spark
To flesh-colored Christs that glow in the dark
It's easy to see without looking too far
That not much
Is really sacred.

While preachers preach of evil fates
Teachers teach that knowledge waits
Can lead to hundred-dollar plates
Goodness hides behind its gates
But even the president of the United States
Sometimes must have
To stand naked.

An' though the rules of the road have been lodged
It's only people's games that you got to dodge
And it's alright, Ma, I can make it.

Advertising signs that con you
Into thinking you're the one
That can do what's never been done
That can win what's never been won
Meantime life outside goes on
All around you.

You lose yourself, you reappear
You suddenly find you got nothing to fear
Alone you stand with nobody near
When a trembling distant voice, unclear
Startles your sleeping ears to hear
That somebody thinks
They really found you.

A question in your nerves is lit
Yet you know there is no answer fit to satisfy
Insure you not to quit
To keep it in your mind and not fergit
That it is not he or she or them or it
That you belong to.

Although the masters make the rules
For the wise men and the fools
I got nothing, Ma, to live up to.

For them that must obey authority
That they do not respect in any degree
Who despise their jobs, their destinies
Speak jealously of them that are free
Cultivate their flowers to be
Nothing more than something
They invest in.

While some on principles baptized
To strict party platform ties
Social clubs in drag disguise
Outsiders they can freely criticize
Tell nothing except who to idolize
And then say God bless him.

While one who sings with his tongue on fire
Gargles in the rat race choir
Bent out of shape from society's pliers
Cares not to come up any higher
But rather get you down in the hole
That he's in.

But I mean no harm nor put fault
On anyone that lives in a vault
But it's alright, Ma, if I can't please him.

Old lady judges watch people in pairs
Limited in sex, they dare
To push fake morals, insult and stare

While money doesn't talk, it swears
Obscenity, who really cares
Propaganda, all is phony.

While them that defend what they cannot see
With a killer's pride, security
It blows the minds most bitterly
For them that think death's honesty
Won't fall upon them naturally
Life sometimes
Must get lonely.

My eyes collide head-on with stuffed graveyards
False gods, I scuff
At pettiness which plays so rough
Walk upside-down inside handcuffs
Kick my legs to crash it off
Say okay, I have had enough
What else can you show me?

And if my thought-dreams could be seen
They'd probably put my head in a guillotine
But it's alright, Ma, it's life, and life only.

WEB RESOURCES FOR PART FOUR

SITES FEATURING A NUMBER OF THE DISSENTERS IN PART FOUR:

John Howard Lawson
http://historymatters.gmu.edu/d/6441/

The FBI's files on communist infiltration of the film industry can be found at:

http://foia.fbi.gov/compic.htm

And for the HUAC testimony of two friendly witnesses—Ronald Reagan and Walt Disney—on this topic, see:

http://historymatters.gmu.edu/d/6458/

Paul Robeson
www.princeton.lib.nj.us/robeson/links.html

Margaret Chase Smith
www.mcslibrary.org

Pete Seeger
http://home.earthlink.net/~jimcapaldi/
http://historymatters.gmu.edu/d/6457/

Harry Hay

www.radfae.org/harry.htm

www.instepnews.com/harryhaydead.html

www.geocities.com/WestHollywood/Heights/5347/

Allen Ginsberg

www.levity.com/corduroy/ginsberg/home.htm

Martin Luther King Jr.

www.stanford.edu/group/King/

www.martinlutherking.org/

http://seattletimes.nwsource.com/mlk/

http://www.toptags.com/aama/voices/speeches/vietnam.htm

Malcolm X

www.brothermalcolm.net/

www.malcolm-x.org/

Fannie Lou Hamer

www.ibiblio.org/sncc/hamer.html

Stokely Carmichael

www.spartacus.schoolnet.co.uk/USA carmichael.htm

SNCC

For the historical background of the Student Nonviolent Coordinating Committee, see:

www.ibiblio.org/sncc/

The Black Panther Party

www.stanford.edu/group/blackpanthers/index.shtml

Students for a Democratic Society

http://barksdale.uta.edu/undergrad2a.htm

http://riseup.net/sds/index.htm

www.tomhayden.com/

Betty Friedan

www.pbs.org/fmc/interviews/friedan.htm

Bob Dylan

http://www.bobdylan.com/

Phil Ochs

http://www.cs.pdx.edu/~trent/ochs/

http://www.fortunecity.com/tinpan/parton/2/ochs.html

OTHER DISSENTING VOICE OF THE TIME:

Aldo Leopold

See this link for information about ecologist Aldo Leopold:

www.aldoleopold.org/

Rachel Carson

For information about this noted environmentalist pioneer, see:

http://www.rachelcarson.org/

Lawrence Ferlinghetti

For information about beat writer and publisher Lawrence Ferlinghetti, see:

www.citylights.com/CLlf.html

Gary Snyder

For information on Beat poet and Zen master Gary Snyder, see:

www.english.uiuc.edu/maps/poets/s_z/snyder/snyder.htm

Diane Di Prima

For links and information on this Beat poet, see:

www.levity.com/corduroy/diprima.htm
http://dianediprima.com/

Lenny Bruce

Information about social critic and comedian Lenny Bruce can be found at:

www.trialsoflennybruce.com/related.htm

Joan Baez

See this link for information about this influential 1960s folksinger and activist:

http://baez.woz.org/

James Baldwin

Information, about African American writer James Baldwin can be found at:

http://falcon.jmu.edu/~ramseyil/baldwin.htm

Ralph Ellison

For information on this African American author, see:

www.levity.com/corduroy/ellison.htm

Jo Ann Robinson

For information about this Montgomery bus boycott organizer, see:

http://www.aaregistry.com/african_american_history/2012/Jo_Ann_Gibson_Robinson_was_
an_unsung_activist

Ella Baker

For links on civil rights activist Ella Baker, see:

www.virtualology.com/virtualmuseumofhistory/hallofwomen/ELLABAKER.COM/
www.ellabakercenter.org/

Anne Moody

For information about civil rights activist Anne Moody, see:

www.olemiss.edu/depts/english/ms-writers/dir/moody_anne/

Dick Gregory

Information on civil rights activist and comedian Dick Gregory can be found at these sites:

www.africanamericans.com/DickGregory.htm
www.dickgregory.com/

Eldridge Cleaver

Information on this former Black Panther can be found at these sites:

www.who2.com/eldridgecleaver.html
www.pbs.org/wgbh/pages/frontline/shows/race/interviews/ecleaver.html

H. Rap Brown

For one of SNCC leader H. Rap Brown's speeches, see:

www.historychannel.com/speeches/archive/speech_397.html

PART FIVE

Mobilization: Vietnam and the Counterculture, 1964–1975

The March on the Pentagon, October 21, 1967. A group of anti–Vietnam War demonstrators, led by activist Dr. Benjamin Spock, leaving the Lincoln Memorial on the way to the Pentagon.

Introduction: The Movement

The radical 1960s was not a period confined to the boundaries of the actual decade. The seeds were sown in the 1950s and early 1960s, but the era of "doing your own thing," believing "we can change the world," and demanding an end to the Vietnam War and the draft really did not begin until the mid-1960s, and it did not suddenly end on January 1, 1970. Indeed the second wave of the movement, according to historian Terry Anderson, the most radical phase, took place primarily in the early 1970s.

In 1964 and 1965, in the aftermath of the Kennedy assassination, as mentioned in Part Four, the fight against segregation in the South peaked. The culmination of the civil rights movement overlapped the emerging issue of Vietnam, and as discussion of the war heated up and took center stage by 1967, many of the civil disobedience tactics of the civil rights movement were adopted by antiwar activists. Although it appeared on the surface to American foreign policy experts that Vietnam was simply another front line of the cold war in which the United States was committed to containing the spread of communism, the fact remains that Vietnam was a far thornier and more complex issue. Vietnamese nationalist Ho Chi Minh had been agitating for Vietnamese independence from France throughout most of the twentieth century. In Paris at the end of the First World War, Ho Chi Minh had tried to gain an audience with President Woodrow Wilson in an effort to win the U.S. president's support for an independent Vietnam. Ignored in 1919, Ho Chi Minh refused to give up. Throughout the 1920s and 1930s, he lived in the Soviet Union and China, during which time he helped found the Indochinese Communist Party. In 1941, after the Japanese overran the French colony of Indochina (Vietnam, Laos, and Cambodia), Ho founded a new Vietnamese communist party dedicated to Vietnamese independence, the Vietminh. During the war, as the Vietminh fought against the Japanese occupiers, their efforts were supported by U.S. aid. When the Japanese surrendered, Ho declared the new independent Democratic Republic of Vietnam and hoped that now, surely, the United States would support Vietnamese independence. Indeed, he had taken to heart many of President Roosevelt's comments about the ending of colonialism and imperialism in the postwar world. However, Roosevelt did not survive to see the postwar world, and his successor, Harry S Truman, believed that France's wishes were far more important to the security of Europe and the United States than the hopes of the Vietnamese. The French regained control in Vietnam, and war with Ho Chi Minh's forces ensued. In 1954, after the French defeat at Dien Bien Phu, France decided to abandon the colony.

An agreement was reached in Geneva that Vietnam would be split at the 17th parallel into North and South Vietnam. Ho would lead a communist government in the north, and, after a brief interval with Emperor Bao Dai, Ngo Dinh Diem, an ardent anticommunist nationalist, would lead the south. The agreement also called for elections two years hence, in which the Vietnamese people could vote to reunite the country under one government. In 1956, however, the election was canceled because South Vietnamese leaders and the United States realized that the very popular Ho Chi Minh would easily win the election. It was from this point on that the United States began to be drawn ever more deeply into what was to become a quagmire.

With the clarity of hindsight, we can see that central to the problem was that the United States was never able to see Ho Chi Minh for what he was—a nationalist first and foremost, whose primary goal was a free and independent Vietnam. When we looked at him, we only saw red, so to speak; we saw him only as a communist and that meant, according to the cold war paradigm, that he was a pawn of Soviet and Chinese communist expansionists. Under Eisenhower, the United States poured billions of dollars in aid to support the anticommunist Diem in South Vietnam. When Eisenhower left office, there were approximately 900 U.S. military advisors in South Vietnam. Under Kennedy, this number jumped to 16,000. The plot thickened when, in the summer of 1963, the Kennedy administration, embarrassed by Diem's brutal oppression of Buddhists after several monks protested Diem's policies through the shocking tactic of self-immolation, gave tacit approval to a cadre of South Vietnamese generals who were plotting a coup against Diem. The coup took place at the beginning of November, Diem was assassinated and replaced by the generals, Kennedy was distraught that Diem had been murdered (he had, perhaps naively, expected that Diem would be sent into exile), and the United States found itself morally bound up with the outcome.

This was the situation Lyndon Johnson inherited three weeks later, when Kennedy was assassinated. In the atmosphere of grief that engulfed the nation in the aftermath of November 22, Johnson felt bound to carry on Kennedy's policies exactly as Kennedy would have carried them on. "Let us continue," Johnson had said in a speech to the joint houses of Congress the day after Kennedy's funeral. The two most visible legacies Kennedy left behind were civil rights and the commitment in Vietnam. Johnson urged a quick and swift passage to the Civil Rights Bill for which the slain president "had so long worked" (certainly a stretch, in that JFK finally introduced the bill in June 1963). As far as Vietnam was concerned, Johnson believed that withdrawing the U.S. military advisors would be seen as a rejection of Kennedy's policy, even though Kennedy's ambiguous comments in a September 1963 interview with Walter Cronkite indicated that he himself was undecided as to whether to strengthen or reduce our commitment in Vietnam. Furthermore, Johnson's policy in Vietnam was entirely consistent with 25 years of the policy of containment. Like so many others, Johnson accepted as true the "domino principle," that if one nation would fall to communism, then, like a row of toppling dominoes, the neighboring nations would fall, too. In August 1964, after the U.S. destroyer the *Maddox* was fired on in the Gulf of Tonkin, Johnson asked for, and Congress passed, the Gulf of Tonkin Resolution, which gave the president the necessary authority to protect American interests in Vietnam. This resolution, based, it turns out, on a somewhat fictionalized incident, was the authority on which the "war" was fought. Vietnam was not a declared war. This was the beginning of the escalation. Step by step, the United States was inexorably drawn into a conflict that it could not back out of without appearing weak or unreliable to its allies.

The late summer of 1964 was a pivotal moment. Not only did the Gulf of Tonkin Resolution signal the beginning of a deeper involvement in Vietnam but also it coincided with the end of one of the most significant civil rights operations, Freedom Summer. As many of the student volunteers who had worked in Mississippi that summer registering African Americans to vote returned to their campuses, they brought with them an extraordinarily high level of idealism and commitment to making the United States a better place. Setting up tables on campuses and distributing brochures and leaflets urging other students to get involved in the southern struggle for civil rights, young activists spread the word that "the times were a-changin'." At the University of California at Berkeley, students were dismayed when the university told them they could *not* disseminate political information on campus. The resulting uproar led to the Berkeley Free Speech Movement, which rather quickly spread to other campuses around the country. The student movement was born. At first, students demonstrated for free speech, for civil rights, and against the university policy of *in loco parentis,* in which university officials attempted to control student behavior and morals. Vietnam became part of the mix in March 1965, when the University of Michigan inaugurated the first teach-in, in which professors and students examined, discussed, and debated the historical background of Vietnam. Also in 1965, the New Left group, Students for a Democratic Society, which had been founded in 1960, issued a statement condemning "American imperialism" in Vietnam. Within a year, Vietnam became the focus of most student activism.

Simultaneously with the rise of a left-wing political consciousness, many young people also developed a concern with inner values. If, as it was perceived, the older generation was responsible for policies that led the nation into a questionable war in Southeast Asia and a policy of racial discrimination at home, and if these policies were all being severely condemned, then, it was reasoned, the moral values decreed by society should also be called into question. Perhaps the origin of the so-called counterculture can be traced to an event that, at the time, did not seem historically significant—the Beatles' appearance on the Ed Sullivan Show. "Beatlemania" had a profound influence on the youth of America and eventually influenced popular culture to such an extent that rock and roll and folk rock, along with the lifestyles and fashions of popular musicians, became central features in a rapidly evolving counterculture. Within days of the Beatles' February 1964 television appearance, teenage boys around the nation began to let their hair down, literally. The "mop top" hairstyle was here to stay—at least for a while. It was only a foretaste of things to come. The arrival of the Beatles on the American cultural scene coincided with the height of the civil rights movement, the aftermath of the Kennedy assassination, the launch of the student movement, and the first hints at the escalation of the Vietnam War. During a 1965 tour in the United States, the Beatles met Bob Dylan, and there seems little doubt that the English rock group and the American folk singer influenced each other. In the summer of that year, at the Newport Folk Festival, Bob Dylan made his historic appearance on stage with an electric guitar and a backing group rather than his trademark acoustic guitar and harmonica. Singing the surrealistic "Like a Rolling Stone," Dylan seemed to be abandoning the political protest songs that had brought him national prominence. Many diehard folk purists felt betrayed and accused their idol of having sold out to pop culture. But from this point on, Dylan began paving a new way for himself and for other musicians. Folk rock was born. Also in 1965, the Beatles began writing and recording rock and roll songs with meaningful political and social lyrics, like "Eleanor Rigby" and "Nowhere Man." Within two years the Beatles recorded *Sergeant Pepper's Lonely Hearts Club Band*—arguably the most influential rock album ever—which contained "A Day in the Life," "She's Leaving Home," "Lucy in the Sky with Diamonds," and other songs of social meaning. By the late 1960s, rock and roll in the United States and England had been so radically transformed that it little resembled the teenybopper, bubble-gum music that had been popular earlier in the decade. The Fugs, The Mothers of Invention, The Doors, The Grateful Dead, Jimi Hendrix, Janis Joplin, Jefferson Airplane, and The Rolling Stones all began releasing songs filled with meaningful content. Some songs were thought provoking, some extolled drugs and free love, some were humorous parodies of the establishment, and others were filled with scathing, sarcastic comments on the state of the world. To be sure, many folk singers such as Pete Seeger, Phil Ochs, and Arlo Guthrie still performed protest songs without significantly changing their style, but popular music in America would never be the same.

While music was taking on a political character and heightening a sense of generational solidarity, other ideas became part of the evolving counterculture. Timothy Leary and others began to argue for the mind-expanding benefits of such drugs as LSD; drugs were a path to self-discovery and self-fulfillment. Sex, too, was being touted as a path to self-fulfillment. Many thinkers, taking the theories of Freud about sexual repression as a departure point, urged people to be conscious of their sexual repression and then through this awareness develop a healthier attitude about sex that would help them lead a more fulfilled life. These ideas, along with the invention of the birth control pill in 1960, triggered the "sexual revolution." Other trends developed. The 1950s Beat Movement's interest in Zen and Eastern thought also spread among members of the counterculture, who were very willing to experiment and try out any idea that might lead toward self-knowledge and spiritual growth. Alan Watts, Maharishi Mahesh Yogi, and Ram Dass among others espoused meditation as the way to enlightenment. In this way, the spiritual, the erotic, the intellectual, and the emotional qualities of the individual began to be viewed as political. All facets of life, all relationships, were political. The old set of values, the ideas about fitting in and being respectable, were jettisoned in favor of the view that it was what was inside each person that mattered. And since the inner person was what counted, it became central to the "hippie" mind-set that people should look like they did not care what they looked like. Thus long hair and beards, unshaven legs and armpits, thrift shop clothing and tie-dye expressed a new set of values.

The United States that emerged at the end of the watershed year of 1968 had drastically changed from the United States of a year earlier. The Tet Offensive in Vietnam, although it was a defeat for the communists, revealed that much of what the media and the administration was reporting about the war was overly optimistic and that the "light at the end of the tunnel" was nowhere in sight. (One pundit commented that the "light at the end of the tunnel" was the headlight of an oncoming, speeding locomotive.) As a result many ordinary middle-class citizens began to join with student activists in opposing the war. When Senator Eugene McCarthy of Minnesota, running in the Democratic primaries as an antiwar candidate, won more than 40 percent of the vote in the New Hampshire primary, many of the party faithful were shocked that in a conservative state like New Hampshire such a large minority would vote against Johnson's policy. Shortly after the primary, Senator Robert F. Kennedy threw his hat into the ring, declared his candidacy, and vowed to end the war in Vietnam. On March 31, President Johnson, painfully aware of Robert Kennedy's appeal to liberals, African Americans, Latinos, students, and labor, announced during a nationally televised address that he would neither seek nor accept his party's nomination for president. Antiwar activists around the nation were overjoyed, believing as they did that their antiwar posture had convinced the president to abdicate. But their joy perished four days later, on April 4, when an assassin gunned down Martin Luther King Jr. Grief and fear swept over much of the nation. Blacks rioted in many urban centers, extra security was implemented in Washington to protect the Capitol and the White House from violence, and dozens were killed. Robert Kennedy, in a speech the evening of King's assassination, urged restraint and invited blacks and whites to come together. "It is not the end of violence," he said, "but we can, and we must, stand for what King stood for and go beyond violence to cultivate love for each other as a people.

In May, students at Columbia University in New York City took over the university and forced it to close down for the academic year. A wave of demonstrations swept around the world—Berlin, London, Paris. In France, students from the Sorbonne united with workers and forced the DeGaulle government to call for elections. The youth movement and the impetus for change spread behind the Iron Curtain as Czechoslovakia celebrated its Prague Spring—featuring an awakening of free speech and a critical reassessment of communism after the freeze of Stalinism.

In early June, moments after winning the California Democratic primary, Senator Kennedy, the man who had said only two months before that it was not the end of violence, was himself assassinated. By the time the Democratic convention met in Chicago, with demonstrators on the street being clubbed by police all the while chanting "the whole world is watching," it seemed that the United States was on the verge of revolution or maybe self-destruction. The United States did not self-destruct, but the Democratic Party did. The Republican candidate Richard Nixon won the November election, the war in Vietnam would continue for another six years, and many of the student activists who had, as recently as March, believed they could change the world had given up on the political process. By 1969, many had opted out and gone off to live on communes to explore alternative peaceful lifestyles, while others became more radical, like the Weathermen, who broke off from the disintegrating SDS and set out on a campaign of bombing and violence against the establishment.

Although 1968 was a dividing point, the movement continued on until the mid-1970s. In 1969, there were the rock festivals at Woodstock and at Altamont, and there were international moratorium days against the war in October and November—two of the largest antiwar demonstrations of the entire era. In 1970, when the *New York Times* reported on the Nixon administration's secret bombing of Cambodia, another huge wave of demonstrations swept the country. At Kent State University in Ohio, the National Guard fired on students, killing four and wounding several others. Though students were appalled, many Americans applauded the killings, boldly declaring the students deserved what they got. As Nixon stepped up the process of withdrawing American troops ("Vietnamization"), the antiwar demonstrations did begin to subside. As the antiwar movement declined, activists got more involved in local issues and the problems of specific minority groups. The lesson many people had learned from the 1960s is that activism led to empowerment, and empowerment gave groups and individuals some influence in forcing local governments to confront important local issues. In some places, for example, demonstrations were held and petitions signed against building interstate highways through inner-city neighborhoods, forcing local ruling bodies to comply with the public will. In 1969 gays in New York City took to the streets to demand the end of police raids on gay bars and nightclubs. The Gay Liberation Front was born. Cesar Chavez led Chicano migrant workers in California to unionize and demand fair treatment. The American Indian Movement formed and, demanding Red Power, occupied Alcatraz Island and the town of Wounded Knee, South Dakota. Hundreds of thousands of citizens, troubled by industrial pollution and the harm being done to the environment, joined together to compel the government to deal with ecological concerns. In the late 1960s and early 1970s, women, who can hardly be called a "minority," campaigned to raise consciousness and awareness of the inequality of women in American society and pushed the women's movement in a more radical direction. The 1973 *Roe v. Wade* decision finally won for women the right to have control over their own bodies. Even conservatives learned from the protestors by employing the same tactics in marches supporting U.S. troops in Vietnam, in massive demonstrations against federally mandated busing, and at antiabortion rallies at Planned Parenthood clinics around the nation.

When Nixon became president, many observers believed his victory was the result of the Democratic Party having splintered between the doves and the hawks, between its peace faction and its war faction. However, in retrospect, recent historians have viewed Nixon's election as the beginning of a deeply conservative trend in the United States, a trend signifying that the middle class was fed up with the radical excesses of the 1960s. In some ways this view is accurate, but the legacy of the 1960s, the idea that people can and should stand up for issues and concerns that they believe are important, still survives. Whether conservative or liberal, reactionary or radical, people have no qualms about participating in demonstrations or signing petitions for redress of grievances. Though most dissenters have criticized the American mainstream from the left, it is not principally a left-wing phenomenon. Dissent encompasses all political persuasions because the essence of dissent is that it is beyond politics. Dissent is neither Democratic nor Republican. From the end of the Vietnam War in 1975 to the present, even during quiescent times, dissent continues to flourish. The triumph of conservatism did not and does not mean the silencing of dissent.

Mario Savio (1942–1996)

The Berkeley Free Speech Movement grew out of the aftermath of Freedom Summer. When a number of students from the University of California at Berkeley returned home after working for SNCC and CORE in Mississippi, they were understandably very enthusiastic about their experiences there. With evangelical fervor, they began spreading news about the voter registration drive and began recruiting other students for future activities in the South. The University of California announced that they could not set up tables on university property to promote civil rights. To students who believed that civil rights was the most important issue confronting the nation in 1964, this was unacceptable. When they refused to move, security staff were sent in to remove them. Believing that the university was stifling First Amendment freedom of speech, student organizations of every political persuasion, from the radical left to the radical right, began demonstrating against the university policy. Events escalated. During the fall of 1964, the demonstrations grew, many students were arrested, and daily university operations were greatly impaired. In December, one of the Free Speech Movement student leaders, Mario Savio, in an impassioned speech at a demonstration on the steps of Sproul Hall, urged the students to occupy it. The students occupied the building all night, brought the administration of the university to a halt, and remained until the police arrested 800 of them the following day.

Why does Savio argue that students should put their "bodies upon the gears and the wheels"?

Speech at the University of California at Berkeley, December 2, 1964

Now there are at least two ways in which sit-ins and civil disobedience, and whatever, at least two major ways in which it can occur. One when a law exists, is promulgated, which is totally unacceptable to people and they violate it again and again and again until it is rescinded, repealed. All right. But there is another way, . . . Sometimes the pull of the law is such as to render impossible its effective violation as a method to have it repealed. Sometimes the grievances of people **are more,** extend **more,** to more than just the law, extend to a whole mode of arbitrary power, a whole mode of arbitrary exercise of arbitrary power. And that's what we have here.

SOURCE: From a copy in Lynne Hollander Savio's private collection.

We have an autocracy which runs, . . . this university. It's managed. We were told the following: if President Kerr actually tried to get something more liberal out of the regents in his telephone conversation why didn't he make some public statement to that effect? And the answer we received from a well-meaning liberal was the following: He said, "Would you ever imagine the manager of a firm making a statement publicly in opposition to his board of directors? That's the answer! Well I ask you to consider: If this is a firm and if the board of regents are the board of directors and if President Kerr in fact is the manager, then I'll tell you something: the faculty are a bunch of employees and we're the raw materials. But we're a bunch of raw materials that don't mean to **be,** have any process upon us, don't mean to be made into any product, don't mean . . . to end up being bought by some clients of the university, be they the government, be they industry, be they organized labor, be they anyone! We're human beings!

And that . . . brings me to the second mode of civil disobedience. There's a time when the operation of the machine becomes so odious, makes you so sick at heart that you can't take part. You can't even passively take part. And you've got to put your bodies upon the gears and upon the wheels, upon the levers, upon all apparatus, and you've got to make it stop. And you've got to indicate to the people who run it, to the people who own it, that unless you're free the machine will be prevented from working at all!

That doesn't mean—and it will be interpreted to mean unfortunately by the bigots who run *The [San Francisco] Examiner* for example—that doesn't mean that you have to break anything. One thousand people sitting down someplace not letting anybody by, not letting anything happen can stop any machine, including this machine, and it will stop! We're going to do the following and the greater the number of people the safer they'll be and the more effective it will be. We're going once again to march up to the second floor of Sproul Hall. And we're going to conduct our lives for a while in the second floor of Sproul Hall. We'll show movies for example. We tried to get *Une Chante d'Amour.* Unfortunately that's tied up in the courts because of a lot of squeamish moral mothers for a moral America and other people on the outside. The same people who get all their ideas out of *The San Francisco Examiner.* Sad. Sad. But Mr. Landau, . . . has gotten us some other films. Likewise we'll do something . . . which hasn't occurred at this university in a good long time. We're going to have *real classes* up there. There are going to be freedom schools conducted up there. We're going to have classes on [the] First and Fourteenth Amendments. We're going to spend our time learning about the things this university is afraid that we know. We're going to learn about freedom up there. And we're going to learn by doing.

Now we've had some good long rallies. Just one moment. **We've had some good long rallies.** And I think I'm sicker of rallies than anyone else here. It's not going to be long. I'd like to introduce one last person . . . before we enter Sproul Hall. And the person is Joan Baez.

. . . We're going to march in singing "We Shall Overcome." Slowly, there are a lot of us. . . .

Carl Oglesby (1935–)

Students for a Democratic Society (SDS)(see pages 289–294), founded at the beginning of the decade, was by the mid-1960s the leading New Left organization of the student movement. During a major antiwar march on Washington on November 27, 1965, newly-elected SDS president Carl Oglesby delivered a well-received speech denouncing the war and analyzing the dichotomy between U.S. policy in Vietnam and America's revolutionary heritage.

According to Oglesby, were we in Vietnam to fight communism or to promote capitalism? What would U.S. policy be if we were truly a nation that believed in the ideals of the American Revolution? Is Oglesby's position similar to Bryan's and Schurz's stand on American involvement in the Philippines in Part Two?

Speech Denouncing the War in Vietnam, Washington, DC, November 27, 1965

Seven months ago at the April March on Washington, Paul Potter, then President of Students for a Democratic Society, stood in approximately this spot and said that we must name the system that creates and sustains the war in Vietnam—name it, describe it, analyze it, understand it, and change it.

Today I will try to name it—to suggest an analysis which, to be quite frank, may disturb some of you—and to suggest what changing it may require of us.

We are here again to protest a growing war. Since it is a very bad war, we acquire the habit of thinking it must be caused by very bad men. But we only conceal reality, I think, to denounce on such grounds the menacing coalition of industrial and military power, or the brutality of the blitzkrieg we are waging against Vietnam, or the ominous signs around us that heresy may soon no longer be permitted. We must simply observe, and quite plainly say, that this coalition, this blitzkrieg, and this demand for acquiescence are creatures, all of them, of a government that since 1932 has considered itself to be fundamentally *liberal*.

The original commitment in Vietnam was made by President Truman, a mainstream liberal. It was seconded by President Eisenhower, a moderate liberal. It was intensified by the late President Kennedy, a flaming liberal. Think of the men who now engineer that war—those who study the maps, give the commands, push the buttons, and tally the dead: Bundy, McNamara, Rusk, Lodge, Goldberg, the President himself.

They are not moral monsters.

They are all honorable men.

They are all liberals.

SOURCE: Retrieved 3/9/2004 from http://sdsrebels.com/oglesby.htm.

But so, I'm sure, are many of us who are here today in protest. To understand the war, then, it seems necessary to take a closer look at this American liberalism. Maybe we are in for some surprises. Maybe we have here two quite different liberalisms: one authentically humanist; the other not so humane at all.

Not long ago I considered myself a liberal and if, someone had asked me what I meant by that, I'd perhaps have quoted Thomas Jefferson or Thomas Paine, who first made plain our nation's unprovisional commitment to human rights. But what do you think would happen if these two heroes could sit down now for a chat with President Johnson and McGeorge Bundy?

They would surely talk of the Vietnam war. Our dead revolutionaries would soon wonder why their country was fighting against what appeared to be a revolution. The living liberals would hotly deny that it is one: there are troops coming in from outside, the rebels get arms from other countries, most of the people are not on their side, and they practice terror against their own. Therefore: *not* a revolution.

What would our dead revolutionaries answer? They might say: "What fools and bandits, sirs, you make then of us. Outside help? Do you remember Lafayette? Or the three thousand British freighters the French navy sank for our side? Or the arms and men, we got from France and Spain? And what's this about terror? Did you never hear what we did to our own Loyalists? Or about the thousands of rich American Tories who fled for their lives to Canada? And as for popular support, do you not know that we had less than one-third of our people with us? That, in fact, the colony of New York recruited more troops for the British than for the revolution? Should we give it all back?"

Revolutions do not take place in velvet boxes. They never have. It is only the poets who make them lovely. What the National Liberation Front is fighting in Vietnam is a complex and vicious war. This war is also a revolution, as honest a revolution as you can find anywhere in history. And this is a fact which all our intricate official denials will never change.

But it doesn't make any difference to our leaders anyway. Their aim in Vietnam is really much simpler than this implies. It is to safeguard what they take to be American interests around the world against revolution or revolutionary change, which they always call communism—as if that were that. In the case of Vietnam, this interest is, first, the principle that revolution shall not be tolerated anywhere, and second, that South Vietnam shall never sell its rice to China—or even to North Vietnam.

There is simply no such thing now, for us, as a just revolution—never mind that for two-thirds of the world's people the Twentieth Century might as well be the Stone Age; never mind the melting poverty and hopelessness that are the basic facts of life for most modern men; and never mind that for these millions there is now an increasingly perceptible relationship between their sorrow and our contentment.

Can we understand why the Negroes of Watts rebelled? Then why do we need a devil theory to explain the rebellion of the South Vietnamese? Can we understand the oppression in Mississippi, or the anguish that our Northern ghettoes makes epidemic? Then why can't we see that our proper human struggle is not with communism or revolutionaries, but with the social desperation that drives good men to violence, both here and abroad?

To be sure, we have been most generous with our aid, and in Western Europe, a mature industrial society, that aid worked. But there are always political and financial strings. And we have never shown ourselves capable of allowing others to make those traumatic institutional changes that are often the prerequisites of progress in colonial societies. For all our official feeling for the millions who are enslaved to what we so self-righteously call the yoke of communist tyranny, we make no real effort at all to crack through the much more vicious right-wing tyrannies that our businessmen traffic with and our nation profits from every day. And for all our cries about the international Red conspiracy to take over the world, we take only pride in the fact of our six thousand military bases on foreign soil.

We gave Rhodesia a grave look just now—but we keep on buying her chromium, which is cheap because black slave labor mines it.

We deplore the racism of Verwoert's fascist South Africa—but our banks make big loans to that country and our private technology makes it a nuclear power. . . .

This country, with its thirty-some years of liberalism, can send 200,000 young men to Vietnam to kill and die in the most dubious of wars, but it cannot get 100 voter registrars to go into Mississippi.

What do you make of it?

The financial burden of the war obliges us to cut millions from an already pathetic War on Poverty budget. But in almost the same breath, Congress appropriates one hundred forty million dollars for the Lockheed and Boeing companies to compete with each other on the supersonic transport project—that Disneyland creation that will cost us all about two billion dollars before it's done.

What do you make of it?. . .

In 1953 our Central Intelligence Agency managed to overthrow Mossadegh in Iran, the complaint being his neutralism in the Cold War and his plans to nationalize the country's oil resources to improve his people's lives. Most evil aims, most evil man. In his place we put in General Zahedi, a World War II Nazi collaborator. New arrangements on Iran's oil gave twenty-five year leases on forty percent of it to three U.S. firms, one of which was Gulf Oil. The C.I.A.'s leader for this coup was Kermit Roosevelt. In 1960, Kermit Roosevelt became a vice president of Gulf Oil.

In 1954, the democratically elected Arbenz of Guatemala wanted to nationalize a portion of United Fruit Company's plantations in his country, land he needed badly for a modest program of agrarian reform. His government was overthrown in a C.I.A.-supported rightwing coup. The following year, Gen. Walter Bedell Smith, director of the C.I.A. when the Guatemala venture was being planned, joined the board of directors of the United Fruit Company.

Comes 1960 and Castro cries we are about to invade Cuba. The Administration sneers, "poppycock," and we Americans believe it. Comes 1961 and the invasion. Comes with it the awful realization that the United States Government had lied.

Comes 1962 and the missile crisis, and our Administration stands prepared to fight global atomic war on the curious principle that another state does not have the right to its own foreign policy.

Comes 1963 and British Guiana where Cheddi Jagan wants independence from England and a labor law modeled on the Wagner Act. And Jay Lovestone, the AFL-CIO foreign policy chief, acting, as always, quite independently of labor's rank and file, arranges with our Government to finance an eleven-week dock strike that brings Jagan down, ensuring that the state will remain *British* Guiana, and that any workingman who wants a wage better than fifty cents a day is a dupe of communism.

Comes 1964. Two weeks after Undersecretary Thomas Mann announces that we have abandoned the Alianza's principle of no aid to tyrants, Brazil's Goulart is overthrown by the vicious right-winger Ademar Barros, supported by a show of American gunboats at Rio de Janeiro. Within twenty-four hours, the new head of state, Mazzilli, receives a congratulatory wire from our President.

Comes 1965. The Dominican Republic. Rebellion in the streets. We scurry to the spot with twenty thousand neutral Marines and our neutral peacemakers—like Ellsworth Bunker Jr., Ambassador to the Organization of American States. Most of us know that our neutral Marines fought openly on the side of the junta, a fact that the Administration still denies. But how many also know that what was at stake was our new Caribbean Sugar Bowl? That this same neutral peacemaking Bunker is a board member and stock owner of the National Sugar Refining Company, a firm his father founded in the good old days, and one which has a major interest in maintaining the status quo in the Dominican Republic? Or that the President's close personal friend and advisor, our new Supreme Court Justice Abe Fortas, has sat for the past 19 years on the board of the Sucrest Company, which imports black-strap molasses from the Dominican Republic? Or that the rhetorician of corporate liberalism and the late President Kennedy's close friend Adolf Berle, was chairman of that same board? Or that our roving ambassador Averill Harriman's brother Roland is on the board of National Sugar? Or that our former ambassador to the Dominican Republic, Joseph Farland, is a board member of the South Puerto Rico Sugar Co., which owns two hundred and seventy-five thousand acres of rich land in the Dominican Republic and is the largest employer on the island—at about one dollar a day?

Neutralists! God save the hungry people of the world from such neutralists!

We do not say these men are evil. We say, rather, that good men can be divided from their compassion by the institutional system that inherits us all. Generation in and out, we are put to use. People become instruments. Generals do not hear the screams of the bombed; sugar executives do not see the misery of the cane cutters: for to do so is to be that much less the general, that much less the executive.

The foregoing facts of recent history describe one main aspect of the estate of Western liberalism. Where is our American humanism here? What went wrong?

Let's stare our situation coldly in the face. All of us are born to the colossus of history, our American corporate system—in many ways an awesome organism. There is one fact that describes it: With about five percent of the world's people, we consume about half the world's goods. We take a richness that is in good part not our own, and we put it in our pockets, our garages, our split-levels, our bellies, and our futures.

On the *face* of it, it is a crime that so few should have so much at the expense of so many. Where is the moral imagination so abused as to call this just? Perhaps many of us feel a bit uneasy in our sleep. We are not, after all, a cruel people. And perhaps we don't really need this super-dominance that deforms others. But what can we do? The investments are made. The financial ties are established. The plants abroad are built. Our system exists. One is swept up into it. How intolerable—to be born moral, but addicted to a stolen and maybe surplus luxury. Our goodness threatens to become counterfeit before our eyes—unless we change. But change threatens us with uncertainty—at least.

Our problem, then, is to justify this system and give its theft another name—to make kind and moral what is neither, to perform some alchemy with language that will make this injustice seem a most magnanimous gift.

A hard problem. But the Western democracies, in the heyday of their colonial expansionism, produced a hero worthy of the task.

Its name was free enterprise, and its partner was an *illiberal liberalism* that said to the poor and the dispossessed: What we acquire of your resources we repay in civilization: the white man's burden. But this was too poetic. So a much more hard-headed theory was produced. This theory said that colonial status is in fact a *boon* to the colonized. We give them technology and bring them into modern times.

But this deceived no one but ourselves. We were delighted with this new theory. The poor saw in it merely an admission that their claims were irrefutable. They stood up to us, without gratitude. We were shocked—but also confused, for the poor seemed again to be right. How long is it going to be the case, we wondered, that the poor will be right and the rich will be wrong?

Liberalism faced a crisis. In the face of the collapse of the European empires, how could it continue, to hold together, our twin need for richness and righteousness? How can we continue to sack the ports of Asia and still dream of Jesus?

The challenge was met with a most ingenious solution: the ideology of anti-Communism. This was the bind: we cannot call revolution bad, because we started that way ourselves, and because it is all too easy to see why the dispossessed should rebel. So we will call revolution Communism. And we will reserve for ourselves the right to say what Communism means. We take note of revolution's enormities, wrenching them where necessary from their historical context and often exaggerating them, and say: Behold, Communism is a bloodbath. We take note of those reactionaries who stole the revolution, and say: Behold, Communism is a betrayal of the people. We take note of the revolution's need to consolidate itself, and say: Behold, Communism is a tyranny.

It has been all these things, and it will be these things again, and we will never be at a loss for those tales of atrocity that comfort us so in our self-righteousness. Nuns will be raped and bureaucrats will be disemboweled. Indeed, revolution is a *fury*. For it is a letting loose of outrages pent up sometimes over centuries. But the more brutal and longer-lasting the suppression of this energy, all the more ferocious will be its explosive release.

Far from helping Americans deal with this truth, the anti-Communist ideology merely tries to disguise it so that things may stay the way they are. Thus, it depicts our presence in other lands not as a coercion, but a protection. It allows us even to say that the napalm in Vietnam is only another aspect of our humanitarian love—like those exorcisms in the Middle Ages that so often killed the patient. So we say to the Vietnamese peasant, the Cuban intellectual, the Peruvian worker: "You are better dead than Red. If it hurts or if you don't understand why—sorry about that."

This is the action of *corporate liberalism*. It performs for the corporate state a function quite like what the Church once performed for the feudal state. It seeks to justify its burdens and protect it from change. As the Church exaggerated this office in the Inquisition, so with liberalism in the McCarthy time—which, if it was a reactionary phenomenon, was still made possible by our anti-communist corporate liberalism.

Let me then speak directly to humanist liberals. If my facts are wrong, I will soon be corrected. But if they are right, then you may face a crisis of conscience. Corporatism or humanism: which? For it has come to that. Will you let your dreams be used? Will you be a grudging apologist for the corporate state? Or will you help try to change it—not in the name of this or that blueprint or ism, but in the name of simple human decency and democracy and the vision that wise and brave men saw in the time of our own Revolution?

And if your commitment to human values is unconditional, then disabuse yourselves of the notion that statements will bring change, if only the right statements can be written, or that interviews with the mighty will bring change if only the mighty can be reached, or that marches will bring change if only we can make them massive enough, or that policy proposals will bring change if only we can make them responsible enough.

We are dealing now with a colossus that does not want to be changed. It will not change itself. It will not cooperate with those who want to change it. Those allies of ours in the Government—are they *really* our allies? If they *are,* then they don't need advice, they need *constituencies;* they don't need study groups, they need a *movement.* And if they are *not,* then all the more reason for building that movement with the most relentless conviction.

There are people in this country today who are trying to build that movement, who aim at nothing less than a humanist reformation. And the humanist liberals must understand that it is this movement with which their own best hopes are most in tune. We radicals know the same history that you liberals know, and we can understand your occasional cynicism, exasperation, and even distrust. But we ask you to put these aside and help us risk a leap. Help us find enough time for the enormous work that needs doing here. Help us build. Help us shape the future in the name of plain human hope.

The Weather Underground

In 1968, after the assassinations of Martin Luther King Jr. and Robert F. Kennedy and the events in Chicago at the Democratic National Convention, many activists began to give up hope in the political process. Some protestors became more radicalized; others began to "drop out" and to form communes in an effort to achieve personal growth. The idea was to concentrate on reforming oneself and not society—the inner revolution rather than the outer. Students for a Democratic Society itself, the leading New Left student organization, disintegrated.

A splinter group, the Weathermen (taking their name from a line in Bob Dylan's "Subterranean Homesick Blues"), organized itself in 1969 and advocated violent confrontation with the "police state." The Weathermen, (later the gender neutral "Weather Underground"), of course, did not have much chance for success in bringing down the U.S. government, and their membership was never more than two or three hundred, but police forces and the FBI targeted them after their "Days of Rage" campaign in Chicago in October 1969 when they rampaged through the streets breaking store windows.

According to their statement, what is their goal? Are there any valid points in their critique of the United States? How would they view America's role in the world today?

You Don't Need a Weatherman to Know Which Way the Wind Blows, 1969

People ask, what is the nature of the revolution that we talk about? Who will it be made by, and for, and what are its goals and strategy?

The overriding consideration in answering these questions is that the main struggle going on in the world today is between U.S. imperialism and the national liberation struggles against it. This is essential in defining political matters in the whole world: because it is by far the most powerful, every other empire and petty dictator is in the long run dependent on U.S. imperialism, which has unified, allied with, and defended all of the reactionary forces of the whole world. Thus, in considering every other force or phenomenon, from Soviet imperialism or Israeli imperialism to "workers struggle" in France or Czechoslovakia, we determine who are our friends and who are our enemies according to whether they help U.S. imperialism or fight to defeat it.

So the very first question people in this country must ask in considering the question of revolution is where they stand in relation to the United States as an oppressor nation, and where they stand in relation to the masses of people throughout the world whom U.S. imperialism is oppressing.

The primary task of revolutionary struggle is to solve this principal contradiction on the side of the people of the world. It is the oppressed peoples of the world who have created the wealth of this empire and it is to them that it belongs; the goal of the revolutionary struggle must be the control and use of this wealth in the interests of the oppressed peoples of the world.

It is in this context that we must examine the revolutionary struggles in the United States. We are within the heartland of a world-wide monster, a country so rich from its world-wide plunder that even the crumbs doled out to the enslaved

---

Source: From *New Left Notes,* June 18, 1969, in Harold Jacobs, *Weatherman* (Berkeley, CA: Ramparts Press, 1970), 51–53.

masses within its borders provide for material existence very much above the conditions of the masses of people of the world. The U.S. empire, as a world-wide system, channels wealth, based upon the labor and resources of the rest of the world, into the United States. The relative affluence existing in the United States is directly dependent upon the labor and natural resources of the Vietnamese, the Angolans, the Bolivians, and the rest of the peoples of the Third World. All of the United Airlines Astrojets, all of the Holiday Inns, all of Hertz's automobiles, your television set, car, and wardrobe already belong, to a large degree to the people of the rest of the world.

Therefore, any conception of "socialist revolution" simply in terms of the working people of the United States, failing to recognize the full scope of interests of the most oppressed peoples of the world, is a conception of a fight for a particular privileged interest, and is a very dangerous ideology. While the control and use of the wealth of the Empire for the people of the whole world is also in the interests of the vast majority of the people in this country, if the goal is not clear from the start we will further the preservation of class society, oppression, war, genocide, and the complete emiseration of everyone, including the people of the U.S.

The goal is the destruction of U.S. imperialism and the achievement of a classless world: world communism. Winning state power in the U.S. will occur as a result of the military forces of the U.S. overextending themselves around the world and being defeated piecemeal; struggle within the U.S. will be a vital part of this process, but when the revolution triumphs in the U.S. it will have been made by the people of the whole world. For socialism to be defined in national terms within so extreme and historical an oppressor nation as this is only imperialist national chauvinism on the part of the "movement."

John Kerry (1943–)

When John Kerry served in Vietnam, he was awarded the Combat Action Ribbon, the Silver Star, the Bronze Star, the Republic of Vietnam Campaign Medal, the National Defense Service Medal, and three Purple Hearts. By the time he returned to the United States, however, he was a firm opponent of the war and became one of the founders of Vietnam Veterans Against the War. His 1971 testimony before the Senate Foreign Relations Committee was a sobering appraisal of the war in Vietnam. In 1984 Kerry won election to the U.S. Senate from Massachusetts, and in 2004 he sought the Democratic Party nomination for president.

How would patriotic Americans who believed in the war and steadfastly supported our troops in Vietnam react to Kerry's testimony? What prompted Kerry to turn against the war?

Statement to the Senate Committee on Foreign Relations April 23, 1971

. . . I would like to say for the record, and also for the men behind me who are also wearing the uniform and their medals, that my sitting here is really symbolic, I am not here as John Kerry. I am here as one member of the group of 1,000 which is a small representation of a very much larger group of veterans in this country, and were it possible for all of them to sit at this table they would be here and have the same kind of testimony. . . .

I would like to talk on behalf of all those veterans and say that several months ago in Detroit we had an investigation at which over 150 honorably discharged, and many very highly decorated, veterans testified to war crimes committed in Southeast Asia. These were not isolated incidents but crimes committed on a day-to-day basis with the full awareness of officers at all levels of command.

It is impossible to describe to you exactly what did happen in Detroit—the emotions in the room and the feelings of the men who were reliving their experiences in Vietnam. They relived the absolute horror of what this country, in a sense, made them do.

They told stories that at times they had personally raped, cut off ears, cut off heads, taped wires from portable telephones to human genitals and turned up the power, cut off limbs, blown up bodies, randomly shot at civilians, razed villages in fashion reminiscent of Genghis Khan, shot cattle and dogs for fun, poisoned food stocks, and generally ravaged the countryside of South Vietnam in addition to the normal ravage of war and the normal and very particular ravaging which is done by the applied bombing power of this country.

We call this investigation the Winter Soldier Investigation. The term Winter Soldier is a play on words of Thomas Paine's in 1776 when he spoke of the Sunshine Patriots and summertime soldiers who deserted at Valley Forge because the going was rough.

We who have come here to Washington have come here because we feel we have to be winter soldiers now. We could come back to this country, we could be quiet, we could hold our silence, we could not tell what went on in Vietnam, but we feel because of what threatens this country, not the reds, but the crimes which we are committing that threaten it, that we have to speak out. . . .

In our opinion and from our experience, there is nothing in South Vietnam which could happen that realistically threatens the United States of America. And to attempt to justify the loss of one American life in Vietnam, Cambodia or Laos by linking such loss to the preservation of freedom, which those misfits supposedly abuse, is to us the height of criminal hypocrisy, and it is that kind of hypocrisy which we feel has torn this country apart. . . .

SOURCE: "Legislative Proposals Relating to the War in Southeast Asia," *Hearings before the Committee on Foreign Relations, United States Senate, Ninety-Second Congress, First Session, April–May 1971,* (Washington, DC: Government Printing Office, 1971), 180–208 *passim.*

We found that not only was it a civil war, an effort by a people who had for years been seeking their liberation from any colonial influence whatsoever, but also we found that the Vietnamese whom we had enthusiastically molded after our own image were hard put to take up the fight against the threat we were supposedly saving them from.

We found most people didn't even know the difference between communism and democracy. They only wanted to work in rice paddies without helicopters strafing them and bombs with napalm burning their villages and tearing their country apart. They wanted everything to do with the war, particularly with this foreign presence of the United States of America, to leave them alone in peace, and they practiced the art of survival by siding with whichever military force was present at a particular time, be it Viet Cong, North Vietnamese or American.

We found also that all too often American men were dying in those rice paddies for want of support from their allies. We saw first hand how monies from American taxes were used for a corrupt dictatorial regime. We saw that many people in this country had a one-sided idea of who was kept free by the flag, and blacks provided the highest percentage of casualties. We saw Vietnam ravaged equally by American bombs and search and destroy missions, as well as by Viet Cong terrorism—and yet we listened while this country tried to blame all of the havoc on the Viet Cong.

We rationalized destroying villages in order to save them. We saw America lose her sense of morality as she accepted very coolly a My Lai and refused to give up the image of American soldiers who hand out chocolate bars and chewing gum.

We learned the meaning of free fire zones, shooting anything that moves, and we watched while America placed a cheapness on the lives of orientals.

We watched the United States falsification of body counts, in fact the glorification of body counts. We listened while month after month we were told the back of the enemy was about to break. We fought using weapons against "oriental human beings." We fought using weapons against those people which I do not believe this country would dream of using were we fighting in the European theater. We watched while men charged up hills because a general said that hill has to be taken, and after losing one platoon or two platoons they marched away to leave the hill for reoccupation by the North Vietnamese. We watched pride allow the most unimportant battles to be blown into extravaganzas, because we couldn't lose, and we couldn't retreat, and because it didn't matter how many American bodies were lost to prove that point, and so there were Hamburger Hills and Khe Sanhs and Hill 81s and Fire Base 6s, and so many others.

Now we are told that the men who fought there must watch quietly while American lives are lost so that we can exercise the incredible arrogance of Vietnamizing the Vietnamese.

Each day to facilitate the process by which the United States washes her hands of Vietnam someone has to give up his life so that the United States doesn't have to admit something that the entire world already knows, so that we can't say that we have made a mistake. Someone has to die so that President Nixon won't be, and these are his words, "the first President to lose a war."

We are asking Americans to think about that because how do you ask a man to be the last man to die in Vietnam? How do you ask a man to be the last man to die for a mistake? . . . We are here in Washington to say that the problem of this war is not just a question of war and diplomacy. It is part and parcel of everything that we are trying as human beings to communicate to people in this country—the question of racism which is rampant in the military, and so many other questions such as the use of weapons; the hypocrisy in our taking umbrage at the Geneva Conventions and using that as justification for a continuation of this war when we are more guilty than any other body of violations of those Geneva Conventions; in the use of free fire zones, harassment interdiction fire, search and destroy missions, the bombings, the torture of prisoners, all accepted policy by many units in South Vietnam. That is what we are trying to say. It is part and parcel of everything.

An American Indian friend of mine who lives in the Indian Nation of Alcatraz put it to me very succinctly. He told me how as a boy on an Indian reservation he had watched television and he used to cheer the cowboys when they came in and shot the Indians, and then suddenly one day he stopped in Vietnam and he said, "my God, I am doing to these people the very same thing that was done to my people," and he stopped. And that is what we are trying to say, that we think this thing has to end.

We are here to ask, and we are here to ask vehemently, where are the leaders of our country? Where is the leadership? We're here to ask where are McNamara, Rostow, Bundy, Gilpatric, and so many others? Where are they now that we, the men they sent off to war, have returned? These are the commanders who have deserted their troops. And there is no more serious crime in the laws of war. The Army says they never leave their wounded. The marines say they never even leave their dead. These men have left all the casualties and retreated behind a pious shield of public rectitude. They've left the real stuff of their reputations bleaching behind them in the sun in this country. . . .

We wish that a merciful God could wipe away our own memories of that service as easily as this administration has wiped away their memories of us. But all that they have done and all that they can do by this denial is to make more clear than ever our own determination to undertake one last mission—to search out and destroy the last vestige of this barbaric war, to pacify our own hearts, to conquer the hate and fear that have driven this country these last ten years and more. And more. And so when thirty years from now our brothers go down the street without a leg, without an arm, or a face, and small boys ask why, we will be able to say "Vietnam" and not mean a desert, not a filthy obscene memory, but mean instead where America finally turned and where soldiers like us helped it in the turning.

Timothy Leary (1920–1996)

> Harvard psychologist Timothy Leary, fired in 1963 for controversial experimen-
> tation with the effects of LSD (lysergic acid diethylamide) on the human
> nervous system (famously, his own and his students'), became a central figure

in the counterculture of the 1960s. Many well-known figures—Aldous Huxley, Allen Ginsberg, Alan Watts—were also extolling the mind-expanding benefits of LSD, but Leary became the chief apostle. Traveling around the country, Leary urged audiences to "tune in, turn on, and drop out" with LSD. Tuning in to your inner spirit, he declared, and then turning on with one dose of LSD, would inevitably lead to a more meaningful, more evolved relationship to life. After such an experience, individuals would more than likely drop out of the competitive, hollow, materialistic world of shopping malls and suburban developments. Acid, Leary proclaimed, expanded the consciousness to such an extent that it was a spiritual experience not unlike that of Tibetan Buddhist monks.

To young people who were already questioning the suffocating conformity of the "square" 1950s and who were listening to songs like "Little Boxes," Leary's message resonated, and millions wound up taking him seriously. Leary's guide books to the psychedelic experience—*The Psychedelic Experience*, (with co-authors Ralph Meltzer and Richard Alpert), and *The Politics of Ecstasy*, *Confessions of a Hope Fiend*, and *High Priest*, were popular with hippies seeking to expand their minds. Drugs were not to be "abused" as an escape from reality but "used" as a vehicle for self-discovery. "Acid is not for every brain," Leary stressed, "only the healthy, happy, wholesome, handsome, hopeful, humorous, high-velocity should seek these experiences. This elitism is totally self-determined. Unless you are self-confident, self-directed, self-selected, *please abstain*."

In the following essay, Leary outlines useful tips on how to have a safe and successful LSD experience rather than a "bad trip." Does Leary sound like an irresponsible crackpot or a serious scientific researcher? What do you think of his comparison of drugs with spiritual experience? Can an experience be spiritual if it is drug-induced?

Using LSD to Imprint the Tibetan-Buddhist Experience

A GUIDE TO SUCCESSFUL PSYCHEDELIC EXPERIENCE

Having read this preparatory manual one can immediately recognize symptoms and experiences that might otherwise be terrifying, only because of lack of understanding. Recognition is the key word. Recognizing and locating the level of consciousness. This guidebook may also be used to avoid paranoid trips or to regain transcendence if it has been lost. If the experience starts with light, peace, mystic unity, understanding, and continues along this path, then there is no need to remember the manual or have it reread to you. Like a road map, consult it only when lost, or when you wish to change course.

SOURCE: Retrieved on 1/2/2004 from www.deoxy.org/l_impgui.htm.

PLANNING A SESSION

What is the goal? Classic Hinduism suggests four possibilities:

Increased personal power, intellectual understanding, sharpened insight into self
    and culture, improvement of life situation, accelerated learning, professional
    growth.
Duty, help of others, providing care, rehabilitation, rebirth for fellow men.
Fun, sensuous enjoyment, esthetic pleasure, interpersonal closeness, pure
    experience.
Trancendence, liberation from ego and space-time limits; attainment of mystical
    union.

The manual's primary emphasis on the last goal does not preclude other
goals—in fact, it guarantees their attainment because illumination requires that the
person be able to step out beyond problems of personality, role, and professional
status. The initiate can decide beforehand to devote their psychedelic experience to
any of the four goals.

In the extroverted transcendent experience, the self is ecstatically fused with
external objects (e.g., flowers, other people). In the introverted state, the self is
ecstatically fused with internal life processes (lights, energy waves, bodily events,
biological forms, etc.). Either state may be negative rather than positive, depending
on the voyager's set and setting. For the extroverted mystic experience, one would
bring to the session candles, pictures, books, incense, music, or recorded passages
to guide the awareness in the desired direction. An introverted experience requires
eliminating all stimulation: no light, no sound, no smell, no movement.

The mode of communication with other participants should also be agreed on
beforehand, to avoid misinterpretations during the heightened sensitivity of ego
transcendence.

If several people are having a session together, they should at least be aware of
each other's goals. Unexpected or undesired manipulations can easily "trap" the
other voyagers into paranoid delusions.

PREPARATION

Psychedelic chemicals are not drugs in the usual sense of the word. There is no specific somatic or psychological reaction. The better the preparation, the more ecstatic
and revelatory the session. In initial sessions with unprepared persons, set and
setting—particularly the actions of others—are most important. Long-range set
refers to personal history, enduring personality, the kind of person you are. Your
fears, desires, conflicts, guilts, secret passions, determine how you interpret and
manage any psychedelic session. Perhaps more important are the reflex mecha-
nisms, defenses, protective maneuvers, typically employed when dealing with anxiety.
Flexibility, basic trust, philosophic faith, human openness, courage, interpersonal
warmth, creativity, allow for fun and easy learning. Rigidity, desire to control, distrust,
cynicism, narrowness, cowardice, coldness, make any new situation threatening.

Most important is insight. The person who has some understanding of his own machinery, who can recognize when he is not functioning as he would wish, is better able to adapt to any challenge—even the sudden collapse of his ego.

Immediate set refers to expectations about the session itself. People naturally tend to impose personal and social perspectives on any new situation. For example, some ill-prepared subjects unconsciously impose a medical model on the experience. They look for symptoms, interpret each new sensation in terms of sickness/health, and, if anxiety develops, demand tranquilizers. Occasionally, ill-planned sessions end in the subject demanding to see a doctor.

Rebellion against convention may motivate some people who take the drug. The naive idea of doing something "far out" or vaguely naughty can cloud the experience.

LSD offers vast possibilities of accelerated learning and scientific-scholarly research, but for initial sessions, intellectual reactions can become traps. "Turn your mind off" is the best advice for novitiates. After you have learned how to move your consciousness around—into ego loss and back, at will—then intellectual exercises can be incorporated into the psychedelic experience. The objective is to free you from your verbal mind for as long as possible.

Religious expectations invite the same advice. Again, the subject in early sessions is best advised to float with the stream, stay "up" as long as possible, and postpone theological interpretations.

Recreational and esthetic expectations are natural. The psychedelic experience provides ecstatic moments that dwarf any personal or cultural game. Pure sensation can capture awareness. Interpersonal intimacy reaches Himalayan heights. Esthetic delights—musical, artistic, botanical, natural—are raised to the millionth power. But ego-game reactions—"I am having this ecstasy. How lucky I am!"—can prevent the subject from reaching pure ego loss.

SOME PRACTICAL RECOMMENDATIONS

The subject should set aside at least three days: a day before the experience, the session day, and a follow-up day. This scheduling guarantees a reduction in external pressure and a more sober commitment. Talking to others who have taken the voyage is excellent preparation, although the hallucinatory quality of all descriptions should be recognized. Observing a session is another valuable preliminary.

Reading books about mystical experience and of others' experiences is another possibility (Aldous Huxley, Alan Watts, and Gordon Wasson have written powerful accounts). Meditation is probably the best preparation. Those who have spent time in a solitary attempt to manage the mind, to eliminate thought and reach higher stages of concentration, are the best candidates for a psychedelic session. When the ego loss occurs, they recognize the process as an eagerly awaited end.

THE SETTING

First and most important, provide a setting removed from one's usual interpersonal games, and as free as possible from unforeseen distractions and intrusions. The voyager should make sure that he will not be disturbed; visitors or a phone call will often jar him into hallucinatory activity. Trust in the surroundings and privacy are necessary.

The day after the session should be set aside to let the experience run its natural course and allow time for reflection and meditation. A too-hasty return to game involvements will blur the clarity and reduce the potential for learning. It is very useful for a group to stay together after the session to share and exchange experiences.

Many people are more comfortable in the evening, and consequently their experiences are deeper and richer. The person should choose the time of day that seems right. Later, he may wish to experience the difference between night and day sessions. Similarly, gardens, beaches, forests, and open country have specific influences that one may or may not wish. The essential thing is to feel as comfortable as possible, whether in one's living room or under the night sky. Familiar surroundings may help one feel confident in hallucinatory periods. If the session is held indoors, music, lighting, the availability of food and drink, should be considered beforehand. Most people report no hunger during the height of the experience, then later on prefer simple ancient foods like bread, cheese, wine, and fresh fruit. The senses are wide open, and the taste and smell of a fresh orange are unforgettable.

In group sessions, people usually will not feel like walking or moving very much for long periods, and either beds or mattresses should be provided. One suggestion is to place the heads of the beds together to form a star pattern. Perhaps one may want to place a few beds together and keep one or two some distance apart for anyone who wishes to remain aside for some time. The availability of an extra room is desirable for someone who wishes to be in seclusion.

THE PSYCHEDELIC GUIDE

With the cognitive mind suspended, the subject is in a heightened state of suggestibility. For initial sessions, the guide possesses enormous power to move consciousness with the slightest gesture or reaction.

The key here is the guide's ability to turn off his own ego and social games, power needs, and fears—to be there, relaxed, solid, accepting, secure, to sense all and do nothing except let the subject know his wise presence.

A psychedelic session lasts up to twelve hours and produces moments of intense, intense, INTENSE reactivity. The guide must never be bored, talkative, intellectualizing. He must remain calm during long periods of swirling mindlessness. He is the ground control, always there to receive messages and queries from high-flying aircraft, ready to help negotiate their course and reach their destination. The guide does not impose his own games on the voyager. Pilots who have their own flight plan, their own goals, are reassured to know that an expert is down there, available for help. But if ground control is harboring his own motives, manipulating the plane towards selfish goals, the bond of security and confidence crumbles.

To administer psychedelics without personal experience is unethical and dangerous. Our studies concluded that almost every negative LSD reaction has been caused by the guide's fear, which augmented the transient fear of the subject. When the guide acts to protect himself, he communicates his concern. If momentary discomfort or confusion happens, others present should not be sympathetic or show alarm but stay calm and restrain their "helping games." In particular, the "doctor" role should be avoided.

The guide must remain passively sensitive and intuitively relaxed for several hours—a difficult assignment for most Westerners. The most certain way to maintain a state of alert quietism, poised in ready flexibility, is for the guide to take a low dose of the psychedelic with the subject. Routine procedure is to have one trained person participating in the experience, and one staff member present without psychedelic aid. The knowledge that one experienced guide is "up" and keeping the subject company is of inestimable value: the security of a trained pilot flying at your wingtip; the scuba diver's security in the presence of an expert companion.

The less experienced subject will more likely impose hallucinations. The guide, likely to be in a state of mindless, blissful flow, is then pulled into the subject's hallucinatory field and may have difficulty orienting himself. There are no familiar fixed landmarks, no place to put your foot, no solid concept upon which to base your thinking. All is flux. Decisive action by the subject can structure the guide's flow if he has taken a heavy dose.

The psychedelic guide is literally a neurological liberator, who provides illumination, who frees men from their lifelong internal bondage. To be present at the moment of awakening, to share the ecstatic revelation when the voyager discovers the wonder and awe of the divine life-process, far outstrips earthly game ambitions. Awe and gratitude—rather than pride—are the rewards of this new profession.

THE PERIOD OF EGO LOSS OR NON-GAME ECSTASY

Success implies very unusual preparation in consciousness expansion, as well as much calm, compassionate game playing (good karma) on the part of the participant. If the participant can see and grasp the idea of the empty mind as soon as the guide reveals it—that is to say, if he has the power to die consciously—and, at the supreme moment of quitting the ego, can recognize the ecstasy that will dawn upon him and become one with it, then all bonds of illusion are broken asunder immediately: the dreamer is awakened into reality simultaneously with the mighty achievement of recognition.

It is best if the guru from whom the participant received guiding instructions is present. But if the guru cannot be present, then another experienced person, or a person the participant trusts, should be available to read this manual without imposing any of his own games. Thereby the participant will be put in mind of what he had previously heard of the experience.

Liberation is the nervous system devoid of mental-conceptual redundancy. The mind in its conditioned state, limited to words and ego games, is continuously in thought-formation activity. The nervous system in a state of quiescence, alert, awake but not active, is comparable to what Buddhists call the highest state of *dhyana* (deep meditation). The conscious recognition of the Clear Light induces an ecstatic condition of consciousness such as saints and mystics of the West have called illumination.

The first sign is the glimpsing of the "Clear Light of Reality, the infallible mind of the pure mystic state"—an awareness of energy transformations with no imposition of mental categories.

The duration of this state varies, depending on the individual's experience, security, trust, preparation, and the surroundings. In those who have a little practical experience of the tranquil state of non-game awareness, this state can last from 30 minutes to several hours. Realization of what mystics call the "Ultimate Truth" is possible, provided that the person has made sufficient preparation beforehand. Otherwise he cannot benefit now, and must wander into lower and lower conditions of hallucinations until he drops back to routine reality.

It is important to remember that the consciousness-expansion is the reverse of the birth process, the ego-loss experience being a temporary ending of game life, a passing from one state of consciousness into another. Just as an infant must wake up and learn from experience the nature of this world, so a person must wake up in this new brilliant world of consciousness expansion and become familiar with its own peculiar conditions.

In those heavily dependant on ego games, who dread giving up control, the illuminated state endures only for a split second. In some, it lasts as long as the time taken for eating a meal. If the subject is prepared to diagnose the symptoms of ego-loss, he needs no outside help at this point. The person about to give up his ego should be able to recognize the Clear Light. If the person fails to recognize the onset of ego-loss, he may complain of strange bodily symptoms that show he has not reached a liberated state:

Bodily pressure
Clammy coldness followed by feverish heat
Body disintegrating or blown to atoms
Pressure on head and ears
Tingling in extremities
Feelings of body melting or flowing like wax
Nausea
Trembling or shaking, beginning in pelvic region and spreading up torso.

The guide or friend should explain that the symptoms indicate the onset of ego-loss. These physical reactions are signs heralding transcendence: avoid treating them as symptoms of illness. The subject should hail stomach messages as a sign that consciousness is moving around in the body. Experience the sensation fully, and let consciousness flow on to the next phase. It is usually more natural to let the subject's attention move from the stomach and concentrate on breathing and heartbeat. If this does not free him from nausea, the guide should move the consciousness to external events—music, walking in the garden, etc. As a last resort, heave.

The physical symptoms of ego-loss, recognized and understood, should result in peaceful attainment of illumination. The simile of a needle balanced and set rolling on a thread is used by the lamas to elucidate this condition. So long as the needle retains its balance, it remains on the thread. Eventually, however, the pull of the ego or external stimulation affects it, and it falls. In the realm of the Clear Light, similarly, a person in the ego-transcendent state momentarily enjoys a condition of perfect equilibrium and oneness. Unfamiliar with such an ecstatic non-ego state, the average consciousness lacks the power to function in it. Thoughts of personality, individualized being, dualism, prevent the realization of nirvana (the "blowing out of the flame" of fear or selfishness). When the voyager is clearly in a profound ego-transcendent ecstasy, the wise guide remains silent.

Herbert Marcuse (1898–1979)

Philosopher Herbert Marcuse studied under Martin Heidigger at Freiburg University in Germany and later worked at the Frankfurt Institute for Social Research. After Hitler came to power in 1933, he emigrated to the United States, became a citizen in 1940, and worked for the Office of Strategic Services. After the war, he taught at Columbia, Harvard, Brandeis, and the University of California at San Diego. His research led him to combine Freud and Marx in his analysis of capitalist society, taking ideas from *Civilization and Its Discontents*, in which Freud argues that civilization itself is the result of the sublimation of sexual repression. All societies, according to Marcuse, need a level of repression in order to maintain control. In a totalitarian society, the repression is physical terror. You criticized Hitler; you were shot. In capitalist society, however, repression is primarily sexual. By putting restrictions on sexuality, those in control ensure that the people sublimate their libidinal energy into feelings of patriotism and nationalism, and thus control is preserved.

In the United States, Marcuse contends, there is too much sexual repression, and this "surplus repression" is manipulated by the government and business leaders to fuel consumer capitalism. People must cope with the inexplicable emptiness they feel, and they do so through consumerism—drinking, smoking, overeating, buying goods that are unnecessary, gathering possessions, traveling, attending sporting events. In *One-Dimensional Man* and in *Eros and Civilization*, Marcuse argues that being aware of and coping with sexual repression and then developing a healthy attitude about sex is not only a way to find erotic self-fulfillment, but is also an act of revolution against capitalism. If sexual repression is overcome, you consume less. For some people, Marcuse's theory became the intellectual foundation for the so-called sexual revolution that emerged in the 1960s. Sex is political. Relationships are political. "Make love, not war" is both a social statement and a political statement.

In the 1966 preface to *Eros and Civilization*, Marcuse comments on the student movement and its attempt to address these issues. Did the problem of sexual repression decrease because of the 1960s "sexual revolution"? Do you agree or disagree with his assertion that "the fight for life, the fight for Eros, is the *political* fight"? What would he say today about consumerism and the global economy? About the commodification of sex? How would he interpret the "war on terrorism"?

Political Preface to *Eros and Civilization*, 1966

. . . As the affluence of society depends increasingly on the uninterrupted production and consumption of waste, gadgets, planned obsolescence, and means of destruction, the individuals have to be adapted to these requirements in more than the traditional ways. The "economic whip," even in its most refined forms, seems no longer adequate to insure the continuation of the struggle for existence in today's outdated organization, nor do the laws and patriotism seem adequate to insure active popular support for the ever more dangerous expansion of the system. Scientific management of instinctual needs has long since become a vital factor in the reproduction of the system: merchandise which has to be bought and used is made into objects of the libido; and the national Enemy who has to be fought and hated is distorted and inflated to such an extent that he can activate and satisfy aggressiveness in the depth dimension of the unconscious. Mass democracy provides the political paraphernalia for effectuating this introjection of the Reality Principle; it not only permits the people to choose their own masters and to participate (up to a point) in the government which governs them—it also allows the masters to disappear behind the technological veil of the productive and destructive apparatus which they control, and it conceals the human (and material) costs of the benefits and comforts which it bestows upon those who collaborate. The people, efficiently manipulated and organized, are free; ignorance and impotence, introjected heteronomy is the price of their freedom.

It makes no sense to talk about liberation to free men—and we are free if we do not belong to the oppressed minority. And it makes no sense to talk about surplus repression when men and women enjoy more sexual liberty than ever before. But the truth is that this freedom and satisfaction are transforming the earth into hell. The inferno is still concentrated in certain far away places: Vietnam, the Congo, South Africa, and in the ghettos of the "affluent society": in Mississippi and Alabama, in Harlem. . . .

I hesitate to use the word—freedom—because it is precisely in the name of freedom that crimes against humanity are being perpetrated. The situation is certainly not new in history: poverty and exploitation were products of economic freedom; time and again, people were liberated all over the globe by their lords and masters, and their new liberty turned out to be submission, not to the rule of law but to the rule of the law of the others. . . . [T]he general presumption is that aggressiveness in defense of life is less detrimental to the life Instincts than aggressiveness in aggression.

In defense of life: the phrase has explosive meaning in the affluent society. It involves not only the protest against neo-colonial war and slaughter, the burning of draft cards at the risk of prison, the fight for civil rights, but also the refusal to speak the dead language of affluence, to wear the clean clothes, to enjoy the gadgets of affluence, to go through the education for affluence. The new bohéme, the beatniks and hipsters, the peace creeps—all these "decadents" now have become what decadence probably always was: poor refuge of defamed humanity.

SOURCE: Herbert Marcuse, *Eros and Civilization: A Philosophical Inquiry into Freud* (Boston: Beacon Press, 1955, 1966), xii–xiii, xx–xxii, xxiv–xxv.

Can we speak of a juncture between the erotic and political dimension?

In and against the deadly efficient organization of the affluent society, not only radical protest, but even the attempt to formulate, to articulate, to give word to protest assume a childlike, ridiculous immaturity. Thus it is ridiculous and perhaps "logical" that the Free Speech Movement at Berkeley terminated in the row caused by the appearance of a sign with the four-letter word. It is perhaps equally ridiculous and right to see deeper significance in the buttons worn by some of the demonstrators (among them infants) against the slaughter in Vietnam: MAKE LOVE, NOT WAR. On the other side, against the new youth who refuse and rebel, are the representatives of the old order who can no longer protect its life without sacrificing it in the work of destruction and waste and pollution. They now include the representatives of organized labor—correctly so to the extent to which employment within the capitalist prosperity depends on the continued defense of the established social system.

Can the outcome, for the near future, be in doubt? The people, the majority of the people in the affluent society, are on the side of that which is—not that which can and ought to be. And the established order is strong enough and efficient enough to justify this adherence and to assume its continuation. However, the very strength and efficiency of this order may become factors of disintegration. Perpetuation of the obsolescent need for full-time labor (even in a very reduced form) will require the increasing waste of resources, the creation of ever more unnecessary jobs and services, and the growth of the military or destructive sector. Escalated wars, permanent preparation for war, and total administration may well suffice to keep the people under control, but at the cost of altering the morality on which the society still depends. . . .

In the meantime, there are things to be done. The system has its weakest point where it shows its most brutal strength: in the escalation of its military potential (which seems to press for periodic actualization with ever shorter interruptions of peace and preparedness). This tendency seems reversible only under strongest pressure, and its reversal would open the danger spots in the social structure: its conversion into a "normal" capitalist system is hardly imaginable without a serious crisis and sweeping economic and political changes. Today, the opposition to war and military intervention strikes at the roots: it revels against those whose economic and political dominion depends on the continued (and enlarged) reproduction of the military establishment, its "multipliers," and the policies which necessitate this reproduction. These interests are not hard to identify, and the war against them does not require missiles, bombs, and napalm. But it does require something that is much harder to produce—the spread of uncensored and unmanipulated knowledge, consciousness, and above all, the organized refusal to continue work on the material and *intellectual* instruments which are now being used against man—for the defense of the liberty and prosperity of those who dominate the rest.

To the degree to which organized labor operates in defense of the status quo, and to the degree to which the share of labor in the material process of production declines, *intellectual* skills and capabilities become social and political factors. Today, the organized refusal to cooperate of the scientists, mathematicians, technicians, industrial psychologists and public opinion pollsters may well accomplish what a strike, even a large-scale strike, can no longer accomplish but once accomplished, namely, the beginning of the reversal, the preparation of the ground for political action. That the idea appears utterly unrealistic does not reduce the political responsibility involved in the position and function of the intellectual in contemporary industrial society. The intellectual refusal may find support in another catalyst, the instinctual refusal among the youth in protest. It is their lives which are at stake, and if not their lives, their mental health and their capacity to function as unmutilated humans. Their protest will continue because it is a biological necessity. "By nature," the young are in the forefront of those who live and fight for Eros against Death, and against a civilization which strives to shorten the "detour to death" while controlling the means for lengthening the detour. But in the administered society, the biological necessity does not immediately issue in action; organization demands counter-organization. Today the fight for life, the fight for Eros, is the *political* fight.

Abbie Hoffman (1936–1989)

Abbie Hoffman was one of the most visible and colorful figures of the counterculture. He brought his Youth International Party (Yippies) to Chicago in 1968 to confound and confuse the authorities and the American public during the Democratic National Convention. He was as much a showman and comedian as a political activist; most "straight" people (as opposed to "hippies") usually had no idea what he was talking about. He claimed the Yippies were going to put LSD into Chicago's reservoirs in order to turn on the whole city and, astonishingly, many people believed him! He and Jerry Rubin nominated a pig for president in an alternative convention. In 1969, Hoffman went onstage at Woodstock to advise the audience which pills to take and which ones not to take. He published a number of books, notably *Woodstock Nation* and *Steal This Book*.

In the aftermath of the chaotic and violent Chicago Democratic convention, he was one of the "Chicago Seven" who were brought to trial for causing the riots. Hoffman's testimony at the trial was a tour de force. When asked to identify himself, he said he was "an orphan of America." When asked where he lived, he said, "Woodstock Nation." When asked where that was, he replied: "It is a nation of alienated young people. We carry it around with us as a state of mind in the same way as the Sioux Indians carried the Sioux nation around with them. It is a nation dedicated to cooperation versus competition, to the idea that people should have better means of exchange than property or money."

What Hoffman understood very well was how to confuse, hoodwink, and bamboozle. He and the Yippies generated an enormous amount of publicity—far more than their numbers would warrant. As a result, many Americans were convinced that the counterculture was on the verge of causing a revolution in America, never realizing that the Yippie plot was not much more than street theater.

The following introduction to *Steal This Book* provides some insight into Abbie Hoffman's outrageous mind. According to Hoffman, is there freedom of the press in the United States? Why does he spell Amerika with a *k*? Why does he call theft moral? How would you expect the average citizen to react to this? Is he serious?

Introduction to *Steal This Book*, 1970

It's perhaps fitting that I write this introduction in jail—that graduate school of survival. Here you learn how to use toothpaste as glue, fashion a shiv out of a spoon and build intricate communication networks. Here too, you learn the only rehabilitation possible—hatred of oppression.

Steal This Book is, in a way, a manual of survival in the prison that is Amerika. It preaches jailbreak. It shows you where exactly to place the dynamite that will destroy the walls. The first section—SURVIVE!—lays out a potential action program for our new Nation. The chapter headings spell out the demands for a free society. A community where the technology produces goods and services for whoever needs them, come who may. It calls on the Robin Hoods of Santa Barbara Forest to steal from the robber barons who own the castles of capitalism. It implies that the reader already is "ideologically set," in that he understands corporate feudalism as the only robbery worthy of being called "crime," for it is committed against the people as a whole. Whether the ways it describes to rip-off shit are legal or illegal is irrelevant. The dictionary of law is written by the bosses of order. Our moral dictionary says no heisting from each other. To steal from a brother or sister is evil. To not steal from the institutions that are the pillars of the Pig Empire is equally immoral.

Community within our Nation, chaos in theirs; that is the message of SURVIVE!

We cannot survive without learning to fight and that is the lesson in the second section. FIGHT! separates revolutionaries from outlaws. The purpose of part two is not to fuck the system, but destroy it. The weapons are carefully chosen. They are "home-made," in that they are designed for use in our unique electronic jungle. Here the uptown reviewer will find ample proof of our "violent" nature. But again, the dictionary of law fails us. Murder in a uniform is heroic, in a costume it is a crime. False advertisements win awards, forgers end up in jail. Inflated prices guarantee large profits while shoplifters are punished. Politicians conspire to create police riots and the victims are convicted in the courts. Students are gunned down and then indicted by suburban grand juries as the trouble-makers. A modern, highly mechanized army travels 9,000 miles to commit genocide against a small nation of great vision and then accuses its people of aggression. Slumlords allow rats to maim children and then complain of violence in the streets. Everything is topsy-turvy. If we internalize the language and imagery of the pigs, we will forever be fucked. Let me illustrate the point. Amerika was built on the slaughter of a people.

SOURCE: Abbie Hoffman, *Steal This Book* (New York: Pirate Editions, 1971), iii–viii.

That is its history. For years we watched movie after movie that demonstrated the white man's benevolence. Jimmy Stewart, the epitome of fairness, puts his arm around Cochise and tells how the Indians and the whites can live in peace if only both sides will be reasonable, responsible and rational (the three R's imperialists always teach the "natives"). "You will find good grazing land on the other side of the mountain," drawls the public relations man. "Take your people and go in peace." Cochise as well as millions of youngsters in the balcony of learning, were being dealt off the bottom of the deck. The Indians should have offed Jimmy Stewart in every picture and we should have cheered ourselves hoarse. Until we understand the nature of institutional violence and how it manipulates values and mores to maintain the power of the few, we will forever be imprisoned in the caves of ignorance. When we conclude that bank robbers rather than bankers should be the trustees of the universities, then we begin to think clearly. When we see the Army Mathematics Research and Development Center and the Bank of Amerika as cesspools of violence, filling the minds of our young with hatred, turning one against another, then we begin to think revolutionary.

Be clever using section two; clever as a snake. Dig the spirit of the struggle. Don't get hung up on a sacrifice trip. Revolution is not about suicide, it is about life. With your fingers probe the holiness of your body and see that it was meant to live. Your body is just one in a mass of cuddly humanity. Become an internationalist and learn to respect all life. Make war on machines, and in particular the sterile machines of corporate death and the robots that guard them. The duty of a revolutionary is to make love and that means staying alive and free. That doesn't allow for cop-outs. Smoking dope and hanging up Che's picture is no more a commitment than drinking milk and collecting postage stamps. A revolution in consciousness is an empty high without a revolution in the distribution of power. We are not interested in the greening of Amerika except for the grass that will cover its grave.

Section three—LIBERATE!—concerns itself with efforts to free stuff (or at least make it cheap) in four cities. Sort of a quick U.S. on no dollars a day. It begins to scratch the potential for a national effort in this area. Since we are a nation of gypsies, dope on how to move around and dig in anywhere is always needed. Together we can expand this section. It is far from complete, as is the entire project. Incomplete chapters on how to identify police agents, steal a car, run day-care centers, conduct your own trial, organize a G.I. coffee house, start a rock and roll band and make neat clothes, are scattered all over the floor of the cell. The book as it now stands was completed in the late summer of 1970. For three months manuscripts made the rounds of every major publisher. In all, over 30 rejections occurred before the decision to publish the book ourselves was made, or rather made for us. Perhaps no other book in modern times presented such a dilemma. Everyone agreed the book would be a commercial success. But even greed had its limits, and the IRS and FBI following the manuscript with their little jive rap had a telling effect. Thirty "yeses" become thirty "noes" after "thinking it over." Liberals, who supposedly led the fight against censorship, talked of how the book "will end free speech."

Finally the day we were bringing the proofs to the printer, Grove consented to act as distributor. To pull a total solo trip, including distribution, would have been neat, but such an effort would be doomed from the start. We had tried it before and blew it. In fact, if anyone is interested in 4,000 1969 Yippie calendars, they've got a deal. Even with a distributor joining the fight, the battle will only begin when the books come off the press. There is a saying that "Freedom of the press belongs to those who own one." In past eras, this was probably the case, but now, high speed methods of typesetting, offset printing and a host of other developments have made substantial reductions in printing costs. Literally anyone is free to print their own works. In even the most repressive society imaginable, you can get away with some form of private publishing. Because Amerika allows this, does not make it the democracy Jefferson envisioned. Repressive tolerance is a real phenomenon. To talk of true freedom of the press, we must talk of the availability of the channels of communication that are designed to reach the entire population, or at least that segment of the population that might participate in such a dialogue. Freedom of the press belongs to those that own the distribution system. Perhaps that has always been the case, but in a mass society where nearly everyone is instantaneously plugged into a variety of national communications systems, wide-spread dissemination of the information is the crux of the matter. To make the claim that the right to print your own book means freedom of the press is to completely misunderstand the nature of a mass society. It is like making the claim that anyone with a pushcart can challenge Safeway supermarkets, or that any child can grow up to be president.

State legislators, librarians, PTA members, FBI agents, church-goers, and parents: a veritable legion of decency and order already is on the march. To get the book to you might be the biggest challenge we face. The next few months should prove really exciting. . . .

If you have comments, law suits, suggestions or death threats, please send them to: Dear Abbie P.O. Box 213, Cooper Station, New York, NY 10003. Many of the tips might not work in your area, some might be obsolete by the time you get to try them out, and many addresses and phone numbers might be changed. If the reader becomes a participating researcher then we will have achieved our purpose.

Watch for a special edition called Steal This White House, complete with blueprints of underground passages, methods of jamming the communications network and a detailed map of the celebrated room where according to Tricia Nixon, "Daddy loves to listen to Mantovanni records, turn up the air conditioner full blast, sit by the fireplace, gaze out the window to the Washington Monument and meditate on those difficult problems that face all the peoples of this world."

December, 1970
Cook County Jail, Chicago

"Free speech is the right to shout 'theater' in a crowded fire."

A yippie proverb

Ram Dass (1931–)

One of Timothy Leary's colleagues at Harvard and the coauthor of *The Psychedelic Experience* was Richard Alpert. Along with Leary, Alpert experimented with LSD and other hallucinogens as a path to self-discovery. However, after a number of years of "tripping" and searching, during which time he became increasingly dissatisfied with the drug experience, Alpert went to India in 1967. He studied in the Himalayas with Neem Karoli Baba, and in 1968, after a profound spiritual awakening, he returned to the United States renamed Ram Dass ("Servant of God"). Since then, he has lectured to hundreds of thousands of people around the world on such topics as meditation, karma yoga, aging, and death and dying.

This extract from *Be Here Now* details part of the journey of his spiritual awakening. According to Ram Dass, how does one become free? What is "siddhi?" What is "Ahimsa?"

From *Be Here Now*

At one point in the evening I was looking in my shoulder bag and came across the bottle of LSD.

"Wow! I've finally met a guy who is going to Know! He will definitely know what LSD is. I'll have to ask him. That's what I'll do. I'll ask him." Then I forgot about it.

The next morning, at 8 o'clock a messenger comes. Maharaji wants to see you immediately. We went in the Land Rover. The 12 miles to the other temple. When I'm approaching him, he yells out at me, "Have you got a question?"

And I take one look at him, and it's like looking at the sun. I suddenly feel all warm.

And he's very impatient with all of this nonsense, and he says, "Where's the medicine?"

I got a translation of this. He said medicine. I said, "Medicine?" I never thought of LSD as medicine! And somebody said, he must mean the LSD. "LSD?" He said, "Ah-cha—bring the LSD."

So I went to the car and got the little bottle of LSD and I came back.

"Let me see?"

So I poured it out in my hand—"What's that?"

"That's STP. . . . That's librium and that's. . . . " A little of everything. Sort of a little traveling kit.

He says, "Gives you siddhis?"

SOURCE: Ram Dass, *Be Here Now* (New York: Crown, 1971), from the unpaginated preface.

I had never heard the word "siddhi" before. So I asked for a translation and siddhi was translated as "power." From where I was at in relation to these concepts, I thought he was like a little old man, asking for power. Perhaps he was losing his vitality and wanted Vitamin B 12. That was one thing I didn't have and I felt terribly apologetic because I would have given him anything. If he wanted the Land Rover, he could have it. And I said, "Oh, no, I'm sorry." I really felt bad I didn't have any and put it back in the bottle.

He looked at me and extended his hand. So I put into his hand what's called a "White Lightning." This is an LSD pill and this one was from a special batch that had been made specially for me for traveling. And each pill was 305 micrograms, and very pure. Very good acid. Usually you start a man over 60, maybe with 50 to 75 micrograms, very gently, so you won't upset him. 300 of pure acid is a very solid dose.

He looks at the pill and extends his hand further. So I put a second pill—that's 610 micrograms—then a third pill—that's 915 micrograms—into his palm.

That is sizeable for a first dose for anyone!

"Ah-cha."

And he swallows them! I see them go down. There's no doubt. And that little scientist in me says, "This is going to be very interesting!"

All day long I'm there, and every now and then he twinkles at me and nothing—nothing happens! That was his answer to my question. Now you have the data I have.

I was taken back to the temple. It was interesting. At no time was I asked, do you want to stay? Do you want to study? Everything was understood. There were no contracts. There were no promises. There were no vows. There was nothing.

The next day Maharaji instructed them to take me out and buy me clothes. They gave me a room. Nobody ever asked me for a nickel. Nobody ever asked me to spread the word. Nobody ever did anything. There was no commitment whatsoever required. It was all done internally. And that day I met a man who was to become my teacher, Hari Dass Baba.

Hari Dass Baba is quite an incredible fellow, as I found out. I spent five months under his tutelage. He is 48 years old. He weighs 90 pounds. He is a jungle saddhu. He went into the jungle when he was 8 years old. He is silent (mauna). He has been mauna for 15 years. He writes with a chalkboard. He only uses his voice to sing holy songs. He reads and writes six or eight different languages, including Chinese, English, French, Hindi. He taught me always in beautiful English.

This guru—Maharaji—has only his blanket. You see, he's in a place called SAHAJ SAMADHI and he's not identified with this world as most of us identify with it. If you didn't watch him, he'd just disappear altogether into the jungle or leave his body, but his devotees are always protecting him and watching him so they can keep him around. They've got an entourage around him and people come and bring gifts to the holy man because that's part of the way in which you gain holy merit in India. And money piles up, and so they build temples, or they build schools. He will walk to a place and there will be a saint who has lived in that place or cave and he'll say, "There will be a temple here," and then they build a temple. And they do all this around Maharaji. He does nothing.

Hari Dass Baba—this little 90 pound fellow—architecturally designed all of the temples and schools, supervised all the buildings and grounds, had many followers of his own, slept two hours a night. His food intake for the last 15 years had been 2 glasses of milk a day. That's it. His feces are like two small marbles each day. His arms are about this big around, tiny, but when the workmen can't lift a particularly heavy rock, they call for 'Chota Maharaji'—the little great king. As in a comic strip, he goes over and lifts the rock, just with one-pointedness of mind. He had met Maharaji in the jungle 15 years before, and he had become a disciple of Maharaji.

As an example of Maharaji's style, I was once going through my address book and I came to Lama Govinda's name (he wrote *Foundations of Tibetan Mysticism* and *Way of the White Cloud*) and I thought, "Gee, I ought to go visit him. I'm here in the Himalayas and it wouldn't be a long trip and I could go and pay my respects. I must do that some time before I leave."

And the next day there is a message from Maharaji saying, "You are to go immediately to see Lama Govinda."

Another time, I had to go to Delhi to work on my visa and I took a bus. This was the first time after four months that they let me out alone. They were so protective of me. I don't know what they were afraid would happen to me, but they were always sending somebody with me. . . . They weren't giving me elopement privileges, as they say in mental hospitals.

But they allowed me to go alone to Delhi and I took a 12 hour bus trip. I went to Delhi and I was so high. I went through Connaught Place, which is the western hustle part of New Delhi. It's mostly BOAC and American Express and restaurants that serve ice cream sodas. The whole scene, which is right in the middle of India, has nothing to do with India particularly and all the Indians who hustle westerners walk around in this block. And I went through that barefoot, silent with my chalkboard—I was silent all the time. At American Express, writing my words it was so high that not at one moment was there even a qualm or a doubt. I got so high that I went into some stores to buy things—right in Connaught Place, which is designed to hustle westerners. . . . And everybody knew I was a westerner, and yet they insisted on giving me the stuff free!

"You are a saddhu—it's a blessing to me that you'll take my goods." That's how powerful the thing was that I was into at that time.

So after all day long of doing my dramas with the Health Department and so on, it came time for lunch. I had been on this very fierce austere diet and I had lost 60 lbs. I was feeling great—very light and very beautiful—but there was enough orality still left in me to want to have a feast. I'll have a vegetarian feast. I thought. So I went to a fancy vegetarian restaurant and I got a table over in a corner and ordered their special deluxe vegetarian dinner, from nuts to nuts, and I had the whole thing and the last thing they served was vegetarian ice cream with 2 english biscuits stuck into it. And those biscuits . . . the sweet thing has always been a big part of my life, but I knew somehow, maybe I shouldn't be eating those. They're so far out from my diet. It's not vegetables—it's not rice. And so I was almost secretly eating the cookies in this dark corner. I was feeling very guilty about eating these cookies. But nobody was watching me. And then I went to a Buddhist monastary for the night and the next day took the bus back up to the mountain.

Two days later, we heard Maharaji was back—he had been up in the mountains in another little village. He travels around a lot, moves from place to place. I hadn't seen him in about a month and a half—I didn't see much of him at all. We all went rushing to see Maharaji and I got a bag of oranges to bring to him and I came and took one look at him, and the oranges went flying and I started to cry and I fell down and they were patting me. Maharaji was eating oranges as fast as he could, manifesting through eating food the process of taking on the karma of someone else.

Women bring him food all day long. He just opens his mouth and they feed him and he's taking on karma that way. And he ate eight oranges right before my eyes. I had never seen anything like that. And the principal of the school was feeding me oranges and I was crying and the whole thing was very maudlin, and he pulls me by the hair, and I look up and he says to me, "How did you like the biscuits?"

I'd be at my temple. And I'd think about arranging for a beautiful lama in America to get some money, or something like that. Then I'd go to bed and pull the covers over my head and perhaps have a very worldly thought; I would think about what I'd do with all my powers when I got them; perhaps a sexual thought. Then when next I saw Maharaji he would tell me something like, "You want to give money to a lama in America." And I'd feel like I was such a beautiful guy. Then suddenly I'd be horrified with the realization that if he knew that thought, then he must know that one, too . . . ohhhhh . . . and that one, too! Then I'd look at the ground. And when I'd finally steal a glance at him, he'd be looking at me with such total love.

Now the impact of these experiences was very profound. As they say in the Sikh religion—Once you realize God knows everything, you're free. I had been through many years of psychoanalysis and still I had managed to keep private places in my head—I wouldn't say they were big, labeled categories, but they were certain attitudes or feelings that were still very private. And suddenly I realized that he knew everything that was going on in my head, all the time, and that he still loved me. Because who we are is behind all that.

I said to Hari Dass Baba, "Why is it that Maharaji never tells me the bad things I think?" and he says, "It does not help your sadhana—your spiritual work. He knows it all, but he just does the things that help you."

The sculptor had said he loved Maharaji so much, we should keep the Land Rover up there. The Land Rover was just sitting around and so Maharaji got the Land Rover after all, for that time. And then one day, I was told we were going on an outing up in the Himalayas for the day. This was very exciting, because I never left my room in the temple. Now in the temple, or around Maharaji, there were eight or nine people. Bhagwan Dass and I were the only westerners. In fact, at no time that I was there did I see any other westerners. This is clearly not a western scene, and in fact, I was specifically told when returning to the United States that I was not to mention Maharaji's name or where he was, or anything.

The few people that have slipped by this net and figured out from clues in my speech and their knowledge of India where he was and have gone to see him, were thrown out immediately . . . very summarily dismissed, which is very strange. All I can do is pass that information on to you. I think the message is that you don't need to go to anywhere else to find what you are seeking.

So there were eight or nine people and whenever there was a scene, I walked last. I was the lowest man on the totem pole. They all loved me and honored me and I was the novice, like in a karate or judo class, where you stand at the back until you learn more. I was always in the back and they were always teaching me.

So we went in the Land Rover. Maharaji was up in the front—Bhagwan Dass was driving. Bhagwan Dass turned out to be very high in this scene. He was very very highly thought of and honored. He had started playing the sitar; he was a fantastic musician and the Hindu people loved him. He would do bhajan—holy music—so high they would go out on it. So Bhagwan Dass was driving and I was way in the back of the Land Rover camper with the women and some luggage.

And we went up into the hills and came to a place where we stopped and were given apples, in an orchard and we looked at a beautiful view. We stayed about 10 minutes, and then Maharaji says, "We've got to go on."

We got in the car, went further up the hill and came to a Forestry camp. Some of his devotees are people in the Forestry department so they make this available to him.

So we got to this place and there was a building waiting and a caretaker—"Oh, Maharaji, you've graced us with your presence." He went inside with the man that is there to take care of him or be with him all the time—and we all sat on the lawn.

After a little while, a message came out, "Maharaji wants to see you." And I got up and went in, and sat down in front of him. He looked at me and said.

"You make many people laugh in America?"

I said, "Yes, I like to do that."

"Good . . . You like to feed children?"

"Yes. Sure."

"Good."

He asked a few more questions like that, which seemed to be nice questions, but. . . ? Then he smiled and he reached forward and he tapped me right on the forehead, just three times. That's all.

Then the other fellow came along and lifted me and walked me out the door. I was completely confused. I didn't know what had happened to me—why he had done it—what it was about.

When I walked out, the people out in the yard said that I looked as if I were in a very high state. They said tears were streaming down my face. But all I felt inside was confusion. I have never felt any further understanding of it since then. I don't know what it was all about. It was not an idle movement, because the minute that was over, we all got back in the car and went home.

I pass that on to you. You know now, what I know about that. Just an interesting thing. I don't know what it means, yet.

Hari Dass Baba was my teacher. I was taught by this man with a chalkboard in the most terse way possible. I would get up early, take my bath in the river or out of a pail with a lota (a bowl). I would go in and do my breathing exercises, my pranayam and my hatha yoga, meditate, study, and around 11:30 in the morning, this man would arrive and with chalkboard he would write something down:

"If a pickpocket meets a saint, he sees only his pockets."

Then he'd get up and leave. Or he'd write,

"If you wear shoeleather, the whole earth is covered with leather."

These were his ways of teaching me about how motivation affects perception. His teaching seemed to be no teaching because he always taught from within . . . that is, his lessons aroused in me just affirmation . . . as if I knew it all already.

When starting to teach me about what it meant to be "ahimsa" or non-violent, and the effect on the environment around you of the vibrations—when he started to teach me about energy and vibrations, his opening statement was "Snakes Know Heart." "Yogis in jungle need not fear." Because if you're pure enough, cool it, don't worry. But you've got to be very pure.

So his teaching was of this nature. And it was not until a number of months later that I got hold of Vivekananda's book "Raja Yoga" and I realized that he had been teaching me Raja Yoga, very systematically—an exquisite scientific system that had been originally enunciated somewhere between 500 BC and 500 AD by Patanjali, in a set of sutras, or phrases, and it's called Ashtanga Yoga, or 8-limbed yoga—and also known as Raja or Kingly yoga. And this beautiful yogi was teaching me this wisdom with simple metaphor and brief phrase.

Now, though I am a beginner on the path, I have returned to the West for a time to work out karma or unfulfilled commitment. Part of this commitment is to share what I have learned with those of you who are on a similar journey. One can share a message through telling "our-story" as I have just done, or through teaching methods of yoga, or singing, or making love. Each of us finds his unique vehicle for sharing with others his bit of wisdom.

For me, this story is but a vehicle for sharing with you the true message . . . the living faith in what is possible.

Protest Music II

By mid-decade folk music had begun to have an impact on popular music. Many rock and roll musicians, in the aftermath of the Beatles invasion and Bob Dylan's going electric at Newport in the summer of 1965, began to write songs with political content. As these songs proliferated on the airways and young people flocked to record stores to buy the latest albums, the effect was to unify student activists around the country. Students from New York or Chicago or San Francisco—when they arrived in Washington for an antiwar demonstration—all shared familiarity with the songs of The Doors, Bob Dylan, Country Joe and the Fish, Simon and Garfunkel, Jefferson Airplane, and the Beatles. And, as in the civil rights movement, many songs would be sung during the demonstrations, adding further to a sense of unity and common purpose. Along with "We Shall Overcome" and "Where Have All the Flowers Gone," protestors sang John Lennon's "All We Are Saying, Is Give Peace a Chance" and Country Joe McDonald's "I-Feel-Like-I'm-Fixin'-to-Die Rag."

In addition to antiwar compositions, rock bands also explored social and cultural themes. The Mothers of Invention's "Plastic People," for example, ridicules middle-class consumerist values. The Doors' "The End," Jim Morrison's surrealistic, primal outburst, seemed so suited to disintegration of a society consumed by the madness in Vietnam that Francis Ford Coppola featured it in his 1978 film *Apocalypse Now*. More conventional protest songs were still being written. Pete Seeger's "Waist Deep in the Big Muddy" is his comment on Johnson's escalation of the Vietnam War. Seeger sang this on the *Smothers Brothers Comedy Hour* in 1968, and it was so controversial that CBS eventually canceled the popular show. Country Joe McDonald's "I-Feel-Like-I'm-Fixin'-to-Die Rag"—the most famous Vietnam War protest song—electrified the crowd at Woodstock in 1969. Creedence Clearwater Revival's "Fortunate Son" highlights the age-old historical truism that the poor fight and die in wars for the rich. As dissent and protest took center stage during the civil rights movement, other groups were encouraged to demand their rights. Buffy Sainte-Marie, a Cree Indian, for example, compellingly sang of the plight of Native Americans in "My Country 'Tis of Thy People You're Dying."

What do these songs reveal about American attitudes in the 1960s? Is anything sacred to these songwriters? Are these songs patriotic or unpatriotic? Would songs like these find popularity today?

"Waist Deep in the Big Muddy"

It was back in nineteen forty-two,
I was a member of a good platoon.
We were on maneuvers in Loozianna,
one night by the light of the moon.
The Captain told us to ford a river,
That's how it all begun.
We were—knee deep in the Big Muddy
But the big fool said to push on.

The Sergeant said, "Sir, are you sure
This is the best way back to the base?"
"Sergeant, go on, I forded this river
'Bout a mile above this place.
It'll be a little soggy but just keep slogging.
We'll soon be on dry ground."
We were—waist deep in the Big Muddy
but the big fool said to push on.

The Sergeant said, "Sir, with all this equipment
No man will be able to swim."
"Sergeant, don't be a nervous Nellie,"
The Captain said to him.
"All we need is a little determination;
Men, follow me, I'll lead on."
We were—neck deep in the Big Muddy
but the big fool said to push on.

SOURCE: *Waist Deep in the Big Muddy (The Big Muddy), words and music by Pete Seeger.* TRO— © copyright 1967 (renewed) Melody Trails, Inc., New York, NY. Used by permission.

All at once, the moon clouded over,
We heard a gurgling cry.
A few seconds later, the captain's helmet
Was all that floated by.
The Sergeant said, "Turn around men!
I'm in charge from now on."
And we just made it out of the Big Muddy
With the captain dead and gone.

We stripped and dived and found his body
Stuck in the old quicksand.
I guess he didn't know that the water was deeper
Than the place he'd once before been.
Another stream had joined the Big Muddy
'Bout a half mile from where we'd gone.
We were lucky to escape from the Big Muddy
When the big fool said to push on.

Well, I'm not going to point any moral;
I'll leave that for yourself
Maybe you're still walking, you're still talking
You'd like to keep your health.
But every time I read the papers
That old feeling comes on;
We're—waist deep in the Big Muddy
And the big fool says to push on.

Waist deep in the Big Muddy
And the big fool says to push on.
Waist deep in the Big Muddy
And the big fool says to push on.
Waist deep! Neck deep! Soon even a
Tall man'll be over his head, we're
Waist deep in the Big Muddy!
And the big fool says to push on!

"I-Feel-Like-I'm-Fixin'-to-Die Rag"

Yeah, come on all of you, big strong men,
Uncle Sam needs your help again.
He's got himself in a terrible jam
Way down yonder in Vietnam
So put down your books and pick up a gun,
We're gonna have a whole lotta fun.
And it's one, two, three,

SOURCE: Country Joe and The Fish, *I Feel Like I'm Fixin' to Die*, Vanguard Records 1967.

What are we fighting for?
Don't ask me, I don't give a damn,
Next stop is Vietnam;
And it's five, six, seven,
Open up the pearly gates,
Well there ain't no time to wonder why,
Whoopee! we're all gonna die.

Well, come on generals, let's move fast;
Your big chance has come at last.
Gotta go out and get those reds—
The only good commie is the one who's dead
And you know that peace can only be won
When we've blown 'em all to kingdom come.
And it's one, two, three,
What are we fighting for?
Don't ask me, I don't give a damn,
Next stop is Vietnam;
And it's five, six, seven,
Open up the pearly gates,
Well there ain't no time to wonder why
Whoopee! we're all gonna die.

Well, come on Wall Street, don't move slow,
Why man, this is war au-go-go.
There's plenty good money to be made
By supplying the Army with the tools of the trade,
Just hope and pray that if they drop the bomb,
They drop it on the Viet Cong.
And it's one, two, three,
What are we fighting for?
Don't ask me, I don't give a damn,
Next stop is Vietnam.
And it's five, six, seven,
Open up the pearly gates,
Well there ain't no time to wonder why
Whoopee! we're all gonna die.

Well, come on mothers throughout the land,
Pack your boys off to Vietnam.
Come on fathers, don't hesitate,
Send 'em off before it's too late.
Be the first one on your block
To have your boy come home in a box.
And it's one, two, three
What are we fighting for?
Don't ask me, I don't give a damn,

Next stop is Vietnam.
And it's five, six, seven,
Open up the pearly gates,
Well there ain't no time to wonder why,
Whoopee! we're all gonna die.

"My Country 'Tis of Thy People You're Dying"

Now that your big eyes have finally opened
Now that you're wondering how must they feel,
Meaning them that you've chased across America's movie screens.
Now that you're wondering how can it be real
That the ones you've called colorful, noble and proud
In your school propaganda
They starve in their splendor?
You've asked for my comment I simply will render:
My country 'tis of thy people you're dying.

Now that the longhouses breed superstition
You force us to send our toddlers away
To your schools where they're taught to despise their traditions.
You forbid them their languages, then further say
That American history really began
When Columbus set sail out of Europe, then stress
That the nation of leeches that conquered this land
Are the biggest and bravest and boldest and best.
And yet where in your history books is the tale
Of the genocide basic to this country's birth,
Of the preachers who lied, how the Bill of Rights failed,
How a nation of patriots returned to their earth?
And where will it tell of the Liberty Bell
As it rang with a thud
O'er Kinzua mud,
And of brave Uncle Sam in Alaska this year?
My country 'tis of thy people you're dying.

Hear how the bargain was made for the West:
With her shivering children in zero degrees,
Blankets for your land, so the treaties attest,
Oh well, blankets for land is a bargain indeed,
And the blankets were those Uncle Sam had collected
From smallpox-diseased dying soldiers that day.
And the tribes were wiped out and the history books censored,
A hundred years of your statesmen have felt it's better this way.

SOURCE: Buffy Sainte-Marie, *Little Wheel Spin and Spin,* Vanguard Records 1966.

And yet a few of the conquered have somehow survived,
Their blood runs the redder though genes have paled.
From the Grand Canyon's caverns to Craven's sad hills
The wounded, the losers, the robbed sing their tale.
From Los Angeles County to upstate New York
The white nation fattens while others grow lean;
Oh the tricked and evicted they know what I mean.
My country 'tis of thy people you're dying.

The past it just crumbled, the future just threatens;
Our life blood's shut up in your chemical tanks.
And now here you come, bill of sale in your hands
And surprise in your eyes that we're lacking in thanks
For the blessings of civilization you've brought us,
The lessons you've taught us, the ruin you've wrought us—
Oh see what our trust in America's brought us.
My country 'tis of thy people you're dying.

Now that the pride of the sires receives charity,
Now that we're harmless and safe behind laws,
Now that my life's to be known as your "heritage,"
Now that even the graves have been robbed,
Now that our own chosen way is a novelty—
Hands on our hearts we salute you your victory,
Choke on your blue white and scarlet hypocrisy
Pitying the blindness that you've never seen
That the eagles of war whose wings lent you glory
They were never no more than carrion crows,
Pushed the wrens from their nest, stole their eggs, changed their story;
The mockingbird sings it, it's all that he knows.
"Ah what can I do?" say a powerless few
With a lump in your throat and a tear in your eye—
Can't you see that their poverty's profiting you.
My country 'tis of thy people you're dying.

"Fortunate Son"

Some folks are born to wave the flag,
Ooh, they're red, white and blue.
And when the band plays "Hail to the chief",
Ooh, they point the cannon at you, Lord,

It ain't me, it ain't me, I ain't no senator's son, son.
It ain't me, it ain't me; I ain't no fortunate one, no,
Yeah!

SOURCE: Creedence Clearwater Revival. *Willy and the Poor Boys*, Fantasy 1969.

Some folks are born silver spoon in hand,
Lord, don't they help themselves, oh.
But when the taxman comes to the door,
Lord, the house looks like a rummage sale, yes,

It ain't me, it ain't me, I ain't no millionaire's son, no.
It ain't me, it ain't me; I ain't no fortunate one, no.

Some folks inherit star spangled eyes,
Ooh, they send you down to war, Lord,
And when you ask them, "How much should we give?"
Ooh, they only answer More! more! more! yoh,

It ain't me, it ain't me, I ain't no military son, son.
It ain't me, it ain't me; I ain't no fortunate one, one.
It ain't me, it ain't me, I ain't no fortunate one, no no no,
It ain't me, it ain't me, I ain't no fortunate son, no no no,

Redstockings

After women got the vote in 1920, many people assumed that there was no further need for women to agitate for their rights. Alice Paul introduced the Equal Rights Amendment in 1923, but by the 1960s most people had forgotten about it. Betty Friedan's *Feminine Mystique* and the founding of the National Organization of Women, in conjunction with women's experience participating in civil rights and antiwar activism, reawakened the feminist movement. As a result, by the late 1960s, many women were becoming very serious about change.

The earlier movement had concentrated on political and, to some extent, on economic rights. The second wave of feminism now began to emphasize attitudes and consciousness. It was not enough for women to be able to vote; they needed also to be viewed and treated as equal members of society. Ironically, one of the forces that radicalized the women's movement was the counterculture and New Left itself. Women who attended Students for a Democratic Society (SDS) meetings found that after an evening of discussing Marx and Marcuse or analyzing race and class issues in the United States or examining the historical background of the war in Vietnam, they were usually expected to make sandwiches and coffee for their male comrades. One woman observed at the 1965 national SDS convention that "women only made peanut butter sandwiches, waited on tables, cleaned up and got laid. That was their role." Being treated as objects by left-wing men, who should have known better, was a wake-up call that radicalized many women. Feminists began setting up caucuses and workshops where they gathered to discuss *women's* problems in a classist, racist, sexist society. Before the decade was out, many radical women's groups had formed. Some believed that women should completely separate from male-dominated society; others believed that women would only achieve liberation if the entire class structure of society was first eliminated.

Redstockings was a group formed by Ellen Willis and Shulamith Firestone (the name is a left-wing play on "Blue Stockings," a pejorative term for intelligent women) that called for consciousness-raising sessions to enable women to see through the artificial roles that had been forced on them by men. They asked: Are women really more nurturing than men and consequently more suited to be the caregiver in a family? Is this biologically determined or a social construct? Redstockings also participated in demonstrations along with many other more radical feminist groups. Some picketed the Miss America contest in Atlantic City in 1968. Another group, W.I.T.C.H. (Women's International Terrorist Conspiracy from Hell) held a witches' dance on Wall Street in October 1968 and put a hex on the Stock Exchange.

According to this manifesto, in what way are women an oppressed class? Is it true, as the manifesto claims, that all forms of oppression, "racism, capitalism, imperialism," are extensions of male supremacy? Why are male-female relationships political?

The Redstockings Manifesto, 1969

I. After centuries of individual and preliminary political struggle, women are uniting to achieve their final liberation from male supremacy. Redstockings is dedicated to building this unity and winning our freedom.

II. Women are an oppressed class. Our oppression is total, affecting every facet of our lives. We are exploited as sex objects, breeders, domestic servants, and cheap labor. We are considered inferior beings, whose only purpose is to enhance men's lives. Our humanity is denied. Our prescribed behavior is enforced by the threat of violence.

Because we have lived so intimately with our oppressors, in isolation from each other, we have been kept from seeing our personal suffering as a political condition. This creates the illusion that a woman's relationship with her man is a matter of interplay between two unique personalities, and can be worked out individually. In reality, every such relationship is a "class" relationship, and the conflicts between individual men and women are political conflicts that can only be solved collectively.

III. We identify the agents of our oppression as men. Male supremacy is the oldest, most basic form of domination. All other forms of exploitation and oppression

---

SOURCE: "Redstockings Manifesto" (Notes from the Second Year, 1970), reprinted in full in *Feminism in Our Time: The Essential Writings, World War II to the Present*, Miriam Schneir, Ed. (New York: Vintage Books, 1994), 125–129.

(racism, capitalism, imperialism, etc.) are extensions of male supremacy; men dominate women, a few men dominate the rest. All power structures throughout history have been male-dominated and male-oriented. Men have controlled all political, economic, and cultural institutions and backed up this control with physical force. They have used their power to keep women in an inferior position. All men receive economic, sexual, and psychological benefits from male supremacy. All men have oppressed women.

IV. Attempts have been made to shift the burden of responsibility from men to institutions or to women themselves. We condemn these arguments as evasions. Institutions alone do not oppress; they are merely tools of the oppressor. To blame institutions implies that men and women are equally victimized, obscures the fact that men benefit from the subordination of women, and gives men the excuse that they are forced to be oppressors. On the contrary, any man is free to renounce his superior position provided he is willing to be treated like a woman by other men.

We also reject the idea that women consent to or are to blame for their oppression. Women's submission is not the result of brainwashing, stupidity, or mental illness but of continual, daily pressure from men. We do not need to change ourselves, but to change men.

The most slanderous evasion of all is that women can oppress men. The basis for this illusion is the isolation of individual relationships from their political context and the tendency of men to see any legitimate challenge to their privileges as persecutions.

V. We regard our personal experience, and our feelings about that experience, as the basis for an analysis of our common situation. We cannot rely on existing ideologies as they are all products of male supremacist culture. We question every generalization and accept none that are not confirmed by our experience.

Our chief task at present is to develop female class consciousness through sharing experience and publicly exposing the sexist foundation of all our institutions. Consciousness-raising is not "therapy," which implies the existence of individual solutions and falsely assumes that the male-female relationship is purely personal, but the only method by which we can ensure that our program for liberation is based on the concrete realities of our lives.

The first requirement for raising class consciousness is honesty, in private and in public, with ourselves and other women.

VI. We identify with all women. We define our best interest as that of the poorest, most brutally exploited woman. We repudiate all economic, racial, educational, or status privileges that divide us from other women. We are determined to recognize and eliminate any prejudices we may hold against other women. We are committed to achieving internal democracy. We will do whatever is necessary to ensure that every woman in our movement has an equal chance to participate, assume responsibility, and develop her political potential.

VII. We call on all our sisters to unite with us in struggle. We call on all men to give up their male privileges and support women's liberation in the interest of our humanity and their own. In fighting for our liberation, we will always take the side of women against their oppressors. We will not ask what is "revolutionary" or "reformist," only what is good for women.

The time for individual skirmishes is passed. This time we are going all the way.

S.C.U.M.
Society for Cutting Up Men

Valerie Solanas was an intriguing figure. She was abused as a child, went to live in New York, made a living as a prostitute, appeared in a couple of Andy Warhol films, and put a lot of effort into a script she wrote, "Up Your Ass," that she hoped Warhol would produce. Warhol, however, after praising her typing (!), misplaced the script and, affronted, she walked into his studio in June 1968 and shot him. The year before, she founded S.C.U.M., the Society for Cutting Up Men, and wrote a manifesto in which she claimed that the male was a biological accident, a mistake of nature. Her notoriety after she shot Warhol and was sent to prison led to the publication of the manifesto, which was avidly read by many feminists (although most did not take her statements seriously). It remains, however, an excellent example of extreme dissent.

Do you think she is sincere in her assertions, or is there a bizarre sense of humor at work here? Are any of her points valid?

From "SCUM Manifesto," 1968

Life in this society being, at best, an utter bore and no aspect of society being at all relevant to women, there remains to civic-minded, responsible, thrill-seeking females only to overthrow the government, eliminate the money system, institute complete automation and destroy the male sex.

It is now technically feasible to reproduce without the aid of males (or, for that matter, females) and to produce only females. We must begin immediately to do so. Retaining the male has not even the dubious purpose of reproduction. The male is a biological accident: the Y (male) gene is an incomplete X (female) gene, that is, it has an incomplete set of chromosomes. In other words, the male is an incomplete female, a walking abortion, aborted at the gene stage. To be male is to be deficient, emotionally limited; maleness is a deficiency disease and males are emotional cripples.

SOURCE: Valerie Solanas, *SCUM Manifesto*, (Oakland, CA: AK Press, 1968) passim.

The male is completely egocentric, trapped inside himself, incapable of empathizing or identifying with others, or love, friendship, affection or tenderness. He is a completely isolated unit, incapable of rapport with anyone. His responses are entirely visceral, not cerebral; his intelligence is a mere tool in the services of his drives and needs; he is incapable of mental passion, mental interaction; he can't relate to anything other than his own physical sensations. He is a half-dead, unresponsive lump, incapable of giving or receiving pleasure or happiness; consequently, he is at best an utter bore, an inoffensive blob, since only those capable of absorption in others can be charming. He is trapped in a twilight zone halfway between humans and apes, and is far worse off than the apes because, unlike the apes, he is capable of a large array of negative feelings—hate, jealousy, contempt, disgust, guilt, shame, doubt—and moreover, he is *aware* of what he is and what he isn't.

Although completely physical, the male is unfit even for stud service. Even assuming mechanical proficiency, which few men have, he is, first of all, incapable of zestfully, lustfully, tearing off a piece, but instead is eaten up with guilt, shame, fear and insecurity, feelings rooted in male nature, which the most enlightened training can only minimize; second, the physical feeling he attains is next to nothing; and third, he is not empathizing with his partner, but is obsessed with how he's doing, turning in an A performance, doing a good plumbing job. To call a man an animal is to flatter him; he's a machine, a walking dildo. It's often said that men use women. Use them for what? Surely not pleasure.

Eaten up with guilt, shame, fears and insecurities and obtaining, if he's lucky, a barely perceptible physical feeling, the male is, nonetheless, obsessed with screwing; he'll swim through a river of snot, wade nostril-deep through a mile of vomit, if he thinks there'll be a friendly pussy awaiting him. He'll screw a woman he despises, any snaggle-toothed hag, and furthermore, pay for the opportunity. Why? Relieving physical tension isn't the answer, as masturbation suffices for that. It's not ego satisfaction; that doesn't explain screwing corpses and babies.

Completely egocentric, unable to relate, empathize or identify, and filled with a vast, pervasive, diffuse sexuality, the male is psychically passive. He hates his passivity, so he projects it onto women, defines the male as active, then sets out to prove that he is ("prove that he is a Man"). His main means of attempting to prove it is screwing (Big Man with a Big Dick tearing off a Big Piece). Since he's attempting to prove an error, he must "prove" it again and again. Screwing, then, is a desperate compulsive, attempt to prove he's not passive, not a woman; but he *is* passive and *does* want to be a woman.

Being an incomplete female, the male spends his life attempting to complete himself, to become female. He attempts to do this by constantly seeking out, fraternizing with and trying to live through and fuse with the female, and by claiming as his own all female characteristics—emotional strength and independence, forcefulness, dynamism, decisiveness, coolness, objectivity, assertiveness, courage, integrity, vitality, intensity, depth of character, grooviness, etc.—and projecting onto women all male traits—vanity, frivolity, triviality, weakness, etc. It should be said, though, that the male has one glaring area of superiority over the female—public relations. (He has done a brilliant job of convincing millions of women that men are women and women are men). The male claim that females find fulfillment through motherhood and sexuality reflects what males think they'd find fulfilling if they were female.

Women, in other words, don't have penis envy; men have pussy envy. When the male accepts his passivity, defines himself as a women (males as well as females think men are women and women are men), and becomes a transvestite he loses his desire to screw (or to do anything else, for that matter; he fulfills himself as a drag queen) and gets his cock chopped off. He then achieves a continuous diffuse sexual feeling from "being a woman." Screwing is, for a man, a defense against his desire to be female. Sex is itself a sublimation. . . .

He is responsible for:

War: The male's normal compensation for not being female, namely, getting his Big Gun off, is grossly inadequate, as he can get it off only a very limited number of times; so he gets it off on a really massive scale, and proves to the entire world that he's a "Man." Since he has no compassion or ability to empathize or identify, proving his manhood is worth an endless amount of mutilation and suffering and an endless number of lives, including his own—his own life being worthless, he would rather go out in a blaze of glory than to plod grimly on for fifty more years.

Niceness, Politeness, and 'Dignity': Every man, deep down, knows he's a worthless piece of shit. Overwhelmed by a sense of animalism and deeply ashamed of it; wanting, not to express himself, but to hide from others his total physicality, total egocentricity, the hate and contempt he feels for other men, and to hide from himself the hate and contempt he suspects other men feel for him; having a crudely constructed nervous system that is easily upset by the least display of emotion or feeling, the male tries to enforce a "social" code that ensures perfect blandness, unsullied by the slightest trace or feeling or upsetting opinion. He uses terms like "copulate," "sexual congress," "have relations with" (to men sexual relations is a redundancy), overlaid with stilted manners; the suit on the chimp. . . .

Gloria Steinem (1934–)

Gloria Steinem has had a critical influence on the feminist movement. In 1963 she wrote an article about her experience working in a Playboy Club, "I Was a Playboy Bunny," and by the late 1960s she was a regular columnist for New York magazine. Her influence became more significant in 1971, when, with Betty Friedan, Shirley Chisholm, and Bella Abzug, she cofounded the National Woman's Caucus. Before the year was over, she had published the first issue of Ms. Magazine, which became a leading instrument in raising women's consciousness about feminist issues. Steinem, more radical than feminist Betty Friedan, is famous for her comment that "a woman needs a man like a fish needs a bicycle."

In this article, which first appeared in the Washington Post in 1970 and was later reprinted several times in different versions, Steinem presents the case for feminism. What are the goals of the feminist movement? In what way will women's liberation emancipate men as well as women? Why is consciousness raising important? In what ways have women's roles changed since 1970?

"Women's Liberation 'Aims to Free Men, Too,'" June 7, 1970

This is the year of Women's Liberation. Or at least, it's the year the press has discovered a movement that has been strong for several years now, and reported it as a small, privileged, rather lunatic event instead of the major revolution in consciousness—in everyone's consciousness, male or female—that I believe it truly is.

It is a movement that some call "feminist" but should more accurately be called humanist; a movement that is an integral part of rescuing this country from its old, expensive patterns of elitism, racism and violence.

The first problem for all of us, men and women, is not to learn, but to unlearn. We are filled with the popular wisdom of several centuries just past, and we are terrified to give it up. Patriotism means obedience, age means wisdom, woman means submission, black means inferior: these are preconceptions imbedded so deeply in our thinking that we honestly may not know that they are there.

Unfortunately, authorities who write textbooks are sometimes subject to the same popular wisdom as the rest of us. They gather their proof around it, and end by becoming the theoreticians of the status quo. Using the most respectable of scholarly methods, for instance, English scientists proved definitively that the English were descended from the angels while the Irish were descended from the apes.

It was beautifully done, complete with comparative skull measurements, and it was a rationale for the English domination of the Irish for more than 100 years. I try to remember that when I'm reading Arthur Jensen's current and very impressive work on the limitations of black intelligence, or when I'm reading Lionel Tiger on the inability of women to act in groups.

It wasn't easy for the English to give up their mythic superiority. Indeed, there are quite a few Irish who doubt that they have done it yet. Clearing our minds and government policies of outdated myths is proving to be at least as difficult, but it is also inevitable. Whether it's woman's secondary role in society or the paternalistic role of the United States in the world, the old assumptions just don't work any more.

Part of living this revolution is having the scales fall from our eyes. Every day we see small obvious truths that we had missed before. Our histories, for instance, have generally been written for and about white men. Inhabited countries were "discovered" when the first white male set foot there, and most of us learned more about any one European country than we did about Africa and Asia combined.

SOURCE: Gloria Steinem, "Women's Liberation 'Aims to Free Men, Too.'" *Washington Post,* Sunday, June 7, 1970.

I confess that, before some consciousness-changing of my own, I would have thought that the women's history courses springing up around the country belonged in the same cultural ghetto as home economics. The truth is that we need Women's Studies almost as much as we need Black Studies, and for exactly the same reason: too many of us have completed a "good" education believing that everything from political power to scientific discovery was the province of white males.

We believed, for instance, that the vote had been "given" to women in some whimsical, benevolent fashion. We never learned about the long desperation of the women's struggle, or about the strength and wisdom of the women who led it. We knew a great deal more about the outdated, male supremacist theories of Sigmund Freud than we did about societies where women had equal responsibility, or even ruled.

"Anonymous," Virginia Woolf once said sadly, "was a woman."

A BLACK PARALLEL

I don't mean to equate our problems of identity with those that flowed from slavery. But, as Gunnar Myrdal pointed out in his classic study *An American Dilemma,* "In drawing a parallel between the position of, and feeling toward, women and Negroes, we are uncovering a fundamental basis of our culture."

Blacks and women suffer from the same myths of childlike natures; smaller brains; inability to govern themselves, much less white men; limited job skills; identity as sex objects, and so on. Ever since slaves arrived on these shores and were given the legal status of wives—that is, chattel—our legal reforms have followed on each other's heels—with women, I might add, still lagging considerably behind.

President Nixon's Commission on women concluded that the Supreme Court sanctions discrimination against women—discrimination that it long ago ruled unconstitutional in the case of blacks—but the commission report remains mysteriously unreleased by the White House. An equal rights amendment now up again before the Senate has been delayed by a male-chauvinist Congress for 47 years. Neither blacks nor women have role-models in history: models of individuals who have been honored in authority outside the home.

As Margaret Mead has noted, the only women allowed to be dominant and respectable at the same time are widows. You have to do what society wants you to do, have a husband who dies, and then have power thrust upon you through no fault of your own. The whole thing seems very hard on the men.

Before we go on to other reasons why Women's Liberation Is Men's Liberation, too—and why this incarnation of the women's movement is inseparable from the larger revolution—perhaps we should clear the air of a few more myths—the myth that women are biologically inferior, for instance. In fact, an equally good case could be made for the reverse.

Women live longer then men. That's when the groups being studied are always being cited as proof that we work them to death, but the truth is that women live longer than men even when the groups being studied are monks and nuns. We survived Nazi concentration camps better, are protected against heart attacks by our female hormones, are less subject to many diseases, withstand surgery better and are so much more durable at every stage of life that nature conceives 20 to 50 percent more males just to keep the balance going.

The Auto Safety Committee of the American Medical Association has come to the conclusion that women are better drivers because they're less emotional than men. I never thought I would hear myself quoting the AMA, but that one was too good to resist.

I don't want to prove the superiority of one sex to another: that would only be repeating a male mistake. The truth is that we're just not sure how many of our differences are biological and how many are societal. What we do know is that the differences between the two sexes, like the differences between races, are much less great than the differences to be found within each group.

CHAINS OF MINK

A second myth is that women are already being treated equally in this society. We ourselves have been guilty of perpetuating this myth, especially at upper economic levels where women have grown fond of being lavishly maintained as ornaments and children. The chains may be made of mink and wall-to-wall carpeting, but they are still chains.

The truth is that a woman with a college degree working full time makes less than a black man with a high school degree working full time. And black women make least of all. In many parts of the country—New York City, for instance—a woman has no legally guaranteed right to rent an apartment, buy a house, get accommodations in a hotel or be served in a public restaurant. She can be refused simply because of her sex.

In some states, women get longer jail sentences for the same crime. Women on welfare must routinely answer humiliating personal questions; male welfare recipients do not. A woman is the last to be hired, the first to be fired. Equal pay for equal work is the exception. Equal chance for advancement, especially at upper levels or at any level with authority over men, is rare enough to be displayed in a museum.

As for our much-touted economic power, *we* make up only 5 percent of the Americans receiving $10,000 a year or more, and that includes all the famous rich widows. We are 51 per cent of all stockholders, a dubious honor these days, but we hold only 18 per cent of the stock—and that is generally controlled by men.

In fact, the myth of economic matriarchy in this country is less testimony to our power than to resentment of the little power we do have.

You may wonder why we have submitted to such humiliations all these years; why, indeed, women will sometimes deny that they are second-class citizens at all. The answer lies in the psychology of second-classness. Like all such groups, we come to accept what society says about us. We believe that we can make it in the world only by "Uncle Tom-ing," by a real or pretended subservience to white males.

Even when we come to understand that we, as individuals, are not second class, we still accept society's assessment of our group—a phenomenon psychologists refer to as internalized aggression. From this stems the desire to be the only woman in an office, an academic department or any other part of the man's world. From this also stems women who put down their sisters—and my own profession of journalism has some of them.

INHUMANITY TO MAN

I don't want to give the impression, though, that we want to join society exactly as it is. I don't think most women want to pick up briefcases and march off to meaning-less, depersonalized jobs. Nor do we want to be drafted—and women certainly should be drafted; even the readers of Seventeen magazine were recently polled as being overwhelmingly in favor of women in national service—to serve in a war like the one in Indochina.

We want to liberate men from those inhuman roles as well. We want to share the work and responsibility, and to have men share equal responsibility for the children. Probably the ultimate myth is that children must have fulltime mothers, and that liberated women make bad ones. The truth is that most American children seem to be suffering from too much mother and too little father.

Women now spend more time with their homes and families than in any other past or present society we know about. To get back to the sanity of the agrarian or joint family system, we need free universal day care. With that aid, as in Scandinavian countries, and with laws that permit women equal work and equal pay, man will be relieved of his role as sole breadwinner and stranger to his own children.

No more alimony. Fewer boring wives. Fewer childlike wives. No more so-called "Jewish mothers," who are simply normally ambitious human beings with all their ambitiousness confined to the house. No more wives who fall apart with the first wrinkle because they've been taught that their total identity depends on their out-sides. No more responsibility for another adult human being who has never been told she is responsible for her own life, and who sooner or later says some version of, "If I hadn't married you, I could have been a star." Women's Liberation really is Men's Liberation, too.

The family system that will emerge is a great subject of anxiety. Probably there will be a variety of choices. Colleague marriages, such as young people have now, with both partners going to law-school or the Peace Corps together, is one alternative. At least they share more than the kitchen and the bedroom. Communes; marriages that are valid for the child-rearing years only—there are many possibilities.

The point is that Women's Liberation is not destroying the American family. It is trying to build a human compassionate alternative out of its ruins.

SIMPLY INCORRUPTIBLE

One final myth that women are more moral than men. We are not more moral; we are only uncorrupted by power. But until the old generation of male chauvinists is out of office women in positions of power can increase our chances of peace a great deal.

I personally would rather have had Margaret Mead as President during the past six years of Vietnam than either Lyndon Johnson or Richard Nixon. At least she wouldn't have had her masculinity to prove. Much of the trouble this country is in has to do with the masculine mystique: The idea that manhood somehow depends on the subjugation of other people. It's a bipartisan problem.

The challenge to all of us is to live a revolution, not to die for one. There has been too much killing, and the weapons are now far too terrible. This revolution has to change consciousness, to upset the injustice of our current hierarchy by refusing to honor it. And it must be a life that enforces a new social justice.

Because the truth is that none of us can be liberated if other groups are not. Women's Liberation is a bridge between black and white women, but also between the construction workers and the suburbanites, between Mr. Nixon's Silent Majority and the young people it fears. Indeed, there's much more injustice and rage among working-class women than among the much publicized white radicals.

Women are sisters; they have many of the same problems, and they can communicate with each other. "You only get radicalized," as black activists always told us, "on your own thing." Then we make the connection to other injustices in society. The women's movement is an important revolutionary bridge, and we are building It.

Stonewall

The movement of the 1960s led to the mobilization of minorities around the country. Chicanos, Native Americans, homosexuals, lesbians, and many others were inspired to stand up for their rights. In June 1969, the dissenting impulse spawned the gay rights movement. After one of the routine police raids at the Stonewall Inn in Greenwich Village (a bar frequented by gays), a succession of demonstrations broke out. Many gay men decided they were no longer going to take the harassment, and by the end of the summer the Gay Liberation Front was born. The following flyers were distributed during the summer of 1969 to spread the word and encourage more people to join the movement.

How does a minority group effect change? Will rights ever be granted to people if they don't act proactively to claim those rights?

Stonewall Documents, 1969

FLYER 1

Get the mafia and the cops out of gay bars.

The nights of Friday, June 27, 1969 and Saturday, June 28, 1969 will go down in history as the first time that thousands of Homosexual men and women went out into the streets to protest the intolerable situation which has existed in New York City for many years—namely, the Mafia (or syndicate) control of this city's Gay bars in collusion with certain elements in the Police Dept. of the City of New York. The demonstrations were triggered by a Police raid on the Stonewall Inn late Friday night, June 27th. The purported reason for the raid was the Stonewall's lack of a liquor license. Who's kidding whom here? Can anybody really believe that an operation as big as the Stonewall

---

SOURCE: Donn Teal, *The Gay Militants* (New York: St. Martin's Press, 1971), 24–25, 36, 37.

could continue for almost three years just a few blocks from the 6th Precinct house without having a liquor license? No! The Police have known about the Stonewall operation all along. What's happened is the presence of new "brass" in 6th Precinct which has vowed to "drive the fags out of the Village."

Many of you have noticed one of the signs which the "management" of the Stonewall has placed outside stating "Legalize Gay bars and lick the problem." Judge Kenneth Keating (a former US Senator) ruled in January 1968 that even close dancing between Homosexuals is legal. Since that date there has been nothing illegal, per se, about a Gay bar. What is illegal about New York City's Gay bars today is the Mafia (or syndicate) stranglehold on them. Legitimate Gay businessmen are afraid to open decent Gay bars with a healthy social atmosphere (as opposed to the hell-hole atmosphere of places typified by the Stonewall) because of fear of pressure from the unholy alliance of the Mafia and elements in the Police Dept. who accept payoffs and protect the Mafia monopoly.

We at the Homophile Youth Movement (HYMN) believe that the only way this monopoly can be broken is through the action of Homosexual men and women themselves. We obviously cannot rely on the various agencies of government who for years have known about this situation but who have refused to do anything about it. Therefore we urge the following:

1. That Gay businessmen step forward and open Gay bars that will be run legally with competitive pricing and a healthy social atmosphere.

2. That Homosexual men and women boycott places like the Stonewall. The only way, it seems, that we can get the criminal elements out of gay bars is simply to make it unprofitable for them.

3. That the Homosexual citizens of New York City, and concerned Heterosexuals, write to mayor Lindsay demanding a thorough investigation and effective action to correct this intolerable situation.

FLYER 2

July 24th
Do you think homosexuals are revolting?
You bet your sweet ass we are.

We're going to make a place for ourselves in the revolutionary movement. We challenge the myths that are screwing up this society. MEETING: Thursday, July 24th, 6:30 PM at Alternate U, 69 West 14th Street at Sixth Avenue.

FLYER 3

Homosexuals are coming.
Together at last.

To examine how we are oppressed and how we oppress ourselves. To fight for gay control of gay businesses. To publish our own newspaper. To these and other radical ends. . . .

Cesar Chavez (1927–1993)

Cesar Chavez spent most of his early life traveling around the southwest as a migrant farm worker with other Chicanos (Americans of Mexican heritage), eking out a subsistence living by going from farm to farm during harvest season. In the early 1960s, inspired by the civil rights movement and Martin Luther King Jr.'s leadership, he began to organize the first farm workers' union in America. "If you're outraged at conditions, then you can't possibly be free or happy until you devote all your time to changing them and do nothing but that," he said. In 1965 his union, the National Farm Workers Association, with about 1200 members, joined with another union in a grape strike in Delano. The strike (*La Huelga*) wound up lasting five years, during which time millions of supporters and sympathizers around the country showed their solidarity by boycotting California grapes. From the beginning, the NFWA (United Farm Workers after 1966), under Chavez's direction, adhered to the principles of nonviolence espoused by Gandhi and King. In fact, Chavez, emulating Gandhi, went on a hunger strike in 1968 for 25 days. Robert Kennedy, who by that time had thrown his full support behind Chavez, flew to California to be the one to give Chavez bread when he broke the fast. Economic pressure finally forced the growers to negotiate with the UFW in 1970, and Chavez's long campaign finally achieved its goal.

Chavez's efforts were not the only ones to promote the rights of Chicanos and Latinos. In 1969, a new organization La Raza Unida (the United Race), influenced by Chavez's struggle and the optimistic activism of the 1960s, spread throughout the southwest. In Texas, Colorado, New Mexico, and California, chapters of La Raza Unida opened, each emphasizing the issues of its locality, each working to elect their own representatives in their own districts, and each working to overturn anti-Chicano/Latino discrimination.

According to Chavez in this 1970 interview, why is nonviolence more effective than violence? What would happen if those struggling for their rights resorted to violence, even in self-defense?

Interview with Cesar Chavez, Apostle of Non-Violence, May 1970

OBSERVER: *Why do you insist on non-violent means in this struggle?*

CHAVEZ: Our conviction is that human life and limb are a very special possession given by God to man and that no one has the right to take that away, in any cause, however just. We also find that violence is contagious; it is uncontrollable.

SOURCE: *The Observer,* May 1970.

If we use it, then the opposition is going to respond in kind and it is going to be escalated.

Also we are convinced that non-violence is more powerful than violence. We are convinced that non-violence supports you if you have a just and moral cause. Non-violence gives the opportunity to stay on the offensive, which is of vital importance to win any contest. Suppose we are striking and the opponent appears to be getting the best of us and we resort to violence. Then he will bring in other forces and one of two things happens: violence has to be escalated, or there is total demoralization of the workers. Non-violence works in exactly the opposite manner: when for every violent action committed against us, we respond with non-violence, we tend to attract people's support; we have a chance of attracting other people who are not involved because they are workers, but are involved because they have a conscience and because they would rather see a non-violent solution to things.

OBSERVER: *So it is a good strategy.*

CHAVEZ: Yes, but that alone is not reason enough. If you have no basis for non-violence other than a strategy, a tactic, then when it fails your only alternative is completely the reverse and that's violence. So you have to balance the strategy with a clear understanding of what you are doing. However important the struggle is and however much misery and poverty and degradation exist, we know that it cannot be more important than one human life. That's basic. Second, we operate on the theory that men who are involved and truly concerned about people are not by nature violent. If they were violent they couldn't have that love and that concern for people. That sort of man becomes violent when that deep concern he has for people is frustrated, when he's faced with overwhelming odds against what he is trying to do. Then sometimes he feels that violence is really a short-cut or a sort of miracle to end everything and bring about a solution. We don't want to get into that trap.

OBSERVER: *What if violence is a short-cut?*

CHAVEZ: It isn't. It has never been proved in the history of mankind that it is a short-cut.

OBSERVER: *You're using a very broad perspective.*

CHAVEZ: Well, let me tell you—if I were to tell the workers: "All right, we're going to be violent; we're going to burn the sheds and we're going to dynamite the grower's homes and we're going to burn the vineyards," provided we could get away with it, the growers would sign a contract. But you see that that victory came at the expense of violence; it came at the expense of injuring. I think that once that happens it would have a tremendous impact on us. We would lose our perspective and we would lose the regard we have for human beings—and then the struggle would become a mechanical thing.

OBSERVER: *If you lose a sense of justice in your cause, you lose a lot of strength.* . . .

CHAVEZ: Nothing can replace that strength. And the victory is not total. If you use violence, you have to sell part of yourself for that violence, either because of your own self-guilt or because you have to incorporate people who are extremists and violent or whatever it might be. Then you are no longer the master of your own struggle, and the important thing is that for poor people to be able to get a clean victory is something you don't often see. If we get it through violence, then the employers will just wait long enough until they can get even with you—and then the workers will respond, and then—

OBSERVER: *So a violent resolution to a problem is never a resolution, just a cessation?*

CHAVEZ: Let me give you an example: the armed revolutions we have. What happens? Once you set up an army or militia to gain independence you have to maintain that army. You know against whom? Against your own people.

OBSERVER: *All violence is necessarily an oppression then?*

CHAVEZ: That's right. If we were to become violent and we won the strike, as an example, then what would prevent us from turning violence against opponents in the movement who wanted to displace us? Say they felt they had more leadership and they wanted to be the leaders. What would prevent us from turning violence against them? Nothing. Because we had already experienced that violence awarded us victory. If we are concerned about human beings and if we are concerned about respecting man, then we have to be concerned about the consequences.

Another thing is that people think non-violence is really weak and non-militant. These are misconceptions that people have because they don't understand what non-violence means. Non-violence takes more guts, if I can put it bluntly, than violence. Most violent acts are accomplished by getting the opponent off guard, and it doesn't take that much character, I think, if one wants to do it. I am confronted frequently by people who say, "So-and-so tried non-violence and it didn't work." That's not really so. Non-violence is very weak in the theoretical sense; it cannot defend itself. But it is most powerful in the action situation where people are using non-violence because they want desperately to bring about some change. Non-violence in action is a very potent force and it can't be stopped. The people who are struggling have the complete say-so. No man-made law, no human ruler, no army can destroy this. There is no way it can be destroyed, except by those within the non-violent struggle. And so, if we have the capacity to endure, if we have the patience, things will change.

OBSERVER: *What do you say to the honest activist who feels that so many of the channels to change in this society are closed that he has no choice but to take up arms? I'm thinking of people like Camillo Torres in Columbia.*

CHAVEZ: There is no question that they have tremendous love for people and they want to bring about change. In the case of Torres, we see very clearly how he went from a life of priesthood to the extreme of using violence. And I'm sure he felt he had no other way of doing it. But I'm sure that if we examine the development of this man, and if we examine the reasons for which he worked, we would find that he probably was a failure as an organizer, an organizer of masses of people. . . .

OBSERVER: *Then for you non-violence is a universal approach regardless of the degree of oppression?*

CHAVEZ: The greater the oppression, the more leverage you have. What I'm trying to say is violence didn't work and it's not going to work, and if it works it replaces, as in Latin America, one violent government with another that is more violent. People are abused with violence. In Latin America, who gets killed in case of a revolution? The poor people, the workers. Who gets nothing but crumbs when another force comes into power? Take the Mexican revolution, take any revolution—the people of the land are the ones who give their bodies, who get killed, and they really don't gain that much from it. I think it's too big a price to pay for not getting anything. They are being exploited as much by the ones who "help" them as by the others. To call men to arms with a lot of promises and to ask them to give their lives for a cause, and then not produce for them afterward is the most vicious sort of oppression. And we've seen it happen.

OBSERVER: *Has Christianity affected your philosophy of non-violence?*

CHAVEZ: Very definitely. Christianity is not the only religion, but it is the one that I am a believer in. It has taught us the message of Christ with regard to loving our neighbor and with regard to respecting one another and exhorting us to be able to forgive. Now these are very difficult things and, of course, we are not even approaching that. But we have seen very little action in a dramatic form by Christians in our world. There is a lot of good will, and they talk a lot about that—but people sacrificing themselves—very little.

Gandhi is an example. He was not a Christian but in my estimation he probably personifies a Christian more than most men. He showed us not by talking, not by what he wrote as much as by his actions, his own willingness to live by truth and by respect for mankind and accepting the sacrifices. You see non-violence exacts a very high price from one who practices it. But once you are able to meet that demand then you can do most things, provided you have the time. Gandhi showed how a whole nation could be liberated without an army. This is the first time in the history of the world when a huge nation, occupied for over a century, achieved independence by non-violence. It was a long struggle and it takes time.

OBSERVER: *You speak of patience and determination as a necessary part of non-violent politics. The grape workers' strike is one of the longest in American history. What keeps you going?*

CHAVEZ: I think that it is a conviction in what we are doing—that we are involved in a just cause. We know that most likely we are not going to do anything else in the rest of our life except this. We know that if we weren't doing this we wouldn't be doing anything we would like to do more than this. We know really there is nowhere else to go and although we would like to see victory come soon we are willing to wait. Non-violence calls for hard-nosed organizing, for a minimum of dramatics and a great deal of understanding of what the situation is—being able to assess the opposition, being able to win by winning small victories constantly, and by not letting yourself be locked into a position where you can't move because you're cornered.

OBSERVER: *Do you see your struggle as having historical significance?*

CHAVEZ: All successful struggles tend to set precedents, but I think more important than that, perhaps for the first time in the history of the richest nation in the world, it would give those people who work at producing food some food for themselves. . . . And also it would point out very concretely that this came about because of the determination of the people in the struggle, and more important because of the way the people conducted themselves through the struggle.

The American Indian Movement

In the aftermath of the civil rights movement's call for black power, red power became the rallying cry of American Indians. A new organization, the American Indian Movement (AIM), was founded in 1968. From November 1969 to June 1971, approximately a hundred Indians from several different tribes joined AIM in reclaiming and occupying Alcatraz Island. Wanting to call attention to the plight of Native Americans, they occupied the island in the name of Indians of All Tribes, demanded the deed for the island, and insisted that they be allowed to set up an Indian university, a museum, and a cultural center. After fruitless negotiations between the Indians and the federal government, President Nixon ordered the island retaken. On June 11, 1971, a force of FBI agents and federal marshals forcibly removed them.

In 1972, AIM sponsored a march on Washington billed as the Trail of Broken Treaties. AIM members occupied the Bureau of Indian Affairs (BIA) headquarters and issued a 20-point proposal for President Richard Nixon to consider. The following year, elders from the Lakota Sioux nation requested AIM's assistance in dealing with BIA and tribal council corruption in South Dakota. This led to AIM's occupation of Wounded Knee (site of the last armed Indian resistance in 1890) and an infamous 71-day standoff between armed Indians and federal marshals. The Indians demanded that the 1868 Fort Laramie Treaty guaranteeing the Black Hills to the Lakota be honored. They also wanted an end to the strip mining at the Pine Ridge Reservation. At the end of the siege, however, the federal government made no concessions, and the Indians were removed.

Though the Alcatraz and Wounded Knee occupations were thwarted, were the Indians successful in achieving their main goal of calling attention to their cause? In the following proclamation, how valid are their arguments for reclaiming Alcatraz? Which of AIM's 20 proposals in the second proclamation are justifiable?

A Proclamation: To the Great White Father and All His People, 1969

We, the Native Americans, reclaim the land known as Alcatraz Island in the name of all American Indians by right of discovery.

We wish to be fair and honorable in our dealings with the Caucasian inhabitants of this land, and hereby offer the following treaty:

We will purchase said Alcatraz Island for $24 in glass beads and red cloth, a precedent set by the white man's purchase of a similar island about 300 years ago. We know that $24 in trade goods for these 16 acres is more than was paid when Manhattan Island was sold, but we know that land values have risen over the years.

Our offer of $1.24 per acre is greater than the 47 cents per acre that the white men are now paying the California Indians for their land. We will give to the inhabitants of this land a portion of that land for their own, to be held in trust by the American Indian Affairs and by the bureau of Caucasian affairs to hold in perpetuity—for as long as the sun shall rise and the rivers go down to the sea.

We will further guide the inhabitants in the proper way of living. We will offer them our religion, our education, our lifeways, in order to help them achieve our level of civilization and thus raise them and all their white brothers up from their savage and unhappy state.

We offer this treaty in good faith and wish to be fair and honorable in our dealings with all white men.

We feel that this so-called Alcatraz Island is more than suitable for an Indian Reservation, as determined by the white man's own standards. By this we mean that this place resembles most Indian reservations in that:

1. It is isolated from modern facilities, and without adequate means of transportation.
2. It has no fresh running water.
3. It has inadequate sanitation facilities.
4. There are no oil or mineral rights.
5. There is no industry and so unemployment is very great.
6. There are no health care facilities.
7. The soil is rocky and non-productive; and the land does not support game.
8. There are no educational facilities.
9. The population has always exceeded the land base.
10. The population has always been held as prisoners and kept dependent upon others.

Further, it would be fitting and symbolic that ships from all over the world, entering the Golden Gate, would first see Indian land, and thus be reminded of the true

---

SOURCE: Retrieved on 5/10/2004 from http://cwis.org/fwdp/Americas/alcatraz.txt

history of this nation. This tiny island would be a symbol of the great lands once ruled by free and noble Indians.

What use will we make of this land?

Since the San Francisco Indian Center burned down, there is no place for Indians to assemble and carry on tribal life here in the white man's city. Therefore, we plan to develop on this island several Indian institutions:

1. A Center for Native American Studies will be developed which will educate them to the skills and knowledge relevant to improve the lives and spirits of all Indian peoples. Attached to this center will be travelling universities, managed by Indians, which will go to the Indian Reservations, learning those necessary and relevant materials now about.

2. An American Indian Spiritual Center, which will practice our ancient tribal religious and sacred healing ceremonies. Our cultural arts will be featured and our young people trained in music, dance, and healing rituals.

3. An Indian Center of Ecology, which will train and support our young people in scientific research and practice to restore our lands and waters to their pure and natural state. We will work to de-pollute the air and waters of the Bay Area. We will seek to restore fish and animal life to the area and to revitalize sea-life which has been threatened by the white man's way. We will set up facilities to desalt sea water for human benefit.

4. A Great Indian Training School will be developed to teach our people how to make a living in the world, improve our standard of living, and to end hunger and unemployment among all our people. This training school will include a center for Indian arts and crafts, and an Indian restaurant serving native foods, which will restore Indian culinary arts. This center will display Indian arts and offer Indian foods to the public, so that all may know of the beauty and spirit of the traditional Indian ways.

Some of the present buildings will be taken over to develop an American Indian Museum which will depict our native food and other cultural contributions we have given to the world. Another part of the museum will present some of the things the white man has given to the Indians in return for the land and life he took: disease, alcohol, poverty, and cultural decimation (as symbolized by old tin cans, barbed wire, rubber tires, plastic containers, etc.). Part of the museum will remain a dungeon to symbolize both those Indian captives who were incarcerated for challenging white authority and those who were imprisoned on reservations. The museum will show the noble and tragic events of Indian history, including the broken treaties, the documentary of the Trail of Tears, the Massacre of Wounded Knee, as well as the victory over Yellow-Hair Custer and his army.

In the name of all Indians, therefore, we reclaim this island for our Indian nations, for all these reasons. We feel this claim is just and proper, and that this land should rightfully be granted to us for as long as the rivers run and the sun shall shine.

We hold the rock!

American Indian Movement 20 Point Proposal
October 1972, Minneapolis, Minnesota

"TRAIL OF BROKEN TREATIES": FOR RENEWAL OF CONTRACTS, RECONSTRUCTION OF INDIAN COMMUNITIES & SECURING AN INDIAN FUTURE IN AMERICA!

RESTORATION OF CONSTITUTIONAL TREATY-MAKING AUTHORITY: The U.S. President should propose by executive message, and the Congress should consider and enact legislation, to repeal the provision in the 1871 Indian Appropriations Act which withdrew federal recognition from Indian Tribes and Nations as political entities, which could be contracted by treaties with the United States, in order that the President may resume the exercise of his full constitutional authority for acting in the matters of Indian Affairs—and in order that Indian Nations may represent their own interests in the manner and method envisioned and provided in the Federal Constitution.

ESTABLISHMENT OF TREATY COMMISSION TO MAKE NEW TREATIES: The President should impanel and the Congress establish, within the next year, a Treaty Commission to contract a security and assistance treaty of treaties, with Indian people to negotiate a national commitment to the future of Indian people for the last quarter of the Twentieth Century. Authority should be granted to allow tribes to contract by separate and individual treaty, multitribal or regional groupings or national collective, respecting general or limited subject matter . . . and provide that no provisions of existing treaty agreements may be withdrawn or in any manner affected without the explicit consent and agreement of any particularly related Indian Nation.

AN ADDRESS TO THE AMERICAN PEOPLE & JOINT SESSIONS OF CONGRESS: The President and the leadership of Congress should make a commitment now and next January to request and arrange for four Native Americans—selected by Indian people at a future date—and the President of the United States and any designated U.S. Senators and Representatives to address a joint session of Congress and the American people through national communications media regarding the Indian future within the American Nation, and relationships between the Federal Government and Indian Nations—on or before June 2, 1974, the first half century anniversary of the 1924 "Indian Citizenship Act."

COMMISSION TO REVIEW TREATY COMMITMENTS & VIOLATIONS: The President should immediately create a multi-lateral, Indian and non-Indian Commission to review domestic treaty commitments and complaints of chronic violations and to recommend or act for corrective actions including the imposition of mandatory sanctions or interim restraints upon violative activities, and including formulation of legislation designed to protect the jeopardized Indian rights and eliminate the unending patterns of prohibitively

SOURCE: Retrieved on 10/3/2002 from www.aimovement.org/archives/index.html

complex lawsuits and legal defenses—which habitually have produced indecisive and interment results, only too frequently forming guidelines for more court battles, or additional challenges and attacks against Indian rights. (Indians have paid attorneys and lawyers more than $40,000,000 since 1962. Yet many Indian people are virtually imprisoned in the nation's courtrooms in being forced constantly to defend their rights, while many tribes are forced to maintain a multitude of suits in numerous jurisdictions relating to the same or a single issue, or a few similar issues. There is less need for more attorney assurances than there is for institution of protections that reduce violations and minimize the possibilities for attacks upon Indian rights.)

RESUBMISSION OF UNRATIFIED TREATIES TO THE SENATE: The President should resubmit to the U.S. Senate of the next Congress those treaties negotiated with Indian nations or their representatives, but never heretofore ratified nor rendered moot by subsequent treaty contract with such Indians not having ratified treaties with the United States. . . .

ALL INDIANS TO BE GOVERNED BY TREATY RELATIONS: The Congress should enact a Joint Resolution declaring that as a matter of public policy and good faith, all Indian people in the United States shall be considered to be in treaty relations with the Federal Government and governed by doctrines of such relationship.

MANDATORY RELIEF AGAINST TREATY RIGHTS VIOLATIONS: The Congress should add a new section to Title 28 of the United States Code to provide for the judicial enforcement and protection of Indian Treaty Rights. Such section should direct that upon petition of any Indian Tribe or prescribed Indian groups and Individuals claiming substantial injury to, or interference in the equitable and good faith exercise of any rights, governing authority or utilization and preservation of resources, secured by Treaty, mandatorily the Federal District courts shall grant immediate enjoinder or injunctive relief against any non-Indian party or defendants, including State governments and their subdivisions or officers, alleged to be engaged in such injurious actions, until such time as the District U.S. Court may be reasonably satisfied that a Treaty Violation is not being committed, or otherwise satisfied that the Indians' interests and rights, in equity and in law, are preserved and protected from jeopardy and secure from harm.

JUDICIAL RECOGNITION OF INDIAN RIGHT TO INTERPRET TREATIES: The Congress should by law provide for a new system of federal court jurisdiction and procedure, when Indian treaty or governmental rights are at issue, and when there are non-Indian parties involved in the controversy, whereby an Indian Tribe or Indian party may by motion advance the case from a federal District Court for hearing, and decision by the related U.S. Circuit Court of Appeals. . . .

CREATION OF CONGRESSIONAL JOINT COMMITTEE ON RECONSTRUCTION OF INDIAN RELATIONS: The next Congress of the United States, and its respective houses, should agree at its outset and in its organization to withdraw jurisdiction over Indian Affairs and Indian-related program authorizations from all existing Committees except Appropriations of the House and Senate, and create a Joint House-Senate "Committee on Reconstruction of Indian Relations and Programs" to assume such jurisdiction and responsibilities for recommending new legislation and program authorizations to both houses of Congress—including consideration and action upon all proposals presented herewith by the "Trail of Broken Treaties Caravan," as well as matters from other sources. The Joint Committee membership should consist of Senators and Representatives who would be willing to commit considerable amounts of time and labors and conscientious thought to an exhaustive review and examining evaluation of past and present policies, program and practices of the Federal Government relating to Indian people, to the development of a comprehensive broadly-inclusive "American Indian Community Reconstruction Act," which shall provide for certain of the measures herein proposed, repeal numerous laws which have oppressively disallowed the existence of a viable "Indian Life" in this country, and affect the purposes while constructing the provisions which shall allow and ensure a secure Indian future in America.

LAND REFORM AND RESTORATION OF A 110-MILLION ACRE NATIVE LAND BASE: The next Congress and Administration should commit themselves and effect a national commitment implemented by statutes or executive and administrative actions, to restore a permanent non-diminishing Native American land base of not less than 110-million acres by July 4, 1976. . . .

REVISION OF 25 U.S.C. 163; RESTORATION OF RIGHTS TO INDIANS TERMINATED BY ENROLLMENT AND REVOCATION OF PROHIBITIONS AGAINST "DUAL BENEFITS": The Congress should enact measures fully in support of the doctrine that an Indian Nation has complete power to govern and control its own membership—but eradicating the extortive and coercive devices in federal policy and programming which have subverted and denied the natural human relationships and natural development of Indian communities, and committed countless injuries upon Indian families and individuals. . . .

REPEAL OF STATE LAWS ENACTED UNDER PUBLIC LAW 280 (1953): State enactment's under the authority conferred by the Congress in Public Law 280 has posed the most serious threat to Indian sovereignty and local self-government of any measure in recent decades. Congress must now nullify those State statutes. . . .

RESUME FEDERAL PROTECTIVE JURISDICTION FOR OFFENSES AGAINST INDIANS: The Congress should enact, the Administration support and seek passage of, new provisions under Titles 18 and 25 of the U.S. Code, which shall extend the protective jurisdiction of the United States over Indian persons wherever situated in its territory and the territory of the several States, outside of Indian Reservations or Country, and provide the prescribed offenses of violence against Indian persons shall be federal crimes, punishable by prescribed penalties through prosecutions in the federal judiciary, and enforced in arrest actions by the Federal Bureau of Investigation. . . .

ABOLITION OF THE BUREAU OF INDIAN AFFAIRS BY 1976: A New Structure: The Congress working through the proposed Senate-House "Joint Committee on Reconstruction of Indian Relations and Programs," in formulation of an Indian Community Reconstruction Act should direct that the Bureau of Indian Affairs shall be abolished as an agency on or before July 4, 1976. . . .

CREATION OF AN "OFFICE OF FEDERAL INDIAN RELATIONS AND COMMUNITY RECONSTRUCTION": The Bureau of Indian Affairs should be replaced by a new unit in the federal government which represents an equality of responsibility among and between the President, the Congress, and the Governments of the separate Indian Nations (or their respective people collectively), and equal standing in the control of relations between the Federal Government and the Indian Nations. . . .

PRIORITIES AND PURPOSE OF THE PROPOSED NEW OFFICE: The central purpose of the proposed "Office of Federal Indian Relations and Community Reconstruction" is to remedy the break-down in constitutionally-prescribed relationships between the United States and Indian Nations and people and to alleviate the destructive impact that distortion in those relationships has rendered upon the lives of Indian people. . . .

INDIAN COMMERCE AND TAX IMMUNITIES: The Congress should enact a statute or Joint Resolution certifying that trade, commerce, and transportation of Indians remain wholly outside the authority, control, and regulation of the several States. Congressional acts should provide that complete taxing authority upon properties, use of properties and incomes derived therefrom, and business activities within the exterior boundaries of Indian reservations, as well as commerce between reservations and Indian Nations, shall be vested with the respective or related tribal governments, or their appropriate to subdivisions—or certify that consistent with the Fourteenth Amendment, Section 2 statehood enabling acts, prevailing treaty commitments, and the general policy of the United States, that total Indian immunity to taxing authority of states is reaffirmed and extended with uniformity to all Indian Nations as a matter of established or vested right. . . .

PROTECTION OF INDIANS' RELIGIOUS FREEDOM AND CULTURAL INTEGRITY: The Congress shall proclaim its insistence that the religious freedom and cultural integrity of Indian people shall be respected and protected throughout the United States, and provide that Indian religion and culture, even in regenerating or renaissance or developing stages, or when manifested in the personal character and treatment of one's own body, shall not be interfered with, disrespected, or denied. (No Indian shall be forced to cut their hair by any institution or public agency or official, including military authorities or prison regulation, for example.). . .

NATIONAL REFERENDUMS, LOCAL OPTIONS, AND FORMS OF INDIAN ORGANIZATION: The Indian population is small enough to be amenable to voting and elective processes of national referendums, local option referendums, and other elections for rendering decisions, approvals, or disapproval on many issues and matters. The steady proliferation of Indian and Indian-interest organizations and Indian advisory boards and the like, the multiplication of Indian officials and the emergence of countless Indian "leaders," represent a less preferable form for decision-making a state of disorganization, and a clear reflection of deterioration in the relations between the United States and Indian people as contracting sovereigns holding a high standard of accountability and responsibility. Some Indians seem to stand by to ratify any viewpoints relating to any or all Indians; others conditioned to accept any viewpoint or proposal from official sources. Whereas Indian people were to be secure from political manipulation and the general political system in the service of Indian needs, political favor, and cutthroat competition for funds with grants made among limited alliances of agency-Indian friends have become the rule—while responsibilities and accountability to Indian people and Indian communities have been forgotten. While the treaty relationship allows that we should not be deprived by power what we are possessed of by right—little personal power and political games are being played by a few Indians while we are being deprived our rights. This dissipation of strength, energies, and commitment should end. We should consolidate our resources and purpose to restore relations born of sovereignty and to resume command of our communities, our rights, our resources, and our destiny. (The National Council on Indian Opportunity Association on American Indian Affairs, and the National Tribal Chairman's Association are examples of government, non-Indian directed, and Indian organizations which are among many which could and should be eliminated). (At least none should be funded from federal sources.)

HEALTH, HOUSING, EMPLOYMENT, ECONOMIC DEVELOPMENT, AND EDUCATION: The Congress and Administration and proposed Indian Community Reconstruction Office must allow for the most creative, if demanding and disciplined forms of community development and purposeful initiatives. . . . Death remains a standard cure for environmentally induced diseases afflicting many Indian children without adequate housing facilities, heating systems, and pure water sources. Their delicate bodies provide their only defense and protection—and too often their own body processes become allies to the quickening of their deaths as with numerous cases of dysentery and diarrhea. Still, more has been spent on hotel bills for Indian-related problem-solving meetings, conferences, and conventions, than has been spent on needed housing in recent years. More is being spent from federal and tribal fund sources on such decision-making activities that is being committed to assist but two-thirds of Indian college students having desperate financial need. Rather, few decisions are made, and less problems solved, because there has developed an insensitivity to conscience which has eliminated basic standards of accountability. Indian communities have been fragmented in governmental, social, and constitutional functions as they have become restructured or de-structured to accommodate the fragmentation in governmental programming and contradictions in federal policies. There is a need to reintegrate these functions into the life and fabric of the communities. Of treaty provisions standard to most treaties, none has been breached more viciously and often as those dealing with education—first by withdrawing education processes from jurisdiction and responsibility of Indian communities, and from the power of Indian self-government—and failing yet to restore authority to our people, except through increased funding of old advisory and contract-delegation laws, or through control to conduct school in the conditioned forms and systems devised by non-Indians, or otherwise commended by current popularity. At minimum, Indian Nations have to reclaim community education authority to allow creative education processes in forms of their free choice, in a system of federally-sanctioned units or consolidated Indian districts, supported by a mandatory recognition of accreditation in all other systems in this land.

WEB RESOURCES FOR PART FIVE

SITES FEATURING A NUMBER OF THE DISSENTERS IN PART FIVE:

Berkeley Free Speech Movement
http://bancroft.berkeley.edu/FSM/
www.fsm-a.org/

Mario Savio
www.fsm-a.org/#Mario

Carl Oglesby
http://riseup.net/sds/index.htm

The Weather Underground
http://foia.fbi.gov/weather.htm
www.upstatefilms.org/weather/main.html

Vietnam Vets Against the War
www.vvaw.org/
www.pbs.org/greatspeeches/timeline/j_kerry_s.html

Abbie Hoffman
http://theaction.com/Abbie/
http://users.lmi.net/bblackie/ahb/

Timothy Leary
www.deoxy.org/leary.htm
www.leary.com/

Ram Dass
www.ramdasstapes.org/index.htm
www.ramdass.org/

Herbert Marcuse
www.marcuse.org/herbert/
www.marxists.org/reference/archive/marcuse/

Modern Women's Liberation Movement
http://scriptorium.lib.duke.edu/wlm/

National Organization for Women
www.now.org/

Gloria Steinem
www.nwhp.org/tlp/biographies/steinem/steinem_bio.html

www.msmagazine.com/index.asp

Redstockings
www.afn.org/~redstock/

Valerie Solanas
www.geocities.com/WestHollywood/Village/6982/solanas.html

Stonewall and the Gay Liberation Front
www.columbia.edu/cu/lweb/eresources/exhibitions/sw25/case1.html

Cesar Chavez
www.sfsu.edu/%7Ececipp/cesar_chavez/chavezhome.htm

American Indian Movement
www.aimovement.org/

OTHER DISSENTING VOICES OF THE TIME:

Amira Baraka
For African American writer Amira Baraka, see:

www.english.uiuc.edu/maps/poets/a_f/baraka/baraka.htm

Richard Fariña
Although he died at the age of 29, writer-folksinger Richard Fariña had an important impact on 1960s counterculture.

www.richardandmimi.com/

David Dellinger
Peace activist David Dellinger was one of the Chicago 7. See this site for Information.

www.law.umkc.edu/faculty/projects/ftrials/Chicago7/DellingerD.html

Ron Kovic
Anti-Vietnam War veteran Ron Kovic is still active in antiwar protest.

http://myhero.com/hero.asp?hero=Kovic

Ken Kesey
To learn more about Ken Kesey and the "Merry Pranksters," see:

www.key-z.com/
www.lib.virginia.edu/speccol/exhibits/sixties/kesey.html

Hunter S. Thompson
See this link for information about "gonzo" journalist Hunter S. Thompson.

www.geocities.com/SoHo/Lofts/5752/

Mary King and Casey Hayden
One of the first documents of the modern radical feminist movement was written by SNCC and SDS organizers Mary King and Casey Hayden.

www.cwluherstory.com/CWLUArchive/memo.html
http://t3.preservice.org/T0301022/hayden.html

Kate Millett

For a chapter of Kate Millett's Sexual Politics, *see:*

www.marxists.org/reference/subject/philosophy/works/us/millett.htm

Shulamith Firestone

See this link for the writings of radical feminist Shulamith Firestone:

www.marxists.org/reference/subject/philosophy/works/us/fireston.htm

Robin Morgan

For an interview with feminist Robin Morgan, see:

http://womensissues.about.com/cs/feminism/a/aarobinmorgan.htm

Jo Freeman

See these sites for writings on and information about feminist Jo Freeman:

http://flag.blackened.net/revolt/hist_texts/structurelessness.html
www.jofreeman.com/

Angela Davis

For information about this radical Marxist activist, see:

www.spartacus.schoolnet.co.uk/USAdavisAN.htm

Alice Walker

See this link for material about literary figure Alice Walker:

www.library.csi.cuny.edu/dept/history/lavender/walker.html

Arlo Guthrie

Woody Guthrie's son, Arlo, also had an influence on 1960s protest music, especially with his celebrated antidraft song, "Alice's Restaurant."

www.arlo.net/
www.pbs.org/americanrootsmusic/pbs_arm_oralh_arloguthrie.html
www.fortunecity.com/tinpan/parton/2/alice.html

The Berrigan Brothers

See these sites dedicated to radical Catholic priests and peace activists Daniel and Philip Berrigan.

http://rmc.library.cornell.edu/EAD/htmldocs/RMM04602.html
www.cmi.k12.il.us/~capiech/thoreau/dpb.htm

Peter Matthiessen

For information about writer, environmentalist, and spiritual seeker Peter Matthiessen, see:

www.albany.edu/writers-inst/matsnsa.html
www.tibet.org/Tibet100/voices/matthiessen.html

Barry Commoner

For information about environmentalist Barry Commoner see:

www.geocities.com/combusem/COMMONER.HTM
www.findarticles.com/cf_0/PI/search.jhtml?key=%22Barry%20Commoner%22

N. Scott Momaday

For information about Native American writer and cultural critic N. Scott Momaday, see:

www.coh.arizona.edu/inst/eng102-lolita/momaday/momaday.htm
www.english.uiuc.edu/maps/poets/m_r/momaday/momaday.htm

Maggie Kuhn

Maggie Kuhn was the founder of the Gray Panthers, an organization devoted to securing the rights of senior citizens.

http://mtmt.essortment.com/maggiekuhn_rfxw.htm

PART SIX

Contemporary Dissent, 1975–Present

To protest the Pacific Lumber Company's plan to cut down a 1000-year-old giant redwood in a forest in Humboldt County, California, Julia Butterfly Hill lived in the tree for two years. Hill passionately believes that environmental issues are deeply entwined with social justice issues. "The destroyer and the hero lies within the hearts of each and every one of us," she said, "Who are you going to choose to be?"

Introduction: Crossing the Threshold into the New Millennium—Globalization vs. Jihad

Throughout the nation's history, there was always the assumption that politicians were corruptible, but generally speaking people tended to have faith in the president and in his pronouncements. When FDR, Ike, or JFK spoke to the public, people believed them. The Johnson administration's deceptions, however, revealed by the publication of the Pentagon Papers in the *New York Times,* began to change that. When Richard Nixon was forced to resign over the Watergate scandal, what remaining faith the majority had in the integrity of Washington evaporated. Ford and Carter were honest men and did help to restore some confidence in the political process, but ever since the 1970s, the American people are far more cynical about government.

After the excitement of the 1960s and Watergate, many people simply wanted to have a breather and return to some sense of business as usual. Dissent and protest did continue, but with the big issues apparently solved, activists concentrated on specific local concerns. Ecology, of course, is a global issue, but environmentalists generally acted locally by demonstrating against industrial polluters, such as General Electric in New York, in an effort to get laws passed that would restrict the amount of toxic waste companies were allowed to dump in rivers and streams or release into the atmosphere. Pete Seeger, whose activism spans several decades and multiple causes, organized the Clearwater Hudson River Revival, an annual folk festival dedicated to putting pressure on the industries that were polluting the Hudson River. The success of this local movement was quite apparent by the 1980s, when sturgeon appeared again in the cleaner waters of the Hudson after an absence of a century. Greenpeace, founded in the early 1970s, concentrated its activities on specific incidents perpetrated by companies and countries that were damaging the environment. Environmentalists also were opposed to the proliferation of nuclear power plants, and many thousands of people participated in anti-nuke demonstrations, especially after the near meltdown at Three Mile Island in 1979.

Later, in the 1990s, environmentalist Julia Butterfly Hill performed an unusual act of civil disobedience in order to save a thousand-year-old giant redwood tree from the Pacific Lumber Company—she climbed 180 feet up into the tree and proceeded to live in its branches for the next 738 days until the lumber company finally agreed not to cut it down. "I gave my word," she said, "to this tree, the forest, and all the people, that my feet would not touch the ground until I had done everything in my power to make the world aware of this problem and to stop the destruction." Unlike the Earth Liberation Front, which does not shrink from using violence to preserve the environment, "tree hugger" Julia Butterfly Hill called on people to unite together in love for all living things.

When Reagan became president, there was hope that the economy, which had stagnated as a result of Vietnam and the OPEC oil embargoes of 1973 and 1978, would rebound. Tax cuts and the revenue poured into defense spending and the Strategic Defense Initiative, a program designed to create an antimissile defense system, did create more wealth for many industries, but the predicted "trickle down" effect, whereby prosperity would trickle down to the working class through more job opportunities, did not take place.

As far as foreign policy was concerned, Reagan was determined to fight communism around the globe. The United States must stand firm against the Soviet Union, which he referred to as the "evil empire." This strategy in effect reversed the détente process that Nixon had begun to relieve tensions between the United States and the Soviet Union and the People's Republic of China. After the Soviet Union invaded Afghanistan, President Jimmy Carter and National Security Advisor Zbigniew Brzezinski began to provide assistance to the mujahedin. As the Soviets became more embroiled in the war, it became Reagan's policy to do everything possible to thwart and frustrate them and to make Afghanistan into the Soviet Union's Vietnam. With congressional approval, Reagan expanded this effort by authorizing the CIA to aid, equip, and train Muslim fundamentalists in their fight against the Soviets. The training, the supplies, the money, and the Stinger missiles were highly effective in frustrating the Soviet attempt to subdue Afghanistan, prolonged the war until 1989, and eventually led to the Soviet withdrawal. The U.S. involvement also gave rise to the Taliban and the career of Osama bin Laden. Later the CIA would refer to bin Laden's subsequent terrorist campaign against the U.S. as "blowback," a term signifying unexpected consequences of CIA operations. Reagan was also concerned about communist inroads in Central America, especially in Nicaragua and El Salvador. American efforts to undermine the left-wing Sandinista regime in Nicaragua, primarily by training counterrevolutionaries to overthrow the Sandinistas, raised concerns that the United States might get entangled in another Vietnam. There were some scattered protests, but they did not become widespread because Congress passed legislation forbidding the CIA to train the "Contras."

In 1988, the last full year of his term, Reagan began to moderate his anticommunist rhetoric, mostly because of the influence of Mikhail Gorbachev. Gorbachev had come to power in the Soviet Union in 1985, and his policies of *glasnost* and *perestroika* began opening up Soviet society and paving the way for the end of the cold war. In one of the ironies of history, the Soviet Union's anti-American propaganda efforts in the 1960s helped bring this about. During the 1960s, the Soviet press had a field day with the antiwar and civil rights protests in America, which were depicted as proof of the "anti-imperialist struggle under capitalism." According to cold war scholar Vladislav Zubok, this was a serious miscalculation on the part of the Soviet propaganda machine. One of the reasons communism failed in the Soviet Union and Eastern Europe is that people living under communism became painfully aware that the American people could at least march, protest, and dissent. This proved that the United States was indeed a freer society than the Soviet Union. As a result, many Soviet citizens began to overcome their distrust of the United States. When they saw protestors and demonstrators in the streets, they saw democracy at work and therefore realized that the United States, despite its faults, was a democratic society. In this way the United States as early as the 1960s unwittingly motivated a minority of dissidents and educated youth in the eastern bloc countries to strive for democracy. "We knew," a Soviet citizen once told Zubok, "*we* had to create democracy when we saw American protestors take to the streets."

In November 1989, one of the most memorable events of the twentieth century took place. The East German government, after months of unrest and economic crisis, opened the Berlin Wall. It was the moment the cold war disintegrated. Thousands of Germans flocked to Berlin. From east and west, they came, and they brought their sledgehammers and chisels, and the wall came down. Within months, each of the Soviet satellite nations abandoned communism and voted in new democratic regimes. The Soviet Union itself, in December 1991, was dissolved. Mikhail Gorbachev, who had intended to allow dissent and discussion to build "socialism with a human face" along the model of the Prague Spring of 1968, had instead opened a Pandora's box that wound up being far more momentous than anyone could have imagined, and by doing away with the Soviet Union, Gorbachev no longer had a job.

At first Americans were jubilant, believing, as many did, that "we won the cold war," and that now the terrible threat of a nuclear confrontation that could potentially destroy civilization was gone. The world, it was assumed, was a safer place. Indeed, when Saddam Hussein invaded neighboring Kuwait, the unity of the coalition that fought the Persian Gulf War to remove the Iraqis from Kuwait boosted this optimistic view. But within a few years a new reality emerged, and grave doubts began to creep in.

The Clinton administration concentrated on the economy, which did indeed rebound during his two terms in office. In fact, the economy soared so high that most Americans considered that Clinton was doing such an excellent job of running the country that they were able to overlook the Monica Lewinsky scandal that swamped his administration. The domestic issue that proved controversial enough to arouse dissenters was globalization. Clinton had backed the North American Free Trade Agreement and the General Agreement on Tariffs and Trade. Antiglobalists were vehemently opposed to this spreading of free enterprise, claiming that it was merely an updated version of capitalist imperialism. A wide variety of diverse groups came together to oppose the World Trade Organization: Labor unions were concerned that more American jobs would disappear; environmentalists were alarmed that moving industrial plants and factories to third world nations, where environmental standards were laxer than they were in the United States, would exacerbate the problems of global warming and the destruction of the environment; human rights activists were troubled about the exploitation of children and poor people in third world sweatshops. Criticizing the pro-business collaboration of both Republicans and Democrats, Ralph Nader ran for president in 1996 and in 2000 as the standard-bearer of the Green Party.

Other dissenters made their voices heard in the 1990s. Along with the continuation of pro-life activists picketing abortion clinics and pro-choice advocates demanding the safeguarding of a woman's right to choose, various right-wing groups protested what they viewed as too much government intrusion into their lives. The Michigan Militia, the Freemen in Montana, and other groups called for individuals to arm themselves and be ready to resist any attempt by the government in Washington to undermine the Bill of Rights. Timothy McVeigh was responsible for the single most devastating act of domestic terrorism in American history when he detonated a bomb at the Alfred P. Murrah Federal Building in Oklahoma City that killed 168 people. Theodore Kaczynski, the Unabomber, killed people with letter bombs because he believed technology, and those promoting it, was a disaster for the human race. There was also a proliferation of right-wing talk-show hosts like Rush Limbaugh, who protested zealously and effectively against the Clinton administration. Such critics, although they might appear on the surface to be part of the dissenting tradition, are not actually genuine protestors advocating social change but instead the cutting edge of a well-organized, well-funded, and ultimately successful Republican offensive to regain power.

In the post–cold war world, Clinton's foreign policy had to feel its way along as diplomats were forced to learn the new rules of engagement. Confrontation between two superpowers was a thing of the past, but new, more complex realities surfaced. The United States continued to maintain a military presence in Saudi Arabia after the Persian Gulf War had come to an end. This fact, along with U.S. support of Israel, angered many Arabs. The inexorable spread of American mass culture and con- sumerist values around the world also created resistance from people who believed their own values and culture would be subverted and eventually destroyed. Political Scientist Benjamin R. Barber has called this confrontation between traditional soci- eties and American globalism "Jihad vs. McWorld."

Terrorism has been around for centuries, but in the 1970s and 1980s it began to be employed more frequently by disempowered groups who felt there was no other alternative for them to get their point across. Palestinians in particular, knowing the most powerful nation in the world supported Israel, felt helpless. Regularly, members of the Palestinian Liberation Organization (PLO) or the Popular Front for the Liberation of Palestine (PFLP) would hijack a commercial jet, make their demands (perhaps the release of other terrorists who were serving prison sentences), and, after the demands were met, escape. By the 1990s, however, terrorism had begun to have a new, more terrifying face. Increasingly, terrorists used suicide mis- sions. As early as 1983, suicide bombers struck in Lebanon, when a truck filled with explosives rammed into the U.S. Marine barracks in Beirut, killing 241 Marines. During Clinton's presidency, in 1996, suicide bombers struck at the American embassies in Tanzania and Kenya, killing 224 people. The terrorists behind this were not Palestinians but Saudis linked to Osama bin Laden's Al Qaeda network. Clinton's response was to order a missile attack on reputed Al Qaeda training camps in Afghanistan and a chemical plant in Somalia. Some observers believe this retribution only exacerbated the problem. Chalmers Johnson, for instance, in his book *Blowback,* published a year before September 11, suggests that the appropriate response would have been to remove American military personnel from Saudi Arabia. If bin Laden was behind the embassy bombings, Johnson wrote, then we still do not know what the blowback will be from Clinton's missile attack in Afghanistan. Perhaps the response occurred in 2000, when Al Qaeda suicide bombers blew a hole in the side of the U.S. destroyer *Cole* in Yemen, killing 17 sailors.

At first, after George W. Bush was declared the winner of the contested 2000 elec- tion, the new president concentrated on resurrecting the defense projects of the Reagan administration, specifically the missile defense shield. But on September 11, 2001, it became devastatingly apparent that such highly sophisticated methods of national security were helpless in the face of a relatively low-tech type of attack. The terrorists who hijacked four jetliners—turning them into highly explosive missiles that brought down the twin towers of the World Trade Center, ripped open the

Pentagon, and killed more than 3000 innocent people—were able to accomplish their feat using box cutters.

In the aftermath of the attacks, the United States has been forced to face a different truth. It is not simply that the "world changed" on September 11. The world was pretty much the same on the twelfth as it was on the tenth. What had changed is that Americans had lost their innocence (or perhaps we should say naiveté). They awoke to the fact that the perception many others around the world, including our allies, have about America does not match the way we see ourselves. The aftermath of September 11 saw the advent of the war on terrorism. For many people, this has meant fighting back and making our nation more secure against such threats. For some people, it has also meant a time of self-reflection and reevaluation of America's priorities. Dissent, which had seemed subdued in the 1990s with the exception of the World Trade Organization demonstrations, once again reared its head. As the United States bombed Afghanistan, thousands of protestors took to the streets. When the PATRIOT Act was passed, many more feared that in our quest for security we were eroding the basic constitutional principles that has made this country great. Even before the United States invaded Iraq in 2003, millions of people took to the streets to demonstrate against such a war.

We cannot know what lies in store. We *do* know that as long as the United States is the United States, there will always be differences of opinion on social, political, diplomatic, and military issues and that people from all walks of life, from all political persuasions, Republicans, Democrats, Socialists, Libertarians, will speak their minds. In a time of war, however, when national security itself is threatened, is it unpatriotic to dissent? Have those who protest given up on the American dream? Are dissenters undermining the very society that guarantees the right to dissent? What takes precedence, national security or civil liberties? Or is dissent itself an expression of patriotism?

Edward Abbey (1927–1989)

In 1948 Edward Abbey hitchhiked through the American West. He felt himself irresistibly attracted to the desert and finally settled in Arizona. He wrote several novels about loners and would-be anarchists, as well as nonfiction works that have since become classics of the environmental movement. For a time he worked as a park ranger in Utah at Arches National Monument. His journal of his two years of solitude in the wilderness (*Desert Solitaire*) was published in 1968 and is considered by many a twentieth-century *Walden*. His most celebrated book is *The Monkey Wrench Gang*, a tongue-in-cheek, wildly funny novel about a gang of misfit environmental terrorists who travel about the American Southwest blowing up dams and bridges, sabotaging road construction sites, and otherwise wreaking havoc in an attempt to save the wilderness from the developers. Writer Larry McMurtry called Abbey the "Thoreau of the West," a title that Abbey himself belittled. However, like Thoreau, Abbey was a champion of nonconformity and a sworn enemy of hypocrisy, sanctimoniousness, and smug intellectualism. "I hate intellectual discussion," he once said. "When I hear the words 'phenomenology' or 'structuralism,' I reach for my buck knife."

Along with the mobilization of minority groups, environmentalism was another outgrowth of the 1960s. Greenpeace, one of the most effective and visible organizations, was founded in 1971 and dedicated to save the forests, protect the oceans, stop global warming, and oppose nuclear power. During the Reagan years, when Secretary of the Interior James Watt opened up millions of acres of public land for development, the environmental movement and such organizations as Greenpeace expanded and strengthened. Realizing that the future of humanity was dependent on a sane ecological policy millions of Americans, regardless of political affiliation, vowed to "save the planet."

Though Abbey is known as one of the heroes of the environmental movement, ranking alongside John Muir, John Burroughs, and Rachel Carson, it would not be accurate to look at a man so irreverently original and anarchistic as Abbey as a product of the activism that emerged from the 1960s. He had no tolerance for anyone who belonged to any movement. Nothing escaped his withering sarcasm regardless of political orientation. Reaganites, feminists, television evangelists, hippies, corporate executives, Indians, lumberjacks, tree-huggers, tourists, and Sierra Clubbers all were targets of his scorn. He hated seeing the wilderness being developed, but part of his reasoning had nothing to do with environmentalism; it was because he still believed in the frontier myth that open spaces had created the American character and American democracy—a myth that has largely been discredited by historians. The settlement of the American West depended on federal grants and subsidies for railroads in the nineteenth century and irrigation projects in the twentieth, as well as federal land grants to homesteaders and stationing the U.S. army to protect settlers from the Indians. Abbey also hated the fact that national parks enticed so many tourists to drive through them in their campers and Winnebagos. In *Desert Solitaire* he demanded that cars be prohibited from national parks.

> Let the people walk. Or ride horses, bicycles, mules, wild pigs—anything— but keep the automobiles and the motorcycles and all their motorized relatives out. We have agreed not to drive our automobiles into cathedrals, concert halls, art museums, legislative assemblies, private bedrooms and the other sanctums of our culture; we should treat our national parks with the same deference, for they, too, are holy places.... [T]he forests and mountains and desert canyons are holier than our churches. Let us behave accordingly.

The fictional ecoterrorists in *The Monkey Wrench Gang* subsequently inspired acts of sabotage and vandalism against ski lodges, tourist enclaves, lumber companies, and power companies by a group calling themselves Earth First! Abbey, while not actually endorsing such actions, had proclaimed that ecoterrorism was "illegal but ethically imperative."

In this excerpt from *Desert Solitaire*, Abbey extols the virtues of the wilderness. What does this passage reveal about the state of the environment? Abbey always insisted that development for the benefit of the growing urban centers of the West was detrimental to human freedom. In fact, in his view, it was the government's method of maintaining control and keeping Americans subjugated. Is this true, or does development, as many politicians and developers insist, actually enhance individual opportunity and freedom?

From *Desert Solitaire*, 1968

Once upon a time there was a continent covered with beautiful pristine wilderness, where giant trees towered over lush mountainsides and rivers ran wild and free through deserts, where raptors soared and beavers labored at their pursuits and people lived in harmony with wild nature, accomplishing every task they needed to accomplish on a daily basis using only stones, bones and wood, walking gently on the Earth. Then came the explorers, conquerors, missionaries, soldiers, merchants and immigrants with their advanced technology, guns, and government. The wild life that had existed for millennia started dying, killed by a disease brought by alien versions of progress, arrogant visions of manifest destiny and a runaway utilitarian science.

In just 500 years, almost all the giant trees have been clear-cut and chemicals now poison the rivers; the eagle has faced extinction and the beaver's work has been

Source: Edward Abbey, *Desert Solitaire* (New York: Simon & Schuster, 1968), 155–156.

supplanted by the Army Corps of Engineers. And how have the people fared? What one concludes is most likely dependent on how well one is faring economically, emotionally and physically in this competitive technological world and the level of privilege one is afforded by the system. But for those who feel a deep connection to, a love and longing for, the wilderness and the wildness that once was, for the millions now crowded in cities, poor and oppressed, unable to find a clear target for their rage because the system is virtually omnipotent, these people are not faring well. All around us, as a result of human greed and a lack of respect for all life, wild nature and Mother Earth's creatures are suffering. These beings are the victims of industrial society. . . .

Cutting the bloody cord, that's what we feel, the delirious exhilaration of independence, a rebirth backward in time and into primeval liberty, into freedom in the most simple, literal, primitive meaning of the word, the only meaning that really counts. The freedom, for example, to commit murder and get away with it scot-free, with no other burden than the jaunty halo of conscience.

(My God! I'm thinking, what incredible shit we put up with most of our lives— the *domestic* routine, (same old wife *every* night), the stupid and useless and degrading *jobs,* the *insufferable* arrogance of elected officials, the crafty *cheating* and the *slimy* advertising of the businessmen, the tedious wars in which we kill our buddies instead of our *real* enemies back home in the capital, the foul, diseased and *hideous* cities and towns we live in, the constant *petty* tyranny of the automatic washers, the automobiles and TV machines and telephones! ah *Christ*! . . . what *intolerable* garbage and what utterly *useless crap* we bury ourselves in day by day, while patiently enduring at the same time the creeping strangulation of the clean white *collar* and the rich but *modest* four-in-hand garrote!)

Such are my thoughts—you wouldn't call them thoughts would you?—such are my feelings, a mixture of revulsion and delight, as we float away on the river, leaving behind for a while all that we most heartily and joyfully detest. That's what the first taste of the wild does to a man, after having been penned up for too long in the city. No wonder the Authorities are so anxious to smother the wilderness under asphalt and reservoirs. They know what they are doing. Play safe. Ski only in a clockwise direction. Let's all have fun together.

Paul Weyrich (1941–)

Paul Weyrich, founder of the American Legislative Exchange Council, chairman and CEO of the Free Congress Foundation, and founder (with Joseph Coors) of the Heritage Foundation, is a persuasive, passionate conservative. An advocate of free trade and family values and the coiner of the term "moral majority," he has been called "one of the conservative movement's more vigorous thinkers." He has written perceptive policy reports and numerous articles, all espousing a conservative, religious viewpoint. In 1987, in response to the Iran-Contra affair, he wrote "A Conservative's Lament," condemning the manner in which the Reagan administration was contravening the Constitution in the way it was conducting its covert foreign policy. Weyrich believes that the United States must live up to its ideals of preserving freedom.

According to this article, why is our national strategy outdated, and what must be done? What is wrong with the process of choosing our leaders? Have conservatives heeded Weyrich's advice?

"A Conservative's Lament: After Iran, We Need to Change Our System and Grand Strategy," 1987

As proponents of a strong foreign policy and defense, conservatives have a special responsibility. Our advocacy brings with it the burden of doing the job competently. We must be leaders in thinking deeply and carefully about America's role in the world, about relating goals to means and about our national strengths and weaknesses and the opportunities and constraints they impose. If we fail to do this, we lose our legitimacy as advocates.

In the Iran-contra mess, conservatives have failed. Obviously, they failed in the way the matter was handled. But the failure is really much more profound than that. The scandal is not a disease, but a symptom. It is a symptom of some underlying contradictions in our national strategy and national institutions.

Conservatives should have identified and addressed these long ago, but we did not. Now, conservative leaders seem to be looking little if at all beyond the details of the scandal—and how to distance themselves from it. That merely compounds the failure.

Instead, as conservatives, we should be taking the lead in looking for the roots of the crisis. There are three.

First, our national strategy is outdated, dysfunctional and insupportable. Essentially it is still containment, a strategy developed in the late 1940s. It was an arguable strategy even then. But at least we had the power to carry it out. We had only one rival: the Soviet Union. Europe and Asia were both power vacuums. We moved to fill those vacuums, lest the Soviets do so.

Today, the situation is vastly different. Europe, Asia and the Middle East are power centers, not vacuums. The concept of a superpower is waning rapidly. The world includes many other forces—China, Islamic nationalism, Polish Catholicism—which are more powerful locally than either the United States or the Soviet Union.

In pursuit of containment, we still thrust ourself into everything that happens around the world. But what we put forward, increasingly, is weakness, not strength.

Source: Paul M. Weyrich, "A Conservative's Lament: After Iran, we Need to Change Our System and Grand Strategy," in the *Washington Post*, March 8, 1987, B-5.

In a world where we control far less of the total sum of power than we did forty years ago, we cannot do otherwise. The real strength is no longer there. We are propping up a hollow facade, vast commitments unsupported by either capabilities or popular will. So we stumble from failure to failure; in Southeast Asia, in Iran, in Lebanon and now in the Iran-contra mess.

It is time for a new national grand strategy. Nothing less will address the real problem. Conservatives have a responsibility to take the lead in developing one.

Second, there is a basic contradiction between the structure of our government and our role as a great power. Our government was designed not to play great-power politics but to preserve domestic liberty. To that end—at which it has been remarkably successful—it was structured so as to make decisions difficult. Separation of powers, congressional checks on executive authority, the primacy of law over *raison d'tat*—all of these were intentionally built into our system. The Founding Fathers knew a nation, with such a government could not play the role of great power. They had no such ambition for us—quite the contrary.

For about 20 years after World War II, we were able to act as a great power without running into this contradiction. We could do so because we had only one serious rival, and even over that rival, our superiority was immense. Now, we have to play on a much more crowded and competitive field. Our institutions are not adequate to the game. If the executive does what it must in the international arena, it violates the domestic rules. If the Congress enforces those rules, as it is supposed to do, it cripples us internationally.

Since Watergate, some 140 measures have been passed by Congress to restrict the president's power to conduct foreign policy.

Third, our current system institutionalizes amateurism. Unlike European parliamentary democracies, we have no "shadow cabinet," no group of experts who are groomed by their party for decades before they take high office. Our presidents can be peanut farmers or Hollywood actors. They can choose their top advisors either from among "professionals" who may not share their goals or supporters who often have no background or expertise in policy. Either way, they lose, and so does the country.

The current crisis could not make the point better; our foreign policy was set by an admiral and a Marine lieutenant colonel, neither of whom had any background in the field. The resulting failure is not their fault. The system by which they were chosen is defective.

If we are going to be a serious nation, we need a serious system for selecting our leaders and advisors. We need some type of shadow government, in which leaders and top advisors can be identified and developed, and through which our politics can be better focused on policy choices. The world is a professional league, and we cannot win fielding amateur teams.

If the crisis leads us to get at the systemic problems it manifests, it will, on the whole, have been a good thing. But that is not what we are doing. We are letting ourselves be captured by the symptoms and ignoring the disease.

We—especially conservatives—owe the country something better. On foreign policy and the institutions that make it, it is a time for us to show some leadership—or give it over to someone who can do a better job.

ACT UP

In 1987, when the AIDS crisis was exploding across the nation, many gays and lesbians were outraged that the Reagan administration was doing nothing to deal with the epidemic. AIDS was viewed by Washington as a problem that concerned only homosexuals and intravenous drug users and was of no concern to the white, middle-class, heterosexual majority. Politicians often conveyed an attitude that such people simply deserved what they got. In response to this cavalier indifference, the AIDS Coalition to Unleash Power (ACT UP) was formed as an in-your-face, direct-action organization that would coordinate protests in an effort to force the do-nothing federal government to do something about the epidemic. Although ACT UP was formed by gay men, the organization, from the beginning, welcomed others who were affected by AIDS (e.g., drug users, hemophiliacs), as well as anyone else who felt that all people should be treated with fairness and respect. Adopting the tactics of the civil rights and antiwar movements, ACT UP held its first demonstration on March 24, 1987, on Wall Street, where they singled out the pharmaceutical companies that were withholding vital AIDS drugs in order to increase profits, as well as the homophobia that lay behind the government's unwillingness to act. Within a few months, ACT UP demonstrations were attracting hundreds and even thousands of participants, whose pressure eventually induced the Food and Drug Administration to grant approval for the release of the controversial AIDS drugs.

The documents included here are the flyer for the first demonstration, one demonstrator's reasoning for participating in a civil disobedience action, and a speech delivered by Vito Russo at a 1988 demonstration. According to ACT UP, what needs to be done? What is the reason for the Reagan administration's inaction?

_____

ACT UP Activist Aldyn Mckean Explains Civil Disobedience

I have an arrest record for civil disobedience that spans 23 years and covers seven states, the District of Columbia, and one foreign country. However, I never go to a demonstration to get arrested; I go to demonstrations to bring about change, and am willing to risk arrest to produce that desired change.

Any group that wishes to use civil disobedience or direct action to achieve change must:

1. make absolutely clear what change is desired, usually by listing specific demands;
2. target a group or individual with the power to bring about the desired change;
3. design actions so that the cost of resisting change is perceived by the person/group in power to be greater than the cost of giving in.

_____

SOURCE: Retrieved on 1/3/2004 from www.actupny.org/documents

NO MORE BUSINESS AS USUAL!

**Come to Wall Street in front of Trinity Church
at 7AM Tuesday March 24 for a**

MASSIVE AIDS DEMONSTRATION

To demand the following

1. Immediate release by the Federal Food & Drug Administration of drugs that might help save our lives.

   These drugs include: Ribavirin (ICN Pharmaceuticals); Ampligen (HMR Research Co.); Glucan (Tulane University School of Medicine); DTC (Merieux); DDC (Hoffman-LaRoche); AS 101 (National Patent Development Corp.); MTP-PE (Ciba-Geigy); AL 721 (Praxis Pharmaceuticals).

2. Immediate abolishment of cruel double-blind studies wherein some get the new drugs and some don't.
3. Immediate release of these drugs to everyone with AIDS or ARC.
4. Immediate availability of these drugs at affordable prices. Curb your greed!
5. Immediate massive public education to stop the spread of AIDS.
6. Immediate policy to prohibit discrimination in AIDS treatment, insurance, employment, housing.
7. Immediate establishment of a coordinated, comprehensive, and compassionate national policy on AIDS.

President Reagan, nobody is in charge!

AIDS IS THE BIGGEST KILLER IN NEW YORK CITY OF YOUNG MEN AND WOMEN.

**Tell your friends. Spread the
word. Come protest together.**

**7 AM . . . March 24 . . . You must be
on time!**

AIDS IS EVERYBODY'S BUSINESS NOW.

The AIDS Network is an ad hoc and broad-based community of AIDS-related organizations and individuals.

SOURCE: Retrieved on 1/3/2004 from www.actupny.org/documents/1stFlyer.html

The classic type of civil disobedience advocated by Gandhi and Martin Luther King Jr. is one in which an unjust law is deliberately and openly violated. Most of the demands of AIDS activists do not lend themselves to the classic Gandhi/King style of civil disobedience. Nevertheless, the same basic principles apply: Make it more costly for those in power to resist than to give in.

This is done in one of two ways:

1. create problems for those in power that will not go away until they give in (for example, occupy their offices or zap their phone lines), and/or

2. educate the public in ways that both cause embarrassment to those in power and cause them to be fearful that the popular movement for change may grow strong enough to threaten their power (for example, interrupt news broadcasts or hang banners).

We should be thinking and talking about what we do much more carefully. For example, when we sat down and blockaded the entrance to the New York State Senate last year in Albany, we were very clear about what we were doing. We did not say we were there to get arrested. We said we had a set of demands and that if Ralph Marino (the Senate Majority Leader) and Governor Cuomo would agree to our demands, we would go home because we were there to pursue a specific set of demands; those demands were picked up and publicized by the media covering the arrests. That helped to educate people, embarrassed Cuomo and Marino, and contributed to the building of our movement and the achievement of change. Other ACT UP members who were in Albany that same day apparently told a local newspaper reporter that they were "going to get arrested." That reporter then wrote a column that described people who were intent on getting arrested, as if getting arrested were an end in itself. There was no mention in this column of the specific issues that drove people to commit civil disobedience.

If these individuals had instead told the reporter that they were willing to risk arrest in order to bring about X, Y and Z, the action might have been more powerful. My point is simply this: When we engage in civil disobedience, we do so to achieve change, not to get arrested. Getting arrested is of little significance in and of itself. We're not out to accumulate arrests like merit badges. Arrests result from our commitment to achieve change; they are the means to an end, not the end in themselves.

Aldyn Mckean (d. 1994)

Vito Russo, "Why We Fight," 1988

A friend of mine in New York City has a half-fare transit card, which means that you get on buses and subways for half price. And the other day, when he showed his card

SOURCE: Video transcript of speech delivered at the ACT UP Demonstration, Albany, NY, May 9, 1988, and the ACT UP Demonstration at the Department of Health and Human Services, Washington, DC, October 10, 1988. Retrieved on 1/3/2004 from www.actupny.org/ documents/whfight.html to the token attendant, the attendant asked what his disability was and he said, I have AIDS. And the attendant said, no you don't, if you had AIDS, you'd be home dying. And so, I wanted to speak out today as a person with AIDS who is not dying.

You know, for the last three years, since I was diagnosed, my family thinks two things about my situation. One, they think I'm going to die, and two, they think that my government is doing absolutely everything in their power to stop that. And they're wrong, on both counts.

So, if I'm dying from anything, I'm dying from homophobia. If I'm dying from anything, I'm dying from racism. If I'm dying from anything, it's from indifference and red tape, because these are the things that are preventing an end to this crisis. If I'm dying from anything, I'm dying from Jesse Helms. If I'm dying from anything, I'm dying from the President of the United States. And, especially, if I'm dying from anything, I'm dying from the sensationalism of newspapers and magazines and television shows, which are interested in me, as a human interest story—only as long as I'm willing to be a helpless victim, but not if I'm fighting for my life.

If I'm dying from anything—I'm dying from the fact that not enough rich, white, heterosexual men have gotten AIDS for anybody to give a shit. You know, living with AIDS in this country is like living in the twilight zone. Living with AIDS is like living through a war which is happening only for those people who happen to be in the trenches. Every time a shell explodes, you look around and you discover that you've lost more of your friends, but nobody else notices. It isn't happening to them. They're walking the streets as though we weren't living through some sort of nightmare. And only you can hear the screams of the people who are dying and their cries for help. No one else seems to be noticing.

And it's worse than a war, because during a war people are united in a shared experience. This war has not united us, it's divided us. It's separated those of us with AIDS and those of us who fight for people with AIDS from the rest of the population.

Two and a half years ago, I picked up *Life* magazine, and I read an editorial which said, "it's time to pay attention, because this disease is now beginning to strike the rest of us." It was as if I wasn't the one holding the magazine in my hand. And since then, nothing has changed to alter the perception that AIDS is not happening to the real people in this country.

It's not happening to us in the United States, it's happening to them—to the disposable populations of fags and junkies who deserve what they get. The media tells them that they don't have to care, because the people who really matter are not in danger. Twice, three times, four times—*The New York Times* has published editorials saying, don't panic yet, over AIDS—it still hasn't entered the general population, and until it does, we don't have to give a shit.

And the days, and the months, and the years pass by, and they don't spend those days and nights and months and years trying to figure out how to get hold of the latest experimental drug, and which dose to take it at, and in what combination with other drugs, and from what source? And, how are you going to pay for it? And where are you going to get it? Because it isn't happening to them, so they don't give a shit.

And they don't sit in television studios, surrounded by technicians who are wearing rubber gloves, who won't put a microphone on you, because it isn't happening to them, so they don't give a shit.

And they don't have their houses burned down by bigots and morons. They watch it on the news and they have dinner and they go to bed, because it isn't happening to them, and they don't give a shit.

And they don't spend their waking hours going from hospital room to hospital room, and watching the people that they love die slowly—of neglect and bigotry, because it isn't happening to them and they don't have to give a shit. They haven't been to two funerals a week for the last three or four or five years—so they don't give a shit, because it's not happening to them.

And we read on the front page of *The New York Times* last Saturday that Anthony Fauci now says that all sorts of promising drugs for treatment haven't even been tested in the last two years because he can't afford to hire the people to test them. We're supposed to be grateful that this story has appeared in the newspaper after two years. Nobody wonders why some reporter didn't dig up that story and print it 18 months ago, before Fauci got dragged before a Congressional hearing.

How many people are dead in the last two years, who might be alive today, if those drugs had been tested more quickly? Reporters all over the country are busy printing government press releases.

They don't give a shit, it isn't happening to them—meaning that it isn't happening to people like them—the real people, the world-famous general public we all keep hearing about.

Legionnaire's Disease was happening to them because it hit people who looked like them, who sounded like them, who were the same color as them. And that fucking story about a couple of dozen people hit the front page of every newspaper and magazine in this country, and it stayed there until that mystery got solved.

All I read in the newspapers tells me that the mainstream, white heterosexual population is not at risk for this disease. All the newspapers I read tell me that IV drug users and homosexuals still account for the overwhelming majority of cases, and a majority of those people at risk.

And can somebody please tell me why every single penny allocated for education and prevention gets spent on ad campaigns that are directed almost exclusively to white, heterosexual teenagers—who they keep telling us are not at risk!

Can somebody tell me why the only television movie ever produced by a major network in this country, about the impact of this disease, is not about the impact of this disease on the man who has AIDS, but of the impact of AIDS on his white, straight, nuclear family? Why, for eight years, every newspaper and magazine in this country has done cover stories on AIDS only when the threat of heterosexual transmission is raised?

Why, for eight years, every single educational film designed for use in high schools has eliminated any gay positive material, before being approved by the Board of Education? Why, for eight years, every single public information pamphlet and videotape distributed by establishment sources has ignored specific homosexual content?

Why is every bus and subway ad I read and every advertisement and every billboard I see in this country specifically not directed at gay men? Don't believe the lie that the gay community has done its job and done it well and educated its people.

The gay community and IV drug users are not all politicized people living in New York and San Francisco. Members of minority populations, including so called sophisticated gay men are abysmally ignorant about AIDS.

If it is true that gay men and IV drug users are the populations at risk for this disease, then we have a right to demand that education and prevention be targeted specifically to these people. And it is not happening. We are being allowed to die, while low risk populations are being panicked—not educated, panicked—into believing that we deserve to die.

Why are we here together today? We're here because it is happening to us, and we do give a shit. And if there were more of us AIDS wouldn't be what it is at this moment in history. It's more than just a disease, which ignorant people have turned into an excuse to exercise the bigotry they have always felt.

It is more than a horror story, exploited by the tabloids. AIDS is really a test of us, as a people. When future generations ask what we did in this crisis, we're going to have to tell them that we were out here today. And we have to leave the legacy to those generations of people who will come after us.

Someday, the AIDS crisis will be over. Remember that. And when that day comes—when that day has come and gone, there'll be people alive on this earth—gay people and straight people, men and women, black and white, who will hear the story that once there was a terrible disease in this country and all over the world, and that a brave group of people stood up and fought and, in some cases, gave their lives, so that other people might live and be free.

So, I'm proud to be with my friends today and the people I love, because I think you're all heroes, and I'm glad to be part of this fight. But, to borrow a phrase from Michael Callen's song: all we have is love right now, what we don't have is time.

In a lot of ways, AIDS activists are like those doctors out there—they're so busy putting out fires and taking care of people on respirators, that they don't have the time to take care of all the sick people. We're so busy putting out fires right now, that we don't have the time to talk to each other and strategize and plan for the next wave, and the next day, and next month and the next week and the next year.

And, we're going to have to find the time to do that in the next few months. And, we have to commit ourselves to doing that. And then, after we kick the shit out of this disease, we're all going to be alive to kick the shit out of this system, so that this never happens again.

Vito Russo, 1988

Jeff Paterson (1968–)

There has not been a war in American history that has not seen opposition, even from within the military. Operation Desert Storm, the first Gulf War in 1991, although enthusiastically supported by the American people was no exception. In August 1990, Marine Corps Corporal Jeff Paterson refused to board the troop transport that would take him to Saudi Arabia. He was the first of many military resisters during the Gulf War and has recently been very active in the antiwar demonstrations protesting the 2003 Iraq War. Marine Glen Motil and West Point graduate Dave Wiggins also opposed the first Gulf War while serving, and Andrew McGuffin, Charles Sheehan-Miles, and Alan Gunderson have claimed that their service in Desert Storm irrevocably changed them and convinced them to become antiwar activists.

In January 2001, the tenth anniversary of the commencement of Operation Desert Storm, the *Revolutionary Worker* (a fiercely anticapitalist weekly that supports radical causes and worldwide communist revolution) interviewed Mr. Paterson. What was Paterson's chief objection to the war? If he is a conscientious objector, why would he join the U.S. Marines in the first place? Do you think many other soldiers would endorse his views?

Interview with Jeff Paterson, January 2001

UP AGAINST THE WAR MACHINE

RW: January 2001 is the 10th anniversary of the start of the U.S. war in the Persian Gulf. Many long-time readers of the RW remember the stand you took in 1990, as the first GI to refuse orders to fight in the war. But newer readers may not have heard about this. Could you run down what happened to you?

JP: Ten years ago the U.S. launched a protracted bombing campaign against Iraq, but for me the war began four months before that. In the days following the Iraqi invasion of Kuwait a small number of troops were already being prepared for deployment and I was part of that deployment force of Marines. At that point I had been in the Marine Corps for almost four years of my four-year enlistment. I only had a couple of weeks left, and I was looking forward to getting out in a couple of weeks and signing up for community college and getting on with my life.

I came from a small rural town in northern California. I lived on a ranch outside of town. My mom could barely make ends meet. We had one car. There was no bus to get into town. The only real option was being a ranch hand, and the Marine Corps seemed like a good alternative to that. I liked punk music, I thought it was kind of in your face. At the same time I thought the Marine Corps mystique was kind of in your face too.

Source: *The Revolutionary Worker Online.* Retrieved on 12/20/2003 from http://rwor.org

I found myself stationed in Okinawa, Japan, isolated on a small island, where, for reasons unknown to me, the local population despised us. Many of my so-called friends, their main thing in life was getting drunk and purchasing prostitutes. I was really feeling down. I couldn't relate to anybody or anything.

About that time I decided to check out the base library. On a dusty bottom shelf there were books about El Salvador and Nicaragua. During this time I was in an artillery unit and Central America was headline news. We were mainly training and preparing to help overthrow the Sandinista government in Nicaragua, or to "save" El Salvador from the FMLN rebels. I started checking out those books and reading about the armed struggles taking place in those countries and the peasants organizing and standing up against U.S. intervention. I didn't understand all the politics at the time of those particular groups but I dug what they were doing—fighting U.S. intervention. I came to have more sympathy for them than the organization I was a part of.

The U.S. military, particularly the Marine Corps, tells you there's no point in talking to anyone about what you've been through because they could just never understand. What are they talking about? About how we fucked over all the people in the countries that we were in. How it's perfectly acceptable to purchase a woman for a week or give their parents a dishwasher in exchange for a servant and a sex slave. How it is perfectly fine to blow up somebody's house with a 155 mm Howitzer artillery—which we did a couple of times—and then pay off these peasants with canned foods from our mess hall. They told us that people on the outside wouldn't understand all this. They're right.

All this really laid the basis for a couple of years later when I was ordered to pack my bags for Saudi Arabia. I put all of the pieces together: what I saw in Okinawa, Japan, how we treated people and how we were looked at by the local people as an occupying force, being stationed briefly near Subic Bay in the Philippines, in South Korea. I started to see that all of these things are not the exception but the rule. Although I had never been to the Middle East, I was rather certain that what we were going to do there would not be in the interests of the people there, but more of the same—controlling the resources of these countries for U.S. interests.

I was serving out the last months of my enlistment in Hawaii when I checked out the scene around the university to better understand what was really happening in Central America, and the bigger picture of what the U.S. was up to in all of these places around the world. I soon hooked up with activists around the university—Refuse & Resist!, CISPES, and others—who turned me on to the struggle of the Hawaiian people against the destruction of their homeland. While I was in Hawaii I was ordered to be part of a bombing campaign against one of the islands there called Kahoolawe, similar to what's going on in Puerto Rico right now in Vieques. Connecting all these experiences with the activist scene around the university gave me the strength to take a stand against this war.

RW: On August 16, 1990, you had a press conference where you said, "I will not be a pawn in America's power plays for profit and oil in the Middle East." You said you would refuse to board the plane and if dragged out to the Saudi desert you would refuse to fight. What was happening at that point and what was the response of the authorities to that?

JP: All this happened very quickly. In early August Iraq invaded Kuwait and 48 hours later Bush was on TV saying we couldn't let this stand. Forty-eight hours after that I was told to pack my bags and be ready to catch a plane within 48 hours. I was not sure what to do. I asked friends. Most of them said the situation sucks but what can you do, you have to go. But there were a handful of friends, one in particular from Refuse & Resist!, who said, "Just do what's right." That's what made me seriously consider what I was going to do. For four years I had followed orders, done what I was told to do. But now for the first time I was being challenged to do what was right and that was something very new to me.

Once I knew that I had a small core of people who were going to take up my case, help me, or at least visit me while I was in jail, that gave me strength to do what was right. Once I decided to do what was right, all my feelings for the last three or four years—all the stuff that I had seen that was so fucked up came to the surface. I decided I wasn't going to go. What I said at that first press conference was those four years of pent-up frustration and anger—to make amends for all the things I participated in as part of the military.

One night I was introduced to a well-known activist lawyer, Eric Seitz, who, during the Vietnam War, had defended many GI resisters. The next day, instead of reporting for regular duty, I wrote a statement and held a press conference in his office. I returned to the base that evening and ran into a guard who was watching the barracks. He told me that everybody had seen me on TV and the officers had a big meeting and they were saying that they needed to make an example out of me so other people won't have crazy ideas.

I came back the next morning to my unit—160 Marines. The commanding officer was giving a speech and saying that he could understand why people might want to kick my ass and rip off my head but that would be illegal and technically people shouldn't do that but if anybody did do that he could understand that too.

After that day there was a whole month of back and forth with the military. The military was telling people on the outside, in response to my support committee, that I wasn't going to Saudi Arabia, they would never make anybody go, that I was a coward, that I was bad, that I would be thrown in jail or whatever. But all the while the military was telling me that there was no way they could let me not go. If other Marines got the idea that they could choose what's right and wrong, that was something they couldn't stand for. They told me they were going to make me go, even if I was just going to dig ditches or peel potatoes.

And all during that time there were at least two sides—officers and what we called lifers, people who actually believed all the propaganda vs. the huge number of people in the military who joined just like me, confused 18-year-olds who didn't know what they wanted to do with their lives, young Black men escaping the inner cities of Chicago or Compton, poor white people from Louisiana who didn't want to live their father's life on the farm. Most of them didn't understand what I was saying politically about the situation in the Middle East but I struck a chord with them. They looked at me as someone who was going up against the military. For years we sat around drinking beers and talking about how everything was fucked up. They saw me as going up against all the stuff that we'd talk about over beers, bringing it out into the open.

RW: What was your situation after the press conference? Did they throw you in the brig?

JP: Not yet. They were undecided about what they wanted to do with me. There was a train of thought that the best thing that could happen was that I would just go along with the program. They thought that even if people saw me on TV saying that I would not go, they could turn that around if they had movie footage showing that I went after all.

There was a three week period of dealing back and forth. I filed to be discharged as a conscientious objector. I stated that there was no conceivable war that this military would fight that would serve any good for mankind. On questioning, I refused to put down those people around the world who were resisting the same war machine. They used my refusal to condemn those just armed struggles as the basis to deny my discharge.

During those three weeks I went on a hunger strike. The military was telling the whole world that I was not going to be forced to go to Saudi Arabia but I knew the opposite was true. So I stopped eating as a way of saying that even if they forced me to go I would be more of a burden than an asset.

During this time my case gained more publicity. Some of the rebellious Black Marines kind of took me under their wing and gave me some cover. There were a couple of rednecks—goons—they came to get me and said something like "Your n****r friends ain't going to help you." And that made things a lot easier for me because the battle lines were clearly drawn.

During this time I was under room arrest so I wouldn't "infect" other people with my ideas. One night, in the middle of the night, these four guys climbed through the window and woke me up poking me with broomsticks and one guy was playing with his bayonet. I was half asleep and I heard them say something like "We're going to kill you, motherfucker." And my response was, "Why? What's the reasoning behind that?" Their response was, "You're a chicken shit coward, motherfucking faggot, that's why."

I thought that I better wake up quickly and engage these guys. I ran down all the things that I had read about. I asked them if they knew about how Iraq had gassed the Kurdish people, while the U.S. continued to supply them with arms, how the U.S. played off Iraq and Iran during their war. What exactly was this dictatorship in Kuwait that we were protecting? Their response was like, "Nobody had ever told us what was really going on." After a couple of hours of this, at least it seemed like a couple of hours, they declared that they were not going to kick my ass because I was doing this for a reason and I wasn't a coward after all.

Two days later one of the same guys came up to me in the hallway and he snuck me this funky looking leaflet that he had done on his office computer. He had taken my photograph from the newspaper and scribbled "Free Jeff Paterson." He told me that he made a few copies and that he spread them around the PX and the commissary. I asked him why he did this and his reply was that he wanted to "blow their minds." He said, "The general will shit when he sees this."

I thought that incident was pretty amazing. I think at first they thought they were rebelling against the stated official policy of "hands off the coward," but they saw that there was something bigger to rebel against and they dug that even more.

Almost every day something like that happened. One of the charges brought against me was "giving away classified information to potential enemies." This was supposedly my statement that I was going to be deployed to the Middle East because I had a classified security clearance due to my training in nuclear weapons. For some reason they dropped that charge. Later I learned from a clerk in the general's office that he shredded my clearance files to get back at the fucking general who made his life miserable.

RW: The picture of you sitting on the tarmac, refusing to fight in the Gulf War, made national headlines. Did you have a sense of the kind of impact your case was having more broadly outside the military?

JP: At the time I didn't really have a sense of how things would develop. I thought there would be a headline in the local paper that said 10,000 troops deployed and at the bottom it would say one guy says no. I thought that would be a great success. People would know that one guy protested.

All this was in August, four months before the actual bombing began. But from where I was at the bombing was imminent, it was going to happen, all the talk about negotiated settlement that was not real. We were loading our cannons onto the boats and we weren't doing it for a show. We were doing it to kill a lot of people. One of the things that really moved me was when the colonel gathered our battalion on the base. People were worried; they wanted to be home by Christmas. And his reassurance was that if anything goes wrong we're going to let loose the "silver bullet"—which was what I was trained to work with, artillery fired nuclear warheads—and "nuke those fucking rag heads." And just hearing that pushed me a long way toward refusing to have any part of that war.

RW: Then you were ordered to go to the Middle East. How did that come down?

JP: A week into my hunger strike on August 30 my unit was gathered and my commanding officer said we need a dozen volunteers that would be leaving immediately. About a third of the lifers and others raised their hands. A lot more people volunteered than they needed but the CO made a point of "volunteering" me. We were told to pack our bags, that we would be leaving immediately.

They let me leave the base to store my car off the base. And the person they had to escort me was a close friend of mine who let me contact my supporters and set up a press conference. So, upon returning to the base, I participated in a large press conference at the gates to the air station. The press asked me what I was going to do. I hadn't thought about what I was going to do if they actually tried to put me on a plane. I said I would have to sit down or something. And a few hours later, that's exactly what happened. I was ordered onto the transport plane and I sat down on the runway and watched people that I knew get on the plane.

While I was sitting there on the runway, various lifers—my master sergeant, CO, and a naval investigator—jumped around me yelling shit about me being chicken shit, that they would hunt me down when they got back from the war. I just sat there, ignoring them, looking straight ahead. That just pissed them off more.

RW: After they removed you from the runway what happened next?

JP: I was taken to the military brig at Pearl Harbor to await my court-martial trial which began in late November. The prosecution was asking for five years in Leavenworth. I was thinking about what people around the world go up against to oppose the U.S., and what the people of Iraq were facing. My personal sacrifice didn't seem that big in comparison.

As the trial started we took every opportunity to publicize my case and use it as an organizing means, not just to challenge the charges against me but to also mobilize against the war. Every day my trial went on people protested outside the gates, people chained themselves to the gate, people hung banners over freeways leading into the base. One day the judge was an hour late and he was joking about how there was a "Free Jeff Paterson" banner blocking the freeway and he had to sit in the tunnel for a half-hour choking on fumes because of that.

My case was becoming such an issue and point of debate that eventually the military decided that they had a war to fight and it was in their interest to get rid of me as quickly as possible. So they just discharged me. One day I was facing five years. Then, because of our strategy of mobilizing as many people as possible around my case and against the war, 48 hours later I was back in California. And a few days after that I was part of the mobilization of hundreds of thousands of people in the SF Bay Area and the bigger movement to stop the war.

During a so-called "victory parade" in San Francisco I was arrested for climbing on a five-ton truck while others disrupted the parade. A week later I was arrested for trying to chain myself to the turret of a tank during the Oakland parade. I shared a cell that day with dozens of activists who unmasked that parade of shame.

RW: Can you talk about other GI resisters during the Persian Gulf War?

JP: People told me of the legacy of resistance among GI's during the Vietnam War— organizations like Vietnam Veterans Against the War. I got calls from Vietnam veterans like Brian Willson who had his legs cut off by a train during a protest against U.S. intervention in Central America. So I had some frame of reference. I was able to get some strength from feeling a part of that legacy.

After my initial press conference, my support committee began receiving calls from other people around the country who were reservists in the Army or Marine Corps, active duty Air Force. People put me in touch with dozens and later hundreds of people who were going through the same decision that I had gone through regarding what to do and what was right. There was a committee set up in New York City that defended dozens of people, most of them from just one military reserve unit based there. There were news articles, hidden in the press, about two or three people refusing to fight and being put in the brig in Arizona. Here in the SF Bay Area there were local reservists who refused to fight, held press conferences and were imprisoned by the Marine Corps for two years each. The Marine Corps took a lesson from my case. They saw I was able to get support in the surrounding community, which made them uneasy. They began identifying resisters and sending them to places where they thought they could isolate them from their community, from their base of support, or from lawyers who might take up their cases.

After the war I spent two years publishing a newsletter called *The Anti-Warrior*. It gave voice to these resisters. It was a way they could have their stories and poems published so people knew what was going on.

One hundred fifty people in the military publicly made statements against the war. Over 100 of those were sentenced and did some time in prison. Several did a year or more at Leavenworth prison. The military released numbers indicating 7,500 GIs officially filed for discharge as conscientious objectors during the Gulf War. Beyond that, I heard numerous accounts of commanding officers tearing up these petitions in front of a GI.

RW: For 10 years the war against the people of Iraq has continued. Could you talk about that?

JP: There's no doubt that the war has never ended against the people of Iraq. UN studies show that 1.5 million Iraqi people have died, not mainly from the war, but from the U.S. sanctions, from malnutrition and preventable diseases. They are dying from contaminated water supplies after the U.S. deliberately and systematically destroyed Iraq's water treatment facilities. The U.S. continues to pound Iraq, during some periods averaging a bombing every other day. And this hardly makes the news.

A couple of years ago the U.S. was again threatening a large scale bombing of Iraq. I had just spoken at a protest rally when a Marine Corps vet, Andrew McGuffin, told me about some of the shit he was a part of in Iraq during the war—the burned bodies, miles and miles of smoldering cars, flesh cooking. He said, back then, I thought people like you were a big wuss—but those smells have changed me forever. I pushed him up to the microphone at that rally and we did a radio show together in Berkeley that night. Tens of thousands of Gulf War vets are now suffering from Gulf War Syndrome, and the reality that they are disposable is setting in. One in seven Gulf War vets have already filed for disability. That's twice the rate of the Vietnam War or World War II!

Recently I signed on to "A Call from Veterans: End the U.S./UN Sanctions— Stop the U.S. War Against the People of Iraq!" petition which is being circulated by Vietnam Veterans Against the War Anti-Imperialist.

Ten years later, the U.S. war machine continues to pound the people of Iraq. The same things that jarred me awake while I was in the military are still happening. But people around the world are seeing what this U.S. new world order-globalization is all about and people are fighting back, like the Seattle WTO meeting being shut down. Like in the Philippines, where I was stationed, there is an armed struggle and the New People's Army is fighting against U.S. imperialism. In Peru, the People's War is continuing. I've been reading about the Maoist revolution in Nepal, like the great series that Li Onesto did in the *RW*. All of this can't help but give people hope for the future. Many of us who have been in the military, especially Vietnam vets, know better than anyone else that the U.S. war machine can be defeated.

Anita Hill (1956–)

In the autumn of 1991, the nation was mesmerized by the televised Senate confirmation hearings for Judge Clarence Thomas. When President George Bush appointed Thomas to succeed retiring Supreme Court Justice Thurgood Marshall, a good deal of controversy erupted. Many thought it appropriate that an African American would succeed another African American, although many liberals and civil rights activists opposed Clarence Thomas's conservatism. The controversy, however, reached the boiling point when University of Oklahoma law professor Anita Hill testified at the hearings that Judge Thomas had sexually harassed her. Her testimony was so lucid, so clear that many people—especially women who had experienced similar treatment but remained silent about it—wholeheartedly believed her. The fact that the white male senators on the committee browbeat her to punch holes in her testimony reinforced the perception that Hill was telling the truth. Although Clarence Thomas was confirmed and became a Supreme Court justice, the hearings had a huge impact on the nation. Since 1991, the federal government, state and local governments, companies, and universities have all implemented sexual harassment training workshops to eradicate the problem.

Why is sexual harassment so compelling that, overnight, this hearing inflamed the entire nation? What is the underlying issue in sexual harassment?

Opening Statement at the Clarence Thomas Confirmation Hearings, October 11, 1991

Mr. Chairman, Senator Thurmond, members of the committee, my name is Anita F. Hill, and I am a professor of law at the University of Oklahoma. I was born on a farm in Okmulgee County, Oklahoma, in 1956. I am the youngest of 13 children. I had my early education in Okmulgee County. My father, Albert Hill, is a farmer in that area. My mother's name is Irma Hill. She is also a farmer and a housewife.

My childhood was one of a lot of hard work and not much money, but it was one of solid family affection, as represented by my parents. I was reared in a religious atmosphere in the Baptist faith, and I have been a member of the Antioch Baptist Church in Tulsa, Oklahoma, since 1983. It is a very warm part of my life at the present time.

For my undergraduate work, I went to Oklahoma State University and graduated from there in 1977. I am attaching to this statement a copy of my resume for further details of my education.

Source: Retrieved on 8/27/2003 from http://gos.sbc.edu/h/hill.html

I graduated from the university with academic honors and proceeded to the Yale Law School, where I received my JD degree in 1980. Upon graduation from law school, I became a practicing lawyer with the Washington, DC, firm of Ward, Hardraker, and Ross.

In 1981, I was introduced to now Judge Thomas by a mutual friend. Judge Thomas told me that he was anticipating a political appointment, and he asked if I would be interested in working with him. He was, in fact, appointed as Assistant Secretary of Education for Civil Rights. After he had taken that post, he asked if I would become his assistant, and I accepted that position.

In my early period there, I had two major projects. The first was an article I wrote for Judge Thomas' signature on the education of minority students. The second was the organization of a seminar on high-risk students which was abandoned because Judge Thomas transferred to the EEOC where he became the chairman of that office.

During this period at the Department of Education, my working relationship with Judge Thomas was positive. I had a good deal of responsibility and independence. I thought he respected my work and that he trusted my judgment. After approximately three months of working there, he asked me to go out socially with him.

What happened next and telling the world about it are the two most difficult things—experiences of my life. It is only after a great deal of agonizing consideration and sleepless number—a great number of sleepless nights that I am able to talk of these unpleasant matters to anyone but my close friends.

I declined the invitation to go out socially with him and explained to him that I thought it would jeopardize what at the time I considered to be a very good working relationship. I had a normal social life with other men outside of the office. I believed then, as now, that having a social relationship with a person who was supervising my work would be ill-advised. I was very uncomfortable with the idea and told him so.

I thought that by saying no and explaining my reasons my employer would abandon his social suggestions. However, to my regret, in the following few weeks, he continued to ask me out on several occasions. He pressed me to justify my reasons for saying no to him. These incidents took place in his office or mine. They were in the form of private conversations which would not have been overheard by anyone else.

My working relationship became even more strained when Judge Thomas began to use work situations to discuss sex. On these occasions, he would call me into his office for reports on education issues and projects, or he might suggest that, because of the time pressures of his schedule, we go to lunch to a government cafeteria. After a brief discussion of work, he would turn the conversation to a discussion of sexual matters.

His conversations were very vivid. He spoke about acts that he had seen in pornographic films involving such matters as women having sex with animals and films showing group sex or rape scenes. He talked about pornographic materials depicting individuals with large penises or large breasts involved in various sex acts. On several occasions, Thomas told me graphically of his own sexual prowess.

Because I was extremely uncomfortable talking about sex with him at all and particularly in such a graphic way, I told him that I did not want to talk about these subjects. I would also try to change the subject to education matters or to nonsexual personal matters such as his background or his beliefs. My efforts to change the subject were rarely successful.

Throughout the period of these conversations, he also from time to time asked me for social engagements. My reaction to these conversations was to avoid them by eliminating opportunities for us to engage in extended conversations. This was difficult because at the time I was his only assistant at the Office of Education—or Office for Civil Rights.

During the latter part of my time at the Department of Education, the social pressures and any conversation of his offensive behavior ended. I began both to believe and hope that our working relationship could be a proper, cordial, and professional one.

When Judge Thomas was made chair of the EEOC, I needed to face the question of whether to go with him. I was asked to do so, and I did. The work itself was interesting, and at that time it appeared that the sexual overtures which had so troubled me had ended. I also faced the realistic fact that I had no alternative job. While I might have gone back to private practice, perhaps in my old firm or at another, I was dedicated to civil rights work, and my first choice was to be in that field. Moreover, the Department of Education itself was a dubious venture. President Reagan was seeking to abolish the entire department.

For my first months at the EEOC, where I continued to be an assistant to Judge Thomas, there were no sexual conversations or overtures. However, during the fall and winter of 1982, these began again. The comments were random and ranged from pressing me about why I didn't go out with him to remarks about my personal appearance. I remember his saying that some day I would have to tell him the real reason that I wouldn't go out with him.

He began to show displeasure in his tone and voice and his demeanor and his continued pressure for an explanation. He commented on what I was wearing in terms of whether it made me more or less sexually attractive. The incidents occurred in his inner office at the EEOC.

One of the oddest episodes I remember was an occasion in which Thomas was drinking a Coke in his office. He got up from the table at which we were working, went over to his desk to get the Coke, looked at the can and asked, "Who has pubic hair on my Coke?" On other occasions, he referred to the size of his own penis as being larger than normal, and he also spoke on some occasions of the pleasures he had given to women with oral sex.

At this point, late 1982, I began to feel severe stress on the job. I began to be concerned that Clarence Thomas might take out his anger with me by degrading me or not giving me important assignments. I also thought that he might find an excuse for dismissing me.

In January of 1983, I began looking for another job. I was handicapped because I feared that, if he found out, he might make it difficult for me to find other employment and I might be dismissed from the job I had. Another factor that made my search more difficult was that there was a period—this was during a period of a hiring freeze in the government. In February of 1983, I was hospitalized for five days on an emergency basis for acute stomach pain which I attributed to stress on the job.

Once out of the hospital, I became more committed to find other employment and sought further to minimize my contact with Thomas. This became easier when Allison Duncan became office director, because most of my work was then funneled through her and I had contact with Clarence Thomas mostly in staff meetings.

In the spring of 1983, an opportunity to teach at Oral Roberts University opened up. I participated in a seminar—taught an afternoon session and seminar at Oral Roberts University. The dean of the university saw me teaching and inquired as to whether I would be interested in furthering—pursuing a career in teaching, beginning at Oral Roberts University. I agreed to take the job in large part because of my desire to escape the pressures I felt at the EEOC due to Judge Thomas.

When I informed him that I was leaving in July, I recall that his response was that now I would no longer have an excuse for not going out with him. I told him that I still preferred not to do so. At some time after that meeting, he asked if he could take me to dinner at the end of the term. When I declined, he assured me that the dinner was a professional courtesy only and not a social invitation. I reluctantly agreed to accept that invitation, but only if it was at the very end of a working day.

On, as I recall, the last day of my employment at the EEOC in the summer of 1983, I did have dinner with Clarence Thomas. We went directly from work to a restaurant near the office. We talked about the work I had done, both at education and at the EEOC. He told me that he was pleased with all of it except for an article and speech that I had done for him while we were at the Office for Civil Rights. Finally, he made a comment that I will vividly remember. He said that if I ever told anyone of his behavior that it would ruin his career. This was not an apology, nor was it an explanation. That was his last remark about the possibility of our going out or reference to his behavior.

In July of 1983, I left Washington, DC, area and have had minimal contact with Judge Clarence Thomas since. I am of course aware from the press that some questions have been raised about conversations I had with Judge Clarence Thomas after I left the EEOC. From 1983 until today, I have seen Judge Thomas only twice. On one occasion, I needed to get a reference from him, and on another he made a public appearance in Tulsa.

On one occasion he called me at home and we had an inconsequential conversation. On one occasion he called me without reaching me, and I returned the call without reaching him, and nothing came of it. I have on at least three occasions, been asked to act as a conduit to him for others.

I knew his secretary, Diane Holt. We had worked together at both EEOC and education. There were occasions on which I spoke to her, and on some of these occasions undoubtedly I passed on some casual comment to then Chairman Thomas. There were a series of calls in the first three months of 1985, occasioned by a group in Tulsa, which wished to have a civil rights conference. They wanted Judge Thomas to be the speaker and enlisted my assistance for this purpose.

I did call in January and February to no effect, and finally suggested to the person directly involved, Susan Cahal, that she put the matter into her own hands and call directly. She did so in March of 1985. In connection with that March invitation, Ms. Cahal wanted conference materials for the seminar and some research was needed. I was asked to try to get the information and did attempt to do so.

There was another call about another possible conference in July of 1985. In August of 1987, I was in Washington, DC, and I did call Diane Holt. In the course of this conversation, she asked me how long I was going to be in town and I told her. It is recorded in the message as August 15. It was, in fact, August 20th. She told me about Judge Thomas's marriage and I did say to congratulate him.

It is only after a great deal of agonizing consideration that I am able to talk of these unpleasant matters to anyone except my closest friends. As I've said before these last few days have been very trying and very hard for me and it hasn't just been the last few days this week. It has actually been over a month now that I have been under the strain of this issue.

Telling the world is the most difficult experience of my life, but it is very close to having to live through the experience that occasion this meeting. I may have used poor judgment early on in my relationship with this issue. I was aware, however, that telling at any point in my career could adversely affect my future career. And I did not want early on to burn all the bridges to the EEOC.

As I said, I may have used poor judgment. Perhaps I should have taken angry or even militant steps, both when I was in the agency, or after I left it. But I must confess to the world that the course that I took seemed the better as well as the easier approach.

I declined any comment to newspapers, but later when Senate staff asked me about these matters I felt I had a duty to report. I have no personal vendetta against Clarence Thomas. I seek only to provide the committee with information which it may regard as relevant.

It would have been more comfortable to remain silent. I took no initiative to inform anyone. But when I was asked by a representative of this committee to report my experience, I felt that I had to tell the truth. I could not keep silent.

Gay Liberation

During the 1980s and 1990s, many gays and lesbians demonstrated passionately for their rights, and the gay liberation movement became far more visible. In 1994 the House of Representatives held hearings, during which a number of gay activists testified to urge Congress to pass legislation that would end discrimination against gays in the workforce.

Are antidiscrimination laws necessary? Do such laws give an unfair advantage to those they are meant to protect, as some critics argue?

Statement of Ernest Dillon

I would like to thank the panel for inviting me to this hearing. I would like to thank you for inviting me to this affair. I am just here to tell a story. I wish I didn't have a story to tell, and I wish panels like this were not necessary. But they are necessary because people in the workplace are being discriminated against because of sexual orientation.

My story started in 1980. I began working for the Post Office in 1980, and I was a pretty good postal employee. I was a teamworker and I worked hard. And I worked with other individuals when my work was done. I worked in that kind of environment for about four years. Then an individual, a coworker of mine, began to verbally shout sexual epithets about my sexual orientation towards me and to verbally harass me.

I apprised my supervisors of this situation, and I also apprised my union of the situation. My supervisors told me that nothing could be done to this individual until he did something to me. The union, on the other hand, told me that I should keep notes about the things that had been written about me and the things that they were saying about me. People heard those things, and so I did that.

Then in 1985, in May of 1985, I walked into the restroom during the washup period to get washed up to go to lunch and this individual was in the restroom. And he—as I washed my hands and turned to dry them at the paper towel rack, he assaulted me. He knocked me out, knocked me unconscious. When I came to, there was blood all over the floor. I sustained several injuries, a bruised sternum and two black eyes and I required several stitches in my forehead.

I was off from work for a period of three weeks because of those injuries. And when I returned to work, I learned that that individual had been fired but there were two other individuals in the same work area who kind of picked up the ball and started rolling with it again. And I again began to apprise my supervisors and other management personnel of what was going on and that I was afraid that another assault was going to ensue. They told me the same thing. There was nothing they could do about it.

That was in 1985. I dealt with that for three years, until 1988, and finally an individual came over into my work area and made another violent, threatening remark to me. I asked to be sent to the nurse's office and I asked to be sent home. She saw that I was pretty upset and so she sent me home.

That was on a Friday and on that following Monday, I made an appointment to see a mental health consultant. I saw a therapist and explained my situation. He took down what was going on with me on the job. He immediately took me off the job and advised me to file an equal opportunity claim and a worker's compensation claim. So I did both of those things. Eventually, the worker's compensation claim was accepted and EEOC began to investigate and we went through the channels and the procedures necessary.

SOURCE: Congress, House, Committee on Education and Labor, *Employment Discrimination Against Gay Men and Lesbians*, 103d Congress, 2d Session, June 20, 1994 (Washington, D.C.: U.S. Government Printing Office, 1994). Retrieved on 12/27/2003 from http://historymatters.gmu.edu/d/6463/

I won the case at the initial level but when we got out of the internal system and into the court system, I lost on every level. I lost because there was no law that protected people from such a harassment because of sexual orientation.

I am now back with the Post Office after being off of work for four years. I returned to the Post Office in 1992, but at a different postal installation. So far everything there is okay.

I just think that a law needs to be passed so that people will not have to go through the kind of thing that I had to go through. . . .

Statement of Daniel Miller

My name is Dan Miller. I am a Certified Public Accountant living in Harrisburg, Pennsylvania. I operate my own CPA firm. I am an employer, homeowner, landlord, and church member. I derive much enjoyment from close family relationships with my parents, siblings, and my personal partner, Carl, and his two young children.

In most respects I am a typical middle-class American. Unlike most Americans, I am a victim of blatant discrimination and the experience has radically changed my life.

Prior to owning my own CPA firm, I was employed by Donald L. DeMuth Professional Management Consultants. It was Mr. Donald DeMuth's firm that irrationally discriminated against me on the basis of my sexual orientation. . . .

My story begins late in the summer of 1990. Several incidents of anti-gay violence occurred in Harrisburg and I was one of several community leaders informing city council and requesting action. Eventually, I appeared on several local TV news programs asking for increased police protection for gay and lesbian residents.

On Wednesday, October 17, 1990, at 10 a.m., my boss, Donald L. DeMuth, called me into his office. I was fired effective immediately. I sat in his office in stunned silence. "You are fired" kept ringing over and over in my mind. I was devastated. DeMuth continued: I would receive no severance pay or vacation pay, no benefits. Nothing.

And then he went for the final and most severe blow, asking, "What do you want me to tell our clients?" He assumed that I was humiliated and embarrassed at being gay. Apparently DeMuth expected me to leave his firm and hang my head in shame.

I was enraged. I told him, "Tell them the truth: Tell them you fired me because I'm gay." In front of the entire office staff, I cleaned out my desk and left the office of DeMuth Professional Management Consultants for the last time.

At home I didn't know what to do next. I didn't know how being fired would affect future job prospects. My life was in turmoil. How was I going to pay my bills, my mortgage, my taxes? I signed up for unemployment compensation, but DeMuth contested benefit payment. He claimed firing me for homosexuality was just cause. I was forced to return to the unemployment office for several additional interviews before benefits were approved. It was humiliating.

At home, I became depressed. I couldn't eat and I just barely slept. My life was collapsing and it had all happened because I am gay and not willing to deny it.

In fact, I had never publicly acknowledged that I was gay. I had only exercised my freedom of speech and spoke in support of increased protection from anti-gay violence. Speaking on this issue cost me my job. My boss automatically assumed I was gay and fired me without even knowing the facts.

The following trial testimony displays the pure bigotry espoused by Donald DeMuth when questioned by my attorney Daniel Sullivan.

"Now, as of October 17, 1990, Mr. Miller was properly discharging his duties?"

DeMuth responds: "I consider homosexuality as cause that incapacitated him from properly discharging his duties."

"Was he properly discharging his duties with respect to his services as a professional financial consultant as of October 17, 1990?"

DeMuth: "Not if he is a homosexual." . . .

I then went to the Pennsylvania Human Relations Commission. I was even more disappointed. The law didn't include the term "sexual orientation" and there was nothing they could do. They even refused to record my case for use as a statistical reference. I was forced to accept the fact that with no legal protection, I had to move on as best I could.

Six weeks passed and on December 1, 1990, I opened my own CPA office in downtown Harrisburg. Approximately one-third of DeMuth's former clients engaged me as their accountant. Although the future looked promising, my troubles with DeMuth were not over. In some ways they were just beginning.

At the end of my first tax season, I began receiving letters from DeMuth and his attorney demanding compensation for his former clients that had hired me. It wasn't enough that he fired me solely for being gay. Now he wanted to be compensated for his costly business decision.

DeMuth based this claim on a contract I was required to sign six months after I began working with him. The contract in effect punished me for being gay. It stated that if I was fired for just cause and I opened a competing CPA firm, I was required to pay DeMuth for former clients that retained my services. It further defined homosexuality as just cause.

Appalled at this clause, I sought legal advice. Believing that the contract was illegal and unenforceable, I signed the contract.

One year after opening my firm, in November 1991, DeMuth filed suit against me for $124,000. He claimed that I had breached our contract and sought to have the courts enforce his personal prejudice. In June 1993, our case was heard before a jury in Cumberland County presided by Judge Kevin Hess.

Lacking a specific law prohibiting employment discrimination on the basis of sexual orientation, Judge Hess refused to let us argue that the firing was unconstitutional or against public policy, and subsequently the jury awarded DeMuth a total judgment plus interest of $130,000. The entire experience has cost me a considerable amount of emotional turmoil and just under $200,000 in judgment, interest, appeal costs and attorney's fees.

Later, juror Mary Warner wrote in the Harrisburg Patriot News, "DeMuth took the witness stand, thrust out his jaw and said unapologetically that he had fired a good employee for being gay." She goes on to say, "It was outrageous to hear intolerance like that in a court of law where people come to seek protection from intolerance. But the law was silent."

In a separate editorial, the paper wrote, "Until the civil rights of all Americans, homosexual and heterosexual, are given equal authority under the law, discrimination shall infect the Land of the Free." . . .

I ask you, as leaders of this country, to stop this injustice. You have the power to help stop anti-gay discrimination by passing civil rights legislation. Unless such legislation is passed, anti-gay employment discrimination will continue to occur in America and the law will be silent. . . .

Statement of Nancy McDonald

I am Nancy McDonald and I am a retired educator, school administrator, and educational consultant from Tulsa, Oklahoma. My husband and I have four children. Our youngest daughter is a lesbian.

We are copresidents of the Tulsa Chapter of Parents, Friends and Families of Lesbians and Gays, and I also serve as a regional director and a member of the national board of directors.

I am here today to speak to you about workplace discrimination against our gay, lesbian and bisexual children.

Our lesbian daughter is a teacher and she specializes in bilingual education, and as any parent, we would love to have her return to Oklahoma to teach. But in Oklahoma, if a teacher is perceived to be gay, by a parent, a coworker or an administrator, the charge can be used to initiate an investigation or dismissal.

I do not want to subject her to that. This is included in the State of Oklahoma's school reform passed by the State legislature in 1990. Gay, lesbian or bisexual educators must remain in the closet. And yet I know from my experience that they are the most creative, talented and dedicated educators any school system could employ, and it is unfortunate that they must hide their sexual orientation.

On the other hand, there are no role models, gay or lesbian role models, in our schools for our gay, lesbian and bisexual children. They have no one to turn to for factual information.

This produces very low self-esteem and puts our children at risk for suicide. Consequently 30 percent—30 percent—of all suicides committed by youth are by our gay and lesbian children. This was reported in the study on youth suicide conducted by the Federal Government.

Gay educators are employed in our public schools, in our colleges, in our universities, and they are victims of discrimination. As in most cases, grounds for dismissal are contrived. Many of them are minor infractions of the rules, subjective opinions, not adequately validated. Gay, lesbian, or bisexual teachers find it extremely difficult to combat these allegations because they will have to identify themselves, and when they do, they can be dismissed. It is a Catch-22 situation.

I would like to share with you some additional examples that I know of personally in Tulsa, Okalhoma. . . .

I know a lesbian who was employed as a caregiver in a community home for the retarded. She was dismissed because there was concern that she would molest the persons residing in the home. She has an excellent work record and was never, ever, given any negative evaluations. She is very fearful of being identified and not being able to get another job. . . .

A young woman, a lesbian, was dismissed from a fast food restaurant. Here coworkers had told the owners that she was a lesbian, and he was concerned that she would keep customers away from the store. She had worked at this fast food restaurant for 18 months. . . .

A minister of a mainline Christian denominational church is dismissed because he performed a commitment ceremony for two gay men. The ceremony took place away from the church. The denomination declares that it is accepting of gays and lesbians. This minister has served this church for over 20 years, and only now accusations of his inability to serve that congregation have come forth. The church board of directors does not want to be perceived as a congregation encouraging gays and lesbians to attend this particular church. He is terribly concerned about losing his retirement benefits.

A social worker with outstanding credentials in working with families and child abuse was dismissed because the board of directors of the agency, after learning that she is a lesbian, was concerned about her working with children. The reason that they gave in her dismissal: She had poor work habits. . . .

I want you to know that our children live with fear, fear that if they are honest about their sexual orientation they will be dismissed. For the most part, sexual orientation will not be identified as the main reason for dismissal. They will be dismissed because of trumped-up, minor infractions of the rules.

They are trapped. If they are honest, as we have taught them to be as parents, they are dismissed. If they remain in the closet, they live with the fear, the stress, that every day someone will snitch on them.

Discrimination on the basis of sexual orientation is prohibited by statute in only eight States and the District of Columbia. While a growing number of cities are enacting local nondiscrimination codes, there is also a growing movement to repeal or prohibit State or municipal nondiscrimination provisions.

We have just gone through this in Tulsa. It is not a pleasant experience. Only a Federal law will ensure that all individuals are protected from discrimination on the basis of sexual orientation. . . .

Statement of Phill Wilson, Director of Public Policy, AIDS Project Los Angeles

Thank you, and good afternoon. My name is Phill Wilson. I am Director of Public Policy for AIDS Project Los Angeles, one of the largest AIDS service organizations in the country. I am also the founder of the Black Gay and Lesbian Leadership Forum.

A national climate of fear and discrimination has thrust APLA into the role of having to preserve and protect the dignity and self-respect of persons affected by

HIV and AIDS. We provide critically needed education to the public, health care providers, educators, business and religious leaders, the media, public officials and other opinion leaders.

It is within this framework that I address this panel today. I thank you for this invitation. I am honored to speak to you on an issue of paramount importance to me personally as a black gay man who is living with AIDS. That issue is the elimination of discrimination against gay and lesbians in general, and particularly the eradication of prejudice faced by people of color in this country.

Too often I am faced with young black men who carry with them the promise and the dreams of their family. Often they are the first ones in their families to go to college. I meet them when they have their first bout of pneumocystis or they find a Kaposi's sarcoma lesion. I always ask them, "Why didn't you come forward sooner? Why didn't you find out your HIV status? Why didn't you exercise the possibility of accessing treatment?" All too often the response is, "I didn't want anyone to know that I way gay. I was afraid to lose my job." All too often this fear around losing their job has cost them their lives.

We have a crisis in America that affects all our communities, not just African Americans and other people of color, not just lesbians and gay men, but every person who has ever come to the table in search of justice, but was met with discrimination. . . .

A recent court ruling in the State of Arizona attests to this fact. In the case of Blaine vs. Golden State Container Company, the Arizona Court of Appeals held that gays and lesbians are not protected from discrimination by private employers.

In addition to this ruling, a proposed amendment to the Nevada State constitution says that objection to homosexuality based upon one's convictions is a liberty and right of conscience and shall not be considered discrimination related to civil rights.

Both of these examples highlight a troubling situation in this country. States categorically deny basic civil rights to a group of their own law-abiding, tax-paying residents. Basic civil rights such as protection from harassment in the workplace and wrongful termination, granted as a matter of course to the majority of citizens, are legally denied to lesbians and gay men in most States.

A widespread misconception is that lesbians and gay men have legal recourse when discrimination occurs in the workplace. We do not. There is no Federal law against discrimination based on sexual orientation.

We need a Federal bill enacted that explicitly protects gays and lesbians from discrimination in all aspects of life, especially in the workplace. . . .

This country is a special place. It is special because at our core is the ideal of equality. At our core is the understanding that equality, equal rights, are not special.

Special rights is the banner under which opponents to a Federal bill will rally. There is nothing special about the right to a job for which you are qualified. There is nothing special about the right to perform your job free of harassment and fear. There is nothing special about the right to life, liberty, and the pursuit of happiness.

In 1968, an act of violence took the life of Dr. Martin Luther King, Jr. I was 11 years old, but I remember the day clearly. More importantly, I remember Dr. King's words as he told of his dream.

"I have a dream today," he said, and when he spoke about the sons of former slaves and the sons of former slave owners, he made no distinction between the gay ones and the straight ones. When Dr. King sang, "Free at last, free at last, thank God almighty, we are free at last," he included all of us.

I am the great-grandson of a slave. I was a part of that dream, as all of us are. From the floor of the Democratic national convention, I quote Mel Boozer: "I have been called a nigger and I have been called a faggot and I can describe for you the difference in the marrow of my soul. I can describe difference in one word: None."

Many people compare the discrimination based on sexual orientation to the discrimination based on race. I do not believe they are the same. I do not think it is important that they be the same. The tragedies that happen in Mogadishu are not the tragedies that are happening in Sarajevo, and yet we understand that the tragedies in Mogadishu and the tragedies in Sarajevo are both wrong.

When you deny someone a job because they are gay or you deny someone a job because they are a woman or you deny someone a job because they are black, when you deny someone a home because they are gay or lesbian, or you deny someone a home because they are black or you deny someone a home because they are a woman, in the end, you have people who are jobless, you have people who are homeless. . . .

Statement of Letitia Gomez, Executive Director, Latino/a, Lesbian and Gay Organization

Good afternoon. I want to start by thanking you, Congressman Owens, and the other members of the committee for attending. My name is Letitia Gomez and I am Executive Director of the National Latino Lesbian and Gay Organization, LLEGO. LLEGO is committed to educating the public, in general, as well as the gay and lesbian Latino community, in particular, about the contributions of gay and lesbian Latinos in the U.S.

Our mission is to work toward providing resources to the gay and lesbian Latino community that will facilitate self-empowerment and enable gay and lesbian Latinos to deal effectively with the issues of civil rights, health and culture. . . .

I am glad to testify before you today about employment discrimination against gay men, lesbians and bisexual people who are Latinos. Unlike gays, lesbians and bisexual people who are white or African American, lesbians and gay Latinos are viewed as foreigners, although a majority of Latinos in the United States are U.S. born. The gay and lesbian Latino community is a mirror of the larger Latino community in that we are young and growing in population and in the work force.

Gay, lesbian and bisexual Latinos work in the government and private sector as professionals, technicians, and administrative staff in many service jobs. We are unlike the larger Latino community in that many times it is difficult for us to separate discrimination against us based on sexual orientation from racial discrimination, because when you are a person of multiple oppressions you have to wonder if the discrimination is about your race, gender, if you are a woman, or sexual orientation.

Discrimination forces some gay, lesbian and bisexual Latinos to live in a climate of fear that their livelihood could be jeopardized and therefore perpetuates self-hatred that has an adverse impact on their psychological, economic and social well-being. I would like to provide you with a specific example of what I am talking about.

In 1986 Angela Romero, a veteran of the Denver police department and a member of the Denver police department's School Resource Program was called out of a lecture at one of her assigned schools and told to report to her supervisor's office immediately. When she arrived at his office, her supervisor told her that her division chief and sergeant had information that would damage her work integrity. While they did not say so in the meeting, the implication was that her lesbianism made her a threat to children. She would later learn that the session was raised because she had stopped one day to buy a book at a lesbian book store. Her supervisor asked Angela if she had anything to say to him about this.

Angela didn't know quite what to make of her supervisor's inquiry. Up to this point in her career, she received outstanding reviews from all the schools; however, she and her sergeant had had a difficult relationship during the previous year. Angela thought his behavior towards her was because she was a Mexican. Her supervisor's inquiries started her to think about the damaging information that her sergeant purported to have.

Alcohol and drugs were not a part of her life and she had never discussed her sexual orientation with any of her fellow police officers. When she confronted her supervisor with the nature of the information, he refused to say what it was.

The next thing Angela knew, she was asked to transfer out of the School Resource Program to the ID unit. She refused, even though she was guaranteed that she could keep her recent promotion. After she protested her transfer, Angela was relieved of her duties with the schools and was assigned to street patrol. Sometime later, she learned that the underlying reason for the personnel action was because she was suspected of being a lesbian.

Angela decided to come out to protect her job so that she could do the work she most wanted to do. Angela spent more than four years fighting the system, virtually alone. She had nowhere to turn inside of the police department that would offer her protection or support. She consulted outside agencies.

One equal employment opportunity specialist told her that it was too bad her case was not based on the fact that she was Hispanic, because it would be a lot tougher to get support for discrimination against her based on sexual orientation. The local American Civil Liberties Union would not take her case. The Denver gay and lesbian community was not in a position to support or help her.

When she finally found a private practice lawyer who specialized in employment discrimination, this lawyer told her that the statute of limitations for a case based on sexism or racism had expired. She was determined not to quit her job, but make the State change its sexual harassment policy.

During this process, Angela continued to work. And as I stated earlier, she was assigned to work street patrol. There were several occasions when her fellow officers would not respond to her calls for backup. She began to fear for her life.

During roll call, disparaging remarks were made about homosexuals and lesbians in her presence and about her. She found herself calling her superiors on their homophobia and sexism and she documented all the retaliation. One aspect of her superior's response was to place unmarked cars in front of her house and the houses of the friends she visited in off-duty hours.

Just when the system seems to be shutting down on her, the City of Denver passed its civil rights ordinance. Shortly afterwards, the Denver Police Department amended its sexual harassment policies to include sexual orientation. Today, Angela is still an officer for the Denver Police Department, but the memory of this series of events is still difficult for her to talk about. However, she is proud of the fact that she decided not to compromise who she is as a Latino lesbian for the job she loves, being a police officer.

I have to emphasize, however, that this discrimination did exact a price on Angela that she could almost not pay. She paid a high personal price for the emotional and mental torment that she endured as a result of the unprofessional behavior of her fellow police officers. She also came close to losing her life or risking severe injury several times because of the failure to get backup on high risk calls. This failure also resulted in dangerous criminals staying on the street longer than they should have because her only recourse at times was to retreat. . . .

Therefore, I ask this committee to seriously consider the merit of legislation that will protect the rights of gay men, lesbians and bisexual people and our friends to work regardless of their sexual orientation. And please do not be led into the discussion that we, lesbians, gay men and bisexual people, want special rights. This is about the equal right to work in the U.S. As we are all painfully aware in this day and time, we need to be about keeping people employed and providing safe workplace environments so that they can carry out their jobs. . . .

The Michigan Militia

After the destruction of the Alfred P. Murrah Federal Building in Oklahoma City, many newspaper articles were written about the Michigan Militia and numerous other right-wing organizations and militias. Timothy McVeigh, who set off the bomb that killed 168 people, had had some ties with the militia, as did his partner, Terry Nichols. The Michigan Militia denied having any involvement with the bombing, but concern heightened about the climate of hate and distrust that such extralegal militias were breeding around the country. Militias are particularly angry about heavy-handed, violent federal responses to groups that have set themselves apart from American society, especially the 1992 FBI shootout with members of a white supremacist group at Ruby Ridge, Idaho, and the 1993 ATF confrontation with David Koresh's Branch Davidians in Waco, Texas. But even if armed confrontations between the government and such groups did not occur, many militias, especially in the western states, remain adamantly opposed to any governmental interference in their lives. American citizens, they believe, should be allowed to free themselves of the constraints of the federal government and return to the days of "rugged individualism." Their argument, however, overlooks the fact that much of the land that was supposedly settled by pioneering rugged individualists was given to the settlers at nominal prices by the federal government, that the railroads that took settlers west were built with federal subsidies, that the irrigation projects that made much of the land arable were constructed with federal funds, and that even the interstate highway system was built by the federal government. To be sure, only a very small minority of people want to return to a (mythical) simpler existence, but the fact that they have armed themselves in an effort to protect the Constitution has caused some concern—especially in the aftermath of the Oklahoma City bombing. Some observers claim that the militia ideology is just a smokescreen for racism and that their objection to the federal government derives more from their perception that the government, through welfare legislation and entitlements, favors minorities, primarily African Americans.

The "Statement of Purpose" and "In Defense of Liberty II" are posted on the Michigan Militia Web site. What is the purpose of the militia? Is it realistic for them to expect that, like the minutemen of Lexington and Concord, they would be able to resist the invasion of a foreign power? What foreign power are they preparing to fight?

Statement of Purpose and Mission, 1995

As it becomes increasingly obvious that the Constitution of the State of Michigan and the Constitution of the United States are being ignored, violated, and trampled on, we find it necessary to establish the Southern Michigan Regional Militia.

It shall be the sworn duty of this Militia to protect, defend, support, uphold and obey the Constitutions of the State of Michigan and the United States of America. Notice is hereby given that violations of either the State or National Constitution, by any alliance, nation, power, state, organization, agency, office, or individual shall be met with a fierce and determined resistance.

It shall also be the duty of this Militia to provide each member with a thorough working knowledge of Constitutional rights and a good understanding of State, Local, and Federal Government. The Militia shall at all times assist members who wish to contact their elected representatives. The command staff of the brigade shall inform the unit of any pending legislative action that may be of concern to the Militia.

SOURCE: Retrieved on 8/20/2003 from www.michiganmilitia.com/literature/in_defense _of_liberty.htm

It shall also be the duty of the Militia to continually strive for a high state of preparedness for a number of situations that may arise. These situations include, but are not limited to: invasion by a foreign power, invasion by foreign soldiers under multinational command, suspension of Constitutional rule, natural and man-made disasters, support of Constitutionally legitimate State and Local Government agencies, search and rescue situations, and any other number of emergencies.

The Militia shall, at all times, act with the highest standards of decency and honor.

In Defense of Liberty II, 1995

The concept of "In Defense of Liberty" was originated by Dave Franey in response to the Oklahoma City bombing. This updated edition has been put together on account of the changes that have occurred over the years. We have not softened any of the questions; they are presented in the same manner in which they were asked. We hope this will assist you in understanding a little more about the militia, and what we represent. Many thanks to all the dedicated patriots who helped!

1. What is the militia?
The militia is: all able-bodied citizens who are capable of bearing arms; the absolute last line of defense against any threat to the State or Country, whether that threat is natural or man made, foreign or domestic.

Our motivation is patriotism and a sincere desire to defend the Constitution. Our goal is to encourage all citizens to achieve a high level of preparedness for a wide variety of possible emergencies.

We support a Constitutionally limited government and defend the American ideals of Life, Liberty and the pursuit of Happiness. We are open to all citizens regardless of race, sex, religion, or political affiliation. Groups not open to public membership and/or which are organized for any other purposes are not militias. The militia, as an organization, has no religious theme; is not racial in nature; nor does it advocate terrorism or violence.

2. Why would you want to join an extremist organization like the militia?
The militia as an organization, represents beliefs in: the inalienable right to keep and bear arms; the American ideals of Life, Liberty, and the pursuit of Happiness; freedom and love of country. If being a patriot has become so unfashionable with the general populace as to be considered extreme, then so be it. We joined because these qualities, whether popular or not, are honorable.

3. Is militia activity legal?
Yes, we all have the inalienable rights of self-defense; to keep and bear arms; freedom of speech; and to peaceably assemble. These cover the majority of militia activities. The Constitution of the United States prohibits government, at any level, from interfering or infringing on these rights. Additionally, the Geneva Convention, Hague Protocols, International Law, Laws of Land Warfare, as well as Michigan State Law and Federal Law, all specifically provide for citizen militias, with or without state recognition.

4. Is the government going to target me if I join the militia?

If you are asking this question there is obviously something enormously wrong; it places emphasis on the fact that people are fearful of government reprisal for engaging in legal activities. Law-abiding American citizens participating in legal activities are afraid of their government! Unfortunately, we cannot answer this question for you, we can only speculate. You will have to ask the government, as we do not speak for them. However, the fear behind this question should compel you to at least look into the patriot movement. . . .

6. Are you racists?

No, we welcome Americans of all races, cultures, and beliefs; we gain nothing from turning anyone away, regardless of the hue of their skin. We do not side ourselves with, advocate, or discriminate against any one particular race or culture; the militia is as diverse as the general population.

There are, however, individuals or groups that claim to be militias that say they are of a superior race fighting the "great race war . . . to annihilate the mud people". These individuals or groups are not militias—they are racists.

7. Are you militant?

No, the nature and purpose of a citizen militia is defensive and concerns itself with the preservation of Life, Liberty and the pursuit of Happiness. We may be regarded as serious and ever vigilant, but we are not militant.

However, there are individuals or groups that claim to be militias that are determined to be engaged in combat and are aggressively active. These individuals or groups are not militias—they are militant. . . .

9. The members of the Army, Navy, Air Force, Marines, Coast Guard and the state and local police are all sworn to protect and uphold the Constitution. Why do we need militias or even armed citizens?

As Americans, it is "everyone's" responsibility to uphold and defend the Constitution; this is a requirement of a free people.

The militia is needed as the absolute last line of defense against any threat, whether natural or man-made, foreign or domestic; it is everyone's responsibility to be prepared to protect and defend state and country.

As to the need for armed citizens, as a human being you have the right to live for your own sake, and while living, you are responsible for defending the life of you and yours.

It is irresponsible, unwise, cowardly, and just plain un-American to deny these responsibilities. "If a people expect to be ignorant and free, they expect what never was and never will be."

10. Are you terrorists?

No, the militia does not advocate terrorism or violence. Only lunatics, including those in government, destroy buildings full of men, women, and children. The militia is a dedicated group of citizen patriots who volunteer their time and energy to further the cause of freedom. The only thing we blow to pieces are bowling pins; and if we are ever attacked by them, we will win! (Bowling pins are commonly used for target practice at militia training.)

11. What good does the militia do? What is your contribution to society?
The militia fulfills a long established American tradition as the ultimate and final guarantor of freedom; it establishes that as a free people we are ready, willing and able to defend our lives and country.

We hold informative monthly meetings, update those in attendance on topics such as: pending legislation, civic activities, current events, safety bulletins; and we offer training opportunities in the areas of: weapons safety, CPR, first aid, land navigation, and other useful field techniques. We strongly encourage everyone to vote and become involved in the safeguarding of rights within their local communities. We believe that the educated, responsible citizen is the best possible guarantee of all our freedoms. . . .

Theodore Kaczynski (1942–)

Harvard graduate Theodore Kaczynski, better known as the Unabomber, was a brilliant mathematician who, after teaching briefly at the University of California at Berkeley, left academia in 1971 and began his reclusive life in Montana. Kaczynski can be viewed as a twentieth-century Luddite, but instead of breaking factory machines, as did the eighteenth-century British Luddites opposing the industrial revolution, he began mailing letter bombs to universities and research laboratories. In 1978 he sent off his first letter bomb (to a professor at the University of Chicago), which, when it was opened, injured a police officer. For the next 18 years, he sent more sophisticated, more lethal bombs to academics who specialized in technological subjects at universities and to research and development people at high-tech companies. The FBI doggedly pursued him without much success. The break came when he insisted that his "Manifesto" denouncing technology and progress be published in several mainstream newspapers (like the *New York Times*). When his younger brother read the manifesto, he immediately recognized the style and phrasing, as well as many of the ideas, as his brother's. He tipped off the FBI, and in 1996 Kaczynski was arrested in his cabin in the Montana woods.

Here are a few passages from his long, rambling manifesto, along with an excerpt from an interview Kaczynski gave to a reporter from *Earth First! Journal*. Why are industrialization and technology a "disaster for the human race"? Are these the ravings of a lunatic or the sober reflections of a scientific intellect concerned with the fate of humanity? Why would he resort to violence?

The Unabomber Manifesto, 1996

INTRODUCTION

1. The Industrial Revolution and its consequences have been a disaster for the human race. They have greatly increased the life-expectancy of those of us who live in "advanced" countries, but they have destabilized society, have made life unfulfilling, have subjected human beings to indignities, have led to widespread psychological suffering (in the Third World to physical suffering as well) and have inflicted severe damage on the natural world. The continued development of technology will worsen the situation. It will certainly subject human beings to greater indignities and inflict greater damage on the natural world, it will probably lead to greater social disruption and psychological suffering, and it may lead to increased physical suffering even in "advanced" countries.

2. The industrial-technological system may survive or it may break down. If it survives, it MAY eventually achieve a low level of physical and psychological suffering, but only after passing through a long and very painful period of adjustment and only at the cost of permanently reducing human beings and many other living organisms to engineered products and mere cogs in the social machine. Furthermore, if the system survives, the consequences will be inevitable: There is no way of reforming or modifying the system so as to prevent it from depriving people of dignity and autonomy.

3. If the system breaks down the consequences will still be very painful. But the bigger the system grows the more disastrous the results of its breakdown will be, so if it is to break down it had best break down sooner rather than later.

4. We therefore advocate a revolution against the industrial system. This revolution may or may not make use of violence: it may be sudden or it may be a relatively gradual process spanning a few decades. We can't predict any of that. But we do outline in a very general way the measures that those who hate the industrial system should take in order to prepare the way for a revolution against that form of society. This is not to be a POLITICAL revolution. Its object will be to overthrow not governments but the economic and technological basis of the present society.

5. In this article we give attention to only some of the negative developments that have grown out of the industrial-technological system. Other such developments we mention only briefly or ignore altogether. This does not mean that we regard these other developments as unimportant. For practical reasons we have to confine our discussion to areas that have received insufficient public attention or in which we have something new to say. For example, since there are well developed environmental and wilderness movements, we have written very little about environmental degradation or the destruction of wild nature, even though we consider these to be highly important. . . .

207. An argument likely to be raised against our proposed revolution is that it is bound to fail, because (it is claimed) throughout history technology has always progressed, never regressed, hence technological regression is impossible. But this claim is false.

208. We distinguish between two kinds of technology, which we will call small-scale technology and organization-dependent technology. Small-scale technology is

SOURCE: Retrieved on 8/11/2003 from www.panix.com/~clays/Una/

technology that can be used by small-scale communities without outside assistance. Organization-dependent technology is technology that depends on large-scale social organization. We are aware of no significant cases of regression in small-scale technology. But organization-dependent technology DOES regress when the social organization on which it depends breaks down. Example: When the Roman Empire fell apart the Romans' small-scale technology survived because any clever village craftsman could build, for instance, a water wheel, any skilled smith could make steel by Roman methods, and so forth. But the Romans' organization-dependent technology DID regress. Their aqueducts fell into disrepair and were never rebuilt. Their techniques of road construction were lost. The Roman system of urban sanitation was forgotten, so that until rather recent times did the sanitation of European cities equal that of Ancient Rome.

209. The reason why technology has seemed always to progress is that, until perhaps a century or two before the Industrial Revolution, most technology was small-scale technology. But most of the technology developed since the Industrial Revolution is organization-dependent technology. Take the refrigerator for example. Without factory-made parts or the facilities of a post-industrial machine shop it would be virtually impossible for a handful of local craftsmen to build a refrigerator. If by some miracle they did succeed in building one it would be useless to them without a reliable source of electric power. So they would have to dam a stream and build a generator. Generators require large amounts of copper wire. Imagine trying to make that wire without modern machinery. And where would they get a gas suitable for refrigeration? It would be much easier to build an icehouse or preserve food by drying or picking, as was done before the invention of the refrigerator.

210. So it is clear that if the industrial system were once thoroughly broken down, refrigeration technology would quickly be lost. The same is true of other organization-dependent technology. And once this technology had been lost for a generation or so it would take centuries to rebuild it, just as it took centuries to build it the first time around. Surviving technical books would be few and scattered. An industrial society, if built from scratch without outside help, can only be built in a series of stages: You need tools to make tools to make tools to make tools. . . . A long process of economic development and progress in social organization is required. And, even in the absence of an ideology opposed to technology, there is no reason to believe that anyone would be interested in rebuilding industrial society. The enthusiasm for "progress" is a phenomenon particular to the modern form of society, and it seems not to have existed prior to the 17th century or thereabouts. . . .

Interview with Theodore Kaczynski, June 1999

TK: . . . I read Edward Abbey in mid-eighties and that was one of the things that gave me the idea that, 'yeah, there are other people out there that have the same attitudes that I do.' I read *The Monkey Wrench Gang*, I think it was. But what first

SOURCE: Dr. Theodore Kaczynski, in an interview with the *Earth First! Journal*, Administrative Maximum Facility Prison, Florence, Colorado, USA, June 1999. Retrieved on 5/10/2004 from http://www.primitivism.com/Kaczynski.htm. Also see www.earthfirstjournal. org.

motivated me wasn't anything I read. I just got mad seeing the machines ripping up the woods and so forth. . . .

EF: Why, I asked, did he personally come to be against technology? His immediate response was,

TK: Why do you think? It reduces people to gears in a machine, it takes away our autonomy and our freedom. . . . The honest truth is that I am not really politically oriented. I would have really rather just be living out in the woods. If nobody had started cutting roads through there and cutting the trees down and come buzzing around in helicopters and snowmobiles I would still just be living there and the rest of the world could just take care of itself. I got involved in political issues because I was driven to it, so to speak. I'm not really inclined in that direction. . . .

Unquestionably there is no doubt that the reason I dropped out of the technological system is because I had read about other ways of life, in particular that of primitive peoples. When I was about eleven I remember going to the little local library in Evergreen Park, Illinois. They had a series of books published by the Smithsonian Institute that addressed various areas of science. Among other things, I read about anthropology in a book on human prehistory. I found it fascinating. After reading a few more books on the subject of Neanderthal man and so forth, I had this itch to read more. I started asking myself why and I came to the realization that what I really wanted was not to read another book, but that I just wanted to live that way. . . .

I don't think it [fixing the system] can be done. In part because of the human tendency, for most people, there are exceptions, to take the path of least resistance. They'll take the easy way out, and giving up your car, your television set, your electricity, is not the path of least resistance for most people. As I see it, I don't think there is any controlled or planned way in which we can dismantle the industrial system. I think that the only way we will get rid of it is if it breaks down and collapses. That's why I think the consequences will be something like the Russian Revolution, or circumstances like we see in other places in the world today like the Balkans, Afghanistan, Rwanda. This does, I think, pose a dilemma for radicals who take a non-violent point of view. When things break down, there is going to be violence and this does raise a question, I don't know if I exactly want to call it a moral question, but the point is that for those who realize the need to do away with the techno-industrial system, if you work for its collapse, in effect you are killing a lot of people. If it collapses, there is going to be social disorder, there is going to be starvation, there aren't going to be any more spare parts or fuel for farm equipment, there won't be any more pesticide or fertilizer on which modern agriculture is dependent. So there isn't going to be enough food to go around, so then what happens? This is something that, as far as I've read, I haven't seen any radicals facing up to. . . .

The big problem is that people don't believe a revolution is possible, and it is not possible precisely because they do not believe it is possible. To a large extent I think the eco-anarchist movement is accomplishing a great deal, but I think they could do it better. . . . The real revolutionaries should separate themselves from the reformers. . . . And I think that it would be good if a conscious effort was being made to get as many people as possible introduced to the wilderness. In a general way, I think what has to be done is not to try and convince or persuade the majority of people that we are right, as much as try to increase tensions in society to the point where things start to break down. To create a situation where people get uncomfortable enough that they're going to rebel. So the question is how do you increase those tensions? I don't know. . . .

Protest Music III

By the mid-1970s, the innovative and political aspect of popular music had succumbed to commercialism. Songs were losing their power. With the Vietnam War coming to an end, songwriters were no longer writing antiwar songs. Disco came on the scene, and rock and roll seemed stale. Punk and later grunge were efforts to inject some life into music, but the jaded messages that were being put across lacked the passion and freshness of earlier protest music. African American rap music and hip hop brought more fervor and excitement in its lyrical condemnation of life in a racist society and has recently begun to take on broader issues. This is most notably seen in Mos Def's "New World Water," which departs from the racial theme and touches on the issues of globalization and the "new world order."

By the 1990s, Dead Prez, The Roots, Talib Kweli, Common, Rage Against the Machine, Mos Def, The Coup, and Public Enemy were just a few of the artists who churned out scores of protest songs that made no attempt whatsoever at subtlety.

According to these performers, what are the biggest problems facing the United States at the end of the twentieth century? What role does economics play in these problems? What role does race play? Can songs with such merciless and raw lyrics be effective in convincing people of the validity of a cause?

"Know Your Enemy"

> *Huh*
> *Yeah, we're comin' back then with another bombtrack*
> *Think ya know what it's all about*
> *Huh*
> *Hey yo, so check this out*

Source: Rage Against the Machine, *Rage Against the Machine*, Sony Records 1992.

Yeah
Know your enemy

Come on

Born with insight and a raised fist
A witness to the slit wrist, that's with
As we move into '92
Still in a room without a view
Ya got to know
Ya got to know
That when I say go, go, go
Amp up and amplify
Defy
I'm a brother with a furious mind
Action must be taken
We don't need the key
We'll break in

Something must be done
About vengeance, a badge and a gun
'Cause I'll rip the mike, rip the stage, rip the system
I was born to rage against 'em

Fist in ya face, in the place
And I'll drop the style clearly
Know your enemy . . . Know your enemy

Yeah

Hey yo, and dick with this . . . uggh
Word is born
Fight the war, fuck the norm
Now I got no patience
So sick of complacence
With the D the E the F the I the A the N the C the E
Mind of a revolutionary
So clear the lane
The finger to the land of the chains
What? The land of the free?
Whoever told you that is your enemy?

Now something must be done
About vengeance, a badge and a gun
'Cause I'll rip the mike, rip the stage, rip the system
I was born to rage against 'em

Now action must be taken
We don't need the key
We'll break in

I've got no patience now
So sick of complacence now
I've got no patience now
So sick of complacence now
Sick of sick of sick of sick of you
Time has come to pay . . .
Know your enemy

Come on
Yes I know my enemies
They're the teachers who taught me to fight me
Compromise, conformity, assimilation, submission
Ignorance, hypocrisy, brutality, the elite
All of which are American dreams

"Mathematics"

[Mos Def]
Booka booka booka booka booka booka
Ha hah
You know the deal
It's just me yo
Beats by Su Primo for all of my peoples negroes and latinos
and even the gringos

Yo check it one for Charlie Hustle two for Steady Rock
Three for the fourth comin live future shock
It's five dimensions six senses
Seven firmaments of heaven to hell 8 Million Stories to tell
Nine planets faithfully keep in orbit
with the probable tenth, the universe expands length
The body of my text posess extra strength
Power-liftin powerless up, out of this, towerin inferno
My ink so hot it burn through the journal
I'm blacker than midnight on Broadway and Myrtle
Hip-Hop past all your tall social hurdles
like the nationwide projects, prison-industry complex
Broken glass wall better keep your alarm set
Streets too loud to ever hear freedom sing
Say evacuate your sleep, it's dangerous to dream
but you chain cats get they CHA-POW, who dead now
Killin fields need blood to graze the cash cow

Source: Mos Def, *Black on Both Sides*, Priority Records 1999.

It's a number game, but shit don't add up somehow
Like I got, sixteen to thirty-two bars to rock it
but only 15% of profits, ever see my pockets like
sixty-nine billion in the last twenty years
spent on national defense but folks still live in fear like
nearly half of America's largest cities is one-quarter black
That's why they gave Ricky Ross all the crack
Sixteen ounces to a pound, twenty more to a ki
A five minute sentence hearing and you no longer free
40% of Americans own a cell phone
so they can hear, everything that you say when you ain't home
I guess, Michael Jackson was right, "You Are Not Alone"
Rock your hardhat black cause you in the Terrordome
full of hard niggaz, large niggaz, dice tumblers
Young teens and prison greens facin life numbers
Crack mothers, crack babies and AIDS patients
Young bloods can't spell but they could rock you in PlayStation
This new math is whippin motherfuckers ass
You wanna know how to rhyme you better learn how to add
It's mathematics

Chorus: scratched by DJ Premier (repeat 2X)

"The Mighty Mos Def.."
"It's simple mathematics" -> Fat Joe
"Check it out!"
"I revolve around science . . . "
"What are we talking about here?"

.. "Do your math" -> Erykah Badu (2X)..
.. "One.. t-t-two.. three, four" -> James Brown ..
.. "What are we talking about here?" ..

[Mos Def]
Yo, it's one universal law but two sides to every story
Three strikes and you be in for life, manditory
Four MC's murdered in the last four years
I ain't tryin to be the fifth one, the millennium is here
Yo it's 6 Million Ways to Die, from the seven deadly thrills
Eight heroes gettin found with 9 mill's
It's 10 P.M., where your seeds at? What's the deal
He on the hill puffin krill to keep they belly filled
Light in the ass with heavy steel, sights on the pretty shit in life
Young soldiers tryin to earn they next stripe
When the average minimum wage is $5.15
You best believe you gotta find a new ground to get cream
The white unemployment rate, is nearly more than triple for black

so frontliners got they gun in your back
Bubblin crack, jewel theft and robbery to combat poverty
and end up in the global jail economy
Stiffer stipulations attached to each sentence
Budget cutbacks but increased police presence
And even if you get out of prison still livin
join the other five million under state supervision
This is business, no faces just lines and statistics
from your phone, your zip code, to S-S-I digits
The system break man child and women into figures
Two columns for who is, and who ain't niggaz
Numbers is hardly real and they never have feelings
but you push too hard, even numbers got limits
Why did one straw break the camel's back? Here's the secret:
the million other straws underneath it—it's all mathematics

Chorus
{closing scratch} "Mathematics."

"New World Water"

[Mos Def]
There's nothing more refreshing (that cool refreshing drink)
Than a cool crisp clean glass of water
On a warm summer's day (That cool refreshing drink)
Try it with your friends

New World Water make the tide rise high
Come in and it'll make your house go "Bye" (My house!)
Fools done upset the Old Man River
Made him carry slave ships and fed him dead nigga
Now his belly full and he about to flood somethin
So I'ma throw a rope that ain't tied to nothin
til your crew use the H2 in wise amounts since
it's the New World Water; and every drop counts
You can laugh and take it as a joke if you wanna
But it don't rain for four weeks some summers
And it's about to get real wild in the half
You be buying Evian just to take a fuckin bath
Heads is acting wild, sippin poor, puffin dank
Competin with the next man, but how your playa rank?
See I ain't got time try to be Big Hank,
Fuck a bank; I need a twenty-year water tank

Source: Mos Def, *Black on Both Sides*, Priority Records 1999.

Cause while these knuckleheads is out here sweatin they goods
The sun is sitting in the treetops burnin the woods
And as the flames from the blaze get higher and higher
They say, "Don't drink the water! We need it for the fire!"
New York is drinkin it (New World Water)
Now all of California is drinkin it (New World Water)
Way up north and down south is drinkin it (New World Water)
Used to have minerals and zinc in it (New World Water)
Now they say it got lead and stink in it (New World Water)
Four carbons and monoxide
Push the water table lopside
Used to be free now it cost you a fee
Cause all things fully loaded they roam cross the sea
Man, you gotta cook with it, bathe and clean with it (That's right)
When it's hot, summertime you fiend for it (Let em know)
You gotta put it in the iron you steamin with (That's right)
It's what they dress wounds and treat diseases with (Shout it out)
The rich and poor, black and white got need for it (That's right)
And everybody in the world can agree with this (Let em know)
Assumption promotes health and easiness (That's right)
Go too long without it on this earth and you leavin it (Shout it out)
Americans wastin it on some leisure shit (Say word?)
And other nations be desperately seekin it (Let em know)
Bacteria washing up on they beaches (Say word?)
Don't drink the water, son they can't wash they feet with it (Let em know)
Young babies and professional neediness (Say word?)
Epidemics hoppin up off the petri dish (Let em know)
Control centers try to play it all secretive (Say word?)
To avoid public panic and freakiness (Let em know)
There are places where TB is common as TV
Cause foreign-based companies go and get greedy
The type of cats who pollute the whole shore line
Have it purified, sell it for a dollar twenty-five
Now the world is drinkin it
Your moms, wife, and baby girl is drinkin it
Up north and down south is drinkin it
You just have to go to your sink for it
The cash registers is goin to chink for it
Four carbons and monoxide
Got the fish lookin cockeyed
Used to be free now it cost you a fee
Cause it's all about gettin that cash (Money)

Said it's all about gettin that cash (Money) (x9)
Johny cash (Money)
Roseland cash (Money)

Give me cash (Money)
Cold cash (Money)
(Repeat to fade)

Cash rules everything around me,
Move!

"Son of a Bush"

oh no
struck by greased lightning
F'd by the same last name, you know what?
China ain't never givin back that gottdamn plane
must got this ol nation trained
on some kennel ration
refrain
the same train
fulla cocaine
froze the brain
have you forgotten
i been thru the first term of rotten
the father, the son
and the holy Bush-it we all in
dont look at me
i aint callin for no assassination
im just sayin who voted for this asshole of the nation

deja Bush
crushed by the head rush
15 years back
when i wrote the first bum rush
saw you salute
to the then
vice prez
who did what Raygun said
and then became prez
himself went for delf
knee deep in his damn self
stuck in a 3 headed bucket
of trilateral Bush-it
sorry ain't no better way of puttin it
no you cannot freestyle this

Source: Public Enemy, *Revolverlution*, Koch Records 2002.

cause yo ass still ain't free
if fight for yall
and they get me
how many of yall is comin to get me?
none
cause its easier to forget me

ain't that a Bush
son of a Bush is here
all up in your zone
you aint never heard so much soul to the bone
i told y'all when the first Bush was tappin my phone
spy vs spy
can't truss em
as you salute to the Illuminati
take your ass to your 1 millionth party
now here's the pitch
high and inside
certified genocide
ain't that a Bush repeat ain't that a Bush
out of nowhere
headed to the hothouse?
killed 135 at the last count . . . Texas bounce
cats in the cage
got a ghost of a chance
of comin back
from your whack ass killin machine

son of a Bush ain't that a son of a Bush
cats doin bids
for doin the same Bush shit that you did
serial killer kid uh serial killer kid
Coke its the real thing
used to make you swing
used to be your thing
daddy had you under his wing
bringin kilos to fill up silos
you probably sniffed piles
got inmates in Texas scrubbin tiles
that shit is wild
CIA child
that shit is wild
CIA child

Ralph Nader (1934–)

In the year 2000, the Green Party nominated Ralph Nader for president. Nader and his followers believed that the Democratic and Republican parties no longer responded to the needs of the people, but instead only answered to corporate interests that were the single biggest threat to American democracy. The United States, as Nader often put it, was a government "of the Exxons, by the General Motors and for the DuPonts." In 1965 his book *Unsafe at Any Speed* took on General Motors and launched the Princeton- and Harvard-educated lawyer's long career as the nation's leading consumer advocate. Nader's book detailed how the quest for profit led to faulty automobile design, especially in GM's Corvair, which frequently had lethal results. Like Upton Sinclair's *The Jungle*, which swayed Congress to pass the Pure Food and Drug Act 60 years earlier, the uproar over the book resulted in the passage of the Traffic and Motor Vehicle Safety Act, shifting the power to determine motor vehicle safety from the automobile manufacturers to the federal government. Over the subsequent decades, Nader and the activist attorneys he employed, Nader's Raiders, put pressure on the government to pass protective legislation and create several watchdog agencies: the Environmental Protection Agency, the Occupational Safety and Health Administration, the Consumer Product Safety Commission, and others. However, in the 1980s, President Reagan cut the funding for many of these regulatory agencies, and as a result corporations had more leeway to exploit the environment and workers. Profits soared, the gap between the rich and the poor widened, and Nader found much of what he had worked for slipping away.

In the 1990s, Nader shifted his focus away from congressional regulation to the growing issue of globalization, which he believed was endangering democracy by concentrating wealth and power in the hands of a few multinational corporations. When the Clinton administration sponsored the North Atlantic Free Trade Agreement (NAFTA), creating a free-trade zone linking the United States with Canada and Mexico, and the General Agreement on Tariffs and Trade (GATT), establishing the World Trade Organization, Nader became convinced that the Democrats were just as much a tool of big business as the Republicans and that therefore the time had come to create a third party that would look after the interests of the people. He ran for president in 1996 and again in 2000, but never got more than 2.7 percent of the popular vote. The impact in 2000, however, had long-range consequences that are still unfolding. Because many of Nader's supporters were disillusioned Democrats, the Greens drew enough votes away from Al Gore in Florida that George W. Bush wound up winning the election, even though Gore had won the popular vote nationally. Many people therefore believed that the Green Party was culpable for the Republican victory.

The first document here is Nader's attack on "corporate welfare"; the second is the preamble and key values of the Green Party platform. What is the major threat that business poses for democracy? What solution do Nader and the Green Party offer? Are these ideas too far removed from the mainstream that the Greens could never hope to achieve electoral success? How does this platform compare with the 1892 Populist and the 1912 Socialist platforms? Which of the three is the most radical?

——————————

It's Time to End Corporate Welfare As We Know It, 1996

The issue of concentration of power and the growing conflict between the civil society and the corporate society is not a conflict that you read about or see on television. So unfortunately, most of us grow up corporate; we don't grow up civic.

If I utter the following words, what images come to mind: crime, violence, welfare and addictors? What comes to mind is street crime; people lining up to get their welfare checks; violence in the streets; and drug dealers—the addictors.

And yet, by any yardstick, there is far more crime, and far more violence, and far more welfare disbursement (and there are far more addictors) in the corporate world than in the impoverished street arena. The federal government's corporate welfare programs number over 120. They are so varied and embedded that we actually grow up thinking that the government interferes with the free enterprise system, rather than subsidizing it.

It's hard to find a major industry today whose principal investments were not first made by the government—in aerospace, telecommunications, biotechnology and agribusiness. Government research and development money funds the drug and pharmaceutical industry. Government research and development funds are given freely to corporations, but they don't announce it in ads the next day.

Corporate welfare has never been viewed as debilitating. Nobody talks about imposing workfare requirements on corporate welfare recipients or putting them on a program of "two years and you're out." Nobody talks about aid to dependent corporations. It's all talked about in terms of "incentives."

At the local community level, in cities that can't even refurbish their crumbling schools—where children are without enough desks or books—local governments are anteing up three, four, five hundred million dollars to lure very profitable baseball, football and basketball sports moguls who don't want to share the profits. Corporate sports are being subsidized by cities.

Corporations have perfected socializing their losses while they capitalize on their profits. There was the savings-and-loan debacle—and you'll be paying for that until the year 2020. In terms of principal and interest, it was a half-trillion-dollar bailout of 1,000 savings-and-loans banks. Their executives looted, speculated and defrauded people of their savings—and then turned to Washington for a bailout.

Foreign and domestic corporations can go on our land out West. If they discover gold, they can buy the acreage over the gold for no more than $5 an acre. That's been the going rate since the Mining Act of 1872 was enacted. That is taking inflation-fighting too far.

——————————

SOURCE: Ralph Nader, *The Ralph Nader Reader* (New York: Seven Stories Press, 2000), 154–158.

There's new drug called Taxol to fight ovarian cancer. That drug was produced by a grant of $31 million of taxpayer money through the National Institutes of Health, right through the clinical testing process. The formula was then given away to the Bristol-Myers Squibb company. No royalties were paid to the taxpayer. There was no restraint on the price. Charges now run $10,000 to $15,000 per patient for a series of treatments. If the patients can't pay, they go on Medicaid, and the taxpayer pays at the other end of the cycle, too.

Yet what is the big issue in this country and in Washington when the word "welfare" is spoken? It is the $300 monthly check given a welfare mother, most of which is spent immediately in the consumer economy. But federal corporate welfare is far bigger in dollars. At the federal, state and local levels there is no comparison between the corporate welfare and poverty welfare programs.

We have 179 law schools and probably only 15 of them (and only recently) offer a single course or seminar on corporate crime. You think that's an accident? Law school curricula are pretty much shaped by the job market, and if the job market has slots in commercial law, bankruptcy law, securities and exchange law, tax law or estate planning law, the law schools will oblige with courses and seminars.

One professor studying corporate crime believes that it costs the country $200 billion a year. And yet you don't see many congressional hearings on corporate crime. You see very few newspapers focusing on corporate crime. Yet 50,000 lives a year are lost due to air pollution, 100,000 are lost due to toxics and trauma in the workplace, and 420,000 lives are lost due to tobacco smoking. The corporate addictor has a very important role here, since it has been shown in recent months that the tobacco companies try to hook youngsters into a lifetime of smoking from age 10 to 15.

When you grow up corporate, you don't learn about the reality of corporate welfare. The programs that shovel huge amounts of taxpayer dollars to corporations through inflated government contracts via the Pentagon, or through subsidies, loan guarantees, giveaways and a variety of clever transfers of taxpayer assets get very little attention.

We grow up never learning what we own together, as a commonwealth. If somebody asks you what you and your parents own, you'd say: homes, cars and artifacts. Most of you would not say that you are owners of the one-third of America that is public land or that you are part owners of the public airwaves.

When you ask students today who owns the public airwaves you get the same reply—"the networks," or maybe "the government." We own the public airwaves and the Federal Communications Commission is our real estate agent. The radio and TV stations are the tenants who are given licenses to dominate their part of the spectrum 24 hours a day, and for four hours a day they decide who says what.

You pay more for your auto license than the biggest TV station pays for its broadcast license. But if you, the landlord, want in on its property, the radio and TV stations say, "Sorry, you're not going to come in." These companies say they've got to air trash TV—sensual TV, home shopping and rerun movies.

We have the greatest communications system in the world and we have the most demeaning subject matter and the most curtailed airing of public voices (known in the trade as the "sound bite"). The sound bite is down to about five seconds now.

You and your parents also may be part owners of $4 trillion in pension funds invested in corporations. The reason this doesn't get much attention is that although we own it, corporations control it. Corporations, banks and insurance companies invest our pension money. Workers have no voting mechanism regarding this money. If they did, they'd have a tremendous influence over corporations that have major pension trust investments.

Not controlling what we own should be a public issue, because if we begin to develop control of what we own, we will marshal vast existing assets that are legally ours for the betterment of our society. That will not happen unless we talk about why people don't control what they own.

All of the reforms require a rearrangement of how we spend our time. The women who launched the women's right-to-vote movement decided to spend time—in the face of incredible opposition. The people who fought to abolish slavery also decided to spend time. The workers who formed trade unions gave time.

Historically, how have we curbed corporate power? By child labor prohibition, by occupational health and safety rules, by motor vehicle standards and food and drug safety standards. But the regulatory agencies in these areas are now on their knees. Their budgets are very small—far less than 1 percent of the federal budget.

Their job is to put the federal cop on the corporate beat against the illegal dumping of toxics. But these laws do not get high compliance by corporations, and the application of regulatory law and order against corporate crime, fraud, abuse and violence is at its lowest ebb. I've never seen some of these agencies as weak as they are now. President Ronald Reagan started it and President George Bush extended it. And now we have "George Ronald Clinton" making the transition very easy.

The dismantling of democracy is perhaps now the most urgent aspect of the corporatization of our society. And notice, if you will, two pillars of our legal system—tort law and contract law.

The principle of tort law is that if you are wrongfully injured, you have a remedy against the perpetrator. That's well over 200 years old. And now, in state legislatures and in Congress, laws have been passed, or are about to be passed, that protect the perpetrators, the harm-doers—that immunize them from their liability.

When the physicians at the Harvard School of Public Health testify that about 80,000 people die in hospitals every year from medical malpractice—a total larger than the combined fatalities in motor vehicle accidents, homicides and death by fire each year in the U.S.—it raises the issue of why our elected representatives are vigorously trying to make it more difficult for victims of medical malpractice to have their day in court.

As in the Middle Ages, 1 percent of the richest people in this country own 90 percent of the wealth. The unemployment rate doesn't take into account the people who looked for a job for six months and gave up, and it doesn't take into account the underemployed who work 20 hours a week. Part of growing up corporate is that we let corporations develop the yardsticks by which we measure the economy's progress.

Democracy is the best mechanism ever devised to solve problems. That means the more we refine it—the more people practice it, the more people use its tools—the more likely it is we will not only solve our problems or at least diminish them, we also will foresee and forestall risk levels. When you see corporations dismantling democracy, you have to take it very seriously and turn it into a public political issue.

Among the five roles that we play, one is voter-citizen, another is taxpayer, another is worker, another is consumer and another is shareholder through worker pension trusts. These are critical roles in our political economy. Yet they have become weaker and weaker as the concentration of corporate power over our political and cultural and economic institutions has increased year by year.

We're supposed to have a government of, by and for the people. Instead we have a government of the Exxons, by the General Motors and for the DuPonts. We have a government that recognizes the rights and liabilities and privileges of corporations, which are artificial entities created by state charters, against the rights and privileges of ordinary people.

Jefferson warned us that the purpose of representative government is to counteract "the excesses of the monied interests"—then the merchant class; now the corporations. Beware of the government that doesn't do that.

Green Party Platform, 2000

PLATFORM PREAMBLE

As the new century dawns, we look back with somber reflection at how we have been as a people and as a nation. Realizing our actions will be judged by future generations, we ask how with foresight and wisdom, we can renew the best of our past, calling forth a spirit of change and participation that speaks for a free and democratic society.

We submit a bold vision of our future, a PLATFORM on which we stand:

An ethic of KEY VALUES leading to a POLITICS OF ACTION.
A hopeful, challenging plan for A PROSPERING, SUSTAINABLE ECONOMY.
A call to CREATE and CONSERVE a rich, DIVERSE environment characterized by
    a sense of COMMUNITY.

What we are proposing is a vision of our common good that goes beyond special interests and the business of politics.

What we are proposing is an INDEPENDENT POLITICS, a democratic vision that empowers and reaches beyond background and political loyalty to bring together our combined strengths as a people.

We, the GREEN PARTY, see our political and economic progress, and our individual lives, within the context of an evolving, challenging world.

As in nature, where adaptation and diversity provide key strategies of survival, a successful political strategy is one that is diverse, adaptable to changing needs, and strong and resilient in its core values:

Democracy, practiced most effectively at the grassroots level and in local communities.
SOCIAL JUSTICE and EQUAL OPPORTUNITY, emphasizing personal and social
    responsibility, accountability, and non-violence.
ENVIRONMENTAL and ECONOMIC SUSTAINABILITY, balancing the interests
    of market- and value-driven business, of the community and land, of living and
    future generations.

Source: Retrieved on 8/11/2003 from www.gp.org

Looking to the future with hope and optimism, we believe we can truly change history—that together we can make a real difference in the quality of our lives and environment. Our common destiny brings us together across our nation and around the globe. It is for us to choose how we will be remembered. It is for us to choose the future we are creating today.

GREEN KEY VALUES

1. Grassroots democracy: Every human being deserves a say in the decisions that affect their lives and not be subject to the will of another. Therefore, we will work to increase public participation at every level of government and to ensure that our public representatives are fully accountable to the people who elect them. We will also work to create new types of political organizations which expand the process of participatory democracy by directly including citizens in the decision-making process.

2. Social justice and equal opportunity: All persons should have the rights and opportunity to benefit equally from the resources afforded us by society and the environment. We must consciously confront in ourselves, our organizations, and society at large, barriers such as racism and class oppression, sexism and homophobia, ageism and disability, which act to deny fair treatment and equal justice under the law.

3. Ecological wisdom: Human societies must operate with the understanding that we are part of nature, not separate from nature.

We must maintain an ecological balance and live within the ecological and resource limits of our communities and our planet. We support a sustainable society which utilizes resources in such a way that future generations will benefit and not suffer from the practices of our generation. To this end we must practice agriculture which replenishes the soil; move to an energy efficient economy; and live in ways that respect the integrity of natural systems.

4. Non-violence:
It is essential that we develop effective alternatives to society's current patterns of violence. We will work to demilitarize, and eliminate weapons of mass destruction, without being naive about the intentions of other governments.

We recognize the need for self-defense and the defense of others who are in helpless situations. We promote non-violent methods to oppose practices and policies with which we disagree, and will guide our actions toward lasting personal, community and global peace.

5. Decentralization:
Centralization of wealth and power contributes to social and economic injustice, environmental destruction, and militarization. Therefore, we support a restructuring of social, political and economic institutions away from a system which is controlled by and mostly benefits the powerful few, to a democratic, less bureaucratic system. Decision-making should, as much as possible, remain at the individual and local level, while assuring that civil rights are protected for all citizens.

6. Community-based economics and economic justice: We recognize it is essential to create a vibrant and sustainable economic system, one that can create jobs and

provide a decent standard of living for all people while maintaining a healthy ecological balance. A successful economic system will offer meaningful work with dignity, while paying a "living wage" which reflects the real value of a person's work.

Local communities must look to economic development that assures protection of the environment and workers' rights; broad citizen participation in planning; and enhancement of our "quality of life." We support independently owned and operated companies which are socially responsible, as well as co-operatives and public enterprises that distribute resources and control to more people through democratic participation.

7. Feminism and gender equity: We have inherited a social system based on male domination of politics and economics. We call for the replacement of the cultural ethics of domination and control with more cooperative ways of interacting that respect differences of opinion and gender. Human values such as equity between the sexes, interpersonal responsibility, and honesty must be developed with moral conscience. We should remember that the process that determines our decisions and actions is just as important as achieving the outcome we want.

8. Respect for diversity: We believe it is important to value cultural, ethnic, racial, sexual, religious and spiritual diversity, and to promote the development of respectful relationships across these lines. We believe that the many diverse elements of society should be reflected in our organizations and decision-making bodies, and we support the leadership of people who have been traditionally closed out of leadership roles. We acknowledge and encourage respect for other life forms than our own and the preservation of biodiversity.

9. Personal and global responsibility: We encourage individuals to act to improve their personal well-being and, at the same time, to enhance ecological balance and social harmony. We seek to join with people and organizations around the world to foster peace, economic justice, and the health of the planet.

10. Future focus and sustainability: Our actions and policies should be motivated by long-term goals. We seek to protect valuable natural resources, safely disposing of or "unmaking" all waste we create, while developing a sustainable economics that does not depend on continual expansion for survival. We must counterbalance the drive for short-term profits by assuring that economic development, new technologies, and fiscal policies are responsible to future generations who will inherit the results of our actions.

QUALITY OF LIFE

Our overall goal is not merely to survive, but to share lives that are truly worth living. We believe the quality of our individual lives is enriched by the quality of all of our lives. We encourage everyone to see the dignity and intrinsic worth in all of life, and to take the time to understand and appreciate themselves, their community and the magnificent beauty of this world.

Ani DiFranco (1970–)

Ani DiFranco, self-described feminist, bisexual, and "righteous babe," is one of the most creative and electrifying voices on the contemporary singer-songwriter-poet scene. She has performed in numerous venues all over the world, from the Hudson River Clearwater Revival and Carnegie Hall in New York to the Fuji Rock Festival in Japan. Her recordings are all self-produced so that she can maintain complete autonomy over her work. In spite of not being signed by a major label (she has turned down offers), she has achieved astonishing success over the past decade. Her songs and poetry deal with feminist, political, and social issues.

Shortly after September 11, 2001, she posted the following poem on her Web site. Although she specifically blasts President George W. Bush, the poem is not merely a partisan anti-Republican diatribe. DiFranco, in looking for the cause of the September 11 terrorist attacks, lays blame on American energy policy and foreign policy in general, and therefore just as much of the culpability can be assigned to the Clinton administration as well as those of George H. W. Bush, Ronald Reagan, and every administration since the onset of the cold war.

What specific causes, according to DiFranco, lay behind the attacks? Does she give any indication of how we should handle the "war on terrorism"?

———————

"self evident," 2001

yes,
us people are just poems
we're 90% metaphor
with a leanness of meaning
approaching hyper-distillation
and once upon a time
we were moonshine
rushing down the throat of a giraffe
yes, rushing down the long hallway
despite what the p.a. announcement says
yes, rushing down the long stairs
with the whiskey of eternity
fermented and distilled

SOURCE: Retrieved   on   9/12/2002   from   www.righteousbabe.com/ani/l_self_evident. html.

to eighteen minutes
burning down our throats
down the hall
down the stairs
in a building so tall
that it will always be there
yes, it's part of a pair
there on the bow of noah's ark
the most prestigious couple
just kickin back parked
against a perfectly blue sky
on a morning beatific
in its indian summer breeze
on the day that america
fell to its knees
after strutting around for a century
without saying thank you
or please

and the shock was subsonic
and the smoke was deafening
between the setup and the punch line
cuz we were all on time for work that day
we all boarded that plane for to fly
and then while the fires were raging
we all climbed up on the windowsill
and then we all held hands
and jumped into the sky

and every borough looked up when it heard the first blast
and then every dumb action movie was summarily surpassed
and the exodus uptown by foot and motorcar
looked more like war than anything i've seen so far
so far
so far
so fierce and ingenious
a poetic specter so far gone
that every jackass newscaster was struck dumb and stumbling
over 'oh my god' and 'this is unbelievable' and on and on
and i'll tell you what, while we're at it
you can keep the pentagon
keep the propaganda
keep each and every tv
that's been trying to convince me
to participate
in some prep school punk's plan to perpetuate retribution
perpetuate retribution

even as the blue toxic smoke of our lesson in retribution
is still hanging in the air
and there's ash on our shoes
and there's ash in our hair
and there's a fine silt on every mantle
from hell's kitchen to brooklyn
and the streets are full of stories
sudden twists and near misses
and soon every open bar is crammed to the rafters
with tales of narrowly averted disasters
and the whiskey is flowin
like never before
as all over the country
folks just shake their heads
and pour

so here's a toast to all the folks who live in palestine
afghanistan
iraq

el salvador

here's a toast to the folks living on the pine ridge reservation
under the stone cold gaze of mt. rushmore

here's a toast to all those nurses and doctors
who daily provide women with a choice
who stand down a threat the size of oklahoma city
just to listen to a young woman's voice

here's a toast to all the folks on death row right now
awaiting the executioner's guillotine
who are shackled there with dread and can only escape into their heads
to find peace in the form of a dream

cuz take away our playstations
and we are a third world nation
under the thumb of some blue blood royal son
who stole the oval office and that phony election
i mean
it don't take a weatherman
to look around and see the weather
jeb said he'd deliver florida, folks
and boy did he ever

and we hold these truths to be self evident:
#1 george w. bush is not president
#2 america is not a true democracy
#3 the media is not fooling me

cuz i am a poem heeding hyper-distillation
i've got no room for a lie so verbose
i'm looking out over my whole human family
and i'm raising my glass in a toast
here's to our last drink of fossil fuels
let us vow to get off of this sauce
shoo away the swarms of commuter planes
and find that train ticket we lost
cuz once upon a time the line followed the river
and peeked into all the backyards
and the laundry was waving
the graffiti was teasing us
from brick walls and bridges
we were rolling over ridges
through valleys
under stars
i dream of touring like duke ellington
in my own railroad car
i dream of waiting on the tall blonde wooden benches
in a grand station aglow with grace
and then standing out on the platform
and feeling the air on my face

give back the night its distant whistle
give the darkness back its soul
give the big oil companies the finger finally
and relearn how to rock-n-roll
yes, the lessons are all around us and a change is waiting there
so it's time to pick through the rubble, clean the streets
and clear the air
get our government to pull its big dick out of the sand
of someone else's desert
put it back in its pants
and quit the hypocritical chants of
freedom forever

cuz when one lone phone rang
in two thousand and one
at ten after nine
on nine one one
which is the number we all called
when that lone phone rang right off the wall
right off our desk and down the long hall
down the long stairs
in a building so tall
that the whole world turned
just to watch it fall

and while we're at it
remember the first time around?
the bomb?
the ryder truck?
the parking garage?
the princess that didn't even feel the pea?
remember joking around in our apartment on avenue D?

can you imagine how many paper coffee cups would have to change their design
following a fantastical reversal of the new york skyline?!

it was a joke, of course
it was a joke
at the time
and that was just a few years ago
so let the record show
that the FBI was all over that case
that the plot was obvious and in everybody's face
and scoping that scene
religiously
the CIA
or is it KGB?
committing countless crimes against humanity
with this kind of eventuality
as its excuse
for abuse after expensive abuse
and it didn't have a clue
look, another window to see through
way up here
on the 104th floor
look
another key
another door
10% literal
90% metaphor
3000 some poems disguised as people
on an almost too perfect day
should be more than pawns
in some asshole's passion play
so now it's your job
and it's my job
to make it that way
to make sure they didn't die in vain
sshhhhhh. . . .
baby listen
hear the train?

Amnesty International

As would be expected in the aftermath of the September 11 terrorist attacks, many people were detained and questioned. Amnesty International (AI), founded in London in 1961, is an international organization that investigates alleged human rights abuses around the globe. In the weeks and months following the attacks, AI received testimony from many sources that rights abuses were occurring in the United States. AI issued a report, which is here excerpted.

Where do the need for security and the need to secure rights come into conflict? What rights, if any, need to be temporarily suspended to ensure the nation's safety?

Amnesty International's Concerns Regarding Post–September 11 Detentions in the U.S.

. . . In the two months following the September 11 attacks on the World Trade Center and Pentagon, more than 1,200 non-U.S. nationals were taken into custody in the USA, in nationwide sweeps for possible suspects. Partial data released by the government last November revealed that most were men of Arab or South Asian origin detained for immigration violations. Another 100 or so were charged with criminal offences, none directly relating to the events of 11 September.

Six months on, some 300 people arrested in the post September 11 (post 9.11) sweeps are believed to remain in the custody of the Immigration and Naturalization Service (INS); an unknown number of others have been deported or released on bail, sometimes after months in custody. . . .

There continues to be a disturbing level of secrecy surrounding the detentions, which has made it difficult to monitor the situation. To date, the government has provided only limited data, which includes neither the names nor the places of detention of those held in post 9.11 INS custody, and immigration proceedings in many such cases have been ordered closed to public scrutiny. However, AI has gathered information from various sources, including a recent visit to two jails identified as housing detainees and extensive interviews with attorneys, detainees, relatives and former detainees.

Amnesty International's findings confirm many of the organization's earlier concerns and suggest that a significant number of detainees continue to be deprived of certain basic rights guaranteed under international law. These include

SOURCE: Retrieved on 8/11/2003 from www.amnestyusa.org/waronterror/9.11. detentions2.rtf, 1–2, 43–44.

the right to humane treatment, as well as rights which are essential to protection from arbitrary detention, such as the right of anyone deprived of their liberty to be informed of the reasons for the detention; to be able to challenge the lawfulness of the detention; to have prompt access to and assistance from a lawyer; and to the presumption of innocence.

According to immigration attorneys, many post 9.11 detainees have been charged with routine visa violations for which they would not normally be detained. While technically in INS custody, some have been held for weeks or months pending security "clearance" by the Federal Bureau of Investigation (FBI), a process shrouded in secrecy. Lack of information given to detainees or their attorneys as to why they are being held has made it difficult for them effectively to challenge their detention.

Amnesty International recognizes that governments need to be vigilant in investigating potential "terrorist" links. However, the secrecy surrounding the current proceedings creates the potential for abuse. There is also concern that the immigration system is being used to hold non-nationals on flimsy evidence pending broad criminal probes, without the safeguards which are present in the criminal justice system.

For example, unlike people detained in the context of criminal procedures, INS detainees have no right to court-appointed attorneys. Contrary to assertions made by Attorney General Ashcroft in November 2001 that all INS detainees had the opportunity to seek legal assistance through probono legal service providers if necessary, AI has learned that many detainees have been without access to lawyers for far longer than was initially reported. This is of particular concern given that some are being simultaneously investigated by the FBI and subjected to lengthy—and possibly indefinite—detention. . . .

Amnesty International also remains deeply concerned that, although they are not charged with crimes, many post 9.11 detainees are held in punitive conditions in jails, sometimes alongside people charged or convicted of criminal offences. AI has received reports of cruel treatment, including prolonged solitary confinement, heavy shackling of detainees (including use of chains and leg shackles) during visits or court appearances and lack of adequate outdoor exercise. There have also been allegations of physical and verbal abuse.

. . . Amnesty International fully recognizes the government's obligation to take all necessary measures to protect its borders and investigate crimes and potential threats to national security. However, the organization is concerned that the government has used its expanded powers to detain non-nationals in the wake of September 11 without the necessary safeguards under international law. AI is concerned that the detentions in some cases may amount to arbitrary deprivation of liberty in violation of Article 9(1) of the ICCPR [International Covenant on Civil and Political Rights]. The secrecy surrounding the detention process has, further, created a serious lack of public accountability. Transparency in the process is necessary to ensure that all persons deprived of their liberty can fully exercise their rights under US and international law. Amnesty International urges the U.S. Government to:

Provide in full the information requested under the FOIA [Freedom of Information Act]; make public information on the number and nationalities of those still detained; the reasons for their detention; the date and place of arrest; date and charges; and place of detention; provide information on the numbers and nationalities of those deported or removed under voluntary departure arrangements and the countries to which they have been returned.

Ensure that all persons in federal custody, including those held in local or county jails, are treated humanely in accordance with international standards and that no-one is subjected to torture or other cruel, inhuman or degrading treatment. The Department of Justice should fully investigate all allegations of ill-treatment of detainees or prisoners and take appropriate action in the case of those found guilty of misconduct.

Ensure respect for the rights of everyone arrested or detained as set out under international standards, including Article 9 of the ICCPR and the Body of Principles. Such rights include the right to be informed of the reasons for arrest and to be given prompt access to attorneys and relatives and consular officials or representatives of relevant international organizations as requested. Ensure that all detained persons are provided with written notification of their rights as guaranteed by international standards and U.S. law, in a language they understand.

Ensure that all arrested or detained persons are brought promptly before a judge and have access to the courts and a procedure in which they may challenge the lawfulness of their detention.

Ensure that no-one is detained on national security grounds unless charged with a recognizable offence or action is being taken to deport within a reasonable period. There must be a realistic possibility of deportation being effected.

Ensure that no-one is removed or deported to a country where they risk being subjected to serious human rights abuses.

Ensure that asylum seekers are not generally detained and that anyone claiming asylum is allowed a full and fair hearing of their claim as provided under the 1951 Refugee Convention and the 1967 Protocol.

The UN High Commissioner for Refugees should be granted access to all asylum seekers and refugees in detention.

Ensure that restraints are applied only when strictly necessary as a precaution against escape, on medical grounds or to prevent damage or injury, in accordance with international standards. Under no circumstances should detainees be shackled when appearing before immigration judges. . . .

Earth Liberation Front

According to the FBI, the radical Earth Liberation Front (ELF), which preaches a policy of "ecoterrorism," is one of the top domestic terrorist organizations in the United States. ELF has taken credit for many acts of sabotage and arson against lumber companies, ski lodges, and even the U.S. Forestry Service in an effort to thwart industrial and tourist encroachment into the natural habitat of endangered species. ELF claimed, for example, that the reason it torched a Vail, Colorado, ski lodge in 1998 was to prevent the ski company from expanding into 885 acres of forest that was the habitat for the Canada lynx. Though little is known about the origins of ELF, which is said to be an offshoot of Earth First!, it does issue press releases taking responsibility for its members' actions. One of the people associated with ELF is "spokesperson" Craig Rosebraugh. Rosebraugh claims that he is merely an "intermediary" between the organization and the media who reports information that was passed on to him about ELF activities. In 2002, while the United States was stepping up its antiterrorism campaign, domestic terrorism, too, became a significant target of federal law enforcement agencies and congressional investigations. The following testimony was submitted by Rosebraugh to a congressional hearing on ecoterrorism. Also reprinted here is one of the Earth Liberation Front's press releases. This one is from September 2002, after a fire severely damaged a U.S. Forestry Service facility in Irvine, Pennsylvania.

How does Rosebraugh justify acts of sabotage and destruction against property? Does ecoterrorism successfully focus attention on the issues that ELF wants addressed, or does such violence create a backlash? What will be the result, according to Rosebraugh, if groups like ELF do not commit such acts of sabotage?

Written Testimony Supplied to the U.S. House of Representatives for the February 12, 2002, Hearing on "Ecoterrorism"

Submitted to the House on February 7, 2002

> *When a long train of abuses and usurpations, pursuing invariably the same object, evinces a design to reduce [the people] under absolute despotism, it is their right, it is their duty, to throw off such government, and to provide new guards for their future security.*

> *The oppressed should rebel, and they will continue to rebel and raise disturbance until their civil rights are fully restored to them and all partial distinctions, exclusions and incapacitations are removed.*

> Thomas Jefferson, 1776

. . . Throughout my childhood and adolescent years, the education I received from my parents, schools, popular media and culture instilled in me a pride for my country, for my government, and everything the United States represented. I was taught

------

Source: Retrieved on 8/29/2003 from www.earthliberationfront.com.

about the great American history, our Constitution, Bill of Rights, and our legacy of being at the forefront of democracy and freedom. I considered myself to be just an average boy taking an active part in the popular American pastimes of competitive sports, consumer culture, and existing within a classic representation of the standard, middle-class suburban lifestyle . . . .

Particularly, with the advent of the industrial revolution in the United States, the destruction of the natural world took a sharp turn for the worse. The attitude, more so than ever, turned to one of profits at any cost and a major shift from sustainable living to stockpiling for economic benefit. This focus on stockpiling and industrial productivity caused hardship on communities, forcing local crafters and laborers to be driven out of business by overly competitive industries. Additionally, with this new focus on sacrificing sustainable living for financial gain, natural resources were in greater demand than ever. Semi-automatic to automatic machinery, production lines, the automobile, the roadway system, suburbs, and the breakup of small, fairly self-sufficient communities all came about, at least in part, due to the industrial revolution. This unhealthy and deadly transgression of course was supported and promoted by the U.S. government, always eager to see growth in the domestic economy.

All of this set the stage for the threatening shortage of natural resources and the massive environmental pollution and destruction present today in the United States. In cities such as Los Angeles, Detroit, and Houston, the air and soil pollution levels are so extreme people have suffered and continue to face deadly health problems. Waterways throughout the country, including the Columbia Slough in my backyard, are so polluted from industries it is recommended that humans don't even expose themselves to the moisture let alone drink unfiltered, unbottled water. The necessary and crucial forests of the Pacific Northwestern region of the country have been systematically destroyed by corporations such as Boise Cascade, Willamette Industries, and others within the timber industry whose sole motive is profits regardless of the expense to the health of an ecosystem. In Northern California, the sacred old growths, dreamlike in appearance, taking your breath away at first glance, have been continuously threatened and cut by greedy corporations such as Pacific Lumber/Maxxam. The same has occurred and still is a reality in states including Washington, Oregon, Idaho, and Colorado.

The first National Forests were established in the United States more than a century ago. One hundred fifty-five of them exist today spread across 191 million acres. Over the years, the forest products industry has decimated publicly owned National Forests in this country, leaving a horrendous trail of clearcuts and logging roads. Commercial logging has been responsible for annihilating nearly all of the nation's old growth forests, draining nutrients from the soil, washing topsoil into streams, destroying wildlife habitat, and creating an increase in the incidence and severity of forest fires. Only an estimated 4 percent of old growth forests in the United States are remaining.

The National Forests in the United States contain far more than just trees. In fact, more than 3,000 species of fish and wildlife, in addition to 10,000 plant species, have their habitat within the National Forests. This includes at least 230 endangered plant and animal species. All of these life forms co-exist symbiotically to naturally create the rich and healthy ecosystems needed for life to exist on this planet.

The benefits of a healthy forest cannot be overrated. Healthy forests purify drinking water, provide fresh clean air to breathe, stabilize hillsides, and prevent floods. Hillsides clearcut or destroyed by logging roads lose their ability to absorb heavy rainfall. If no trees exist to soak up moisture with roots to hold the soil, water flows freely down slopes, creating muddy streams, polluting drinking water, strengthening floods, and causing dangerous mudslides. Instead of valuing trees and forests for being necessary providers of life, the U.S. Forest Service and commercial logging interests have decimated these precious ecosystems.

The timber corporations argue that today in the United States more forests exist than perhaps at any time in the last century or more. It doesn't take a forestry specialist to realize that monoculture tree farms—in which one species of tree, often times non-native to the area, is grown in mass in a small area for maximum production— do not equate to a healthy forest. Healthy forests are made up of diverse ecosystems consisting of many native plant and animal species. These healthy ecosystems are what grant humans and all other life forms on the planet with the ability to live. Without clean air, clean water, and healthy soil, life on this planet will cease to exist. There is an overwhelming battery of evidence that conclusively shows that we are already well on our path toward massive planetary destruction.

The popular environmental movement in the United States, which arguably began in the 1960s, has failed to produce the necessary protection needed to ensure that life on this planet will continue to survive. This is largely due to the fact that the movement has primarily consisted of tactics sanctioned by the very power structure that is benefiting economically from the destruction of the natural world. While a few minor successes in this country should be noted, the overwhelming constant trend has been the increasingly speedy liquidation of natural resources and annihilation of the environment.

The state sanctioned tactics, that is, those approved by the U.S. government and the status quo and predominantly legal in nature, rarely, if ever, actually challenge or positively change the very entities that are responsible for oppression, exploitation, and, in this case, environmental destruction. Throughout the history of the United States, a striking amount of evidence indicates that it wasn't until efforts strayed beyond the state sanctioned that social change ever progressed. In the abolitionist movement, the Underground Railroad, public educational campaigns, in addition to slave revolts, forced the federal government to act. With the Suffragettes in the United States, individuals such as Alice Paul acting with various forms of civil disobedience added to the more mainstream efforts to successfully demand the vote for women. Any labor historian will assert that in addition to the organizing of the workplace, strikes, riots, and protests dramatically assisted in producing more tolerable work standards. The progress of the civil rights movement was primarily founded upon the massive illegal civil disobedience campaigns against segregation and disenfranchisement. Likewise, the true pressure from the Vietnam anti-war movement in this country only came after illegal activities such as civil disobedience and beyond were implemented. Perhaps the most obvious, yet often overlooked, historical example of this notion supporting the importance of illegal activity as a tool for positive, lasting change, came just prior to our war for independence. Our educational systems in the United States glorify the Boston Tea Party while simultaneously failing to recognize and admit that the dumping of tea was perhaps one of the most famous early examples of politically motivated property destruction.

In the mid-1990s, individuals angry and disillusioned with the failing efforts to protect the natural environment through state sanctioned means, began taking illegal action. At first, nonviolent civil disobedience was implemented, followed by sporadic cases of nonviolent property destruction. In November 1997, an anonymous communiqué was issued by a group called the Earth Liberation Front claiming responsibility for their first-ever action in North America.

Immediately, the label of *ecoterrorism* appeared in news stories describing the actions of the Earth Liberation Front. Where exactly this label originated is open for debate, but all indications point to the federal government of the United States in coordination with industry and sympathetic mass media. Whatever the truth may be regarding the source of this term, one thing is for certain—the decision to attach this label to illegal actions taken for environmental protection was very conscious and deliberate. Why? The need for the U.S. federal government to control and mold public opinion through the power of propaganda to ensure an absence of threat is crucial. If information about illegal actions taken to protect the natural environment were presented openly to the public without biased interpretation, the opportunity would exist for citizens to make up their *own* minds about the legitimacy of the tactic, target, and movement. By attaching a label such as "terrorism" to the activities of groups such as the Earth Liberation Front, the public is left with little choice but to give in to their preconceived notions negatively associated with that term. For many in this country, including myself, information about terrorism came from schools and popular culture. Most often times, the definition of terrorism was overtly racist associated frequently in movies and on television shows with Arabs and the *others* our government told us were threatening. Terrorism usually is connected with violence, with politically motivated physical harm to humans.

Yet, in the history of the Earth Liberation Front, both in North America and abroad in Europe, no one has ever been injured by the group's many actions. This is not a mere coincidence, but rather a deliberate decision that illustrates the true motivation behind the covert organization. Simply put and most fundamentally, the goal of the Earth Liberation Front is to save life. The group takes actions directly against the property of those who are engaged in massive planetary destruction in order for all of us to survive. This noble pursuit does not constitute terrorism, but rather seeks to abolish it.

A major hypocrisy exists when the U.S. government labels an organization such as the Earth Liberation Front a terrorist group while simultaneously failing to acknowledge its own terrorist history. In fact, the U.S. government by far has been the most extreme terrorist organization in planetary history. Some, but nowhere near all, of the examples of domestic terrorism were discussed earlier in this writing. Yet, further proof can be found by taking a glimpse at the foreign policy record of the United States even as recently as from the 1950s. In Guatemala (1953–1990s) the CIA organized a coup that overthrew the democratically elected government led by Jacobo Arbenz. This began some 40 years of death squads, torture, disappearances, mass executions, totaling well over 100,000 victims. The U.S. government apparently didn't want Guatemala's social democracy spreading to other countries in Latin America.

In the Middle East (1956–1958) the United States twice tried to overthrow the Syrian government. Additionally, the U.S. government landed 14,000 troops to purportedly keep the peace in Lebanon and to stop any opposition to the U.S. supported Lebanese government. The U.S. government also conspired to overthrow or assassinate Nasser of Egypt. . . .

Here in the United States, the growth of the empire, of capitalism, and of industry, has meant greater discrepancies between the wealthy and poor, a continued rise in the number of those considered to be a threat to the system, as well as irreversible harm done to the environment and life on the planet. Corporations in the United States literally get away with murder, facing little or no repercussions due to their legal structures. The U.S. government, which sleeps in the same bed as U.S. corporations, serves to ensure that the "business as usual" policies of imperialism can continue with as little friction as possible. Anyone questioning the mere logic of this genocidal culture and governing policy is considered a dissident and, more often than not, shipped off to one of the fastest growing industries of all, the prison industrial complex. . . .

U.S. imperialism is a disease, one that continues to grow and become more powerful and dangerous. It needs to be stopped. One of the chief weapons used by those protecting the imperialist policies of the United States is a slick, believable propaganda campaign designed to ensure U.S. citizens do not question or threaten the "American way of life." Perhaps the strongest factor in this campaign is the phenomenon of capitalism. By creating a consumer demand for products, corporations, greatly aided by the U.S. government, can effectively influence people's dreams, desires, wants, and life plans. The very American Dream promoted throughout the world is that anyone can come to the United States, work hard, and become happy and financially secure. Through the use of the propaganda campaign designed, promoted, and transmitted by the U.S. ruling class, people are nearly coerced into adopting unhealthy desires for, often times, unreachable, unneeded, and dangerous consumer goods. Through impressive societal mind control, the belief that obtaining consumer products will equal security and happiness has spread across the United States, and much of the planet at this point, like some extreme plague. The fact that the policies of the United States murder people on a daily basis is unseen, forgotten, or ignored, as every effort is made by people to fit into the artificial model life manufactured by the ruling elite. . . .

I was asked originally if I would voluntarily testify before the House Subcommittee on Forests and Forest Health at a hearing focused on "ecoterrorism." I declined in a written statement. U.S. Marshals then subpoenaed me on October 31, 2001 to testify at this hearing on February 12, 2002, against my will. Is this hearing a forum to discuss the threats facing the health of the natural environment, specifically the forests? No, clearly there is not even the remotest interest in this subject from the U.S. government or industry. The goal of this hearing is to discuss methodologies to improve the failed attempts law enforcement have made since the mid-1990s in catching and prosecuting individuals and organizations who take nonviolent, illegal direct action to stop the destruction of the natural environment. I have no interest in this cause or this hearing. In fact, I consider it a farce.

Since 1997, the U.S. government has issued me seven grand jury subpoenas, raided my home and work twice, stealing hundreds of items of property, and, on many occasions, sent federal agents to follow and question me. After this effort, which has lasted nearly five years, federal agents have yet to obtain any information from me to aid their investigations. As I have never been charged with one crime related to these so-called ecoterrorist organizations or their activities, the constant harassment by the federal government constitutes a serious infringement on my Constitutional right to freedom of speech. This Congressional Subcommittee hearing appears to be no different, harassing and targeting me for simply voicing my ideological support for those involved in environmental protection.

I fully praise those individuals who take direct action, by any means necessary, to stop the destruction of the natural world and threats to all life. They are the heroes, risking their freedom and lives so that we as a species as well as all life forms can continue to exist on the planet. In a country so fixated on monetary wealth and power, these brave environmental advocates are engaging in some of the most selfless activities possible.

It is my sincere desire that organizations such as the Earth Liberation Front continue to grow and prosper in the United States. In fact, more organizations, using similar tactics and strategies, need to be established to directly focus on U.S. imperialism and the U.S. government itself. For, as long as the quest for monetary gain continues to be the predominant value within U.S. society, human, animal, and environmental exploitation, destruction, and murder will continue to be a reality. This drive for profits at any cost needs to be fiercely targeted, and those responsible for the massive injustices punished. If there is any real concern for justice, freedom, and, at least, a resemblance of a true democracy, this revolutionary ideal must become a reality.

All power to the people. Long live the earth liberation front. Long live the animal liberation front. Long live all the sparks attempting to ignite the revolution. Sooner or later the sparks *will* turn into a flame!

Press Release, September 3, 2002

The ELF Press Office received the following communique September 1, 2002:

The Earth Liberation Front is claiming responsibility for the 8/11/02 arson attack on the United States Forest Service Northeast Research Station in Irvine, Pennsylvania.

The laboratory was set ablaze during the early morning hours, causing over $700,000 damage, and destroying part of 70 years worth of research. This lesson in "prescribed fire" was a natural, necessary response to the threats posed to life in the Allegheny Forest by proposed timber sales, oil drilling, and greed driven manipulation of Nature.

This facility was strategically targeted, and if rebuilt, will be targeted again for complete destruction. Furthermore, all other U.S. Forest Service administration and research facilities, as well as all DCNR buildings nationwide should now be considered likely targets.

These agencies continue to ignore and mislead the public, at the bidding of their corporate masters, leaving us with no alternative to underground direct action. Their blatant disregard for the sanctity of life and its perfect Natural balance, indifference to strong public opposition, and the irrevocable acts of extreme violence they perpetrate against the Earth daily are all inexcusable, and will not be tolerated. If they persist in their crimes against life, they will be met with maximum retaliation.

In pursuance of justice, freedom, and equal consideration for all innocent life across the board, segments of this global revolutionary movement are no longer limiting their revolutionary potential by adhering to a flawed, inconsistent "non-violent" ideology. While innocent life will never be harmed in any action we undertake, where it is necessary, we will no longer hesitate to pick up the gun to implement justice, and provide the needed protection for our planet that decades of legal battles, pleading, protest, and economic sabotage have failed so drastically to achieve.

The diverse efforts of this revolutionary force cannot be contained, and will only continue to intensify as we are brought face to face with the oppressor in inevitable, violent confrontation. We will stand up and fight for our lives against this iniquitous civilization until its reign of TERROR is forced to an end—by any means necessary.

In defense of all life,
Pacific E.L.F.

Not in Our Name

As the United States prepared for war with Iraq in the winter of 2003, despite overwhelming popular support for the administration, a wave of dissent swept across the nation. One group, Not in Our Name, NION, circulated an antiwar petition on the Internet. A remarkable thing about the antiwar movement in 2003 was that a large minority of American citizens were opposed to a war that had not even begun. It took four years of fighting in Vietnam before the antiwar movement began to attract such numbers in the late 1960s.

The NION Statement of Conscience is the petition that was signed by more than 65,000 people. However, it had no effect on deterring the administration's decision to go to war. Is it fair to accuse the United States itself of terrorism? Why do U.S. policies "pose grave dangers to the people of the world"? What are the perceived dangers inherent in the PATRIOT Act? Is this statement fully within the American tradition of dissent, as the writers claim?

Statement of Conscience, 2003

Let it not be said that people in the United States did nothing when their government declared a war without limit and instituted stark new measures of repression.

The signers of this statement call on the people of the U.S. to resist the policies and overall political direction that have emerged since September 11, 2001, and which pose grave dangers to the people of the world.

We believe that peoples and nations have the right to determine their own destiny, free from military coercion by great powers. We believe that all persons detained or prosecuted by the United States government should have the same rights of due process. We believe that questioning, criticism, and dissent must be valued and protected. We understand that such rights and values are always contested and must be fought for.

We believe that people of conscience must take responsibility for what their own governments do—we must first of all oppose the injustice that is done in our own name. Thus we call on all Americans to RESIST the war and repression that has been loosed on the world by the Bush administration. It is unjust, immoral, and illegitimate. We choose to make common cause with the people of the world.

We too watched with shock the horrific events of September 11, 2001. We too mourned the thousands of innocent dead and shook our heads at the terrible scenes of carnage—even as we recalled similar scenes in Baghdad, Panama City, and, a generation ago, Vietnam. We too joined the anguished questioning of millions of Americans who asked why such a thing could happen.

But the mourning had barely begun, when the highest leaders of the land unleashed a spirit of revenge. They put out a simplistic script of "good vs. evil" that was taken up by a pliant and intimidated media. They told us that asking why these terrible events had happened verged on treason. There was to be no debate. There were by definition no valid political or moral questions. The only possible answer was to be war abroad and repression at home.

In our name, the Bush administration, with near unanimity from Congress, not only attacked Afghanistan but abrogated to itself and its allies the right to rain down military force anywhere and anytime. The brutal repercussions have been felt from the Philippines to Palestine, where Israeli tanks and bulldozers have left a terrible trail of death and destruction. The government has waged an all-out war on and

SOURCE: Retrieved on 4/15/2003 from www.nion.us/NION.HTM. Used by permission.

occupied Iraq—a country which has no connection to the horror of September 11. What kind of world will this become if the U.S. government has a blank check to drop commandos, assassins, and bombs wherever it wants?

In our name, within the U.S., the government has created two classes of people: those to whom the basic rights of the U.S. legal system are at least promised, and those who now seem to have no rights at all. The government rounded up over 1,000 immigrants and detained them in secret and indefinitely. Hundreds have been deported and hundreds of others still languish today in prison. This smacks of the infamous concentration camps for Japanese-Americans in World War 2. For the first time in decades, immigration procedures single out certain nationalities for unequal treatment.

In our name, the government has brought down a pall of repression over society. The President's spokesperson warns people to "watch what they say." Dissident artists, intellectuals, and professors find their views distorted, attacked, and suppressed. The so-called Patriot Act—along with a host of similar measures on the state level—gives police sweeping new powers of search and seizure, supervised if at all by secret proceedings before secret courts.

In our name, the executive has steadily usurped the roles and functions of the other branches of government. Military tribunals with lax rules of evidence and no right to appeal to the regular courts are put in place by executive order. Groups are declared "terrorist" at the stroke of a presidential pen.

We must take the highest officers of the land seriously when they talk of a war that will last a generation and when they speak of a new domestic order. We are confronting a new openly imperial policy towards the world and a domestic policy that manufactures and manipulates fear to curtail rights.

There is a deadly trajectory to the events of the past months that must be seen for what it is and resisted. Too many times in history people have waited until it was too late to resist.

President Bush has declared: "you're either with us or against us." Here is our answer: We refuse to allow you to speak for all the American people. We will not give up our right to question. We will not hand over our consciences in return for a hollow promise of safety. We say NOT IN OUR NAME. We refuse to be party to these wars and we repudiate any inference that they are being waged in our name or for our welfare. We extend a hand to those around the world suffering from these policies; we will show our solidarity in word and deed.

We who sign this statement call on all Americans to join together to rise to this challenge. We applaud and support the questioning and protest now going on, even as we recognize the need for much, much more to actually stop this juggernaut. We draw inspiration from the Israeli reservists who, at great personal risk, declare "there IS a limit" and refuse to serve in the occupation of the West Bank and Gaza.

We also draw on the many examples of resistance and conscience from the past of the United States: from those who fought slavery with rebellions and the underground railroad, to those who defied the Vietnam war by refusing orders, resisting the draft, and standing in solidarity with resisters.

Let us not allow the watching world today to despair of our silence and our failure to act. Instead, let the world hear our pledge: we will resist the machinery of war and repression and rally others to do everything possible to stop it.

THE OVER 65,000 SIGNERS INCLUDE . . .

Robert Altman
Edward Asner
Kevin Bacon
Noam Chomsky
Deepak Chopra
Jill Clayburgh
John Cusack
Angela Davis
Ossie Davis
Mos Def
Ani Di Franco
Diane DiPrima
Steve Earle
Barbara Ehrenreich
Daniel Ellsberg
Brian Eno
Fifty-three Maryknoll
    priests and brothers
Jane Fonda
Tom Hayden

Rev. Jesse Jackson
Jim Jarmusch
Spike Lee
Toni Morrison
Graham Nash
Claes Oldenburg
Yoko Ono
Grace Paley
Bonnie Raitt
John Sayles
Kyra Sedgwick
Pete and Toshi Seeger
Martin Sheen
Gloria Steinem
Oliver Stone
Gore Vidal
Alice Walker
Howard Zinn

(*partial list as of 4/15/03*)

Veterans Against the Iraq War

Of the many thousands of Vietnam veterans who were against the Vietnam War, many have resurfaced to oppose the Iraq War in 2003. A smaller number of Desert Storm veterans have also come out strongly against the latest war. A nonpartisan group of U.S. veterans issued the Call to Conscience from Veterans to Active Duty Troops and Reservists, urging all current military personnel to examine their consciences and reevaluate their stance on war with Iraq. The other two selections reprinted here are from West Point graduate David Wiggins. Wiggins, a conscientious objector during the First Gulf War (Operation Desert Storm), is a physician who has been writing and publishing antiwar articles on the Internet aimed at the military. The first is an open letter asking troops to examine whose interests would be served by a war in Iraq; the second is his ruminations about defending freedom. There are already documented cases of soldiers resisting the war. Marine Corps Reservist Stephen Funk, for example, refused to serve and turned himself in to military authorities on April 1, 2003.

Are antiwar activists' efforts aimed at the military acts of subversion or even treason, or are they simply an expression of free speech? Are any of the former soldiers' criticisms valid? What is the main objection to the war expressed by the group of veterans?

Call to Conscience from Veterans to Active Duty Troops and Reservists

We are veterans of the United States armed forces. We stand with the majority of humanity, including millions in our own country, in opposition to the United States' all-out war on Iraq. We span many wars and eras, have many political views and we all agree that this war is wrong.

Many of us believed serving in the military was our duty, and our job was to defend this country. Our experiences in the military caused us to question much of what we were taught. Now we see our REAL duty is to encourage you as members of the U.S. armed forces to find out what you are being sent to fight and die for and what the consequences of your actions will be for humanity. We call upon you, the active duty and reservists, to follow your conscience and do the right thing.

In the last Gulf War, as troops, we were ordered to murder from a safe distance. We destroyed much of Iraq from the air, killing hundreds of thousands, including civilians. We remember the road to Basra—the Highway of Death—where we were ordered to kill fleeing Iraqis. We bulldozed trenches, burying people alive. The use of depleted uranium weapons left the battlefields radioactive. Massive use of pesticides, experimental drugs, burning chemical weapons depots and oil fires combined to create a toxic cocktail affecting both the Iraqi people and Gulf War veterans today. One in four Gulf War veterans is disabled.

During the Vietnam War we were ordered to destroy Vietnam from the air and on the ground. At My Lai we massacred over 500 women, children and old men. This was not an aberration, it's how we fought the war. We used Agent Orange on the *enemy* and then experienced first hand its effects. We know what Post Traumatic Stress Disorder looks, feels and tastes like because the ghosts of over two million men, women and children still haunt our dreams. More of us took our own lives after returning home than died in battle.

If you choose to participate in the invasion of Iraq you will be part of an occupying army. Do you know what it is like to look into the eyes of a people that hate you to your core? You should think about what your "mission" really is. You are being sent to invade and occupy a people who, like you and me, are only trying to live their lives and raise their kids. They pose no threat to the United States even though they have a brutal dictator as their leader. Who is the U.S. to tell the Iraqi people how to run their country when many in the U.S. don't even believe their own President was legally elected?

SOURCE: Retrieved on 1/3/2004 from www.calltoconscience.net/

Saddam is being vilified for gassing his own people and trying to develop weapons of mass destruction. However, when Saddam committed his worst crimes the U.S. was supporting him. This support included providing the means to produce chemical and biological weapons. Contrast this with the horrendous results of the U.S.-led economic sanctions. More than a million Iraqis, mainly children and infants, have died because of these sanctions. After having destroyed the entire infrastructure of their country including hospitals, electricity generators, and water treatment plants, the U.S. then, with the sanctions, stopped the import of goods, medicines, parts, and chemicals necessary to restore even the most basic necessities of life.

There is no honor in murder. This war is murder by another name. When, in an unjust war, an errant bomb dropped kills a mother and her child it is not "collateral damage," it is murder. When, in an unjust war, a child dies of dysentery because a bomb damaged a sewage treatment plant, it is not "destroying enemy infrastructure," it is murder. When, in an unjust war, a father dies of a heart attack because a bomb disrupted the phone lines so he could not call an ambulance, it is not "neutralizing command and control facilities," it is murder. When, in an unjust war, a thousand poor farmer conscripts die in a trench defending a town they have lived in their whole lives, it is not victory, it is murder.

There will be veterans leading protests against this war on Iraq and your participation in it. During the Vietnam War thousands in Vietnam and in the U.S. refused to follow orders. Many resisted and rebelled. Many became conscientious objectors and others went to prison rather than bear arms against the so-called enemy. During the last Gulf War many GIs resisted in various ways and for many different reasons. Many of us came out of these wars and joined with the antiwar movement.

If the people of the world are ever to be free, there must come a time when being a citizen of the world takes precedence over being the soldier of a nation. Now is that time. When orders come to ship out, your response will profoundly impact the lives of millions of people in the Middle East and here at home. Your response will help set the course of our future. You will have choices all along the way. Your commanders want you to obey. We urge you to think. We urge you to make your choices based on your conscience. If you choose to resist, we will support you and stand with you because we have come to understand that our REAL duty is to the people of the world and to our common future.

Message to the Troops: Resist!, October 11, 2002

Dear Soldier of the U.S. Military:

Considering the common practice of talking about "supporting the troops" in times of hostilities, I should let you know how I feel.

With all due respect, I want you to know that if you participate in this conflict, you are not serving me, and I don't support you. Speaking for myself, I feel those

SOURCE: Retrieved on 3/10/2004 from www.strike-the-root.com/archive/wiggins. html.

who participate will be damaging my reputation as an American, and further endangering me and my children by creating hatred that will someday be returned to us—perhaps someday soon. Your actions will not lead to a safer world, but a more dangerous world of pre-emption and unilateral decisions to commit mayhem. I don't support that.

This talk of "supporting the troops" is just another method our government uses to manipulate and control us. I don't support the troops, but I certainly fear for the lives of the troops. I would support the troops staying home. I regret that our so-called leaders have involved the troops in such a foolish, misguided undertaking. I would support the troops disobeying orders. I feel sorry for the troops' families. I would support the troops if they realized that the best way to defend their families would be to stay alive and healthy and resist this war.

The only people the troops are possibly serving are those who agree with this act of military aggression. Perhaps you are not even serving them if they end up suffering retribution for your actions.

Oh yes, and you are serving the President, of course—the man who avoided combat duty and deserted his National Guard unit. You are serving the man who enriched himself through crony capitalism, shady accounting practices and insider trading while running multiple corporations into bankruptcy. You will be serving the man who lost the popular vote for president, but was handed the presidency by a Supreme Court influenced by his father and through voting irregularities in a state governed by his brother. You will be serving the man who, as President, turned the budget surplus into a deficit and presided over the largest stock market decline since the great depression. You will be serving the man who unilaterally withdrew from the Anti-Ballistic Missile Treaty, ignored the Nuclear Non-Proliferation Treaty and rejected the International Criminal Court and Kyoto Protocol on Global Warming.

If you are involved in an invasion of Iraq, you will be faced with some difficult ethical decisions. Are the Iraqi foot soldiers really the guilty party here? Is it reasonable to expect them to refuse orders to defend themselves against an invading force (you)? Is this conflict really necessary at all? If not, why kill these people? If it is, are there other means our Commander-in-Chief and others are not exploring that might prevent you from having to kill these people and possibly civilians too, and possibly die yourself or contribute to your friend's death? I'm glad I don't have to make those decisions.

I feel for you and the difficult decisions you must make. I hope this note frees you of any sense of obligation to serve me you must feel, and helps you make a conscientious decision that you will be proud to accept complete responsibility for making. Please pass the sentiments I expressed in this letter on to your fellow soldiers.

David Wiggins

Defending My Freedom, March 21, 2003

I am sitting here defending my freedom. By that, I mean exercising my freedom. By that, I mean opposing this naked aggression on Iraq. In agreement, freedom is moot. I revel in defiance because defiance makes me free. I defy this Government. I defy this President. I defy these soldiers. I defy; therefore I am free.

It has been said, "Give me liberty or give me death." We will all have death. The question remains; will I live in freedom or in fear? No soldier gives me the ability to think, the ability to express my thoughts, or the ability to act. A soldier may take my arms, my legs, my voice, or my life; but a soldier cannot take me. At best, a soldier is a baby's blanket for freedom that diminishes fear but offers no substantial protection. How can a soldier protect that which he does not possess? No soldier invading Iraq will make me free.

By what twisted logic do soldiers tell me they defend my freedom? First, soldiers, "give up their freedom so that they may defend the freedom of others." This is impossible. By giving up their freedom, soldiers might be used to threaten freedom or to defend freedom. The soldiers follow orders in either case. Attacking and destroying a nation and killing its people "preemptively" on flimsy pretenses and unproven assertions is not defending my freedom.

By voluntarily giving up their own freedom, soldiers damage the cause of freedom for all. To defend freedom, soldiers should refuse to give up their freedom. Soldiers should obey their conscience without question, not their orders without question. Let us, without orders, try to convince the soldiers to leave their families and their lives to fly across an ocean for the purpose of attacking a people that has not attacked us and poses us no palpable threat. Let us, without half-truths, mis-truths, propaganda and lies; convince the soldiers to do this. This would be freedom. This would be the end of soldiers and the end of war. This would be the end of the preemptive attack on Iraq.

Soldiers fly and sail and drive and march and intimidate and destroy and kill. In this way, it is said, they prevent others from causing me fear and harm. Perhaps this makes some feel safer, but those that need to feel safe to feel free are neither safe nor free. Defeating Iraq is but a distraction. Defeat your fears and you will be free.

Consider the soldiers' victims. Are they not encouraged to fly and sail and drive and march and intimidate and destroy and kill in response? Will not the sons and daughters and family and friends and countrymen and all the descendants of those killed, and crippled, and destitute, and diseased cry for revenge? How does this improve my safety? When was the war to end all wars? I must have missed it. This war in Iraq will certainly make me less safe for the rest of my life. I oppose this government that demands my money, and this President who uses it to violate the peace. I oppose this President who assaults those who have not assaulted me. I oppose this President who invades, bombs, kills, assassinates, destroys, and sows fear and death. For every action, there is an equal and opposite reaction. I oppose this President who, by his aggression invites aggression; who by his violence, invites violence; who by causing death, invites death. I declare my independence from this self-destructive system. I wash my hands of this invasion of Iraq.

Why should I rally behind the United States Commander in Chief? Because I am free, I resist. My conscience is my Commander in Chief. Peace, Truth, Justice and Freedom are my generals. This is my land, I was born here. I have no other land. The government of the United States of America, a co-inhabitant of this land, claims sovereignty over me. By claiming me as its own, it purports to make me free. This Government demands the results of my labor so that it might live and act. Though I do not give permission, though I resist, this government uses the fruits of my labor to send soldiers to destroy, to maim, and to kill in my name. By this, it purports to defend my freedom. If I resist, this government may follow me, eavesdrop on my conversations, and keep me under video surveillance, strip search me at airports, keep secret files on my past and present activities, and similarly treat my family and friends. If my peaceful expressions of my freedom make this Government insecure, or if I refuse its demands, this Government will send police and eventually soldiers to my door. Though I resist peacefully and am a danger to no person, though I seek only to act conscientiously and defend my freedom, this Government will place me in handcuffs and imprison me. If I resist, if I protest, this Government, this President, these soldiers promise "serious consequences" and will use "all necessary force" to subdue me. This Government, this President, these soldiers may force me to the ground, kick me and beat me with sticks until I am unconscious, or sodomize me with a broomstick. This Government, this President, these soldiers may shoot and kill me for demonstrating on campus, or they may pump poison gas into my house to choke me, and ignite it to burn me to death. This is how the Government of the United States, the President, and the soldiers defend my freedom. God Bless America.

The American Civil Liberties Union

The mission of the American Civil Liberties Union (ACLU), founded in 1920 during the Red Scare that followed the First World War, is to safeguard the Bill of Rights. Throughout the years, the nonpartisan ACLU has taken on many controversial issues on all sides of the political spectrum. The central concern for the ACLU, though, always comes down to whether it is guaranteed in the Bill of Rights. The ACLU has battled for the right of free speech for everyone, from antiwar protestors and civil rights demonstrators to the Ku Klux Klan.

In May 2003, the ACLU issued a report, Freedom Under Fire: Dissent in Post-9/11 America (a portion of which is here excerpted), detailing some of the civil liberties infractions that have occurred in the aftermath of the terrorist attacks. According to the ACLU, the government, in its efforts to create unanimity of opinion backing the decision to go to war with Iraq, is stifling free speech and dissent and is therefore overstepping its bounds.

What are the state and federal measures that the ACLU views as a threat to civil liberties? What are people doing about it? Where does one draw the line between dissent and patriotism?

Freedom Under Fire: Dissent in Post-9/11 America, May 2003

INTRODUCTION

There is a pall over our country. In separate but related attempts to squelch dissent, the government has attacked the patriotism of its critics, police have barricaded and jailed protesters, and the New York Stock Exchange has revoked the press credentials of the most widely watched television network in the Arab world. A chilling message has gone out across America: Dissent if you must, but proceed at your own risk.

Government-sanctioned intolerance has even trickled into our private lives. People brandishing anti-war signs or slogans have been turned away from commuter trains in Seattle and suburban shopping malls in upstate New York. Cafeterias are serving "freedom fries." Country music stations stopped playing Dixie Chicks songs, and the Baseball Hall of Fame cancelled an event featuring "Bull Durham" stars Tim Robbins and Susan Sarandon, after they spoke out against the war on Iraq.

Compounding the offense is the silence from many lawmakers. There is palpable fear even in the halls of Congress of expressing an unpopular view.

Why should this disturb us? Because democracy is not a quiet business. Its lifeblood is the free and vibrant exchange of ideas. As New York Times columnist and author Thomas L. Friedman has pointed out, the war on terror is also a war of ideas. How are we going to convince holdouts in other countries about the importance of free speech and civil liberties if we show so little faith in our own?

With U.S. forces deployed overseas, and concerns about safety and freedom at home, we ought to be having as robust a debate as possible. . . .

Yes, some government officials, including local police, have come down hard on protesters, as this report makes clear. But in most of the cases that have come to light, protesters have stood firm. Lawsuits alleging excessive force, wrongful arrest and denial of due process have been filed on behalf of hundreds of protesters in New York and Washington alone. Undaunted by suspensions, arrests or other actions taken against them, a high school student in Michigan, a pair of college students in Iowa, a shopkeeper in Colorado and two grandmothers in Tampa are among those stepping forward to challenge those who would violate their First Amendment rights.

These democratic stirrings encourage us. We recall that although some of the greatest names in American liberalism (President Franklin D. Roosevelt and Supreme Court Justices Earl Warren and Hugo Black) supported the Japanese internments after Pearl Harbor, history has exonerated the people of good hearts and minds who opposed them.

Dissenters who take unpopular positions in their own times are often seen as heroes later on. We believe that when future generations look at what was done to our core freedoms and values after 9/11, the voices of dissent will stand out as the true defenders of democracy.

Anthony D. Romero
Executive Director, ACLU

SOURCE: Retrieved on 8/11/2003 from www.aclu.org/SafeandFree/SafeandFree.cfm?ID=12666&c=206, i–ii, 1–3, 5, 7, 10.

FREEDOM UNDER FIRE: DISSENT IN POST-9/11 AMERICA

In the tense time following the Sept. 11, 2001, terrorist attacks on New York and Washington, Attorney General John Ashcroft mocked government critics and assailed their patriotism, calling their concerns "phantoms of lost liberty." And the American Civil Liberties Union shot back with a national ad campaign asserting our right to be "safe and free."

"The nation's highest ranking law enforcement officer is using his bully pulpit to shut down dissent and debate," ACLU Executive Director Anthony D. Romero charged, declaring that free and robust debate is the engine of social and political justice.

But Ashcroft's words were just the opening volley in a war of intimidation. White House spokesman Ari Fleischer also warned Americans to "watch what they say." Conservative commentators like Bill O'Reilly suggested prosecuting war protesters as "enemies of the state." Since 2001, hundreds have been arrested for exercising their constitutionally protected freedoms, and some have lost their jobs or been suspended from school. Many have called on the ACLU for assistance.

We need to stop and consider the direction in which we are going, for we are in danger of allowing ourselves to be governed by our fears rather than our values. We are not the first generation to face this challenge.

Since the administration of President John Adams, who feared that sympathy with the radical ideas of the French Revolution would throw America into upheaval, there have been attempts to silence dissent. The Alien Act of 1798, which gave Adams the power to deport any non-citizen he judged dangerous, was never enforced, but his Sedition Act was used to suppress freedom of the press. President Abraham Lincoln suspended the writ of habeas corpus during the Civil War. And President Woodrow Wilson used the Espionage Act of 1917 not to catch spies but to mount a full-scale assault on free speech.

Faced with strong domestic opposition to the First World War from citizens who believed he was less interested in "making the world safe for democracy" than in protecting the investments of the wealthy, Wilson encouraged "patriotic citizens" to report on neighbors they suspected of disloyalty. His Justice Department prosecuted more than 2,000 critics of the war and judges were quick to hand down harsh punishments. In 1918, Congress also enacted a Sedition Act, restricting criticism of the government, the Constitution, the flag and the military.

The decades that followed ushered in some of the most shameful chapters in American history: the World War II internments of Japanese Americans; the McCarthy hearings; the Pentagon Papers, Watergate and FBI spy scandals. All involved government restrictions on speech, the press and freedom of movement. All were popular at the time, and are now seen as abhorrent to the national interest. . . .

Dissent since 9/11 has taken three principal forms: mass protests and rallies, messages on signs or clothing, and other acts of defiance by communities and individuals. These have ranged from silent vigils in parks to the passage of resolutions by dozens of local governments protesting federal measures that threaten fundamental freedoms.

Some government officials, including local police, have gone to extraordinary lengths to squelch dissent wherever it has sprung up, drawing on a breathtaking array of tactics—from censorship and surveillance to detention, denial of due process and excessive force. Police have beaten and maced protesters in Missouri, spied on law-abiding activists in Colorado and fired on demonstrators in California, and campus police have helped FBI agents to spy on professors and students in Massachusetts. Ashcroft's Justice Department has further asserted the right to seize protesters' assets and deport immigrants under anti-terrorism statutes rushed through Congress after the attacks, and debated whether to revoke U.S. citizenship in some cases. . . .

MASS MOVEMENT IN WASHINGTON

In a class-action lawsuit filed March 27, 2003, the ACLU of the National Capital Area charged police with deliberately violating the constitutional rights of more than 400 peaceful anti-war demonstrators and bystanders by directing them into a police trap and then arresting them—though they had not violated any law.

"In this country, the government is not supposed to arrest you unless you break the law," said local ACLU Legal Director Arthur Spitzer. "But the evidence will show that the police deliberately rounded up hundreds of people who had not broken any law, many of whom were not even involved in the demonstration. No one in the neighborhood was safe from the lawless conduct of the D.C. police."

The arrests occurred on Sept. 27, 2002, in Pershing Park, two blocks from the White House. Arrestees were charged with failing to obey a police order—though no order to disperse was ever given; in fact, people who tried to leave were physically prevented from doing so, according to the ACLU complaint. One demonstrator suffered broken ribs after being knocked down by the police. The true purpose of the mass arrests, the ACLU contends, was to disrupt and prevent peaceful political demonstrations scheduled for that weekend. . . .

DISTRESS SIGNAL AT GRINNELL

The Iowa Civil Liberties Union in December 2002 sued two police officers and a county attorney who threatened to arrest a pair of Grinnell College students for hanging a U.S. flag upside-down from their dormitory window. "People tell me it offends them to see the flag upside-down, but sometimes I tell them it offends me to see one right-side up," said Juan Diaz, 18, who with John Bohman hung the flag Sept. 26, 2002, as a sign of their "displeasure with the policies of the United States Government" toward Iraq.

Flag etiquette says that a flag should be flown upside-down only as a sign of distress. And after the lawsuit was filed in U.S. District Court in Des Moines, authorities agreed that hanging it upside-down was protected under the First Amendment. But officials defended other restrictions in their flag ordinance, which the suit says is unconstitutional in its entirety. The students also seek damages for willful violation of their speech rights.

"Police use this (flag etiquette) law for no other purpose than to silence government critics," ICLU executive director Ben Stone said, citing a 30-year-old Iowa Supreme Court ruling (State v. Kool, 212 N. W. 2d 518 (Iowa 1973)), that displaying an American flag upside-down was protected speech and could not be prosecuted. In 1989, the U.S. Supreme Court threw out the conviction of a protester who was arrested for actually burning a flag during a demonstration (Texas v. Johnson, 491 U.S. 397), declaring that the right of free speech protected symbolic use of the flag. . . .

PEACE OFFENSE IN NEW YORK

Oddly, a T-shirt promoting "Peace" brought out the cavalry at a mall in upstate Guilderland, N.Y., where Stephen Downs, a 61-year-old lawyer, was arrested for refusing to leave or remove a shirt he'd bought there. The New York Civil Liberties Union on March 11, 2003, wrote the operators of the Crossgates Mall after Downs was led away in handcuffs on a trespassing charge. "Give Peace a Chance," his shirt said on one side, and "Peace On Earth" on the other. Downs was accompanied by his 31-year-old son Roger, who also wore an anti-war T-shirt, but was allowed to leave after removing it.

The mall operators later asked the Guilderland Police Department to drop the trespassing charge but the news coverage made Downs a local hero and the NYCLU erected a billboard in protest near the entrance. "Welcome to the mall, you have the right to remain silent," it said. The security officer who called police was way out of line, NYCLU Executive Director Donna Lieberman said; decades earlier, at the height of the Vietnam War, the Supreme Court had even upheld the right of a protester (in Cohen v. California) to wear a jacket emblazoned with "Fuck the Draft" in a county courthouse.

"While the issue of free speech in shopping malls came to a head with Mr. Downs' arrest at Crossgates, it remains an issue at malls across the country," Lieberman said. "When, as here, the mall replaces Main Street as a center of commercial and social activity, the censorship of expression has a devastating effect on the freedom and diversity that is at the heart of a free society." . . .

FULL EXPOSURE IN FLORIDA

A U.S. District Court judge in West Palm Beach, Fla. prohibited officials from blocking a nude anti-war demonstration in a state park. The ACLU of Florida went to court on behalf of T. A. Wayner, a Fort Pierce naturist who planned to choreograph the creation of a peace symbol on Singer Island using nude bodies, and videographer George T. Simon, who planned to observe. Randall Marshall, legal director for the ACLU of Florida, said the intent was "not mere nudity, but political protest against the government's plans for war." For these demonstrators, he said, "nudity is an essential part of their political expression."

Judge Donald M. Middlebrook agreed, calling it "well within the ambit of the First Amendment." (He added that the state was free to put up signs notifying the public that the Feb. 14 demonstration would be taking place, or to erect screens around it.) . . .

WEB RESOURCES FOR PART SIX

SITES FEATURING A NUMBER OF THE DISSENTERS IN PART SIX:

Edward Abbey
www.abbeyweb.net/
www.ecotopia.org/ehof/abbey/

Paul Weyrich
www.freecongress.org/
Also see the media transparency site (a watchdog organization that tracks the funding behind think tanks):

www.mediatransparency.org/people/weyrich.htm

Anita Hill
www.now.org/issues/harass/anitahil.html
http://chnm.gmu.edu/courses/122/hill/hillframe.htm

ACT UP
www.actupny.org/

Right-Wing Militias
There are numerous links and resources here for right-wing militias, as well as just about everything having to do with the right-wing political philosophy. The point of view in these links varies from pro to anti, and from biased to unbiased, so there is the opportunity to view the right wing from various perspectives.

www.publiceye.org/lnk_antidem.html
www.michiganmilitia.com/literature/literature.htm

Unabomber
www.unabombertrial.com

Mos Def
www.mosdefinitely.com/

Public Enemy
www.publicenemy.com/

Julia Butterfly Hill
www.ottermedia.com/LunaJulia.html
www.ecotopia.org/ehof/hill/

Ralph Nader
www.nader.org/

Ani DiFranco
www.columbia.edu/~marg/ani/
www.ani-difranco.net/

Amnesty International
www.amnesty.org/
www.amnestyusa.org/

Earth Liberation Front
www.earthliberationfront.com/about/

Not in Our Name
www.notinourname.net/index.html

Veterans Against the War
Vietnam Veterans Against the War is still active in antiwar protests.

www.vaiw.org/vet/index.php
www.vvaw.org/

The American Civil Liberties Union
www.aclu.org/

OTHER DISSENTING VOICES OF THE TIME:

The Clamshell Alliance
See this link for an article written about the antinuclear power group the Clamshell Alliance:

www.ecologia.org/newsletter/year90/jan90c.html

Irving Kristol
For information on the "Godfather of Neoconservativism," see:

www.wpunj.edu/~newpol/issue23/vieux23.htm
www.pbs.org/arguing/nyintellectuals_krystol.html

Jerry Falwell
For information about this evangelical minister, see:

www.falwell.com/
http://atheism.about.com/library/glossary/western/bldef_falwelljerry.htm

Rush Limbaugh
To examine controversial right-wing talk-show host Rush Limbaugh's philosophy, see his Web site:

www.rushlimbaugh.com/

Jesse Jackson
For information about this civil rights activist, see:

www.pbs.org/wgbh/pages/frontline/jesse/

Robert Byrd
See Senator Robert Byrd's anti–Iraq War speech at:

http://byrd.senate.gov/byrd_speeches/byrd_speeches_2003february/byrd_speeches_2003
   march_list/byrd_speeches_2003march_list_1.html

Audre Lorde
For information about African American lesbian activist and writer Audre Lorde, see:

www.alp.org/
www.emory.edu/ENGLISH/Bahri/RYAN.HTML

Physicians for Social Responsibility

For, information about Physicians for Social Responsibility and the group's founder, Dr. Helen Caldicott, see:

www.speakersandartists.org/People/HelenCaldicott.html
www.dialoguefordemocracy.org/event/caldicott.php
www.shareguide.com/Caldicott.html

Queer Nation

For information about Queer Nation and to view John Dennis and Chris Cooper's radical gay comic Web site, see:

www-2.cs.cmu.edu/~mjw/Queer/MainPage.html
www.queernation.com/

Michael Moore

For information about this controversial film maker, see:

www.michaelmoore.com

TEXT CREDITS

Page 163: From *The Collected Poems of Langston Hughes* by Langston Hughes. Copyright © 1994 by the Estate of Langston Hughes. Used by permission of Alfred A. Knopf, a division of Random House, Inc.

Page 187: "Pretty Boy Floyd," by Woody Guthrie. Copyright © 1958 (renewed) by Sanga Music, Inc. All rights reserved. Used by permission.

Page 188: "Jesus Christ," words and music by Woody Guthrie. TRO – © Copyright 1961 (renewed) 1963 (renewed) Ludlow Music, Inc., New York, NY. Used by permission.

Page 189: J. Saunders Redding, "The Meaning of World War Two for a Negro, 1942" from J. Saunders Redding, "A Negro Looks at This War," *American Mercury 55* (November 1942). Reprinted with permission.

Page 193: David Dellinger from Larry Gara & Lenna Mae Gara, eds., *A Few Small Candles: War Resisters of World War II Tell Their Stories.* Published by Kent State University Press, 1999. Used with permission of The Kent State University Press.

Page 203: From John Tateishi and Roger Daniels, *And Justice for All.* Copyright © 1999 The University of Washington Press. Used by permission.

Page 206: From Minoru Yasui's letters, 1942 and 1943. Obtained from letters in Yuka Yasui Fujikura's Private Collection. Reprinted by permission

Page 209: By Henry Miller, from *Remember to Remember,* copyright © 1961 by Henry Miller. Reprinted by permission of New Directions Publishing Corp.

Page 250: Harry Hay, "Keynote Speech" at the Gay Spirit Visions Conference in Highlands, North Carolina, 1990. Copyright © by the estate of Harry Hay. Reprinted by permission of the estate of Harry Hay and Gay Spirit Visions (www.gayspiritvisions.org).

Page 255: Allen Ginsberg, "America" from *Collected Poems 1947–1980* by Allen Ginsberg. Copyright © 1956, 1959 by Allen Ginsberg. Reprinted by permission of HarperCollins Publishers Inc.

Page 258: "I Ain't Scared of Your Jail" by Lester Cobb. Copyright 1963 (renewed) by Sanga Music, Inc. All rights reserved. Used by permission.

Page 258: "If You Miss Me at the Back of the Bus" by Carver Neblett. Copyright © 1963 (renewed) by Sanga Music, Inc. All rights reserved. Used by permission.

Page 259: Bob Dylan, "Only a Pawn in the Game." Copyright © 1963 by Warner Bros. Inc. Copyright renewed 1991 by Special Rider Music. All rights reserved. International copyright secured. Reprinted by permission.

Page 262: Copyright 1963 Martin Luther King Jr., copyright renewed 1991 Coretta Scott King. Reprinted by arrangement with the Estate of Martin Luther King Jr., c/o Writers House as agent for the proprietor New York, NY.

Page 274: Fanny Lou Hamer, "Testimony" from the records of the Democratic National Committee, Series II, Box 102, Folder: DNC Credentials 1964—Mississippi Credentials Committee, Atlantic City, NJ, August 22, 1964. Used by permission.

Page 276: From Malcolm X, *Two Speeches by Malcolm X.* Copyright © 1965, 1990 by Betty Shabazz and Pathfinder Press. Reprinted by permission.

Page 278: Stokely Carmichael, "Berkeley Speech," October 1966. Used by permission of the Foundation Kwame Ture, Inc.

Page 287: The Black Panther Party, "Platform and Program of The Black Pather Party," October 1966 by Bobby Seale and Huey Newton.

Page 295: "The Problem That Has No Name" from *The Feminine Mystique* by Betty Friedan. Copyright © 1983, 1974, 1973, 1963 by Betty Friedan. Used by permission of W. W. Norton & Company, Inc.

Page 298: Betty Friedan, "Statement of Purpose, National Organization of Women" from *It Changed My Life: Writings On The Women's Movement,* originally published by Random House. Copyright © 1963, 1964, 1966, 1970, 1971, 1972, 1973, 1974, 1975, 1976, 1985, 1991, 1998 by Betty Friedan. Reprinted by permission of Curtis Brown, Ltd.

Page 303: "I Ain't Marching Anymore" by Phil Ochs. Copyright © 1964, renewed 1992 Barricade Music Inc. Administered by Almo Music Corp. All rights reserved. Used by permission.

Page 304: "Little Boxes." Words and music by Malvina Reynolds. Copyright © 1962 by Schroder Music Company, renewed 1990. Used by permission.

Page 305: Bob Dylan, "The Times They Are a Changin." Copyright © 1963 by Warner Bros. Inc. Copyright renewed 1991 by Special Rider Music. All rights reserved. International copyright secured. Reprinted by permission.

Page 306: Bob Dylan, "It's Alright Ma (I'm Only Bleeding." Copyright © 1963 by Warner Bros. Inc. Copyright renewed 1991 by Special Rider Music. All rights reserved. International copyright secured. Reprinted by permission.

Page 320: Speech by Mario Savio, December 2, 1964 at The University of California at Berkeley. Used by permission.

Page 322: Carl Oglesby, Speech, Washington, November 27, 1965. Used by permission.

Page 328: "You Don't Need a Weatherman to Know Which Way the Wind Blows," The Weatherman from *New Left Notes,* June 18, 1969 in Harold Jacobs, *Weatherman* (Ramparts Press, 1970). Used by permission.

Page 333: Timothy Leary, *The Psychedelic Experience: A Manual Based on the Tibetan Book of the Dead.* Reprinted by permission.